D1250593

Interpersonal Helping Skills

A Guide to Training Methods, Programs, and Resources

Eldon K. Marshall
P. David Kurtz
and Associates

Interpersonal
Helping Skills

NOV 1 7 1984

 Jossey-Bass Publishers
San Francisco • Washington • London • 1982

INTERPERSONAL HELPING SKILLS
A Guide to Training Methods, Programs, and Resources
by Eldon K. Marshall and P. David Kurtz and Associates

Copyright © 1982 by: Jossey-Bass Inc., Publishers
433 California Street
San Francisco, California 94104

&

Jossey-Bass Limited
28 Banner Street
London EC1Y 8QE

Copyright under International, Pan American, and Universal Copyright Conventions. All rights reserved. No part of this book may be reproduced in any form—except for brief quotation (not to exceed 1,000 words) in a review or professional work—without permission in writing from the publishers.

Library of Congress Cataloging in Publication Data
Main entry under title:

Interpersonal helping skills.

Includes bibliographies and indexes.
1. Interpersonal relations.   2. Helping behavior.
3. Social skills.   4. Group relations training.
5. Leadership.   I. Marshall, Eldon K.   II. Kurtz,
P. David.
HM132.I55   1982   302.3   82-17275
ISBN 0-87589-551-4

Manufactured in the United States of America

The paper in this book meets the guidelines for permanence and durability of the Committee on Production Guidelines for Book Longevity of the Council on Library Resources.

JACKET DESIGN BY WILLI BAUM

FIRST EDITION

Code 8242

The Jossey-Bass
Social and Behavioral Science Series

To Our Families:
Joy, Mark, Jeffrey, and Tim Marshall
and
Gail, Paul, Adam, and Jon Kurtz

Preface

Since Carl Rogers initiated his inquiry into the helping process, the field of helping skills has grown by leaps and bounds. The primary purpose of this book is to draw together the ever-burgeoning models of helping skills and their accompanying training methods. It is meant to function as an effective tool for practitioners as well as for researchers—for those engaged in teaching and using skills as well as those interested in empirical investigation of skills typologies and training techniques.

While preparing this book, we were impressed with the growth of a variety of eclectic skill models alongside the more established approaches, the infusion of skills training programs into the education of virtually every professional and paraprofessional helping group, the significant refinements in the major skills training models, the development of a program that specifically addresses cross-cultural helping skills training, the burgeoning of multimedia skills training programs, and the quality of skills training research.

Work on this book has also raised our consciousness regarding the less positive developments in the field. Despite the enthusiasm and hope expressed regarding the role of helping skills in facilitating clients' mental health, the question of the effect of skills on client treatment outcomes remains largely unanswered. While this deficit has been acknowledged, few authorities in the field appear interested in tackling it. Furthermore, although the recent development of skills models for group facilitation or leadership is noteworthy, the development of skills models for dyadic helping efforts seems, at least temporarily, to have plateaued. The more recent models appear to be largely derivative, and thus offer no new real innovations. Another issue is the lack of concern for the ethical issues involved in skills training and use.

In this book we attempt to capture the multidisciplinary uses of helping skills. The contributors document the generic applicability of both helping skills models and their accompanying training methods to a wide range of helping fields. Application illustrations were drawn from the fields of education, clinical and counseling psychology, guidance and counseling, special education, vocational rehabilitation, psychiatry, health care, nursing, and social work. The book is intended for those actively engaged in training helpers, whatever their orientation or affiliation. It constitutes a guidebook as well as a reference for graduate and undergraduate courses in helping skills.

The book is organized into six parts. Part One, "Development and Applications of Skills Training," presents a comprehensive survey of skills training research conducted with professional and paraprofessional populations over the past twelve years and an in-depth review of the empirical evidence linking interpersonal skills to therapy outcomes. It outlines the evolution of the field and thoroughly documents the expanding scope of helping skills, typologies, and skills training methods, and presents a sobering picture of the effect of the helper's use of skills on therapy outcomes.

Part Two, "Skills Training Models," presents unique features of the major models of interpersonal skills development in a fashion that enhances comparative understanding of their evolution, underlying theory, training methods and techniques, results of empirical testing, new extensions and adaptations, and projections for future uses. Our intention in Part Two is to present significant systems of skills training side by side so that their relative merits can be compared and better understood.

Skills approaches to group leadership training are clearly on the cutting edge of advances in the field. Part Three, "Group Leadership Skills Training," explores the relevance of a skills approach to training group helpers. Chapters in this part highlight the place of skills in group work and examine the generic and group-specific skills essential to effective leadership of counseling and therapy-oriented groups. Illustrative typologies of group facilitation skills and instructional models for their development are presented.

Part Four, "Designing, Conducting, and Evaluating Skills Training Programs," presents important considerations for those engaged in classroom, workshop, or in-service skills training contexts. It provides guidance regarding: (1) organizational requisites and arrangements necessary for effective program implementation, (2) management of learning conditions to facilitate skills training design and delivery, (3) available resources for skills trainers, including packaged programs, films, audiotapes and videotapes, simulations and organizations, and (4) methods and procedures for the evaluation of skills training programs.

Part Five, "Training Clients in Interpersonal Skills," looks at the use of skills training with client populations. Psychoeducational approaches are fast becoming an important modality of social treatment. Chapters in Part Five present exemplary models of social skills development and explore the overall relevance of a microskills perspective to the treatment of clients.

The Epilogue, "Future Directions for Interpersonal Skills Training," raises critical issues and suggests possible new directions for the field.

With the growing numbers of research reports it is becoming increasingly difficult to stay abreast of the field. To assist investigators we compiled an abstracted review of *all* skills training research publications from 1970 through 1981 (Resource A). Similarly, it is difficult for skills trainers and instructors to be aware of numerous training resources available. Resource B is a comprehensive compilation of existing packaged training programs, films, audiotapes, videotapes, simulations, and organizations offering training and consultation services.

As the contributors to this volume make clear, the field of skills training is fast maturing. Research and practice contribute to an ever-growing body of knowledge regarding the interpersonal dimensions of helping, the process of skills learning, and methods applicable to the training of skilled helpers. In this book we attempt to elucidate the state of the science and art of skills training and key issues that must be confronted if the field is to advance. We hope that it will stimulate new, improved training practices that build upon the best of current models and methods and will encourage continued growth of empirically grounded training practices.

We would like to acknowledge our debt and deep appreciation to all of those who, in many and various ways, have helped to make this book possible. We are particularly grateful to all our authors for their contributions toward a more comprehensive and effective skills training field. The opportunity to know, work with, and learn from them has unquestionably been the most rewarding aspect of preparing this book. We have been most fortunate to have been able to gather together such a creative, productive and influential group of practitioners, educators and researchers. A special acknowledgement is extended to Benjamin Granger and Louie Beasley of the University of Tennessee School of Social Work for their administrative support of this project. Their understanding of the demands of the project was an important source of encouragement. We wish to thank Patricia Pollock for her valuable editorial assistance and Connie Covert and Florence Dufty for their indispensable secretarial and clerical assistance. Special gratitude is extended to our families for their patience, encouragement, and support throughout the development of this book.

Nashville, Tennessee   Eldon K. Marshall
August 1982   P. David Kurtz

Contents

The Authors

ELDON K. MARSHALL is associate professor, Department of Psychiatry and Behavioral Sciences, University of Oklahoma, Health Sciences Center, and staff member in mental health services, Oklahoma Children's Memorial Hospital. From 1972 to late 1982 he served as associate professor of social work at the University of Tennessee. He received his B.A. degree in education from DePauw University (1956), his M.S.W. degree from Wayne State University (1960), and his Ph.D. degree in education from St. Louis University (1972). From 1960 to 1966 Marshall held a variety of social work positions in the public schools and in community mental health and youth serving agencies. From 1966 to 1972 he served as instructor in social work at St. Louis University.

P. DAVID KURTZ is professor of social work and education at the University of Georgia where he chairs the School Social Service Program. He received his B.A. degree in philosophy from the St. Paul Seminary (1964), and his M.S.W. degree (1967) and Ph.D. degree (1971) in educational psychology from the University of Michigan. From 1972–1975 Kurtz served as assistant professor at Pennsylvania State University, College of Human Development, Department of Individual and Family Studies. Subsequently he was associate professor at the University of Tennessee, School of Social Work in Nashville, where he chaired the Treatment Specialization Program.

WILLIAM A. ANTHONY, professor and director of the Center for Rehabilitation Research and Training in Mental Health, Boston University

JERRY AUTHIER, associate professor, Departments of Family Practice and Psychiatry, University of Nebraska Medical Center

JACQUELINE N. BUCK, assistant professor, Department of Psychology, Southern Illinois University at Carbondale

JOHN W. CHARPING, assistant professor, School of Social Work, University of Tennessee

M. HARRY DANIELS, associate professor, Department of Guidance and Educational Psychology, Southern Illinois University at Carbondale

WAYNE D. DUEHN, professor, Graduate School of Social Work, University of Texas at Arlington

GERARD EGAN, professor, Department of Psychology, Loyola University of Chicago

MARYANNE GALVIN, assistant professor, Department of Counselor Education, University of New Hampshire

GEORGE M. GAZDA, research professor of education, University of Georgia, and clinical professor of psychiatry, Medical College of Georgia

BERNARD GUERNEY, JR., professor of human development and head, Individual and Family Consultation Center, Pennsylvania State University

KAY GUSTAFSON, staff clinical psychologist, Omaha Veterans Administration Medical Center, and clinical assistant professor of medical psychology, Department of Psychiatry, University of Nebraska College of Medicine

PAMELA A. HOGWOOD, family service worker, YWCA Try Angle House, Nashville, Tennessee

ALLEN E. IVEY, professor and director of counseling psychology, University of Massachusetts

EILEEN KRIMSKY, psychologist, Office of Counseling and Psychological Services, Denison University

MICHAEL J. LAMBERT, professor of clinical psychology, Brigham Young University

MARTITA A. LOPEZ, assistant professor, Department of Psychology and Social Sciences, Rush-Presbyterian-St. Luke's Medical Center, Chicago

RICHARD P. MCQUELLON, doctoral candidate in counseling, educational psychology, and special education, Michigan State University

NAZNEEN SADA MAYADAS, professor, Graduate School of Social Work, University of Texas at Arlington

JOHN R. MORELAND, clinical associate professor, Department of Psychiatry, Ohio State University Medical School

THOMAS D. MORTON, administrator, Office of Continuing Social Work Education, University of Georgia

EDWARD J. PAWLAK, professor of policy, planning, and administration, School of Social Work, Western Michigan University

PAUL PEDERSEN, professor of education and chairman, Department of Counseling and Guidance, Syracuse University

GERALD L. STONE, professor, College of Education, University of Iowa

DANNY H. THOMPSON, associate professor of policy, planning, and administration, School of Social Work, Western Michigan University

RAPHAEL L. VITALO, clinical director, W. W. Johnson Life Center, Inc., Springfield, Massachusetts

INA F. WAY, family therapist, Family and Children's Center, Mishawaka, Indiana

Interpersonal Helping Skills

A Guide to Training Methods, Programs, and Resources

Part One

Development and Applications of Skills Training

Chapter 1

Evolution of Interpersonal Skills Training

P. David Kurtz
Eldon K. Marshall

The helper-helpee relationship is clearly an important factor in the helping process. As Strupp (1974) noted, "There is no need to dwell on the common observation that all forms of psychotherapy entail a significant human relationship" (p. 2). Ivey and Authier (1978) developed a taxonomy of helper behavior that examined the microcounseling skills from eight treatment approaches—nondirective, Rogerian encounter, behavioral, analytic, Tavistock, family therapy, Gestalt, and eclectic. Although the approaches differ in their goals and techniques, each uses certain microskills in varying combinations.

Although there is consensus that effective helping entails a significant human relationship, what makes a human relationship significant is difficult to identify. In recent years, researchers have posited a range of helper qualities, attitudes, and skills that, they believe, compose the core conditions of the human relationship. Although these core conditions include some commonalities, substantial differences also exist, and no single core attribute or set of

3

core attributes has been identified. The core conditions cannot be construed without examining their interaction with such contextual variables as demographic characteristics (sex and social class); culture (race and religion); helper personality, helping orientation, and level of experience; helpee personality and expectations; and organizational setting (goals and policies). The complexity of these variables, as well as the elusiveness of many helper qualities, makes it exceedingly difficult to determine the factors that influence the helping relationship.

Furthermore, beyond the forming of a helping relationship, helping involves a range of activities that require particular qualities, attitudes, and skills. Many of the recent interpersonal skills training models, for instance, have extended their focus beyond the core skills to include more advanced skills, such as interpretation, direct mutual communiation, goal identification, problem solving, and modeling.

The purpose of this chapter is to summarize the evolution of interpersonal helping skills models and training methods and present a research survey reflecting the current status of the field in general and training models in particular.

Evolution

Rogers (1961) proposed certain relationship conditions as necessary and sufficient to produce personality change. He hypothesized that "If the counselor is congruent or transparent, so that his words are in line with his feelings rather than the two being discrepant; if the counselor likes the client, unconditionally; and if the counselor understands the essential feelings of the client as they seem to the client—then there is a strong probability that this will be an effective relationship" (p. 49). Initial research findings were supportive of Rogers's hypothesis. Based on a review of the literature up to 1970 on this hypothesis Truax and Mitchell (1971) concluded, "These studies taken together suggest that therapists or counselors who are accurately empathetic, nonpossessively warm in attitude, and genuine are indeed effective" (p. 310). Subsequent critiques of this body of research, however, seriously question Rogers's hypothesis (see for example, Chinsky and Rappaport, 1970; Rachman, 1973; Blackwood, 1975).

Nevertheless, Rogers's hypothesis has had a profound impact on making the helping process observable, its practice and training techniques operational, and its outcomes measurable. Prior to the advent of the client-centered approach, psychotherapy was viewed as a private interaction between therapist and patient, the secrecy surrounding the interview prohibited public scrutiny, and the supervisory training process was largely confidential. Although others were conducting significant research on helper-helpee interaction (Kounin and others, 1956; and Polansky and Kounin, 1956), Rogers was the first major figure to shed light on the helping process, posing the question, "Is it possible to state, in terms which are clearly definable and measurable, the psychological conditions which are both necessary and sufficient to bring about constructive personality change?" (1957a, p. 95). He believed that in working with individuals and groups, the attitudes and feelings of helpers are important, rather than their theoretical orientation, procedures, or techniques. According to Rogers, the three most desirable attitudinal characteristics of the therapist are empathy, unconditional positive regard, and genuineness.

One of the key implications of Rogers's position is that training should focus on the development of the proper helper attitudes and should occur in a facilitative context similar to the one the therapist provides for clients. Traditionally, two principal approaches to training were used. One was exclusively didactic, emphasizing direct teaching to facilitate cognitive understanding of pertinent theories. The trainer passed down an accumulated store of knowledge that the learner was required to accept and assimilate into a set of premises applied in conducting treatment. The other was experiential, focusing on providing a safe, secure setting for enabling the student to learn about self and experiment with relating to clients. According to Whitaker (1949), "Teaching psychotherapy differs specifically from every other type of medical teaching. One teaches attitudes rather than facts, and that which is intuitive, abstract, and personal becomes more significant than the factual or historical" (p. 899). Medical education principally used the didactic mode (Schwartz and Abel, 1955), whereas social work largely relied on the supervisor-supervisee relationship (Boehm, 1961; Towles, 1961).

Rogers and his colleagues, departing from conventional trends, developed short training workshops and attempted to evaluate their effectiveness. The approach involved a series of graded experiences in which the student: discriminated between facilitative and nonfacilitative therapists in recorded and live demonstrations; conducted role-played interviews using the newly acquired attitudes; participated in individual and group therapy; and conducted supervised client interviews. Psychotherapy was now open to public inspection, and thus systematic study was possible.

Rogers's framework provided part of the groundwork for the efforts of Truax and Carkhuff (1967). Oriented to the development of empathy, nonpossessive warmth, and genuineness, their didactic-experiential model integrated three elements: a training environment in which the supervisor provides high levels of facilitative helping conditions; didactic and experiential training in discrimination and cultivation of the core conditions; and a quasi group therapy experience in which the learner explores the helping self and allows it to emerge. The didactic-experiential model was the forerunner of Carkhuff's systematic human relations training (SHRT) model. Although Carkhuff (1981) acknowledges the influence of Rogers's approach on his work, he is quick to point out that he was influenced by other theories and that his model is an eclectic one. Systematic human relations training is similar to the Rogerian training program in that it is a person- or trainee-centered, rather than skills-centered, approach that focuses on the personal or emotional difficulties experienced by trainees in their role as helper. However, Carkhuff emphasized more than Rogers the acquisition of specifiable, facilitative qualities that differentiate successful from unsuccessful helpers. Throughout the ongoing development of SHRT, Carkhuff has taken steps to further refine the operational definitions of those helper qualities and has divided them into two categories or dimensions: the responsive, which includes empathy, respect, and specificity of expression; and the initiative, which includes genuineness, self-disclosure, confrontation, and immediacy. Carkhuff outlined the developmental stages of the helping process—self-exploration, self-understanding, and action orientation—and described the differential use of responsive and initiative qualities in each stage. Like Rogers, Truax and Carkhuff (1967) were committed to "erasing the artificial distinction between research training and therapy training . . . [and to] researching the therapeutic process and its outcomes in order to explicate its effective ingredients, training persons to provide higher levels of these ingredients, and researching the resultant process and outcome to determine if indeed there is a significant improvement" (p. 225).

The work of Rogers and of Truax and Carkhuff signaled but the beginning of important advances in the training field. Subsequent innovations contributed to a new and growing body of training technology. Ivey's microcounseling model, for example, is a significant recent innovation in human relations training (Ivey and Authier, 1978), with roots in Allen's (1967) work on microteaching. Like the client-centered and SHRT paradigms, microtraining is a conceptual framework of core interpersonal helping skills, as well as a technology for teaching. Developed out of Ivey's desire to identify and teach the core interpersonal skills of effective interviewing, the model is based on the assumption that interviewer behavior is extremely complex and can best be taught by breaking the interview down into discrete behavioral units. Ivey shifted the focus from helper attitudes and qualities to operationally defined techniques or behaviors and from person- or trainee-centered training to skills-centered training. The microtraining approach, which builds on the didactic-experiential training framework, emphasizes trainee acquisition of identifiable helping skills that can be incorporated into individual helper styles. The initial skills presented in the model include nonverbal attending skills, minimal encouragers, open and closed questions, paraphrases, reflections of feelings, and summarizations. Designed to bridge the gap between theory and practice, the teaching technology of microtraining, although containing didactic elements, is primarily experiential. Based on the proposition that the interviewing process can be taught, microtraining emphasizes development of single skills, self-observation and confrontation, observation of videotaped models, and simulated practice. The model also offers a controlled, systematic research setting in which the interview may be studied under naturalistic conditions.

Emerging somewhat concurrently with microtraining was Kagan's (1975) interpersonal process recall (IPR) model. One of the major video-based approaches to interpersonal skills development, IPR provides instruction in basic communication skills, including exploratory, listening, affective, and honest labeling responses, and emphasizes heightened self-awareness and knowledge of the subtleties of interpersonal interaction. Following IPR came a significant non-media-based system of basic helping skills developed by Danish and Hauer (1973). The "helping skills program" is a skills-centered approach that trains helpers in basic nonverbal and verbal responsive skills, self-involving behavior, and influence responses.

Numerous other models for interpersonal skills development have also emerged, including major adaptations of established models (Gazda, 1973; Gazda and others, 1977); developmental models (Egan, 1982; Schulman, 1974); structured learning training (Goldstein, 1973; Goldstein and Goedhart, 1973); self-instructional and programmed texts (Bullmer, 1975; Evans and others, 1979; Hackney and Nye, 1973); automated, packaged programs (Milnes and Bertcher, 1980; Berzon and Reisel, 1976; Goodman, 1978); and cross-cultural programs (Pedersen, 1976). Matarazzo (1978) concludes that most interpersonal training programs are derived from either the client-centered, SHRT, or microtraining models. However, some, such as Kagan's (1975) interpersonal process recall (IPR) and Pedersen's (1975) triad model for cross-cultural counselor training, appear to have unique roots and methods. The proliferation of training programs has been accompanied by the spread of training from the traditional counseling professions of psychology, psychiatry, and social work to such nontraditional counseling professions as early childhood education, law enforcement, corrections, nursing, nutrition, and foster care.

Another recent trend is the application of skills training to work with groups. Rogers was the first to highlight the importance of core conditions in working with groups, an application later underscored by Carkhuff (1973) and Ivey (1973). Initially, the major focus of the field was on dyadic treatment, and, in those programs dealing with both individuals and groups, group skills tended to be largely an extension of those used in helping individuals. Currently, however, interest has centered on the identification of group-specific skills and the development of programs for their acquisition, an approach well illustrated by contributions in this volume, as well as by the work of Bertcher (1979), Dyer and Vriend (1977), Egan (1976), Moreland and Buck (1979), and Shulman (1979).

In its brief history, the study of the qualities, attitudes, and skills essential to effective helping has moved from the privacy of traditional psychotherapy to the experimental examination of the helping process; from qualitative helper attitudes to discrete behavioral units; from core conditions for facilitating the helping relationship to a broad range of skills for performing numerous helper activities, such as problem exploration, goal identification, decision making, and problem solving; from purely didactic or experiential training paradigms to training approaches that combine both; and from person- or trainee-centered training programs to skills-centered curricula. From this study has emerged a broad-based, skills-focused helper training field. According to Matarazzo (1978), in this young field, the "teaching *method* for interviewing skills seems to be less problematic than the questions of *what* to teach" (p. 961). As the following research report on the current status of skills training makes clear, there is not only little consensus regarding core interpersonal helping skills but also considerable diversity regarding optimal training methods.

Current Status: A Twelve-Year Survey of Research

In the wake of economic, political, and philosophical changes in delivery of mental health and medical services, changes that have increased the commitment to train a wide array of personnel to deliver these services, interpersonal skills training appears to be growing by leaps and bounds. For example, in a survey of all 111 four-year medical schools in the United States, Kahn, Cohen, and Jason (1979) received replies from 79 schools, 76 (97 percent) of which indicated that courses in interpersonal skills development were taught in their programs. Of 61 (out of a possible 85) accredited graduate schools of social work responding to a questionnaire regarding the inclusion of interpersonal skills training in their curricula, 48 (78 percent) were offering skills training (Hines, 1978).

The twelve-year survey presented in this chapter serves to preface the skills models discussed in this volume with a current, comprehensive overview of skills training research conducted with professional and paraprofessional populations in the 1970s and early 1980s. The survey describes the trends in skills training research, analyzes patterns in skills training practice, and explores key issues and their implications for further development of the field.

Survey Design. The survey, conducted by the authors and covering research spanning a twelve-year period from January 1970 through December 1981, is based on a computer search of the Educational Resource Information Center (ERIC) and *Psychological Abstracts,* supplemented by a systematic search of twenty-two professional journals from the fields of counseling, psychology, medicine, and social work. The survey was intended to be exhaustive but did not include reports from *Dissertation Abstracts.* The largest proportion of studies were drawn from *Counseling Psychology* (forty-three studies), *Counselor Education and Supervision* (thirty-three studies), *The Journal of Medical Education* (nineteen studies), and *Journal of Community Psychology* (seven studies). Only experimental, quasi-experimental, and preexperimental studies were included (Campbell and Stanley, 1963); descriptive studies were omitted. In this regard, the analysis does not completely reflect the current level of activity in the skills training area, since numerous descriptive reports of varied training endeavors conducted with different populations have been published. Studies surveyed are listed and summarized in Resource A.

The studies were clustered into four groups: counseling, medicine, social work, and nonprofessional. The first three groups included all training studies oriented to professional practitioners, professional degree students, and paraprofessionals in the fields of counseling, medicine, and social work. The nonprofessional group consisted of paraprofessional helpers and nonprofessional degree students who were not specifically identified as being in either counseling, medicine, or social work. A total of 141 studies were surveyed, of which 33 percent centered on counselors, 25 percent on medical personnel, 9 percent on social workers, and 33 percent on nonprofessional helpers (see Table 1). The paucity of studies of social work training, which does not reflect the widespread inclusion of skills

Table 1. Total Number, Purpose, and Population of Studies Surveyed.

	Counseling	Medicine	Social Work	Nonprofessional	Total
Total Number of Studies	47	35	12	47	141
Purpose of Study					
Program evaluation	13	24	8	18	63
Program comparison	12	8	3	7	30
Component study	22	3	1	22	48
Populations[a]					
Professional practitioner	2	7	1		10
Professional degree student	36	25	10		71
Paraprofessional	11	3	5		19

[a]Some studies involved more than one group of subjects; therefore, the total number of populations is greater than the total number of studies surveyed.

training in social work education (Hines, 1978), probably indicates a relative lack of empirical interest in this area among social workers.

The trends in the number of studies published each year during the twelve-year span of the survey are worth noting. In the years 1970, 1971, and 1972, eight, eleven, and six studies were published, with the nonprofessional group accounting for most (ten), followed by counseling (nine) and medicine (six); the first social work training study did not appear until 1973. The publication rate mushroomed to seventeen reports in 1973 and 16 in 1974, with counseling accounting for most of the investigations (fifteen), followed by nonprofessionals (ten), medicine (seven), and social work (one). This peak period was followed by a leveling off in the number of published studies to eleven or twelve per year from 1976 to 1981. Most (75 percent) of the social work studies were published between 1977 and 1980. The consistent publication record for this field indicates commitment to empirical examination of the training process. Although the skills training models have proved generally successful, significant questions and the need for further development of the field warrant continued investigation.

The framework of Marshall, Charping, and Bell (1979) has been adapted to analyze the research from these investigations in relation to purpose, trainee population, training models, duration, training methods, interpersonal skills at focus, evaluation design, and retention of trained skills.

Purpose of the Studies. Based on statements of intent in the research reports surveyed, studies were classified as program evaluations, program comparisons, or component studies. Studies categorized as program evaluations were aimed primarily at determining whether a specified training program effected change in some designated interpersonal criterion. Program comparisons were concerned with comparing two or more different skills training programs, and component studies used an analytical method to isolate and examine the effect of certain variables, either singly or in combination, on skills acquisition. For example, one study compared the effects of feedback alone with a combined feedback and modeling procedure, and another investigation sought to determine the effectiveness of different modeling formats on skills development. Forty-five percent of the total of 141 studies focused on program evaluation, 21 percent were concerned with program comparisons, and 34 percent were identified as component studies (see Table 1). In addition, the four trainee groups varied considerably in the purpose of their respective studies. For example, 69 percent of the studies in medicine and 67 percent in social work focused on program evaluation, whereas almost half of the studies of counselors and nonprofessionals were component studies. Researchers in the counseling and nonprofessional groups have apparently been more concerned with examining the effectiveness of specific training variables, the other two groups with investigating overall training outcomes.

Characteristics of Trainees. The trainees or subjects in the three professional groups were categorized as either professional practitioners, professional degree students, or paraprofessionals (see Table 1). The vast majority of studies (76 percent) from the three professional groups were conducted with professional degree students; paraprofessionals accounted for 20 percent of the studies, and professional practitioners for a scant 11 percent. Most of the professional practitioners trained were in the field of medicine. The nonprofessional group was composed of a wide array of helpers and students, including resident hall advisers, hotline workers, and undergraduate human services students. Virtually all skills training programs in the four groups were aimed at entry level graduate students in counseling, medicine, and social work, at undergraduates, or at paraprofessionals.

Training Models. Training models refer to the recognized training programs listed in Table 2, which constitute the experimental or treatment conditions in the studies surveyed. The "other" category was established for those investigations having an identifiable model but not falling into any of the listed classifications. The eclectic category includes studies in which either the model was not clearly labeled or a composite of methods from different models was used.

Systematic human relations training is the most frequently used model, with microtraining a distant second. However, these two widely heralded models, when combined, account for less than one-third of the studies surveyed. The other recognized models each make up only a small proportion of the total number studied. Most of the models (46 percent) employed in the studies are eclectic. Among the studies of medical and nonprofessional groups, over half are eclectic. Most of the studies of the IPR model have occurred in medicine, but that model accounts for only 12 percent of the total number of studies in this field. Systematic human relations training accounts for almost one-third of the social work studies and about one-fifth of the studies of counselors and nonprofessionals. Although the behavioral model was cited in only a handful of studies, the majority of the methods component studies investigated variables which emanated from operant learning and social learning principles.

An examination of how many studies of the various models were published each year during the span of the survey reveals a trend away from recognized models toward eclectic training programs. All twelve studies published in 1981 fell into either the eclectic or "other" categories. The most notable decline in publication of research on skills models is found for the SHRT model—during the past five years, only six studies have appeared, in contrast to twenty-two studies published from 1970 to 1977. Interestingly, even though Carkhuff and his associates developed and refined the SHRT model with counseling and nonprofessional groups, of the six recently

Table 2. Training Models and Training Duration of Studies Surveyed.

	Counseling	Medicine	Social Work	Nonprofessional	Total
Training Model[a]					
SHRT	10	5	4	9	28
Microcounseling	6	2		8	16
IPR	3	4			7
Behavioral	3	1	2	1	7
Helping skills training	1		2	3	6
Programmed instruction	2	1		3	6
Structured learning training	1	1			2
Triad model	1				1
Eclectic	19	20	2	24	65
Other	6	2	2	4	14
Duration (in hours)[b]					
Five or less	14	5	1	11	31
Six to ten	3	3		8	14
Eleven to fifteen	1	7	1	3	12
Thirty-six or more	9	5	1	5	20
Not specified	15	14	5	11	45

[a]Some studies used more than one model; therefore, the total number of models is greater than the total number of studies surveyed.
[b]Includes only those duration categories in which a minimum of twelve studies surveyed were included.

published studies, only two focused on counselor training and none on nonprofessional training.

Matarazzo (1978) concludes, "It is no longer possible to draw together all of the burgeoning research in this area, but most of it has been stimulated by only three broad, theoretically based programs: the client-centered, didactic-experiential program; the microcounseling program . . . and the behavior modification paradigm" (p. 961). However, the large proportion of studies categorized as eclectic and "other" suggests that considerable diversity exists among programs and reflects the growing perception that no one model is more effective than the others.

Since component studies frequently examine a set of variables, rather than a complete model, it was thought that these studies might skew the training model data toward the eclectic model category. Therefore, an analysis that included only the program comparison and program evaluation categories was conducted on each group. The analysis revealed this skewing effect in studies of counseling, social work, and nonprofessional training programs, but not in medical studies. When the program comparison and program evaluation data for the first three groups was combined, SHRT accounted for 39 percent and microtraining for 16 percent of the programs—a total of more than half. When combined, the eight training models listed in Table 2 accounted for 80 percent of the studies in the counseling group and 72 percent in the social work and nonprofessional groups. By contrast, 63 percent of the medical training models were eclectic, with SHRT and IPR, the most popular models in medicine, each accounting for only 16 percent of the training studies.

Training duration. The duration tabulations for all groups except social work formed a bimodal curve (see Table 2), revealing a tendency toward either short (under 10 hours) or long (over 36 hours) training programs. Skills training programs would therefore seem to have two predominant forms: workshops of one day or less and complete courses. Some training programs, especially those involved in component studies, ran for short periods (Alssid and Hutchison, 1977; Stone and Vance, 1976). By contrast, several programs by Carkhuff and his associates (Carkhuff, 1971; Carkhuff and Griffin, 1970, 1971) ran over 100 hours. In a review of twenty packaged training programs, Burstein (1979) noted a broad range in length of from three to thirty sessions and from 6 to 100 hours. On the average, these programs ran from six to twelve sessions of 1.5 to 2 hours per session.

Training method. Training method refers to those techniques, activities, and procedures constituting the instructional conditions in the studies surveyed. The most commonly used methods were feedback (78 percent), skills practice (70 percent), and skills demonstration (73 percent). Although videotape replay of trainee performance is an essential component of such models as microtraining and IPR, as indicated in Table 3, only one-fifth of the studies used this form of feedback. Audiotape replay, often used in place of videotape replay, was used in 12 percent of the training programs. When using skills demonstrations, the training sessions

Table 3. Number of Studies Surveyed Using Various Training Methods.

Method	Counseling	Medical	Social Work	Nonprofessional	Total
Lectures	16	20	4	26	66
Practice					
Simulated with role-played clients	17	14	9	20	60
Simulated with coached clients	8	6		5	19
With real clients	6	12	1		19
Demonstration					
Live models	13	11	7	12	43
Videotaped models	17	10	1	15	43
Audiotaped models	7	1		5	13
Scripted models	4				4
Group discussion	14	15	2	12	43
Feedback					
Instructor/trainer	12	9	4	13	38
Peer	4	9	4	5	22
Client	1	4	1		6
Videotape	5	12	3	7	27
Audiotape	8	5	1	3	17
Rating of trainee					
Instructor/trainer	3	1	2		6
Peers	1	3	3	1	8
Client		3			3
Self	11	5		3	19
Exercises					
Structured group exercises	1	1		2	4
Response to simulated client statements	14	8	3	6	31
Written handouts	14	5		5	24
Positive reinforcement					
Peer, social	2		2		4
Trainer, social	8	1	2	2	13
Mechanical	1			3	4
Discrimination/ communication training	6	4	1	2	13
Manuals	3	2		9	14
Supervision	4	2	1	6	13
Readings	4	4		3	11
Group process experience	3	3	1	1	8
Trainee rating of model	3	1	1	2	7

were usually either live or videotaped, thus exposing trainees to both verbal and nonverbal skills. Simulated client situations were the most common practice modes; in only 14 percent of the studies did trainers practice with actual clients. Interestingly, the medical group had a substantially higher proportion of programs that included practice with real clients (34 percent) than did counseling (13 percent), social work (8 percent), or nonprofessional (none). The heavy reliance on simulated and coached clients means that skills practice occurs in contrived circumstances. Since the greater the similarity between training and helping settings, the greater the likelihood that learning will be generalized to the work environment, the use of simulated practice lessens the transferability of skills acquired.

A related issue concerns the interpretation of research results based on simulated or coached client interviews as the dependent measure. The discrepancy between actual and artificial interviews raises the question of whether the real-life use of skills is being measured. The examination of the use of trained skills in real work settings, instead of with coached or simulated clients, is a neglected area of research.

Other training methods used in a substantial proportion of the studies include the rating or assessment of trainee performance by trainers, peers, self, and client; various structured skills practice exercises; lectures; group discussions; and handouts. Given the influence of Carkhuff's SHRT model, it is interesting to note that only a handful of the programs employed structured discrimination-communication training. Similarly, despite the fact that many of the programs draw from the behavioral framework, only 14 percent made explicit use of positive reinforcement—results that may be misleading, however, since training methods like practice feedback and group discussion often entail the implicit use of positive reinforcement.

Interpersonal skills. One of the more revealing aspects of the survey is the range of skills taught and the frequency with which the more commonly recognized skills are included in training programs. Ivey and Authier (1978) distinguish between attending skills in the helping process, which are the more beginning-level, responsive skills, and skills of interpersonal influence, which are the more advanced-level, initiative skills. Carkhuff (1969) speaks of advanced

Table 4. Interpersonal Skills Taught in Studies Surveyed.

Skill	Counseling	Medical	Social Work	Nonprofessional	Total
Empathy	15	11	9	20	55
Questioning	6	8	7	5	26
Genuineness	7	1	6	9	23
Respect	4	0	6	9	19
Attending	5	2	3	7	17
Reflection of feelings	3	2	0	10	15
Confrontation	4	4	1	6	15
Concreteness	5	0	3	4	12
Immediacy	3	1	1	6	11

[a]Includes only skills taught in at least eleven of the studies surveyed.

skills as "additive dimensions of helping," and Egan (1982) talks of "advanced accurate empathy." Table 4 lists the more commonly cited skills and indicates the number of studies making reference to each. Six of the skills were isolated and defined by Truax and Carkhuff (1967) and Carkhuff (1969). The others, such as questioning, attending, and reflection of feelings, emanate from Ivey's microtraining approach (Ivey and Authier, 1978). Of the nine skills listed, four are initiative skills, including genuineness, confrontation, immediacy, and concreteness, and five are responsive skills. Except for genuineness, the initiative skills are less frequently included in training programs than the responsive skills. Overall, training programs emphasized the teaching of the more introductory responsive skills, which focus on relationship building and information gathering, rather than the more advanced, influence-oriented skills, such as information sharing, advice giving, self-disclosure, and interpretation. For example, although microtraining was second only to SHRT in popularity, advanced-level microtraining skills were rarely dependent variables in the studies surveyed. Of the 141 studies, none examined self-expression, directions, influencing summarization, or direct-mutual communication; one focused on expression of content and expression of feelings; two centered on interpretation; and five examined self-disclosure.

These findings, combined with the fact that almost all train-ing programs are directed to either beginning-level professional de-gree students, paraprofessionals, or nonprofessionals, support Matarazzo's (1978) contention that "a noteworthy aspect of the pub-lished research is that it has been done almost exclusively on neo-phyte therapists-professionals or nonprofessional mental health trainees. . . . This seems to be due both to the fact that it is easier to define and measure dimensions of basic skill than more subtle ones and that nonprofessionals are more likely to be trained in suffi-ciently large groups to enable a study of comparative methods to be conducted" (p. 942).

Matarazzo's contention that most training programs are not applicable beyond the first year of graduate training is true; how-ever, her conclusion (1978) that there is "convergence among pro-grams at least on a few basic measured variables" (p. 962) is not valid. Empathy is the only skill that is taught in more than 20 percent of the programs, and the range of skills taught is staggering. One hundred and thirty-eight distinct skills labels were cited in the studies surveyed; of these, 111 were cited in only one study and 18 were named in from two to six studies. Ten studies did not specify the skills taught in their programs. Due to empirical evidence for the positive impact on clients of Rogers's core conditions and to the fact that the more prominent skills training programs have evolved from the client-centered model, the Rogerian core facilitative conditions are incorporated either explicitly or implicitly in most of the recent skills training programs.

Although an examination of the studies summarized in Re-source A reveals a wide range of distinct skills, similarity or overlap does appear to exist among the different skills labels. For example, the skills entitled "expression of affect," "expression of feelings," "sharing of self," "self-referent responses," and "self-disclosure" may in fact represent the same or similar interpersonal processes. However, since the reports of the studies surveyed rarely define the skills taught in their programs, accurate judgments of the equiva-lence of seemingly similar skills labels are not possible.

Conversely, when an identical skill label is reported in differ-ent studies, the definition employed may vary. As Matarazzo (1978) cautions, the most highly analyzed skill of all, empathy, "appar-

Table 5. Evaluation Design Used in Studies Surveyed.

Evaluation Design	Counseling	Medical	Social Work	Nonprofessional	Total
Experimental	27	9	5	25	66
Quasi-experimental	7	7	2	8	24
Preexperimental	13	19	5	14	51

ently is not a unitary variable" (p. 950). Thus, although empathy was taught in almost 40 percent of the programs, variance undoubtedly exists in the way this skill was defined and measured.

Evaluation design. Of all the studies surveyed, 47 percent employed an experimental research design (Campbell and Stanley, 1963) (see Table 5), with counseling and nonprofessional groups accounting for the majority of the experimental design investigations. Clearly, helper training can no longer be characterized as containing "a rarity of research and a plenitude of platitudes" (Rogers, 1957b, p. 76).

Despite the experimental nature of the research designs, skills training research has its limitations. Based on an extensive review of interpersonal skills training research, Marshall, Charping, and Bell (1979) note the need for investigations to establish outcome criteria that are operationally defined, measure interpersonal performance in actual helping situations, and use dependent measures that assess the appropriateness, frequency, and timing of skills usage. Another limitation is the small sample size of most studies. For instance, of the counseling studies with experimental designs, only 15 percent included at least twenty subjects per treatment group, with thirteen as the average experimental group size.

Retention of trained skills. Gormally and Hill (1974) lament that retention of skills, particularly long-term retention, has not been measured. As indicated in Table 6, the studies surveyed bear this out. Approximately one-fourth of the studies collected follow-up data; however, only 18 percent of the programs explicitly intended to measure retention of skills. Of the thirty-five studies that included follow-up measures, the retention measures in twenty-one

Table 6. Number of Surveyed Studies That Evaluate for Retention.

Retention Test Period	Counseling	Medical	Social Work	Nonprofessional	Total
Less than one month	5 (4)[a]	1		5 (3)	11 (7)
One to two months	2 (2)	6 (3)		2 (2)	10 (7)
Two to six months		1	2 (2)	1 (1)	4 (3)
Six to twelve months	3 (3)	1 (1)		2 (2)	6 (6)
Beyond twelve months	1 (1)	1 (1)		3 (1)	5 (3)
Not specified				2	2

[a]Numbers in parenthesis indicate those studies in which retention measurement was expressly stated as one of the research purposes.

studies were given within two months after training terminated, and only ten studies examined whether skills gains were retained beyond six months. Thus, in general, retention, especially long-term retention, of trained skills continues to be a neglected area of research.

Conclusion

Interpersonal skills training continues to be prominent in the fields of its origin, counseling and nonprofessional helping, and has been quickly assimilated into the fields of social work and medicine. Such training appears to be playing an ever-increasing role in training professional degree students and paraprofessionals in these fields, but, except in medicine, little attention has been directed to the training of professional practitioners.

Although the survey reveals various trends in skills training research, perhaps the most notable finding is the diversity in content and teaching mode; eclectic models seem to be growing in popularity. Many of the features of the newer models can be traced to their predecessors, yet, in many of the more recent studies, the models are marked by innovation and improvement. The unique needs of various helping groups and client populations account for some of these adaptations.

The significant studies of recent years indicate that those researchers who seek to advance the state of the science and art of interpersonal helping would do well to consider the following guidelines: (1) focus on questions of educational and practical significance; (2) incorporate research and evaluation into the instructional process to promote better linkage between research and educational practice; (3) investigate the role and effect of advanced-level helping skills and of methods for furthering their acquisition; (4) appraise the nature and extent of the impact on clients and practice outcomes of interpersonal helping skills; (5) determine more precisely the nature and extent of retention and of the generalization of learning; and (6) conduct inquiries that further understanding of the process by which knowledge, values, skills, and professional roles are integrated.

References

Allen, D. (Ed.). *Micro-Teaching: A Description.* Stanford, Calif.: Stanford Teachers Education Program, 1967.

Alssid, L. L., and Hutchison, W. R. "Comparison of Modeling Techniques in Counselor Training." *Counselor Education and Supervision,* 1977, *16,* 36–41.

Bertcher, H. J. *Group Participation: Techniques for Leaders and Members.* Beverly Hills, Calif.: Sage, 1979.

Berzon, B., and Reisel, J. *Effective Interpersonal Relationships.* La Jolla, Calif.: University Associates, 1976.

Blackwood, G. L., Jr. "Accurate Empathy: Critique of a Construct." Unpublished manuscript, Department of Psychology, Vanderbilt University, May 1975.

Boehm, W. "Social Work: Science and Art." *Social Service Review,* 1961, *35,* 144–151.

Bullmer, K. *The Art of Empathy: A Manual for Improving Accuracy of Interpersonal Perception.* New York: Human Sciences Press, 1975.

Burstein, B. *Guidance Formats for Modifying Interpersonal Communication.* Unpublished manuscript, University of California, Los Angeles, 1979.

Campbell, D. T., and Stanley, J. C. *Experimental and Quasi-Experimental Designs for Research.* Chicago: Rand McNally, 1963.

Carkhuff, R. R. *Helping and Human Relations.* Vols. 1 and 2. New York: Holt, Rinehart and Winston, 1969.

Carkhuff, R. R. "Principles of Social Action in Training for New Careers in Human Services." *Journal of Counseling Psychology,* 1971, *8* (2), 147–151.

Carkhuff, R. R. "A Human Technology for Group Helping Processes." *Educational Technology,* 1973, *13* (1), 31–38.

Carkhuff, R. R. Personal communication, October 1981.

Carkhuff, R. R., and Griffin, A. H. "The Selection and Training of Human Relations Specialists." *Journal of Counseling Psychology,* 1970, *17* (5), 443–450.

Carkhuff, R. R., and Griffin, A. H. "Selection and Training of Functional Professionals for Concentrated Employment Programs." *Journal of Clinical Psychology,* 1971, *27,* 163–165.

Chinsky, J. M., and Rappaport, J. "Brief Critique of the Meaning and Reliability of 'Accurate Empathy' Ratings." *Psychological Bulletin,* 1970, *73,* 379–382.

Danish, S., and Hauer, A. *Helping Skills: A Basic Training Program.* New York: Behavioral Publications, 1973.

Dyer, W. W., and Vriend, J. *Counseling Techniques That Work.* New York: Funk & Wagnalls, 1977.

Egan, G. *Interpersonal Living: A Skills/Contract Approach to Human Relations Training in Groups.* Monterey, Calif.: Brooks/Cole, 1976.

Egan, G. *The Skilled Helper.* (Rev. ed.) Monterey, Calif.: Brooks/Cole, 1982.

Evans, D. R., and others. *Essential Interviewing: A Programmed Approach to Effective Communication.* Monterey, Calif.: Brooks/Cole, 1979.

Gazda, G. M. *Human Relations Development: A Manual for Educators.* Boston: Allyn & Bacon, 1973.

Gazda, G. M., and others. *Human Relations Development: A Manual for Educators.* (2nd ed.) Boston: Allyn & Bacon, 1977.

Goldstein, A. P. *Structured Learning Therapy: Towards a Psychotherapy for the Poor.* New York: Academic Press, 1973.

Goldstein, A. P., and Goedhart, A. "The Use of Structured Learning for Empathy Enhancement in Paraprofessional Psychotherapist Training." *Journal of Community Psychology,* 1973, *1* (2), 168–173.

Goodman, G. *Sashatapes User's Manual.* Los Angeles: University of California, Los Angeles, Extension, 1978.

Gormally, J., and Hill, C. E. "Guidelines for Research on Cark-huff's Training Model." *Journal of Counseling Psychology*, 1974, *21*, 539–547.

Hackney, H., and Nye, S. *Counseling Strategies and Objectives.* Englewood Cliffs, N.J.: Prentice-Hall, 1973.

Hines, J. Personal communication. 1978.

Ivey, A. E. "Demystifying the Group Process: Adapting Microcounseling Procedures to Counseling in Groups." *Educational Technology*, 1973, *13* (2), 27–31.

Ivey, A. E., and Authier, J. *Microcounseling: Innovations in Interviewing, Counseling, Psychotherapy, and Psychoeducation.* Springfield, Ill.: Thomas, 1978.

Kagan, N. *Interpersonal Process Recall: A Method of Influencing Human Interaction.* (Rev. ed.) East Lansing, Mich.: Mason Media, 1975.

Kahn, G. S., Cohen, B., and Jason, H. "The Teaching of Interpersonal Skills in U.S. Medical Schools." *Journal of Medical Education*, 1979, *54*, 29–35.

Kounin, J. S., and others. "Experimental Studies of Clients' Reactions to Initial Interviews." *Human Relations*, 1956, *9*, 265–292.

Marshall, E. K., Charping, J. W., and Bell, W. J. "Interpersonal Skills Training: A Review of the Research." *Social Work Research and Abstracts*, 1979, *15*, 10–16.

Matarazzo, R. G. "Research on the Teaching and Learning of Psychotherapeutic Skills." In S. L. Garfield and A. E. Bergen (Eds.), *Handbook of Psychotherapy and Behavior Change.* New York: Wiley, 1978.

Milnes, J., and Bertcher, H. *Communicating Empathy.* San Diego, Calif.: University Associates, 1980.

Moreland, J. R., and Buck, J. N. "Basic Principles of Group Process and Group Facilitation." In V. A. Harren (Ed.), *Career Decision Making for College Students: Facilitators' Handbook.* Carbondale: Southern Illinois University, 1979.

Pedersen, P. "The Triad Model of Cross-Cultural Counselor Training." *Personnel and Guidance Journal*, 1975, *56*, 94–100.

Pedersen, P. "A Model for Training Mental Health Workers in Cross-Cultural Counseling." In J. Westermeyer and B. Maday

(Eds.), *Culture and Mental Health*. The Hague, Netherlands: Mouton, 1976.

Polansky, N. A., and Kounin, J. S. "Clients' Reactions to Initial Interviews: A Field Study." *Human Relations*, 1956, *9*, 237-264.

Rachman, S. J. "The Effects of Psychological Treatment." In H. Eysenck (Ed.), *Handbook of Abnormal Psychology*. New York: Basic Books, 1973.

Rogers, C. R. "The Necessary and Sufficient Conditions of Psychotherapeutic Personality Change." *Journal of Consulting Psychology*, 1957a, *21*, 95-103.

Rogers, C. R. "Training Individuals to Engage in the Therapeutic Process." In C. R. Strother (Ed.), *Psychology and Mental Health*. Washington, D.C.: American Psychological Association, 1957b.

Rogers, C. R. *On Becoming a Person*. Boston: Houghton Mifflin, 1961.

Schulman, E. "Intervention in Human Services." St. Louis, Mo.: Mosby, 1974.

Schwartz, E. K., and Abel, T. M. "The Professional Education of the Psychoanalytic Psychotherapists." *American Journal of Psychotherapy*, 1955, *9*, 253-261.

Shulman, L. *The Skills of Helping Individuals and Groups*. Itasca, Ill.: Peacock, 1979.

Stone, G. L., and Vance, A. "Instructions, Modeling, and Rehearsal: Implications for Training." *Journal of Counseling Psychology*, 1976, *23* (3), 272-279.

Strupp, H. H. "On the Basic Ingredients of Psychotherapy." *Psychotherapy and Psychosomatics*, 1974, *24*, 249-260.

Towles, C. "Roles of the Supervisor in the Union of Cause and Function in Social Work." *Social Service Review*, 1961, *35*, 144-151.

Truax, C. B., and Carkhuff, R. R. *Toward Effective Counseling and Psychotherapy*. Hawthorne, N.Y.: Aldine, 1967.

Truax, C. B., and Mitchell, K. M. "Research on Certain Therapist Interpersonal Skills in Relation to Process and Outcome." In A. E. Bergin and S. L. Garfield (Eds.), *Handbook of Psychotherapy and Behavior Change*. New York: Wiley, 1971.

Whitaker, C. A. "Teaching the Practicing Physician to Do Psychotherapy." *Southern Medical Journal*, 1949, *42*, 889-903.

Chapter 2

Relation of Helping Skills to Treatment Outcome

Michael J. Lambert

This chapter will review research into the effects of therapist interpersonal skills on client outcome. First, therapist relationship factors will be placed in context with other variables that affect outcome. Next, research on client-centered therapy will be reviewed, followed by a review of outcome studies undertaken by those who followed Rogers with their own models of interpersonal influence. Finally, some recommendations for future research will be made. The reader should be aware that the emphasis is on the remote, rather than the immediate, consequences of therapy—that is, on the results of outcome research and posttherapy adjustments, rather than on the in-therapy behavior of clients.

Patient, Therapist, and Technique Factors

That psychotherapy is more effective than no psychotherapy has been adequately demonstrated (Smith, Glass, and Miller, 1980;

Gomes-Schwartz, Hadley, and Strupp, 1978; Bergin and Lambert, 1978). However, despite numerous attempts to show the different effects of various forms of treatments, little evidence exists to correlate theory or technique with treatment outcome; hence, prescriptive psychotherapy remains, for the most part, a promise, rather than a reality.

A review of psychotherapy process and outcome literature strongly suggests that the most powerful predictors of outcome are not therapist or treatment variables but client variables. Among those traits seen as most important are ego strength, expectations, motivation for therapy, initial degree of disturbance, duration of symptoms prior to treatment, and diagnosis. The most severely disturbed, least-skillful, and most broadly impaired patients are less likely to profit from psychotherapeutic interventions than their healthier counterparts. In an earlier paper (Lambert, 1976), for example, obvious differences were noted between the spontaneous recovery rates of different diagnostic groups. Hypochondriasis is a disorder that persists for years with little improvement, whereas anxiety states and depressive illnesses tend to be transient disorders that may improve considerably with the passage of time.

Of course, a complex relationship exists between client variables and psychotherapy outcome, a relationship that depends on the type and source of outcome measures used and on the sample of patients included in a particular study. Although the results of studies correlating client variables with outcome have been inconsistent, certain relationships can be found that are reasonably predictive of later success. For example, there is considerable evidence that initial degree of disturbance is related to both positive and negative outcomes, but only when certain criteria (such as global ratings of improvement) and certain patient samples are studied. Nevertheless, those who are initially the least healthy are the least likely to profit from therapy and are probably the most likely to experience deteriorative consequences from psychotherapy (Lambert, Bergin, and Collins, 1977). Client variables are relatively powerful predictors of outcome.

After client variables, which are also confounded by and interact with environmental factors, most research evidence favors the importance of therapist experience and general relationship factors as predictors, if not causes, of outcome. Specific treatment methods are a distant third in accounting for the effects of psychotherapy. Although new techniques may be supported with great enthusiasm before empirical data are collected, such techniques often turn out to be a source of frustration, if not embarrassment (for example, compare the past and current status of Freudian treatment techniques, the promise of hypnosis, even behavioral techniques). The few exceptions to this general trend provide us with little support for the notion that certain psychotherapeutic procedures are uniquely effective.

A final area of recent interest has been the matching of therapist, client, and technique for optimal outcome. However, the assumption that the best match can be identified has yet to be supported with any reliable results or consistent data.

The preceding summary places the therapist's contribution to psychotherapy outcome into a perspective that seems consistent with empirical research. Figure 1, which graphically expresses the same perspective, is based on the author's review of psychotherapy outcome literature. The percentages portrayed are rough estimates derived from correlational data and controlled research. The error term reflects the primitive nature of current understanding of personality change. Increasing our understanding of the effective ingredients of psychotherapy could dramatically affect the percentages portrayed in this figure. As research is refined the error factor will decrease and the amount of outcome due to techniques or therapist factors may increase markedly.

In general, empirical research suggests that psychotherapies obtain similar results through different methods because they share certain common properties. For example, Marks (1978) has suggested that the similarity of success rates of diverse behavioral therapies with phobias can be attributed to the fact that these behavioral therapies all involve exposure of the patient to the feared object. Another property thought to be shared by different therapies is the therapeutic relationship or the atmosphere created by a skillful clinician. The remaining sections of this discussion will concern the nature and strength of the evidence supporting the importance of therapist relationship factors in facilitating positive and negative

Figure 1. The Relative Contribution of Client, Therapist, and Technique Variables to Psychotherapy Outcome.

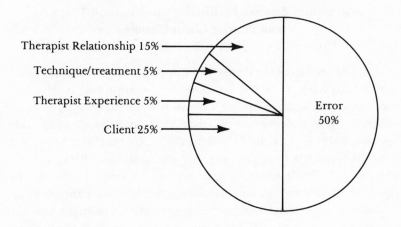

Therapist Relationship 15%

Technique/treatment 5%

Therapist Experience 5%

Client 25%

Error 50%

Client: Included here would be such variables as age, sex, socioeconomic level, IQ, marital status, diagnosis, motivation, ego strength, interaction with environmental factors, therapy readiness, degree of disturbance, and duration of symptoms prior to seeking treatment. Some of these are overlapping variables, but each considered separately interacts with treatment variables to produce outcome.

Therapist relationship variables: Includes such therapist-offered conditions as empathy, genuineness, warmth, and respect.

Therapist experience: Includes such unspecified variables as poise, confidence, good judgment, accurate expectations, personal maturity, and even relationship skills.

Technique and treatment variables: Includes specified procedures that are clearly delineated and distinguishable from other procedures. Included would be such diverse methods as assertive training, EMG feedback, gestalt therapy, and cognitive behavioral therapy. In general, it represents the conclusions drawn from comparative studies.

Error term: Represents unaccounted components of outcome such as measurement error (that is, since most outcome measures have reliabilities that do not exceed .80, 35 percent error could be due to this level of reliability).

Source: Lambert, (Reprinted with permission from Pergamon Press.) 1981.

changes in patient status. In particular, research on client-centered therapy and its derivatives will be explored.

Relationship Between Facilitative Conditions of Therapy and Positive Client Change

The impact of the theoretical formulations and clinical practice of Carl Rogers and his associates has been profound. Many of the constructs and techniques developed by Rogers have been adopted by a wide variety of therapy modalities (Jakubowski-Spector, 1973; Weiner, 1975; Yalom, 1975). Rogers (1959) has stated what he considers to be the necessary and sufficient therapist variables and client characteristics for positive outcome in therapy in much the same way as a mathematician might state theorems or postulates. In a less formal way, Rogers (1962) puts his general hypothesis as follows: "If I can provide a certain type of relationship, the other person will discover within himself the capacity to use that relationship for growth, and change and personal development will occur" (p. 33).

The earliest studies of psychotherapy outcome in client-centered therapy concerned changes in psychotherapy patients as a function of therapy as a whole. Cartwright's (1957) bibliography summarized these early, crude studies, which generally did not involve the specification of therapist behavior and its differential relation to outcome. Even the volume edited by Rogers and Dymond (1954) did not examine the interpersonal skills of therapists but concentrated on the overall effects of treatment. Since Rogers's (1957) specification of the "necessary and sufficient conditions" for personality change, research efforts have been marked by improved methodology and increasing precision in isolating and measuring presumably crucial therapist variables. These variables have generally been measured by interval rating scales with theoremlike definitions for each point on the scale. Several sets of scales have been developed that are similar in both construction and content, the most notable being those of Truax and Carkhuff (1967) and Carkhuff (1969). Generally, the scales attempt to measure the degree to which the following conditions are provided by the therapist in the helping relationship (for a more detailed discussion of these constructs, see Truax and Carkhuff, 1967).

- Accurate empathy (empathic understanding) is the degree to which the therapist is successful in communicating his awareness and understanding of the client's current feelings in language that is attuned to the client.
- Nonpossessive warmth (unconditional positive regard) is the extent to which the therapist communicates nonevaluative caring and positive regard for the client and respect for the client as a person.
- Genuineness (congruence) is the extent to which the therapist is nondefensive and "real" in his interactions with the client.

Soon after Rogers's original specification of these conditions, a study was undertaken to test emerging hypotheses about the importance of therapist attitudes or facilitative conditions. Halkides (1958) has often been quoted as providing evidence that the facilitative conditions offered by therapists are related to positive changes in clients. Halkides sampled interviews from twenty client-therapist pairs and had three judges rate the degree of unconditional positive regard, congruence, and empathic understanding. On the basis of criteria derived from several change measures, the client sample was divided into most- and least-successful cases. Highly significant associations between success and the relationship variables were found.

Rogers and his associates were enthusiastic about the possibilities suggested by this study, and the next fifteen years brought a proliferation of studies on these so-called interpersonal skills or facilitative conditions. The studies in Table 1, which has been reprinted from an earlier review of outcome research on therapist interpersonal skills (Lambert, DeJulio, and Stein, 1978), represent the best available answers to questions about the relationship between facilitative conditions and outcome. These studies have been included because they examined outcomes in actual patients who sought treatment in a wide variety of settings; used measures of symptomatic improvement, rather than in-therapy behavior; and included research designs with clear attention to internal validity.

Table 1. Relationship of Facilitative Conditions to Improvement in Psychotherapy Patients in Selected Outcome Studies.

Study	Therapist orientation (N)[a]	Client population (N)[b]	Source of outcome criteria[c]	Type and source of ratings of therapist facilitative conditions[d]
Barrett-Lennard (1962)	Client centered (21)	College counseling center clients (42)	Client and therapist	BRI,* T
Bergin and Jasper (1969)	Unspecified (36)	Outpatients (36)	Clinician	AE
Beutler and others (1972)	Unspecified (8)	Inpatients (54)	Therapist and other	AE
Beutler and others (1973)	Unspecified (8)	Inpatients (49)	Therapist	AE, NPW, G
Dickenson and Truax (1966)	Client centered (1)	Counseling center clients (24)	Other	AE,* UPR,* G*
Garfield and Bergin (1971)	Mixed (21)	Outpatients (38)	Client, therapist, and clinician	AE, NPW, G
Kurtz and Grummon (1972)	Mixed (31)	Counseling center clients (31)	Client, clinician, and therapist	Other, BRI,* AE*
Mitchell (Note 1)	Mixed (1)	Outpatients (120)	Client, therapist, clinician, and significant others	AE, NPW, G*
Mullen and Abeles (1971)	Mixed (36)	Counseling center clients (36)	Client	AE,* NPW
Rogers and others (1967)	Client centered (8)	Inpatients (16)	Therapist, client, clinician, and other	AE, NPW, G,* BRI
Sloane and others (1975)	Other (6)	Outpatients (30)	Therapist, client, clinician, and significant other	AE, NPW, G
Truax (1963)	Unspecified (—)	Inpatients (14)	Client and clinician	AE, UPR, G, Composite*
Truax (1966)	Unspecified (8)	Delinquent inpatients (69)	Client and other	AE, NPW,* G,* TRQ

Study				
Truax and others (1973)	Other (16)	Outpatients (16)	Client, therapist, significant others, and clinician	AE,* NPW,* G*
Truax, Carkhuff, and Kodman (1965)	Mixed (4)	Inpatients (40)	Client	AE,* UPR,* G*
Truax, Wargo, and Silber (1966)	Unspecified (2)	Delinquents (40)	Client and other	AE,* UPR,* G*
Truax and others (1966)	Unspecified (4)	Outpatients (40)	Client, therapist, and clinician	AE,* NPW,* G*
Truax, Wittmer, and Wargo (1971)	Mixed (15)	Inpatients (160)	Client and other	AE,* NPW, G, Composite*

[a]The therapist's theoretical orientation was classified as client-centered, mixed (when some of the therapists in a study were client-centered), other (which usually meant the therapists were eclectic or analytically oriented), or unspecified.

[b]Patients classified as outpatients were for the most part adult neurotics, whereas those classified as inpatients were hospitalized schizophrenics.

[c]Outcome measures were, for the most part, diverse but common standardized assessment devices. Those that were self-report devices filled out by the client included the Minnesota Multiphasic Personality Inventory, Q-Sort, and Tennessee Self-Concept Scale. Therapist measures included gross ratings of improvement and Target Symptom Complaints. Clinician ratings came from measures such as the Structured and Scaled Interview to Assess Maladjustment and the Psychiatric Status Schedule. Reports of change from significant others included ratings by parents and the Vineland Social Maturity Scale. The "other" category included criteria from diverse sources and involved such diverse indices of change as grade point average and time out of hospital.

[d]The process measures of facilitative conditions consisted of the rating scales devised by Truax or Carkhuff. Trained judges rated samples of therapy process, usually from audiotapes. These ratings are abbreviated as follows: AE = accurate empathy, NPW = nonpossessive warmth, and G = genuineness or congruence. The second most frequently used measures were filled out by the clients themselves and involved either the Truax Relationship Questionnaire (TRQ) or the Barrett-Lennard Relationship Inventory (BRI). Ratings of the quality of the relationship were occasionally made by the therapist (T) or by some other measurement method (Other), such as the Affective Sensitivity Scale.

*Indicates a statistically significant relationship between ratings of facilitative conditions and measures of therapy outcome. It should be noted that there were many nonsignificant correlations. Also, the statistically significant relationships that were found seldom accounted for much of the variance in client improvement.

Source: Lambert, DeJulio, and Stein (1978). Copyright 1978 by the American Psychological Association. Reprinted by permission of the author.

The generally well-designed and well-executed studies cited in Table 1 present only modest evidence in favor of the hypothesis that such factors as accurate empathy, warmth, and genuineness influence outcome, and indicate that other, unaccounted-for variables also contribute to changes in clients. In addition, this evidence does not reveal a cause-effect relationship between facilitative conditions and outcome. Also summarized in Table 1 are other variables that might add to our understanding of the relationship between facilitative conditions and outcome. Some authors suggested that differential effects would result when therapy was offered by therapists who had orientations other than client-centered. Others suggested that, with less disturbed clients, client perception measures of conditions would be better predictors of outcome than measures of empathy based on judgments of taped samples of the therapy process. Therefore, the variables summarized include the theoretical orientation and experience of the therapist, the degree of disturbance noted in clients, the nature and source of outcome data, and the type and source of process ratings. Some data were unobtainable—most notably, an accurate description of the experience level and theoretical orientation of the therapists.

Trends in the data do not support the idea that therapist interpersonal skills and therapy outcome interact with theoretical orientation, type of process measure, type of outcome measure, or patient diagnosis, even though research conducted by Truax and the initial studies tended to show more positive results.

The studies listed in Table 1 do not properly reflect the great enthusiasm generated by the writing, clinical work, and research of those interested in the client-centered hypothesis. The idea that patients were helped most by the quality of the therapist-patient relationship, rather than by the school, technique, or favorite theory of the professional, has had profound implications. Most important, perhaps, has been the possibility that people without professional credentials could provide treatments as beneficial as those provided by professional therapists. As a result, the theory and research of this group have had a remarkable impact on the philosophy and procedures used in a variety of professional and paraprofessional training programs (a topic that will be discussed later in this chapter).

In contrast to research conducted in the late 1960s and early 1970s, more recent research has been less supportive of the causal link between therapist attitudes and patient outcome. Mitchell (1973) has conducted the largest-scale outcome study to date of experienced, practicing psychotherapists. The author randomly chose therapists from across the country and rated segments of their taped interviews using the Carkhuff (1969) scales. Significant correlations between the outcome measures and facilitative conditions were expected but not found. However, two weaknesses should be mentioned that could account for the failure to find any significant relationship between warmth or empathy and outcome (genuineness was modestly related to outcome). The most serious problem was one of inadequate sampling, a limitation currently being studied by Mitchell himself. Facilitative conditions were not measured throughout therapy and therefore may not have accurately represented the therapist's level of responding during the therapy relationship. In fact, although therapy lasted from six months to two years, only five three-minute samples were drawn for each therapist-patient dyad. Furthermore, the ratings themselves were lower and more restricted in range than in other studies employing the same scales, a result that may well be a consequence of the sample of therapists studied—only 7 percent considered themselves Rogerian. Empathy and warmth may not be basic techniques or skills of many eclectic, psychoanalytic, and behavioral therapists; other variables may account for their effectiveness. Certainly, this result also raises questions about possible problems with the ratings themselves.

Sloane and others (1975), in a generally well-designed study with experienced therapists, compared behavioral therapists with psychoanalytically oriented psychotherapists in the treatment of a sample of neurotic patients. Among numerous significant and important findings, these authors examined, but found no significant relationship between, outcome and facilitative conditions. Again, these results may suggest that the scales are inappropriate for schools of therapy other than client-centered. (Interestingly, the behavioral therapists were, on the average, rated higher on Truax-Carkhuff facilitative conditions than the psychoanalytically oriented psychotherapists.)

In addition, ratings of the conditions were noticeably restricted in range, which would not only limit the size of the correlations but also raises questions about the rating procedure. As with
the Mitchell study, samples were taken from only a single interview,
not from all therapy sessions. Further, the sampling procedure was a
peculiar one wherein behavioral therapists' ratings were not
randomly selected but were taken when they were acting like psychotherapists, rather than when they were using behavioral techniques. Thus, the samples rated were not necessarily representative
of the level of facilitative conditions offered throughout the session.
Differences in therapeutic style obviously pose a dilemma for researchers interested in studying diverse therapies.

In addition, several recent studies have cast doubt on the notion that the therapist relationship variables are independent of
client behavior. For example, Lee and others (1979) examined the
differential impact of verbal and nonverbal reinforcement by a client
on counselor behavior. During a short interview, a client-actor reinforced the counselors' reflection-of-feeling statements with a verbal
or a combined verbal and nonverbal response. A control group of
counselors was offered verbal and nonverbal reinforcements as well,
but these were not contingent on counselor reflection-of-feeling
statements. Results showed that counselors who received verbal and
nonverbal reinforcement showed significant increases in their feeling statements, whereas counselors in the control group showed no
significant gains. Futhermore, verbal reinforcement alone was
found to be as potent as verbal-nonverbal reinforcement. The addition of certain key nonverbal behaviors to the client's behavioral
repertoire did not increase the number of feeling statements emitted
by the therapist.

Despite growing doubts about the importance of the client-
centered relationship variables, some recent studies still report positive associations between these variables and outcome. Valle (1981),
for example, assessed the level of interpersonal skills of alcoholism
counselors using the five-point Carkhuff scale. The 244 patients
were undergoing their first known inpatient treatment for alcoholism. Following random assignment to counselors rated high and
low on these skills, differential outcomes as assessed by relapse rates

over a two-year period tended to favor those treated by high-level counselors.

In addition to research that specifically tested the Rogerian hypotheses, a variety of related studies carried out in recent years have examined the Rogerian position without testing it in the traditional manner. Perhaps the best designed of these studies, undertaken at Vanderbilt University by Strupp and Hadley (1979), contrasted the relative contribution to outcome of technical therapist skills and so-called nonspecific relationship factors. Strupp and his colleagues examined the process and outcome of therapy offered by five analytically or experientially oriented psychotherapists to fifteen college students with high MMPI scores on Scales 2, 7, and 0, and compared these results with "therapy" offered by seven nonprofessional college professors to fifteen clients with similar disturbances. Outcomes for the two treatment groups were also contrasted with outcomes obtained by students assigned either to a minimal contact, wait list control group or to a so-called silent control group of students from the college population who had achieved MMPI profiles similar to those of the treatment subjects but who had not sought help for their problems. Change was measured by: the MMPI; patients', therapists', and clinicians' ratings of changes in target complaints; self-rated overall change; and experts' ratings on clinical scales of disturbance. Process analysis was done using the Vanderbilt Process Scale, a scale that measures such therapist dimensions as warmth and empathy.

Comparisons of amount of change among groups revealed that: no significant differences were apparent between groups on any of the six measures based on the patient's own perspective; therapist measures, which apply only to the two treated groups, showed no significant differences between the two groups; ratings made by the independent clinician did not differ significantly between the two treatment groups; and post hoc, pairwise comparisons showed that both treated groups were significantly more improved than the control groups on four of the six variables—on the remaining two variables, only the therapist group was significantly more improved than the controls. Analyses of process indicated that professional therapists (divided into analytically and experientially oriented groups) and alternative therapists behaved quite differently in therapy. Therapists with an analytic orientation tended to maintain distance between themselves and their patients; experiential therapists offered friendlier, more personal relationships; and alternative therapists were generally warm, supportive listeners who offered their patients specific suggestions about how they might change their lives. Therapist behavior that positively related to good outcome on all measures were: facilitating communication, maintaining a current time focus, and talking about the patient's own experiences and feelings.

Just as one can find support for the importance of relationship factors in the Vanderbilt study, even some of the literature on behavioral therapy suggests the importance of these variables. Morris and Suckerman (1974a, 1974b, 1975) and Wolowitz (1975), for example, show that therapist warmth is necessary for effecting positive change in behavioral desensitization. These studies demonstrate that, even with the correct application of a behavioral procedure in the treatment of a simple phobia, a therapist variable such as warmth may play a significant role in mediating change.

These and related studies provide additional support for the position that the relationship is central in the change process and that the teaching and training of relationship skills should be stressed in the education and training of psychotherapists. We turn our attention now to variants on the Rogerian theme, such as microcounseling and human relations training.

Effects of Human Relations Training, Microcounseling, and Other Models

The client-centered school can be credited with the active research interest in therapist attitudes that eventually led to the establishment of training programs teaching a variety of therapist facilitative attitudes and interpersonal skills. This research in turn resulted in increasing specification of the necessary and sufficient conditions for positive therapy outcome. The process of training raters to judge the level of empathy, warmth, congruence, and respect offered by therapists resulted in the application of these same training methods to student therapists themselves.

Truax and Carkhuff (1967) published influential research related to the facilitative conditions, outlined an experiential-didactic training program, and emphasized the importance of measuring changes in trainee skills subsequent to training. Ivey and others (1968) also outlined the use of related methods called microcounseling procedures. During the late 1960s, numerous similar methods were developed and applied in counselor education programs, graduate schools of social work and psychology, and medical schools. For example, in an attempt to analyze interviewing "errors," Matarazzo and her associates (1965) studied such content-free variables as length of utterance, reaction time, and frequency of interruptions. Danish and Hauer (1973), Egan (1975), Gazda and others (1977), Goodman (1972), and Kagan (1975, 1979), all presented interesting variations on the basic methods to be used in training effective counselors. In varying degrees, all these approaches emphasize the central role of the therapist and therapist behavior in mediating change and are characterized by a tendency toward increased specificity and clarity in training goals. Even teaching these facilitative interpersonal skills to those seeking therapy has been considered a preferable treatment method, an approach typified by the work of Robert Carkhuff and his associates.

Carkhuff (1972) argued that training in relationship skills has a powerful effect on the professional adequacy of all trainees. In addition, he suggested that his model for training has clearly demonstrated, positive effects on psychological adjustment and the total functioning of personality. In fact, he emphasized that trainee benefits, which apparently generalize to many life tasks (for example, school performance and work stability), are the most significant outcomes of training.

Since this 1972 report, an even broader variety of studies has been conducted on the impact of the human resources development (HRD) model. This impressive body of research has studied outcome in various types of helping relationships in different populations (teacher-student relationships, marital therapy, and therapy with delinquents, prison populations, chronic, institutionalized mental patients, and related populations) and has continued to emphasize skills deficiency and skills training. On the whole, these studies provide support for the importance of therapist interpersonal skills and suggest that these skills can be systematically taught and learned by the use of HRD programs. Carkhuff and his associates (1972) have shown that clients treated by therapists high in these skills have better posttherapy outcomes than clients treated by therapists rated low in these skills. Anthony (1979) also studied patients treated by therapists identified as high and low in HRD skills and found differential rates of success (including rates of employment) for these client groups.

In an earlier report, Lambert and DeJulio (1977) evaluated the empirical status of Carkhuff's human resource development model, identifying studies used by Carkhuff (1972) to support the effectiveness of interpersonal skills training. Evaluation of this research did not provide strong evidence for the therapeutic value of interpersonal skills training. Major objections to the research included failure to specify the precise nature of treatment; in some cases, failure to include comparative control groups; absence of measures of the training process and its benefit to helpees; questionable validity of dependent measures; and lack of broad generalization of gains made by helpers in the use of interpersonal skills.

In a subsequent article, Anthony and Drasgow (1978) provided a critique of the Lambert and DeJulio (1977) review. The interested reader may wish to study this series of articles, as well as the empirical research already cited in support of the effectiveness of the HRD model. Carkhuff and his associates have undertaken considerable research on the effects of HRD on client outcome, research that supports the idea that the quality of the relationship that develops between client and therapist influences positive personality change. However, the positive results of Carkhuff and his associates should not be accepted uncritically.

Among several other distinct approaches related to the work of Carkhuff and his associates, the approach of Ivey and his associates has been most notable. These professionals have developed extensive training strategies extending well beyond teaching the core conditions suggested by Rogers that teach attending skills, influencing skills, focusing skills, and so-called quality dimensions, such as high levels of concreteness, confrontation, and immediacy. Like Carkhuff, Ivey and his associates have suggested that the skills they teach can be a preferred mode of treatment for a wide variety of clients.

Their training methods involve both a technology and a conceptual framework that have generated a great deal of empirical research. Unlike Rogerian therapy, however, microcounseling does not stand as an independent theory of personality change but is rather a series of strategies for effectively teaching specific skills. Unfortunately, research in this area has not focused on psychotherapy outcome but has focused instead on the effects of microcounseling on trainees (Forsyth and Ivey, 1980). The few therapy outcome studies that have been published in this area have focused primarily on the immediate effects of therapist behaviors on patient in-therapy behavior, rather than on more remote consequences, such as improvement of symptoms.

Kasdorf and Gustafson (1978) have reviewed these studies and have found research suggesting that microtraining results in desirable in-therapy patient behaviors, such as active involvement in treatment, increased personal focus, and increased focus on feelings (Hearne, 1976; Welch, 1976). Unfortunately, Kasdorf and Gustafson (1978), in their literature review, did not find a single outcome study that reported correlations between in-therapy patient and therapist behavior and later patient outcome. Typical of research in this area was a study published by Moreland, Ivey, and Phillips (1973). Twenty-four second-year medical students were randomly assigned to one of two interview training groups. Twelve were taught microcounseling techniques that focused on attending behavior, open-ended questions, minimal encouragers skills, paraphrases, reflection of feelings, and summarization. The twelve control-group trainees were observed by faculty members and provided with feedback in a less focal and systematic format during six group training sessions. Dependent measures were derived from pretraining and posttraining interviews with patients at the hospital. Verbal behavior was then categorized and rated with the Attending Behavior Rating Scale (Ivey, 1971) and the Therapist Error Check List (Matarazzo and others, 1965). Results indicated that both groups of students improved in their skills. Those who received microcounseling improved significantly more on attending behaviors and reflection of feelings and made significantly fewer errors on the Therapist Error Check List. No patient outcome data were collected.

The tendency for research on interpersonal skills training models to be limited to in-therapy behavior is also apparent in the work of Danish and his colleagues. For example, Ehrlich, D'Augelli, and Danish (1979) studied the relationship between counselor verbalization, client in-therapy behavior, and client perception of counselors. This analogue study manipulated such therapist interventions as affective restatements, closed questions, open questions, and advice. As with most of the research in this area, the emphasis was more on the immediate effect of these therapist behaviors on client verbal pattern (for example, the use of self-references, the length of utterance, the use of affective words) than on actual outcome. The study was exemplary of research on the effects of therapist response styles but failed to show (or even test) whether or not the resulting client in-therapy behavior was related to any beneficial personality or behavioral change.

Kagan and his associates at Michigan State have taken a somewhat different tack from the Rogerian group. In an attempt to facilitate human interaction between clients and counselors, they developed a method of supervision and training termed interpersonal process recall (IPR). Since its inception in the early 1960s, IPR has been used with a variety of populations and has been applied for much broader purposes than training therapists. Like Rogers, Carkhuff, Ivey, and their associates, Kagan saw and pursued the possibility of affecting large numbers of people and entire communities. The components of this model have varied over time but usually involve defining effective interpersonal behavior (including empathy or affective sensitivity), reviewing videotaped interviews, identifying the interactional dynamic occurring in the helping relationship, receiving feedback from clients, and learning to use the relationship itself to understand the client in mutual recall sessions.

Kagan (1980) reports that several therapy outcome studies have found this model effective both in terms of in-therapy process and client benefits. This evidence, however, is limited to only three published studies, the results of which can hardly be taken as convincing evidence that IPR training affects client outcome.

One study that explored this issue compared the effects of interpersonal process recall (IPR) and traditional supervision on thirty-six counselors and thirty-six clients who were assigned randomly to groups using one or the other method (Kingdon, 1975). Six supervisors matched on relevant variables were assigned to either group randomly and trained in the respective technique. In the IPR sessions, videotaping of the counseling interview was followed by a client recall session in which the supervisor and client reviewed the session, with the client commenting on various points and the supervisor facilitating client recall of underlying thoughts and feelings, while the counselor-trainee observed from outside the room. After the third counseling session, a mutual recall session was conducted with all three participants, the primary purpose of which was to allow client and trainee to share previously unexpressed feelings and attitudes.

In the comparison group, audiotapes of counseling sessions were played during the supervisory hour. The supervisor focused on the counselor-client interaction and attempted to promote self-understanding and a greater appreciation for the dynamics of the interview. However, the client was not present during these discussions.

Dependent measures involved the Counselor Evaluation Inventory (Linden, Stone and Shertzer, 1965), the Observation Questionnaire (Gelso, 1972), the Counselor Evaluation Rating Scale (Myrick and Kelly, 1971), and ratings of self-exploration and empathy using the Carkhuff scales. The results suggested that the different techniques of supervision did not have differential effects on the development of counselor empathy, client satisfaction with counseling, supervisor ratings of counselor performance, or client inhibition. However, clients who were being seen by an IPR-supervised counselor did show increased self-exploration by the third counseling session. Thus, only slight support for the effectiveness of the IPR method emerged after three supervisory sessions, and even this conclusion is open to other plausible explanations. In addition, the emphasis of this and other studies was not on the measurement of client improvement.

On a more positive note, videotape replay and recall have been shown to be effective in facilitating both the communication and involvement of clients in group therapy, especially clients who were categorized as having low self-esteem or as being socially inactive. In a study conducted by Hartson and Kunce (1973), four groups were evaluated in three areas: self-introspection, self-disclosure, and adequate responding. Two of the groups, one consisting of YMCA volunteers and the other of university students from the testing and counseling services, participated in traditional T-group therapy. The remaining two groups, composed of samples from the same two populations, participated in group therapy with the aid of Kagan's (Kagan, Krathwohl, and Miller, 1963) IPR model.

The results showed that, whereas all four groups improved in the areas of communication and involvement, both IPR groups showed significantly greater improvement, particularly in self-disclosure and self-introspection. Data from three independent sources—subjects' test scores and audiotape and videotape ratings—support the premise that videotape replay and interpersonal process recall were useful techniques in facilitating specific changes. Although subjects in the traditional T-group had higher satisfaction scores, some also seemed to be made worse by the direct confrontation techniques used in this type of treatment. In addition, this study, like others conducted by the Kagan group, did not test the effect of IPR-trained counselors on client outcome, but dealt with the treatment hypothesis and process, rather than with outcome measures.

In addition to the interpersonal skills approaches that have evolved directly from client-centered theory, there has been considerable research on closely related methods. These methods, like those advocated by Carkhuff and his associates, have dealt mainly with the direct treatment of patients through training methods made popular by Ivey. Many of these approaches fall under the heading of social skills or assertiveness training (Twentyman and Zimmering, 1978). These methods have typically been applied either with mildly anxious college students or with schizophrenic in-patients. Dating problems and lack of assertiveness are typical target problems. Thus research on these training (treatment) approaches has been limited in scope. Nevertheless, this research seems to reinforce the conclusions that have been drawn from research on therapist training and the value of the training as treatment paradigm. Recent reviews of these methods have been published by Curran (1977) and Lambert (1982).

The observant reader will notice that when we start to discuss training as treatment, expand the interpersonal skills to more concrete behavioral concepts, and explore related procedures, we have moved a long way from the topic of central interest: Does the therapists' attitudes or relationship orientation positively affect patient outcome? We have moved from a humanistic existential theory and language system to a behavioral conceptualization and language system. We have moved from speaking of "effective moments" in therapy to analyzing highly systematic technical procedures.

Methodological and Conceptual Issues

A few central conceptual and methodological issues must be dealt with before the contribution of therapist attitudes and skills to outcome will be fully understood. As mentioned previously, Rogers has stressed an empathic attitude on the part of the therapist, an attitude well illustrated in his article, "Empathetic: An Unappreciated Way of Being" (Rogers, 1975). In addition, Rogers has recently emphasized the client's need to experience being understood as central to client-centered therapy and central to the therapeutic relationship, in general.

Despite the Rogerian emphasis on client-perceived empathy, Rogers and his coworkers (Rogers and others, 1967) employed ratings by objective judges, as well as measures of client perception of facilitative conditions. These researchers felt that judges naive to the purposes and design of the study could rate the process unobtrusively. On the other hand, some have felt that clients and therapists, as participants, are best able to judge the level of conditions present in their psychotherapy sessions. The question of who should evaluate therapists' warmth, empathy, and genuineness is a central issue in the study of therapy.

Several related issues are also important: What is the relationship between such diverse psychotherapy process measures as the Truax-type rating scales and the Barrett-Lennard Relationship Inventory? What is the relationship between these diverse process measures and therapeutic outcomes? Is there a tendency for a specific process measure to relate to a particular kind of outcome measure? Do these measurement strategies interact with variables related to the client (for example, type or severity of problem), therapist, or treatment modality?

Hill (1974) has reported the most thorough and exhaustive study of this phenomenon to date. She compared the perceptions of a single therapy session by clients, therapists, objective judges using rating scales, and judges who made frequency tabulations. Twenty-four therapists saw forty-eight clients and made audiotapes of the second session. Two judges rated the tapes (N = 144) for empathy and self-exploration. Each client and each therapist filled out a report on satisfaction and progress, including information on what he or she perceived as happening during the session. Many interrelationships were reported among the various measurements and points of view. Empathy as measured by the Carkhuff (1969) scale and rated by objective judges was found to correlate with the frequency count of therapists' empathic responding but was unrelated to the assessment of satisfaction and progress as judged by both clients and therapists.

In short, the four methods of evaluating what went on in the therapy sessions produced rather conflicting and confusing results. Hill (1974) has attempted to deal with this confusion, noting that each view of the therapy process takes into account different information and needs. For example, the client, who is not trained to look at the process of therapy session by session, probably sees it in its totality at the end of treatment and judges it as either good or bad. On the other hand, therapists are able to recall more accurately than clients what went on in each session but are generally less satisfied with the results. Perhaps this discrepancy is a function of therapist and client expectations. Tape-judged empathy ratings and observed frequency counts of empathic behavior were in close agreement but did not relate to perceptions of therapy from other points of view. Objective judges, whose expectations may differ from both clients' and therapists', evaluate the process from yet another point of view, as well as from a different vantage point—usually from audiotapes that exclude the therapist's nonverbal cues (cues that certainly affect the client's perception).

Elsewhere, Lambert, DeJulio, and Stein (1978) have analyzed studies that used diverse measures of therapist skills and psychotherapy outcome. These studies show quite clearly that a strong, consistent relationship does not exist among measures drawn from therapists, clients, and judges in regard to the level of facilitative conditions offered during psychotherapy. In addition, tape-judged measures of therapist interpersonal skills do not show a stronger relationship to outcome than client perception measures (Gurman, 1977; Luborsky and others, 1971; Parloff, Waskow, and Wolfe, 1978).

A recent attempt to explain the failure to obtain a stronger and more consistent relationship between different empathy measures and between empathy measures and outcome was undertaken by Barrett-Lennard (1981). In his view, the lack of consensus among traditional measures of empathy is to be expected on theoretical grounds, since empathy actually comprises at least three distinct phases: an internal, attentional-experiential set (a process occurring in the therapist); an observable attempt by the therapist to communicate this understanding; and the client's perception of the therapist. Thus, empathy can be viewed as a sequence of empathic resonation, expressed empathy, and received empathy. Different measurement methods vary in the degree to which they measure one or more of these phases of empathy and are therefore likely to provide discrepant views of the process.

This clarification of the empathic process may provide guidelines for improved research and training in empathy. However, it leaves unresolved the question of the influence of empathy on outcome and probably implies that the only theoretically consistent measures of empathy will be based on patient perception of the process. Unfortunately, research designs that include patient perceptions of both the process and outcome of therapy fail to meet rigorous scientific standards because they confound the rating source with actual change. High correlations could be due to an underlying factor, such as client hostility or optimism. When client perception measures of empathy are employed by researchers, the most convincing evidence of improvement will be provided by measures of outcome that do not also rely on patient self-report data.

Conclusion

Practicing clinicians from a variety of disciplines and diverse theoretical positions generally accept the importance, if not the central role, of therapist relationship factors in psychotherapy outcome. Scientific analysis of the role of these factors, however, has provided only modest corroboration for this view. Contrary to frequent claims for the efficacy of these facilitative conditions, experimental evidence suggests that neither a clear test nor unequivocal support for the Rogerian hypothesis has emerged. For example, although patients of therapists who have poor interpersonal skills or are rated as being deficient in facilitative attitudes are sometimes made worse by therapy, they also show improvement on some occasions.

A major problem with the models that have followed and modified the Rogerian position is their lack of interest in connecting innovative training in interpersonal skills with improvement in client functioning. A partial exception to this rule has been the research of Carkhuff and his associates; research on this model has shown that clients of the widest diversity profit from exposure to therapists who have been trained in interpersonal skills.

The greatest need at this time is for a model of interpersonal influence that specifies more clearly the relationship between therapist activity, patient response, and patient outcome. More testing is needed to discover when in therapy such qualities as warmth, empathy, and self-disclosure are most and least helpful. This research will be facilitated in turn by a clearer understanding of the types of client change that can be expected and accurately measured. The current models of interpersonal skills lend themselves well to empirical research—they are precise, well organized, time-limited, and highly manageable in experimental designs. Such models have also made it apparent that systematic training in these skills is more effective than nonsystematic training. However, the relative contribution of interpersonal skills and facilitative attitudes to therapy outcome needs to be more carefully explored.

References

Anthony, W. A. "A Skills Training Approach in Psychiatric Rehabilitation." Unpublished manuscript, Boston University, 1979.

Anthony, W. A., and Drasgow, J. "A Human Technology for Human Resource Development." *Counseling Psychologist*, 1978, 7, 58–65.

Barrett-Lennard, G. T. "The Empathy Cycle: Refinement of a Nuclear Concept." *Journal of Counseling Psychology*, 1981, 28, 91–100.

Bergin, A. E., and Lambert, M. J. "The Evaluation of Therapeutic Outcome." In S. L. Garfield and A. E. Bergin (Eds.), *Handbook of Psychotherapy and Behavior Change*. (2nd ed.) New York: Wiley, 1978.

Carkhuff, R. R. *Helping and Human Relations: A Primer for Lay and Professional Helpers*. 2 Vols. New York: Holt, Rinehart and Winston, 1969.

Carkhuff, R. R. "Rejoinder: What's It All About Anyway? Some Reflections on Helping and Human Resource Development Models." *Counseling Psychologist*, 1972, 3, 79–87.

Cartwright, D. S. "Annotated Bibliography of Research and Theory Construction in Client-Centered Therapy." *Journal of Counseling Psychology*, 1957, 4, 82–100.

Curran, J. "Skills Training as an Approach to Treatment of Heterosexual-Social Anxiety: A Review." *Psychological Bulletin*, 1977, 84, 140–157.

Danish, S. J., and Hauer, A. *Helping Skills: A Basic Training Program*. New York: Behavioral Publications, 1973.

Egan, G. *The Skilled Helper*. Monterey, Calif.: Brooks/Cole, 1975.

Ehrlich, R. P., D'Augelli, A. R., and Danish, S. J. "Comparative Effectiveness of Six Counselor Verbal Responses." *Journal of Counseling Psychology*, 1979, 26 (5), 390–398.

Forsyth, D. R., and Ivey, A. E. "Microtraining: An Approach to Differential Supervision." In A. K. Hess (Ed.), *Psychotherapy Supervision: Theory, Research, and Practice*. New York: Wiley, 1980.

Gazda, G. M., and others. *Human Relations Development*. Boston: Allyn & Bacon, 1977.

Gelso, C. J. "Inhibition Due to Recording and Client's Evaluation of Counseling." *Psychological Reports*, 1972, 31, 675–677.

Gomes-Schwartz, B., Hadley, S. W., and Strupp, H. H. "Individual Psychotherapy and Behavior Psychotherapy." *Annual Review of Psychology*, 1978, 29, 435–471.

Goodman, G. *Companionship Therapy: Studies in Structured Intimacy.* San Francisco: Jossey-Bass, 1972.

Gurman, A. S. "The Patient's Perception of the Therapeutic Relationship." In A. S. Gurman and A. M. Razin (Eds.), *Effective Psychotherapy.* Elmsford, N.Y.: Pergamon Press, 1977.

Halkides, G. *An Investigation of Therapeutic Success as a Function of Four Variables.* Unpublished doctoral dissertation, Department of Psychology, University of Chicago, 1958.

Hartson, D. J., and Kunce, J. T. "Videotape Replay and Recall in Group Work." *Journal of Counseling Psychology,* 1973, *20* (5), 437–441.

Hearn, M. "Three Modes of Training Counsellors: A Comparative Study." Unpublished doctoral dissertation, University of Western Ontario, 1976.

Hill, C. E. "A Comparison of the Perceptions of a Therapy Session by Clients, Therapists, and Objective Judges." *JSAS Catalog of Selected Documents in Psychology,* 1974, *4,* 16.

Ivey, A. E. *Microcounseling: Innovations in Interviewing Training.* Springfield, Ill.: Thomas, 1971.

Ivey, A. E., and others. "Microcounseling and Attending Behavior: An Approach to Prepracticum Counselor Training." *Journal of Counseling Psychology, Monograph Supplement,* 1968, *15* (5), 1–12.

Jakubowski-Spector, P. "Facilitating the Growth of Women Through Assertive Training." *Counseling Psychologist,* 1973, *4,* 75–86.

Kagan, N. *Influencing Human Interaction.* Washington, D.C.: American Personnel and Guidance Association, 1975.

Kagan, N. *Influencing Human Interaction—Fifteen Years with IPR.* Unpublished manuscript, Department of Psychology, Michigan State University, 1979.

Kagan, N. "Influencing Human Interaction—Eighteen Years with IPR." In A. K. Hess (Ed.), *Psychotherapy Supervision: Theory, Research, and Practice.* New York: Wiley, 1980.

Kagan, N., Krathwohl, D. R., and Miller, R. "Stimulating Recall in Therapy Using Videotape—A Case Study." *Journal of Counseling Psychology,* 1963, *10,* 237–243.

Kasdorf, J., and Gustafson, K. "Outcome Research in Microcounseling." In A. E. Ivey and J. Authier (Eds.), *Microcounseling:*

Innovations in Interviewing, Counseling, Psychotherapy, and Psychoeducation. Springfield, Ill.: Thomas, 1978.

Kingdon, M. A. "A Cost/Benefit Analysis of the Interpersonal Process Recall Technique." *Journal of Counseling Psychology*, 1975, *22*, 353-357.

Lambert, M. J. "Spontaneous Remission in Adult Neurotic Disorders: A Revision and Summary." *Psychological Bulletin*, 1976, *83*, 107-119.

Lambert, M. J. "Evaluating Outcome Variables in Cross-Cultural Counseling and Psychotherapy." In A. J. Marsella and P. B. Pedersen (Eds.), *Cross-Cultural Counseling and Psychotherapy*. Elmsford, N.Y.: Pergamon Press, 1981.

Lambert, M. J. *The Effects of Psychotherapy*. Vol. 2. New York: Human Sciences Press, 1982.

Lambert, M. J., Bergin, A. E., and Collins, J. L. "Therapist-Induced Deterioration in Psychotherapy." In A. S. Gurman and A. S. Razin (Eds.), *Effective Psychotherapy: The Therapists Contribution*. Elmsford, N.Y.: Pergamon Press, 1977.

Lambert, M. J., and DeJulio, S. S. "Outcome Research in Carkhuff's Human Resource Development Training Programs: Where is the Donut?" *Counseling Psychologst*, 1977, *6*, 79-86.

Lambert, M. J., DeJulio, S. S., and Stein, D. M. "Therapist Interpersonal Skills: Process, Outcome, Methodological Considerations, and Recommendations for Future Research." *Psychological Bulletin*, 1978, *85*, 467-489.

Lee, D. Y., and others. "Client Verbal and Nonverbal Reinforcement of Counselor Behavior: Its Impact on Interviewing Behavior and Postinterview Evaluation." *Journal of Counseling Psychology*, 1979, *26*, 204-209.

Linden, J. D., Stone, S. C., and Shertzer, B. "Development and Evaluation of an Inventory for Rating Counseling." *Personnel and Guidance Journal*, 1965, *44*, 267-276.

Luborsky, L., and others. "Factors Influencing the Outcome of Psychotherapy." *Psychological Bulletin*, 1971, *75*, 145-185.

Marks, I. "Behavioral Psychotherapy of Adult Neurosis." In S. L. Garfield and A. E. Bergin (Eds.), *Handbook of Psychotherapy and Behavior Change*. New York: Wiley, 1978.

Matarazzo, R. G., and others. "Learning the Art of Interviewing: A Study of What Beginning Students Do and Their Pattern of

Change." *Psychotherapy: Theory, Research, and Practice*, 1965, 2, 49–60.

Mitchell, K. M. "Effective Therapist Interpersonal Skills: The Search Goes On." Address presented by Department of Psychology, at Michigan State University, 1973.

Moreland, J. R., Ivey, A. E., and Phillips, J. S. "An Evaluation of Microcounseling as an Interviewer Training Tool." *Journal of Consulting and Clinical Psychology*, 1973, *41*, 294–300.

Morris, R. J., and Suckerman, K. R. "The Importance of the Therapeutic Relationship in Systematic Desensitization." *Journal of Consulting and Clinical Psychology*, 1974a, *42*, 148.

Morris, R. J., and Suckerman, K. R. "Therapist Warmth as a Factor in Automated Systematic Desensitization." *Journal of Consulting and Clinical Psychology*, 1974b, *42*, 214–250.

Morris, R. J., and Suckerman, K. R. "Morris and Suckerman Reply." *Journal of Consulting and Clinical Psychology*, 1975, *43* (4), 585–586.

Myrick, R. D., and Kelly, F. D. "A Scale for Evaluating Practicum Students in Counseling and Supervision." *Counselor Education and Supervision*, 1971, *10*, 330–336.

Parloff, M. B., Waskow, I. E., and Wolfe, B. E. "Research on Therapist Variables in Relation to Process and Outcome." In S. L. Garfield and A. E. Bergin (Eds.), *Handbook of Psychotherapy and Behavior Change*. (2nd ed.) New York: Wiley, 1978.

Rogers, C. R. "A Theory of Therapy, Personality, and Interpersonal Relationships, As Developed in the Client-Centered Framework." In S. Koch (Ed.), *Psychology: A Study of a Science*. Vol. 3: *Formulations of the Person and the Social Context*. New York: McGraw-Hill, 1959.

Rogers, C. R. "The Interpersonal Relationship: The Core of Guidance." *Harvard Educational Review*, 1962, *32*, 416-429.

Rogers, C. R. "Empathetic: An Unappreciated Way of Being." *Counseling Psychologist*, 1975, *5*, 2-10.

Rogers, C. R., and Dymond, D. F. *Psychotherapy and Personality Change*. Chicago: University of Chicago Press, 1954.

Rogers, C. R., and others. *The Therapeutic Relationship and Its Impact: A Study of Psychotherapy and Schizophrenics*. Madison: University of Wisconsin Press, 1967.

Sloane, R. B., and others. *Psychotherapy Versus Behavior Therapy.* Cambridge, Mass.: Harvard University Press, 1975.

Smith, M. L., Glass, G. V., and Miller, T. I. *The Benefits of Psychotherapy.* Baltimore, Md.: Johns Hopkins University Press, 1980.

Strupp, H. H., and Hadley, S. W. "Specific Versus Nonspecific Factors in Psychotherapy: A Controlled Study of Outcome." *Archives of General Psychiatry,* 1979, *36,* 1125–1136.

Truax, C. B., and Carkhuff, R. R. *Toward Effective Counseling and Psychotherapy: Training and Practice.* Hawthorne, N. Y.: Aldine, 1967.

Twentyman, C. T., Jenson, M., and Kloss, J. "Social Skills Training for the Complex Offender: Employment-Seeking Skills." *Journal of Clinical Psychology,* 1978, *34,* 320–325.

Twentyman, C. T., and Zimmering, R. T. "Behavioral Training of Social Skills: A Critical Review." In M. Hersen, R. M. Eisler, and P. M. Miller (Eds.), *Progress in Behavior Modification.* Vol. 7. New York: Academic Press, 1979.

Valle, S. R. "Alcoholism Counselor Interpersonal Functioning and Patient Outcome." *Journal of Alcohol Studies,* 1981, *42,* 206–210.

Weiner, I. B. *Principles of Psychotherapy.* New York: Wiley, 1975.

Welch, C. *Counsellor Training in Interviewing Skills: Interpersonal Process Recall in a Microcounseling Model.* Unpublished doctoral dissertation, Department of Education, McGill University, 1976.

Wolowitz, H. M. "Therapist Warmth: Necessary or Sufficient Conditions in Behavioral Desensitization?" *Journal of Consulting and Clinical Psychology,* 1975, *42,* 584.

Yalom, I. D. *The Theory and Practice of Group Psychotherapy.* (2nd ed.) New York: Basic Books, 1975.

Part Two

======

Skills Training Models

The first section of this book traced the evolution of skills training practice since its inception. Amidst the diverse training methods and techniques in use today, several major models of interpersonal skills development have emerged. Heretofore, discussion of the distinctive features of these models has been scarce and has varied greatly in thoroughness and detail (Ivey and Authier, 1978; Weinrach, 1977; Danish and Brock, 1974; Waters and others, 1976). Although many books, monographs, and articles can be found describing each of these models, no central reference brings them together in a way that makes it easy for readers to discern their similarities and differences. The chapters in this section are organized to make possible such meaningful comparisons. Readers are afforded a unique perspective on the commonalities and differences in focus, origins, underlying theory, and empirical base of each system of training and can see the variance in component skills and training methods and techniques. Discussion of the models also highlights the diverse applications of skills training to a wide range of helping professions.

In Chapter Three, Anthony and Vitalo present the human resources development model, often referred to as systematic human relations training (SHRT), the forerunner of the major models of skills training. The extensive empirical base is detailed, along with the evolution of the responsive (empathy, respect, and concreteness) and initiative (genuineness, self-disclosure, confrontation, and im-

55

mediacy) dimensions considered central to all effective interpersonal helping processes. Through a highly systematic approach to training, helpers are taught the skills of attending, responding, personalizing, and initiating necessary to implement the exploration, understanding, and action phases of helping. Key instructional methods and training aids integral to SHRT are highlighted, as are its many applications for training various groups of professional and paraprofessional helpers.

Using combinations of didactic instruction, videotaped modeling, behavioral practice, self-observation, and focused feedback methods, the microtraining model, which appeared shortly after the development of SHRT, has demonstrated its adaptability for training a wide range of professional and paraprofessional helpers. Distinguished by its emphasis on systematically teaching individual skills, the model has most commonly been applied to teaching mixtures of attending skills (including nonverbal attending, minimal encouragement, verbal following, questioning, reflection of feelings, paraphrasing, and summarization) and influence skills (including directions, expression of content, expression of feelings, interpretation, self-disclosure, and direct mutual communication.) In Chapter Four, Authier and Gustafson present the history, component skills, training methods, and research base of the microtraining approach. Two significant extensions of the model are discussed in detail—enriching intimacy, a relationship enhancement program for professionals, paraprofessionals, and lay persons; and step group therapy, a program for teaching basic communication skills to psychiatric inpatients.

Whereas microtraining develops specific skills without emphasis on the theoretical context of their application, Egan teaches interpersonal skills within a problem-solving model of helping. In Chapter Five, he presents a problem-solving framework for therapy that illuminates the interpersonal skills essential to helping clients define presenting problems, explore alternative solutions, and specify relevant courses of action. Egan outlines his unique training program, which systematically teaches trainees the skills of problem solving through instructional methods that include cognitive input, skills modeling, practice, feedback, and homework assignments.

In addition to acquiring a basic repertoire of communication skills, effective helpers must develop sensitivity to the complex interpersonal dynamics encountered in the helping process and become skillful in responding to affective communication. Interpersonal process recall (IPR) was the first of the major skills training models to concern itself not only with teaching the elements of effective communication but also with developing high levels of helper self-understanding and competence in dealing with human emotion. In Chapter Six, McQuellon reviews the evolution, underlying theory, and key instructional methods of this model and then explores the unique inquiry and recall techniques used to illuminate the important cognitive and affective dynamics that occur in the helping relationship. Research conducted on the model is reviewed, and applications of IPR to therapy and training are discussed.

Structured learning training (SLT) is an interpersonal training procedure applicable both to training helpers and to treating clients. Like microtraining, SLT focuses on single skills; emphasis is on tailoring training programs to the unique needs of the population being trained. Programs focus on ameliorating skills deficits through highly systematic skills training processes that typically include modeling, role playing, corrective feedback and social reinforcement, and transfer training procedures. In Chapter Seven, Lopez reviews the extensive research underlying the model, discusses major features of the approach, and provides a detailed example of a structured learning program.

Despite the advances in skills training models and methods, sufficient attention has not been given to the role of cultural factors in the skills learning and application process. In Chapter Eight, Pedersen discusses the effect of cultural factors on the helping process and highlights some of the important cultural issues in the application of the training models presented in this volume. He then presents his cross-cultural triad training model, a unique training system oriented to developing more culturally aware and sensitive helpers. Following discussion of training methods and evaluation results, Pedersen provides two triad model training designs, along with examples of the model's application.

References

Danish, S. J., and Brock, G. W. "The Current Status of Paraprofessional Training." *Personnel and Guidance Journal,* 1974, *53* (4), 299–303.

Ivey, A. E., and Authier, J. *Microcounseling: Innovations in Interviewing, Counseling, Psychotherapy and Psychoeducation.* Springfield, Ill.: Thomas, 1978.

Waters, E., Fink, S., Goodman, J., and Parker, G. "Strategies for Training Adult Counselors." *Counseling Psychologist,* 1976, *6* (1), 61–65.

Weinrach, S. G. "Training Packages." *Personnel and Guidance Journal,* 1977, *55* (10), 612–618.

Chapter 3

<hr>

Human Resource Development Model

William A. Anthony
Raphael L. Vitalo

In 1963, Robert Carkhuff went to work with Carl Rogers and his Psychotherapy Research Group at the Wisconsin Psychiatric Institute, University of Wisconsin. In less than six months, Carkhuff, in conjunction with Charles Truax, had instituted systematic, step-by-step interpersonal skills training programs for both professional and lay helpers (Carkhuff and Truax, 1965a, 1965b; Truax and Carkhuff, 1967). Carkhuff used straightforward educator's logic: If we can identify and measure the effective ingredients of helping, we can teach those ingredients to prospective helpers.

The early interpersonal training was, to be sure, less systematic and less effective than its later counterpart—for example, the interchangeable response had not yet been formulated. The early training did, however, cover empathy; unconditional positive regard, or nonpossessive warmth; and congruence, or genuineness. The later training emphasized the helper's accurate empathic responses to the helpee's experience and the effective initiative that flows from this responsiveness. In this chapter, we will explore the research base of the human resources development (HRD) model, the evolution of the helping dimensions, the characteristics and applications of the helping skills themselves, and training procedures and techniques.

Research Base

In the early 1960s the helping professions were challenged by numerous studies indicating that counseling and psychotherapy did not make a difference (Eysenck, 1960, 1965; Levitt, 1963; Lewis, 1965). For example, both adults and children in control groups not assigned to professional practitioners were found to gain as much, on the average, as people assigned to professional counselors and therapists. In hospital studies, about two-thirds of the patients improved and remained out of the hospital for a year after treatment whether or not they had received treatment. Similarly, in a recent review of outcome studies of more than fifty treatment settings, Anthony (Anthony and others, 1972, 1978) studied the lasting effects of counseling, rehabilitation, and psychotherapeutic techniques and found that, within three to five years after treatment, 65 to 75 percent of the expatients had become patients again and that, regardless of the follow-up period, the gainful employment of expatients was less than 25 percent.

The major conclusion that might be drawn from these data is that counseling and psychotherapy, as traditionally practiced, are effective in no more than 20 percent of the cases. (Of the two-thirds of the clients and patients who eventually get better, only one-quarter to one-third stayed better, implying that psychotherapy has lasting positive effects in roughly one-fifth of the cases.) To answer these challenges, naturalistic studies of helping were undertaken that led to predictive studies and, in turn, to the generalization and extension of an effective helping skills model.

Naturalistic Studies. Studies of the natural variability of professionally treated clients and patients indicates that they demonstrate a greater range of effects than clients and patients not treated by professionals (Rogers and others, 1967; Truax and Carkhuff, 1967). In other words, some professionally treated clients got significantly better, and some got significantly worse. These findings were both consoling and distressing; counseling and psychotherapy really did have an impact, but that impact could be either helpful or harmful (Bergin and Garfield, 1971).

Furthermore, these studies indicated that one could account, at least in part, for the helpful, neutral, and harmful effects by determining the helpers' levels of functioning in certain interpersonal dimensions—for example, empathy, or empathic understanding. Counselors and therapists who offered high levels of these core interpersonal dimensions facilitated the improvement of their clients on a variety of outcome measures. Clients of helpers offering low levels of empathy stayed the same or became worse (Rogers and others, 1967; Truax and Carkhuff, 1967).

These early naturalistic studies have been replicated in part by other researchers. For example, Bozarth and Rubin (1975), after evaluating audio recordings of the interviews of 160 rehabilitation counselors and 1,000 clients in twelve states, arrived at the following conclusion: "The higher levels of the interpersonal skills, even though only falling on the operational scale definition of minimally facilitative, tended to be related to higher vocational gain at closure, higher monthly earnings at follow-up, positive psychological change ten months or more following intake, and greater job satisfaction at follow-up" (p. 296).

Valle (1981) had similar results in studying the counseling of alcoholics. The level of interpersonal skills of alcoholism counselors was assessed using the Carkhuff Five-Point Rating Scales for empathy, respect, genuineness, and concreteness. The subjects of the study were 244 patients admitted for the first time to an inpatient, hospital-based treatment facility and randomly assigned to counselors rated at different levels of interpersonal skills. Results indicated that the higher the level of interpersonal skills of the counselors, the fewer the times a patient relapsed six, twelve, eighteen and twenty-four months after treatment, the fewer the relapse days, and the less these days cost for follow-up periods of six, twelve, eighteen and twenty-four months.

Predictive Studies. Following these early naturalistic studies, a number of predictive validity studies were conducted, in which the levels of the helper's functioning on interpersonal dimensions like empathy were manipulated, and the effects of these manipulations on the helping process and helping outcomes were measured. In general, the behavior of clients and patients within the helping process changed according to the helpers' level of functioning: when helpers offered high levels of interpersonal dimensions like empathy, helpees explored their problems in meaningful ways; when helpers offered low levels of interpersonal skills, helpees did not explore their problems in meaningful ways (Carkhuff and Alexik, 1967; Holder, Carkhuff, and Berenson, 1967; Piaget, Carkhuff, and Berenson, 1968; Truax and Carkhuff, 1967). Further, studies of helping outcomes found that, in general, helpees whose helpers functioned at high levels of interpersonal dimensions moved toward higher levels of functioning, and helpees whose helpers functioned at low levels of interpersonal dimensions moved toward lower levels of functioning (Pagell, Carkhuff, and Berenson, 1967).

Generalization Studies. The next series of studies sought to generalize the effects of these interpersonal dimensions to other helping and human relationships. The first effort was to study the effects of teachers' levels of interpersonal functioning on learners' development. In one study of student achievement, documented in the book, *Kids Don't Learn From People They Don't Like,* Aspy and Roebuck (1977) divided teachers into high and low levels of interpersonal functioning and found significant relationships between those levels and such student achievement indices as word meaning, paragraph meaning, spelling, word study skills, and language. In a number of subsequent studies conducted to assess the relationship of interpersonal dimensions to a variety of other student outcome indices, the students of teachers offering high levels of these interpersonal dimensions demonstrated significant, constructive gains in emotional, interpersonal and intellectual functioning (Aspy and Roebuck, 1972, 1977).

In further studies, these effects have been generalized in all areas of helping and human relationships where the "more-knowing" person influences the "less-knowing" person: parent-child relationships (Carkhuff, 1971a; Carkhuff and Pierce, 1976); teacher-student relationships (Aspy and Roebuck, 1977; Carkhuff, 1969); counselor-client relationships (Berenson and Carkhuff, 1967); and therapist-patient relationships (Anthony, 1979; Rogers and others, 1967; Truax and Carkhuff, 1967). For example, in the area of counselor supervision, studies directed by Pierce (Pierce, Carkhuff, and Berenson, 1967; Pierce and Schauble, 1970; 1971) found that counseling interns who had supervisors functioning at high levels of empathy, regard, and concreteness changed positively in these dimensions in the course of supervision, whereas interns who had supervisors functioning at low levels of these dimensions did not change over the course of supervison. Similar results were found at follow-up.

In general, "less-knowing" persons will move toward the levels of functioning of "more-knowing" persons over time, depending on both the extensiveness and intensity of contacts: helpees of high-level functioning helpers improve on a variety of process and outcome indices; helpees of low-level functioning helpers become worse.

Extension Studies. Finally, a number of studies were conducted that extended the relevance of those dimensions to other helping tasks. For example, Vitalo (1970) found that the effects of behavior modification programs were contingent in part on the modifiers' levels of interpersonal functioning. And Mickelson and Stevic (1971) found that the success of career information seeking was dependent on the helpers' levels of interpersonal functioning, as well as on the effectiveness of the reinforcement programs. In general, those helpers who functioned at the highest levels and had the most systematic helping programs were most effective.

Simultaneously, the core interpersonal dimensions studied were gradually extended and then factored into responsive and initiative dimensions (Berenson and Mitchell, 1974; Carkhuff, 1969): responsive dimensions respond to the helpee's experience; initiative dimensions, while taking into consideration the helpee's experience, are generated from the helper's experience. In addition, a number of systematic helping programs were developed to extend the helpers' initiative activities and therefore their effectiveness with helpees (Carkhuff, 1969, 1971a).

In summary, certain helping dimensions appearing naturally in a limited number of helpers were found in predictive studies to be related to both helping process and outcome. In addition, the effectiveness of these helping dimensions was generalized to all helping and human relationships. Finally, these dimensions were extended to equip the helpers with more of the ingredients they needed to help others effectively. These ingredients of helping have been widely accepted as fundamental by the professional literature

(Brammer, 1979; Combs, Avila, and Purkey, 1978; Danish and Hauer, 1973; Egan, 1975; Gazda, 1973; Gordon, 1975; Hackney and Cormier, 1979; Johnson, 1972; Okun, 1976; Patterson, 1973).

Evolution of the Dimensions

Over a period of time, the core dimensions of helping have evolved and been extended in an ongoing effort to account for helping effectiveness. What began as a crude definition of the dimension of empathy has evolved into an extensive equation for human resources development. In order to understand these dimensions, we must understand four factors: the sources of the helping dimensions; the helping process that these dimensions influence; the helper skills that actualize these dimensions; and the helpee outcomes these dimensions are intended to achieve.

Helping Sources. There are two fundamental approaches to helping: the insight approach and the action approach. The insight approach has been supported by many traditional therapeutic schools. In particular, psychoanalytic, neoanalytic, and client-centered practitioners have emphasized the client's insight as the basis for the development of an effective set of assumptions about his or her world (Adler, 1927; Freud, 1933; Fromm, 1947; Horney, 1945; Jung, 1939; Rank, 1929; Rogers and others, 1967). The action approach has been promulgated by the learning theory and behavior modification schools, as well as by the trait-and-factor approach for matching people and jobs. These schools have emphasized the client's development and implementation of rational action plans for managing his or her world (Eysenck, 1960; Ginzberg and others, 1951; Krasner and Ullman, 1965; Parsons, 1909; Super, 1949; Watson, 1916; Wolpe, Salter, and Renya, 1964).

Unfortunately, the insight and action approaches are each incomplete without the other. Most insight approaches fail to develop insights programmatically so that the client can "own" them, or they fail to develop systematic action programs based on these insights. Similarly, although the action approaches effectively develop their programs, they fail to consolidate the behavioral changes they have accomplished and neglect to complement the action with insights that enable the client to guide his or her own life (Carkhuff and Berenson, 1976, 1977). In order to assist clients in changing behavior, the insight and action approaches must be integrated into a single effective helping process.

Helping Process. In order to demonstrate a change or gain in behavior, helpees must act differently than they did before. In order to act effectively, helpees must accurately understand their goals and how to achieve them. In order to understand their goals, helpees must explore their world experientially. These three learning or relearning processes are the phases of helping through which help-ees must be guided (Carkhuff and Berenson, 1976): Helpees must first *explore* how well they are functioning in their own environ-ments. They must next *understand* the gap between their present level of functioning and their individual goals. Next they must *act* to get from their present level of functioning to their goals. Once they have acted on their understanding, they begin the helping pro-cess again by exploring the consequences of their actions.

Helper Skills. In order to be effective, therefore, the helper's skills must facilitate the helpee's movement through the three-phase helping process. In the development of the HRD model, the dimen-sion of empathy was later complemented by unconditional positive regard and genuineness (Rogers and others, 1967). These three di-mensions were then redefined as accurate empathy, respect, and gen-uineness (Carkhuff, 1969; Truax and Carkhuff, 1967) and were in turn complemented by other dimensions—specificity, or concrete-ness; self-disclosure; confrontation; and immediacy. All the dimen-sions were then categorized as either responsive or initiative (Berenson and Mitchell, 1974; Carkhuff, 1969).

The responsive dimensions (empathy, respect, specificity of expression) responded to the helpee's experience and thus facilitated the helpee's movement toward understanding. The initiative di-mensions (genuineness, self-disclosure, confrontation, immediacy, and concreteness) were generated from the helper's experience and stimulated the helpee's movement toward action (Berenson and Mitchell, 1974; Carkhuff, 1971a). The initiative dimensions were later extended to incorporate the problem solving and program development skills needed to fully assist helpees in achieving appropriate outcomes (Carkhuff, 1974b, 1975; Carkhuff and Anthony, 1979).

Helpee Outcomes. In the early research, helpee outcome measures emphasized the emotional changes or gains of the helpees. Since the helping methods were insight-oriented, helpee exploration was emphasized, and the outcome assessments measured the changes in the helpee's level of emotional insight (Rogers and others, 1967; Truax and Carkhuff, 1967). Clearly, these emotional outcome studies were limited because they were assessing only one dimension of the helpee's functioning.

The outcomes were later defined more broadly to incorporate all dimensions of human resources development to which the helping process is dedicated. The emotional dimension was extended to incorporate the interpersonal functioning of the helpees (Carkhuff, 1969, 1971a). The dimension of physical functioning was added to measure the helpees' fitness and energy levels (Collingwood, 1972), and the intellectual dimension to measure the helpees' intellectual achievement and capabilities (Aspy and Roebuck, 1972, 1977).

In summary, helping effectiveness is a function of the helper's skill in facilitating the accomplishment of helping outcomes, including the physical, emotional, and intellectual dimensions of human resources development. The helping process by which outcomes are accomplished emphasizes the helpee's exploration, understanding, and action and is facilitated by both responding and initiating skills.

Helping Skills

The responsive and initiative dimensions of helping facilitate the exploration, understanding, and action that culminate in physical, emotional, and intellectual helpee outcomes. As a result of attempts to teach helpers how to accomplish these processes and outcomes, the responsive and initiative dimensions were further refined into concrete helping skills: attending, responding, personalizing, and initiating. Attending skills provide preparation for responding, and personalizing skills act as a transition between responding and initiating.

Attending Skills. Attending skills involve communicating a "hovering attentiveness" to the helpee (Carkhuff, 1973). The helper attends by physically positioning himself or herself in a way that the helpee can directly face and maintain eye contact with the helper. By attending physically, the helper communicates interest in the helpee's welfare; by observing and listening, the helper learns from and about the helpee. Attending is the richest source of learning about the helpee (Barker, 1971; Birdwhistell, 1967; Ekman, Friesen, and Ellworth, 1972; Garfield, 1971; Genther and Moughan, 1977; Genther and Saccuzzo, 1977; Hall, 1959, 1976; Ivey, 1971; Mehrabian, 1972; Schefflen, 1969; Smith-Hanen, 1977). Within the helping process, the helper establishes the conditions for the helpee's involvement by communicating interest in the helpee. Reduced to their minimum, attending skills may be seen as the acts that express concern and respect for the helpee in a world that is often unconcerned and disrespectful (Carkhuff and Berenson, 1976).

Responding Skills. Basic responding skills involve the helper's accurate understanding and communication of the content and feelings of the helpee's experience. When the helper's understanding of the helpee's experience is so complete as to be interchangeable with the helpee's understanding, these skills serve to ensure that the helper is fully in tune with the helpee (Aspy and Roebuck, 1977; Carkhuff, 1969; Carkhuff and Berenson, 1967; Rogers and others, 1967; Truax and Carkhuff, 1967). Responding skills serve to stimulate the helpee's exploration of his or her experience of the world by accurately mirroring that experience and by showing that the helper is fully in tune with the helpee's experience (Carkhuff and Berenson, 1976).

Personalizing Skills. Using personalizing skills, the helper processes the knowledge gained from helpee exploration and initiates movement toward understanding through a consideration of the personal implications of the meaning, problem, feeling, goal that the helpee has expressed in the understanding phase of helping. Personalizing skills culminate in the helpee's personal experience of the problem as the inability to handle difficult situations (Adler, 1927; Anthony, 1971; Berenson and Mitchell, 1974; Binswanger, 1956; Carkhuff, 1969; Carkhuff and Berenson, 1976; Freud, 1933; Fromm, 1947; Heidegger, 1962; Horney, 1945; Jung, 1939; May, 1961; Rank, 1929).

Personalizing skills provide a transition from responding to initiating and from exploring to acting. When employed effectively, they facilitate the helpee's understanding of how he or she wants to be in the world by focusing on his or her goals, which are then taken as the basis for acting (Carkhuff and Berenson, 1976).

Initiating Skills. Most simply, initiating skills foster the development and implementation of the specific steps required to achieve the personally meaningful goals the helpee has established (Authier and others, 1975; Carkhuff, 1969, 1971b, 1974b, 1975; Carkhuff and Anthony, 1979; Collingwood and others, 1978; Goldstein, Sprafkin, and Gershaw, 1976; Ivey, 1976; Sprinthall and Mosher, 1971). The initiating skills conclude the first cycle of the helping process: attending skills serve to involve the helpee in the helping process; responding skills facilitate exploration; personalizing skills facilitate understanding; and initiating skills stimulate action. Using the feedback from action, the helping or learning process is resumed until goals are achieved and problems resolved.

Training Programs

The human resource development model is a skills-based model. In other words, it views all reactions to stress, indeed all pathology, as a consequence of a skills deficit, and its basic goal is to transform such deficits into assets by helping people actualize their physical, emotional, and intellectual resources. Over the last fifteen years, and particularly within the last decade, the Carkhuff training approach, by adopting innovation from educational technology, has evolved into the competency-based HRD model, with observable and measurable training goals, objectives, and procedures.

These evolutionary changes have been based on over 10,000 hours of extensive training experiences with over 50,000 trainees from all kinds of populations (Carkhuff and Pierce, 1977). A recent study (Cash and Vellema, 1979) has shown the current HRD training program to be more effective in producing trainee change than the earlier training approach, which was not as technologically refined. However, both types of training increase skills significantly. In summary, the human resources development model is a skills-based model dedicated to actualizing human potential (Carkhuff and Berenson, 1967, 1976, 1981); in order to understand the model fully, we must understand the philosophy, experiences, and content of training.

Training Philosophy. Since training in helping is one type of interpersonal learning process, the same variables that operate effectively in any learning process will be effective in helping training: the conditions or atmosphere that afford the trainee an experiential base that nourishes his or her self-development; the identification of the trainer as a model for effective functioning; and the use of didactic methods and reinforcement by shaping in an attempt to develop trainee skills. The learning process takes place most effectively when all elements are integrated in an interactional process in which the trainer offers what has proved meaningful and effective in his or her experience, in the context of a relationship that facilitates the trainee's own exploration, understanding, and action.

Implicitly and explicitly, the training is committed to engaging the trainee in a lifelong training process. Just as in helping, the goal in training is to facilitate change in the direction of an individual's optimal personal development. The trainee is being asked to become an ever-changing, ever-evolving person in the process of becoming more effective in his or her world, a person who lives, learns, and works effectively and helps others to do the same (Carkhuff and Berenson, 1967, 1976).

Training Experience. Both training and counseling are experiential—that is, as in all learning processes, the trainee's experience of the process is central. Does the trainee feel understood? Does the trainee feel free to act on, qualify, and modify the teachings received? Does the trainee have the experience of a second, real party to the training relationship and of a truly meaningful interaction?

In addition to offering high levels of helping conditions, the trainer acts as a role model of a person who is living, learning, and working effectively. The training process will be as effective as the trainer is skilled. Indeed, the trainee is limited by the trainer's level of functioning, and the trainer who cannot add to the level of the trainee's responsiveness or help the trainee to develop a more meaningful direction in life cannot be successful (Carkhuff, 1969).

Training Content. The details of the attending, responding, personalizing, and initiating skills necessary for helping comprise the content of the training of these skills. As already mentioned,

Figure 1. The Basic Helping Model.

Phases of Helping

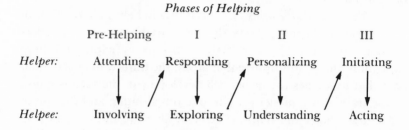

these helping skills are needed to facilitate the helpee's movement through exploration, understanding, and action (see Figure 1) (Carkhuff, 1973; Carkhuff and Berenson, 1967, 1976).

As the basic helping model makes clear, the pre-helping phase involves both helper and helpee; in phase I, the helper responds accurately to the helpee's exploration of his or her experience; in phase II, the helper personalizes the helpee's expression of experience and facilitates his or her understanding; and in phase III, helper initiative stimulates the helpee to act on his or her understanding. Again, environmental feedback serves to recycle the helping process, stimulating more extensive exploration, more accurate understanding, and more effective action. The dynamics of the helping skills involved are illustrated in more detail in Figure 2.

Attending. Attending skills include the following: attending physically, or posturing oneself to be fully attentive to the helpee; observing the context, appearance, and behavior of the helpee for cues to the helpee's physical, emotional, and intellectual state; listening to the helpee in order to hear the content, the feeling, and the meaning—the reasons for the helpee feeling the way he or she does. The attending skills lay the groundwork for helper responses that facilitate helpee exploration.

Responding. Responding skills involve responding to content, feeling, and meaning of the helpee's expression of his or her experience. Responding to content is based on listening for content. In responding to content, the helper may repeat verbatim the content of the helpee's expression when the expression is not too lengthy. When it is lengthy, the helper may attempt to reconstruct the content in the following format: "You say _____ ."

Figure 2. Helping Skills Formats for Basic Helping Model.

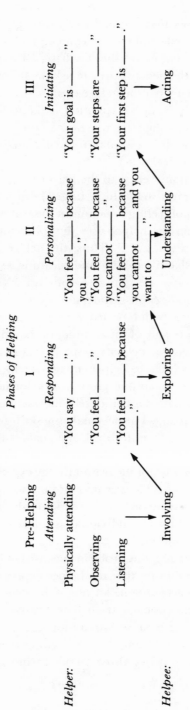

Thus, the helper may respond to a distraught husband as follows: "You say your wife and you are contemplating divorce."

The content establishes the basis for responding to feelings. At this point, the helper learns to ask the following question: "If I had experienced what the helpee expressed, how would it make me feel?" The answer to that question is the feeling word the helper would employ in the reflective format: "You feel _____." Thus, the helper may respond to the distraught husband's feelings as follows: "You feel upset."

Full responsiveness to the helpee's experience must include the meaning or reason for the feeling. The meaning relates the helpee's expression of feeling to action in the real world. In responding to the meaning, the helper uses the following format: "You feel _____ because _____." Thus, the helpee may respond to the distraught husband's feeling and meaning as follows: "You feel upset because you are going to split up." The helper learns to create interchangeable understanding—a common base of communication—with repeated responses. In that way, both helper and helpee can be sure of the accuracy of the helper's responses. The ultimate test of the helper's responsiveness is the level of self-exploration in which the helpee engages. Helper responsiveness and helpee exploration lay the groundwork for helper personalizing, which in turn facilitates helpee self-understanding.

Personalizing. The personalizing skills involve personalizing the meaning, problems, feelings, and goals of the helpee's exploration of experience. Personalizing the meaning makes the helpee directly accountable for the reason for the experience. In personalizing the meaning, the helper may use the following format: "You feel _____ because you _____." Thus, the helper may personalize the meaning for the individual as follows: "You feel upset because you will be alone."

Personalizing the problem means developing the response deficit or vulnerability that the helpee experiences by making the helpee directly accountable for the problem he or she is having. In personalizing the problem, the helper may use the following format: "You feel _____ because you cannot _____." Personalizing the feelings means developing the new feelings that may arise once the problem has been personalized. In other words, the question for the helpee is: "Now that I am accountable for the problem, how does that change my feeling?" In personalizing the feelings, the helper may use the same format as for personalizing the problem, with a new or different feeling: "You feel _____ because you cannot _____ ." Thus, the helper may personalize feelings as follows: "You feel disappointed in yourself because you cannot handle your part of the marriage."

Personalizing the goal means formulating wishes or objectives that may emerge once the problem has been personalized. The helper may simply append the desires of the helpee to the format for personalizing problems and feelings: "You feel _____ because you cannot _____ and you want to _____ ." The helper personalizes the goal for the helpee so that the helpee can then understand where he is in relation to where he wants or needs to be. The ultimate test of the helper's personalizing skills is the level of self-understanding the helpee achieves concerning what he or she wants to achieve in the world. Helper personalizing and helpee understanding lay the groundwork for helper initiating, which leads in turn to helpee action.

Initiating. Using the initiating skills, the helper develops a goal with the helpee from the personalized understanding phase, initiating steps to the goal and assisting the helpee to implement them (Carkhuff, 1975). In order to operationalize the goal in observable and measurable terms, the helpee needs to answer the following questions: Who is doing what to whom, at what level and under what conditions? The answer to these questions will enable the helper to present the goal in the following format: "Your goal is to _____ ." Thus, the helper may initiate a goal response as follows: "Your goal is to learn to be able to respond accurately to your wife's experiences at least once every day at home."

An accurate description of the goal dictates the steps necessary to achieve that goal—the goal is simply the final step. The first step is the smallest step that can be taken toward achieving the goal; the primary steps are the major steps sequenced toward the goal; and the secondary steps are the substeps leading to the primary steps. The steps may be presented to the helpee in the following format: "Your steps are _____ ." Thus, the helper may initiate steps in our example as follows: "Your steps are to attend physically, to observe, to listen and to respond."

When all the primary and secondary steps to the goal have been developed, the helpee sets out to implement the first step. At each stage of implementation, the helpee masters the steps by repeating, reviewing, rehearsing, and reinforcing them. The first step may be presented to the helpee in the following format: "Your first step is _____ ." Thus, the helper may initiate the first step as follows: "Your first step in learning to attend physically is to face the other person." The helper assists the helpee in developing an action program. The ultimate test of the helper's initiating skills is the level of action in which the helpee engages.

Summary. The purpose of training, like the purpose of helping, is to initiate lifelong learning for both trainer and trainee. Both training and helping exemplify effective living and involve interpersonal learning processes that facilitate the development and growth of all persons involved. Training is a way of life.

Training Procedures and Techniques

Just as the helper facilitates the helpee's movement through the exploring, understanding, and acting phases, the trainer provides the trainee with opportunities to explore, understand, and act in relation to the interpersonal skills content. To accomplish these purposes, the basic training model involves both helping and teaching skills (Carkhuff and Berenson, 1976). As Figure 3 makes clear, the helping and teaching skills appropriate to each phase of training are employed simultaneously and in a complementary fashion to achieve the training objectives.

Facilitating Involvement. The goals of the pretraining phase are to facilitate the trainee's involvement in the training process. The trainer facilitates this involvement by using both helping and teaching skills: the helping skills involve attending to the trainee population; the teaching skills involve developing the content to achieve the helping skills objectives—that is, developing the skills and skills steps and providing the supportive knowledge needed for the helper to accomplish those skills (Carkhuff and others, 1977).

Figure 3. The Basic Training Model.

Phases of Training

	Pre-Training	I	II	III
Trainer:				
Helping Skills	Attending	Responding	Personalizing	Initiating
	and	and	and	and
Teaching Skills	Content	Skills	Goal Setting	Teaching
	Development	Diagnosis		Delivery
Trainee:	Involving	Exploring	Understanding	Acting

Facilitating Exploration. The goal of the exploration phase is to give trainees an opportunity to experience their relationship to the content. Here the trainees have an opportunity to discover what they can do (skills) and what they know about the skills content (knowledge). The trainers use their responding helping skills and their diagnostic teaching skills to facilitate this trainee exploration (Carkhuff and others, 1977).

Facilitating Understanding. The goals of the understanding phase are to develop goals for the trainees' implementation of content. To create a clear image of what the trainees will learn, skills must be modeled using any of a number of techniques—reading dialogue, audio taped interactions, videotaped interactions, and live demonstrations by the trainer. Here the trainers use their personalizing helping skills and their goal-setting teaching skills to facilitate trainee understanding of goals (Carkhuff and others, 1977).

Facilitating Action. The goals of the action phase are trainee acquisition and application of skills content. In other words, trainees must first learn the skill and then learn to apply it in actual helping situations. To facilitate skills acquisition, the trainer must describe and demonstrate each skill step and give trainees an opportunity to do, repeat, and apply that step. Here the trainers use their initiative helping skills and their teaching delivery skills to facilitate trainee action (Carkhuff and others, 1977).

Training Aids

The training content is facilitated by the use of books and other training aids. Depending on the level of training, different books may be used to facilitate understanding of the dimensions involved (see Table 1). *Helping and Human Relations* (Carkhuff, 1969) is the basic source book for professionals, and its two volumes, together with *Toward Effective Counseling and Psychotherapy* (Truax and Carkhuff, 1967), remain among the most frequently cited texts in the social sciences. *The Development of Human Resources* (Carkhuff, 1971a) serves as an application in human and community development; *Teaching as Treatment* (Carkhuff and Berenson, 1976) examines the basic principles of psychological education; and *The Principles of Psychiatric Rehabilitation* (Anthony, 1979) extends the principles to psychiatric rehabilitation.

The basic text used in training is *The Art of Helping* (Carkhuff, 1973), a distillation of the models developed in *Helping and Human Relations*. *The Art of Problem Solving* (Carkhuff, 1974b) and *The Art of Program Development* (Carkhuff, 1975) complement and culminate the presentation of helping skills development. *The Skills of Helping* (Carkhuff and Anthony, 1979) serves as a text for advanced undergraduates and includes problem solving and program development skills, as well as helping skills.

In education, *The Skilled Teacher* (Carkhuff and Berenson, 1981) serves as a basic source for graduate students, and *Kids Don't Learn From People They Don't Like* (Aspy and Roebuck, 1977) provides a description of relevant research studies. *The Skills of Teaching Series* (Carkhuff and others, 1977) is used for advanced trainees and incorporates content development, lesson planning, and teaching delivery skills, as well as interpersonal helping skills. At the introductory level, *The Do's and Don'ts of Teaching* (Berenson and others, 1977) serves as a text for beginning trainees.

In addition to books, videotape and audiotape training aids are also available (see Table 2). *The Evolution of Systematic Human Resource Development Models* and *Carkhuff as Person* (listed in Table 2) provide the background knowledge for training, and *The Helping Model Module* introduces the helping skills in the form of attending, responding, personalizing, and initiating modules that concentrate on specific skills. Demonstrations of these helping skills are available in videotaped case studies entitled *The Case of Jane, The Case of Manny,* and *The Case of Jerry.* In addition, audiotapes for selection and training are available in specialty areas, including

Table 1. Published Training Aids for Helping and Teaching.

Levels of Training	Areas of Application	
	Helping	*Teaching*
Graduate	*Helping and Human Relations* (Carkhuff, 1969) *Toward Effective Counseling and Psychotherapy* (Truax and Carkhuff, 1967) *The Development of Human Resources* (Carkhuff, 1971a) *Teaching as Treatment* (Carkhuff and Berenson, 1976) *Principles of Psychiatric Rehabilitation* (Anthony, 1979)	*The Skilled Teacher* (Carkhuff and Berenson, 1981) *Kids Don't Learn From People They Don't Like* (Aspy and Roebuck, 1977)
Advanced (Undergraduate)	*The Skills of Helping* (Carkhuff and Anthony, 1979)	*The Skills of Teaching Series* (Carkhuff and others, 1977, 1978, 1979): *Interpersonal Skills* *Content Development Skills* *Lesson Planning Skills* *Teaching Delivery Skills*
Beginning	*The Art of Helping* (Carkhuff, 1973) *The Art of Problem Solving* (Carkhuff, 1974b) *The Art of Program Development* (Carkhuff, 1975)	*The Do's and Don'ts of Teaching* (Berenson and others, 1977)

Table 2. Videotape and Audiotape Training Aids (available from Human Resource Development Press, Amherst, Mass.).

Levels of Training	Videotapes	Audiotapes
Background	*The Evolution of Systematic Human Resource Development Models* *Carkhuff as Person*	Counselor-Counselee Package Teacher-Student Package Correctional Helper-Inmate Package Human Relations Package

Introductory	*The Helping Model Module:*
	  Attending Skills Module
	  Responding Skills Module
	  Personalizing Skills Module
	  Initiating Skills Module
	The Problem-Solving Skills Module
	The Program Development Skills Module	

Demonstrations	*The Case of Jane* *The Case of Manny* *The Case of Jerry*	

counselor-counselee relations, teacher-student relations, correctional helper-inmate relations, and human relations, in general.

All of these books and tapes present the concrete steps needed to perform the skills involved and provide trainees with an empirical base for making observable and measurable applications and transfers of those skills and for studying their effects.

Training Applications

Helping skills technologies and training systems developed side by side, shaping and refining one another. As helpers were trained in helping skills, the effects of training on helping outcomes was carefully studied and the feedback used in the shaping and refining process. Credentialed counselors and therapists were the first to be trained, followed by lay and indigenous helpers and finally by helpees who were trained to service themselves.

Credentialed Helpers. The first series of training applications demonstrated that professional helpers could be trained to function at the level of "outstanding" practitioners (Truax and Carkhuff, 1967). In a later series, it was established that credentialed professionals could, in the brief time of 100 hours or less, learn to function above minimally effective and self-sustaining levels of interpersonal skills, levels beyond those offered by most "outstanding" practitioners (Carkhuff, 1969). Perhaps most importantly, trained counselors were able to involve their counselees in the helping process at levels that led to constructive change or gain. In one guidance demonstration study, in comparison with a very low base success rate of 13 to 25 percent, the trained counselors were able to demonstrate success rates between 74 and 91 percent.

A series of training applications in teaching soon followed. Hefele (1971), in his study of effects of systematic human relations training on student achievement, found that the training of teachers in helping skills served to improve student achievement. Berenson (1971) found that a group of teachers trained in helping skills were rated significantly higher in interpersonal skills and competency in the classroom than three groups of teachers who were exposed to a variety of control conditions. One control group received didactic training about helping skills; another control group was told it was in a study investigating teachers' relationships with pupils; a third group had no prior knowledge that it was participating in a study. Aspy and Roebuck (1977), building on their earlier work, have continued to employ a variety of teacher training strategies, demonstrating the positive effects of helping skills on student physical, emotional, and intellectual functioning.

Functional Professionals. Interpersonal functioning is clearly not the exclusive province of credentialed professionals. Functional professionals are lay persons who perform the functions of professionals without the typical academic credentials (Anthony and Carkhuff, 1978). With the growing recognition that lay personnel can learn as well as professionals to be caring and empathic in their relations with helpees, a number of training applications using lay personnel were conducted. In most of these applications, staff personnel, such as nurses, hospital attendants, policemen, prison guards, dormitory counselors, and community volunteers, were trained, and their efforts in treatment studied. The effects of training were positive for both staff members and helpees. In general, the lay helpers were able to elicit significant changes in work behaviors, discharge rates, recidivism rates, and a variety of other areas, including self-reports, significant-other reports, and expert reports (Anthony and Carkhuff, 1978; Carkhuff, 1969, 1971a; Carkhuff and Berenson, 1976).

Indigenous Personnel. The difference between functional professional staff and indigenous personnel is the difference between the attendant and the patient, the policeman and the delinquent, the guard and the inmate, the teacher and the student. Indigenous personnel are part of the community being serviced, and it is a natural extension of the lay helper training principle to train helpee recipients, as well as staff.

Here the research indicates that, with systematic selection and training, indigenous helpers can work effectively with the populations from which they are drawn. For example, human relations specialists drawn from recipient ranks have facilitated school and work adjustments for troubled populations. New careers teachers, themselves drawn from the ranks of the unemployed, have systematically helped others to learn the skills they need to get and hold meaningful jobs (Carkhuff, 1971a).

Helpee Populations. The logical culmination of helper training is to train helpee populations directly in the skills they need to service themselves. In 1969, Carkhuff (1969, 1971b) suggested that training clients directly in the skills they need to function in society could be a potent treatment method. In other words, once the helpee has established an effective therapeutic relationship, identified with the helper what specific goals need to be attained, and developed the necessary program steps, the helper can then involve the helpee in skills training programs designed to achieve those goals. These initial attempts in the skills training of clients form the foundation of the teaching-as-treatment process. The main difference between the teaching and training approaches is that, as a helper moves from training individual clients to teaching groups of clients, he or she must become increasingly knowledgeable about the learning management processes and about the teaching skills needed by clients (Carkhuff and Berenson, 1976). Many different attempts at psychological education for clients have followed the teaching-as-treatment model (Authier and others, 1975; Ivey, 1976; Sprinthall and Mosher, 1971).

In addition, skills training programs using an action-oriented, behavioristic approach (for example, see Lazarus, 1971) have been developed for many different clients with many different skills deficits. For example, the literature has reported on such programs as diverse as public speaking for anxious clients (Fremouw and Zitter, 1978); study skills training for students (Lent and Russell, 1978); and migraine headache education (Mitchell and White, 1976). To decrease migraines, Mitchell and White (1976) taught patients environmental analysis skills, self-recording skills, monitoring skills, and relaxation skills. Randhawa (1978) found that interpersonal skills formed a part of job maintenance across occupations and a variety of programs have taught job-related skills. For example, mentally retarded clients were shown to be capable of learning job-interviewing skills (Grinnell and Lieberman, 1977); offenders with psychiatric histories not only changed their perceptions about their chances for employment through skills training but also obtained more jobs than the control group (Twentyman, Jenson and Kloss, 1978); and career decision-making skills have been taught to helpees (Egner and Jackson, 1978).

Other researchers have developed social skills training programs. Socially anxious men have been taught conversational and
dating skills (Curran, 1977), and chronic psychiatric patients taught
social skills exhibited a decreased level of arguing and fighting on
their hospital wards, a change that was maintained over a three-
month follow-up period (Matson and Stephens, 1978). Trower, Bryant, and Argyle (1977) investigated the difference between systematic
desensitization and a social skills training package that included
training in conversational skills and discrimination of nonverbal
cues. Twenty socially unskilled patients and twenty socially phobic
patients were trained. The phobic patients responded equally well
to both forms of intervention, while the socially unskilled patients
were helped more by the social skills training. The social skills
training reduced the anxiety level of both groups, while also changing behaviors. More detailed information about the unique benefits
of a social skills training approach has been described by Trower
and others (1978). Meichenbaum (1977) developed a program to
teach hospitalized schizophrenics self-instruction skills to develop
appropriate social behaviors. Patients were able to learn attending
skills, coping skills to handle frustration, and observing skills to
monitor the effects of their own behavior.

Interestingly, however, some of the most ingenious skills
training programs have been based on insight-oriented approaches.
For example, programs have been developed to systematically teach
clients the same relationship skills that the effective helper uses in
the first two phases of the helping process—that is, to respond to
others and themselves in a skillful manner so that they can function
more effectively in interpersonal situations.

Some of the earliest skills training programs trained psychiatric inpatients in responding skills (Pierce and Dragsow, 1969; Vitalo, 1971). Both of these studies found that such patients could be
trained to function at higher levels of interpersonal skills and
achieve a higher level of interpersonal functioning than patients
exposed to a variety of control and other treatment conditions. Similar results have been found in training parents (Carkhuff and Bierman, 1970; Reed, Roberts, and Forehand, 1977) and mixed racial
groups (Carkhuff and Banks, 1970).

The value of teaching as marital treatment has recently been well explored in the literature (Luber, 1978). In one study, married couples who were experiencing marital difficulties were trained in both the responsive and initiative interpersonal skills, and their therapeutic outcome was then compared with the outcome of couples counseled by a more traditional, insight-oriented approach (Valle and Marinelli, 1975). Therapy-outcome data indicated that the trained group outperformed the traditionally counseled group in all outcome measures. The efficacy of communication skills training in marital dysfuction has been further supported by Epstein and Jackson (1978).

Another recent study employed responding skills training as a means of treating college student clients who had sought help for personal-social problems at a university counseling clinic (Cabush and Edwards, 1976). Compared to a control group of clients who were counseled by a more traditional, insight-oriented approach, the skills training helpees significantly outperformed the control group on six counseling outcome measures. Different approaches have attempted to teach still other interpersonal skills to psychiatric patients (Goldstein, Sprafkin, and Gershaw, 1976).

Perhaps the most comprehensive study of the effects of the training-as-treatment approach has focused on the changeover of an entire institution for delinquent boys from a custodial to a skills training orientation (Carkhuff, 1974). Correctional personnel with no credentials in mental health were trained in the interpersonal, problem-solving, and program development skills outlined in this chapter. Using their program development skills, the correctional personnel helped develop more than eighty skills training programs in a variety of physical, emotional, and intellectual areas of functioning. The results they achieved were quite dramatic, indicating that they were able to bring about a level of inmate change of which credentialed mental health professionals would be justifiably proud. A summary of the various outcome criteria used indicates that the delinquents' physical functioning increased 50 percent, their emotional functioning 100 percent, and their intellectual functioning 15 percent. The physical functioning measure assessed seven categories of physical fitness as developed by the American Association for Health, Physical Education, and Recreation; the measure of emotional functioning involved a rating of the juveniles' human relations skills; and intellectual functioning was measured by the California Achievement Test. In addition to the gains in physical, emotional, and intellectual functioning, during a one-year period, "elopement" status decreased 56 percent, recidivism rates decreased 34 percent, and crime in the community surrounding the institution decreased 34 percent.

Following this study, many programs began utilizing teaching as a preferred mode of treatment with problem youths. For example, delinquent youths with low levels of living, learning, and working skills were trained in those skills. The results yielded recidivism rates of approximately 10 percent after one year and 20 percent after two years, compared with base rates for the control groups of 50 percent and 75 percent, respectively (Collingwood and others, 1978). In another study, in which minority-group high school dropouts were taught skills in learning reading and mathematics, the results indicated that the students were able to gain one year or more in intellectual achievement in twenty-six two-hour sessions (Berenson and others, 1978). Clearly, teaching was a preferred mode of treatment in both preventative and rehabilitative modalities.

Teaching helpees the kinds of skills they need to service themselves is a direct extension of the helper principle. When people are trained in the skills necessary to function effectively in their world, the probability is increased that they will begin to live, learn, and work in increasingly constructive ways.

Conclusion

Several dimensions of the Carkhuff model for helping and human resources development have been presented in this chapter: its research base; its dimensions and extensions; and its operationalization and application. The responsive and initiative skills that have evolved constitute the core of all helping experiences and when learned to a high level of expertise, may be used in all one-to-one and one-to-group relationships. They may be used in conjunction with specialty skills in counseling, teaching, and managing, or in conjunction with any of a number of preferred modes of treatment, drawn from a variety of helping orientations, for meeting the helpee's needs. Finally, the same skills may be taught directly to the helpees to enable them to help themselves; in fact, teaching client skills is the preferred mode of treatment for most helpee populations.

Carkhuff's models for helping and human resources development have served to create a whole new technology of human services—a human technology with human goals and technological means. In this regard, Carkhuff's lasting contributions include the development of the first data-based helping model, the development of the first systems-based approaches to helping, and the development of the first systematic psychoeducational skills approach to helping and mental health.

References

Adler, A. *Understanding Human Nature.* New York: Wolfe and Greenberg, 1927.

Anthony, W. A. "A Methodological Investigation of the 'Minimally Facilitative Level of Interpersonal Function'." *Journal of Clinical Psychology,* 1971, *27,* 156–157.

Anthony, W. A. *The Principles of Psychiatric Rehabilitation.* Baltimore, Md.: University Park Press, 1979.

Anthony, W. A., and Carkhuff, R. R. "The Functional Professional Therapeutic Agent." In A. S. Gurman and A. M. Razin (Eds.), *Effective Psychotherapy: A Handbook of Research.* Oxford, England: Pergamon Press, 1978.

Anthony, W. A., Cohen, M., and Vitalo, R. "The Measurement of Rehabilitation Outcome." *Schizophrenia Bulletin,* 1978, *4* (3), 365–383.

Anthony, W. A., and others. "The Efficacy of Psychiatric Rehabilitation." *Psychological Bulletin,* 1972, *78,* 447–456.

Aspy, D. N., and Roebuck, F. N. "An Investigation of the Relationship Between Levels of Cognitive Functioning and the Teacher's Classroom Behavior." *Journal of Educational Research,* May 1972.

Aspy, D. N., and Roebuck, F. N. *Kids Don't Learn From People They Don't Like.* Amherst, Mass.: Human Resource Development Press, 1977.

Authier, J., and others. "The Psychological Practitioner as a Teacher." *Counseling Psychologist*, 1975, *5*, 31–50.

Barker, L. L. *Listening Behavior*. Englewood Cliffs, N.J.: Prentice-Hall, 1971.

Berenson, B. G., and Carkhuff, R. R. *Sources of Gain in Counseling and Psychotherapy*. New York: Holt, Rinehart and Winston, 1967.

Berenson, B. G., and Mitchell, K. M. *Confrontation: For Better or Worse*. Amherst, Mass.: Human Resource Development Press, 1974.

Berenson, D. H. "The Effects of Systematic Human Relations Training upon the Classroom Performance of Elementary School Teachers." *Journal of Research and Development in Education*, 1971, *4*, 70–85.

Berenson, D. H., and others. "The Physical, Emotional, and Intellectual Effects of Teaching Learning Skills to Minority Group Dropout Learners." *Research Reports, Carkhuff Institute of Human Technology*, Amherst, Mass.: Carkhuff Institute of Human Technology, 1978, *1* (3).

Berenson, S. R., and others. *The Do's and Don'ts of Teaching*. Amherst, Mass.: Human Resource Development Press, 1977.

Bergin, A. E., and Garfield, S. L. (Eds.). *Handbook of Psychotherapy and Behavior Change*. New York: Wiley, 1971.

Binswanger, L. "Existential Analysis and Psychotherapy." In F. Fromm-Reichman and J. L. Moreno (Eds.), *Progress in Psychotherapy*. New York: Grune & Stratton, 1956.

Birdwhistell, R. "Some Body Motion Elements Accompanying Spoken American English." In L. Thayer (Ed.), *Communication: Concepts and Perspectives*. Washington, D.C.: Spartan, 1967.

Bozarth, J. D., and Rubin, S. E. "Empirical Observations of Rehabilitation Counselor Performance and Outcome: Some Implications." *Rehabilitation Counseling Bulletin*, September 1975, pp. 294–298.

Brammer, L. *The Helping Relationship*. (2nd ed.) Englewood Cliffs, N.J.: Prentice-Hall, 1979.

Cabush, D. W., and Edwards, J. J. "Training Clients to Help Themselves: Outcome Effects of Training College Students in Facilitative Self-Responding." *Journal of Counseling Psychology*, 1976, *23*, 34–39.

Carkhuff, R. R. *Helping and Human Relations.* Vols. 1 and 2. New York: Holt, Rinehart and Winston, 1969.

Carkhuff, R. R. *The Development of Human Resources.* New York: Holt, Rinehart and Winston, 1971a.

Carkhuff, R. R. "Training as a Preferred Mode of Treatment." *Journal of Counseling Psychology*, 1971b, *18*, 123–131.

Carkhuff, R. R. *The Art of Helping.* Amherst, Mass.: Human Resource Development Press, 1973.

Carkhuff, R. R. *Cry Twice.* Amherst, Mass.: Human Resource Development Press, 1974a.

Carkhuff, R. R. *The Art of Problem Solving.* Amherst, Mass.: Human Resource Development Press, 1974b.

Carkhuff, R. R. *The Art of Program Development.* Amherst, Mass.: Human Resource Development Press, 1975.

Carkhuff, R. R., and Alexik, M. "The Effects of the Manipulation of Client Depth of Self-Exploration upon High and Low Functioning Counselors." *Journal of Clinical Psychology*, 1967, *23*, 210–212.

Carkhuff, R. R., and Anthony, W. A. *The Skills of Helping.* Amherst, Mass.: Human Resource Development Press, 1979.

Carkhuff, R. R., and Banks, G. "Training as a Preferred Mode of Facilitating Relations Between Races and Generations." *Journal of Counseling Psychology*, 1970, *17*, 413–418.

Carkhuff, R. R., and Berenson, B. G. *Beyond Counseling and Therapy.* New York: Holt, Rinhart and Winston, 1967.

Carkhuff, R. R., and Berenson, B. G. *Teaching as Treatment.* Amherst, Mass.: Human Resource Development Press, 1976.

Carkhuff, R. R., and Berenson, D. H. *The Skilled Teacher.* Amherst, Mass.: Human Resource Development Press, 1981.

Carkhuff, R. R., and Bierman, R. "Training as a Preferred Mode of Treatment of Parents of Emotionally Disturbed Children." *Journal of Counseling Psychology*, 1970, *17*, 157–161.

Carkhuff, R. R., and Pierce, R. M. *Helping Begins at Home.* Amherst, Mass.: Human Resource Development Press, 1976.

Carkhuff, R. R., and Pierce, R. M. *The Art of Helping III: Trainer's Guide.* Amherst, Mass.: Human Resource Development Press, 1977.

Carkhuff, R. R., and Truax, C. B. "Training in Counseling and Psychotherapy." *Journal of Consulting Psychology,* 1965a, *29,* 333–336.

Carkhuff, R. R., and Truax, C. B. "Lay Mental Health Counseling." *Journal of Consulting Psychology,* 1965b, *29,* 426–432.

Carkhuff, R. R., and others. *The Skills of Teaching Series.* 3 Vols. Amherst, Mass.: Human Resource Development Press, 1977, 1978, 1979.

Cash, R. W., and Vellema, C. K. "Conceptual Versus Competency Approach in Human Relations Training Programs." *Personnel and Guidance Journal,* 1979, *58* (2), 91–94.

Collingwood, T. "HRD Model and Physical Fitness." In D. W. Kratochvil (Ed.), *HRD Model in Education,* Baton Rouge, La.: Southern University, 1972.

Collingwood, T., and others. *Developing Youth Resources.* Amherst, Mass.: Carkhuff Institute of Human Technology, 1978.

Combs, A., Avila, D., and Purkey, W. *Helping Relationships: Basic Concepts for the Helping Professions.* Boston: Allyn & Bacon, 1978.

Curran, J. "Skills Training as an Approach to Treatment of Heterosexual-Social Anxiety: A Review." *Psychological Bulletin,* 1977, *84,* 140–157.

Danish, S. J., and Hauer, A. *Helping Skills: A Basic Training Program.* New York: Behavioral Publications, 1973.

Egan, G. *The Skilled Helper.* Monterey, Calif.: Brooks/Cole, 1975.

Egner, J., and Jackson, D. "Effectiveness of a Counseling Intervention Program for Teaching Career Decision-Making Skills." *Journal of Counseling Psychology,* 1978, *25,* 45–52.

Ekman, P., Friesen, W., and Ellworth, P. *Emotion in the Human Face.* Elmsford, N.Y.: Pergamon Press, 1972.

Epstein, N., and Jackson, E. "An Outcome Study of Short-Term Communication Training with Married Couples." *Journal of Consulting and Clinical Psychology,* 1978, *46,* 207–212.

Eysenck, H. J. "The Effects of Psychotherapy." In H. J. Eysenck (Ed.), *The Handbook of Abnormal Psychology,* New York: Basic Books, 1960.

Eysenck, H. J. "The Effects of Psychotherapy." *Journal of Psychotherapy,* 1965, *1,* 99–178.

Fremouw, W., and Zitter, R. A. "A Comparison of Skills Training and Cognitive Restructuring—Relaxation for the Treatment of Speech Anxiety." *Behavior Therapy*, 1978, *79*, 248–260.

Freud, S. *New Introductory Lectures*. New York: Norton, 1933.

Fromm, E. *Man for Himself*. New York: Holt, Rinehart and Winston, 1947.

Garfield, S. "Research on Client Variables in Psychotherapy." In A. E. Bergin and S. L. Garfield (Eds.), *Handbook of Psychotherapy and Behavioral Change*. New York: Wiley, 1971.

Gazda, G. *Human Relations Development*. Boston: Allyn & Bacon, 1973.

Genther, R., and Moughan, J. "Introverts' and Extraverts' Responses to Nonverbal Attending Behavior." *Journal of Counseling Psychology*, 1977, *24*, 144–146.

Genther, R., and Saccuzzo, D. "Accuracy of Perceptions of Psychotherapeutic Content as a Function of Observers' Levels of Facilitation." *Journal of Clinical Psychology*, 1977, *33*, 517–519.

Ginzberg, E., and others. *Occupational Choice*. New York: Columbia University Press, 1951.

Goldstein, A. P., Sprafkin, R. P., and Gershaw, N. J. *Skill Training for Community Living: Applying Structured Learning Therapy*. Elmsford, N.Y.: Pergamon Press, 1976.

Gordon, R. *Interviewing: Strategy, Techniques, and Tactics*. Homewood, Ill.: Dorsey Press, 1975.

Grinnell, R., and Lieberman, A. "Teaching the Mentally Retarded Job-Interviewing Skills." *Journal of Counseling Psychology*, 1977, *24*, 332–337.

Hackney, H., and Cormier, L. *Counseling Strategies and Objectives*. (2nd ed.) Englewood Cliffs, N.J.: Prentice-Hall, 1979.

Hall, E. *The Silent Language*. New York: Doubleday, 1959.

Hall, E. *Beyond Culture*. New York: Doubleday, 1976.

Hefele, T. J. "The Effects of Systematic Human Relations Training upon Student Achievement." *Journal of Research and Development in Education*, 1971, *4*, 52–69.

Heidegger, M. *Being and Time*. London: SCM Press, 1962.

Holder, T., Carkhuff, R. R., and Berenson, B. G. "The Differential Effects of the Manipulation of Therapeutic Conditions upon High and Low Functioning Clients." *Journal of Counseling Psychology*, 1967, *14*, 63–66.

Horney, K. *Our Inner Conflicts.* New York: Norton, 1945.

Ivey, A. E. "The Counselor as Teacher." *Personnel and Guidance Journal,* 1976, *54,* 431–434.

Ivey, A. E. *Microcounseling: Innovations in Interviewing Training.* Springfield, Ill.: Thomas, 1971.

Johnson, D. *Reaching Out: Interpersonal Effectiveness and Self-Actualization.* Englewood Cliffs, N.J.: Prentice-Hall, 1972.

Jung, C. *The Integration of the Personality.* New York: Holt, Rinehart and Winston, 1939.

Krasner, L., and Ullman, L. *Research in Behavior Modification.* New York: Holt, Rinehart and Winston, 1965.

Lazarus, A. *Behavior Therapy and Beyond.* New York: McGraw-Hill, 1971.

Lent, R., and Russell, R. "Treatment of Test Anxiety by Cue-Controlled Desensitization and Study-Skills Training." *Journal of Counseling Psychology,* 1978, *25,* 217–224.

Levitt, E. E. "Psychotherapy with Children: A Further Evaluation." *Behavior Research and Therapy,* 1963, *1,* 45–51.

Lewis, W. W. "Continuity and Intervention in Emotional Disturbance: A Review." *Exceptional Children,* 1965, *31,* 465–475.

Luber, R. "Teaching Models in Marital Therapy: A Review of Research Issues." *Behavior Modification,* 1978, *2,* 77–91.

Matson, J., and Stephens, R. "Increasing the Appropriate Behavior of Explosive Chronic Psychiatric Patients with a Social Skills Training Package." *Behavior Modification,* 1978, *2,* 61–72.

May, R. (Ed.). *Existential Psychology.* New York: Random House, 1961.

Mehrabian, A. *Nonverbal Communication.* Hawthorne, N.Y.: Aldine, 1972.

Meichenbaum, D. *Cognitive Behavior Modification: An Integrative Approach.* New York: Plenum, 1977.

Mickelson, D. J., and Stevic, R. R. "Differential Effects of Facilitative and Nonfacilitative Behavioral Counselors." *Journal of Counseling Psychology,* 1971, *18,* 314–319.

Mitchell, K., and White, R. "Self-Management of Tension Headaches: A Case Study." *Journal of Behavior Therapy and Experimental Psychiatry,* 1976, *7,* 246–254.

Okun, B. *Effective Helping: Interviewing and Counseling Techniques.* North Scituate, Mass.: Duxbury Press, 1976.

Pagell, W., Carkhuff, R. R., and Berenson, B. G. "The Predicted Differential Effects of the Level of Counselor Functioning upon the Level of Functioning of Outpatients." *Journal of Clinical Psychology*, 1967, *23*, 510–512.

Parsons, F. *Choosing a Vocation.* Boston: Houghton Mifflin, 1909.

Patterson, C. *Theories of Counseling and Psychotherapy.* (2nd ed.) New York: Harper & Row, 1973.

Piaget, G., Carkhuff, R. R., and Berenson, B. G. "The Development of Skills in Interpersonal Functioning." *Counselor Education and Supervision*, 1968, *2*, 102–106.

Pierce, R. M., Carkhuff, R. R. and Berenson, B. G. "The Differential Effects of High and Low Functioning upon Counselors in Training." *Journal of Clinical Psychology*, 1967, *23*, 212–215.

Pierce, R. M., and Drasgow, J. "Teaching Facilitative Interpersonal Functioning to Psychiatric Inpatients." *Journal of Counseling Psychology*, 1969, *16*, 295–298.

Pierce, R. M., and Schauble, P. "Graduate Training of Facilitative Counselors: The Effects of Individual Supervision." *Journal of Counseling Psychology*, 1970, *7*, 210–215.

Pierce, R. M., and Schauble, P. "Study on the Effects of Individual Supervision in Graduate School Training." *Journal of Counseling Psychology*, 1971, *18*, 186–187.

Randhawa, B. "Clustering of Skills and Occupations: A Generic Skills Approach to Occupational Training." *Journal of Vocational Behavior*, 1978, *12*, 80–92.

Rank, O. *The Trauma of Birth.* New York: Harcourt Brace Jovanovich, 1929.

Reed, S., Roberts, M., and Forehand, R. "Evaluation of Effectiveness of Standardized Parent Training Programs in Altering the Interaction of Mothers and Noncompliant Children." *Behavior Modification*, 1977, *1*, 323–350.

Rogers, C. R., and others. *The Therapeutic Relationship and Its Impact.* Westport, Conn.: Greenwood Press, 1967.

Schefflen, A. *Stream and Structure of Communication Behavior.* Bloomington, Ind.: Purdue University Press, 1969.

Smith-Hanen, S. "Nonverbal Behavior and Counselor Warmth and Empathy." *Journal of Counseling Psychology*, 1977, *24*, 87-91.

Sprinthall, N., and Mosher, R. "Psychological Education: A Means to Promote Personal Development During Adolescence." *The Counseling Psychologist*, 1971, *2* (4), 3-84.

Super, D. E. *Appraising Vocational Fitness*. New York: Harper & Row, 1949.

Trower, P., Bryant, B., and Argyle, M. *Social Skills and Mental Health*. London: Methuen Press, 1977.

Trower, P., and others. "The Treatment of Social Failure: A Comparison of Anxiety Reduction and Skills Acquisition." *Behavior Modification*, 1978, *2*, 41-60.

Truax, C. B., and Carkhuff, R. R. *Toward Effective Counseling and Psychotherapy*. Chicago: Aldine, 1967.

Twentyman, C., Jenson, M., and Kloss, J. "Social Skills Training for the Complex Offender: Employment-Seeking Skills." *Journal of Clinical Psychology*, 1978, *34*, 320-325.

Valle, S. K., and Marinelli, R. P. "Training in Human Relations Skills as a Preferred Mode of Treatment for Married Couples." *Journal of Marriage and Family Counseling*, 1975, *1*(4), 359-365.

Valle, S. R. "Alcoholism Counselor Interpersonal Functioning and Patient Outcome." *Journal of Alcohol Studies*, 1981, *42*, 783-790.

Vitalo, R. "The Effects of Facilitative Interpersonal Functioning in a Conditioning Paradigm." *Journal of Counseling Psychology*, 1970, *17*, 141-144.

Vitalo, R. "Training in Interpersonal Skills as a Preferred Mode of Treatment." *Journal of Clinical Psychology*, 1971, *27*, 166-171.

Watson, J. B. "Behaviorism and the Concept of Mental Disease." *Journal of Philosophical Psychology*, 1916, *13*, 589-597.

Wolpe, J., Salter, A., and Renya, L. *The Conditioning Therapies*. New York: Holt, Rinehart and Winston, 1964.

Chapter 4

Microtraining: Focusing on Specific Skills

Jerry Authier
Kay Gustafson

Microtraining as discussed in this chapter is a model of instruction that divides complex human behaviors into discrete behavioral units and then teaches those units through didactic instruction, behavioral practice, observation, and immediate concrete feedback (primarily videotape). This cycle is repeated until competency is reached in the particular behavioral unit being emphasized.

Such a model can be used for teaching a wide array of skills. Indeed, the trainer is limited only by his or her ability to analyze complex skills into discrete behavioral units and then to design instructional modalities that help the trainee first learn the behavioral skills and later integrate the component skills into a more meaningful gestalt. However, microtraining will be presented here only as it relates to teaching basic interpersonal communication skills.

Foundations

Microtraining was first applied to the area of training in basic communication skills by the microcounseling program developed by Ivey (1971). Its roots, however, lie in the microteaching program developed by Allen (1967), Aubertine (1967), and their colleagues at Stanford University as part of a teacher education program. Microteaching employs the basic microtraining format outlined above to train student teachers in basic teaching skills. In small, self-contained units, student teachers focus on a specific teaching skill, practice using it while conducting a small (four or five person) class for five to twenty-five minutes, and then review their skill usage with their supervisor. A package of eighteen teaching skills has been developed by Allen and others (1969).

Regardless of the skill taught, the microtraining model itself rests on firm behavioral foundations. The well-tested and validated components of didactic instruction, modeling, feedback, and behavioral practice form the core of the training paradigm. Modeling has long been shown to be a significant factor in the effective teaching and strengthening of skills (Bandura, 1969; Bednar and others, 1974; Dalton, Sundblad, and Hylbert, 1973; Perry, 1975). Repeated evidence has also shown that, as the skills become more complex, a combination of modeling and didactic instruction is more effective than modeling alone (Forti, 1975; Goldberg, 1970; Perkins and Atkinson, 1973; Uhlemann, Lea, and Stone, 1976; Whalen, 1969). Further studies have indicated that practice and feedback are important factors in retention and utilization of complex learning (Hutchcraft, 1970; McDonald and Allen, 1967; Wallace and others, 1975). Finally, the value of teaching single skills in the building of a sense of mastery has received research support (Bank, 1968; Bear, 1968; Gendlin and Rychlak, 1970; Lovaas, 1968).

The full microtraining structure consists of a combination of all the components mentioned. However, one of the virtues of the system is that it easily allows flexibility of emphasis to suit the demands of the particular skill, the setting, and, especially, the training population. In basic interpersonal communication skills training, the major challenge for the microtrainer is to analyze the targeted trainee population in order to select relevant skills and to modify the basic instructional paradigm to fit the existing abilities and needs of trainees.

The microtraining format for teaching interpersonal communication skills can be seen as a continuum, with one end comprised of various helper training programs and the other end comprised of psychoeducational programs for clients. In the middle fall lay public training programs for management personnel and others seeking interpersonal growth. This chapter will present three sample microtraining programs: microcounseling, a helper training program; enriching intimacy, a lay public training program; and step group therapy, a patient training program.

Microcounseling

Target Population. Microcounseling is an adaptation of microtraining for teaching helpers basic interviewing skills (Ivey, 1971). This trainee population has a fairly high entering skills level, if only because of its desire to help others, and is thus likely to realize the importance to its own work identity of developing and mastering new skills. In addition, trainees in the helping professions are generally of above average intelligence, especially those in graduate training, and have a fairly high natural ability to communicate effectively. Thus, the target population is usually well motivated and relatively quick to learn, with a solid skills base and sensitivity on which to build.

Interpersonal Skills. To attempt to delimit skills areas would be a disservice to microtraining, since it can be employed to teach a wide array of skills. Indeed, as mentioned previously, trainers are limited, not by content, but only by their ability to analyze skills into discrete behavioral components that can be taught using a microtraining format. Nevertheless, since training in basic interviewing skills is the foundation of many microtraining programs, some of the main communication skills taught with this approach will be described.

Attending behaviors were among the first communication skills taught using a microtraining model. Indeed, Ivey and others (1968) conducted the first study of the microtraining model to assess the extent to which these behaviors—eye contact and relaxed postural position with appropriate gestures and verbal following—could be learned by beginning counselors. They found that not only were these skills learned but, in every pretraining and posttraining comparison, the client's reactions to the interviewer were significantly positive. Essentially, the effects of attentiveness may be attributed to the fact that these behaviors demonstrate that the interviewer is with the client, respects the client as a person, and is interested in what he or she has to say. The goal of good attending behavior, as well as of the other microcounseling skills, is to facilitate free client expression.

Microcounseling skills called focused attention consist of open invitation to talk, minimal encouragement to talk, reflection of feelings, paraphrase, and summarization. Open invitation to talk consists of the interviewer's using open-ended, rather than closed, questions. Closed questions can usually be answered with a yes or a no or with factual data, whereas open-ended questions provide the interviewee with room for self-expression without imposed structuring by the interviewer. Open-ended questions are designed to help the client clarify his or her view of the problem, rather than provide information for the interviewer. Open invitations to talk are intended to facilitate the client telling his or her own story.

Minimal encouragement to talk is a focused attending behavior in which the interviewer facilitates communication by being minimally active in the interview, both in terms of how much he or she says and in terms of the amount of direction he or she imposes on the content and flow of the interview. Once the client has begun to tell his or her story, the interviewer's goal is to encourage the client to continue exploring and elaborating on the problem. Minimal encouragement to talk allows the interviewer to accomplish this efficiently with a minimum of structuring, which results in a smooth flow of communication from the interviewee.

In reflection of feelings, the interviewer facilitates communication by verbally reflecting his or her empathic understanding back to the client, thus demonstrating that he or she is attempting to understand just how the client feels. Sometimes such behavior actually gives the client permission to openly express his or her own feelings—an important development, since clients often do not think they should talk about the way they feel.

Paraphrasing facilitates communication by showing the patient that the interviewer is following, as well as attempting to understand, the content being discussed. Paraphrasing clarifies confusing content, crystallizing issues by stating them more succinctly. The paraphrase can also be used as a perception check, as it tells the interviewee what is being heard and, if incorrect, allows the interviewee to restate what he or she actually meant.

Summarization entails integration, recapitulation, condensation, and crystallization of the essence of what the interviewee has stated during a previous portion of the interview. This microcounseling skill differs from reflection of feeling and paraphrasing in that it includes both affective and cognitive components of the interviewee's communication. Furthermore, the temporal period covered by the summarization skill is considerably longer than that covered by either the reflection of feelings or paraphrasing skill. Summarization is often used to emphasize important points covered during an ongoing interview, to recap a previous interview, or to terminate the interview by highlighting key areas that were covered during the session. The goals of this particular skill are to serve as a perception check and a stimulus for further exploration of a particular topic area and to crystallize and integrate confusing content or feeling areas.

Skills of interpersonal influence, another category of interpersonal helping skills taught by the microcounseling model, consist of self-expression, direction, expression of feelings, expression of content, influencing summarization, self-disclosure, interpretation, and direct mutual communication. These skills bring a sense of humanness to the helping situation that will enrich the client and promote rapid and solid growth. Such skills are necessary to expedite the helping process and to take full advantage of the helper's expertise. Carkhuff (1969), Brammer (1973), and Egan (1975) discuss "additive dimensions of helping," "advanced accurate empathy," and "advocacy for the client," respectively, as examples of skills of interpersonal influence. Even Rogers (1970), the father of nondirective counseling, has stressed as important elements of the helping process such skills of interpersonal influence as self-disclosure and feedback.

Self-expression is, in essence, how the helper comes across. In this regard, the helper needs to appear confident and self-assured and be able to communicate frankly and honestly, as he or she understands them, the facts of the helpee's situation. Tone of voice, eye fixation patterns, facial expression, and posture are also emphasized in the microtraining of self-expression. Not that the interviewer's particular style of helping must be compromised; rather, training in self-expression is a means of polishing that style.

Perhaps the clearest example of influence in the interview is giving directions. Ivey and Gluckstern (1976) define the skill of giving directions as consisting of four key dimensions: self-expression, structure, concreteness (as opposed to vagueness), and "checkout." Effective self-expression skills consist of being believable by presenting directions with appropriate eye contact, body language, and verbalization. Structure essentially involves the sequencing of the kinds of directions being given to the client. Being concrete, as opposed to vague, means stating specifically what the client is to do. Finally, the check-out phase of effective self-expression involves directly or indirectly asking clients to demonstrate that they understand the directions. Of course, if they repeat the directions to the helper or follow the directions immediately, check-out is not necessary.

Activities for which directions may be given in the helping process range from relaxation procedures to homework assignments. Some of the nondirective or more humanistically oriented therapists may believe strongly that directions on the part of the helper are inappropriate or unwise. However, when appropriate to a particular theory of counseling or intervention, giving directions may be taught by microcounseling.

Expression of feelings and expression of content, two other skills of interpersonal influence often taught in microcounseling training, model what clients are asked to do, communicating that expression of feelings and content is acceptable and thus giving the client tacit permission to engage in such behaviors himself or herself. Expression of content can also take the form of discussing findings and results with the client clearly and concisely, without using psychological jargon or redundancy.

The influencing summarization skill is another skill of interpersonal influence taught in microcounseling. Although similar to the summarization skill of attending, the summarization skill of influencing has the additional component of informing the client of the helper's expectations, whether they be merely the scheduling of the next visit or the completion of some homework assignment.

Such expectations will depend on the type of counseling being conducted. In addition, a summarization can often point out discrepancies that the helper heard over the course of the interview. The influencing summarization, like the paraphrase, can serve as a perception check; further, it can serve as a means of tying things together and redirecting a segment of the interview or of a subsequent therapy session.

Self-disclosure is based on expression of content, expression of feelings, and summarization (Jourard, 1971). It includes consideration of the use of the personal pronoun and the object and tense of the sentence. High levels of self-disclosure are those that occur in the present tense and have the client as their object. When self-disclosure is used in this manner—that is, "my reaction to you is . . ."—it is capable of producing an immediate transference-countertransference experience and thus can be very powerful within a psychotherapeutic exchange. Self-disclosure can also model that it is all right to discuss personal opinions or feelings.

Interpretation, another skill taught in the microcounseling format, is quite broad in that, in addition to having the attending behaviors as its foundation, it also involves some of the skills of interpersonal influence. Conceptually, interpretation as taught in microcounseling is based on Levy's *Psychological Interpretation* (1963) and consists of bringing an alternate frame of reference to bear on a set of observations or behaviors. Accordingly, the content of an interpretation will depend on the theoretical orientation of the helper. Nevertheless, regardless of theoretical orientation, interpretation offers clients a new frame of reference through which they can view and hopefully understand and deal with their problems.

Direct, mutual communication was not originally developed as a microcounseling skill, since it was modeled on behaviors taught in sensitivity, encounter, or T groups. However, since this skill essentially highlights interpersonal openness and directness of expression, it may now be considered a relevant skill for counseling and interviewing training, particularly for those helpers who value open communication. The major difference between the training of these skills and the training of the other microcounseling skills is that both the interviewer and the interviewee receive microtraining. Another difference is the focus on here-and-now—on the process that is going on during the dyadic interaction. The skill may consist of any of the previously discussed microcounseling skills and, in some instances, of a synthesis of a number of these skills. Other specific dimensions taught during training in direct, mutual communication are: frequent use of pronouns *I* and *you;* feedback of personal content and affect; a statement of the helper's experience of the helpee, using self-disclosure of content and affect; present-tense statements; and invitations for the helpee to participate, using the same skills in verbal interactions (for example, "How do you respond to that?"). Emphasis on these dimensions allows for systematic training for two or more people in communicating more fully and effectively.

Training Format. Using the microtraining format, microcounseling attempts to incorporate basic learning theory concepts into a systematic approach to teaching interviewing and counseling skills. The basic model outlined by Ivey and Authier (1978) consists of the following components:

1. Base-line interview of five minutes, on videotape. The trainee interviews a volunteer client about a real or role-played situation or concern. Depending on the situation, a specific issue may be agreed on by both participants before the session begins, or a simple, unstructured, unplanned interview may be held.
2. Training
   a. A written manual describing the single skill to be learned is read by the trainee.
   b. Video models illustrating the specific skill are shown to the trainee and discussed with reference to the single skill being taught.
   c. The trainee views the original base-line interview and compares his or her performance with the modeling tape.
   d. The supervisor, as trainer, maintains a warm, supportive relationship with the trainee, often stressing positive aspects of the performance while constantly focusing on the single skill being taught.
3. Reinterview
   The trainee videotapes another session and gives special emphasis to the single skill being learned. This tape is reviewed with the supervisor or trainer [p. 11].

The process is continued until the trainee reaches an agreed-on level of competency. Learning one skill at a time, rather than being overwhelmed by the necessity of doing everything right in the first interview, facilitates skills mastery. Moreover, the opportunity for immediate feedback through self-observation and supervision serves as a guideline for future interview performance. In addition, observing videotaped models can help the trainee learn through imitation. The trainee not only has the opportunity to read and hear about good techniques in interviewing and counseling but also, by virtue of seeing them in action, may partially acquire those skills through imitation. Finally, the fact that microtraining includes real interviews helps the trainee bridge the gap between training sessions and actual counseling sessions.

Although all the components of the training process provide visual images of the skill being taught, the live modeling of the skill by the trainer during training sessions is especially important. The supervisor must personally incorporate many of the skills into his training repertoire. A supervisor's not attending to the trainee when teaching attending behavior and not noting appropriate emotions or feelings when teaching reflection of feelings are examples of how failing to model these skills can have an inhibitory effect on the learning process. Moreover, the trainer needs to manifest the global skills of respect/warmth, empathy, and genuineness, not only for demonstration purposes but for developing a supportive environment in which learning may occur.

The general assumption is that the most effective context for teaching microcounseling skills is when the trainer and trainee are involved in a supportive relationship while focusing on single skills. However, the acceptable variations in such a relationship, and even the need for a supervisor, have been questioned. Microcounseling skills have been effectively taught by supervisors with varied styles, by multiple supervisors, or even without supervisors (Authier and Gustafson, 1976b; Frankel, 1970; Goldberg, 1970). Moreover, even the single skill emphasis has been varied: with some trainees, it is possible to teach more than one skill at a time, whereas, with others, it is desirable to break the skills into even smaller components. The key is to assess the entry skills level of the trainees and then to tailor both the supervisory style and the skills to be learned to the trainee population.

Microcounseling can be modified to meet the training needs of a wide array of helper populations. Microcounseling has been adapted to training, among others, counselors, paraprofessionals, social workers, medical students, nurses, and resident physicians. For example, medical students need to be trained in a slightly different set of helping skills than personnel and guidance counselors. Their interpersonal skills entry level and even their mindset with regard to the necessity of being trained in basic communication skills differs from counselor trainees. These factors suggest the need for varying not only the skills being emphasized but also the model depicting each skill and the setting in which the training occurs.

The major advantage of the microcounseling-microtraining format is that it allows for these differences and, as a consequence, effectively imparts the necessary skills to the trainee population. For example, a model videotape of a physician using reflection of feelings in a live situation with a real patient was found to be a more effective means of imparting that skill to residents in family practice than a model videotape of a psychologist and a client practicing the same skill. Moreover, model tapes also allowed for teaching a set of interpersonal helping skills unique to the physician, such as consulting a medical chart or making the transition from the medical history to the physical examination. Thus, as stated at the beginning of this chapter, the trainer is limited only by his or her ability to analyze complex skills into discrete behavioral units and then to design instructional modalities that help the trainee first learn the behavioral skills and later integrate the component skills into a more meaningful gestalt.

Enriching Intimacy

Target Population. A relationship skills training program using a modified microcounseling format, enriching intimacy (EI), was initially developed to teach the global interpersonal skills of respect/warmth (R/W), empathy (E) and genuineness (G) to medical personnel—residents, medical students and nurses—but has since been successfully adapted to teach those skills to paraprofessionals and members of the lay public. Trainee populations have included hotline volunteers, new employee assistance counselors in business, members of church groups, and members of adult education classes. The common bond between these trainees is that their main motivation for improving their skills is more personal than vocational, and their goals may combine self-improvement and an improved ability to help others. Trainees' motivations for learning these skills range from interest in taking a stimulating class or going along with a church group to a strongly felt need to improve interpersonal relationships or to work on a crisis hotline. This population is composed of a broader range of intellectual levels and entering skills repertoires than the professional trainee population. In addition, training settings are likely to be less well-equipped and time constraints greater.

The EI program was among the first helper training programs developed with the intention of having trainees apply their skills in their personal communications with others. Authier and Gustafson (1973) state:

> Our conceptualization that genuineness, warmth/respect, and empathy are components of being intimate with one another in all types of relationships is a new emphasis, however, and our approach to training these characteristics is new. That is, these features have long been considered central therapeutic ingredients to be shown by the helper during a therapeutic relationship and, as such, were considered the private domain of the therapist. We want to underscore that even though this is a training program for helpers, we feel that these factors are characteristic of all intimate relationships and, as such, should also occur outside of the therapeutic setting. Ideally, our somewhat grandiose wish would be for a more intimate level of relating in our world in general; more practically, our immediate focus here is on training for the more formal helping relationships with the hope that, as the skills become a part of you, they will enrich your less-formal relationships, as well [p. 3].

Interpersonal Skills. An innovative thrust of the EI program is the use of a microtraining model to teach the behavioral skills related to global therapist characteristics. The global quality of such characteristics made them difficult to teach to beginning therapists. Even though Truax and Carkhuff (1967) and Carkhuff (1969) developed globally focused training programs designed to train therapists to increase their level of respect/warmth, empathy, and genuineness, the effectiveness and efficiency of those programs were questionable. Indeed, of seventeen studies cited by Carkhuff, only two resulted in increased manifestation of the attitudes at above the

minimally facilitative level. Since that time, Carkhuff and Berenson
(1976) have moved from global to behavioral definitions of those
dimensions and have begun systematically teaching their behavioral
components. Until this occurred, however, the single most limiting
aspect of programs designed to teach respect/warmth, empathy, and
genuineness stemmed from the lack of behavioral specificity. The
enriching intimacy program is designed to systematically teach the
behavioral components of each of those three global interpersonal
skills.

The behaviors taught in the enriching intimacy program
were chosen largely on the basis of their face validity, their correspondence with theoretical descriptions of those dimensions, and, in
a few cases, their research-derived relationship. As defined by the EI
program, respect/warmth consists of three major components: communicating interest and a willingness to listen; facilitating the
client's telling his or her own story; and communicating respect for
the individual's worth, integrity, and abilities. Table 1 outlines the
various behaviors that help the trainee to communicate those three
components. The integrative phase of respect/warmth training
helps the trainee incorporate all nineteen behaviors as part of being
respectful and warm toward another.

The empathy section of the EI program is, for the most part,
designed to help trainees learn to convey their perception of how
another person is feeling in a language that the other person can
understand. The behavioral components emphasized during the
empathy portion of the training are divided into the nonverbal and
verbal, as outlined in Table 2.

In addition, being empathic is seen as comprised of two other
major dimensions: the feeling dimension and the intensity-distance
dimension. Since empathy is defined as being attuned to the way a
person is feeling and being able to convey that understanding in a
language he or she can understand, the use of feeling words is
stressed as part of the training. The emphasis is on conveying an
understanding not of facts, contents, or events but of feelings of
varying intensities. For example, feeling irritated is far less intense
than feeling rageful. Further, distance is reduced and the intensity of
the intimacy increased by the use of the present tense, personal pro-

Table 1. Behavioral Components of Warmth-Respect.

Communicating willingness to listen:

1. Varied eye contact
2. Relaxed posture
3. Appropriate, comfortable gestures
4. Rotation toward client
5. Leaning forward client
6. Appropriate seating distance

Communicating interest and facilitating the client's telling of his or her own story:

1. Nodding of head
2. Facial expression of interest
3. Voice tone
4. Avoidance of interruptions
5. Repetition of key words
6. Single questions
7. Open questions
8. Paraphrasing

Communicating respect for the individual's worth, integrity, and abilities:

1. Use of nonevaluative and nonabsolute language
2. Use of the client's name
3. Positive statements about the client
4. Avoidance of stereotyped gestures and responses
5. Leaving options to the client

nouns, and words or expressions that express the true intensity of the feelings being experienced.

Of particular note is the fact that many of the verbal skills are similar to those emphasized in microcounseling. For example, the reflection of feelings skill is identical to focused attention in the microcounseling paradigm. Similarly, the self-disclosure skill is similar to its counterpart in the microcounseling paradigm, although it differs in its inclusion of a check-out phase, whereby the helper specifically ends the self-disclosure by questioning the helpee as to his or her view of the parallels or contrasts that have been drawn between their experiences. This is seen as crucial lest the helper's self-disclosure become the new focus of the conversation, thereby interfering with the helpee's progress. Moreover, the enrich-

Table 2. Behavioral Components of Empathy.

Communicating nonverbally through intensity, congruence of vocal tone, pace, and volume:

1. Extend eye contact longer.
2. Sit closer.
3. Lean forward and possibly touch.
4. Indicate interest through facial expression.
5. Communicate involvement through gestures toward self.

Communicating verbally:

1. Focus comments and questions on the feeling content, rather than on the event or fact content, of the person's verbalizations.
2. Reflect current feelings, particularly those expressed nonverbally.
3. Use words or expressions that express the intensity of the feeling.
4. Use present tense and personal pronouns.
5. Make a statement, rather than ask a question.
6. Self-disclose, with expressions of similarity and awareness of differences.
7. Confront incongruence between verbal and nonverbal behaviors.
8. Give permission to express feelings through direct statements, strength confrontations, and acknowledgment of the difficulty of expressing feelings.

---

ing intimacy program stresses that self-disclosure can sometimes instill hope in the client—for example, by demonstrating that the counselor was able to work through a similar experience. The emphasis on making a statement, rather than asking a question, although somewhat different from the interpretation skill in microcounseling, does sometimes have an interpretive flavor. Perhaps alone among EI skills, confrontation does not have its counterpart in the microcounseling format. As defined in the empathy training phase of the EI program, this skill consists of confronting discrepancies in verbal and nonverbal behaviors in an attempt to get the client to clarify these incongruities, perhaps to the extent of more honestly acknowledging how he or she may be feeling.

The genuineness dimension of the EI training program emphasizes that being genuine involves an accurate awareness and conveyance of one's own feelings. Genuineness is similar to the

Table 3. Behavioral Components of Genuineness.

Evidence genuine willingness to listen:

1. Reemphasize nonverbal aspects of respect showing congruence between interviewer's verbal and nonverbal behaviors:

   1. Match voice tone, gestures, and facial expression with verbal content.
   2. Do not manifest defensive professional facade and language to avoid difficult topics or to avoid awareness and communication of one's own feelings.
   3. Admit lack of understanding.
   4. Ask for clarifications.
   5. Acknowledge limitations, as well as realistic potentials.

Giving feedback:

1. Communicate willingness to look at one's own feelings and reactions by considering one's own role in the immediate interaction.

Responding with confrontation:

1. Emphasize trainee manner in confronting.

---

microcounseling skill of direct mutual communication but differs to the degree that specific behaviors are emphasized, as outlined in Table 3. Feedback, the only verbal skill not also taught in microcounseling, consists of informing the other person of the effect that his or her specific behavior and affect is having on one. Since feedback is a very delicate skill, the phrasing and timing of the reaction are emphasized. Feedback is taught with the understanding that, whether it is negative or positive, it can be given in such a way that it is constructive, rather than destructive.

The skill of confrontation in genuineness training emphasizes method, rather than content. Since confrontation requires an awareness of how the interviewer would feel in the situation being described by the interviewee, the frame of reference confrontation is stressed during the genuineness training phase—for example, the interviewer might say: "You say that your wife walking out on you did not upset you, but I think I'd be upset if my wife walked out on me." The purpose of this form of confrontation is to help the interviewee be more genuine in his or her responses to the interviewer but at the same time to allow the interviewer to clarify feelings and content that do not fit his or her own frame of reference.

Training Format. The training format adheres to the basic microtraining model: reading a training manual that operationally defines the skill to be learned during that session; viewing a three- to five-minute model tape; practicing the skill during a five-minute role play that is simultaneously being videotaped; discussing the videotaped practice session; and repeating the above cycle until competency in the skill is attained. The total program entails about twenty hours of training.

A major deviation from the microtraining format involves the use of model tapes for each of the three global interpersonal skills. Trainees view each of the three global skills prior to and following each training phase and as a precursor to the group integrative phase. Other deviations from microtraining may be noted in the outline of the program presented in Table 4. The most notable deviations are the use of audiotape in identifying verbally expressed feelings, the role-played fantasy situation, and the group integration session.

The group integration phase of the enriching intimacy program is perhaps the most complex. In a group context, trainees are expected to engage in all of the behaviors of each of the global characteristics while discussing issues of personal importance. To successfully implement the integration phase, the trainer must be a competent group facilitator.

The complete EI format as outlined in Table 4 was originally designed for training helping professionals (Gustafson, 1975). As the program has been utilized with the lay public, however, a number of modifications have been necessary. For instance, in settings without videotape recording equipment, the use of triads—in which one person observes and gives feedback while two other persons practice the skill as interviewer and interviewee—has proven an acceptable alternative. In one instance, in which even videotape playback equipment was not available, live modeling by the trainers was substituted.

At times, special needs of the trainee populations dictate modifications in the format. Telephone hotline volunteers, for ex-

Table 4. Enriching Intimacy Program Outline.

I. Respect/Warmth Skills Training

    A. View and discuss model videotape of effective and ineffective global behaviors.
    B. Communicate a willingness to listen.
    C. Communicate interest and facilitate interviewees' telling their own story.
    D. Communicate respect for the individual's worth, integrity, and abilities.
    E. Review model videotape of effective and ineffective global behaviors.
    F. Make and view two-and-a-half- to three-minute videotaped practice interviews that incorporate all of the emphasized behaviors in communicating high levels of respect.

II. Empathy Skills Training

    A. View and discuss model videotape of effective and ineffective global behaviors.
    B. Identify nonverbal components of communicating empathy.
    C. Use audiotaped stimuli to identify verbally expressed feelings.
    D. Identify nonverbal clues to feelings.
    E. Facilitate exploration of hesitant or conflicting expressions of feelings.
    F. Use self-disclosure as a means of communicating empathic understanding.
    G. Review the model videotape of effective and ineffective global behaviors.
    H. Make and view two-and-a-half- to three-minute videotaped practice interviews that incorporate all of the emphasized behaviors in communicating high levels of empathy.

III. Genuineness Skills Training

    A. View and discuss the model videotape of effective and ineffective global behaviors.
    B. Conduct a two-minute videotaped interview that models poor genuineness behavior.
    C. Teach feedback skill using standard microcounseling format.
    D. Ask each trainee to spend a few minutes fantasizing the most difficult topic area and kind of person for him or her to relate to in a helpful, genuine way.
    E. Each person conducts a three- to four-minute videotaped interview with his or her partner, role playing that most feared situation.

Table 4, Cont'd.

IV. Group Integration Training

The purpose of the group sessions is to continue the process, particularly vital to genuine communication, of becoming comfortable with being aware of and expressing one's own feelings and to provide a situation to practice integrating all three global skills while interacting with others for a prolonged period of time.

---

ample, must learn to project respect/warmth, empathy, and gennuineness entirely through verbal channels and to rely on nonvisual signals from their clients. In training, therefore, they must practice the skills with an invisible partner and focus on the audio portion of the recorded interview. Examples in the skills manuals may also be rewritten to better fit the trainees' situation. Lower entry skills levels of trainees may dictate spending longer times on the more basic skills, and time constraints may eliminate the final group integration phase. On the other hand, if trainees represent a stable, ongoing group—for example, church group members who want to improve their relationships—many opportunities for generalization exist, and more time is available for practicing and incorporating skills into interaction patterns.

In all these modifications, the core microtraining format remains intact, and the major elements of skills focus, instruction, modeling, practice sessions, and feedback continue to be utilized. Step group therapy, however, makes even greater changes in the basic microtraining format.

Step Group Therapy

Target Population. The step group therapy program as developed and described by Authier (1973), Authier and Fix (1977), and Gustafson (1979) utilizes a modified microtraining format to teach psychiatric inpatients basic communication skills. Step groups epitomize the psychoeducational model of psychological treatment by teaching psychological self-help to a patient population. The argument might be made that any training in interpersonal skills, regardless of the population, would be psychoeducational. However, for the purpose of this discussion, psychoeducation is conceived of as the teaching of psychological skills with the goal of eliminating aberrant behavior or of developing new behaviors to compensate for deficits due to psychopathological impairment. Step group therapy uses the second approach, since most psychiatric inpatients have been shown to have deficits in basic relationship skills (Coleman, 1965; Libert and Lewinsohn, 1973; Stillman, 1971). Despite widespread recognition of these skills deficits, however, direct training programs for psychiatric inpatients are a recent innovation.

One factor inhibiting the introduction of training in basic communication skills for psychiatric patients stemmed from the belief that psychiatric patients were incapable of learning such skills. However, several studies conducted in the early 1970s demonstrated that this was not the case (Donk, 1972; Freiband and Rudman, 1970; Goldstein, 1973; Higgins, Ivey and Uhlemann, 1970; Ivey, 1973; Orlando, 1974; Pierce and Drasgow, 1969; Vitalo, 1971). Interestingly, all of these studies except the Goldstein investigation used a modified helper training program. The Donk (1972), Freiband and Rudman (1970) and Higgins, Ivey, and Uhlemann (1970) studies are of particular note because they all used a microtraining format to teach basic communication skills to a psychiatric population. For example, Donk (1972) used a microtraining framework to teach hospitalized mental patients the attending behavior skill, demonstrating that patients who had learned that skill showed improved ward adjustment as compared to patients in nontreatment control groups. Freiband and Rudman (1970) combined microtraining with operant conditioning to treat a schizophrenic patient who had been hospitalized for a full year without improvement. Within three weeks after beginning microtraining, the patient was seeking a job in the community.

Other cultural factors mitigating against implementation of a psychoeducational approach include the norm that learning how to communicate effectively is something individuals acquire from their relationship with significant others, especially family members, not from their relationship with health professionals. Teaching basic skills to an adult is usually considered tantamount to putting him or her in the role of a child. Furthermore, health professionals are reluctant to conceive of themselves as trainers or teachers, especially when they value the recognition and status associated with the doctor role in the medical model for curing illness.

Even when all these obstacles are overcome, however, the inpatient psychiatric population and the treatment setting present special challenges requiring changes in the basic microtraining format to make large scale implementation possible. Primary among these is the wide range of social skills deficits present in the population. Not only do most patients have low skills levels but many lack strong motivation to learn the skills. Large numbers of trainees, a relatively rapid turnover, and limited trainer time are other factors that further restrict the application of a psychoeducational program.

The step group program was designed in direct response to these factors. The specific microtraining modifications are covered more fully in the training format section that follows. Suffice it to say that the program consists of three group levels, each of which focuses on three specific skills while incorporating skills learned in the preceding group or groups. All patients on an inpatient psychiatric unit, with the exception of individuals with severe organic impairment, are assigned to the step group program. All start at step 1 and are promoted individually to higher levels based on skills usage.

Interpersonal Skills. The skills of the step group therapy are essentially microcounseling skills. Step 1 skills—eye contact, verbal following, and relaxed posture—are attending behavior skills, and the open question and reflection of feelings skills of step 2 are focused attention skills, all of which are drawn directly from the microcounseling paradigm. The remaining skills—including making questions into statements in step 2 and confrontation, feedback, and self-disclosure in step 3—bear resemblance to other microcounseling skills but are uniquely defined in this program.

The question-into-statement interpersonal skill was included in step 2 because patients tend to ask so many questions that interchanges become interrogations. This skill attempts to break the chain of questions by training the patient to rephrase as a statement what he or she would have asked as a question. In addition, patients are instructed to make these statements using tentative language in order to minimize any defensiveness on the part of the other person involved in the interchange. For example, instead of asking, "Aren't you and your wife getting along?" they are instructed to change that question to a statement by saying, "It sounds like you and your wife aren't getting along very well."

The skills emphasized in step 3 of the step group therapy program often focus on the patient's own feelings. The feedback skill is defined as telling the other person your reaction to his or her behavior. Instructions to the patient while they are learning the feedback skill caution them not to be accusatory, a tendency that can be minimized by using a personal pronoun, tentative language, and a feeling word. For example, instead of saying, "You are making me angry by interrupting me all the time," they would say, "I feel annoyed because it seems like I am getting interrupted before I'm able to finish my point." The patients receive instructions regarding the timing of feedback and the prefacing of feedback with a comment that minimizes the other person's defensiveness—for example, "I don't mean to be offensive . . ." or "I hesitate to bring this up because it may sound harsh. . . ." The complexity of this skill requires several group sessions before patients can effectively use it, and the process of acquiring the skill often leads to vigorous group discussion with open expression of feelings.

The self-disclosure skill, another skill emphasized during step 3 that involves self-awareness, is defined as telling another person how you would think and feel in a situation similar to the one being described by that person. Patients are taught that self-disclosure is most effetcive when their feelings relate to a situation similar to the situation being discussed by the other patient. Emphasis is also given to here-and-now self-disclosure, which makes for the most therapeutic group exchange. For example, if someone has just used the feedback skill to mention that he or she feels uncomfortable discussing certain issues, another group member might self-disclose as follows: "I think I can identify with the way you might be feeling. I know I feel somewhat embarrassed when this topic is discussed. Is that how you feel?" The openness of self-disclosure provides excellent grist for the therapeutic mill.

The main emphasis in the confrontation skill is to teach patients to point out, in a nonattacking manner, an inconsistency that they have just observed. Patients tend to have a layman's definition of confrontation. Thus, it is stressed that confrontation means merely questioning an inconsistency as means of clarifying the inconsistency, rather than as a means of putting the other person in his or her place. For example, instead of saying, "You're lying, because just a few minutes ago you said such and such," they might be instructed to say, "I'm somewhat confused. I thought I heard you saying such and such, but now I hear you saying such and such." Specifically, patients are taught to use a personal pronoun, be specific in the inconsistency that they are seeing or hearing, and use a conjunction as a means of demonstrating that they are seeking to clarify, rather than attack.

In essence, patients are instructed in step 3 to be respectful, empathic, and genuine in the use of various interpersonal skills, rather than disrespectful, nonempathic, and nongenuine. Although minimal instruction is given regarding these more global characteristics, the role of the group facilitator is to model them throughout the group sessions, particularly when he or she is using one of the interpersonal skills of the step group therapy program. In this way, patients quickly learn that the group is a safe, supportive place to practice the various interpersonal skills and are therefore rather open to discussing various personal issues, especially by the time they have been promoted to group 3.

Training Format. The training format as initially developed closely parallels the microtraining format in many respects. At the beginning of each step group session, the three skills to be learned are presented both through didactic instruction and videotaped models. The skills are practiced in a group context, and group members provide feedback regarding how well individual members performed the skills. Since videotaped feedback is not used, group members serve as the eye of the camera. During the remaining portion of the session, members either practice skills or give feedback to others. The topics for discussion are left open, but members are encouraged to use the meeting time to raise important personal issues.

Important differences from the standard microtraining format do exist, however. The single skill emphasis during practice has been replaced by a three-skills emphasis. And most important, extended group practice is utilized, rather than a series of brief, one-to-one practice interactions. These microtraining modifications stem from the need to train large numbers of patients with a minimum of staff time, as well as from the dual therapeutic aim of teaching needed interpersonal skills while providing a setting where these skills can be used to explore meaningful problem areas. A group-based system was deemed the best means to both satisfy the need for practical efficiency and achieve therapeutic aims. The need to cluster skills grew largely from practical considerations, but the choice and arrangements of the skill clusters were made with the goal of enhancing the group facilitation component of the program, particularly in step groups two and three. The presentation of these skills generates discussion of meaningful personal topics that can then be optimally explored in the group context. The step group leader's role requires competence in both training and group facilitation skills.

In the use of group process as a means for enhancing skills acquisition, the program differs from most direct interpersonal skills training programs for psychiatric inpatients (Donk, 1972; Goldstein, 1973; Gutride and others, 1974; Orlando, 1974; Pierce and Drasgow, 1969; Vitalo, 1971). However, clinical research indicates that group processes such as the clarification of norms, goals, and roles have a positive effect on individual improvement (Hanson and others, 1966; Ryan, 1971; Yalom and others, 1967). Gustafson (1979) combined microtraining and group therapy to solidify the step group design.

The stepwise structure also evolved from practical considerations, since it accommodates the wide skills range, rapid turnover rate, and low motivation levels that often characterize the trainee population. The three-group hierarchy automatically sorts a constantly changing population into relatively homogeneous skills level groups with a minimum of staff time, at the same time enhancing both the training and group therapy aspects of each group. The stepwise progression also addresses the problem of low learning motivation by providing the highly visible reward of promotion to the next highest step. In this manner, the program utilizes learning theory, especially operant principles, as a means of shaping increasingly more effective communication skills.

Differences within specific inpatient settings have required further modifications in the basic step group structure (Gustafson, 1979), including the use of cards, rather than videotaped models; increased one-to-one practice; and, for a stable, security unit population, a single skill group, competency-based model in which everyone in a small group set has to be competent in a given skill before the entire group moves on to a new skill.

Evaluation Procedures and Research Findings

An advantage of the microtraining model is that it "appears to be a paradigm that is sufficiently precise for experimental rigor but is simultaneously practical for action research in applied clinical settings" (Kasdorf and Gustafson, 1978, p. 372). To date, hundreds of studies have demonstrated the effectiveness of the microtraining approach to teaching a wide array of skills to diverse training groups. Discussion in this section will focus on the effectiveness of microtraining with helpers, the lay public, and inpatients.

Helping Professionals and Paraprofessionals. Many studies have been conducted supporting the effectiveness of microtraining with helping professionals and paraprofessionals. The first microtraining study involved training beginning counselors in attending behaviors (Ivey and others, 1968). Later, Moreland and others (1970) demonstrated the effectiveness of microcounseling with helping professionals, a study of particular significance because it employed uncoached clients. Moreland and his associates trained ten beginning clinical psychology graduate students in the attending and focused-attention behaviors. Pretraining and posttraining videotapes of thirty-minute interactions with the same clients, rated independently by blind raters, demonstrated significant improvement of the attending behavior skill. The students' use of open invitation, reflection of feelings, and summarization improved according to both quantitative and qualitative measures. The trainees also decreased their number of closed questions and demonstrated a decreased number of errors on the Therapist Error Checklist (Matarazzo and others, 1965). Scroggins and Ivey (1976) employed microcounseling to teach residence counselors attending and focused-attention behaviors. Analysis of pretraining and posttraining tapes revealed that the microcounseling trainees improved significantly in minimal encouragement, paraphrasing, reflection of feelings, and summarization, as well as on an overall rating of empathy, as compared to a no-training control group. However, a one-year follow up, while evidencing retention of the minimal encouragement behavior, demonstrated a decline in the reflection of feelings, open-ended questions, and summarization.

In addition to training in the basic microcounseling skills, counselors and clinical psychology graduate students have received microtraining in a variety of more specialized counseling skills. Elsenrath, Coker, and Martinson (1972), for example, used a microtraining format to train dormitory counselors to decrease the length of their responses and to increase the length of their silence before responding to a student's statement. In addition, global interpersonal characteristics like empathy, positive regard, concreteness, and immediacy are increasingly becoming the focus of behavioral definition and microtraining instruction. Ivey and Authier (1978) and Ivey and Simek-Downing (1980) stress that many, if not most, of the behaviors used by counselors and therapists of differing theoretical orientations can be taught using microtraining.

Microtraining has also been used to effectively train paraprofessional helpers in interpersonal skills. Drug counselors (Authier and Gustafson, 1975a; Gluckstern, 1972, 1973; LaFrance, 1970), campus peer counselors (Dorosin, D'Andrea, and Jacks, 1976; Scroggins and Ivey, 1976), dormitory counselors (Danish, 1970), psychology students (Berg and Stone, 1980), counseling aides (Haase and Dimattia, 1970), day camp leaders (Zeevi, 1970a, 1970b), hotline volunteers (Evans, Uhlemann and Hearn, 1978; Hearn, Uhlemann, and Evans, 1975; Uhlemann, Hearn, and Evans, 1980; Zeevi, 1970a, 1970b), manpower counselors (Greenall, 1969), employee assistance interview counselors (Munz and others, 1976), health educators (Authier and Gustafson, 1975b), nurses (Authier and Gustafson, 1976b), and teaching aides (Collins, 1970) have all been taught interviewing, counseling, and interpersonal skills using some form of microtraining. Although the training effects in some of the above studies were not statistically significant, all demonstrated posttraining improvement. Moreover, Haase and Dimattia (1970), Gluckstern (1972, 1973), Haase, Dimattia, and Guttman (1972), and Guttman and Haase (1972) demonstrated retention of the acquired skills up to one year after training. These findings attest not only to the effectiveness of microtraining in developing interpersonal skills but also to the flexibility of adapting the format to the kinds of skills taught and to trainee populations of varying ages, educational levels, and entry skills levels.

Research on microtraining has expanded to examine the effect of conventional microtraining, modified microtraining, and no training on the acquisition of interpersonal helping skills (Boyd, 1973; Authier and Gustafson, 1976a; Thompson and Blocker, 1979). Authier and Gustafson (1976b) studied the effect of a combination of microtraining and supervision on the development of nurses' verbal communication skills. The trainees in the supervised microtraining group improved more than the nurses in the nonsupervised microtraining group, although not significantly. In a related study designed to teach open-ended questioning and reflection of feelings to undergraduate education students, Thompson and Blocher (1979) discovered that standard microtraining combined with cocounseling was significantly more effective than mere instruction followed by unsupervised practice, but did not differ substantially from standard microtraining without cocounseling. Supervision introduced into both of the microtraining situations had a significant impact on skills learning, but the effect differed among the supervisors.

Berg and Stone (1980), extending this line of microtraining research, examined the effects of trainee conceptual level and degree of supervision structure on the skills development of female introductory psychology students. Self-report measures generally supported the matching model predictions for low-conceptual-level participants. These trainees reported "greater satisfaction with high-structured supervision, perceived high-structured supervision as more helpful, and thought they learned more from this form of supervision than from low-structured supervision" (p. 507). On the other hand, some self-report evidence indicated that persons higher in conceptual level preferred less structure. Behavior measures, however, yielded minimal support for the matching model hypothesis and indicated that, in general, no significant interaction existed between participant conceptual level and degree of supervision structure.

In another line of microtraining research, some investigations have focused on components of the model (Elsenrath, Coker, and Martinson, 1972; Frankel, 1971; Kelly, 1971; Perkins and Atkinson, 1973; Peters, Cormier, and Cormier, 1978). For example, Peters, Cormier, and Cormier (1978) examined the effects of four primary components of the microtraining model on beginning graduate counseling students' acquisition of interpersonal skills. The results revealed that written and videotaped models, role-play practice, peer feedback, and role-play remediation practice were similarly effective in teaching the skills.

Studies comparing microtraining to alternative skills training models have also been conducted (DiMattia and Arndt, 1974; Toukmanian and Rennie, 1975; Evans, Uhlemann and Hearn, 1978; Uhlemann, Hearn and Evans, 1980). Toukmanian and Rennie (1975) compared the effect of microtraining, human relations training, and a no-training control group on undergraduates' development of a series of listening skills. Compared to the control group, both treatment groups increased communication effectiveness. However, the microtraining students gained significantly more on empathy than did their human relations counterparts.

Evans, Uhlemann, and Hearn (1978) compared the effects of microtraining, sensitivity training, and a no-training control condition on the development of skills in beginning hotline workers. The results revealed that, whereas the sensitivity participants responded with more open inquiries than the control group members, microtraining trainers were judged to be more empathic and to give more responses defined as good by the Therapist Error Checklist than members of either of the other two groups. In a similar study, Uhlemann, Hearn, and Evans (1980) compared the influence of three conditions—microtraining, programmed learning with role-play practice and feedback, and no training—on hotline workers' acquisition of a series of interpersonal skills. Compared to the control group, the two treatment groups made equally significant gains in skills development. However, both treatment groups failed to produce noteworthy generalization of the acquired skills, and only the microtraining group scored significantly higher than the no-training group on ratings of empathy.

Lay Public and Outpatients. Toward the interpersonal growth-psychoeducation end of the microtraining continuum, fewer research studies have been conducted, but support for the effectiveness of the model remains high. Haase and others (1971) conducted one of the first microtraining studies with outpatients, adapting the microtraining paradigm to teach accurate expression of feelings to clients prior to initiation of counseling. They found that clients trained in this manner expressed more emotion during the first session of actual counseling than clients who did not undergo microtraining in the interpersonal skill. Aldrige (1971) taught mothers of problem children basic attending skills as part of his family therapy program. Galassi, Galassi, and Litz (1974) and Gormally and others (1975) used microtraining for situational non-assertive clients; in the results of the latter study, clients were objectively rated as more assertive than members of an insight-oriented control group.

Outpatient trainee self-report data also suggest microtraining to be effective (Ivey and Authier, 1978). Most trainees reported that they found the program helpful in improving their interpersonal communication skills and would recommend it to others. On a more clinical level, couples undergoing marital therapy have demonstrated an improvement in their interpersonal communication when microtraining has been utilized to help them with their marital problems. The subjective evidence, coupled with the improvement made by many of the couples, suggests that microtraining, especially the enriching intimacy program, is effective in imparting interpersonal communication skills to marriage partners.

Inpatients. Unfortunately, microtraining of psychiatric inpatients, which invariably occurs in a clinical setting, has been fraught with the difficulty of controlling confounding variables. Thus, thorough study of how effectively group members learn interpersonal skills is difficult. As discussed previously, studies of the use of microcounseling with psychiatric inpatients (Donk, 1972; Freiband and Rudman, 1970; Higgins, Ivey, and Uhlemann, 1970; Ivey, 1973; Orlando, 1974) suggest that direct training in interpersonal communication skills is an effective modality with psychiatric patients.

Petrick (1976) conducted a study of the step group therapy program that included direct behavioral counts of skills usage during videotaped step group meetings and dyadic interactions, combined with a variety of indirect measures of members' communication skills levels as evidenced during other meetings on the ward. The group meeting data demonstrated that step 2 and 3 members made questions into statements more frequently than step 1 members and that step 3 members used open-ended questions more frequently than step 1 and 2 members. In addition, the dyadic interaction data demonstrated that step 1 members used verbal following significantly less frequently than step 2 and 3 members, whereas step 2 and 3 members used open-ended questions significantly more frequently than step 1 members.

The indirect measures of the members' communication skills level in other settings on the ward were even more impressive. These findings revealed that weekly ratings by ward staff members of the overall communication level of individual patients differed significantly in the direction predicted by the step level of the patient. The proportion of step 2 and 3 members on each of the ward treatment teams was also found to be closely related to that team staff's rating of satisfaction with the quality and quantity of the members' discussion in daily team meetings. These findings demonstrated at least partial support for the effectiveness of the step group program.

In summary it appears that Carkhuff's (Ivey, 1971) statement regarding the effectiveness of microtraining appears to be accurate: "It is a preferred technique of skills acquisition, for it is based on the principle of practicing that which you wish to affect" (p. ix). Microtraining does impart interpersonal communication skills, in some instances more effectively than other helper training formats (Di-Mattia and Arndt, 1974; Hearn, 1976; Toukmanian and Rennie, 1975). However, the combination of microtraining and other training formats may be even more effective than microtraining alone (Fletcher, 1972; Welch, 1976).

Future Directions

A variety of research and development opportunities await the future microtrainer, regardless of the population emphasis chosen. Basic research on specific structural components, skills, and populations can, of course, continue. Skills generalization and retention need considerably more attention. In general, microtraining for the lay public and for psychiatric inpatients has received less research attention than microtraining for helpers; thus, the development of innovative programs to train management personnel and persons seeking self-growth offers exciting possibilities. Within the helper training area, the delineation of new skills or patterns of skills to represent different theoretical therapy models has begun (Ivey and Authier, 1978; Ivey and Simek-Downing, 1980), and evaluative studies exploring the effectiveness of teaching these therapy models through microtraining are needed. In psychoeducation, further evaluation of the combination of microtraining and other therapy approaches—for example, the use of a microtraining component with the behavioral treatment of depression—is warranted. Many promising combinations await clinical and research trial.

The use of the microtraining format for training life skills other than the basic interpersonal communication skills is another area of growing interest. These skills might focus on specific interpersonal interactions, such as assertiveness on the job or parenting, but a novel innovation would be to microtrain cognitive (intrapersonal) skills. Many of the cognitive-behavioral methods seem adaptable to a microtraining format.

A final area of interest across the population continuum is the investigation of culturally relevant factors both in the skills taught and in the instructional components used. Sue (1977), Katz and Ivey (1977), and Ivey and Authier (1978) have made preliminary studies in this area.

The microtraining technology has been proven effective; the trainer is only limited by his or her ability to define the behavioral skills components of the complex behavior he or she wishes to teach and by his or her ability to modify the structural format to accommodate the needs and demands of the trainees.

References

Aldrige, E. "The Microtraining Paradigm in the Instruction of Junior High School Students in Attending Behavior." Unpublished dissertation, Department of Education, University of Massachusetts, Amherst, 1971.

Allen, D. (Ed.). *Micro-Teaching: A Description.* Stanford, Calif.: Stanford Teacher Education Program, 1967.

Allen, D., and others. *Teaching Skills for Elementary and Secondary School Teachers.* New York: General Learning, 1969.

Aubertine, H. "The Use of Microteaching in Training Supervising Teachers." *High School Journal,* 1967, *51,* 99–106.

Authier, J. "A Step Group Therapy Program Based on Levels of Interpersonal Communication." Unpublished manuscript, University of Nebraska Medical Center, 1973.

Authier, J., and Fix, A. "A Step Group Therapy Program Based on Levels of Interpersonal Communication." *Small Group Behavior,* 1977, *8,* 101–108.

Authier, J., and Gustafson, K. "Enriching Intimacy: A Behavioral Approach." Unpublished training manual, University of Nebraska Medical Center, 1973.

Authier, J., and Gustafson, K. "Application of Supervised and Nonsupervised Microcounseling Paradigms in the Training of Paraprofessionals." *Journal of Counseling Psychology,* 1975a, *22,* 74–78.

Authier, J., and Gustafson, K. "Developing Relationship Skills in Medical Educators." *Biomedical Communications,* 1975b, *3,* 18, 29, 35, 38.

Authier, J., and Gustafson, K. "Step Group Therapy Training: A Theoretical Ideal." Unpublished paper, University of Nebraska Medical Center, 1976a.

Authier, J., and Gustafson, K. "The Application of Supervised and Nonsupervised Microcounseling Paradigms in the Training of Registered and Licensed Practical Nurses." *Journal of Consulting and Clinical Psychology,* 1976b, *44,* 704–709.

Bandura, A. *Principles of Behavior Modification.* New York: Holt, Rinehart and Winston, 1969.

Bank, P. "Behavioral Therapy with a Boy Who Had Never Learned to Walk." *Psychotherapy,* 1968, *5,* 150–153.

Bear, D. "Some Remedial Uses of the Reinforcement Contingency." In J. Shlein (Ed.), *Research in Psychotherapy.* Vol. 3. Washington, D.C.: American Psychological Association, 1968.

Bednar, R. L., and others. "Empirical Guidelines for Group Therapy: Pretraining, Cohesion, and Modeling." *The Journal of Applied Behavioral Science,* 1974, *10,* 149–165.

Berg, K., and Stone, G. "Effects of Conceptual Level and Supervision Structure on Counselor Skill Development." *Journal of Counseling Psychology,* 1980, *27,* 500–509.

Boyd, J. D. "Microcounseling for a Counseling-like Verbal Response Set: Differential Effects of Two Micromodels and Two Methods of Counseling Supervision." *Journal of Counseling Psychology,* 1973, *20,* 97–98.

Brammer, L. *The Helping Relationship.* Englewood Cliffs, N.J.: Prentice-Hall, 1973.

Carkhuff, R. R. *Helping and Human Relations.* Vols. 1 and 2. New York: Holt, Rinehart and Winston, 1969.

Carkhuff, R. R., and Berenson, B. G. *Teaching as Treatment: An Introduction to Counseling and Psychotherapy.* Amherst, Mass.: Human Resource Development Press, 1976.

Coleman, J. *Abnormal Psychology and Modern Life.* Glenview, Ill.: Scott, Foresman, 1965.

Collins, E. Personal communication. Miami, Fla.: 1970.

Dalton, R., Jr., Sundblad, L., and Hylbert, K. "An Application of Principles of Social Learning to Training in Communication of Empathy." *Journal of Counseling Psychology,* 1973, *20,* 378–383.

Danish, S. J. Personal communication. Carbondale, Ill.: 1970.

DiMattia, D. J., and Arndt, G. M. "A Comparison of Microcounseling and Reflective Listening Techniques." *Counselor Education and Supervision,* 1974, *14,* 61–64.

Donk, L. "Attending Behavior in Mental Patients." *Dissertation Abstracts International,* 1972, *33,* 569.

Dorosin, D., D'Andrea, V., and Jacks, R. "A Peer Counselor Training Program: Rationale, Curriculum, and Evaluation." Unpublished paper, Cowell Student Health Center, Stanford University, Palo Alto, Calif., 1976.

Egan, G. *The Skilled Helper.* Monterey, Calif.: Brooks/Cole, 1975.

Elsenrath, D., Coker, D., and Martinson, W. "Microteaching Interviewing Skills." *Journal of Counseling Psychology,* 1972, *19,* 150–155.

Evans, D. R., Uhlemann, M. R., and Hearn, M. T. "Microcounseling and Sensitivity Training with Hotline Workers." *Journal of Community Psychology*, 1978, *6*, 139–146.

Fletcher, J. "Increasing Skills of Offering Acceptance." Unpublished doctoral dissertation, Department of Education, University of Washington, Seattle, Wash., 1972.

Forti, L. "Media Therapy: An Evaluation of the Effects of Programmed Instruction and Videotaped Models on Microcounseling Behaviors." Unpublished doctoral dissertation, Department of Education, American University, Washington, D.C., 1975.

Frankel, M. "Videotape Modeling and Self-Confrontation Techniques: An Evaluation of Their Effects on Counseling Behavior." Unpublished doctoral dissertation, Department of Education, University of Rochester, Rochester, N.Y., 1970.

Frankel, M. "Effects of Videotape Modeling and Self-Confrontation Techniques on Microcounseling Behavior." *Journal of Counseling Psychology*, 1971, *18*, 465–471.

Freiband, W., and Rudman, S. Personal communication. Northampton, Mass.: 1970.

Galassi, J., Galassi, M., and Litz, M. "Assertive Training in Groups Using Video Feedback." *Journal of Counseling Psychology*, 1974, *5*, 390–394.

Gendlin, E., and Rychlak, J. "Psychotherapeutic Processes." In P. Mussen, and M. Rosenzweig, (Eds.), *Annual Review of Psychology*. Palo Alto, Calif.: Annual Reviews, 1970.

Gluckstern, N. "Parents as Lay Counselors: The Development of a Systematic Parent Program for Drug Counseling." Unpublished doctoral dissertation, Department of Education, University of Massachusetts, 1972.

Gluckstern, N. "Training Parents as Drug Counselors in the Community." *Personnel and Guidance Journal*, 1973, *51*, 676–680.

Goldberg, E. "Effects of Models and Instructions on Verbal Behavior: An Analysis of Two Factors of the Microcounseling Paradigm." Unpublished doctoral dissertation, Department of Education, Temple University, 1970.

Goldstein, A. P. *Structured Learning Therapy: Toward a Psychotherapy for the Poor*. New York: Academic Press, 1973.

Gormally, J., and others. "A Microtraining Approach to Assertion Training." *Journal of Counseling Psychology*, 1975, *22*, 299–303.

Greenall, D. "Manpower Counselor Development Program." Unpublished manual, Vancouver, British Columbia, Department of Manpower and Immigration, 1969.

Gustafson, K. "An Evaluation of Enriching Intimacy—A Behavioral Approach to the Training of Empathy, Respect-Warmth, and Genuineness." Unpublished doctoral dissertation, Department of Psychology, University of Massachusetts, 1975.

Gustafson, K. "Step Group Therapy: A Behavioral Group Approach for Short-Term Psychiatric Inpatients." In D. Upper and S. Ross (Eds.), *Behavioral Group Therapy*. Champaign, Ill.: Research Press, 1979.

Gutride, M., and others. "Structured Learning Therapy with Transfer Training for Chronic Inpatients." *Journal of Clinical Psychology*, 1974, *30*, 277–279.

Guttman, M.A.J., and Haase, R. F. "The Generalization of Microcounseling Skills from Training Period to Actual Counseling Setting." *Counselor Education and Supervision*, 1972, *12*, 98–107.

Haase, R. F., and DiMattia, D. J. "The Application of the Microcounseling Paradigm to the Training of Support Personnel in Counseling." *Counselor Education and Supervision*, 1970, *10*, 16–22.

Haase, R. F., DiMattia, D. J., and Guttman, M.A.J. "Training of Support Personnel in Three Human Relations Skills: A Systematic One-Year Follow-Up." *Counselor Education and Supervision*, 1972, *11*, 194–199.

Haase, R. F., and others. "Client Training Prior to Counseling: An Extension of the Microcounseling Paradigm." *Canadian Counsellor*, 1971, *5*, 9–15.

Hanson, P., and others. "Autonomous Groups in Human Relations Training for Psychiatric Patients." *Journal of Applied Behavioral Science*, 1966, *2*, 305–324.

Hearn, M. "Three Modes of Training Counsellors: A Comparative Study." Unpublished doctoral dissertation, University of Western Ontario, 1976.

Hearn, M., Uhlemann, M., and Evans, D. "Microcounseling and Sensitivity Training with Hotline Workers." Paper presented to the annual general meeting of the Canadian Psychological Association, Quebec City, June, 1975.

Higgins, W., Ivey, A. E., and Uhlemann, M. "Media Therapy: A Programmed Approach to Teaching Behavioral Skills." *Journal of Counseling Psychology*, 1970, *17*, 20-26.

Hutchcraft, G. "The Effects of Perceptual Modeling Techniques in the Manipulation of Counselor Trainee Interview Behavior." Unpublished doctoral dissertation, Department of Education, Indiana University, 1970.

Ivey, A. E. *Microcounseling: Innovations in Interviewing Training*. Springfield, Ill.: Thomas, 1971.

Ivey, A. E. "Media Therapy: Educational Change Planning for Psychiatric Patients." *Journal of Counseling Psychology*, 1973, *20*, 338-343.

Ivey, A. E., and Authier, J. *Microcounseling: Innovations in Interviewing Counseling, Psychotherapy, and Psychoeducation*. (2nd ed.) Springfield, Ill.: Thomas, 1978.

Ivey, A. E., and Gluckstern, N. *Basic Influencing Skills: Leader and Participant Manuals*. North Amherst, Mass.: Microtraining Associates, 1976.

Ivey, A. E., and Simek-Downing, L. *Counseling and Psychotherapy*. Englewood Cliffs, N.J.: Prentice-Hall, 1980.

Ivey, A. E.,, and others. "Microcounseling and Attending Behavior: An Approach to Prepracticum Counselor Training." *Journal of Counseling Psychology*, 1968, *15*, 1-12.

Jourard, S. *Self-Disclosure: An Experimental Analysis of the Transparent Self*. New York: Wiley, 1971.

Kasdorf, J., and Gustafson, K. "Research Related to Microtraining." In A. E. Ivey and J. Authier (Eds.), *Microcounseling: Innovations in Interviewing, Counseling, Psychotherapy, and Psychoeducation*. Springfield, Ill.: Thomas, 1978.

Katz, J., and Ivey, A. E. "White Awareness: The Frontier of Racism Awareness Training." *Personnel and Guidance Journal*, 1977, *55*, 485-489.

Kelly, J. D. "Reinforcement in Microcounseling." *Journal of Counseling Psychology*, 1971, *18*, 268-272.

LaFrance, R. Personal communication. Amherst, Mass., 1970.

Levy, L. *Psychological Interpretation.* New York: Holt, Rinehart and Winston, 1963.

Libert, J., and Lewinsohn, P. "Concept of Social Skill with Special Reference to the Behavior of Depressed Persons." *Journal of Consulting and Clinical Psychology,* 1973, *40,* 304-312.

Lovaas, O. "Some Studies in Childhood Schizophrenia." In J. Shlein (Ed.), *Research in Psychotherapy,* Vol. 3. Washington, D.C.: American Psychological Association, 1968.

McDonald, F., and Allen, D. "Training Effects of Feedback and Modeling Procedures on Teaching Performance." Unpublished report, Stanford University, 1967.

Matarazzo, R., and others. "Learning the Art of Interviewing: A Study of What Beginning Students Do and Their Patterns of Change." *Psychotherapy: Theory, Research, and Practice,* 1965, *2,* 49-60.

Moreland, J., and others. "A Study of the Microtraining Paradigm with Beginning Clinical Psychologists." Unpublished paper, University of Massachusetts, 1970.

Munz, V., and others. "Public Health Employee Assistance Program: Interviewer/Counselor Training Workshop." Unpublished manual, Roy Little John Associates, Washington, D.C., 1976.

Orlando, N. "The Mental Patient as Therapeutic Agent: Self-Change, Power, and Caring." *Psychotherapy: Theory, Research, and Practice,* 1974, *11,* 58-62.

Perkins, S., and Atkinson, D. "Effect of Selected Techniques for Training Resident Assistants in Human Relations Skills." *Journal of Counseling Psychology,* 1973, *20,* 89-94.

Perry, M. "Modeling and Instructions in Training for Counselor Empathy." *Journal of Counseling Psychology,* 1975, *22,* 173-179.

Peters, G., Cormier, L., and Cormier, W. "Effects of Modeling, Rehearsal, Feedback, and Remediation on Acquisition of a Counseling Strategy." *Journal of Counseling Psychology,* 1978, *25,* 231-237.

Petrick, S. "An Evaluation of a Combined Group Therapy and Communication Skills Training Program for Psychiatric Inpatients." Unpublished dissertation, Department of Psychology, University of Nebraska, 1976.

Pierce, R. M., and Drasgow, J. "Teaching Facilitative Interpersonal

Functioning to Psychiatric Patients." *Journal of Counseling Psychology*, 1969, *16*, 295–298.

Rogers, C. R. *Carl Rogers on Encounter Groups*. New York: Harper & Row, 1970.

Ryan, W. *Blaming the Victim*. New York: Random, 1971.

Scroggins, W., and Ivey, A. E. "An Evaluation of Microcounseling as a Model to Train Resident Staff." Unpublished manuscript, Department of Education, University of Alabama, 1976.

Stillman, S. "Mental Illness and Peer Group Popularity." *Journal of Clinical Psychology*, 1971, *27*, 202–203.

Sue, D. W. "Counseling the Culturally Different." *Personnel and Guidance Journal*, 1977, *55*, 422–425.

Thompson, A., and Blocher, D. "Cocounseling Supervision in Microcounseling." *Journal of Counseling Psychology*, 1979, *26*, 413–418.

Toukmanian, S., and Rennie, D. "Microcounseling Versus Human Relations Training: Relative Effectiveness with Undergraduate Trainees." *Journal of Counseling Psychology*, 1975, *22*, 345–352.

Truax, C. B., and Carkhuff, R. R. *Toward Effective Counseling and Psychotherapy: Training and Practice*. Hawthorne, N.Y.: Aldine, 1967.

Uhlemann, M., Hearn, M., and Evans, D. "Programmed Learning in the Microtraining Paradigm with Hotline Workers." *American Journal of Community Psychology*, 1980, *8*, 603–612.

Uhlemann, M., Lea, G., and Stone, G. "Effects of Modeling and Instructions on Low-Functioning Trainees." *Journal of Counseling Psychology*, 1976, *23*, 509–513.

Vitalo, R. "Teaching Improved Interpersonal Functioning as a Preferred Mode of Treatment." *Journal of Consulting and Clinical Psychology*, 1971, *35*, 166–171.

Wallace, W., and others. "Incremental Effects of Modeling and Performance Feedback in Teaching Decision-Making Counseling." *Journal of Counseling Psychology*, 1975, *22*, 570–572.

Welch, C. "Counselor Training in Interviewing Skills: Interpersonal Process Recall in a Microcounseling Model." Unpublished doctoral dissertation, Department of Education, McGill University, 1976.

Whalen, C. "Effects of a Model and Instructions on Group Verbal

Behaviors." *Journal of Consulting and Clinical Psychology,* 1969, *33,* 509-521.

Yalom, I. D., and others. "Preparation of Patients for Group Therapy: A Controlled Study." *Archives of General Psychiatry,* 1967, *17,* 416-427.

Zeevi, S. "Development and Evaluation of a Training Program in Human Relations." Unpublished doctoral dissertation, Department of Education, University of Massachusetts, 1970a.

Zeevi, S. "Microtraining in a Community Center." Unpublished paper, Department of Education, University of Massachusetts, 1970b.

Chapter 5

Integrative Problem Solving

Gerard Egan

Skilled helpers are people who can help others manage their lives more effectively. In order to be helpful, they need a systematic and congruent model of helping and the skills and techniques to make this model operative. Since dozens of different models or approaches to helping exist, both neophyte and established helpers may well ask themselves what approach or combination of approaches has the most to offer. Or, if they choose to be eclectic, they may wonder how they might pursue an integrative and systematic, rather than a hodgepodge, eclecticism.

In the *Handbook of Psychotherapy and Behavior Change,* Mahoney and Arnkoff (1978) suggest that problem-solving approaches to helping offer a great deal of promise in a field—that is, counseling and psychotherapy—that is often criticized for lack of effectiveness. "Among the cognitive learning therapies, it is our opinion that the problem-solving perspectives may ultimately yield the most encouraging clinical results. This is due to the fact that—as a broader clinical endeavor—they encompass both the cognitive re-

Note: This chapter draws on the author's book, *Skilled Helping: An Integrative Problem-Solving Approach to the Stages, Techniques, and Skills of Helping.* Monterey, Calif.: Brooks/Cole, 1982.

structuring and the coping skills therapies (not to mention a wide range of 'noncognitive' perspectives)" (p. 709). Indeed, the problem-solving model of helping can be called a folk model in that, in one form or another, it can be found even in the earliest philosophical writings, such as those of Aristotle. The general problem-solving model, although it may take different forms in the works of different writers, remains basically the same, for it is part of the logic of being human to want to solve problems. Many, if not most, of us often ignore this logic when faced with the problems and crises of everyday life, that is, we either resist solving them, hoping they will go away, or we use a hit-and-miss rather than a systematic approach to managing them. Therefore, the problem-solving model has the advantage of belonging to no specific school of helping and thus avoids some of the unfortunate limitations of school approaches—for instance, overconcern with the writings and helping style of the founder of the school and a reluctance to assimilate other useful approaches into the theory and methodologies of the school.

Problem Solving: A Framework for Helping

The problem-solving approach described here is framework, or map, of the helping process. This framework logically outlines the goals of successful helping, providing, as it were, the "geography" of helping. A skilled helper is one who "knows the territory" of helping and can therefore provide direction for the client. Another way of putting it is that a problem-solving framework outlines the tasks of helping and indicates the relationships that exist among these tasks.

The framework used by this author both to train helpers and to provide help for clients consists of four stages and eight steps or tasks, two for each stage. The underlying hypothesis is that, in all effective helping, no matter what model or school of helping is being used, the goals or accomplishments indicated by all eight of these tasks are achieved by clients working both with their helpers and on their own. Helpers are seen as consultants to their clients—that is, they help their clients accomplish one or more of the eight tasks of the problem-solving process. With this help, clients complete the process on their own, using resources in their day-to-day environments. Needless to say, some clients need more help, others less. Skilled helpers are capable of determining, in consultation and collaboration with their clients, precisely at what step and to what extent help is needed.

The four stages of the helping process are:

1. *Problem identification and clarification.* Problems cannot be handled if they remain vague and unspecific. For instance, a woman examines her life and finds that drinking actually aggravates her problems, rather than solving them or giving her a respite from them.

2. *Goal setting.* Once a problem is seen clearly, or at least more clearly than before, clients can be helped to decide what they want to do about it. For instance, the woman decides to stop drinking completely for at least six months.

3. *Program development.* Once clients decide what they want to do, they must then determine precisely how they are going to do it—that is, they must concretely delineate the step-by-step behaviors by which they will accomplish their goals. For instance, the woman, after reviewing a number of possibilities, decides to join Alcoholics Anonymous and follow the steps of that organization's programs.

4. *Implementation.* Finally, clients need to act, need to put their programs into effect in order to reach their goals. The woman actually joins Alcoholics Anonymous and, with the help of its programs and of her fellow members, puts liquor out of her life.

In its briefest outline, the problem-solving process is a simple, straightforward program for facing and handling problem situations. It is perhaps the perversity of human nature, or what Maslow (1968) calls the "psychopathology of the average," that most people do not seem either to think about or to use this logic when actually confronted with problem situations. "In ordinary affairs, we usually muddle ahead, doing what is habitual and customary, being slightly puzzled when it sometimes fails to give the intended outcome but not stopping to worry much about the failures because there are still too many other things . . . to do. Then circumstances conspire against us and we find ourselves caught failing where we must succeed—where we cannot withdraw from the field or lower our self-imposed standards or ask for help or throw a tantrum. Then we may suspect that we have a problem. . . . An ordinary person almost never approaches a problem systematically and exhaustively unless he has been specifically educated to do so" (Miller, Galanter, and Pribram, 1960, pp. 171, 174).

Paradoxically, if the rudiments of problem solving are explained to people, they often respond, "Oh sure, I know that." The logic of problem solving seems to be an ability all human beings share, but somehow it does not always influence our behavior. Still, the fact that people share this logic is one of the advantages of using a problem-solving framework with clients. At some level of their being, they understand the model. In fact, at the beginning of the helping process, when a contract is being drawn up between helper and client, this framework can be shared with clients in a way that does not confuse or overburden them, thereby preparing them for the movement of the helping process.

What follows is an expanded, eight-step version of the basic problem-solving process consisting of four broad stages. The first step in each stage can be seen as an expanding or, in some ways, a data-gathering step; the second is more or less a contracting, decision-making step. Since the approach to training consists, for the most part, in having trainees learn the model by actually applying it to themselves and their concerns, this framework provides an overview of the principal stages of the training process, as well.

Problem awareness. Helpers cannot be of service to clients if the clients are unaware of problems or difficulties in their lives. Presumably, most people grapple with most problems in living by themselves or with the informal help of family and friends. They live without professional help. On the other hand, people who find that they are not able to cope with their problems and either do not want to share those problems with family and friends or feel that family and friends are not competent enough to help might turn to some kind of professional helper—clergyperson, teacher, coach, supervisor, doctor, counselor, social worker, nurse, psychologist, psychotherapist, psychiatrist, lawyer. They will usually turn to such a person if the problem is serious or disturbing enough and if they have some expectation that the person to whom they are turning can actually help them.

Not all clients find themselves in a helping relationship voluntarily. "Involuntary clients [those who, for some reason or another, have been sent to a helper] may well account for the majority of caseloads throughout the land" (Dyer and Vriend, 1975, p. 102). Two classes of persons are sent to helpers involuntarily— those who are unaware that they are doing harm to themselves or others and those who do not seem to care. Persons in the first category need to be helped to become aware of their behavior and its consequences; those in the second category need to face their not caring. The problem-solving framework is useful with both voluntary and involuntary clients.

Problem Situation, Rather Than Problem. Needless to say, problems in living are quite different from mathematical or engineering problems. D'Zurilla and Goldfried (1971), in discussing problems in living, prefer the term *problematic situation,* and I tend to use the term *problem situation:* "The term *problem* will refer here to a specific situation or set of related situations to which a person must respond in order to function effectively in his environment. . . . [T]he term *problematic situation* will be used in most instances in place of *problem.* In the present context, a situation is considered problematic if no effective response alternate is immediately available to the individual confronted with the situation" (p. 107-108). Problems in living are messier than mathematical problems with clear-cut solutions, principally because strong human feelings and emotions are often involved. Further complexity arises from the fact that problem situations exist not only between people but also between people and the social settings and systems of their lives (see Egan and Cowan, 1979). Because of this complexity, helpers face a difficult task. On the one hand, they need to understand and appreciate the complexity of any given problem situation and help clients do the same. Oversimplification of problems, followed by superficial solutions, helps no one. On the other hand, they need to avoid and help clients avoid being overwhelmed by the complexity of the clients' problem situations. Even in the face of apparent chaos, they must be able to help clients do something. Nevertheless, problem situations, unlike problems, are not solved; rather, they are managed to a greater or lesser degree. Helpers are successful if they help their clients manage problem situations more effectively.

Stage I: Clarification of the Problem Situation

John Dewey once suggested that a question well asked is a question half-answered. Similarly, clients that have a clear idea of precisely what is going wrong in their lives are in a better position to discover ways of managing their lives more effectively.

Step 1: General or Current Life-Style Assessment. When clients first come to helpers, they may have specific problems—"My drug habit and drinking are messing me up in school, at work, and with my family"—or they may come with general feelings of dissatisfaction—"I just seem so tired and listless lately. I'm depressed, but I don't know why." Whether the problem presented is specific or general, it can be helpful if both counselor and client are able to see it in a wider perspective. For example, if a person goes to a doctor with a pain in her chest, the doctor does not merely deal with that particular pain but also gives her a physical examination in order to assess the pain in the context of her present state of physical functioning. A life-style assessment—that is, an assessment of current personal, interpersonal, and social functioning—whether relatively brief or quite detailed, provides a background or context that helps clarify the client's problem situation. In Gestalt terms, the presenting problem situation is figure and the current life-style of the client is the ground against which the figure is seen. The ground serves to highlight and clarify the figure. Assessment, then, can be considered an expanding step in the helping process, for it deals with life-style, the context of problem situations, the larger picture. An initial assessment can serve several purposes:

- *Identifying the real problem.* When clients are helped to place their concerns in perspective, they sometimes come to realize that the presenting problems are really symptoms of more fundamental problems.

    Cora came to the counseling center complaining of headaches and poor motivation in school. A brief general assessment soon made it clear that her struggle for independence from her parents probably had a great deal to do with both headaches and motivation.

• *Clarifying problem situations.* If a client's problems are vague, a life-style assessment can help make them more concrete and specific.

Jethro talked to his clergyman about losing interest in almost everything, including participating in church activities. A brief assessment indicated that he was in a job and a marriage that depressed him and, now that he was thirty-nine, he was beginning to face some of the common issues associated with the midlife crisis.

• *Helping put order in chaos.* Sometimes clients will come to helpers and tell long and highly emotional stories of the difficulties they are facing. Rather than presenting one problem, they present a series of interrelated or seemingly disconnected problems—that is, a complicated problem situation. In this case, the assessment step finds an inherent order in what might otherwise seem like chaos.

Assessment in its fullest sense is not a mere first step in the helping process that can be completed at the beginning of helping. Rather, it is a process that permeates all of the steps of helping. Skilled helpers keep an assessment eye out and an assessment ear open whenever they are with clients. For instance, they are always sensitive to whether the issue at hand is the most important one for the client, and they are always trying to identify and help clients identify both unperceived areas of deficit and unappreciated resources. Such ongoing assessment can also be used to help make clients aware of the values they are enacting in their lives and of the stress that might be arising from unrecognized value conflicts.

Heath (1980a, 1980b) urges helpers to develop and use a comprehensive and valid model of human development and psychological maturity. Traditionally, helpers have been introduced to models of psychosocial dysfunctioning and left to their own devices in understanding problems in living against the background of normal functioning. As a result, some helpers have tended to see psychopathology everywhere and have become more adept at categorizing social-emotional disorders than at helping clients identify personal and environmental resources and set realistic goals based on a working knowledge of normal human development. A "people-in-systems" model has been developed (Egan, 1982b; Egan and Cowan,

1979) to provide helpers with a framework for helping clients assess their present life-styles and develop goals in keeping with both personal and environmental resources. This model deals with the stages of human development and the normative tasks and crises of each stage; with the social settings and systems of life and the ways in which these affect both development and day-to-day functioning; and with the kinds of working knowledge and life skills needed by individuals to carry out developmental tasks and invest themselves in their social setting.

Assessment models enable helpers to listen in focused ways to what clients are saying. Focused rather than haphazard listening is, of course, completely different from biased or stereotypical listening. Effective assessment models, such as Egan and Cowan's people-in-systems model, are based on the comprehensive life experiences of clients. Trainees in the people-in-systems approach learn this model by using it to listen to and understand their own life experiences and those of their fellow trainees.

Step 2: Focusing and Exploration. Since all problems cannot be dealt with at once, the helper needs to focus on issues that seem to require immediate attention, seem to be common to a number of the client's problems, or can be handled with available resources. For instance, if an assessment reveals that Vincent is having trouble with his wife, his children, his boss, those who work under his direction, and the men at the local bar, it would make sense not to consider each of these as separate problems but to focus on the behavioral characteristics of his interpersonal style and the patterns of his interpersonal communication.

Focusing means helping clients choose to explore an issue or an interrelated group of behaviors that seems central, in one way or another, to the presenting problem situation. This contracting step moves away from a consideration of a person's total life-style and from a general consideration of a complex problem situation to concentrate on specific areas, issues, and behaviors. Helpers do not unilaterally decide what issues are to be explored further or considered first, but only do so in consultation with their clients.

In the second part of step 2, the helper assists clients to explore and clarify the issues that seem most worthy of attention. Once it has been determined what area needs investigation, counselors help clients delineate the problem situation in terms of concrete and specific experiences, behaviors, and feelings—that is, what is happening to the client, what is the client doing or not doing, and how is the client reacting emotionally to his or her experiences and behaviors. At this stage, the goal is to help clients develop as concrete and clear a picture as possible of the problem situation, at least from their own point of view.

Problem clarification deals with both overt and covert behavior. Covert behavior refers to the client's "inner life"—that is, thoughts, imaginings, memories, attitudes, and opinions insofar as the client chooses to engage in and direct these. For instance, harboring a grudge would be an example of a covert behavior. Many clients become involved in self-defeating patterns of thinking about themselves, others, and their environment. For instance, they may keep telling themselves in a variety of ways that they are inadequate or incapable of coping with crisis situations or with situations like the one they are presently facing. As we shall see, once such patterns are uncovered and clarified, they must be challenged.

Steps 1 and 2 of the helping process do not always immediately uncover the most critical problems of a client's life. Frequently what seems to be an important issue in the beginning proves later on to be either a symptom or a relatively inconsequential problem. Some clients, in their initial visits with a helper, bring up only safe issues, minor problems. Later, when they trust the helper's competence, they raise the real issues. Needless to say, helpers must be sensitive to the emergence of more central issues or problems.

Some clients feel unable to handle problem situations because they become so preoccupied with the associated feelings and emotions that they fail to take action. If this is the case, then the kind of listening and exploring that takes place in these first steps helps give vent to their emotions. Once they are freed from the burden of unmanageable emotions, they find themselves capable of action once again. A substantial amount of counseling provides precisely this kind of service, and if clients need do no more to remobilize their resources, so much the better. However, most clients require more help than this.

Skills of Stage I. The principal skills helpers need to be effective consultants at this stage of the helping process are active listening (including the use of assessment models to help focus their listening), the communication of empathy, and probing. These skills are instruments or tools for achieving the goals of stage I, the establishment of a working relationship with the client, and the clarification of the problem situation. Skilled helpers not only listen well but also interweave probing and empathy to help clients define and clarify their problem situations. Although there is an ongoing argument about the usefulness or even the existence of empathy as a helping skill (see Anthony, 1978; Bellingham, 1978; Chinsky and Rappaport, 1970; Gladstein, 1977; Hackney, 1978; Rappaport and Chinsky, 1972; Truax, 1972), the assumption here is that the communication of accurate empathy is both a relationship-building and a data-gathering skill. Since many clients appreciate being listened to and understood, empathy can contribute to building a working relationship. Empathy is also an instrument of social influence. Clients who feel understood tend to explore issues more fully and in greater depth. In this sense, empathy contributes to gathering the kind of data that can help clients define and clarify problem situations.

In an earlier version of this helping framework (Egan, 1975), respect and genuineness were considered stage I skills. In this discussion, they are seen as foundation qualities that should permeate the entire helping process. However, these qualities need to be expressed behaviorally. If they remain mere attitudes, they do little good. Respect and genuineness are expressed in different ways at different stages of helping. For instance, initial warmth may eventually give way to a kind of "tough love" that demands action from clients.

Finally, a word of caution at this stage of the helping process: Helping is an organic process with an inherent movement, and the goal of counseling is to help clients move toward behavior that enables them to cope with and manage problem situations more effectively. All the stages and steps of the helping process are designed to contribute to this goal. Therefore, problem exploration and clarification are not goals in themselves. Rather, the assumption is that clients will be able to act intelligently and effectively only if an understanding of the problem situation enables them to decide just what they want to do.

Stage II: Deciding What to Do to Manage the Problem Situation

Once clients get a clear picture of what is going wrong, they need to determine what can be done to manage the situation better. By the end of stage I, they should have a clearer picture of the problem situation or of one or more of the major issues of the problem situation. However, they still may not have a complete-enough picture to decide what they are going to do, in which case they must work with the helper to achieve the clarity necessary to set reasonable goals for situation management.

Step 3: Acquiring the New Perspectives Needed to Set Meaningful Goals. Quite often clients do not manage problem situations well because they view both themselves and their relationship to the problem situation in narrow or even distorted ways. Their inability to see the whole situation clearly and their distorted thinking about self and others limits them either to inaction or to uncreative, futile attempts to manage the problem situation. In other words, clients often need to develop new possibly more objective and realistic perspectives on themselves, others, the environment, and the problem situation if they are to make a reasonable decision about what to do. In step 3, clients are challenged to develop such perspectives. Ideally, helpers are consultants who assist clients in challenging themselves. However, when clients do not challenge themselves or are unsuccessful in their attempts to develop more objective views of their problems, challenge from the helper and from others can be very beneficial.

In this way, step 3 is an expanding step, encouraging the client to reach out for new and more objective perspectives on his or her problems. A sign that this step is successful is that clients begin to take more and more responsibility for challenging themselves and begin to see, at least in a general way, actions they must take to handle their problems. For instance, Jane, in exploring her relationship with her fiance, talks about her inability to communicate her anger to him directly—she communicates it in oblique, obstructive ways. The counselor, who has been listening carefully not only to what Jane is saying but also to what she is only half-saying or implying, may help her see that it is her hurt, not her anger, that she finds difficult to discuss with her fiance. If she did not disguise her anger, she would be forced to deal with her hurt, which would make her feel vulnerable. Once this becomes clear, she makes the decision to talk to her fiance about the entire self-defeating pattern.

Skills for Acquiring New Perspectives. The skills needed by helpers to be effective consultants at this stage may be called challenging skills. Ideally, this means that helpers invite and enable clients to challenge themselves. However, skilled helpers are also capable of using the following challenging skills directly to help clients move toward the kind of problem clarification that leads to meaningful goal setting.

- *Information as challenge.* Helpers can either give or help clients find the kind of information needed to see the problem situation more clearly and more fully. For instance, if a college student of modest talents is depressed because some of his friends have been accepted into graduate school while he has been rejected, it may help him to discover just what percentage of college graduates do go on to graduate school, what percentage of these actually finish, how going to graduate school relates to the subsequent job market, and what normative problems are usually associated with the developmental transition he is facing. Sometimes just being better informed enables clients to manage more effectively. Note that helping clients acquire information needed to get a fuller understanding of the problem situation is not the same as giving advice.
- *Advanced empathy.* This skill enables helpers to share hunches that may help clients see dimensions of themselves or of the problem situation that they have been overlooking. In the example cited earlier, once Jane realized it was her hurt that she was afraid to talk about and not just her anger, she decided to share this larger perspective with her fiance in order to open up clearer channels of communication between them.
- *Confrontation.* Clients sometimes fail to understand their problem situations clearly because they fail to see that they are incapacitated by certain discrepancies in their lives. For instance,

parents would like to see their twenty-five year old son get a job
and become more independent, yet they provide him with whatever funds he needs, discourage him from taking jobs that are
"below his level," and so on. Once they see that they are actually
reinforcing his dependence, they are in a better position to do
something about it.

• *Helper self-sharing.* Helpers can, with discretion, share their
own experiences with clients if the self-sharing does not distract
clients from their own problem situations, does not merely add
another burden to an already overburdened client, and is so
closely related to a client's problem situation that it actually
helps the client see that situation with a clarity suggestive of
some useful action.

• *Immediacy.* A skilled helper may discuss with a client what is
happening between them in the helping relationship itself if this
discussion helps the client understand and collaborate more
fully with the helping process or if it helps the client understand
the problem situation more clearly so that he or she can manage
the problem situation more effectively. Sometimes the kinds of
interpersonal problems that plague clients in their day-to-day
relationships also arise in the counseling relationship. For instance, a client may be having trouble discussing his problems
with a helper because he is afraid of the intimacy this entails.
The helper can then explore with him the fear of intimacy that is
blocking the counseling process itself. Understanding his fear of
intimacy in the counseling relationship can help him to see
more clearly the ways in which he fears intimacy in his everyday
life.

   Neither problem clarification nor challenging are goals in
themselves in the helping process. Rather, they are sub-goals. Challenging as described here is effective if it enables clients to understand critical areas of problem situations more clearly; problem
clarity itself—insight, if you wish—has value only insofar as it enables a client to make an informed decision about what to do to
manage a problem situation more effectively.

   Step 4: Setting Problem-Related Goals. Steps 1, 2, and 3 are
all related to problem definition and clarification, but, once blind

spots are eliminated and the problem is clearly defined, helper and client need to move on. Steps 1, 2, and 3 are successful if they lead to the establishment of realistic goals for active problem handling. Some clients, once they are helped to overcome the blind spots that inhibit effective action, know precisely what they want to do. Others realize, at the end of step 3, that they need to act, but are still not sure what to do. That is, they need help in setting goals.

Goals, if they are to be translated into accomplishments, need to be clear, concrete, realistic, time-limited, adequately related to the presenting problem, within the control of the client, and in keeping with his or her values.

Skills of Goal Setting. The skills discussed in steps 1, 2, and 3—assessment, active listening, accurate empathy, probing, and all the challenging skills—are needed throughout the rest of the helping process. The particular mix of skills required at any given moment depends on the client, the problem situation, the relationship between helper and client, and other, related variables. A skilled helper is one who uses the proper mix of skills and techniques to help clients achieve the goals of each step of the helping process. Although clients need to set goals for themselves, helpers can assist in the process. To do this, helpers need goal-setting skills.

Effective goal-setting skills help clients shape goals that have the characteristics described in the previous section. An important part of the shaping process is to help clients move through the following four stages:

1. *Mere statements of intent:* "Now that I see this whole situation more clearly, I want to do something about it."
2. *Mission statements:* "I'd like to be a better father."
3. *Specific aims:* "I'd like to spend more time with the children."
4. *Concrete and specific goals:* "I plan to spend three nights per week and at least two weekends per month at home with the children."

Goal-setting skills also include the ability to help clients see that problem situations can be handled in more than one way, as well as to help them assess the consequences of a given goal. For instance, if a client thinks of handling an unwanted pregnancy by having an abortion, the helper can make sure that the client appreciates the various consequences of such a decision. Finally, goal-setting skills include the ability to choose a goal or goals that meet the client's specific situation, abilities, limitations, and values.

In a sense, goal setting is at the center of the helping process. Everything done to this point has been oriented toward setting problem-managing goals; everything that follows is done to ensure that these goals are actually accomplished. A goal is a client's way of saying, "This is what I want to do to manage the problem situation more effectively." The client might not know yet exactly how he or she is going to accomplish that goal, but at least the goal itself is clear.

Stage III: Program Development

Whereas goals deal with what is to be done to handle a problem situation, programs deal with how these goals are to be carried out. Goals are ends; programs are the means for achieving those ends. Some clients, once they establish clear and reasonable goals, know exactly what to do. For instance, a father might say, "I know precisely how I must rearrange my work schedule in order to keep three nights per week and two weekends per month free for my children." Many clients, however, still need some help to fashion reasonable programs.

Step 5: Helping Clients Discover Program Possibilities. In this step, counselors help their clients develop a census or list of concrete, realistic programs that will lead to the accomplishment of the goal or goals set in step 4. One reason people fail to achieve goals is that they do not explore the different ways in which the goals can be accomplished. They choose one means or program without a great deal of exploration or reflection, try it, and, when it fails, conclude that they just cannot achieve that particular goal. Suggesting as many ways of achieving a goal as possible raises the probability that one or a combination will suit the resources of a particular client. At this stage of the problem-solving process, as many means as possible, within time and other constraints, should be uncovered. Furthermore, time need not be wasted criticizing them—even seemingly outlandish programs may provide clues for more realistic programs.

For instance, Susan may want to stop drinking—that is, to stop drinking may be an accomplishment she believes will help her manage a problem situation in her life, in some substantial way—but she may not be familiar with the various ways in which people have helped themselves stop drinking. If she is at a loss, the counselor can help her generate a list of possibilities. Ideally, clients generate their own list, but, in fact, they may need more or less help in doing so. Susan, in collaboration with the helper, then generates the following list:

- Join Alcoholics Anonymous and follow their program.
- Get rid of all the alcohol in the house.
- Stop "cold turkey."
- Gradually reduce the amount of alcohol consumption per day or week.
- Take Antabuse, a drug that causes headaches and nausea if followed by alcohol.
- Find activities that can be substituted for drinking.
- Find ways other than the ingestion of alcohol for handling stress.
- Rearrange social life—for example, do not go to bars after work and avoid the three-martini lunch crowd.

Needless to say, the list can be extended, and even the wildest possibilities often contribute something to the final program.

The first three or four steps of the helping process may often be drudgery. However, helping clients establish goals and work out viable programs can be enjoyable for both helper and client, a time when helpers have an opportunity to stimulate the client's creativity and exercise some of their own.

Skills and Techniques for Discovering Program Possibilities. The skills and techniques useful in helping clients at this stage center around creativity and the stimulation of the client's creativity. People who are mired in problem situations often lose what little creativity they have, becoming, even more than the rest of us, victims of what Maslow (1968) has called the "psychopathology of the average." Therefore, they can often benefit greatly from the stimulation of a creative helper. Appropriate skills include:

- *Stimulating divergent thinking.* Although both convergent (one-right-answer) and divergent (multiple-right-answer) thinking are useful in their place, clients have often allowed themselves to become victims of excessive convergent thinking. Stimulating them to become divergent thinkers with respect to their problem situations can help them develop a variety of ways for achieving their goals.
- *Brainstorming.* Brainstorming, a well-established technique for generating practical ideas, includes suspending judgment on the value of the possibilities generated—an especially helpful approach if the client is the kind of person who plays the "yes, but . . ." game.
- *Scenario writing.* Clients can be asked to imagine some other person going about achieving the chosen goal. How does this other person do it? What does it look like? This approach helps some clients gain sufficient distance or objectivity to generate program possibilities.
- *Using fantasy.* Helpers can stimulate clients to use their imagination in a variety of ways—for example, by having them relax and imagine themselves under optimal conditions carrying out their goals.

This step is obviously one of expansion and data gathering. The literature on creativity is filled with techniques for helping people to expand the ways in which they approach problems. Many of these techniques can be applied by helpers, with a little ingenuity, to the problem situations of clients.

Throughout the helping process, but especially from step 4 on, clients can be asked to do writing assignments as a way of keeping them involved in and responsible for the process. For instance, one homework assignment might be to have them write out as many goals or as many program ideas as possible. Sometimes a blackboard can be used during the helping session itself, with helper and client working together on the list of possibilities generated. That most of the writing is left to the client symbolizes that he or she is taking responsibility for managing his or her own problem situation.

Step 6: Choosing a Suitable Program. Ordinarily, helping clients generate many different program possibilities makes it easier to help them choose a program that best fits their abilities, resources, preferences, and level of motivation and is in keeping with the resources and constraints of their environment. Client and helper, in collaboration, review the programs or program elements developed in the previous step and try to choose the best single program or combination of programs.

Skills of Program Choice and Structure. There are two sets of program-choosing skills. The skills of the first set are similar to the skills used in goal setting. Counselors help clients shape programs by choosing and combining program elements that are concrete and specific, verifiable, realistic (within the resources of the client and the constraints of the environment), adequate to the accomplishment of the goal, in keeping with the values of the client, and cast in a reasonable time frame. The second set of skills refers to the ordering of the elements chosen. Once the client has chosen the elements of a program, he or she may need help putting them into some reasonable order. Ideally, programs are step-by-step processes that lead to accomplishment of the goal. Care must be taken that no step is too large or too complicated—larger steps can be broken down into smaller ones, complicated steps can be simplified. Clients should have a clear idea of precisely when they are going to do what. Months of dedicated helping can be ruined when a client tries unsuccessfully to put a poorly constructed and sequenced program into action, only to return defeated and disheartened.

A third set of skills useful at this stage involves the ability to help clients formulate action contracts, in which clients tell themselves what they want to do and when and commit themselves to follow through. Although action contracts are agreements clients make with themselves, counselors can help clients draw up and monitor them. Contacts can be powerful stimuli to action because clients often find keeping to the contract rewarding.

Stage IV: Implementation and Evaluation

Some clients, once they know what they want to do and how they want to do it, move quickly and easily into action and need little help thereafter. However, some clients at this stage still need the kind of direction, support, and challenge that helpers can provide. They also need help in evaluating both the quality of their participation in the helping process itself and the quality of their implementation of problem-managing strategies they work out in conjunction with the helper.

Step 7: Implementation of the Program. At last, planning turns into action. The fruit of helping is behavioral change leading to valued accomplishments that contribute substantially to handling a problem situation. Implementation has two phases: the first takes places when the client is about to put an action program into effect, the second during the program itself.

For the first phase, the saying "forewarned is forearmed" is apt. Most clients run into difficulties and obstacles of greater or lesser seriousness as they carry out the steps of a program. Sometimes it is helpful to review with clients predictable obstacles to the kind of program they are undertaking. To use military language, goals are objectives, programs are the strategies for achieving those objectives, and tactics are the actual ways in which those strategies are put into practice in the field—that is, in the client's everyday life. Previewing with clients some of the possible pitfalls that may be encountered in the execution of a program can help make them better tacticians by helping them develop contingency plans to be used if first-line plans fail. For instance, a person who wants to stop drinking and therefore chooses not to go out to lunch with co-workers who drink rather heavily might find that his change in style puzzles, annoys, or upsets them. They may not accept such simple explanations as, "I want to cut down on calories," "I've decided to drink less," or, "Liquor is taking too much out of my budget." If he meets hostility or is pressured to drop his resolution, knowing in advance how to deal with such difficulties can spell the difference between success and failure.

Force-field analysis is a method of identifying both the forces that restrain people from moving toward desirable goals and the forces that facilitate such movement. Skilled counselors not only help clients identify and prepare for possible pitfalls on the path but also help clients identify resources available along the way. For the person who has joined Alcoholics Anonymous, for example, a telephone number he or she may call anytime, day or night, is such a resource.

During the second phase of implementation, helpers can provide support and challenge for clients in a variety of ways. The ability to help clients apply behavioral principles—such as reinforcement, punishment, extinction, aversive conditioning, modeling, and shaping—is especially useful. For instance, the failure of clients to participate in the programs to which they have committed themselves may mean that the incentives for nonparticipation are stronger than the incentives for participation. Counselors can help clients reduce the strength of restraining incentives and search for more effective incentives for participation only if they are familiar with and capable of using the basic behavioral principles. Learning to use these principles is an important part of the training process.

Finally, all the skills of stages I and II are still important during the implementation phase. For example, simply listening to clients discuss the difficulties they are experiencing in trying to implement programs can be very supportive and, as in stage I, can help clients untangle themselves from self-defeating feelings and emotions. Encouragement to action is a form of challenge that may also be useful at this point.

Step 8: Evaluation. Some clients find it easy to monitor their progress once they embark on a program. Others need the assistance of skilled helpers. Clients can benefit from asking themselves at least three major evaluation questions as they implement programs:

- "To what degree am I participating in the program—fully, partially, or not at all?" Counselors can help clients monitor both the degree and the quality of program participation. The program is not necessarily a poor one just because the client is not participating in it. If the answer to this first question is "partially" or "not at all," the client may need encouragement or challenge, or the program itself may need fine tuning. If clients sincerely want to do something about managing problem situations more effectively and yet resist participating in a particular program, the goal may have been poorly chosen, and the client may not see it as a substantial response to his or her problem situation. In this case, it is necessary to return to step 4.

However, if the answer to this first evaluation question is, "I am participating adequately in the program," then a second question is in order.

- "Am I achieving my goal by participating in the program?" If the answer here is no, the program probably needs major or minor reworking. It is either a poor program in itself or a poor fit for this particular client. In either case, steps 5 and 6 need to be repeated. If, however, the answer to this second evaluation question is yes, a third question is in order.

- "Is the fact that I am achieving my goal contributing in some substantial way to managing the original problem situation?" If the answer is no, then the goal was not chosen wisely and step 4 needs to be repeated. If the answer is yes, the client must decide whether he or she is satisfied with how the problem situation is now being managed and whether the helping relationship needs to continue.

The Skills of Evaluation. First, evaluation skills consist in the ability to help clients become aware of these questions as soon as possible so that, in some sense, the questions inform the planning process. For instance, when a client chooses a goal, he or she must ask whether it will contribute in a substantial and realistic way to handling some dimension of the problem situation. Second, evaluation means helping the client gather the data needed to answer the evaluation questions. If a client asks herself, "To what degree am I participating in this program?" she may need help identifying the behaviors that will provide an answer. Third, evaluation involves helping the client analyze the data and then base decisions on that analysis. For instance, if a client sees that he is now managing a problem situation adequately, although not perfectly, it is time to decide whether to terminate the helping relationship.

This section, then, has provided an overview of a problem-solving approach to helping. The way in which helpers use such a framework is most important. In the hands of unskilled helpers, this framework can be either overly simplistic or complicated and self-defeating.

Training Potential Helpers in the
Problem-Management Framework

Since the problem-management framework suggests that training clients is preferred mode of treatment, two kinds of training will be considered: training potential helpers in the skills and techniques that make the model work and training potential helpers to train clients in relevant life skills. (The complete training process is spelled out in a detailed step-by-step process in the Trainer's Manual which accompanies *Skilled Helping*.)

Training as Personal Development. As noted earlier, helpers learn the framework by applying it to themselves and by using it with one another. The form, then, is the steps of the problem-management model, including training in the individual skills and techniques that make the model work; the content includes the real concerns, problem situations, and developmental issues of trainees. Role playing in training sessions is not as effective as having potential helpers use the training process to learn what it feels like to be a client and to deal with their own personal issues and concerns—concerns that could affect the way in which they will deliver services to others. For instance, if a potential helper is fearful of people he or she sees as strong, the trainee should probably deal with that issue in the training group, since he or she is likely to encounter such people as fellow trainees and as clients.

Internship Method. The small group, in this author's estimation, is the ideal vehicle for training. An internship program in the training groups, which allows supervised trainees to train others in turn in the skills and techniques they have learned, makes it possible to keep groups small. In this way, trainees learn training skills and techniques that prove useful later in training-as-treatment approaches to helping.

Steps in Microskills Training. As the helping model indicates, trainees have to learn a number of individual skills, such as primary-level empathy, the use of probes, advanced empathy, confrontation, and immediacy. The following process indicates the steps in microskills training:

1. *Cognitive input for conceptual understanding.* In this step, trainees are given a conceptual understanding of the skill

through lectures and readings. One approach that has proven effective is to have trainees read about the skill first and then hear a short lecture in the training session that further defines the skill.

2. *Cognitive clarification.* In this step, trainees are given an opportunity to make sure that they understand the concept presented by asking questions or by discussing or explaining the skill.

3. *Modeling for behavioral understanding.* In this step, trainees are given a picture of someone actually using the skill in question, either live or on film or videotape, and are then encouraged to ask questions about what they have seen. In a sense, this is behavioral as well as cognitive input.

4. *Behavioral clarification.* In this step, trainers make sure that trainees have a behavioral, not just a cognitive, understanding of the skill in question by giving them a structured opportunity to show that they are capable of handling the rudiments of the skill. Consider the following example with the skill of primary-level accurate empathy. A trainer makes a statement about herself: "I just don't know what got into me last night. I got into a fight with my mother and ended up calling her a bitch! I don't believe what I did." She then asks the group how she feels and elicits responses from group members. Basing their responses both on what she has said and on how she has said it—her nonverbal and paralinguistic behavior—trainees may say "guilty," "amazed," "ashamed," "depressed," and so on. The trainer reinforces adequate responses and points out the ways in which poor responses fail to hit the mark. She then asks trainees why she feels the way she does, and trainees try to identify the content of her statement by saying, for instance, "because you lost control of yourself" or "because you were disrespectful to her." Once more she reinforces adequate responses and points out the flaws of inappropriate responses. The trainer repeats this process several times until each member of the group shows that he or she has a behavioral feeling for the skill.

5. *Practice.* In this step, the members of the group are divided into subgroups of three, with three roles in each subgroup: speaker, responder, and observer. One member reveals some concern or

issue, the second provides empathy, and the third observes so that he or she can give feedback later. Trainers supervise practice in the subgroups, trainees take turns trying each of the three roles.

6. *Feedback.* After each response or group of responses, the observer and the speaker give feedback to the responder regarding the quality of his or her responses. Effective feedback—clear, behavioral, and concise—is one of the most important aspects of the training process. Trainees must learn to tell one another what was done right, what was done wrong, and what might have been done instead. The tendency toward rambling, philosophical, long-winded feedback, in which an ounce of interaction is followed by a pound of feedback, needs to be carefully monitored.

Feedback should also be delivered in the spirit of cooperative learning. Training groups are, ideally, small communities in which the members are invested in one another's learning. Feedback that is aggressive or indifferent, on the one hand, or overly cautious and sympathetic, on the other, creates a climate that is either too harsh or too soft for effective learning.

If a tape recorder is used in the subgroup, responders can be given the opportunity to criticize their own responses first. Once the speaker gives a brief, behavioral evaluation of his or her own responses, the observer and the speaker can add to or modify what the responder has said. Giving trainees an opportunity for self-feedback can help stimulate them to become more responsible for their own learning.

7. *Time for processing: taking care of maintenance needs.* Effective trainers give trainees an opportunity to discuss how they feel about themselves and about what is happening in the training group, time to celebrate their successes and deal with their frustrations. In the beginning, time can be set aside specifically for these activities. As trainees become more adept at communication and assertiveness skills, taking care of maintenance needs can be combined with the training process itself.

Challenging Skills: A Special Word. Challenging skills constitute "stronger medicine" than the other helping skills and need to be treated with special respect. In the training groups, it is best not to allow trainees to challenge one another until they have shown the ability to use these skills to challenge themselves. Therefore, as trainees explore their own issues and concerns, they are expected both to challenge themselves and to invite others to participate in this process. Each trainee, however, is to remain in charge of his or her own confrontational process, thereby demonstrating that self-challenge, even with real clients, is still the ideal approach.

Inductive and Deductive Learning. The seven steps of microskills training constitute an example of a deductive approach. At times, however, an inductive approach to microskills training can also be used. In inductive approaches, trainees are asked to identify skills that are presented to them either directly or through the method of contrasts. For instance, the method of contrasts can be used to demonstrate empathy in the following way. The trainer tells the trainees that he is going to counsel a coworker in two different ways and wants them to note the differences. First, he spends a few minutes counseling the coworker ineffectively—he does not listen well, asks a lot of questions, challenges some of the things the coworker says, and so on. Then the trainer demonstrates effective helping. He listens well, uses a great deal of empathy and an occasional probe followed by empathy. After the demonstration, he asks the trainees to analyze the two vignettes, point out differences, tell what they did and did not like, and indicate which approach seemed the most useful. Once the skills that best contribute to the helping process are identified and clarified, trainees practice them and receive feedback.

The most effective kind of training includes elements of both inductive and deductive training. Deductive training has the advantage of being very clear and precise. Inductive training, on the other hand, although more cumbersome and time-consuming, can actively engage trainees from the start.

Training Homework: Exercises. Trainees should come to training sessions prepared for what is to take place. Therefore, exercises have been developed to be completed outside the training session (Egan, 1982a). In a sense, these exercises fit between step 4 and step 5 of the training process—once trainees have both a conceptual and a behavioral feeling for a given skill or technique, they then practice it in private, using the written exercises. In the training session, the trainer can do one or two of the items of any exercise with the trainees before asking them to complete the exercise at home. Part of the next training session can be spent in small groups sharing responses to the exercises. This approach is an opportune starting point for practice in the skill or technique in question.

Trainees should have substantial material to talk about in practicing the skills and techniques. The quality of their self-disclosure as they deal with their own difficulties, concerns, and developmental issues significantly influences the quality of the training sessions. Therefore, they are asked to develop personal self-disclosure themes that are worth exploring as they practice the skills and techniques. For example, one trainee, in examining his interpersonal style, soon came to realize that he was very controlling in his relationships to others. He used the training sessions to explore this theme and to do something about his controlling behavior. All the steps of the helping process can be used to explore and work on these themes. If the issues revealed are of little consequence, the training sessions are trivialized, as if powerful tools were being used to work on flimsy material. Therefore, trainees should be encouraged early in the training process to search for themes that will be worthy of exploration.

The Use of Formulas. Formulas can be useful in helping trainees learn and sequence the elements of a skill or technique. By using these formulas, trainees can walk themselves through a given skill in order to become familiar with it. A typical formula is the one for primary-level accurate empathy suggested by Carkhuff (1973).

1. First, give yourself time to assimilate what the client has said. Do not feel pressured to speak immediately.
2. If you have not understood what the client has said, say so. Do not pretend that you have.
3. In the beginning, use the following format in responding to what the client has said: "You feel _____ because _____ ." In describing the feeling, use the right family of emotions and the proper intensity of emotion; in describing the cause, indicate specific experiences or behaviors that underlie the person's feelings.

4. Present an adequate response, but be brief, rather than long-winded.
5. Use language that makes sense to the client, but avoid using language that is foreign to you.

Trainers can also use similar step-by-step formulas to walk trainees through skills they are finding difficult. These formulas are found in the latest book of exercises developed for this helping model.

Learning by Doing: Moving Through the Steps of the Helping Process. Once trainees have acquired the basic communication skills—and, in so doing, have talked about their own concerns—and once they have been exposed to case studies of the application of the helping model to people involved in a variety of problem situations, they are ready to apply the model more systematically to the issues of their own lives. That is, with the help of their trainers, they learn to set goals for themselves, to help one another set goals, to develop programs, to deal with the problems that arise during the implementation phase, and to evaluate the use of the model. Case studies used to illustrate a helping model give trainees an opportunity to point out what has been done right, what has gone wrong, and what else could have been done. However, if trainees are deluged with case studies without the benefit of analytical and critical tools like the helping model outlined in this chapter—or if they are provided with an overabundance of such tools—the case study method can become confusing.

Training Clients in Skills as a Form of Helping

One reason people find themselves in trouble is that they do not have the skills needed to cope with problem situations. As Carkhuff (1971), Carkhuff and Berenson (1976), and others have suggested, clients can be helped not only by being trained in the specific skills they need to handle a given problem situation—for instance, communication skills to help them cope with marital problems—but also by being trained in the rudiments of the problem management process itself. Then helping in its training-as-treatment form becomes the mirror-image of helper training—that is, the form of the helping process is training in the skills and techniques of problem management, and the content is the clients' problem situations.

Needless to say, the training of clients can be a matter of degree. Most approaches to helping, if examined carefully, contain elements of training. Even in psychoanalysis, for example, clients are trained in the skill of free association. Other forms of helping, such as transactional analysis, Gestalt therapy, and rational-emotive therapy, provide more explicit forms of training. Since helping, then, can include a great deal of education (for working knowledge) and training (for skills) as a way of helping clients manage problem situations, potential helpers need to know how to educate and train. In the internship method, trainees not only are trained but also know from the beginning that they are going to train others. Therefore, even while being trained in the skills and techniques of helping, they pay attention to how they are being trained, and their trainers point out the major elements of training. Later, trainees become trainers themselves under supervision, preferably with a relatively experienced trainer in a cotraining situation.

Introducing Trainees to Other Approaches to Helping

A problem-solving or problem situation management approach to helping need not ignore the contributions of the other contemporary approaches to helping, such as Gestalt therapy, rational-emotive therapy, and transactional analysis—quite the contrary. The problem-solving framework specifies concretely and specifically the tasks to be accomplished in effective helping but places no limitations on how these tasks are to be accomplished. Any technique or methodology that is ethical and suited to the needs of both client and counselor can be used to achieve a given task. Potential helpers can be trained to use the problem-solving framework both to organize the contributions of other approaches to helping and to draw from them concepts, strategies, methodologies, techniques, exercises, and skills that contribute to each of the eight helping tasks. This framework, by helping make sense of the welter of approaches found in the helping literature, can become the principal instrument of a systematic and integrative eclecticism.

References

Anthony, W. A. "A Human Technology for Human Resource Development." *Counseling Psychologist,* 1978, 7 (3), 58-65.

Bellingham, R. L. "On Researching the Researchers." *Counseling Psychologist,* 1978, 7 (3), 55-58.

Carkhuff, R. R. "Training as a Preferred Mode of Treatment." *Journal of Counseling Psychology,* 1971, *18,* 123-131.

Carkhuff, R. R. *The Art of Problem-Solving.* Amherst, Mass.: Human Resource Development Press, 1973.

Carkhuff, R. R., and Berenson, B. G. *Teaching as Treatment.* Amherst, Mass.: Human Resource Development Press, 1976.

Chinsky, J. M., and Rappaport, J. "Brief Critique of the Meaning and Reliability of 'Accurate Empathy' Ratings." *Psychological Bulletin,* 1970, *73,* 379-382.

Dyer, W. W., and Vriend, J. *Counseling Techniques That Work: Applications to Individual and Group Counseling.* Washington, D.C.: American Personnel and Guidance Association, 1975.

D'Zurilla, T. J., and Goldfried, M. R. "Problem Solving and Behavior Modification." *Journal of Abnormal Psychology,* 1971, *78,* 107-126.

Egan, G. *The Skilled Helper: A Model for Systematic Helping and Interpersonal Relating.* Monterey, Calif.: Brooks/Cole, 1975.

Egan, G. *Exercises in Helping Skills.* (2nd ed.) Monterey, Calif.: Brooks/Cole, 1982a.

Egan, G. "People-in-Systems: A Comprehensive Model for Counselor Training." In D. Larson (Ed.), *Giving Psychology Away: Innovations in Psychoeducation, Skills Training, and Human Development.* Monterey, Calif.: Brooks/Cole, 1982b.

Egan, G., and Cowan, M. A. *People in Systems: A Model for Development in the Human-Service Professions and Education.* Monterey, Calif.: Brooks/Cole, 1979.

Gladstein, G. "Empathy and Counseling Outcome: An Empirical and Conceptual Review." *Counseling Pyschologist,* 1977, *6* (4), 70-79.

Hackney, H. "The Evolution of Empathy." *Personnel and Guidance Journal,* 1978, *57,* 35-38.

Heath, D. H. "The Maturing Person." In G. Walsh and D. Shapiro (Eds.), *Beyond Health and Normality*. New York: Van Nostrand Reinhold, 1980a.

Heath, D. H. "Wanted: A Comprehensive Model of Healthy Development." *Personnel and Guidance Journal*, 1980b, *58*, 391–399.

Mahoney, M. J., and Arnkoff, D. B. "Cognitive and Self-Control Therapies." In S. L. Garfield and A. E. Bergin (Eds.), *Handbook of Psychotherapy and Behavior Change*. (2nd ed.) New York: Wiley, 1978.

Maslow, A. H. *Toward a Psychology of Being*. (2nd ed.) New York: Van Nostrand Reinhold, 1968.

Miller, G. A., Galanter, E., and Pribram, K. H. *Plans and the Structure of Behavior*. New York: Holt, Rinehart and Winston, 1960.

Rappaport, J., and Chinsky, J. M. "Accurate empathy: Confusion of a Construct." *Psychological Bulletin*, 1972, *77*, 400–404.

Truax, C. B. "The Meaning and Reliability of Accurate Empathy: A Rejoinder." *Psychological Bulletin*, 1972, *77*, 397–399.

Chapter 6

Interpersonal Process Recall

Richard P. McQuellon

The interpersonal process recall (IPR) model, a film-based training program, consists of specific techniques and procedures for recalling thoughts, feelings, intentions, expectations, and images that occur during an interaction. The basic IPR format has interview participants watch a videotape replay of their interaction and attempt to arrive at a deeper understanding of the interaction through individual or mutual recall in the presence of a third party called an inquirer. The inquirer helps the subject, or recaller, examine and recall underlying interpersonal and intrapersonal processes by asking nonjudgmental, noninterpretive questions from a relatively neutral frame of reference. The general goal of the entire model is the development of specific communication skills and interpersonal self-awareness. More than a skills training program, IPR is "a curriculum in human relations" (Brammer and Allmon, 1977, p. 616).

The model has been developed and researched over the past twenty years by Norman Kagan and his colleagues and students at Michigan State University and is described in numerous publica-

Note: I am grateful to Dr. Norman Kagan for his time and concerted efforts over the past three years in explicating many of the concepts described in this chapter. I would also like to thank Michael Cowan for his constructive observations on an earlier draft of this chapter.

tions (Kagan and others, 1967; Burke and Kagan, 1976; Kagan, 1978, 1981). The technique of recall was originally applied in graduate counselor education and training and was rapidly expanded to include a variety of professional and paraprofessional care givers—psychologists, ministers, social workers, physicians, teachers, and dormitory advisers—in a number of different settings. The process has also been used as an adjunct to psychotherapy (Kagan and McQuellon, 1981).

Origins

The IPR method of using videotape replay has technological as well as philosophical precursors. Early applications of audio recordings were reported by Covner (1942, 1944) and Rogers (1942) as aids in the practice of counseling and in research and teaching, and closed circuit television was used experimentally in psychiatric hospitals as early as 1953 to allow patients to watch ongoing group psychotherapy sessions (Tucker and others, 1957). Bloom and his associates (1954) used a technique similar to IPR with audio recordings, recording students in classroom discussion periods and then asking individual students to listen to selected segments of the tape. The investigator would stop the tape at what appeared to be a significant point and ask the subject to recall what was going through his or her mind at the time. Nielsen (1964) successfully used a similar process with 16 mm film in studying self-confrontation.

The philosophical roots of the recall technique, including the inquirer role and function, can be found in the Socratic method, in which questions are posed as a way of stimulating learning. Socrates used questions as a method for helping students think through complex problems or for bettering opponents in debate. The crucial difference between the Socratic and inquirer methods of questioning is that the inquirer does not have a logical solution in mind, nor does he or she seek to better the recaller. The inquirer's central role is to pose questions that facilitate the recaller's exploration of the interpersonal and intrapersonal processes that occurred during the videotaped session. The goal is self-knowledge through an increased awareness and verbalization of the thoughts and feelings that accompany interpersonal behavior, the assumption being that the recaller is the best source of knowledge about his or her own behavior.

The first known scientific study of mental processes began in the experimental laboratory of Wilhelm Wundt in the late 1870s. Along with other early structuralists, he defined psychology as human experience studied from the perspective of the experiencing person. These first experimental psychologists trained subjects in introspection in efforts to understand mental processes and observed that their subjects, when asked to recall specific events, forgot much of what had taken place. The use of recording aids in IPR allows psychologists to employ a form of introspection as a refined procedure. Video recording and the use of an inquirer stimulates much more introspective analysis than memory alone. Kagan observed that viewing a videotape replay with the help of a probing, nonevaluative inquirer who allowed the viewer full responsibility for stopping the tape was a powerful stimulus for self-examination and growth. This observation led to the development of the IPR training method.

Key Assumptions

The basic assumption of the IPR model is that people are their own best source of knowledge about themselves. In his theory of personality and behavior, Rogers (1951) stated a related proposition when he suggested that "the best vantage point for understanding behavior is from the internal frame of reference of the individual himself" (p. 494). In IPR, the inquirer seeks not to actively pursue the recaller's frame of reference but rather to help the recaller explore this frame of reference in relation to specific moments on the tape. For example, the recaller might stop the tape and comment, "I seem to be avoiding eye contact there, and I look very nervous. I was thinking that what I was saying wasn't making any sense. I sound stupid." The inquirer would not reflect back the feeling and content of what was being said but would attempt to help the recaller explore his or her reactions further with a number of questions. Implicit in this assumption is the idea that people are inclined toward self-discovery and awareness, a notion central to the philosophy of human growth articulated by Maslow (1968, 1971). To see oneself interacting leads to self-evaluation and the potential for change. This potential varies widely among individuals, although some empirical evidence supports the hypothesis that self-evaluation is the initial reaction to self-focused attention (Wicklund, 1978). Videotape replay provides a powerful stimulus for self-focused attention.

A second assumption of the IPR model is that all people act as naive psychologists with implicit theories of interpersonal behavior. Simply stated, most people, without having studied psychology, have ideas about what they and other people are like. Wegner and Vallacher (1977) point out that "commonsense theories of psychology" have been discussed by such influential psychologists and philosophers as Kelly (1955), Schutz (1970) and Heider (1958). Heider suggests that "the ordinary person has a great and profound understanding of himself and of other people, which, though unformulated or only vaguely conceived, enables him to interact with others in more or less adaptive ways" (p. 2). These vaguely conceived theories are explored and verbalized more fully in the recall sessions, the assumption being that, provided with the proper stimulation, ordinary people are able to explore their own intuitive psychology and how it influences interpersonal relations. The shortcomings of the "intuitive psychologist" have been discussed elsewhere (Ross, 1978).

A third assumption of the model is that verbal labeling of interpersonal and intrapersonal processes serves an ordering function. Describing physiological reactions, cognitions, affects, and fantasies gives the person a sense of mastery not only over vague sources of anxiety or fear but also over sources of joy and happiness. Dollard and Miller (1950) describe the powerful function of language in helping people change feelings and attitudes. Verbal labeling is a necessary prerequisite to thinking about an emotional response, as well as about events and behaviors. Kagan (1981) has described the process by suggesting that "finding labels, finding words for what had been vague thoughts, finding words for what had been prelanguage feelings, helps us know ourselves in language. We may be literally informing one part of the brain about the content of another, . . . having a language, having words, makes our fears more manageable, less frightening. It's almost as if the fero-

cious wolf, on close examination, is found to be very old and tooth-
less" (p. 103).

A fourth assumption is that beginning counselors need to
accomplish interpersonal developmental tasks in order to become
skillful at influencing human interaction (Kagan, 1981). In the
model, these tasks are located in sequential order, from the least to
the most threatening. First, the counselor must learn specific communication skills or response modes; second, the counselor must
study himself or herself in action, using individual counselor recall;
third, the counselor must obtain feedback from the client with individual client recall, thereby initiating the study of others; and, finally, the counselor must study interactions using mutual recall.

Theoretical Foundations of the IPR Training Model

IPR assumptions and theory did not grow out of any specific
personality theory but rather emerged from the recall sessions of
hundreds of subjects, which were guided by a form of inductive
logic. As a method of exploring interpersonal communication, IPR
can be explained from a variety of theoretical perspectives.

Two basic dynamics have been observed in the application of
the IPR method. First, people need each other for more than physical survival—they need an optimum level of interpersonal stimulation, a level that varies among individuals and fluctuates over time.
Interpersonal relationships are potentially the most satisfying sources of stimulation available to humans, but such relationships can
also be the source of intense emotional suffering. This creates a
second dynamic: people learn to fear each other, recognizing that,
like fire, relationships have the capacity to both warm and scorch
the spirit. Such vague fears and occasional feelings of helplessness
are called "interpersonal allergies or nightmares" by Kagan. These
fears and feelings are probably developed early in life as a result of
lengthy childhood dependence, which would account for the fact
that so many of the intense feelings described by subjects in the IPR
sessions seem infantile, like lingering vestiges of childhood fears.
Most often, these amorphous feelings have not been verbalized in
day-to-day interaction. Consequently, they remain unlabeled and
inaccessible to the logic and the ordering function of language.

These gut-level feelings have been observed repeatedly in the course of hundreds of IPR sessions and usually cluster around four basic themes:

1. *You will hurt me:* If we develop an intimate relationship, you will do something that will cause me pain.
2. *I will hurt you:* In like manner, I could hurt you.
3. *You will engulf me:* If we relate intimately, you will somehow overwhelm me, negate who I am. My sense of self will be engulfed in who you are.
4. *I will engulf you:* In a similar manner, I could engulf you.

These basically opposed states can be seen throughout the ethnological, anthropological, sociological, and psychological literature and probably have roots in biological survival. They are evident in a variety of interpersonal behaviors. For example, most human interactions are characterized by some degree of approach-avoidance behavior. Dollard and Miller (1950) have explained this concept and its variants in terms of approach and avoidance goal gradients that can be used to explain interpersonal behavior. People both approach and retreat from simple direct intimacy with others in a cyclical fashion. Relationships ebb and flow according to the whim and fancy of the interactants and are dependent on a host of variables, both internal (thoughts, feelings, needs) and external (propinquity, circumstances, physical appearance). Attempts at intimacy are followed by relative isolation, followed by new bids for intimacy. This process appears to establish a specific range of safe interpersonal distance unique to each individual. Communication theorists (Argyle and Dean, 1965) have proposed an equilibrium model in which the physical distance, as evidenced in a variety of nonverbal behaviors, balances the two opposed states. The establishment of a predictable psychological distance allows for some level of intimacy, as well as a feeling of safety from the potential risks accompanying such intimacy. This safe range, which is unique to the situation and the relationship, serves to minimize both the pain of boredom and interpersonal deprivation when people are kept at a distance and the experience of anxiety when they are too close. The stronger the fear, the less likely the person will be to seek intimacy. Conversely, if fear is minimal and people feel safe, they will be more able to achieve sustained, intimate contact.

The way in which people send and receive messages is an example of the approach-avoidance dynamic. Much communication is not directly acknowledged by the sender or the receiver. When people interact, they sense each other on many levels, but they consciously acknowledge only a very limited range of what they send or perceive. This feigning of naiveté is a part of many human interactions and reduces the potential for mutuality and the level of genuine intimacy in human relationships, as well as the possibility of being hurt.

Kagan (1980) suggests that people demonstrate basic interpersonal typologies. These manifestations of the approach-avoidance dynamic are seen in the interpersonal pattern or style that individuals develop in order to survive emotionally in a social world that is perceived as dangerous, yet needed. Kagan organizes these patterns into a two-stage model. The first stage consists of the responses of immediate interaction—the way a person acts in daily encounters. These behaviors differ widely and depend on a variety of situational factors. The second stage is characterized by a long-term interpersonal posture, an interpersonal style, a habitual, generalized way of relating to people. The recurrent use of specific interpersonal behaviors (stage 1) leads to the development of a pattern of interaction (stage 2). Thus, an interpersonal style evolves out of characteristic patterns of interpersonal behavior made up of specific interactional units.

The basic interpersonal response modes in stage 1 are characterized by three behavioral manifestations:

1. *Attack:* a continuum of aggressive behavior ranging from assertiveness to hostile attacking.
2. *Withdrawal:* a continuum of behavior ranging from a mild manner to habitual withdrawal from interaction.
3. *Conformity:* a continuum ranging from productive cooperation to total conformity.

The long-term (stage 2) interpersonal style may be different from what the immediate behavior implies. An attacking style may take the form of assertive aggressiveness but, with an appropriate partner, could lead to increased intimacy, an engaging, lively interaction. The interpersonal function of the behavior is of primary concern. What purpose does the behavior serve? Does an attacking style serve to drive people away or to help establish closeness?

In the second stage of the model, six interpersonal styles have been defined, utilizing the attacking, withdrawing, and conforming typology.

1. *Attack may serve a withdrawal function.* A person's immediate and most frequently used response to others may be along the aggressive continuum. Surface attacks serve to keep others at a distance. The aggressive, hostile, attacking person achieves a long-term pattern of withdrawal by driving others away.

2. *Attack may serve to promote conforming behavior.* One may attack others in order to define oneself in terms of a particular group or set of norms or to maintain an unchallenged loyalty to a family or a set of beliefs about interpersonal behavior. Attacking serves to enhance interpersonal conformity and reduce options for involvement with different others. This life-style serves to maintain a degree of safety by insulating one from involvement with others who do not conform to one's own belief system.

3. *Withdrawal may serve an attacking function.* To disengage another through passive withdrawal is a subtle but powerful aggressive act. Under pressure of immediate interpersonal encounter, one may seek to pull back, to escape. The term passive-aggressive has been used to describe this long-term interactional pattern.

4. *Withdrawal may result in conforming.* Here, withdrawal is not aggressive, in that there is no effort to attack through passive demonstrations of hostility. The person simply goes limp interpersonally, nodding and agreeing with everything.

5. *Conforming may serve an attacking function.* This manifestation is most evident in the pseudoconformist, who strikes out when others' backs are turned.

6. *Conforming may lead to withdrawal.* One can conform to maintain distance and safety, but often boredom and loneliness result.

All of these interpersonal styles serve to maintain a degree of safety, a familiar behavior pattern that, for the most part, serves to reduce the imagined fears associated with intimacy.

Fully functioning people are able to draw on a wide range of interpersonal behaviors in developing intimate relationships and are flexible in their use of interactional behaviors, depending on situational determinants (Mischel, 1968). Less-effective people rely on a particular interpersonal pattern and posture, a limited behavioral repertoire. They are unable to take interpersonal risks, prefer old, familiar patterns of interactions, and appear quite fearful of intimacy.

The concepts presented in this section comprise the theory discussion of the IPR training model. The response modes and long-term interpersonal styles are similar to Horney's (1945, 1950) pathology-based perspective of interpersonal typologies. Kagan (1980) clearly points out that these ideas are offered to students as one—and by no means the only or even the best—cognitive map, or set of constructs, for explaining interpersonal behavior. The IPR model relies heavily on the exploration of each individual's experience, behavior, and unique way of viewing the world. Although it attempts to provide a structure, it is an organic model, relying on the emergent discoveries of participants and strongly supporting the notion that there are a variety of ways to describe and perceive one's own and another's experience.

Theoretical Foundations of the Recall Process

A description of the theory underlying the recall process helps to explain why the session is a potentially powerful learning experience. Kagan (1979) suggests that recall provides "the opportunity for 'stepping outside oneself' during or after an interview and examining the session" (p. 477), thereby encouraging the development of that process of self-observation described as the "self as knower," the "I," the "pure ego" (James, 1890), the "observer" in participant observation (Sullivan, 1953), and the "I that is aware of the social me" (Mead, 1977). The uniquely human and paradoxical capacity to be at once in an interaction and outside of it observing can itself be observed and explored. The recaller has the opportunity to view the self as object, to be both the I and the social me of Mead, to step outside the interaction and understand it from the perspective of another who, in this case, is the self at a different time.

The process of observing the "I that is aware of the me" is facilitated by the role of the inquirer, who implicitly defines for the recaller a social-psychological theory of interaction that holds that the defining of the situation is crucial in social interaction (McHugh, 1968). The persons involved in any social encounter produce a definition of the situation in response to the question "What is going on here?"—a question Goffman (1974) suggests occurs implicitly in any face-to-face encounter. The inquirer overtly defines the taped interview as a situation in which many unexpressed reactions were experienced by the recaller. The recall session is defined as an opportunity for discovering and expressing covert aspects of interpersonal behavior by explicitly defining the implicit assumptions operating for the participants in the face-to-face interaction and by stimulating recall with the videotape replay and the inquirer's nonjudgmental attitude and probing questions. These factors help create an expectation or a mental set for the discovery of censored or undiscovered material and stimulate the recaller to ask, "What is going on here in terms of my implicit thoughts, feelings, and beliefs?" In this manner, the basic assumption that the recaller is the best source of information about himself or herself shapes the IPR process.

Influencing Human Interaction: The IPR Program

The IPR program is presented in seven sequential units, with accompanying films and videotapes and an instructor's manual that includes typescripts of each film and an introductory chapter describing a variety of instructional variables. As noted earlier, the sequencing of the units is based on the strategy of having counselor developmental tasks proceed through communication skills training to the study of self, others, and interpersonal interactions. The films and videotapes provide didactic presentations, demonstrations, and time for practice of the skills in response to vignettes and for discussion of questions posed by the narrator.

Elements of Effective Communication

The second unit—unit 1 of the instruction manual consists of introductory material—presents four verbal response modes: exploratory, listening, affective, and honest labeling. Research with mental health therapists has shown that these responses are employed by effective interviewers (Kagan and others, 1967). Kagan (1977) has described these as the most basic of interpersonal skills. Their purpose is to elicit information, promote a sense of trust in the client-counselor interaction, encourage communication of affect, and facilitate open examination of the most personal and intimate areas of a client's life. In the following descriptions of the responses, the context is one in which an interviewer responds to a person who presents a concern.

Exploratory responses take the form of open-ended questions or statements. Their purpose is to encourage elaboration and to help a person stay involved in communicating while allowing him or her freedom to respond. Exploratory responses invite the client to become an active participant in the interaction, rather than a passive recipient of advice. They invite the client to explore more deeply, to expand, to elaborate, and to take a good deal of responsibility for the direction and content of the interview. The exploratory response resembles an essay question, giving latitude for full examination of whatever issue is raised and thereby facilitating discovery of new regions of what may be complex territory. Examples would be: "Tell me more about that," "I'm interested in hearing you say more," or "Go on." More specific examples emerge from the content of the interaction.

Exploratory responses serve to facilitate the development of an egalitarian partnership, in which interviewer and interviewee collaborate in deeper exploration of the concerns presented. The structure of the exploratory response produces the metacommunicative message "I want to understand this concern with you, rather than for you," which follows the basic assumption that people are the best source of information about themselves. Nonexploratory responses further a relationship characterized by authoritarian leadership, in which the interviewer becomes the source of knowledge about the interviewee. Both participants in the interaction can produce this result, but it is less likely to occur with the use of effective exploratory responses.

Listening responses clarify and paraphrase the client's statement, communicating a sense of active and deliberate hearing in a climate of genuine interest. Paraphrasing serves to check out the interviewer's understanding by reflecting back the content of what has been heard. "What I hear you saying is . . . . Am I hearing you right?" Paraphrasing serves the function of providing feedback cues for both interviewer and interviewee, so that the listener can continue to "track" the concern of the interviewee. Asking for clarification usually occurs when the interviewer is confused about what has been said. For example, "I am not sure I understand. . . . Could you say more?" The focus is on hearing the other person and avoiding interpretive, authoritative responses. In contrast, nonlistening responses rarely seek clarification and frequently jump to conclusions prematurely.

Affective responses focus on the feeling quality, the bodily states, and the moods conveyed verbally and nonverbally in the client's message. The purpose of an affective response is to help the client get in touch with feelings, underlying attitudes, gut reactions, and values. While most people recognize intense emotions when experiencing them, especially when their level of physiological arousal is high, these feelings are seldom labeled or discussed directly. Affective responses facilitate the full expression of the other's feeling state. Frequently moods are only vaguely understood and are consequently puzzling or even frightening. Affective responses help the other to recognize and explore the depths of feeling and perhaps to label previously undifferentiated mood states in the presence of an empathic listener. A response may be as simple as "How does that make you feel?" or more complex—for example, "I noticed your voice became low, trailed off, and you stared out the window. You seem to have some feelings about that."

Honest labeling responses are unusually candid without being brutal or rejecting. Their purpose is to encourage a dialogue of content and feelings that are usually difficult to disclose. Such responses communicate a willingness to deal directly with what has been heard and encourage clients to squarely confront their own perceptions, attitudes, and values. Honest labeling responses involve risk, for they do not seek to clean up, modify, or politely distort what has been heard. But not to engage in honest labeling can also be risky, since the client may feel that some of his or her innermost thoughts and feelings are shameful if the interviewer only refers to them obliquely. The interactants may be so polite and diplomatic that they continually avoid the real issue.

All messages exist on at least two levels. On one level, the content of the message refers to the facts that are transmitted verbally. A transcript of a conversation provides a pure example of message content, the acknowledged story line or official statement. On another level, process refers to the manner in which a message is conveyed. Voice tone, facial expression, speech speed, body posture, and nonverbal gestures typically contain cues to what we are feeling for or from the other person. Honest labeling responses go beyond the acknowledged story line to address content and process directly and frankly. This response is potentially the most confrontive of the four. The effort is to engage the other person in actively examining interpersonal behavior and cycling to deeper levels of communication by honestly labeling perceptions and discussing them.

For the sake of clarity and ease of acquisition, these four response modes have been described as distinct entities. However, in most cases, elements of each are combined in a single response. They are not discrete responses to be mechanically repeated but are rather broad categories of responses that have demonstrated effectiveness when used with sincerity and respect (Kagan and others, 1967).

The instructional methods and activities employed in IPR training are grounded in a philosophy of experiential learning and center around the interactions of participants. Typically, training begins with a brief description of the rationale and development of IPR, followed by the introduction of participants. The film *Elements of Communication*, the central focus of unit 2, then presents the four response modes, their purpose, and examples of effective and ineffective responses. The film is frequently stopped, and participants are asked to address issues raised by the narrator and practice the various response modes in relation to specific statements made by the film's characters. Exchange of ideas and opinions occurs in large and small group and dyadic exchange. The trainer monitors the responses, providing guiding feedback and facilitating interaction.

Affect Simulation Process

The third unit consists of a series of short vignettes showing individuals communicating messages directly to the viewer. The messages are provocative and convey intense feelings, such as anger, fear, sadness, and affection. The vignettes can be stressful and are designed to stimulate thoughts, feelings, images, and reactions in the viewer in order to increase sensitivity to his or her own responses. Sensitivity to one's idiosyncratic reactions—especially to "interpersonal allergies," noxious responses to certain behaviors— can be helpful in overcoming fears of interpersonal involvement. The assumption is that participants bring their own stereotypes and prejudices about age, sex, race, body size and shape, and good and bad psychological problems, which can function as obstacles to the intense involvement often necessary for therapeutic interaction.

The trainer has the option of augmenting the film presentation by first describing the rationale for self-study in the training process. Participants are asked to imagine that they are alone with the character in the film, who faces the camera directly and makes a provocative statement. For example, an older woman says admonishingly, "I know I can trust you to do what is right. I know you wouldn't do anything that I wouldn't approve of . . . . I know I can trust you" (Kagan, 1981, p. 84). Following the vignette, reactions are discussed in a variety of formats, including dyads, small groups, and the entire class.

Recall Process and Methodology

The recall session is the core of the IPR training model. During this session, the videotape replay, the active presence of the inquirer, and the recaller's inclination toward self-discovery combine to form a potentially powerful learning experience. A classic example of the material that the recall session seeks to explore can be seen in novels like *Crime and Punishment* or *Native Son,* which provide the reader with a window into the mind of the protagonist.

We have no way of knowing the thoughts of Raskalnikov or Bigger Thomas; only through the depth of exploration unfolded by Dostoyevsky or Wright can we begin to see the world from the protagonist's point of view. The purpose of recall is to provide the recaller with the possibility of discovering a similar window into his or her own mind. The story narrated is the recaller's own.

Individual Recall—Self-Study. The purpose of unit 4 is to describe and demonstrate the recall process as a further method for self-study and to introduce the inquirer role. The trainer typically begins by selecting one of a series of films that depict several therapists, a resident advisor, and a curriculum director recalling reactions to their videotaped interaction. These films of actual, rather than enacted, encounters stimulate questions and discussion about recall sometimes referred to as inquiry, or the inquiry session.

Once recall is understood by the participants, the trainer may demonstrate the process by soliciting volunteers to conduct an interview followed by the interviewer recall session, with the trainer acting as an inquirer. The trainer models the inquirer role and stimulates discussion about the utility of that role. When they have learned the subtleties of the inquirer role and function, participants are ready to conduct their own recall sessions.

Inquirer Role Function. Unit 5 describes the heart of the IPR process, since it is the inquirer who guides the recall session. The ability and willingness of the trainee to recall interpersonal process events depends largely on a skilled inquirer, whose primary task is to facilitate stimulated recall and trainee self-observation and exploration. Lab experiences of one to two hours begin once the inquirer role and function is understood.

When the recaller stops the tape to make observations, the inquirer poses brief, exploratory questions about thoughts, feelings, images, and bodily reactions from a neutral frame of reference. Effective questions emerge from careful, sensitive, deep listening by the inquirer. For example, questions like "How did you feel about that?" "Do you recall what you were feeling?" and "Does that feeling have special meaning for you?" can stimulate affective exploration. Examination of cognitions could be encouraged by "What were you thinking there?" "What thoughts were you having about the other person there?" or "Any ideas about what you wanted to say there?" In addition, certain questions have been found effective in stimulating awareness of bodily sensations—"Any physical sensation with that feeling?" or "Were you having any fantasies at that moment?"; in searching out expectations—"What did you want from him or her"; in exploring mutual perceptions—"How do you think he or she was seeing you there?"; in exploring hidden agendas—"What did you want to say at that point?"; and in leading to other associations—"Did she or he remind you of anyone in your life?"

Effective inquiring requires gentle, assertive probing, a nonjudgmental attitude, and an interest in learning from the recaller's self-observations. The emphasis is on the recaller learning by self-discovery, rather than on evaluative feedback from the inquirer. Kagan suggests that the most effective inquirers are well trained, empathic counselors who are able to listen with polite but assertive questioning attitudes. The inquirer role includes introducing the recall process and posing probing questions that serve to aid the recaller's discovery and elaboration of overt and covert interpersonal processes.

The film *The Inquirer Role and Function* presents some theoretical constructs underlying the role, depicts examples of the inquiry process, poses questions for discussion, and asks participants to practice inquirer questioning behavior following short vignettes. The trainer varies the format and the time spent practicing the role, depending on the needs of the group. The first lab emphasizes training through practice and feedback, rather than through a critique of the behaviors in the recorded session.

Individual Recall—The Study of Others. Unit 6 is designed to help trainees learn about client dynamics directly from the client. The process is similar to the interviewer recall described in unit 4, except that the person presenting the concern does the recalling, rather than the interviewer. The client in the training session is actually a fellow trainee, who has the opportunity to experience presenting a concern to a counselor.

Since the heart of the program is the recalling of interpersonal processes, authentic dyadic interaction in the lab sessions is a central experience for all trainees. The trainer needs to stress the importance of selecting meaningful topics for the interviews. Discussion of personal concerns, such as an impending job change or a difficult relationship, usually leads to rich recall experiences and self-discovery. By this stage of the class, participants hopefully know and trust their lab partners enough to increase the depth of exploration.

The study of others is illustrated by films showing actual interactions, followed by a recall session in which the recaller describes reactions to the interview from his or her perspective. The participants watch the filmed interview with real clients and discuss the impact of learning about the interview directly from these clients. In the teaching setting, fellow trainees will serve in the role of client.

Mutual Recall—The Study of Interactions. Unit 7 is designed to help participants study interactions and use the here and now of interaction as content for discussion. In contrast to the individual recall sessions described in units 4 and 6, both participants are present with the inquirer. Following videotape replay of their interaction, the inquirer encourages both participants to talk about their unexpressed thoughts, feelings, intentions, and expectations. The inquirer's function in mutual recall is to help the participants talk with one another and listen to each other express deeper levels of meaning, as well as to examine perceptions of each other developed during the videotaped interaction. As in individual recall, mutual recall sessions have as content the original interaction itself.

Again, a series of films is available for selection by the trainer, who chooses on the basis of the group's needs and interests. Lab sessions continue, with a shift in emphasis to studying the interactants' relationship as it unfolds in the interview sessions. Lab partners have the opportunity to talk directly to each other about the replayed interaction, to explore their differing perceptions and to engage in general mutual exchange.

Recall Session—Methodology. The following steps are utilized in applying IPR to counseling and psychotherapy training. First, adequate videotape facilities are necessary. The equipment is located in one room, where both the videotaping and recall take place. Next, if the recaller is unfamiliar with the recall and taping procedures, their format and rationale are explained, and questions are answered by the interviewer. The third step is the taping of an interview, which may be as brief as fifteen minutes or as long as the traditional fifty-minute hour. When the interview is finished, the recall session can begin. In interviewer recall, the client leaves the room and the inquirer enters and instructs the recaller in the specifics of individual recall, including the following principles of face-to-face interaction derived from Kagan and others (1967):

1. The mind works faster than the voice. We can think much more quickly than we can speak.
2. Everyone has thoughts during a conversation that are not verbalized. We do not say all that we think or feel.
3. At times, we like what others say, and, at other times, we are annoyed with what is said. We feel both understood and not understood at various times in conversations.
4. At times, we are concerned about another's perception of us and want to be seen and thought of in a particular way.
5. If you were asked now to describe when you felt understood or not understood in the session or when you were making a certain kind of impression, it would be difficult for you to remember. With the videotape replay you will be able to recall these thoughts and feelings in detail. Stop the tape as often as you like, whenever you recall thoughts and feelings that occurred during the interview or observe something that you were unaware of during the interview.
6. When you stop the tape and recount your recollections, I (the inquirer) will ask questions to help you explore your memories and associated reactions.

Typically, responsibility for stopping the tape rests with the recaller. However, in some applications the inquirer may also stop the tape to make observations and provide feedback (Kagan, Krathwohl, and Miller, 1963).

The following individual therapist recall session (Kagan, 1981) illustrates the application of the IPR technique in the supervision of psychotherapy, with the supervisor acting as inquirer. The client had been seeing the therapist for a few months prior to this session. Part of the recorded session is presented first, followed by some of the therapist's recall.

Interview Session

Client:	That was like a slap in her face. I got a big kick out of it, and it finally got to her—got back *at* her, I guess. There aren't too many times that I get to do that.
Therapist:	Do you think it sunk in?
Client:	Oh, yeah, she started crying. Yeah, she started crying and carrying on, and so I said, "Hey, I don't need the hassle," and I hung up on her. And I never hang up on my mother. But I've hung up on her now . . . .
Therapist:	Something this time enabled you to do something that's really been hard to do, and I wonder what it is. What's changed?
Client:	I guess I'm being allowed to grow up. Uh . . . I see things in a different perspective. I feel that I'm getting . . . how do I say it—stronger? I'm getting to see these people that I didn't see before and . . . I don't like what I have had to see in order to become stronger, but I've benefited from it. And even if they were my parents and still are, that doesn't mean I have to cater to them. I mean, why? I used to hop every time they said boo. And I don't need that.
Therapist:	. . . no more hopping?
Client:	No . . . at least, not a whole lot. (Pause.) When I get, you know, tired or vulnerable or whatever, then the odds are greater for me to get back, like, you know—weaker, to be more susceptible to them, I guess.
Therapist:	I wonder if they can kind of sense it when you're weak? You know, you've told me sometimes that it's almost as if they had kind of a radar that—especially your ex-husband—that seems to have happened. You'd be weak and somehow something would come across that he'd know that this was a time to take advantage of you.
Client:	They know exactly where to take advantage of me.
Therapist:	They know your weak spots?
Client:	They know them better than I do. (Pause.) At least, they seem to always be able to hit on it. (Sighs.) I mean,

yesterday, when I told the kids' father that there wasn't going to be any more hassle—I'd asked him to buy boots for the kids because he makes $1400 a month—you know? And I know that I'm still on ADC, and so, anyway, this is why the kids have tried to call him . . . so that he would help out. And he never did get anything for the kids. (Pause.) She went to school and she started crying in the bathroom—she wouldn't go into the classroom because the teacher the day before had told them that they definitely had to have boots and everything, and so anyway I got a call from the school stating, you know, that she really needed them. Well, the teacher said that she would try to ask somebody that she knew of, some of her friends, if she could get a pair of boots, and she didn't but she took up a collection.

Therapist: That really gets to you. Her kind of asking for charity like that, and here's your ex-husband with all this money . . . your kid's father.

Client: Yeah . . . so I went down to the school and picked up the money and I got her some boots—they're really nice. But here they have a father that puts on . . . a beautiful front that he cares, and he ignores them completely. I don't really like to ask him for money, but, my heaven, it seems like he would really want to start doing something. You know, the big show is there . . . .

Therapist: All show and no go . . . .

Client: Yeah. I don't really like to take anything from anybody. It's not the—I mean, I really appreciate it, you know, what they did, but . . . it wouldn't really have been necessary if he had played his part.

Therapist: And his part is what?

Client: Uh . . . being a father and being concerned and caring whether they . . . (Pause.) He gets things first—it's always been that way, and I don't know why I keep thinking that, you know, sometime that he would really start changing.

Therapist: It's hard to give up a hope like that, isn't it?
Client: Yeah, I guess I've hoped all my life. And I can see the
                kids going without—I don't like to see it.

Recall Session

Client: . . . got back at her, I guess. There's not too many
                times that I get to do that. (Stop tape.)
Therapist: I knew there was something bothering her. I knew we
(Recall)   could have a regular session here—that it wouldn't
                take too long. I wanted that to happen, but still in my
                mind there was, "Gee, I hope we're not wasting
                tape"—you know? And also wasting Wanda's time.
                You know, she did have something that just happened.
                You know, coming in to the studio here she said,
                "A lot happened," and I said, "Well, let's wait
                till—well, let's not have a session out in the hallway."
                So I was really saying to her, "We're going to get some-
                thing accomplished today." I think that being in
                therapy with Wanda in a sense can be seen in this
                interview. The whole course of therapy is aimed
                towards freeing herself from needing the approval
                from parental figures.
Client: When I get, you know, tired or vulnerable or whatever,
                then the odds are greater for me to get back, like, you
                know—weaker, to be more susceptible to them, I guess.
Therapist: I wonder if they can kind of sense it when you're weak?
                You know, you've told me sometimes that it's almost
                as if they had kind of a radar . . . (Stop tape.)
Therapist: I do have a tendency to lead a little too much in ther-
(Recall)   apy, although I'm getting over it, or maybe I'm just
                doing it in more subtle ways. I have to learn about
                that. So I want to steer clear of that, especially with
                somebody that really needs to own their accomplish-
                ments in therapy.
Inquirer: That brings up an interesting question—of risks. Were
                there any risks that you were perceiving other than that
                or in addition to that? That note of caution?

Therapist: Uh . . . the risks, I think, the risk that the caution is
(Recall)   involved with is simply producing a model, "cure," so
                to speak. You know—where the person did intellectu-
                alize and they don't own it themselves, it's all tied in
                with therapy—"My therapist really did this," in-
                stead of, "I did it myself."

Therapist: —especially your ex-husband—that seems to have
                happened. You'd be weak and somehow something
                would come across that he'd know that this was a time
                to take advantage of you.

Client: They know exactly where to take advantage of me.

Therapist: They know your weak spots?

Client: They know them better than I do. (Pause.) At least,
                they seem to always be able to hit on it. (Stop tape.)

Therapist: I see that as the dilemma that she has. "How do they
(Recall)   know?" The self-defeating answer to that question that
                she'd tell herself is that they know because they know
                what's best for me. You know, parents are always right
                and this sort of thing. And what I'm trying to get her to
                look at now and I don't think really succeed in this
                session, but will eventually, is they have that radar for
                other reasons than caring about you. Yet you can see
                the perplexed look on her face—"How the hell do they
                know? How do they know when I'm weak?" And I
                think the answers that she tells herself are very weak
                and "I radiate weakness." And they comment, "give me
                my due," and kind of the notion that for anyone else,
                when you're weak, sympathy is appropriate. But for
                her, when you're weak, you're supposed to get stomped
                on. You know, she lies down in front of the door,
                somebody comes in, they're supposed to walk over her.
                If it were anyone else, they'd say, "Why are you lying
                down in front of the door? I don't want to step on
                you." And that's again the dilemma that I think that
                she feels. Why her? "Why me?" And then she answers
                it, "Because I'm rotten."

Inquirer: And you, what are you feeling at that moment?

Therapist: (Recall)	Oh, a sense of . . . well, I'm feeling pretty good because she's building a foundation. We've gone over this before, we'll go over it again and again and again in different ways, from different angles. But she's working it out rationally. She's approaching coming to the understanding . . . that really there are no villains in this place, just a lot of people with a lot of problems who sometimes inadvertently and sometimes deliberately have hurt each other. And she's tended to be the victim. And there are people who gravitate towards victims.
Client:	. . . she didn't but she took up a collection.
Therapist:	That really gets to you. Her kind of asking for charity like that, and here's your ex-husband with all this money . . . your kid's father.
Client:	Yeah . . . (Pause.) So I went down to the school and picked up the money and I got her some boots—they're really nice. (Stop tape.)
Therapist: (Recall)	The sense at that time was, "She's got to feel that hurt, that humiliation"—in a sense, maybe even wallow in it a little. And I know I was helping her do that, I was pointing out things. And not in an angry way, like, "He's your kid's father, damn it, and he has a responsibility to them"—I didn't say it that way. I said it with a little more sadness, because I feel—and it's a hard thing to do—but she's got to go and feel that sadness and really feel that pain. You just can't pluck her out of the pain and say, "Get mad." She'll get mad. But I think she also has to be very much aware of the pain that that man has inflicted on her.
Inquirer:	Do you recall any feelings you were having?
Therapist: (Recall)	Well, it goes through my mind, "That bastard, here he's making $1400 a month and you're on ADC and your kids have to take a collection to get the necessities of life. It's winter and it's getting slushy and snowy out and they can't even have boots, and he's going to dangle those boots and make you jump." And so there's an

anger in there toward him. That occurs to me, but that's not that relevant to her. Except that she can look at me, I suppose, perhaps as a model. But at this point, she's not even there yet. And there's a profound sense of responsibility when I lead her to feel sadness more intensely. And I don't do that glibly.

Inquirer: What does that feel like for you?

Therapist: Well, there are two feelings. One is that I know I have
(Recall) to do it. Because for me that's the way therapy works. And yet people that I work with change. I know that in my head, and that's what I have to do. But there's a sense of, "I wish I didn't have to do it the painful way," you know. I don't see any virtue in pain, particularly. And if there was a way that I could think of to ease it and still have the person own it . . . You know, we get into the whole thing of why do doctors give so many tranquilizers? Well, it eases the pain. But they don't own that—anybody can take the pill.

Inquirer: What does it do to you?

Therapist: It makes me feel just in awe of my responsibility. Of the
(Recall) feelings that I don't particularly have to take home with me and she does. There's an unfairness in that, I suppose, but as long as I feel the inequity of me eliciting very intense feelings and feeling them in a session—sure I'm involved in a session, but not afterwards. Generally, I leave it behind and either go on to seeing my next client or, you know, go home or do something and put it aside. And all these people that I work with, they can't do that [pp. 138–149.]

Theory Discussion. The purpose of unit 8 is to give the trainee a conceptual framework for understanding interpersonal styles and behaviors. This unit was added to the basic IPR training model when Rowe (1972) found that, if students were taught theoretical constructs in addition to the experiential procedures of the model, their skills development was significantly augmented. The typologies described in the section on the foundations of the IPR model are presented in unit 8 as one way in which to develop a beginning understanding of the functions of interpersonal behavior. Fully functioning individuals, it is suggested, are capable of a wide range of interpersonal behavior.

Role of Instructor and Participants. The primary role of the instructor is to ensure the overall quality of the learning experience by facilitating an atmosphere of trust in which skills building and self-discovery can occur. This atmosphere can be more easily maintained by attention to a number of tasks. First, the instructor should make an accurate assessment of the developmental needs and expectations of the trainees. For example, undergraduate nursing majors need clear structure and direction to get the full benefit from lab experiences, whereas professional mental health workers need less direction to participate profitably. Second, the instructor should provide leadership by explicating concepts, demonstrating skills where necessary, and giving written and verbal feedback to the participants. Third, basic physical necessities should be provided—for example, adequate space, film and equipment, and time to conduct the sessions without pressure. Fourth, reference materials, handouts, workbooks, and articles should be supplied as needed. Fifth, films should be stopped frequently to encourage discussion and debate, allow note taking, and challenge the ideas presented. Sixth, the training roles of interviewer, interviewee, inquirer, and recaller should be clearly defined. Finally, and perhaps most important, it is crucial that the instructor learn to minimize lecturing and allow ample time for practicing the response skills, appreciating that participants learn best through experience and discussion.

Design Variations. The basic training activities can be accomplished in approximately thirty hours in groups of eighteen to twenty-four. Although a single trainer can effectively handle a group this size, training in inquiry requires more direct feedback and is ideally facilitated by one trainer for each group of six. Undergraduates typically require the recommended full thirty hours plus six to eight hours of lab time, while more psychologically sophisticated professionals learn the technique in as few as eighteen hours, including lab experiences. One of the virtues of the IPR model is the flexibility it allows the trainer. Numerous design variations can be employed, since there are three film series illustrating interviewer, client, and mutual recall, as well as four separate films for skills building and concept presentation. Selected units may be presented with a variety of film combinations. For example, the *Elements of Communication, Affect Simulation,* and *Theory Discussion* films can be used individually as separate training experiences, and films depicting the various types of recall can be shown to illustrate particular kinds of interactions, such as therapist-client, administrator-teacher, physician-patient, teacher-student, husband-wife, and interdisciplinary health care team. Variations on the basic IPR training format are limited only by the availability of essential materials, the creativity of the trainer, and the cooperation of the participants. As mentioned earlier, the format generally proceeds from didactic presentation of information to increasing involvement in affect simulation exercises, discussion of filmed recall sessions, and lab experiences.

Key Characteristics of IPR

Why is IPR an effective training program? Kagan (1980) suggests a number of reasons. First, the program provides a structure for skills development that encourages intimate interpersonal encounter in a relatively safe environment. Since intimacy is not a dominant theme of life in our society, nonthreatening activities allow for opportunities to experiment with behavior that can facilitate intimate involvement. But skills are not enough; if people are frightened of intense involvement, they are unlikely to seek it with others. Filmed, simulated encounters with such fears can be viewed from a position of safety. Simulation enables trainees to encounter potentially overwhelming experiences without in fact being overwhelmed. Labeling and cognitive analysis can result in mastery over fears that were previously vague and unknown. Interpersonal nightmares (described earlier in this chapter) can be viewed from a safe position, examined, and understood.

Second, small group discussions of reactions to simulated situations allow participants the opportunity to learn about the inner lives of others and to share their own inner life with some degree of intimacy, thereby expanding their descriptive language for the world of private feelings and thoughts.

Third, the interviewer recall format in the lab experience gives the interviewer the opportunity to make explicit his or her thoughts, feelings, aspirations, and perceptions while watching the session in the presence of the questioning inquirer. The interviewer can observe his or her own interpersonal distancing and gain increased awareness of idiosyncratic interactional tendencies. Watching the videotape replay allows the recaller to be conscious of himself or herself while minimizing self-consciousness. Also, the recall provides a chance to practice new behavior—verbalizing what was withheld—without the fear of facing the interpersonal nightmare in the interaction itself.

Fourth, the inquirer role assists participants in developing the skill of helping another learn by self-discovery. People do not naturally possess the skills necessary to help human beings struggle through complexities in their lives. The assertive, nonpunitive, nonhostile relationship skills characteristic of good inquirer behavior facilitate the process of self-examination and discovery. Interpersonal courage can be nurtured in the inquirer, who learns that probing questions do not have to be received as hostile.

Fifth, when the program is used to train counselors, the client recall provides the opportunity to learn about the nature of helping directly from the client. Previous hunches are confirmed or denied. Participants begin to learn that, while discussing their concerns, clients may focus a lot of their energy on how they feel about the counselor and how the counselor may be perceiving them.

Finally, the mutual recall format provides an opportunity for the participants to discuss the "there and then" of the videotaped interaction in the here and now of the recall session. In the presence of the third person inquirer, the participants are usually able to risk describing the perceptions of each other that occurred during the taped interaction. The conversation in mutual recall is characterized by a you-and-me, here-and-now quality, described as the skill of immediacy by Egan (1982). When used with significant others or with people from the population in which participants will be working, this can be a powerful learning experience facilitating increased depth and mutuality in relationship development.

Applications of the IPR Model

The IPR training program has evolved and expanded over the past twenty years as numerous applications in a variety of settings have shaped the thinking of Kagan and his associates. IPR training has been used with psychologists, social workers, physicians, teachers, counselors, undergraduate and graduate students, prison personnel, medical students and residents, and nurses.

Following training, Robbins and others (1979) report greater emphasis on psychosocial issues, an increased level of empathy, and more affective responses in interviews conducted by house officers in an internal medicine residency program employing a modification of the IPR method. Strohlein and others (1977) at the UCLA School of Dentistry describe the recall process as a teaching tool that has produced valuable learning experiences for dental students and faculty. Modifications of the IPR model have produced promising results with policemen (Danish and Brodsky, 1970), with graduate students in counseling programs (Boltuch, 1975; Spivack, 1972), and with undergraduates in nursing, dietetics, music therapy, and other areas (Kagan and Burke, 1976). Medical, pharmacy, and law schools, hospitals, secondary schools, mental health centers, and other agencies have been introduced to IPR in workshop sessions. The IPR model has been used not only in the United States but also in Canada, Australia, Sweden, Denmark, Norway, Germany, Puerto Rico, Israel, Malaysia, and England (Kagan and Byers, 1973, 1975). Because of the flexibility of its training methods and its use of filmed illustrations of interaction and recall from many areas, such as teaching, medicine, psychotherapy, family therapy, and health care, the model has broad applicability and utility in introducing basic interpersonal skills and concepts to both psychologically sophisticated and psychologically unsophisticated populations.

Survey data indicate that the vast majority of medical schools, nursing programs, family practice residencies, and physician's assistant programs include interpersonal skills training in their curricula (Cohen and Friel, 1978). Many of these courses have been influenced by the pioneering work of the College of Human Medicine at Michigan State University, where the doctor-patient interaction course for first-year medical students, structured around the IPR training format, is currently a central component in the clinical science curricula. This course was initially developed under the direction of Hilliard Jason (Jason and others, 1971), who modified the IPR model to meet the needs of medical education. Actors and actresses were recruited as patient models and trained to present themselves as friendly or unfriendly, communicative or uncommunicative, forthright or deceptive, and in specified conditions of health or illness. The patient models described health concerns that were familiar to the students or that required no knowledge of specific diseases. Following didactic and film presentation of the basic concepts of the IPR model, interviews with patient models were conducted, videotaped, and replayed to the medical students using the general recall format. Physicians from the local community trained in IPR often served as inquirers for the recall process. The goal of the interview and the following recall was to help students begin to integrate their nascent medical knowledge with the practice of basic interviewing and counseling skills. Werner and Schneider (1974) detail the course structure and evaluate the effectiveness of this program in the early 1970s. Currently, modifications have been made that use trained faculty members as instructors in groups of six students each. Details of the modifications are described in the second edition of Kagan's *Influencing Medical Interaction* (1981).

That the IPR training model is simple enough to be understood and practical enough to be implemented in a wide variety of settings is a direct result of the broad applicability of its basic concepts and methods; the placing of responsibility for learning directly in the hands of the participants; and the sensitive guidance of competent trainers.

Research and Evaluation

The impact of the IPR training program has been evaluated in many controlled experimental studies, reviewed (Lee, 1973), and compared with several other skills-training models (Brammer and Allmon, 1977). Most studies have before-and-after evaluations of the effect of all or major segments of the model. The literature can be roughly categorized into three areas: research on training application, in which the impact of the entire model is measured; research on acceleration of client progress in psychotherapy applications; and intramodel studies. Several representative studies from each area will be cited, along with summary statements of relevant research.

Research on Training Applications. Kagan and others (1967) report a series of studies supported by the National Institute of Mental Health (NIMH) on the early version of the model, a model that did not include the affect simulation unit and many of the recall films. Results produced preliminary data validating the efficacy of the recall technique in counselor education and supervision and in the elucidation of specific elements of effective communication leading to the development of the four response modes described earlier. In addition to the procedures for counselor education and for accelerating client progress in counseling, several other areas were studied, including the measurement and characteristics of affective sensitivity, nonverbal behavior, and the communication of affect, and teaching-learning strategies. The Affective Sensitivity Scale, further developed by Kagan, Schneider, and Werner (1977), has been used in numerous studies to measure post-IPR training gains.

The elucidation of specific elements of communication grew out of efforts to develop a behavioral counseling rating scale, eventually named the Counselor Verbal Response Scale. The scale response categories were developed by analyzing videotapes of counselors whose skills usually led to positive client comments during recall sessions. These videotapes were compared with videotapes of counselors who seemed ineffective to their clients. The subjective reports of clients, the ratings of experts, and a review of the literature combined to form the data base supporting the efficacy of the four response modes. The response modes were then used as a basis for rating subsequent trainee-client interviews. Using the Counselor Verbal Response Scale as a measure of therapist effectiveness, the research efforts focused on the validation of effective procedures in counselor education and supervision. One such study (Goldberg, 1967), which compared IPR-based supervision with intensive traditional supervision, provided evidence that the IPR methodology could be used to train counselors effectively. When the audiotapes of counselor trainees were rated (double blind) by independent judges, statistically significant differences in counseling skills were found that favored the IPR groups. This pattern of change was consistently observed in each of the three successive academic quarters during which the study was conducted.

In a controlled study, Spivack (1972) analyzed the comparative effectiveness of two prepracticum methods on the interviewing skills of master's degree candidates in counseling. With some design modifications, this study replicated the positive results of the Goldberg study in comparing the IPR supervisory technique with a traditional classroom training experience using lectures, demonstrations, tape critiques, and discussions. The statistically significant results of the study favoring the IPR treatment group indicate that media techniques can be incorporated into a training model within the time and financial limitations of an ongoing master's-level program. Grzegorek (1970) provides further evidence in support of the effectiveness of the model for use in counselor supervision.

Following the early IPR research, studies were conducted applying the model in a variety of ways. Dendy (1971) used the model in a fifty-hour training program for undergraduates (resident assistants). Results revealed significant improvement in interviewing skills and growth in affective sensitivity, with no loss of skills during a subsequent three-month period of no training. This finding is particularly significant for mental health workers interested in the training of paraprofessionals in basic counseling skills.

In a follow-up study, Archer and Kagan (1973) found that, after training, these same undergraduates could effectively train fellow students. The peer-instructed students scored significantly higher on measures of affective sensitivity and self-actualization than did other students who participated in an encounter group of similar duration. In evaluating this study, Kagan (1980) points out that the students were carefully selected and highly motivated and that the results must be considered in this light. He goes on to cite several studies where nonsignificant gains were found in a population of court case workers (Heiserman, 1971) and alcoholics (Munoz, 1971) and generally cautions against making claims for IPR training that cannot be supported with data.

Acceleration of Client Progress in Psychotherapy. Kagan and McQuellon (1981) summarize the literature on the use of IPR in the second major area of research—acceleration of client progress in counseling and psychotherapy. The theoretical rationale, as in training applications, is the study of self through observation and discussion of interpersonal behavior and the exploration of concomitant covert processes. Controlled experimental studies (Hartson and Kunce, 1973; Hurley, 1967; Schauble, 1970; Tomory, 1979; Van Noord, 1973) and case studies (Kagan, Krathwohl, and Miller, 1963;

Kagan and others, 1967; Resnikoff, Kagan, and Schauble, 1970) provide evidence for the effectiveness of the IPR technique.

Schauble (1970) found promising results on several outcome measures when comparing traditional counseling with IPR techniques. Van Noord (1973) conducted a similar investigation with some design improvements, most notably the adoption of different outcome measures. No significant differences were found between groups on the objective measures, although subjective comments by clients favored the IPR group. Tomory (1979) built on these studies by introducing flexibility into the treatment design, allowing therapists to introduce segments of the IPR model, within certain guidelines, when they found it appropriate—for example, he cautioned that they had to use the various components of the model a certain number of times in order to insure meaningful comparisons. He compared a group of traditionally counseled individuals with clients counseled with a combination of IPR and traditional methods and found no significant differences on a series of objective measures, even though clients and therapists alike offered positive feedback on the IPR techniques.

Hartson and Kunce (1973) employed a combination of stimulus films and dyadic and group recall techniques in a study that assessed the effectiveness of IPR in accelerating group psychotherapy with college students. In six sessions, clients in the IPR treatment group showed significantly higher changes in self-disclosure and "readiness-for-group" behavior and participated in more therapeutic interchanges than clients in traditional T groups. However, the T-group clients did show significantly higher satisfaction scores. Differential treatment effects were also observed in separate sample groups. Among socially inactive subjects with low self-esteem (clients at the counseling center), the IPR self-confrontation methods were helpful, whereas the direct confrontation methods of the T group had an adverse effect. Socially active subjects with high self-esteem (participants in a YMCA social skills training group) demonstrated no treatment differences. The authors concluded that direct confrontation by another person in the T group method may have an adverse effect on those with inadequate social skills and low self-esteem. IPR videotaped self-confrontation may provide a less-threatening experience.

Intensive case studies have generally yielded positive results in the application of recall techniques. However, it should be noted that, in each of the case studies cited, variations of the recall process were introduced at different times in the counseling process by expert counselors familiar with IPR techniques. In the first case study of the use of IPR, Kagan, Krathwohl, and Miller (1963) report on a thirty-eight-year-old married woman complaining of depression and an unsatisfactory marital relationship. She had been in treatment with one of the authors for five months prior to her exposure to a single recall session and was described by her therapist as rationalizing her behavior in long, cognitive descriptions. In the procedure utilized, both client and counselor simultaneously viewed the session with different inquirers in separate recall rooms. Any inquirer or recaller could stop the replay to discuss recalled feelings and elaborate on meanings. Whenever the replay was stopped by one member of either team, it automatically stopped for the other team. The recall session seemed to help stimulate movement through a therapeutic impasse by helping the client recognize her excessive rationalizing and by facilitating affective exploration. Following this procedure, marked progress was noted, culminating in a successful termination after eight months of treatment.

Resnikoff, Kagan, and Schauble (1970) report a case study with a highly intelligent, eighteen-year-old male high school senior suffering from mild to acute psychotic reactions. A single IPR session was introduced at session twelve of a twenty-week, twice-weekly contract. The authors chose to utilize the IPR intervention when the client was showing clear signs of depression in order to "get at the dynamics underlying the depression" (p. 103). Client recall was used with both inquirer and client stopping the tape, and the impact of the process was assessed on four broad characteristics of client growth: (1) owning the discomfort—the client admits the feeling of discomfort and begins to specify the locus of concerns, fears, and discomfort; (2) being committed to change—the client cooperates with, rather than resists, the efforts designed to help facilitate change; (3) differentiating stimuli—the client learns to perceive more and more of the external stimuli and reacts to these as discrete, rather than stereotyped, factors; (4) behaving differently—the client reports new behaviors outside the counseling relationship and tries out new behaviors with the counselor. The client's progress in each area was discussed and linked with the impact of the IPR session. The authors conclude "This pattern of resulting gains suggests that this form of stimulus intervention has broad application in the counseling and psychotherapeutic treatment of clients experiencing a variety of personal difficulties with various degrees of severity" (p. 110).

Additional case studies have been reported (Woody and others, 1965), many having been conducted during early research on the process. Other studies have investigated the effects of varying the frequency of videotape feedback during short-term counseling (Grana, 1977) and have attempted a cost-benefit analysis of IPR in terms of the inhibitory effects of using videotape on client self-exploration (costs) and the increased client satisfaction and counselor and supervisor empathy ratings (benefits) (Kingdon, 1975). The clients in this study who were treated by counselors using IPR supervisory methods—that is, client, counselor, and mutual recall—increased their level of self-exploration over time and demonstrated no inhibitory effects of videotape intervention.

In summary, the results of controlled experimental research are mixed. The case study reports are generally supportive of IPR intervention, suggesting that individuals may benefit from the use of specific recall techniques at particular points in the counseling process. Efforts to apply structured programs without regard to the wide variety of client problems and the highly idiosyncratic nature of interaction with different therapists, however, yield only suggestive evidence. More intensive case studies may yield clues to the conditions under which clients respond most favorably to IPR intervention.

Intramodel Studies. Intramodel studies have focused on the effects of several major elements of the entire IPR program. Archer and others (1972) report the results of a pilot study designed to illustrate the potential application of the IPR technique and to examine the impact of the affect simulation vignettes. Clinical observation revealed noticeable physiological reactions during the viewing of the films and the videotape review. Grossman (1975) conducted another study whose results supported the basic premise that the affect simulation vignettes have an impact on viewers.

Katz and Resnikoff (1977) used a systematic, controlled method to test the basic validity of the recall process. Subjects were trained to provide an ongoing record of the intensity of their feelings during dyadic interactions and then asked to repeat the process during a videotape recall of the recorded interaction. All four of the experimental groups demonstrated significant correlates between ongoing and recalled affect. Other studies report the validity and reliability of employing videotapes to stimulate recall (Young, 1980).

Measurement of the qualities that IPR seeks to influence is a challenging, complex task. Generally, following exposure to the IPR training program, subjects are better able to recognize and report affect as shown in filmed vignettes, to use more affective responses in interviews, and to demonstrate increased levels of empathy in interaction. Although the specific components of the IPR model that effect these changes are difficult to isolate, the overall program seems to produce in participants an increased sensitivity to the richness of interpersonal exchange and an awareness that much more is experienced in human interaction than can ever be described. Future research on cognitive styles and personality traits may lead to further specification of how individual differences affect responsiveness to the overall training program and to the recall process specifically.

Conclusion

Because of its adaptability, the IPR model can be used to train people not involved in the helping professions to relate to others more directly and to develop more intense involvements with those in their immediate environment. Currently, funding is being sought to make basic training procedures available to the general public, an effort that could prove to be the most innovative to date in "giving away" the knowledge and skills of counseling psychology. By helping individuals discover for themselves their own basic psychological concepts and guiding assumptions and perceptions of interpersonal interaction, the IPR model provides a methodology for addressing Adler's (1927) dictum that the study of human nature "cannot be pursued with the sole purpose of developing occasional experts. Only the understanding of human nature by every human being can be its proper goal" (p. 3). The exploration of interaction with interpersonal process recall is one method for helping people understand themselves and others in the context of human relationship.

References

Adler, A. *Understanding Human Nature.* New York: Wolfe and Greenberg, 1927.

Archer, J., Jr., and Kagan, N. "Teaching Interpersonal Relationship Skills on Campus: A Pyramid Approach." *Journal of Counseling Psychology,* 1973, *20,* 535–541.

Archer, J., Jr., and others. "A New Methodology for Education, Treatment, and Research in Human Interaction." *Journal of Counseling Psychology,* 1972, *19,* 275–281.

Argyle, M., and Dean, J. "Eye Contact, Distance, and Affiliation." *Sociometry,* 1965, *28,* 289–304.

Bloom, B. S. "The Thought Processes of Students in Discussion." In S. French (Ed.), *Accent on Teaching.* New York: Harper & Row, 1954.

Boltuch, B. S. "The Effects of a Prepracticum Skill Training Program, 'Influencing Human Interaction,' on Developing Counselor Effectiveness in a Master's-Level Practicum." Unpublished doctoral dissertation, Department of Counselor Education, New York University, 1975.

Brammer, L., and Allmon, D. "Reviews: Training Packages." *Personnel and Guidance Journal,* 1977, *55*(10), 612–618.

Burke, J. B., and Kagan, N. "Influencing Human Interaction in Public Schools: Studies of IPR Effectiveness as an In-Service Teacher Training Program." NIMH Project MH13526-02, Michigan State University, 1976.

Cohen, B., and Friel, T. *Teaching Interpersonal Skills to Health Professionals.* Amherst, Mass.: Carkhuff Associates, 1978.

Covner, B. J. "The Use of Phonographic Recordings in Counseling Practice and Research." *Journal of Counseling Psychology,* 1942, *6,* 105–113.

Covner, B. J. "Written Reports of Interviews." *Journal of Applied Psychology,* 1944, *28,* 89–98.

Danish, S., and Brodsky, S. "Psychology in Action: Training of Policemen in Emotional Control and Awareness." *The American Psychologist*, 1970, *25* (4), 368-369.

Dendy, R. F. "A Model for the Training of Undergraduate Residence Hall Assistants as Paraprofessional Counselors Using Videotape Techniques and Interpersonal Process Recall (IPR)." Unpublished doctoral dissertation; Department of Counseling, Personnel Services, and Educational Psychology; Michigan State University, 1971.

Dollard, J., and Miller, N. E. *Personality and Psychotherapy*. New York: McGraw-Hill, 1950.

Egan, G. *The Skilled Helper*. Monterey, Calif.: Brooks/Cole, 1982.

Goffman, E. *Frame Analysis: An Essay on the Organization of Experience*. Cambridge, Mass.: Harvard University Press, 1974.

Goldberg, A. D. "A Sequential Program for Supervision of Counselors Using the Interpersonal Process Recall Technique." Unpublished doctoral dissertation; Department of Counseling, Personnel Services, and Educational Psychology; Michigan State University, 1967.

Grana, R. K. "Videotape Feedback: Frequency of Usage and Its Value as a Counseling Technique." Unpublished doctoral dissertation, Department of Counselor Education, University of Akron, 1977.

Grossman, R. "Limb Tremor Responses to Antagonistic and Informational Communication." Unpublished doctoral dissertation, Department of Physiology, Michigan State University, 1975.

Grzegorek, A. A. "A Study of the Effects of Two Emphases in Counselor Education." Unpublished doctoral dissertation; Department of Counseling, Personnel Services, and Educational Psychology; Michigan State University, 1970.

Hartson, D. J., and Kunce, J. T. "Videotape Replay and Recall in Group Work." *Journal of Counseling Psychology*, 1973, *20*, 437-441.

Heider, F. *The Psychology of Interpersonal Relations*. New York: Wiley, 1958.

Heiserman, M. "The Effect of Experiential-Videotape Training Procedures Compared to Cognitive-Classroom Teaching Methods on the Interpersonal Communication Skills of Juvenile Court

Caseworkers." Unpublished doctoral dissertation; Department of Counseling, Personnel Services, and Educational Psychology; Michigan State University, 1971.

Horney, K. *Our Inner Conflicts.* New York: Norton, 1945.

Horney, K. *Neuroses and Human Growth.* New York: Norton, 1950.

Hurley, S. "Self-Disclosure in Counseling Groups as Influenced by Structural Confrontation and Interpersonal Process Recall." Unpublished doctoral dissertation; Department of Counseling, Personnel Services, and Educational Psychology; Michigan State University, 1967.

Ivey, A. *Microcounseling: Innovations in Interviewing Training.* Springfield, Ill.: Thomas, 1971.

James, W. *Principles of Psychology.* 2 vols. New York: Henry Holt, 1890.

Jason, H., and others. "New Approaches to Teaching Basic Interview Skills to Medical Students." *American Journal of Psychiatry,* 1971, *127,* 1404–1407.

Jourard, S. *Self-Disclosure: An Experimental Analysis of the Transparent Self.* New York: Wiley, 1971.

Kagan, N. "Can Technology Help Us Toward Reliability in Influencing Human Interaction?" *Educational Technology,* 1973, *13,* 44–51.

Kagan, N. "American Psychological Association Presidential Address, Division 17." *The Counseling Psychologist,* 1977, *2,* 4–7.

Kagan, N. "Interpersonal Process Recall: Media in Clinical and Human Interaction Supervision." In M. Berger (Ed.), *Videotape Techniques in Psychiatric Training and Treatment.* (Rev. ed.) New York: Brunner/Mazel, 1978.

Kagan, N. "Counseling Psychology, Interpersonal Skills, and Health Care." In G. C. Stone and Associates, *Health Psychology— A Handbook: Theories, Applications, and Challenges of a Psychological Approach to the Health Care System.* San Francisco: Jossey-Bass, 1979.

Kagan, N. "Influencing Human Interaction: Eighteen Years with IPR." In A. K. Hess (Ed.), *Psychotherapy Supervision: Theory, Research and Practice,* New York: Wiley, 1980.

Kagan, N. *Influencing Medical Interaction.* Unpublished manuscript, University of Michigan, College of Human Medicine, 1981.

Kagan, N. *Interpersonal Process Recall: A Method of Influencing Human Interaction.* (Rev. ed.) Film series and instructor's manual. East Lansing, Mich.: Mason Media, 1981.

Kagan, N., and Burke, J. B. *Influencing Human Interaction Using Interpersonal Process Recall (IPR): A Student Manual.* Michigan State University, 1976.

Kagan, N., and Byers, J. "IPR Workshops Conducted for the United Nations World Health Organization in New Guinea and Australia." World Health Organization, Manila, 1973, 1975.

Kagan, N., Krathwohl, D., and Miller, R. "Stimulated Recall in Therapy Using Videotape—A Case Study." *Journal of Counseling Psychology,* 1963, *10,* 237-243.

Kagan, N., and McQuellon, R. "Interpersonal Process Recall." In R. Corsini (Ed.), *Handbook of Innovative Psychotherapies.* New York: Wiley, 1981.

Kagan, N., Schneider, J., and Werner, A. "The Development of a Measure of Empathy: The Affective Sensitivity Scale." Paper presented at American Psychological Association, San Francisco, Aug. 1977.

Kagan, N., and others. *Studies in Human Interaction: Interpersonal Process Recall Stimulated by Videotape.* Research report, Educational Publication Services, Michigan State University, 1967.

Katz, D., and Resnikoff, A. "Televised Self-Confrontation and Recalled Affect: A New Look at Videotape Recall." *Journal of Counseling Psychology,* 1977, *24,* 150-152.

Kelly, G. A. *The Psychology of Personal Constructs.* New York: Norton, 1955.

Kingdon, M. A. "A Cost/Benefit Analysis of the Interpersonal Process Recall Technique." *Journal of Counseling Psychology,* 1975, *22,* 353-357.

Lee, J. "Book Reviews: Influencing Human Interaction." *Personnel and Guidance Journal,* 1973, *51* (6), 428-430.

Lieberman, M. "A Study of the Relationship Between Physiological Ability and Measures of Tested, Rated, and Perceived Empathy." Unpublished doctoral dissertation; Department of Counseling, Personnel Services, and Educational Psychology; Michigan State University, 1981.

McHugh, P. *Defining the Situation: The Organization of Meaning in Social Interaction.* Indianapolis, Ind.: Bobbs-Merrill, 1968.

Maslow, A. H. *Toward a Psychology of Being.* (2nd ed.) New York: D. Van Nostrand, 1968.

Maslow, A. H. *The Farther Reaches of Human Nature.* New York: Viking, 1971.

Mead, G. *George Herbert Mead on Social Psychology.* (Rev. ed.) (A. Strauss, ed.) Chicago: University of Chicago Press, 1977.

Mischel, W. *Personality and Assessment.* New York: Wiley, 1968.

Munoz, D. "The Effects of Simulated Affect Films and Videotape Feedback in Group Psychotherapy with Alcoholics." Unpublished doctoral dissertation; Department of Counseling, Personnel Services, and Educational Psychology; Michigan State University, 1971.

Nielsen, G. *Studies in Self-Confrontation.* Copenhagen: Munksgaard, 1964.

Resnikoff, A., Kagan, N., and Schauble, P. G. "Acceleration of Psychotherapy Through Stimulated Videotape Recall." *American Journal of Psychotherapy,* 1970, *24* (1), 102-111.

Robbins, A., and others. "Interpersonal Skill Training: Evaluation in an Internal Medicine Residency." *Journal of Medical Education,* 1979, *54,* 885-894.

Rogers, C. R. "The Use of Electrically Recorded Interviews in Improving Psychotherapeutic Techniques." *American Journal of Orthopsychiatry,* 1942, *12,* 429-434.

Rogers, C. R. *Client Centered Therapy.* Boston: Houghton Mifflin, 1951.

Ross, L. "The Intuitive Psychologist and His Shortcomings: Distortion in the Attribution Process." In L. Berkowitz (Ed.), *Cognitive Theories in Social Psychology.* New York: Academic Press, 1978.

Rowe, K. K. "A Fifty-Hour Intensified IPR Training Program for Counselors." Unpublished doctoral dissertation; Department of Counseling, Personnel Services, and Educational Psychology; Michigan State University, 1972.

Schauble, P. G. "The Acceleration of Client Progress in Counseling and Psychotherapy Through Interpersonal Process Recall (IPR)." Unpublished doctoral dissertation; Department of Counseling, Personnel Services, and Educational Psychology; Michigan State University, 1970.

Schutz, A. *On Phenomenology and Social Relation—Selected Writings.* (H. Wagner, Ed.) Chicago: University of Chicago Press, 1970.

Spivack, J. "Laboratory to Classroom: The Practical Application of IPR in a Masters-Level Prepracticum Counselor Education Program." *Counselor Education and Supervision,* 1972, *12,* 3–16.

Strohlein, A., and others. "Total Recall: Using the IPR Method and Video to Teach Dental Students." *Biomedical Communications,* Nov. 1977, pp. 8–12.

Sullivan, H. S. *Interpersonal Theory of Psychiatry.* New York: Morton, 1953.

Tomory, R. E. "The Acceleration and Continuation of Client Growth in Counseling and Psychotherapy: A Comparison of Interpersonal Process Recall (IPR) and Traditional Counseling Methods." Unpublished doctoral dissertation, Michigan State University, 1979.

Tucker, H., and others. "Television Therapy: Effectiveness of Closed Circuit TV for Therapy and Treatment of the Mentally Ill." *Archives of Neurology and Psychiatry,* 1957, *77,* 57–69.

Van Noord, R. "Stimulated Recall with Videotape and Simulation in Counseling and Psychotherapy: A Comparison of Effects of Two Methodologies with Undergraduate Student Clients." Unpublished doctoral dissertation; Department of Counseling, Personnel Services, and Educational Psychology; Michigan State University, 1973.

Wegner, D. M., and Vallacher, R. R. *Implicit Psychology: An Introduction to Social Cognition.* New York: Oxford University Press, 1977.

Werner, A., and Schneider, J. M. "Teaching Medical Students Interactional Skills." *New England Journal of Medicine,* 1974, *290,* 1232–1237.

Wicklund, R. A. "Objective Self-Awareness." In L. Berkowitz (Ed.), *Cognitive Theories in Social Psychology.* New York: Academic Press, 1978.

Woody, R. W., and others. "Stimulated Recall in Psychotherapy Using Hypnosis and Videotape." *American Journal of Clinical Hypnosis*, 1965, 7, 234–241.

Young, D. "Reliability of Videotape-Assisted Recall in Counseling Process Research." Unpublished manuscript, Oregon State Hospital, Salem, 1980.

Chapter 7

Structured Learning

Martita A. Lopez

Structured learning is an interpersonal skills training procedure that has been used since about 1970 both for training helpers and for treating clients. This chapter will focus on its application to helpers, although both uses share a common theoretical, procedural, and research foundation.

The structured learning approach is generally used with groups of eight to twelve trainees and two trainers who meet several times a week for two or three hours. The major goal of the program is for trainees to learn helping skills appropriate to their particular situation—police officers, for example, do not learn the same skills as mental health workers. This flexibility has allowed the program to be easily tailored to a variety of helpers, including nurses, teachers, police officers, counselors, parents, home aides, and managers.

The tailoring of skills to trainees and several procedures built into the method make it more likely that helpers will apply the acquired skills in the work setting. This transfer of training is another major goal of structured learning—many training and treatment programs do not in fact result in transfer (Goldstein and Kanfer, 1979; Kazdin, 1980).

Four major procedures constitute structured learning: modeling, role playing, corrective feedback–social reinforcement, and transfer training. During modeling, the skill is demonstrated to trainees either by the trainers or on audiotape or videotape. Since the skill has already been broken down into small behavioral steps, the performance of each step can be isolated and pointed out during modeling. Trainees are given cards on which these steps are printed to facilitate learning and role playing. Following modeling, trainees are asked for instances from their own jobs in which this skill would be useful. One of these examples is selected for use in the first role play, and the trainee who presented the situation is asked to choose another group member to participate also. After the role play, other trainees and then the trainers provide corrective feedback and social reinforcement. When the skill has been role played correctly using all behavioral steps, another modeling example is demonstrated, and a new trainee role plays. This procedure is followed until all participants have correctly role played at least once. Transfer of training is promoted through the inclusion of such transfer enhancers as using trainees' own experiences, having the trainees practice repeatedly, making the training setting as similar as possible to the work setting, and giving homework assignments. Interspersed with the basic procedures are discussions of the situations in which it would be appropriate to use the skill.

Theoretical and Research Foundations

Arnold P. Goldstein at Syracuse University has been the primary developer of the structured learning model. During the 1960s, Goldstein and others became concerned about the inapplicability of traditional psychotherapy to many types of clients, especially those of the lower socioeconomic classes (Goldstein, Heller, and Sechrest, 1966; Magaro, 1969). Concurrently, paraprofessionals began to be used in therapeutic and quasi-therapeutic roles, and a variety of approaches were employed to train them (Guerney, 1969). In this atmosphere of interest in prescriptive treatment and training, Goldstein began a program of research that focused on the development of an effective treatment method with lower- and working-class clients. He based his early studies on a body of literature suggesting that, for these clients, a successful approach would need to be brief and authoritatively administered, have a behavioral emphasis, involve conformity to concrete example, include role-taking training, and provide early, continuing, and frequent reinforcement (Goldstein, 1973). Also influential was another set of studies on communication patterns of lower- and middle-class persons that indicated that the two groups used different linguistic patterns and that, for the lower-class individual, communication should be less dependent on complex and abstract verbalization and more concrete and action-oriented (Goldstein, 1973). These desirable treatment characteristics identified by both sets of studies pointed to the usefulness of modeling and role playing, which are concrete, action-oriented, structured, behavioral techniques. Although Bandura (1969) and others had demonstrated the efficacy of modeling and social reinforcement, and investigators such as Lazarus (1966) had combined modeling and role playing, most studies had been conducted with middle-class clients or students. Goldstein (1973) describes in detail three series of studies carried out by him and his colleagues using modeling and role playing with lower-class inpatients, outpatients, and paraprofessionals. These studies will be reviewed here to provide some insight into the development of the structured learning approach.

Inpatient Studies. In accord with Goldstein's incremental research strategy, the inpatient investigations began with examinations of the modeling component alone. The first study (Liberman, 1970) involved eighty-four male alcoholic inpatients and used six experimental conditions, four modeling and two control. The modeling conditions were operationalized in terms of four audiotapes of initial psychotherapy interviews with varying degrees of patient disclosure and attraction to therapist. After hearing one of these tapes, each subject participated in an individual, intake-like interview during which he was asked exactly the same questions that had been asked on the tape. These interviews were content-analyzed for disclosure, and attraction to interviewer was assessed by means of a questionnaire. Results of the study revealed no attraction but significant disclosure. Thus, in this study, self-disclosure was enhanced by means of modeling.

The second modeling study, conducted by Friedenberg (1971), sought to investigate the effects on an actual interview of modeling verbal and nonverbal cues of attraction. Subjects were sixty male psychiatric inpatients who were randomly assigned to four experimental conditions (in a 2 x 2 factorial design) involving two levels of attraction to interviewer modeled nonverbally and two levels modeled verbally. Four modeling videotapes were used to operationalize these conditions. After viewing the assigned tape, each subject participated in an interview similar to the one he had seen on tape. Data analysis indicated that exposure to a high-attraction model, whether the model was verbally or nonverbally expressive, led to significantly greater postmodeling attraction and less silence. However, the attraction effect was weak and several components did not transfer to the interview.

The third modeling study was an attempt to strengthen the attraction effect by using conformity pressure, in addition to modeling (Walsh, 1971). Subjects were sixty female psychiatric inpatients who were randomly assigned to five experimental conditions (in a 2 x 2 plus control factorial design) with presence or absence of high-attraction modeling and presence or absence of high-attraction conformity pressure. Subjects heard an interview between a therapist and a client, were or were not exposed to conformity pressure oriented toward attraction to the therapist, and then rated the attractiveness of the therapist. Next, all subjects participated in a live interview with the therapist they had heard on the tape and rated him again for attractiveness. Once again, results showed significant effects for modeling and conformity, but no transfer to the postmodeling interview. Also, there were no additive effects of modeling and conformity.

Goldstein (1973) summarized his conclusions after these three studies as follows: "What may be necesary for more substantial, enduring, and transferable patient change is a more powerful implementation of modeling procedures, perhaps oriented towards more behavioral and less attitudinal skill targets and . . . augmented by opportunities for the patient observers to behaviorally rehearse what they have seen and receive social approval as their rehearsal enactments increasingly approximate the behavior of the model" (p. 112).

At this point, skills taught with structured learning were shifted to those more directly useful to clients in their daily functioning—for example, social interaction—and the components of role playing and social reinforcement were added. Gutride, Goldstein, and Hunter (1973) used modeling, role playing, and social reinforcement to teach social interaction skills to eighty-seven asocial psychiatric inpatients. Subjects were assigned to training and no-training conditions and were also dichotomized according to acute or chronic status and presence or absence of psychotherapy. Modeling videotapes were used, and subjects' role playing was itself videotaped and played back for corrective feedback. Results revealed that participants in structured learning groups performed significantly better on four of the seven social interaction behaviors rated. However, on a test of extended transfer of training, no training effects were in evidence. Acute patients generally performed better than chronic patients, although the training was effective with both groups. Finally, the presence or absence of psychotherapy had no effect on social interaction behavior.

The next study by Gutride, Goldstein, and Hunter (1974) used a group receiving a combination of structured learning and transfer training; an attention control group; a regular structured learning group; a longer structured learning group; and a no-treatment control group. Five modeling videotapes were used to teach social skills during mealtime to 106 psychiatric inpatients. Again, role playing was videotaped and immediately played back. Analysis of the data showed that all three structured learning groups were more socially interactive than the control groups but that the addition of this specific form of transfer training or of extra structured learning had no effect over and above the effect of the basic program.

The final two early studies with inpatients both dealt with affective skills. Orenstein (1972) taught two groups of fifteen female inpatients a skill called focusing-experiencing by using either structured learning or the focusing manual (Gendlin, 1969). There were three control groups, each composed of fifteen inpatients. Results showed no differences across the five groups on the skill. The second affective skill study is reported by Goldstein (1973). He sought to teach role taking to ten female inpatients, each with a history of marital problems. One structured learning group and two control groups were used in the study; each group was composed of ten inpatients. Modeling scenes were presented on videotape. Again, no differences between groups were demonstrated. Goldstein concluded that both training attempts failed because target skills were not adequately broken down into subskills and because training did not last long enough for the teaching of these abstract and therefore more difficult skills.

   Outpatient Studies. As in his early inpatient research, Goldstein's initial focus with outpatients was on the modeling component. The training target skills for lower- and working-class clients in the first three investigations were related to independent or assertive behavior. This area was chosen largely in response to a group of studies suggesting that overdependence on external authority is particularly characteristic of lower-class individuals (Kohn, 1969). For the first study (Goldstein and others, 1973), ninety psychiatric outpatients, half of them women, were selected to participate in three experimental conditions: independence modeling, dependence modeling, and no-modeling control. Modeling situations were presented on audiotape, and subjects' subsequent responses were also audiotaped. The study revealed a significant effect for both sexes for independence modeling and an effect for dependence modeling for females only. The second study, also reported by Goldstein and others (1973), included sixty male and female outpatients in an attempt to enhance the modeling effect. Trait structuring of the therapist as warm or cold was combined with independence modeling in the following groups: warm-independent, cold-independent, no structuring–independent, and no treatment–control. Results indicated an overall modeling effect, with evidence that cold structuring of the model yielded less modeling than warm or no structuring but with no evidence that warm structuring was a modeling enhancer.

   In another investigation of modeling enhancement, Ben (1973) examined the effectiveness of role induction and modeling as a means of altering selected mood states. Role induction is a pretherapy procedure designed to clarify clients' expectations and to provide specific client role training (Hoehn-Saric and others, 1964). Subjects for this study were seventy lower-class men who had sought psychotherapeutic assistance at a community clinic for alcoholics. The design format (2 x 2 plus control) involved the presentation of audiotaped intake interviews displaying the presence or absence of role induction combined with the presence or absence of model client mood improvement or with a no-tape control condition. Clients were given a mood measure before and after hearing the tapes and were then interviewed individually and retested. Analysis of the data revealed that role induction did indeed function as a modeling enhancer: clients exposed to both manipulations displayed a greater decrease of negative mood than those hearing only one or the other.

The inpatient studies described above suggest that the effects of modeling with clients can be enhanced by combining it with activities that help the client rehearse alternative responses and by providing social reinforcement to the client for doing so. The investigations with outpatients indicate that a structuring, role induction procedure can also serve as a modeling enhancer. A structured combination of these components—modeling, role playing, and social reinforcement—form the backbone of structured learning.

Paraprofessional Studies. While comparisons of different components were being conducted with various client populations, the same type of building-block research strategy was being carried out with different groups of paraprofessional psychotherapists and other helpers. The earliest of these studies was a therapy analogue in which 135 nurses and attendants employed at a state mental hospital were used as the sample (Goldstein and others, 1971). The primary dependent variables were attraction to client, empathy, and warmth. The design was a 3 x 3 consisting of three levels of the two independent variables: modeling of attraction to client (high, low, and neutral) and social class of client (middle, lower, and no information). Subjects first read instructions that contained social class information, then listened to a modeling tape of an initial therapy session in which models displayed one of the three levels of attraction to the client. Each subject was asked what he or she would say at various points during the modeling tape. Content analysis of subjects' statements showed that modeling high attraction significantly increased the warmth and empathy of these statements and modeling low attraction decreased warmth and empathy. Social class structuring, however, had little effect on subjects' attraction to clients.

The second investigation of the effectiveness of modeling procedures with paraprofessionals used therapist self-disclosure as a major dependent variable (Lack, 1971). Subjects were sixty female psychiatric attendants randomly assigned to one of four groups in a 2 x 2 factorial design involving the presence and absence of both modeling and instructions for self-disclosure. The method was similar to that just described for the study on empathy, except that a live interview with an actor-client was added at the end to assess minimal transfer of training. Content analysis of trainee statements found that subjects exposed to both modeling and instructions self-disclosed more than those receiving one or the other or none. During the live interview, however, only trainees in modeling conditions self-disclosed more; the effect of instructions did not transfer. This second finding is congruent with results of an earlier study with a client sample in which instructions also had no effect on increasing independent behavior (Goldstein, 1973). Apparently, the simplicity of the skill enabled it to transfer through modeling alone; studies on modeling more complex skills, described later in this chapter, found that additional procedures were required for any transfer to take place.

The third paraprofessional therapist study (Perry, 1970) focused on empathy as the target skill and again examined the effects of modeling and instructions as skill training procedures. A 2 x 3 factorial design was employed, with two levels of instructions and three levels of displayed empathy. Subjects were sixty-six clergymen who volunteered to participate. As in the self-disclosure study, participants either heard or did not hear taped empathy instructions and then listened to one of three modeling audiotapes. Each tape portrayed a therapeutic interview, and subjects were asked at different points what they would say if they were treating the client. Following exposure to instructions and tape, each subject conducted a fifteen-minute interview with an actor-client. Results revealed several main effects for modeling and one for instructions, but no evidence of any transfer of training. The next investigation of empathy training also resulted in a modeling effect without transfer of training. In her study, Sutton (1970) also made an attempt to look at social class bias among paraprofessional helpers. Subjects were sixty psychiatric attendants at a state mental hospital. The 2 x 2 factorial design involved structuring a taped client as middle-class or lower-class and presenting as a model high or low taped therapist empathy, using a method similar to that just described for the Perry (1970) study. Once again, the study revealed a significant modeling effect that did not transfer, but no effect for social class structuring. After reflecting on these four helper-training studies, Goldstein (1973) concluded, as he had with the inpatient and outpatient studies, that modeling was a useful but weak training technique and that more powerful procedures would have to be added to obtain transfer.

The next study described was the first in which modeling, role playing, and social reinforcement were combined for structured learning with helpers. In this evaluation of empathy training (Goldstein and Goedhart, 1973), seventy-four student nurses employed at a public psychiatric hospital participated in a ten-hour course spread over two days in groups consisting of two trainers and six to eight trainees. A no-treatment control group was also used. The method for this early structured learning program involved the following: (1) the nature and meaning of empathy was discussed, with particular attention paid to Carkhuff's (1969) empathy levels; (2) thirty common problem situations were presented in which a nurse and a client interacted, with trainers modeling empathic nurse responding; (3) the thirty situations were again presented, this time with trainees required to devise empathic responses and with social reinforcement given for appropriate responding; (4) the thirty situations were used as the basis for more extended nurse-client conversations that were modeled and then role played with social reinforcement; and (5) all situations were modeled and role played a second time. Results indicated that subjects in structured learning groups provided more empathic responses than controls in the situations used in training and in new, unfamiliar situations and that this effect still existed at a one-month follow-up testing. Four head nurses who had just completed the course then gave the identical training to control group members, who performed as well on dependent measures after the program as the original trainees had. Therefore, structured learning proved useful as both a helper-training and a trainer-training approach. However, a major weakness of the study was that all dependent measures were written and therefore provided more evidence for durability than transfer of training.

Goldstein and Goedhart (1973) conducted another investigation—in essence, a replication and extension of their first—designed
to partially overcome this problem. Subjects were ninety psychiatric
hospital staff members divided into three groups: structured learning plus transfer training, structured learning, and no-training control. Procedures for the latter two groups were identical to those in
the first study. The first group, however, in addition to participation
in the ten-hour program, engaged in activities designed to increase
the probability that the empathic skills learned in the program
would transfer to the ward. For two hours per day over a two-week
period, trainers observed interactions between these group members
and clients on the ward and met with each subject daily to give
specific performance feedback regarding use of empathy and to provide modeling or social reinforcement where appropriate. As predicted, data analysis revealed that both structured learning groups
used higher levels of empathy than controls and that the subjects
receiving structured learning plus transfer training performed better
than the other groups on a tape-recorded measure of empathy skill
administered two weeks after training ended. This study provided
further support for the notion that transfer enhancement must usually be added to modeling, role playing, and social reinforcement in
order to obtain adequate skill acquisition and transfer.

The last paraprofessional study to be described in this section
(Schneiman, 1972) was a departure from previous work in that a
different skill, a different subject sample, and more applied dependent measures were used. Sixty teacher aides were administered the
first pretraining measure, a written questionnaire asking what they
would say in specific problem classroom situations. The second
premeasure was a thirty-minute observation of each subject in the
classroom required for the Classroom Observation Instrument
(Krumboltz and Goodwin, 1966), a measure of various teacher behaviors. Three skills included among the behaviors—rules, disapproval, and praise—were selected as targets for the training
program. Subjects were assigned to either a structured learning
group, a didactic learning group (learning and discussion), or a
no-treatment control group. For both types of training, participants
met for three hours in groups of ten. In structured learning, the
standard modeling, role playing, and social reinforcement proce-

dures were used, with no specific transfer enhancers. Posttraining testing included the two premeasures and a live individual test with a child actor who engaged in disruptive behaviors for five minutes to give the trainee the opportunity to perform the acquired skills. Analysis of the questionnaire data found that both training programs increased trainees' scores above those of control subjects. In the other two measures, however, only structured learning subjects performed the skills better than controls. Perhaps these skills transferred without the inclusion of specific transfer enhancers because they were simpler and more concrete, as suggested earlier.

In summary, early studies with three different types of subject samples have been reviewed, and several conclusions may be drawn. First, a group skills-training procedure using modeling, role playing, and social reinforcement was effective for skills acquisition. Second, none of these components alone was as effective as the three combined. Third, for training most skills, specific transfer enhancers had to be added in order to obtain skills transfer. Finally, this structured learning procedure, with its four components, was useful for teaching a variety of skills to a variety of trainee groups, including inpatients, outpatients, and paraprofessional helpers.

Structured Learning Skills

One of the major goals of structured learning is to tailor the training program to the needs of the group being trained. Consequently, the range of skills trained with this method has been as broad as the variety of helpers with which it has been used. Once a general area of skills deficit has been identified for a particular group, the skills needed must be delineated in concrete, behavioral terms and broken down into small steps. Identification of skills deficits may be accomplished by the administration to potential trainees and their supervisors of a questionnaire such as the Structured Learning Skill Checklist, in which a number of specific skills are listed and instructions are given to rate level of performance of each skill on a five-point scale. This questionnaire may easily be tailored to any group of helpers. Once a set of skills has been selected, a pilot program should be run to evaluate the usefulness of newly developed skills and their behavioral steps.

The following is a representative sample of skills and their behavioral steps that have been taught in structured learning training. The first skill was developed to improve the supervisory capabilities of industrial management personnel (Goldstein and Sorcher, 1974).

Skill: Motivating a poor performer.
1. Focus on the problem, not the employee.
2. Ask for his or her help and discuss his or her ideas on how to solve the problem.
3. Come to agreement on the behavioral steps to be taken by each of you.
4. Plan a specific follow-up date.

This next skill was taught to police officers being trained in hostage negotiation skills (Miron and Goldstein, 1978).

Skill: Building rapport.
1. Stall for time.
2. Disclose information about yourself to the perpetrator, as it may help build rapport.
3. Show high levels of empathy in your response to what the perpetrator says and does.
4. Show high levels of warmth in your response to what the perpetrator says and does.
5. Help the perpetrator save face.
6. Avoid talking down to the perpetrator.
7. Do not criticize, threaten, or act impatient toward the perpetrator.

The next two skills are simpler and may be appropriate for use with helpers or clients (Goldstein, Sprafkin, and Gershaw, 1976).

Skill: Setting problem priorities.
1. List all the problems that are currently pressuring you.
2. Arrange this list in order, from most to least urgent.
3. Take steps to decrease temporarily the urgency of all problems but the one that is most pressing (delegate, postpone, avoid).
4. Concentrate on the most pressing problem.

Skill: Listening.
1. Look at the other person.
2. Show interest in the other's statement.
3. Ask questions on the same topic.
4. Add your feelings and thoughts on the topic.

The latter two skills are taken from a package of fifty-nine skills for community living developed by Goldstein, Sprafkin, and Gershaw (1976). A modeling audiotape has been made for each. Skills vary widely in complexity and include some, such as job seeking, that combine several other, simpler skills. A similar set of fifty skills developed specifically for use with adolescents (Goldstein and others, 1980) includes beginning social skills, advanced social skills, skills for dealing with feelings, skills as alternatives to aggression, skills for dealing with stress, and planning skills.

What Makes Structured Learning Work?

Perhaps first and foremost, structured learning is effective because it has a solid empirical base; the usefulness of its four major components has been extensively documented in the research literature. In addition, Goldstein and his colleagues, as described earlier, used the building-block strategy to develop this model by demonstrating incrementally the efficacy of each component. The flexibility of the approach allows a wide range of skills to be taught to a variety of helpers and clients from virtually all age groups, socioeconomic classes, and levels of education. Skills that have been taught successfully range from the very simple (starting a conversation) to the very complex (negotiating for hostages) and have been tailored for helpers as diverse as nurses, mental health workers, police officers, industrial supervisors, parents, home aides, teachers, counselors, and teacher aides. The concrete, structured, behavioral format of the method allows people without a professional background to function effectively as trainers after a relatively brief preparation program and facilitates evaluation of trainee skills acquisition and transfer. By means of modeling and role playing, trainees learn how to perform the skill, not just what the skill consists of or why it is of value. The major goal of the program is for trainees to learn to apply the skills in the real-life environment, and this emphasis, operationalized in a variety of transfer enhancers throughout training, leads to a relatively acceptable level of transfer. Finally, the group format of structured learning makes the approach more cost-effective than individualized training and provides such additional advantages for trainees as group support for new behaviors, acknowledgment of common problems, and increased socialization.

Training Program

Length and Duration of Sessions. Assuming an optimal group size of two trainers and eight to twelve trainees, a structured learning program may last just long enough to teach one skill (two to three hours) or may go on for a year or more if many skills are to be trained, especially if trainees require extensive role playing to master them. Duration of the total program, then, is extremely flexible and should be directly related to participants' skills deficits. Length of each session is more fixed; two hours is considered ideal for the average trainee, although sessions have been as brief as one-half hour or as long as ten consecutive days. Regarding spacing of sessions, Goldstein and others (1979) have strongly advocated either two or three meetings per week, preferably two. If sessions are very short, then more frequent meetings are desirable. Adequate spacing of sessions is considered important because it gives trainees time to do their transfer-training homework, that is, to trying out newly learned skills in real-life situations.

Key Training Activities. Every effort is made to actively involve trainees in the structured learning program. Didactic teaching is kept to a minimum and all group members are required to participate in training procedures. For this reason, groups are kept fairly small and have two trainers, rather than one.

The four major components of structured learning comprise its key training activities. The first of these is modeling, during which the skill is correctly performed using all behavioral steps in order. Modeling may be enacted by the two trainers or may be presented on audiotape or videotape. Whichever mode of presentation is selected, certain model, display, and trainee characteristics are stressed to increase trainee imitation of the model (Goldstein, Hoyer, and Monti, 1979). Modeling is enhanced when the model is friendly and helpful, highly competent, of high rank or status, of the same sex, in control of resources desired by the trainee, and rewarded for performing the skill. As for the display, greater imitation will take place if the models are shown performing in a vivid and detailed manner, in order from least to most difficult, with considerable repetition, and with a minimum of irrelevant details. And greater imitation will occur when the trainee is instructed to imitate, is similar to the model in background or attitudes, likes the model, and is rewarded for performing the skill. A variety of models and modeling situations are used when feasible to increase skill transfer.

Role playing is the second key training activity. As with modeling, several trainee characteristics have also been found to increase trainee learning from role playing, including the following: the trainee feels he or she has some choice about whether or not to participate in the role playing; the trainee is committed to the role in the sense that he or she role plays in front of others who know him or her; the trainee improvises, rather than following a script; and the trainee is rewarded for his or her performance (Goldstein, Hoyer, and Monti, 1979). In structured learning, each participant is the main actor in a role play scene at least once, and role plays must be repeated until they are correct—that is, until all behavioral steps are followed. If time permits, trainees role play more often to increase overlearning, a transfer enhancer. Usually participants provide their own problem situation for the role play, thus increasing similarities between the training situation and the situation in which the skill is likely to be used—another way to enhance transfer. As trainees role play, others are seeing a variety of additional modeling displays, and transfer is thereby promoted through an increase in stimulus variability and overlearning.

The third major training procedure is social reinforcement, another transfer enhancer, combined here with performance feedback. Goldstein, Hoyer, and Monti (1979) point out the often-noted distinction between learning and performance. Modeling teaches what to do, role playing teaches how to do it, but social reinforcement leads people to actually perform what they have learned. In structured learning, adherence to the skill's behavioral steps is usually what is reinforced, both by trainers and other participants. For some trainees, an aspect of the role play may receive social reinforcement, even if the steps are not followed, in order to make the experience a positive one. The main actor may be praised for a good attempt, his or her level of enthusiasm, a good approach for a difficult situation, and so on. An attempt is also made to incorporate those characteristics that increase the effect of social reinforcement on performance (Goldstein, Hoyer, and Monti, 1979). This increase occurs when the reward is delivered as soon as possible after the behavior, when it is made clear to the trainee which specific behaviors are being reinforced, when the nature of the reinforcement is actually seen as a reward by the trainee, when the amount of the reinforcement constitutes a reward for the trainee, and when the trainer reinforces only some performance of the behavior.

Transfer training is the fourth key training activity. A number of transfer enhancers are interspersed throughout the program, including several already mentioned: identical elements, stimulus variability, overlearning, homework, and performance feedback. Another way to enhance transfer is to provide the trainee with the general rules or principles underlying the skill being taught. In structured learning, this enhancer is usually presented during the introduction and may be repeated later in training.

Goals of Training. Acquisition and transfer of specified skills have previously been mentioned as major goals of structured learning. Trainees must also realize that the steps portrayed by the model are not the only way to enact the skill effectively. Since the overall goal of the program is to help build a flexible selection of effective and satisfying behaviors that trainees can adjust to the demands of each situation, participants must understand the purpose, or general principles, of the skill and must appreciate how the skill can benefit them personally—on the job, with family, and so on. This long-term perspective increases the likelihood of transfer, reduces resistance, and encourages participants to willingly and actively join group procedures.

Role of Trainer and Trainee. In most structured learning groups, at least one of the two trainers is someone familiar with the trainee population, such as a fellow nurse, police officer, or teacher.

The presence of an indigenous trainer is designed to increase the probability that the program will be appropriate for trainees' needs. Trainers need not be professionals, but they should exhibit the skills required in almost any group training effort, what Miron and Goldstein (1978) have termed general trainer skills: oral communication and leadership of group discussion; flexibility and capacity for resourcefulness; physical energy; ability to work under pressure; empathic ability; listening skill; and broad knowledge of human behavior. Of course, trainers must also have specific trainer skills for conducting the group's component procedures. These skills, which should be learned in a structured learning group for potential trainers, include (Miron and Goldstein, 1978):

1. In-depth knowledge of structured learning, its background, procedures, and goals.
2. Skill in orienting both trainees and supporting staff to structured learning.
3. Skill in initiating and sustaining role playing.
4. Ability to present material in concrete, behavioral form.
5. Skill in reducing and transforming trainee resistance.
6. Procedures for effective feedback.
7. Group management skills, such as building cohesiveness.

Trainees for a given group should be relatively homogeneous, based on a common need for training in similar skills areas at similar levels of deficiency. Trainees' degrees of ability to think concretely or abstractly should also be considered, since this variable is important for grouping. Trainees should also be similar in their potential for resembling those persons in the real interpersonal environment with whom they will be using the skill. For example, if trainees are working on interpersonal relationship skills in marriage, the group should include both men and women in the same general age range.

The role of the trainee includes regular attendance at sessions, ability to sustain attention during the session, adequate hearing and vision, ability to understand the procedures and goals of structured learning, ability to remember from one session to the next, and willingness to role play in front of the group. Also helpful are the willingness to complete homework assignments and to bring in real-life situations for role play and discussion in the group.

Possible Design Variations. The flexibility of the method makes possible numerous design variations to tailor each program to different trainee populations. Sessions may be held in school classrooms, hospital wards, activity rooms—wherever there is privacy, quiet, and space for role playing. Ideally, the training setting should be similar to the real-life setting in which the skills will be applied. Duration and number of sessions also vary widely, depending on the number and abilities of trainees in the group and the level of skill complexity. Groups may range in size from as few as four trainees to as many as twenty-five or thirty, but optimum size remains eight to twelve. Number and type of skills trained can range from one to fifty or more, from the simple to the complex, from the abstract to the concrete, from empathy to contingency management. Trainers may be professionals, paraprofessionals—in fact, almost anyone except the very young, the physically ill, and those out of touch with reality. Transfer enhancers may also vary, but should be used as extensively as possible.

Training Materials. Structured learning requires only the simplest materials: chairs and a blackboard. However, for many types of skills, especially those oriented toward clients, written and taped materials have been developed to facilitate training. For groups designed to prepare potential trainers, two teaching aids have been developed: the *Trainer's Manual* (Goldstein, Gershaw, and Sprafkin, 1976), a twenty-four-page booklet containing theoretical and research background material, specific instructions for conducting the group itself, and additional information on the trainee's notebook, homework reports, and modeling tapes; and the three trainer preparation audiotapes, which contain an introductory session with a client group, a session using modeling and role playing, an advanced session in which several transfer enhancers are applied, and a number of examples in which trainee resistance is reduced. Materials to facilitate training helpers or clients include the *Trainee's Notebook* (Sprafkin, Gershaw, and Goldstein, 1976), a twenty-nine-page manual providing basic information and background for the major training components and emphasizing homework preparation and reporting. For groups with adult clients, two skills surveys have been developed to help identify the skills in which a client is deficient and the degree of deficiency (Goldstein, Sprafkin, and Gershaw, 1976). One of the surveys is to be completed by a staff person or someone else who knows the client; the other is to be filled out by the client himself or herself. For adolescents, a Structured Learning Skills Checklist is available (Goldstein and others, 1980), in which someone who knows the client rates his or her performance of fifty skills, and a Skills Checklist Summary has also been developed for this same sample to assess change in skills performance as a result of training. Also available for use with adolescents are a skills training grouping chart to help identify groups of clients who are deficient in the same skills and a skill training class mastery record to help keep track of each group member's participation in training procedures. These materials for adolescent groups can easily be adapted for other trainee populations.

Modeling displays of a variety of skills have been recorded on audiotape and videotape for many types of trainees. The major available set of these tapes, containing displays of fifty-nine skills developed for use with client trainees, is part of a larger package containing a text by Goldstein, Sprafkin, and Gershaw (1976), trainer's manuals, trainee's notebooks, trainer preparation tapes, and a set of skill cards for each skill.

Evaluation procedures. Evaluation of structured learning training may be divided into midtraining, posttraining, and followup phases. During the program, trainees' progress is constantly being monitored through their role playing. Each participant role plays the skill correctly at least once, and usually two or three times. Participants are also reporting on their homework, which indicates their level of skill performance outside the training setting. Immediately following training, any one or a combination of several methods have been used to assess progress: trainees may fill out questionnaires, role play an unfamiliar situation with an unfamiliar person in a new setting, respond verbally to taped situations, or be observed while they are in a position to perform the skill in the real world. Follow-up evaluations may involve reports of skill enactment by supervisors or others who know the trainee, trainee self-report, readministration of some of the measures used earlier, observation of the trainee in a natural setting, or reports from people with whom the trainee was to have applied the skill. When training police officers, for example, people who had been visited by police trainees were surveyed after training and asked about performance of the skills. Clients may be asked to rate their attraction to therapists who were formerly trainees. In structured learning, evaluation emphasizes transfer of the skill, as transfer is a major program goal.

Example of a Structured Learning Program

The following program, described in greater detail by Goldstein and others (1979), was implemented in Syracuse, New York, in 1974. Many of a police officer's calls require crisis intervention involving family fights, mentally disturbed or intoxicated citizens, suicide attempts, and victims of accidents, assault, rape, or other offenses. Officers are often not trained for this type of duty, and these situations are frequently dangerous. Recognizing the need for specialized training, the Syracuse Police Department developed and implemented a Law Enforcement Assistance Administration (LEAA) funded training program aimed at teaching proficiency in crisis intervention skills to Syracuse police. Conducted with 225 police officers, the project used structured learning procedures and materials. Participants met in groups of eight to twelve trainees and two trainers all day for ten consecutive days, with additional on-the-job transfer training for several half-days. Sections of the training rooms were made to resemble common settings in which skills might be used, such as a bar or a kitchen. Trainers for each group consisted of one police officer and one other individual experienced in structured learning.

The first training session began with the trainers' introducing themselves. Trainees were then asked to do the same and to tell the group something about their backgrounds and their training goals. Next, participants were provided with a brief description of the program's rationale, training procedures, and target skills. Other topics briefly covered were the importance of the skills for effective and satisfying police work with a wide variety of people, the value of skills knowledge and flexibility to the trainees themselves, and the manner in which training focuses on altering specific behaviors and not attitude. The trainers then prefaced and summarized the first modeling videotapes with the following statements:

Introduction to Observing and Protecting Against Threats to Your Safety. Today you are going to view a videotape which will demonstrate a skill which is very important in effectively dealing with police calls. This skill is observing and protecting against threats to your safety. When you are dispatched to a call, you must prepare yourself in order to respond quickly and effectively. In the good examples which you will now observe, the officer does three basic things:

1. Considers his prior experience in similar situations.
2. Anticipates that the unexpected may actually happen.
3. Forms a tentative plan of action.

When the officer does these three things, he is better prepared to approach the situation with confidence in his professional skill and to take the most effective action. If the officer does not consider his prior experience in similar situations, anticipate that the unexpected may actually happen, and form a tentative plan of action, he will not be well prepared. The situation may take him by surprise, the outcome being ineffective use of his skill, or worse, personal injury.

You will now see and listen to examples of officers preparing to respond to a call by observing and protecting against threats to their safety. The people on these tapes are not professional actors, but are police officers in the Syracuse Police Department. We would like you to learn these three steps in order to get the benefits of being an effective police officer, so please pay close attention.

(Play tapes.)

You have just seen and heard what experienced police officers do and think as they prepare to respond to a call. In observing and protecting against threats to their safety, they: first, consider their prior experience in similar situations; second, anticipate that the unexpected may actually happen; and, third, form a tentative plan of action. In order to help you refine these skills, the training staff will now direct your attention to specific features of these skills and prepare you for rehearsing this technique. (Goldstein and others, 1979, p. 153. Reprinted with permission from Pergamon Press.

The modeling videotapes themselves are composed of a narrator's introduction, the modeling displays, and the narrator's summary. The narrator, who is the Chief of Police, names and describes the skill, gives the behavioral steps, tells how skill performance may be rewarding and skill absence unrewarding, and repeats the skill steps. After the narrator's request for attention to what follows, the modeling displays are presented. The vignettes, presented in the order of increasing complexity, use all behavioral steps, reflect real-life environments, and end with the model being reinforced for enacting the skill. A variety of models and situations are used, with models similar to trainees in such characteristics as age, sex, and socioeconomic level. After the modeling displays, the narrator repeats the behavioral steps, describes rewards to models and trainees for skill performance, and urges trainees to use the skill steps in the session that follows and in their real-life environment.

A discussion following the playing of the modeling tape focused on the behavioral steps, the actors, and how the skill situation occurs in their own work. After this, trainees were divided into groups of four and were prepared for role playing so that the enactments would be as realistic as possible. Each group of four was asked to develop a crisis event, planning the specific roles of disputant, victim, offender, and other citizens. They were then instructed to role play this crisis as realistically as possible to two other trainees who had been directed to deal with the crisis by following the behavioral steps illustrated on the modeling tape and written on the blackboard. The following specific instructions were given to trainees preparing the crisis enactment (Goldstein and others, 1979):

Your task during this preparation period will be to design a skit in which a dispute occurs (the disputants' relationship will be designated by a trainer). Afterwards, the skit will be performed with members of your group portraying the disputants, while one or more members of another group portray a police officer intervening in that dispute. Representatives of your group will then participate in the critique which follows the skit.

The skit will require careful preparation for effectiveness as a learning/teaching method. We suggest you cover the following steps:

1. Talk about cases you've known that fit the designation; and, select one that can be effectively portrayed, and that promises to be a good learning vehicle for the audience.
2. Discuss the personalities and situations involved.
3. Select group members to portray the roles.
4. Help the actors become familiar with their roles, with what they will say and do before the "police" arrive.
5. Help the actors practice and become "natural" in their roles. Discourage overacting! It is essential that after the police arrive, your actors react naturally to what the "police" do, and not according to some script.

Remember, when your skit is presented, after the intervening officer(s) arrive, the actors should respond to the officer(s) as they think their characters would respond. (p. 157)

Directions to trainers for role playing and corrective feedback–social reinforcement were given as follows:

Before the given role play actually begins, you should deliver the following instructions:

1. To the two trainees responding to the call (responders): In responding to the call you are about to hear, follow and enact the learning points. Do not leave any out, and follow them in the proper sequence.
2. To the trainees enacting the crisis situation (disputants): React as naturally as possible to the behavior of the responding officers. Within the one limitation of not endangering anyone's physical safety, it is important that your reactions to the responding officers be as real-life as possible.
3. To all other trainees (observers): Carefully observe how well the responding officers follow the learning points, and take notes on this for later discussion and feedback.

One of the trainers then instructs the role players to begin. It is your main responsibility at this point to be sure responders keep role playing, and that they try to follow the learning points while doing so. If they "break role," and begin making comments or explaining background events, etc., you should firmly instruct them to resume their roles. One trainer should position himself near the chalkboard and point to each learning point in turn, as the role play unfolds, being sure none are missed or enacted out of order. If either responder feels the role play is not progressing well and wishes to start it over, this is appropriate. Do not permit interruptions of any kind from the group until the role play is completed.

The role playing should be continued until all the skits have been presented and all trainees (responders) have had an opportunity to participate, even if the same skill and learning points must be carried over to a second or third session. Note that while the framework (learning points) of each role play in the series remains the same, the actual content should change from role play to role play. It is crises as they actually occur or could occur which should be the content of the given role play. When completed, each trainee should be better armed to act appropriately in the given reality situations.

After completing each role play, you should have a brief feedback period. The goals of this activity are to let the responders know how well they "stayed with" the learning points, or in what ways they departed from them. It also lets them know the psychological impact of their enactment

on the disputants, and encourages them to try out the role-play behaviors in
real life. To implement this feedback process we suggest you follow a sequence of eliciting comments from:

1. The role-play disputants, i.e., "How did the officers (responders) make
   you feel?" "What are you likely to do now?"
2. The observing trainees, i.e., "How well were the learning points followed?" "What specific behaviors did you like or dislike?"
3. The trainers, who comment, in particular, on how well the learning
   points were followed; and who provide social reinforcement (praise,
   approval, encouragement) for them.
4. The role-play responders themselves, who comment on their own
   enactment, on the comments of others, and on their specific expectations regarding how, when, and with whom they might attempt the
   learning points in their work environment.

In all these critiques, it is crucial that you maintain the behavioral
focus of structured learning. Comments must point to the presence or
absence of specific, concrete behaviors, and not take the form of general
evaluative comments or broad generalities. Feedback, of course, may be
positive or negative in content. At minimum, you can praise a "poor"
performance (major departures from the learning points) as "a good try" at
the same time you criticize its real faults.

If at all possible you should give trainees who fail to follow the
relevant learning points in their role play, the opportunity to re-role play
these same learning points after they've received corrective feedback. As a
final feedback step, after all role playing and discussion of it is completed,
you should replay the modeling tape, or repeat the live demonstration of the
particular skill. This step, in a sense, summarizes the session and leaves the
trainees with a final overview of the learning points. [pp. 158–160]

After modeling, role playing, and feedback-reinforcement
were completed for the first skill, the entire procedure was repeated
for each of the three remaining skills. Presented below are the skill
introductions given by trainers before the modeling tapes were
played (Goldstein and others, 1979).

Introduction to Calming the Situation. You will recall that the behavioral skill illustrated on the first videotape was observing and protecting
against threats to your safety. The tape you will now see illustrates appropriate police behavior in a second phase of the intervention: calming the
situation. The specific learning points which make up skillfully calming
the situation include:

1. Observe and neutralize threats to your safety.
2. Create a first impression of nonhostile authority.
3. Calm the emotional citizen.

How successful you will be in resolving the conflict or crisis depends heavily on your actions soon after you arrive at the crisis scene. The first step in the actual intervention is calming the situation or restoring order. Before intervening can begin to get at the source of the problem, the situation must be calm. Note carefully the techniques used by the officers in combining officer authority with professional procedure and personal concern, to effectively calm the situation.

Introduction to Gathering Relevant Information. In the previous tapes, you have seen police officers preparing to respond to a call and beginning to intervene by calming the situation. Specific techniques have varied, and situations have required different actions. We have emphasized flexibility. Today you will observe the skills used by the officers in carrying out the necessary investigation. Again, we will emphasize techniques and the types of helpful responses exhibited by the officers. Specifically, the major points illustrated in this tape on gathering relevant information are:

1. Explain to the citizen what you want him to discuss with you and why.
2. Interview the citizen so as to gain details of the crisis as clearly as possible.
3. Show that you understand the citizen's statements and give accurate answers to his questions.
4. Revise your plan of action, if appropriate.

The success of your crisis intervention depends heavily on how well you have carried out your investigation. Good investigation is at the heart of police procedure. A police officer always takes action, and that action depends on what he sees, hears, and believes about the situation. This phase of the training will help you in developing your skills as an investigator.

Introduction to Taking Appropriate Action. The skills we have worked with up to this point have all been geared toward handling the crisis situation in such a way that it ends with appropriate police action being taken. If the officer protects himself, calms the persons involved, and determines in sufficient detail what is happening, he will be in a position to deal with the crisis in a professional, competent manner. Today you will observe the specific skills involved in taking such appropriate action. These skills are:

1. Carefully explain your plan of action to the citizen.
2. Check that the citizen understands and agrees with your plan of action.
3. Carry out your plan of action.

Following these steps will enable you to make optimal use of the information you have gathered, and bring the crisis to an appropriate resolution. [pp. 155–156]

Transfer training in this structured learning program was accomplished by means of the transfer enhancers described earlier, such as identical elements, stimulus variability, and overlearning. In addition, to help trainees bridge the considerable gap between the training setting and the squad car, one of the program trainers rode with each trainee on the job for a few hours each week to give further real-life instruction and feedback. Results of an evaluation of this project will be presented in the following section.

Evaluation of the Model

Evaluation studies of structured learning training usually reveal skills-acquisition and at least minimal transfer. For this approach to training, as for most others, transfer to the work setting has presented the greatest challenge; some investigations have revealed adequate transfer, and others have not. The phenomenon of transfer appears to be influenced by such factors as the nature of the skill, the particular characteristics of the trainers and trainees, and the interaction of these factors with various transfer enhancers. Much of the current and planned research on structured learning is an examination of these complex relationships.

The earliest paraprofessional training studies were reviewed toward the beginning of this chapter to illustrate the incremental research design Goldstein and his colleagues employed to develop the structured learning approach. This review of helper training investigations will now be extended to the present and will begin with a brief presentation of the results of the police crisis intervention skills study described in the previous section. Davis (1974) conducted the evaluation and found clear-cut results. Questionnaires given to trainees immediately after training and eight months later showed that they continued to hold the program in high regard and felt better prepared for crisis calls. Trainees were also videotaped in role plays toward the end of training, and a sample of actual interventions were observed. Ratings of both situations by police judges found effective use of good intervention techniques. A group of citizens involved in crisis calls were then surveyed regarding their treatment by police (former trainees), and again results were clearly positive. Unfortunately, no control group was used in this investigation, a defect remedied in the following studies.

In another study, empathy was taught to twenty-nine lower-class home aide trainees using either structured learning or a didactic approach (Robinson, 1973). After training, results demonstrated a stronger effect for structured learning than for the didactic and the no-treatment control methods, an effect that held on several measures of transfer involving simulated interactions. Thirty-seven mothers of early adolescents attended a structured learning program designed to teach empathy (Guzzetta, 1974). To maximize transfer, one group brought their children with them to sessions; in another group, mothers and children participated separately; and, in the third group, only mothers received training. The final group was a no-training control. All three structured learning groups evidenced greater skill acquisition and simulated transfer than the control group, but no other differences were apparent.

Goldstein and Sorcher (1974) applied structured learning with industrial foremen and workers; both a pilot study and a complete program were evaluated. For the pilot, thirty-nine employees, mostly young and black, were divided into either a structured learning or a discussion control group for job orientation. The training group learned eight skills designed to help them adapt to the work situation more effectively—such skills as "not quitting" and "how to react to ostracism." Six months after completion of training, the rate of voluntary quitting was three times higher for control than for structured learning employees. The more complete program trained foremen in supervisory skills, evaluating the effectiveness of training by the productivity of the workers who reported to those foremen. Ten foremen each were assigned to a structured learning group and to a control group. Control group members had previously received traditional supervisory training. After twenty hours of training on five supervisory skills, workers supervised by foremen who had participated in the skills training program had a significantly higher level of productive efficiency. Again significant transfer was accomplished.

Berlin (1974), Healy (1975), and Lopez (1978) investigated the use of structured learning to enhance the recognition of three emotions—anxiety, anger, and sadness, respectively—by mental

hospital nurses and attendants. Approximately fifty subjects participated in each group. Participants were taught either vocal cues for
the emotion, vocal plus facial cues, or vocal cues plus exposure to
facial cues (but no teaching); some participants received no training
at all. The anxiety data analysis revealed no differences between
groups. In the anger study, structured learning subjects acquired the
skill but showed little transfer. Results from the sadness investigation revealed both acquisition of the recognition skill and transfer to
videotaped recognition situations. These discrepancies may reflect
the complexity of the emotional cues trained. For example, cues for
anxiety are more variable and fleeting than those for anger and
sadness. In general, with a variety of subjects, structured learning
training of affective skills has proven more difficult and has resulted
in less acquisition and transfer than training of concrete behavioral
skills.

In another program with nurses and attendants, Lack (1975)
used structured learning to train sixty participants in contingency
management skills. She then compared the basic program with an
expanded program that included problem-solving training, and
both of these were compared with similar didactic programs designed to teach the same information. The structured learning plus
problem-solving training program was found superior to all others
for acquisition of the skills.

In an attempt to further prescribe structured learning for specific trainees, Rosenthal (1975) investigated the training of confrontational skills with sixty student-counselors. He blocked on
conceptual level and compared the efficacy of trainer-led structured
learning with a self-instructional structured learning format and an
attention control. Results indicated significant interaction effects on
confrontational skills for type of structured learning (leader-led versus self-instructional) by conceptual level (high versus low). All
training groups were superior to the attention control. The same
experimental design and variables were used in an investigation by
Gilstad (1977) to see if these interesting and provocative results
would hold up with a different population, sixty elementary
school teachers participating in an empathy-training program. Unlike the previous study, this study revealed no interactions between
conceptual level and type of structured learning. However, struc-

tured learning subjects performed the skill at a higher level than control subjects on both acquisition and transfer measures. Studies such as these, which attempt to identify variables that enhance the ability to match certain trainers, trainees, and skills, are worthy of further attention in programs with helpers. Already a great deal of the recent research on structured learning with clients has focused on this goal.

To briefly summarize the structured learning studies with helpers that have been carried out during the past ten years, most of which have been reviewed in this chapter, it should first be stated that the method has proven successful overall. Participants rate the program highly and especially like the method's concreteness and attention to performing skills in a variety of real-life situations. Virtually all evaluations demonstrate skills acquisition by trainees, and a number of studies have found transfer from the training to the natural setting. However, transfer remains a problem for structured learning, as for most programs, and continues to be a concern of Goldstein and his colleagues and a major issue in structured learning research, both ongoing and planned.

New Applications and Future Directions

Most newer applications have focused on one or both of the following goals, in addition to skills training: identification of transfer enhancers and how to use them effectively; and refinement of current knowledge regarding the matching of trainers, trainees, programs, and skills. Recent studies have also branched out and examined the use of the method with adolescents and elderly persons.

Many recent applications of structured learning have been with adolescents; in fact, an entire program for use with adolescent trainees has been developed, complete with skills, modeling vignettes, and examples of session transcripts (Goldstein and others, 1980). In a variety of investigations, adolescents have participated in programs designed to train them in such skills as assertiveness, cooperation, negotiation, helpfulness, and self-control (reviewed in Goldstein and others, 1980). Often the trainees had been labeled aggressive, acting out, or withdrawn. Generally, the efficacy of one or two transfer enhancers is also examined. As with helpers, skills are usually acquired but transfer with varying degrees of success.

Another focus of recent and planned studies is the prescription of trainers—that is, choosing the type of trainer best suited to a particular trainee population. For example, Cross (1977) divided trainers into those who were task-motivated and those who were relationship-motivated, then paired them with either task-related or relationship-related trainee stress. One of his findings was that relationship-motivated trainers were better with trainees experiencing task-related stress. In another investigation, Robertson (1978) found that trainers high on need to control were more competent with actively resistant trainees than those low on the same need.

Several studies have applied structured learning with elderly persons and have concomitantly examined the effect of transfer enhancers. Lopez (1980) taught a simple social skill to long-term institutionalized elderly persons, varied levels of overlearning as a transfer enhancer, and attempted to tailor the method to the elderly by providing a type of role induction to some groups before training. The role induction was not successful, but subjects given moderate overlearning were the only trainees to exhibit significant skill transfer. In a follow-up study with institutionalized elderly, overlearning was again varied, and this time trainee incentive was manipulated by paying certain groups for performance of correct skill steps (Lopez and others, 1980). Data analysis revealed that only a high level of overlearning led to skill transfer and that monetary reinforcement of skill performance actually decreased the level of acquisition and transfer—perhaps because trainees had come to expect this reward but did not receive it in real-life situations. Several other investigations with elderly persons recently completed or planned involve further exploration of transfer enhancers and of trainee characteristics associated with learning and transfer.

Another recent development has been the publication of a book entitled, *I Know What's Wrong but I Don't Know What to Do About It*, in which Goldstein, Sprafkin, and Gershaw (1979) present a self-help structured learning program for lay people who have behaviors they would like to change. Forty-three skills are included, with behavioral steps, examples, directions for role playing or practice, and instructions for making contracts for behavioral change.

In brief, this chapter has described the development of an approach to skill training known as structured learning. This model is based on a program of research that has included investigations of the efficacy of each component, prescriptions for specific trainers with specific trainees, and applications with new populations for the development of appropriate skills. Results of this research indicate that structured learning is a viable skill-training method for use with helpers and a variety of other groups. Much remains to be learned about this approach and continuing tests of its efficacy are necessary, but the method itself is alive and well.

References

Bandura, A. *Principles of Behavior Modification.* New York: Holt, Rinehart and Winston, 1969.

Ben, D. "Mood Change in Lower-Class Alcoholic Outpatients as a Function of Role Induction and Reward to Model." Unpublished doctoral dissertation, Department of Psychology, Syracuse University, 1973.

Berlin, R. J. "Training of Hospital Staff in Accurate Affective Perception of Fear-Anxiety from Vocal Cues in the Context of Varying Facial Cues." Unpublished master's thesis, Department of Psychology, Syracuse University, 1974.

Carkhuff, R. R. *Helping and Human Relations.* New York: Holt, Rinehart and Winston, 1969.

Cross, W. "An Investigation of the Effects of Therapist Motivational Predispositions in Structured Learning Therapy Under Task Versus Relationship Stress Conditions." Unpublished doctoral dissertation, Department of Psychology, Syracuse University, 1977.

Davis, C. "Training Police in Crisis Intervention Skills." Unpublished manuscript, Syracuse University, Department of Psychology, 1974.

Friedenberg, W. P. "Verbal and Nonverbal Attraction Modeling in an Initial Therapy Interview Analogue." Unpublished master's thesis, Department of Psychology, Syracuse University, 1971.

Gendlin, E. T. "Focussing." *Psychotherapy: Theory, Research, and Practice,* 1969, *6*, 4–15.

Gilstad, R. "Acquisition and Transfer of Empathic Responses by Teachers Through Self-Administered and Leader-Directed Structured Learning Training and the Interaction Between Training Method and Conceptual Level." Unpublished doctoral dissertation, Department of Psychology, Syracuse University, 1977.

Goldstein, A. P. *Structured Learning Therapy: Toward a Psychotherapy for the Poor.* New York: Academic Press, 1973.

Goldstein, A. P., Gershaw, N. J., and Sprafkin, R. P. *Trainers Manual for Structured Learning Therapy.* Elmsford, N.Y.: Pergamon Press, 1976.

Goldstein, A. P, and Goedhart, A. W. "The Use of Structured Learning for Empathy Enhancement in Paraprofessional Psychotherapist Training." *Journal of Community Psychology*, 1973, *1*, 168–173.

Goldstein, A. P., Heller, K., and Sechrest, L. B. *Psychotherapy and the Psychology of Behavior Change.* New York: Wiley, 1966.

Goldstein, A. P., Hoyer, W. J., and Monti, P. J. (Eds.). *Police and the Elderly.* Elmsford, N.Y.: Pergamon Press, 1979.

Goldstein, A. P., and Kanfer, F. H. *Maximizing Treatment Gains: Transfer Enhancement in Psychotherapy.* New York: Academic Press, 1979.

Goldstein, A. P., and Sorcher, M. *Changing Supervisor Behavior.* Elmsford, N. Y.: Pergamon Press, 1974.

Goldstein, A. P., Sprafkin, R. P., and Gershaw, N. J. *Skill Training for Community Living: Applying Structured Learning Therapy.* Elmsford, N. Y.: Pergamon Press, 1976.

Goldstein, A. P., Sprafkin, R. P., and Gershaw, N. J. *I Know What's Wrong but I Don't Know What to Do About It.* Englewood Cliffs, N. J.: Prentice-Hall, 1979.

Goldstein, A. P., and others. "The Effects of Modeling and Social Class Structuring in Paraprofessional Psychotherapy Training." *Journal of Nervous and Mental Disease*, 1971, *153*, 47–56.

Goldstein, A. P., and others. "The Use of Modeling to Increase Independent Behavior." *Behavior Research and Therapy*, 1973, *11*, 31–42.

Goldstein, A. P, and others. *Police Crisis Intervention.* Elmsford, N. Y.: Pergamon Press, 1979.

Goldstein, A. P., and others. *Skill-Streaming the Adolescent: A Structured Learning Approach to Teaching Prosocial Skills.* Champaign, Ill.: Research Press, 1980.

Guerney, B. G. *Psychotherapeutic Agents: New Roles for Non-professionals, Parents, and Teachers.* New York: Holt, Rinehart and Winston, 1969.

Gutride, M. E., Goldstein, A. P., and Hunter, G. F. "The Use of Modeling and Role Playing to Increase Social Interaction Among Schizophrenic Patients." *Journal of Consulting and Clinical Psychology*, 1973, *40*, 408–415.

Gutride, M. E., Goldstein, A. P., and Hunter, G. F. "Structured Learning Therapy with Transfer Training for Chronic Inpatients." *Journal of Clinical Psychology*, 1974, *30*, 277–280.

Guzzetta, R. A. "Acquisition and Transfer of Empathy by Parents of Adolescents Through Structured Learning Training." Unpublished doctoral dissertation, Department of Psychology, Syracuse University, 1974.

Healy, J. A. "Training of Hospital Staff in Accurate Affective Perception of Anger from Vocal Cues in the Context of Varying Facial Cues." Unpublished master's thesis, Department of Psychology, Syracuse University, 1975.

Hoehn-Saric, R., and others. "Systematic Preparation of Patients for Psychotherapy. I. Effects on Therapy Behavior and Outcome." *Journal of Psychiatric Research*, 1964, *2*, 267–281.

Kazdin, A. E. *Behavior Modification in Applied Settings.* Homewood, Ill.: Dorsey Press, 1980.

Kohn, M. L. *Class and Conformity.* Homewood, Ill.: Dorsey Press, 1969.

Krumboltz, J. D., and Goodwin, D. L. *Increasing Task-Oriented Behavior: An Experimental Evaluation of Training Teachers in Reinforcement Techniques.* Stanford, Calif.: Stanford University School of Education, 1966.

Lack, D. Z. "The Effects of a Model and Instructions on Psychotherapist Self-Disclosure." Unpublished master's thesis, Department of Psychology, Syracuse University, 1971.

Lack, D. Z. "Problem-Solving Training, Structured Learning Training, and Didactic Instruction in the Preparation of Paraprofessional Mental Health Personnel for the Utilization of

Contingency Management Techniques." Unpublished doctoral dissertation, Department of Psychology, Syracuse University, 1975.

Lazarus, A. A. "Behavior Rehearsal vs. Non-directive Therapy vs. Advice in Effecting Behavior Change." *Behavior Research and Therapy*, 1966, *4*, 209–212.

Liberman, B. "The Effect of Modeling Procedures on Attraction and Disclosure in a Psychotherapy Analogue." Unpublished doctoral dissertation, Department of Psychology, Syracuse University, 1970.

Lopez, M. A. "Recognizing Non-verbal Cues of Emotion: A Training Program for Paraprofessionals." Paper presented to the Southeastern Psychological Association, Atlanta, March 1978. (ERIC/CAPS Clearinghouse #ED176144).

Lopez, M. A. "Social Skills Training with Institutionalized Elderly: Effects of Precounseling Structuring and Overlearning on Skill Acquisition and Transfer." *Journal of Counseling Psychology*, 1980, *27*, 286–293.

Lopez, M. A., and others. "Effects of Overlearning and Incentive on the Acquisition and Transfer of Interpersonal Skills with Institutionalized Elderly." *Journal of Gerontology*, 1980, *35*, 403–408.

Magaro, P. A. "A Prescriptive Treatment Model Based upon Social Class and Premorbid Adjustment." *Psychotherapy: Theory, Research, and Practice*, 1969, *6*, 57–70.

Miron, M., and Goldstein, A. P. *Hostage.* New York: Pergamon Press, 1978.

Orenstein, R. "Effect of Training Patients to Focus on Their Feelings on Level of Experiencing in a Subsequent Interview." Unpublished doctoral dissertation, Syracuse University, 1972.

Perry, M. A. "Didactic Instructions for and Modeling of Empathy." Unpublished doctoral dissertation, Department of Psychology, Syracuse University, 1970.

Robertson, B. "The Effects of Structured Learning Trainer's Need to Control on Their Group Leadership Behavior with Aggressive and Withdrawn Trainees." Unpublished master's thesis, Department of Psychology, Syracuse University, 1978.

Robinson, R. "Evaluation of a Structured Learning Empathy Training Program for Lower Socioeconomic Status Home-Aide

Trainees." Unpublished master's thesis, Department of Psychology, Syracuse University, 1973.

Rosenthal, N. "Matching Counselor Trainees' Conceptual Level and Training Approaches: A Study in the Acquisition and Enhancement of Confrontation Skills." Unpublished doctoral dissertation, Department of Psychology, Syracuse University, 1975.

Schneiman, R. "An Evaluation of Structured Learning and Didactic Learning as Methods of Training Behavior Modification Skills to Lower and Middle Socioeconomic Level Teacher-Aides." Unpublished doctoral dissertation, Department of Psychology, Syracuse University, 1972.

Sprafkin, R. P., Gershaw, N. J., and Goldstein, A. P. *Trainee's Notebook for Structured Learning Therapy.* New York: Pergamon Press, 1976.

Sutton, K. "Effects of Modeled Empathy and Structured Social Class upon Level of Therapist Displayed Empathy." Unpublished master's thesis, Department of Psychology, Syracuse University, 1970.

Walsh, W. "The Effects of Conformity Pressure and Modeling on the Attraction of Hospitalized Patients Toward an Interviewer." Unpublished doctoral dissertation, Department of Psychology, Syracuse University, 1971.

Chapter 8

Cross-Cultural Triad Model

Paul Pedersen

The goal of cross-cultural training is to heighten a counselor's intentionality through increased knowledge and awareness of, as well as skill in handling, those basic, culturally learned assumptions that control the behavior, attitudes, and insights of both counselors and clients. Cross-cultural training seeks to increase a person's intentional and purposive control over those assumptions in two ways. First, training can increase our awareness of our own cultural biases and unexamined assumptions that help determine, explain, and define normal behavior. Second, training can increase awareness of culturally different alternatives, so that counselors can adapt their knowledge and skills to a variety of culturally different populations, thereby enlarging their skills repertoire. Cultural expertise in the use of intentionality is defined by Ivey (1980) as the ability to generate a maximum number of verbal and nonverbal sentences to communicate with self and others, to communicate with diverse groups within a culture, and to formulate plans and possibilities in a cultural context. The importance of intentionality for all counseling has been emphasized by Ivey (1980) and, to the extent that the

Note: This chapter has been developed with assistance from NIMH grant 1-T24-MH15552 and the East-West Culture Learning Institute.

counseling relationship is mediated by cultural differences, intentionality is especially important.

Effect of Cultural Differences

Many intercultural situations arise in counseling (Wohl, 1981): members of one culture work with members of a host culture to learn about the host culture, as in research; members of a majority culture work with members of a minority culture within the same society; counselors in their home culture work with culturally different clients, as with immigrants, foreign students, or visitors; counselors apply methods of therapy from their own culture in foreign cultures as consultants or visitors; counselors apply methods developed in another culture to clients in their home culture; counselors work with clients from another culture in the context of a third culture, possibly with methods developed in a fourth culture; and clients work with bicultural persons who have lived so long in their host culture that they have developed a unique third culture different from both the home and host cultures. If we then include age, sex role, life-style, and socioeconomic status in the definition of *cultural*, it becomes apparent that all counseling and therapy has an intercultural dimension.

When cultural differences are overemphasized, stereotyping results; when the differences are underemphasized, insensitivity results. A balance must be found that is both authentic to the client in the client's own cultural context and sensitive to the complexities of counseling. Kuhn (1962) describes an "immature science" as characterized by a great variety of explanatory paradigms and a lack of agreement on theoretical principles. The intercultural aspects of counseling demonstrate counseling's immaturity through the extreme variability of research findings, in which positions on identical questions differ, contradictory explanations are given for the same findings, and the same explanations are given for contradictory findings (King, 1978; Strauss, 1979). The differing cultural perspectives of the counselor, the client, the problem, and the socioeconomic-political setting demonstrate the complexity of contrary points of view in a counseling relationship.

The "contact hypothesis" assumes that simply bringing together different groups of people results in more positive intergroup relations. Amir (1969) demonstrates that this hypothesis is only true under carefully prepared, favorable conditions and that spontaneous intergroup contact is in fact more likely to occur under unfavorable conditions that result in disharmony. These unfavorable conditions are best illustrated by relations between the dominant, majority culture and minority groups that have come to be defined by the very condition of being oppressed (Atkinson, Morton, and Sue, 1979). With the civil rights movement of the 1950s, minority groups in the United States became more militant, encouraged by the popular antiwar dissent of the 1960s and the feminism of the 1970s. Mental health became associated with the oppressor, as evidence revealed that minority groups terminated counseling earlier and were otherwise underserved by mental health services.

Attempts to provide more equitable mental health services through the community health movement of the 1960s and through testing reforms to develop "culture fair" measures proved inadequate. Efforts to change social policy through statements by the American Psychological Association (Korman, 1974), the American Psychiatric Association (Wintrob and Harvey, 1981), and the recent President's Commission on Mental Health (Fields, 1979)—all of which have emphasized the counselor's ethical responsibility to consider cultural differences—have been somewhat more successful. However, problems still exist in meeting federal standards for admitting more minority applicants to counseling (Atkinson, Staso and Hosford, 1978) and in retraining school personnel, students, and counselors in racially mixed schools (Jaslow, 1978).

Mental health research has failed to agree on the effects of cultural differences for several reasons: (1) the research emphasis has been on abnormal behavior, rather than normal behavior, across cultures (Katz and Sanborn, 1976); (2) data on pancultural patterns for schizophrenia and affective psychoses have only become available in the 1970s; (3) complex cultural variables are difficult to quantify (Draguns, 1981a, 1981b); (4) available research has neglected practical and applied concerns of services and techniques (Draguns, 1980); (5) interdisciplinary cooperation in mental health research has been lacking (Favazza and Oman, 1977); and (6) most research has emphasized the symptom to the neglect of the interaction of contextual variables (Ivey, 1980).

The most promising theoretical structure for intercultural mental health emphasizes the interaction of persons and environment, going back to Lewin (1935) and applying a holistic environmental emphasis to counseling (Ivey, 1980; Higginbotham and Tanaka-Matsumi, 1981; Endler and Magnusson, 1976). Traditional definitions of counseling have reflected the individualistic bias of the dominant, Western, middle-class perspective, substituting symbiotic model stereotypes for real clients, disregarding cultural variations among clients, and dogmatizing technique-oriented definitions of counseling and therapy (Wrenn, 1962). Non-Western systems place more emphasis on achieving a psychological balance and less emphasis on solving problems or "curing" illness by separating the person from the presenting problem. Alternative systems show less tendency to locate the difficulty inside the isolated individual but rather relate the individual's difficulty to units of interaction in a social context. Health, according to these systems, describes a condition of order and predictability in a context where all elements, even problems and pain, serve a useful and necessary function (Pedersen, in press). The emphasis is more holistic, acknowledging both the positive and negative aspects of the interaction of persons and environment. In the context of balance, therapy in non-Western systems is perceived as continuous and not episodic, a process and not a conclusive event. The contrasting assumptions of such a balanced approach and the "unbalanced," Western approach to mental health might account for the contradictory conclusions of therapy-outcome studies in different cultures.

The therapist needs to establish a facilitative relationship that enables culturally different clients to experience warm acceptance and understanding as the necessary but not sufficient condition of successful therapy (Lambert, 1981). The client must perceive the counselor as well informed, capable, intelligent, trustworthy, and credible from the client's cultural viewpoint; the counselor needs to accommodate wide ranging role expectations from clients without losing his or her own cultural integrity (Sue, 1977, 1978, 1981a, 1981b). When these conditions are not met, the client may be exposed to appropriate process but inappropriate goals, to appropriate goals but inappropriate process, or to inappropriate process and inappropriate goals (Ivey, 1981).

In searching for special, quick, and easy intercultural techniques, counselors may abandon the fundamentals of counseling and therapy in favor of unorthodox methods presumed to be cross-cultural (Patterson, 1978; Wohl, 1981). Insecure counselors may refer clients to culturally similar counselors on the grounds that counselors who are most different from their clients in ethnicity and social class have greatest difficulty effecting constructive changes (Carkhuff and Pierce, 1967; LeVine and Campbell, 1972). In fact, however, the client's preference for a particular counseling style may be more significant than racial, ethnic, or socioeconomic similarity. For example, an active intervention style for positive change is more valued than rapport building in many minority groups (Atkinson, Maruyama, and Matsui, 1978; Peoples and Dell, 1975). Tseng and Hsu (1980) point out how, in a highly organized sociocultural system with regulation and control, an institutionalized catharsis is needed, whereas, in less tightly organized societies lacking goal regulation and guidance, control might be the preferred therapeutic approach.

The counselor can also work through a mediator from the client's culture. Bolman (1968) advocates including a cotherapist from the client's culture; Weidman (1975) has developed the use of a "culture broker" as intermediary for working with culturally different clients; and Slack and Slack (1976), working with chemically dependent clients, advocate the use of a coclient who has already solved a similar problem. Mediators have been used in family therapy (Satir, 1964) to reorganize pathogenic coalitions and relating styles among family members. Zuk (1971) describes counseling as a "go-between" process where the therapist mediates conflict between the client and the community. And Ruiz and Casas (1981) describe a bicultural counseling model for helping counselors work with clients whose identity combines majority and minority cultural values.

Mediation involves problems, however. Miles (1976) points out that boundary-spanning activities can result in role ambiguity and role diffusion for either the client or the counselor, leading to problems of marginality and anomie. Yet, as compared with persons from a single culture, bicultural individuals are described as having higher potential to function with cognitive flexibility, are more creatively adaptive to either culture (Berry, 1975), and are better adjusted to perform at a higher level in either of their two cultures (Szapocznik and Kurtines, 1980). As a mediator, the bicultural counselor serves to interpret either culture and, to be effective, must be accepted in a well-defined role by both cultures (MacKinnon and Michels, 1971). In developing the personality mediation approach, LeVine and Padilla (1980) describe such an individual as standing between the culture of the past, to which he or she has been socialized, and the culture of the future, which he or she can change and create. An understanding of individual and cultural variables can facilitate the growth of counseling relationships by focusing on the interaction between an individual and the cultural environment as they change one another.

Although cultural labels are normally associated with national or ethnic categories, the perspectives of cross-cultural training can also be applied to groups defined by physical, economic, or behavioral characteristics (Kinloch, 1979). Physical types can be divided by sex role, age, or handicap; economic types include lower, middle, and upper classes; and behavioral types include deviants, geniuses, addicts, and so forth. These special groups resemble cultures in many ways. For example, Ambrowitz and Dokecki (1977) suggest that class membership is more significant than race or sex role in determining outcomes of interaction. Erickson (1975) likewise suggests that these subcultural affiliations, based on similar communication styles, intelligence, temperament, class, and identity, might be more important than ethnic or racial similarity. Triandis (1977) has developed an elegant model that sees behavioral intentions as determined by such social cognitions as roles, norms, self-concept, interpersonal agreements, emotional attachments, and the perceived value of the consequences of behavior. Interpersonal behavior is then described as the interaction of these variables. Hines and Pedersen (1980) have developed the notion of roles as cultures into a cultural grid for analyzing the full spectrum of social system variables and cultural perspectives. Seeing roles as cultures, although complicating the definition of culture, does not reduce the level of analysis to individual differences. Rather, it emphasizes the

dynamic patterns of interaction between multiple cultural affiliations, patterns that change for each person from one situation and
time to another, irrespective of more limited ethnic and national
categories. As a consequence, all counseling is to some extent cross-
cultural (Roberts, 1975; Pedersen, in press).

Intercultural Skills Training Models

Persons who have learned to relate to their client in the
client's host culture will presumably function more effectively and
intentionally than previously. Furthermore, persons who have
adapted effectively to one cultural environment will have to change
their approach to adapt effectively in a different cultural environment. To the extent that they are finely tuned to the nuances of one
culture, they may have a more difficult time adapting to a different
culture. Triandis (1975) describes training as familiarizing persons
of one culture with significant dimensions of another culture.
Transfer of learning can be improved by decreasing stimulus generalization and increasing stimulus differentiation toward isomorphic
attributions (the attribution of the same cause or explanation by two
persons from different cultures for events and situations).

A variety of training approaches have been developed to prepare counselors to work with culturally different clients (Bryson,
Renzaglia, and Danish, 1974; Lewis and Lewis, 1970; Mitchel, 1970;
Arrendondo-Dowd and Gonslaves, 1980). Ivey (1980) points out,
however, that these approaches share no uniform theoretical basis,
no systematic development of method, no comparisons of training
outcomes, and no agreed-on outcome criteria. Basically, there is a
criterion problem in measuring intercultural adjustment. Much research was sponsored by the Peace Corps between 1962 and 1970 on
the training and selection of volunteers for service in foreign cultures. Clinical interviews by psychologists and psychiatrists, personality inventories, aptitude tests, peer assessments, self-ratings,
background assessments and situational tests were used, but results
were inconclusive and were unsuccessful in predicting adjustment
or success of volunteers overseas (Hawes and Kealey, 1980; Tucker,
1974; Brislin and Pedersen, 1976).

If we are unable to predict success for persons going from one culture to another, it is not surprising that we should have difficulty training people to work in other cultures. Such training usually takes one of two forms: it emphasizes culturally specific skills related to the unique values of a particular culture or it emphasizes culturally general skills that would apply to many cultural settings. While many skill training approaches, such as those presented elsewhere in this book, for example, may appear to be generalizable to a variety of culturally different settings, at least some of the values underlying those skills are likely to be encapsulated by the particular Euro-American, middle-class culture in which they were originally identified.

Human relations training is focused on the qualities of empathy, warmth, and genuineness as essential training and therapy skills. Therapies characterized in this way by personal growth and self-exploration have in some cases led to increased adaptational difficulties as clients have become more aware of and dissatisfied with their own oppressive context (Wohl, 1981; Halleck, 1971). Seward (1970) argues that many traditional theories of psychotherapy emphasize the individual as an isolated biosocial unit without acknowledging the complex cultural effect on nonindividualistic clients. Therapy's individualistic self-scrutiny and critical analysis assume that mental health originates and is maintained in the individual, rather than the social unit (Lasch, 1978). In considering the person-environment transaction, the counselor must match the counseling style to the cultural values of clientele. Human relations training assumes the value of openness and direct communication, when in fact information considered public by one culture might be considered quite private in another (Barnlund, 1975).

Human relations training disregards the way in which the qualities of empathy, warmth, and genuineness are conveyed to another culture, as well as whether those qualities are in fact valued by that culture (Pedersen, 1977a, 1978a). Rather, human relations training tends to reflect Western, middle-class values that may even be offensive to members of many non-Western cultures.

Microtraining introduces one skill at a time with expert modeling and the opportunity to rehearse the skill. Ivey (1980) suggests that attending and influencing behaviors are presented using a middle-class, verbal approach. Although Ivey readily acknowledges the importance of attending to cultural differences in a client's environment, he has not yet developed guidelines for adapting each of the microskills to a variety of contrasting cultural settings. The values of an individualistic, Western perspective continue to be primary assumptions in the microtraining approach in its present form. Ivey (1980) accepts this implicit cultural bias as a necessary limitation in order to meet the needs of Western audiences. However, to the extent that microtraining is being promoted in non-Western settings, both the content and the process need to be adapted to the requirements of particular cultures. Culturally universal criteria are not yet available for adapting microtraining techniques in a culturally universal mode. Therefore, although it is the most promising design for adaptation in this way, microtraining runs the risk of being misinterpreted and oversimplified by culturally insensitive trainers.

Life development training emphasizes increased understanding of oneself, some knowledge of helping skills, and experience in applying those skills. Many of the same problems cited earlier exist also in the Western value assumptions of this approach, with its focus on the needs of the individual. Alternative therapy models rely instead on a more culturally inclusive perspective, in which all events are interrelated and connected and manifest the same ultimate reality. In a world of inseparable, interacting, and ever-changing roles, the therapist includes past, present, and future perspectives in a transpersonal perspective approaching religious goals (Tart, 1975). The Western notion of development by stages toward the goal of adulthood, in achieving which one attains self-reliance, power, achievement, responsibility, sexual fulfillment, and independence from others, is satirized by Pande (1969), who describes cultural settings where longings for independence are considered neurotic and dependency does not have the negative connotations of immaturity (Pedersen, 1977a, 1978a).

The emphasis on life development disregards the cosmological, spiritual context essential to many non-Western cultures and assumes a linear stage theory of development that is frequently devalued in other cultures. The culturally complex differences in value priorities are not sufficiently recognized to allow life development training skills to generalize beyond their original cultural context. In addition, many cultures do not recognize individual or group talk therapy as the preferred mode of helping.

Structured learning emphasizes modeling, role playing, and social reinforcement and performance feedback for the transfer of training skills. Goldstein's (1981) approach is sensitive to the client's cultural expectations, offering a "reformity prescription" that reformulates treatment to fit those expectations, rather than a "conformity prescription" that expects the client to conform to the therapist's own therapeutic preferences. Goldstein distinguishes between unidifferential, bidifferential, and tridifferential levels of expectancy effects between counselor, client, and environment and uses a behavioral approach to match client and counselor expectations. However, congruent role expectations are not sufficient to predict successful counseling outcomes (Duckro, Beal, and George, 1979). Higginbotham and Tanaka-Matsumi (1981) demonstrate how behavioral approaches to therapy, such as structural learning, can account for the interacting factors of therapy, cultural conceptions of problem behaviors, client expectations, and relevant support networks. However, behaviorism is not a "culture-free" position and maintains its own implicit cultural assumptions with little regard for the interpretation or source of that behavior.

Structured learning faces the problem of cultures that resist the intervention of a stranger from outside the immediate family or unit who seeks to modify behavior. Persons from such cultures might also be offended by the levels of self-disclosure and intrusiveness required in structured learning. Finally, appropriate rewards cannot always be identified in each culture to reinforce a behavior once it is deemed socially desirable.

Interpersonal process recall (Kagan, 1981) emphasizes the use of stimulus affect, films, reviewing interviews, debriefing by an inquirer, mutual recall, and process feedback from the client to facilitate the development of trainee response modes. Kagan led the way for many of the other helping skills training programs by focusing on specific training goals for counseling and by combining the experiential and didactic modes for increased self-discovery. Abundant research has demonstrated IPR's effectiveness with a wide range of cultural and social groups since the idea's inception in 1962. As with subsequent skills training models, its cross-cultural effectiveness depends largely on how it is used and interpreted in relation to the trainee's culture. The variety of approaches incorporated into the IPR skills training program assumes that insight will result in changed behaviors, that a direct, rather than an indirect, teaching of skills is more appropriate, and that the desired outcome of training is greater independence and autonomy for the trainee—assumptions that are not universally endorsed by all cultures.

IPR requires a level of self-disclosure that conflicts with the values of more private cultures; by contrast, these cultures might prefer indirection and implicit communication, perceiving self-disclosure and explicit recall as increasing, rather than decreasing, the stress levels and difficulties of a situation. In addition, the process of IPR training requires more time, technical facilities, and resources than are normally available in many cultures.

Other skills training methods share similar problems when applied to multicultural settings. The whole notion of separating training from real-life interaction is seriously questioned in many cultures, where training is thought to result in oversimplification and abstraction. Many objections to training in intercultural contact have also been raised. One point of view contends that intercultural training is a waste of time and money, that any intelligent individual should be able to adjust to another culture without special preparation. Failure to make such an adjustment is therefore considered a sign of weakness and mental instability unlikely to be prevented by training. Along similar lines, others suggest that regardless of culture each situation requires a single correct response that does not change from time to time or place to place: "You don't have to learn about a foreign culture once you get the feel of the way they do things."

A second point of view contends that intercultural training may in fact do harm. The trainee may learn half-truths and develop stereotypes that have to be unlearned when he or she arrives in the foreign culture. If, for example, the trainee becomes less sensitive to a simulated embarrassing situation, he or she will be less caring when the real situation presents itself. Some say it is a waste of time to focus on one's own cultural assumptions and biases. Rather, more time should be spent learning the values of the foreign culture.

A third point of view contends that, although training may be helpful, it is more often misguided because it emphasizes process rather than content. Only training programs that teach content or factual information about the foreign culture are valuable in learning what to expect. According to this point of view, once trainees are living in the foreign culture, they will be able to identify rewarding experiences that help them adjust. Finally, just being in contact with another culture is assumed to enable the trainee to learn about that culture, although in fact this only happens under favorable conditions.

Different cultural groups have different needs and different constraints for fulfilling those needs. The skills training approach emphasizes the manipulative role of counselors or helping professionals as outside experts. In many cultures, it would be inappropriate to share problems with outsiders. People in these cultures would prefer their own family or "natural" support system, in which people in the same core group rely on one another.

Need for a Cross-Cultural Training Model

Research indicates that counselors who differ from their clients in race, culture, or social class have difficulty effecting constructive changes, whereas counselors who are similar to their clients in these respects have a greater facility for appropriate intervention (Pedersen and others, 1981; Pedersen, Lonner, and Draguns, 1976; Pedersen, 1974b; Marsella and Pedersen, 1981). Barriers of language, class-bound values, and culture-bound goals have a tendency to weaken the counselor-client coalition and disrupt the counseling relationship. Clients and counselors from different cultures risk mutual misunderstanding of one another's assumptions, mutual misperception of one another's reality, and the counselor's misinterpretation of the client's problems. As a consequence, the cross-cultural counselor is likely to experience increased negative transference from the client and to label as neurotic transference what is in fact a culturally normal response (Pedersen, 1976).

The usual system of selecting, training, and certifying counselors may reflect and even reinforce a cultural bias, disregarding cultural variations among clients and adhering to some universal notion of technique-oriented truth. Therapists unable to adjust their own attitudes, beliefs, and style of behavior to those of another culture are likely to substitute their own criteria of desired social effectiveness for alternative criteria more appropriate to the client's environment.

A comprehensive training approach should emphasize a balance of awareness, knowledge, and skill. By increasing awareness of personal bias and culturally contrasting alternatives, the counselor is able to articulate more culturally intentional interventions. Weeks, Pedersen, and Brislin (1976) describe experiential exercises for developing intercultural awareness and for becoming more articulate about the ethnocultural context. Kleinman (1978, 1979) has developed an ethnoscience, which requires that a client's behavior be interpreted from within the client's cultural context. He goes on to specify those skills in an approach to intercultural therapy he calls ethnomethodology. By learning how to incorporate a client's culture into therapy, the counselor can translate helping skills appropriately from one culture to another. This chapter describes one approach to teaching intercultural knowledge, awareness, and skills.

A cross-cultural training program for mental health professionals is needed for a number of reasons. (1) The cultural bias of traditional systems of mental health services, which favors the dominant social classes, can be counter-productive to an equitable distribution of services. (2) Various cultural groups have discovered indigenous modes of coping and treatment that suit their particular needs and may be usefully applied to other groups. (3) Community health services are expensive when they fail, and cross-cultural training can reduce the incidence of failure. (4) The constructs of healthy and normal that guide the delivery of mental health services are not the same for all cultures and may make culturally encapsulated counselors tools of a particular political, social, or economic system. (5) Increased interdependence across national, ethnic, and sociocultural group boundaries requires direct attention to the range of mental health services provided. (6) Most therapists come from dominant cultural groups, whereas most clients do not.

Cross-Cultural Triad Training Model

The triad model for cross-cultural training has been developed to train mental health professionals in working with culturally different clients through a microcounseling laboratory design in which a therapist from one culture is matched with a team consisting of a coached client and a resource person from a contrasting culture for a videotaped simulation of a cross-cultural therapy session. The most frequently used role for the resource person is as an "anticounselor." The therapist seeks to build rapport with the culturally different coached client, offering him or her a counseling solution; the anticounselor seeks to represent the problem element from the client's cultural viewpoint. As a result of the role-played interaction, the therapist learns to articulate the problem explicitly from the client's cultural viewpoint; to anticipate resistance to counseling by clients from a particular culture; to diminish therapist defensiveness while working with a culturally different client; and to practice recovery skills for reestablishing rapport after inappropriate counselor responses.

The triad model describes counseling as occurring in a force field consisting of the goals of the counselor, the goals of the client, and the constraints of the culturally different environment represented by the anticounselor. Counseling, according to this model, is a three-way interaction between counselor, client, and problem, in which the counselor seeks fulfillment in being helpful, the client seeks to reconcile internalized ambiguity, and the problem seeks its own survival through increased power over the client. The function of counseling is essentially to establish a temporary, means-oriented coalition with the client against the problem. Unless such a coalition can be established, the problem will continue to control the client and isolate the counselor. The greater the cultural differences between client and counselor, the less likely the counselor is to establish a coalition with the client against the problem.

Role of the Anticounselor. The unique element in this model is the personified role of the problem, or anticounselor, who actively tries to prevent the counselor from collaborating with the client in solving the problem. The anticounselor may be seen as a third presence, almost in the sense of a demonic possession with a secret strategy of its own. The anticounselor's function in the simulated interview is to use cultural similarity of class, culture, and language to disrupt the counselor-client coalition by explicitly articulating those cultural aspects of the force field that oppose counseling. In this way, the triad model offers numerous advantages that complement other training models (Ivey and Authier, 1978). (1) It provides an opportunity for persons of different ethnic groups to role play critical incidents likely to arise in cross-cultural counseling under controlled conditions that maximize safety. (2) The use of an anti-counselor makes the cultural problems and values less abstract and diffuse for the culturally naive counselor. (3) Inappropriate counselor intervention is identified immediately by the anticounselor's direct and explicit feedback to the trainee. (4) The counselor trainee becomes more aware of the unspoken thoughts and feelings of the client. (5) The simulated interviews can be videotaped to analyze specific ways in which cultural differences affect counseling.

The triad model seems to work best when the client and the resource person offer both positive and negative feedback to the counselor during or after the interview. For this reason, alternatives to the anticounselor role have been developed for the client's partner, including the roles of procounselor and interpreter. When the client-anticounselor team is highly motivated and feels strongly about the issue under discussion, and when the anticounselor has a high degree of empathy for and acceptance by the client, more relevant insights about intercultural counseling result. The anticounselor needs to provide direct, immediate, and articulate feedback to the trainee, with the client being free to reject an inauthentic anticounselor. The simulated interview is spontaneous and not scripted.

Selecting and Training Resource Teams. Selection and training of coached client–anticounselor teams is of primary importance. Resource persons should be as similar to clients as possible, matching ethnicity, socioeconomic group, age, life-style, sex role, and other significant variables, and should be both authentic and articulate representatives of their culture. Resource persons might not be able to verbalize guidelines for cross-cultural counseling; however, when placed in the role of an anticounselor, they are generally quick to demonstrate significant rules and values. The client-anticounselor teams are trained by viewing and discussing one-hour model videotapes and then rehearsing their roles, with the trainer as counselor.

Several adaptations of the triad model are being developed that coach the resource person from the client's culture in one of five adaptive roles in addition to the role of anticounselor. In each case, the resource person is matched as closely as possible with the client in culture and values. As a procounselor, the third person attempts to facilitate a coalition within the interview by reinforcing and encouraging positive counselor behaviors. As an interpreter, the third person attempts to increase the accuracy of communication between counselor and client, irrespective of positive or negative outcomes for counseling. As a third person friendly to counseling, the third person becomes a friend or relative who is encouraging the counseling relationship in a naturalistic mode. As a third person hostile to counseling, the third person becomes a friend or relative who is discouraging the counseling relationship. Sometimes the incorporation of a resource person as an actual third person in the naturalistic mode is less confusing or abstract than having a disembodied anticounselor, procounselor, or interpreter who represents an idea, rather than a real person. A sixth training adaptation being developed includes both a procounselor and an anticounselor in a four-member simulated interview. The interaction between four persons can become quite complicated but clearly demonstrates both positive and negative aspects of the force field in a cross-cultural interview.

In each adaptation, the feedback from the client and resource person to the counselor being trained is continuous and immediate. In addition, a videotape of the interview is analyzed during a debriefing session. Future applications will focus on the cultural differences between clients and counselors, on how those differences affect a discussion of specific problem areas, and on how to teach the counselor skills in monitoring positive and negative feedback from culturally different clients.

Role of the Problem in Counseling. The triad model makes several assumptions about the problem as it becomes a framework for the culturally defined environment of counseling. (1) The problem is seen as both good and bad, especially from the client's point of view; each problem has rewarding as well as punishing features, which define it as a problem. (2) The problem is complex, like a personality, and not limited to the fact that the client drinks too much, gets low grades, is homesick, or deviates from standards of so-called normal behavior. (3) The problem is active, rather than passively accepting, drawing its identity from the client and the client's cultural environment. In the struggle toward a solution, the problem sometimes resembles a personified enemy with a secret strategy of its own, articulated through the resource person in the role of anticounselor. (4) The problem is concrete and not abstract, able to speak for itself, and defined by its own potent threats and promises. (5) The problem is partly cultural, with the third person from the client's culture more likely to know about its complex nuances than a counselor from some other culture.

Assumptions About Intercultural Training. The triad model also makes several assumptions about the intercultural training of counselors. First, it is assumed that the problem element can be effectively treated as if it were the third member of a counseling relationship. This assumption draws from perceptual field theory, which states that people behave according to how things seem to them (Coombs, Richards, and Richards, 1976). Since the client accepts the problem as real, it affects the client's behavior. Therefore, if the counselor is going to participate in a coalition against the problem, he or she will need to work within the client's perceptual field. The anticounselor is similar to the alter ego of psychodrama or Gestalt psychotherapy, except that the anticounselor is not neutral but is deliberately subversive, attempting to disrupt the counseling interview. The counselor is pulling in one direction toward a solution; the anticounselor is pulling in exactly the opposite direction, attempting to maintain the problem; and the client chooses which alternative offers the most meaningful approach.

A client-counselor coalition against the anticounselor becomes the vehicle of effective counseling; ineffective counseling results in a client-anticounselor coalition that isolates the ineffective counselor. The role of the anticounselor is not the role of a person with a problem; it has a negative function in the counseling relationship, just as the counselor's role has a positive function.

Second, the triad model assumes that direct contact with resource persons from another culture in a favorable setting is the most efficient means of training counselors to work with clients from that culture. The role-played interaction provides an opportunity for persons from different ethnic or cultural groups to interact under controlled conditions for the accomplishment of limited training goals to their mutual advantage. The resource persons are often able to teach more about cultural barriers through modeling than through abstract, theoretical discussions, and can do so in a setting that minimizes the dangers of either client or counselor becoming overly defensive or threatened. The anticounselor role clearly and concretely articulates the cultural aspects of the problem. Videotaped simulations of the exchange between counselor, client, and anticounselor provide material that can be used to illustrate specific ways in which cultural differences affect counseling. In this way, the triad model allows members of the culture being served to participate in the training of counselors who will later be serving them.

Third, the three-way interaction provides immediate and continuous feedback to the counselor in a counseling context, which has more powerful training impact than delayed feedback following a simulated interview. A careful analysis of interaction transcripts identifies implicit and explicit, inadvertent and deliberate cultural bias in both the definition of problems and the identification of specific forms of resistance. Such cultural bias prevents counselors from working with certain problems in cross-cultural situations. The separation of idiosyncratic from patterned or cultural differences, a skill necessary in cross-cultural counseling, can be taught by analysis of the arguments and polarized conflicts of the three-way interaction. Cultural differences tend to exaggerate and magnify the effect of inappropriate counseling interventions, providing immediate feedback to trainees in areas of inadequacy that might be less obvious in counseling persons from the counselor's own culture. Even when only a counselor and a culturally different client are involved in the interview, the client's environment continues to feed positive and negative messages that are audible to the client's "inner ear" but inaudible to a cultural outsider. The third resource person makes those implicit messages explicit within the course of the interview itself.

Fourth, the triad model models a style of communication through mediators and go-betweens that is often used in counseling by members of many non-Western cultures, especially when they are being served by a counselor from outside their own culture. Frequently the client will bring a third person into the interview for support and help in articulating the problem. Such a third person may be positively or negatively disposed toward the counseling process. If the counselor is unfamiliar with the client's language, a third person may also be brought in to act as an interpreter, a frequent source of problems for cross-cultural counselors. To some extent, counseling through a translator resembles an adaptation of the triad model, especially when the culture as well as the language needs to be translated. Even in the absence of a language problem, a third person may be required to help the counselor work more sensitively and effectively in another culture and to reduce the client's anxiety about the unfamiliar process of counseling. Such a third person might increase or decrease the comfort of the client, depending on the counselor's ability to select an appropriate go-between and to facilitate the more complex dynamic of a three-way exchange of information in the counseling interview (Pedersen; 1968, 1972, 1973, 1974a, 1975, 1979a, 1979b).

Triad Training Activities and Procedures

The first step in setting up a triad model training program is to locate a suitable resource person. Since the resource person needs to be matched with the client to form a team, they should be from similar cultures and should communicate well enough to anticipate what the other may be thinking and feeling. The client's partner needs to provide accurate insight into what the client is actually experiencing. The resource person should therefore be authentic, as well as articulate enough to represent experiences meaningfully to a cultural outsider. Since the members of the resource team are the teachers in the triad model, much of the model's effectiveness depends on the selection and training of appropriate resource persons.

The second step in setting up the triad model is training the resource persons. Resource persons are instructed to be either consistently negative in an anticounselor mode or consistently positive in a procounselor mode. In this way, the counselor working with a culturally different client will know how to interpret the role of the resource person and will become better able to differentiate between positive and negative categories of feedback in the client's culture. The triad model can be demonstrated by means of videotaped interviews or live modeling showing the resource person as anticounselor, procounselor, or interpreter. The resource persons are then encouraged to practice interviewing using the triad model until they are comfortable with the various roles. Resource persons from different cultures will develop their own adaptations of the roles according to the verbal and nonverbal communication styles of their culture. The feedback to a counselor should be as unambiguous and as immediate to the counselor's action as possible. The counselor, having identified a good or bad intervention, can then correct the intervention and recover rapport immediately.

The third step in using the triad model is selecting the problems to be simulated. Resource persons need to feel comfortable with the problems and knowledgeable about the issues they represent within the cultural setting. Ideally, the problems should illustrate unique issues within the client's culture that might otherwise be unfamiliar to an outsider. The problem should be complex, rather than simple; without an easy solution; frequently encountered in the client's culture; and likely to result in serious consequences if left unresolved. Resource persons should not select problems of serious concern to themselves for which they themselves might seek therapy; otherwise, the training session will become an actual, rather than a simulated, counseling session.

Since, in preparing the training team, the trainer needs to coach the resource persons to be articulate in representing their culture to trainees, he or she must also become minimally familiar with the client's culture. The trainer needs to structure the counselor's interaction with the resource persons so that more information about the client's culture will become explicitly available during the training session. The trainer can do this by means of guided debriefing, thereby developing the counselor's ability to learn in a simulated—and eventually in a real-life—counseling setting.

Counselors need to develop a facility for dealing with complex cultural data within the context of an interview by processing feedback from both the client and the client's partner. Through contrast with the client's culture, the trainee becomes increasingly aware of his or her own cultural viewpoints and values. As the client responds to the counselor's preferred style of counseling, the client will learn about the client's culture, as well. Ultimately the trainee will need to generalize awareness, knowledge, and skills from the simulated interviews to actual counseling.

Since the consistently negative feedback provided by the anticounselor role was contrary to the values of some cultures and became at times so adverse that the simulated interviews were not conducive to learning, procounselor roles were developed for the client's resource person. The procounselor helps a counselor articulate the presenting problem, provides a mediating bridge between the counselor and the client, emphasizes the counselor's positive interventions, and leads the counselor trainee toward increasingly appropriate interventions. The procounselor is not a cotherapist and does not take over the counselor role but facilitates the counselor trainee's own increased effectiveness.

To emphasize the resource persons' potential for enhancing teaching and transfer of knowledge, a third role was developed, the interpreter, or teacher. The interpreter is a neutral participant in the counseling triad, although the same skills are required as for the procounselor and anticounselor roles. The interpreter facilitates communication without regard for positive or negative outcomes, enabling the counselor and client to accurately understand one another's meaning. The interpreter seeks to clarify and interpret the counseling process by rephrasing the thoughts and feelings being communicated, elaborating on what has been said, or identifying misunderstandings as they occur. The cultural interpreter role parallels the role of the language interpreter in counseling and resembles Loo's (1979) "cultural contextualizer" model for cross-cultural training.

Since the anticounselor, the procounselor, and even the interpreter were too abstract for some trainees, a variation was developed in which resource persons role play a friend or relative who is either hostile or friendly to the counselor. The communication resembles that of the anticounselor or procounselor, except that the third person, hostile or friendly, is an actual person related to the client in some way.

To accentuate the force field effect of the triad model, in which both positive and negative feedback interact, a quartet variation was developed matching the counselor with three resource persons role playing client, anticounselor, and procounselor. This variation is more complex than the previously described alternatives and presumes an acquaintance with both the procounselor and anticounselor roles. The combination of roles in a quartet has advantages in introducing both positive and negative feedback immediately and continuously within the context of the same interview.

In order to demonstrate the variety of styles in counseling, a time-sharing variation was developed in which relay interviews were conducted by several counselors, each working with the same resource team for a short period of time as part of one continuous simulated interview. In this way, counselors can identify the ways in which their style differs from the style of their peers.

As the resource persons have become more sophisticated and the counselors have become more skilled, additional variations have been tried. For instance, the resource person can begin an interview as an anticounselor and gradually move toward the role of procounselor. In this way, both roles can be experienced within the context of the same interview. Another variation, used for cultures in which the individual would be unlikely to provide negative feedback outside a group context, entails having more than one resource person take on the collective role of anticounselor (Sananikone, 1980).

Triad Training Materials and Evaluation

The idea for a triad model grew out of work with Indonesian students from 1962 to 1965 in which the problem element of counseling was viewed much more realistically than I had previously experienced. With guidance from Clyde Parker and Donald Blocher, the model was developed during graduate study in counseling psychology at the University of Minnesota (Pedersen, 1966). During three subsequent years of teaching in Asia and several years of counseling foreign students at the University of Minnesota, the model continued to evolve.

Recent research with prepracticum counseling students at the University of Hawaii reveals that students trained with the triad model showed significantly higher scores on a written multiple-choice test designated to measure counselor effectiveness, had lower levels of discrepancy between real and ideal self-descriptions as counselors, and chose greater numbers of positive adjectives in describing themselves as counselors than students who were not trained with the triad model. Students also showed significant gains on the Carkhuff measures of empathy, respect, and congruence, as well as on the seven-level Gordon scales measuring communication of affective meaning (Pedersen, Holwill, and Shapiro, 1978).

A National Institute of Mental Health (NIMH) proposal grew out of the work in Hawaii and resulted in a three-year program for developing interculturally skilled counselors that was housed at the University of Hawaii and the East West Center in Honolulu (Pedersen, 1978b). During this period, general descriptions of the triad model (Pedersen, 1977b, 1979a, 1979b, 1981) and a description of four intercultural skills areas being developed through triad model training (Pedersen, 1978a) were published. The four skills areas included: perceiving the problem from the client's cultural perspective; reducing counselor defensiveness in intercultural confrontation; recognizing resistance in specific, rather than general, terms; and learning recovery skills for getting out of trouble after a culturally insensitive intervention. During the course of the NIMH-funded project, several discussions of the importance of intercultural training and education for mental health professionals were published (Pedersen and others, 1981; Marsella and Pedersen, 1981).

Several researchers have compared the triad model with other training methods. Ivey and Authier (1978) discussed "cultural-environmental-contextual" implications of the triad model and conclude that "the most powerful and direct method for cross-cultural training appears to be that of the cross-cultural triad model of Pedersen" (p. 215). At the same time, they also point out that the triad model is not appropriate for all trainees and that naive trainees benefit more from triad model training after learning the basic microcounseling skills.

Holwill-Bailey (1979) compared the relative efficacy of three training approaches—dyad, triad, and lecture discussion—among seventy-seven prepracticum counseling students. The dyad approach matched each trainee with a coached client, who provided feedback on simulated interviews. The triad approach matched the trainee with a coached client and a third person, who provided feedback as an anticounselor. Participants completed the Budner Tolerance of Ambiguity scale, the Shapiro Adjective Checklist, and a revised Truax-Carkhuff scale of empathy, respect, and congruence. Students from the dyad and triad groups were significantly more effective in communicating empathy, respect, and congruence than students from the lecture-discussion group, although no significant differences were found between dyad and triad training groups.

Sue (1979) field-tested the anticounselor and procounselor training models with thirty-six counseling students, reporting that students felt the anticounselor model to be more effective than the procounselor model in achieving self-awareness, developing cultural sensitivity for contrasting cultural values, and understanding the political and social ramifications of cross-cultural counseling. "The anticounselor model tended to be most effective with having participants achieve awareness of their cultural values and biases, obtaining cultural sensitivity to other ethnically defined groups, and helping them understand the political-social ramifications of counseling. The procounselor model was most effective in helping them obtain specific knowledge of the history experiences and cultural values of ethnic groups and helping them acquire and develop cross-cultural counseling skills and intervention strategies" (p. 60). Students were more comfortable with the procounselor model; the anticounselor model was more anxiety provoking. "When asked to rate the most effective model for learning about cross-cultural counseling in the shortest period of time, however, the anticounselor model was seen as far superior" (p. 61). Whereas confrontation by the anticounselor brought out issues of racism, bias, and conflicting values through immediate feedback to the counselor trainees, the procounselor tended to facilitate acquisition of skills. Whereas the anticounselor pointed out what was wrong, the procounselor helped refocus what could be done to improve a counselor's intercultural style. Ideally, training programs should incorporate complementary procounselor and anticounselor modes.

Evaluation data from more than twenty workshops sponsored through the NIMH-funded training program have tended to confirm these findings (Sue, 1979; Brough, 1980). Videotapes demonstrating the anticounselor, procounselor, interpreter, and other variations of the triad model are being developed through the NIMH project, and evaluation data are being tabulated to determine the model's effectiveness as a cross-cultural training mode for counselors and therapists. Other research is using the triad model to train interviewers (LaFromboise, 1981) and rehabilitation counselors (Anderson, 1978).

A variety of evaluation procedures have been used to collect data on the triad model. The most frequent method has been self-report evaluations by persons who have experienced the model through workshops, classes, and other forms of training. Pre and post work samples of counseling interviews on audiotape and videotape have been used by Holwill-Bailey (1979), Sue (1979), and Pedersen, Holwill, and Shapiro (1978); however, measures of interculturally skilled counseling are still being developed. A promising approach is pretraining and posttraining analysis of critical incidents in cross-cultural counseling (Sue, 1979).

The NIMH grant allows for long-range follow-up of trainees to determine the individual and institutional impact of training (Brough, 1980). For example, reports of supervisors and coworkers following training are used in evaluating the use of triads in training mental health professionals at the Cross-Cultural Training Center in the Department of Psychiatry at the University of Miami's School of Medicine (Lefley, 1980). Another measure is the trainee's ability to teach the model to new trainees, an approach that has been used in courses on cross-cultural counseling at the University of Minnesota and the University of Hawaii. Resource persons have also been used in evaluating students of cross-cultural counseling courses. However, no published data are yet available on these last two modes of evaluation.

Two Triad Model Training Designs

The first training design to be described is appropriate for a small group of about ten or twelve counselors working together in a one-day intensive training experience. The second training design is appropriate for a larger group of about thirty or forty counselors working together in a two-day workshop experience. Each design has its advantages and disadvantages, but the key element in each is the selection and training of culturally matched, coached client-resource person teams. In previous workshops, teams of prisoners have been used to train social workers, and teams of handicapped persons have been used to train rehabilitation counselors. These teams should be acknowledged as the cultural authorities and teachers in the workshop. Since they must be both articulate and authentic to their cultural group, team members should be trained in their coached roles with demonstration videotapes and supervised role rehearsals. Each of the training designs described is led by a facilitator who is already familiar with the triad model.

One-Day Workshop for Small Groups of Trainees. This format requires three trained client–resource person teams from three different cultures; one large meeting room for viewing videotapes and a small nearby video lab for videotaping triads; and ten rolls of videotape, two video recording decks, one camera, and at least one TV monitor. Following an introduction and video demonstrations showing examples of the triad model, the facilitator answers questions while one of the counselors leaves the room with a client–resource person team to make the first videotape. The counselor and team return to the group after having produced a ten-minute videotape of a simulated counseling interview and a five-minute videotape of the three persons debriefing one another. The fifteen-minute videotape is then shown to the larger group for comments and discussion. While this tape is being viewed, another counselor leaves the room with the second team to produce a second tape. By the time the group has discussed the first tape, the second counselor and team have returned with a second tape. While the second tape is being viewed, a third counselor leaves the room with the third team to make a third tape. Each counselor participant takes a turn in making a tape with one of the teams in sequence. After all the counselor participants have had a chance to make, view, and receive feedback on their videotape, a plenary session is held to summarize insights from the various videotapes and to answer questions.

Advantages. Assembling counselors interested in cross-cultural training to discuss the special circumstances of cultural differences is likely to result in ongoing contacts and a network of professional relationships that will be useful to support continued learning after the workshop has concluded. Allowing each participant to produce a tape and receive feedback from colleagues ensures that the experience is intensive and specific to the individual counselor. The three culturally different teams permit the counselors some flexibility in matching themselves with a particular culture. At the same time, counselors are able to compare and contrast how counseling clients from one culture is different from counseling clients from another culture. The videotapes produced during such a workshop also provide a valuable resource if participants and client-resource person teams are willing to allow the videotapes to be used by other trainee groups.

Disadvantages. Facilities to run such a workshop may be difficult to secure. The design requires considerable videotaping equipment, one large meeting room, and a nearby videotaping studio. In this particular design, participants miss one group feedback session while producing their own videotape. However, the advantages of discussing their own videotape while it is still fresh in their mind outweighs the disadvantages of missing one session.

Resource teams must be selected and trained with extreme care and must be paid and acknowledged as professionals whose roles are central to the instructional function of the workshop. Preferably, team members should select one another to ensure cultural closeness and facility in mutual communication and should be verbally articulate—although some teams have used nonverbal approaches very effectively. Some teams are able to role play more easily than others, but, in all cases, team training includes viewing videotaped models on resource person functioning, as well as an opportunity to rehearse roles to meet a criterion of competence as judged by the facilitator. The resource team then preselects several problems to role play during the training.

Two-Day Workshop for Large Groups of Trainees. Requirements for this format include one trained resource person team of the same culture for every eight counselor trainees; one room large enough for everyone to meet and adjoining smaller rooms for groups of ten persons to meet with a minimum of distraction from other groups; and one videotape replay deck and monitor. The first session begins with an introduction of the resource person teams to the participants, a statement of the agenda and goals for the workshop, and time for questions. Then the video demonstrations of the triad model are shown to the total group, followed by questions and some discussion. After the discussion, the facilitator and a resource team demonstrate the triad model, or the entire group may be divided into triads to practice the model under the supervision of the facilitator and coached resource teams.

Once group participants have a clear idea of the model, they are divided into groups of eight according to prearranged criteria to ensure that each group is as heterogeneous as possible in terms of culture, age, sex role, life-style, training, socioeconomic status, and other characteristics. One coached team is then assigned to each of the groups for a period of forty-five minutes and elects a volunteer from the group to function as counselor. The three participants role play the interview for five or ten minutes using one of the problems prepared in advance by the team and then end role playing to debrief one another. After they have given one another feedback, they call on the other group members for additional observations and discussion. The coached team then elects a second volunteer from among the participants and repeats the cycle of simulated interview, debriefing, and discussion. The team should have time to complete at least two interviews during the forty-five minute period, at the end of which time the team rotates to another group for a second forty-five minute session. The entire first day is spent in this way, except that, during the last thirty minutes, all participants gather to share their experiences and ask questions.

The second day begins with a plenary session, with opportunity to ask questions and suggest insights that might be useful to other participants. Groups then continue meeting with resource teams until each of the teams has met with each of the small groups. By this time, all participants have had a chance to role play the counselor in triads.

At this point, the entire group comes together for a discussion, and participants are asked to form their own triads with one another and with members of the resource teams and to assume any of the three roles of counselor, client, or resource person. Participants not wishing to role play are encouraged to observe one of the triads in session. Active participants are instructed to simulate problems they have identified from their own background and cultural group.

Next, the resource teams assemble as a panel in front of the total group, and each team member is given a chance to briefly speak on what he or she has observed during the training process. After each team member has spoken, participants ask questions and discuss the training process within the larger group. By this time, participants usually have numerous questions on the specific ways that cultural differences between coached teams affect the counseling relationship. At the end of the discussion, participants fill out evaluation forms.

Advantages. Alternating small group and large group experiences allows intense interaction, in which participants can learn from one another's style in some detail, and still gives participants the benefit of insights by other participants outside their immediate small group. By having an opportunity to work with more than one team, participants are able to see how different cultures approach the same problems. During the course of the two days, participants have the opportunity to assimilate the training data and to think about questions they might want to ask during the final session. Each participant plays the counselor in a simulated interview at least once and can also experience the roles of client and anticounselor, procounselor and interpreter. Finally, participants are encouraged to present counseling problems they have actually experienced for feedback and suggestions on appropriate intervention strategies.

Disadvantages. Participants do not have the opportunity to make videotapes to observe themselves working with clients from other cultures. Furthermore, the logistics of assembling small groups, assigning participants, and rotating the teams is complicated. At times, small groups become so involved in discussion that they avoid role playing and need to be reminded to save the discussion of issues until the last session. Although the facilitator can circulate among the groups to help involve them in role playing, he or she is not equally accessible to all participants. In any case, the interaction is extremely intense, and liberal allowance should be made for coffee breaks between sessions, at the same time keeping as much pressure on the participants as possible. Another disadvantage is that, since participants are sometimes not able to attend the workshop for the full two days, the small groups may fluctuate in size.

Examples of Applications with the Triad Model

Many of the applications of the triad model to training counselors and therapists have already been discussed. Since cultural differences have been defined to include differences of age, sex role, socioeconomic status, life-style, and group affiliation, a large variety of populations either have been or could be involved in triad model training. Some examples of contrasting populations will suggest how the model might be applied.

In a prepracticum seminar, thirty graduate counseling students were divided into ten triads in which two persons were similar and one person as different as possible in sex role and ethnicity. During the first phase of training, one student in each triad was assigned to the counselor role, one to the client role, and one to the anticounselor role. They met for three hours in the same roles, simulating and discussing three different cross-cultural interviews that were videotaped and reviewed for debriefing. During the next two weeks, the same procedure was followed, but the students rotated roles in the triad (Pedersen, Holwill, and Shapiro, 1978). When compared with the previous class, triad model–trained students achieved significantly higher scores (F = 5.90; p < .01) on the multiple choice test of counseling knowledge and developed a significantly more positive (F = 5.65; p < .05) and congruent (F = 6.03; p < .01) self-image on the adjective checklist. In addition, significant increases in empathy (F = 17.40; p < .005), respect (F = 20.68; p < .005), and congruence (F = 4.50; p < .005) and significant increases on the Gordon scales (F = 12.47; p < .005) were found in work samples taken before and after training.

In a two-day in-service training workshop with thirty-nine Asian-American counselors from the Department of Social Welfare on Maui who were working with largely Caucasian counterculture clients, twenty-eight of the counselors indicated that triad training helped them anticipate resistance from culturally different clients, twenty-five said that training helped them articulate the problem from the client's point of view, and twenty-two indicated that they wanted more training with the model. In a similar two-day workshop with forty social welfare counselors in Hilo, thirty-two indicated that triad training helped them anticipate resistance, thirty said that it helped them articulate the problem from the client's point of view, and twenty-eight said that they would like additional training with the model.

The triad model has been used as an in-service training mode with a number of different populations. Students in the graduate program in international advising at the Experiment for International Living in Brattleboro, Vermont, indicated that the training increased their effectiveness in working with persons from other cultures. A group of twenty-eight CETA counselors working with other ethnic groups in Hawaii indicated that they gained skill in articulating problems, recognizing resistance, and reducing defensiveness in working with culturally different clients. The model was used in training mental health professionals in cross-cultural skills in one-day sessions of a seven-day workshop at the Cross-Cultural Training Center of the University of Miami's Department of Psychiatry and was evaluated as one of the most valuable training approaches in the workshop. In training prisoners to work with social workers at Stillwater Penitentiary in Minnesota, the model was so effective in preparing new social workers at the prison that the prisoners aborted the program, claiming that the trained social workers were becoming more difficult to manipulate. Other populations trained have been counselors working with alcoholics, counselors working with handicapped clients, advisers working with foreign students, medical personnel working with cancer patients, and social welfare workers helping low-income clients.

As examples of how the triad model is applied to training situations, selected portions of transcripts are presented demonstrating how the various roles interact. In the first excerpt, a white counselor is working with a black female client who is experiencing prejudice, racial jokes, and bias with peers, and with a black male anticounselor who has been pointing out the counselor's stereotypical statements and articulating the resistance a black client might experience working with a white counselor.

Anticounselor: We've been here five or six minutes, and how much trust do we have in him? What has he done so far that can make us say that we can trust him to deal with the whole situation? You heard him hesitate. You heard him stumble around, we've heard him take the uniqueness out of the problem . . .

Counselor: Terry . . .

Anticounselor:	We've heard him say, "Deal with the jokes." How much trust can we put in this man?
Counselor:	Terry, why don't you, uh . . . try to, uh . . . eliminate . . . (pause). Not eliminate, certainly not eliminate . . .
Anticounselor:	I'm beginning to think trust is getting less and less.
Counselor:	I asked you a question and . . .
Client:	Well, it's like the questions you are asking don't stick in my mind as well as what he is saying to me. It's like he can relate with what I'm, you know, the thing I'm going with and you gave me a lot of stuff about how a lot of black people are approaching the same problem. But the thing is, what I want to know is how do I deal with it?

An accumulation of counselor mistakes and interventions has contributed to the client's overall perception.

In another interview, a white male counselor is working with a Chinese male client who had never been in counseling before on how his relationship with his fiancee was interferring with his school work. A Chinese female anticounselor emphasized the difficulty a Chinese client might have with just going to counseling and, in particular, with talking about family problems.

Counselor:	Why did you come here today? Can you tell me something about what concerns you?
Client:	Um . . . I come . . .
Anticounselor:	What's the use of coming anyway?
Client:	I don't know how to put it, this . . .
Counselor:	Uh huh. It's difficult to talk about?
Anticounselor:	He probably won't understand.
Client:	I don't know what to say.
Counselor:	I guess, in a way, you are thinking, "What good does it do me right now? Whatever I say is going to be kind of confusing for him."
Client:	Yeah, yeah.

Counselor: Why don't you try and tell me something of what concerns you and let's see if I can try to understand.

Anticounselor: It's too complicated. (Pause.)

Client: Perhaps it isn't.

Counselor: Well . . .

Client: I have a fiancee in Michigan, and we have been separated for quite a long time and we don't have much time to meet. You see, she is doing graduate work there, and it will take her four years to finish her degree. And it will take me two years to finish my degree . . .

Anticounselor: What can you do about it?

Client: I don't know.

In explicating the problem later in the same interview, the anticounselor tended to attack the client as well as the counselor to keep the interview off balance and retain control. The anticounselor can focus on distracting elements of a client's problem to demonstrate cultural resistance to both the client and the counselor.

Anticounselor: You chose to be in graduate school. Since you chose to be in graduate school, why complain about it?

Client: Yeah, I know about it, and she knows about it, as well, but, I mean that . . . we don't know that it is going to turn out like that.

Counselor: Uh huh. You don't deny the fact that you put these pressures on yourself. You accept that.

Client: Yeah, yeah.

Counselor: But at this point you're saying, "My God! I didn't think, when I was taking these responsibilities on myself, that it would lead to this."

Client: And, moreover, when you are in graduate school, you have all kinds of pressure on you that you have to pass this prelim and that and, uh . . .

Anticounselor: School is more important than love affairs.

Client: That's what they think, but . . .

Anticounselor: Your parents won't want you to lose yourself over a love affair and give up your work.

In an example in which a white male counselor is working with a Latin American female client who is having difficulty with male relationships and a Latin American female anticounselor, the emphasis is on clarifying the goal of counseling.

Counselor: Could you tell me some details of what that's like in your country?

Anticounselor: You know what he is trying to do? He is going to try to get everything out of you and then convince you that you have to be the way Americans are and just screw around . . .

Counselor: Well, I'm just thinking that you . . . I don't understand much about your country, what you have been used to . . .

Anticounselor: . . . and you know what will happen when you go back home . . .

Later in the same interview, the counselor is trying to deal with his own discomfort, as well as that of the client, and is scrambling to establish a comfortable rapport. The harder he struggles to regain the client's confidence, the more anxious the client becomes.

Counselor: Would you feel better if I got back behind the desk, and we sort of had that between us?

Client: No, then you remind me of my father.

Counselor: Okay, I don't want to do that. (Laughs). Okay, is this more comfortable?

Client: Yeah, it is.

Counselor: Okay. (Pause.)

Client: Then you make me feel like you are rejecting me. You are not rejecting me?

Counselor: I'm in a box here. On the one hand, I want to do the things that will make you comfortable, and, on the other, I don't want to get too distant and make you feel like I'm rejecting you.

Anticounselor:	He's manipulating you little by little till he gets to a point that he's going to say that you got to be just like American girls. That's the best way.
Counselor:	How do you feel now as opposed to when you came in?
Client:	Well, I'm kind of feeling uncomfortable. It was okay for awhile, and now I feel like, I don't know . . . I feel like I want to go.

If a counselor is not making mistakes in counseling with a client from an unfamiliar culture, the counselor may not be taking enough personal risks. The task of counselor training is not merely to prevent mistakes but also to recover from mistakes once they have been made. The triad model provides opportunities for the counselor to make mistakes and experiment with various strategies for recovering. One example of recovery skills is shown in the interaction between the Latin American female and the counselor, in which the counselor remained nondefensive and stayed on course.

Counselor:	This is, I might say, a problem not just for foreign girls; American girls have this problem also.
Client:	No! You know, they don't have that problem! They seem to enjoy that type of thing, and they don't seem to have a problem with it!
Counselor:	I don't want to argue about that. What we want to do is deal with your problem.
Client:	That's right.

An interchange between the white counselor and the Chinese client demonstrates the use of self disclosure and openness, rather than bluffing, as a recovery strategy when the counselor really does not understand the client's situation.

Anticounselor:	I was saying that, since you are not from our culture, you are no use to him.
Counselor:	Uh huh, I think that's right at this point. I don't know what it means yet. But what I would like to

	do is develop an appreciation and an understanding so that I am in a position to help Sung.
Anticounselor:	I think that you are getting frustrated!
Counselor:	Not yet . . . I could. (Pause.) Could you tell me . . . You see, you're right. I really don't know a great deal about your culture at all, and, in order to help you, I really have to have more of an appreciation of it.

In addition to the anticounselor design, we have discussed the role of a procounselor as an appropriate resource person role to accompany the client. In contrast to the anticounselor, the procounselor is reassuring to the counselor, either just by being present or by offering nonverbal reinforcement. In an interview between a male counselor and a secretly lesbian female client who is having difficulty working with men, a female procounselor demonstrates how a procounselor might provide encouragement and support.

Counselor:	Sounds like you're saying that you really need to get help from a woman, that a man cannot relate to your concerns.
Client:	Uh huh . . .
Procounselor:	Find out what those concerns are that men cannot relate to.
Client:	And, ah . . . I guess, you know, I've heard some things too about, you know, psychiatrists and psychologists and, you know, I think it pays to be careful.
Procounselor:	Maybe you ought to tell him what those are.
Counselor:	What kinds of things are you concerned about?
Client:	Well, just in general, I don't think that male psychiatrists or psychologists can really . . . ah, you know, I just think they don't have the same point of view, they just aren't going to look at it, ah . . . they're not going to have the same kinds of values, and so men might not even hear things the same way.

Counselor:	So you think, for example, you think my biases might really be different than a woman's or than your biases? My values might be different?
Client:	Oh, of course. Certainly! Yes. It is not anything personal, but just, ah, you know, by virtue of being a man, the things that you must do to be a man preclude any sort of possible, really deep understanding of my position.

Later, the client revealed her perception of the experience: "The procounselor was intent on getting to the root of my presenting problem as a basis for the development of trust." The procounselor likewise shared her perception: "I was attempting to facilitate problem clarification by focusing on the here-and-now situation through comments on the client's expectation, first providing data to the therapist and then supporting the client."

An interpreter acts as a teacher, helping the counselor and client to understand one another's language. Usually this requires the interpreter to restate or clarify counselor and client statements. An example of the interpreter role is provided by a black counselor working with a Laotian client and a Laotian interpreter on the adjustment problems of a newly arrived immigrant.

Client:	I do not know what to do, so I spend days and nights thinking about what I am going to do with myself. And I could not eat, as I said before, I could not sleep, so I kind of stay half-awake all the time. And this leads to a lot of things that I have in my mind. At times, I can see my grandparents who died many years ago or my friend who was in the army with me and has been killed. And they are all there happily, and they keep calling my name and waiting to see me.
Interpreter:	What he is saying is that he's stuck because he worries so much about his life, and so, for that, you know . . . in this culture, when you start seeing things, especially your family members and close friends who died, that means that his life is

also going to end. Then he will die soon. If it were back home, that's what would happen.

Later, in clarifying a counselor statement, the interpreter explained to the client that there were resources in this country to help him.

Interpreter: What he is saying is that things like that happen in this country also, but it is not treated as seriously as it would be if it happened in our country. Here, they can do things so that persons with that kind of problem can be helped . . .

The roles of anticounselor, procounselor, and interpreter complement one another, emphasizing significantly different goals for obtaining feedback from the client's resource person. Each resource person, each culture, develops its own unique style, both in the content and the process of that feedback.

Conclusion

To the extent that a counselor and a client come from different cultures, their assumptions are likely to contrast and even conflict with one another. Lambert (1981) suggests that intercultural counseling describes those very conditions that are most unfavorable for successful therapy. The focus of training, then, is to enable counselors to be intentional in their interventions by making them aware of their own assumptions and the culturally contrasting assumptions of their clients. There are no universally accepted criteria for normal behavior; rather, a multitude of culturally learned perspectives have led to apparent confusion as dominant cultures seek to impose their perspectives on minority groups. Although there is considerable rhetorical support for intercultural awareness and abundant research evidence of culturally relevant knowledge, most intergroup contact continues to occur under "unfavorable" conditions and frequently results in disharmony or misunderstanding. Although theories of helping acknowledge the need for intercultural skills, practical applications in the training or implementation of helping skills have been minimal.

The most promising research emphasizes a more holistic perspective on the importance of person-environment interaction. The counselor in a multicultural setting needs mediation skills to translate his or her perspective on mental health into contrasting cultural patterns. Existing models for training helpers emphasize skills appropriate to the dominant white, Western, middle-class culture in which those models originate. To the extent that the client or trainee shares the assumptions of the counselor or trainer, the standard helping skills training approaches work effectively. However, to the extent that all counseling occurs in a multicultural environment, counselors must learn to match the appropriate method with the appropriate situation in an appropriate way, keeping in mind that each training design has its own unique strengths and weaknesses and that none of the alternatives, including the triad model, is the preferred model in all helping skills training programs.

References

Ambrowitz, C., and Dokecki, P. "The Politics of Clinical Judgment: Early Empirical Returns." *Psychological Bulletin,* 1977, *84,* 460–476.

Amir, Y. "Contact Hypothesis in Ethnic Relations." *Psychological Bulletin,* 1969, *71* (5), 319–342.

Anderson, G. B. "The Effects of the Triad Model of Cross-Cultural Counselor Training on Rehabilitation Counselor Interpersonal Functioning with Black Deaf Clients." Research proposal, Department of Rehabilitation Counseling, New York University, 1978.

Arrendondo-Dowd, P., and Gonslaves, J. "Preparing Culturally Effective Counselors." *Personnel and Guidance Journal,* June 1980, *58,* 657–661.

Atkinson, D., Maruyama, M., and Matsui, S. "Effects of Counselor Race and Counseling Approach on Asian Americans' Perceptions of Counselor Credibility and Utility." *Journal of Counseling Psychology,* 1978, *25,* 76–83.

Atkinson, D., Morton, G., and Sue, D. W. *Counseling American Minorities: A Cross-Cultural Perspective.* Dubuque, Iowa: Brown, 1979.

Atkinson, D., Staso, D., and Hosford, R. "Selecting Counselor Trainees with Multicultural Strengths: A Solution to the Bakke Decision Crisis." *Personnel and Guidance Journal,* 1978, *56* (9), 546-549.

Bailey, F. S. "Cross-Cultural Counselor Education: The Impact of Microcounseling Paradigms and Traditional Classroom Methods on Counselor Trainee Effectiveness." Unpublished doctoral dissertation, Department of Guidance and Counseling, University of Hawaii, Aug. 1981.

Barnlund, D. C. *Public and Private Self in Japan and the United States: Communication Styles of Two Cultures.* Tokyo: Simul Press, 1975.

Berry, J. W. "Ecology, Cultural Adaptation, and Psychological Differentiation: Traditional Patterning and Acculturative Stress." In R. Brislin, S. Bochner, and W. Lonner (Eds.), *Cross-Cultural Perspectives on Learning.* New York: Wiley, 1975.

Bolman, W. "Cross-Cultural Psychotherapy." *The American Journal of Psychiatry,* 1968, *124* (9), 1237-1243.

Brislin, R., and Pedersen, P. *Cross-Cultural Orientation Programs.* New York: Wiley, 1976.

Brough, J. *Annual Evaluation Report, Fiscal Year 1979-1980: Developing Interculturally Skilled Counselors.* Honolulu: University of Hawaii, 1980.

Bryson, S., Renzaglia, G. A., and Danish, S. "Training Counselors Through Simulated Racial Encounters." *Journal of Non-White Concerns in Personnel and Guidance,* 1974, *3,* 218-223.

Carkhuff, R. R., and Pierce, R. "Differential Effects of Therapist Race and Social Class upon Patient Depth of Self-Exploration in the Initial Clinical Interview." *Journal of Consulting Psychology,* 1967, *31,* 632-634.

Coombs, A. W., Richards, A. C., and Richards, F. *Perceptual Psychology.* New York: Harper & Row, 1976.

Draguns, J. G. "Psychological Disorders of Clinical Severity." In H. C. Triandis and J. G. Draguns (Eds.), *Handbook of Cross-Cultural Psychology.* Vol. 6: *Psychopathology.* Boston: Allyn & Bacon, 1980.

Draguns, J. G. "Counseling Across Cultures: Common Themes and Distinct Approaches." In P. Pedersen, J. G. Draguns, W. Lonner, and J. Trimble (Eds.), *Counseling Across Cultures*. (2nd ed.) Honolulu: University Press of Hawaii, 1981a.

Draguns, J. G. "Cross-Cultural Counseling and Psychotherapy: History, Issues, and Current Status." In A. Marsella and P. Pedersen, *Cross-Cultural Counseling and Psychotherapy*. Elmsford, N.Y.: Pergamon Press, 1981b.

Duckro, P., Beal, D., and George, C. "Research on the Effects of Disconfirmed Client Role Expectations in Psychotherapy: A Critical Review." *Psychological Bulletin*, 1979, *86*, 80–92.

Endler, N. S., and Magnusson, D. (Eds.). *Interactional Psychology and Personality*. Washington, D.C.: Hemisphere, 1976.

Erickson, R. "Gatekeeping and the Melting Pot." *Harvard Educational Review*, 1975, *45*, 44–71.

Favazza, A. F., and Oman, M. *Anthropological and Cross-Cultural Themes in Mental Health: An Annotated Bibliography 1925–1974*. Columbia: University of Missouri Press, 1977.

Fields, S. "Mental Health and the Melting Pot." *Innovations*, 1979, *6* (2), 2–3.

Goldstein, A. "Expectancy Effects in Cross-Cultural Counseling." In A. J. Marsella and P. Pedersen (Eds.), *Cross-Cultural Counseling and Psychotherapy*. Elmsford, N.Y.: Pergamon Press, 1981.

Halleck, S. L. *The Politics of Therapy*. New York: Harper & Row, 1971.

Hawes, F., and Kealey, D. "An Empirical Study of Canadian Technical Assistance: Adaptation and Effectiveness on Overseas Assignments." Occasional paper, Canadian International Development Agency, 1980.

Higginbotham, H. N., and Tanaka-Matsumi, J. "Behavioral Approaches to Counseling Across Cultures." In P. Pedersen and others (Eds.), *Counseling Across Cultures*. (2nd ed.) Honolulu: University Press of Hawaii, 1981.

Hines, A., and Pedersen, P. "The Cultural Grid: Matching Social System Variables and Cultural Perspectives." *Asian Pacific Training Development Journal*, 1980, *1* (1), 247–274.

Holwill-Bailey, F. Personal communication, 1979.

Ivey, A. E. *Counseling and Psychotherapy: Connections and Applications*. Englewood Cliffs, N.J.: Prentice-Hall, 1980.

Ivey, A. E. "A Person-Environment View of Counseling and Psychotherapy: Implications for Social Policy." In A. Marsella and P. Pedersen (Eds.), *Cross-Cultural Counseling and Psychotherapy.* Elmsford, N.Y.: Pergamon Press, 1981.

Ivey, A. E., and Authier, J. *Microcounseling: Innovations in Interviewing Training.* (2nd ed.) Springfield, Ill.: Thomas, 1978.

Jaslow, C. "Exemplary Programs, Practices, and Policies." In G. Waltz and L. Benjamin (Eds.), *Transcultural Counseling: Needs, Programs and Techniques.* New York: Human Sciences Press, 1978.

Kagan, N. *Interpersonal Process Recall: A Method of Influencing Human Interaction.* (Rev. ed.) East Lansing, Mich.: Mason Media, 1981.

Katz, M., and Sanborn, K. "Multiethnic Studies of Psychopathology and Normality in Hawaii." In J. Westermeyer (Ed.), *Anthropology and Mental Health.* The Hague, Netherlands: Mouton, 1976.

King, L. M. "Social and Cultural Influences on Psychopathology." *Annual Review of Psychology,* 1978, *29,* 405–433.

Kinloch, G. *The Sociology of Minority Group Relations.* Englewood Cliffs, N.J.: Prentice-Hall, 1979.

Kleinman, A. "Problems and Prospects in Comparative Cross-Cultural Medical and Psychiatric Studies." In A. Kleinman and others (Eds.), *Culture and Healing in Asian Societies.* Cambridge, Mass.: Schenkman, 1978.

Kleinman, A. *Patients and Healers in the Context of Culture.* Berkeley: University of California Press, 1979.

Korman, M. "National Conference on Levels and Patterns of Professional Training in Psychology: Major Themes." *American Psychologist,* 1974, *29,* 441–449.

Kuhn, T. S. *The Structure of Scientific Revolutions.* Chicago: University of Chicago Press, 1962.

LaFromboise, T. Personal communication. Department of Counseling, University of Nebraska, 1981.

Lambert, M. J. "The Implications of Psychotherapy Outcome Research on Cross-Cultural Psychotherapy." In A. Marsella and P. Pedersen (Eds.), *Cross-Cultural Counseling and Psychotherapy.* Elmsford, N.Y.: Pergamon Press, 1981.

Lasch, C. *The Culture of Narcissism.* New York: Norton, 1978.

Lefley, H. Unpublished evaluation report on a National Institute of Mental Health cross-cultural training project, fiscal year 1979–1980. Cross-Cultural Training Center, Department of Psychiatry, University of Miami, 1980.

LeVine, R., and Campbell, D. *Ethnocentrism: Theories of Conflict, Ethnic Attitudes, and Group Behavior.* New York: Wiley, 1972.

LeVine, E., and Padilla, A. *Crossing Cultures in Therapy: Pluralistic Counseling for the Hispanic.* Monterey, Calif.: Brooks/Cole, 1980.

Lewin, K. *A Dynamic Theory of Personality.* New York: McGraw-Hill, 1935.

Lewis, M. D., and Lewis, J. A. "Relevant Training for Relevant Roles: A Model for Educating Inner-City Counselors." *Counselor Education and Supervision,* 1970, *10* (1), 31–38.

Loo, C. Personal communication. University of California, Santa Barbara, 1979.

MacKinnon, R. A., and Michels, R. *The Psychiatric Interview in Clinical Practice.* Philadelphia: Saunders, 1971.

Marsella, A., and Pedersen, P. (Eds.). *Cross-Cultural Counseling and Psychotherapy.* Elmsford, N.Y.: Pergamon Press, 1981.

Miles, R. H. "Role Requirements as Sources of Organizational Stress." *Journal of Applied Psychology,* 1976, *61* (2), 172–179.

Mitchel, H. "The Black Experience in Higher Education." *The Counseling Psychologist,* 1970, *2,* 30–36.

Pande, S. K. "The Mystique of Western Psychotherapy: An Eastern Interpretation." *Journal of Nervous and Mental Disorders,* 1969, *146,* 425–432.

Patterson, C. H. "Cross-Cultural or Intercultural Psychotherapy." *International Journal for the Advancement of Counseling,* 1978, *1,* 231–248.

Pedersen, P. "Anticipated Outcomes of Counseling When Viewed as an Instance of Coalition." Unpublished master's thesis, University of Minnesota, 1966.

Pedersen, P. "A Proposal: That Counseling Be Viewed as an Instance of Coalition." *Journal of Pastoral Care,* September 1968.

Pedersen, P. "Simulating the Problem Role in Cross-Cultural Counseling." Paper presented at the American Psychological Association, Honolulu, September 1972.

Pedersen, P. "A Conceptual System Describing the Counseling Relationship as a Coalition Against the Problem." Paper presented at the American Psychological Association, Montreal, Canada, 1973.

Pedersen, P. "Cross-Cultural Communications Training for Mental Health Professionals." *The International and Intercultural Communication Annual*, 1974a, *1*, 53–64.

Pedersen, P. (Ed.). *Readings in Intercultural Communication: Cross-Cultural Counseling*. Chicago: Intercultural Network, 1974b.

Pedersen, P. "A Two-Week International Workshop in Cross-Cultural Counseling." *The International and Intercultural Communication Annual*, 1975, *2*, 102–108.

Pedersen, P. "A Model for Training Mental Health Workers in Cross-Cultural Counseling." In J. Westermeyer and B. Maday (Eds.), *Culture and Mental Health*. The Hague, Netherlands: Mouton, 1976.

Pedersen, P. "Asian Theories of Personality." In R. Corsini (Ed.), *Contemporary Theories of Personality*. Itasca, Ill.: Peacock, 1977a.

Pedersen, P. "The Triad Model of Cross-Cultural Counselor Training." *Personnel and Guidance Journal*, 1977b, *56* (2), 94–100.

Pedersen, P. "Four Dimensions of Cross-Cultural Skill in Counselor Training." *Personnel and Guidance Journal*, 1978a, *56* (8), 480–484.

Pedersen, P. "Training Interculturally Skilled Counselors." Proposal to the National Institute of Mental Health, 1978b.

Pedersen, P. *Basic Intercultural Counseling Skills*. Honolulu: Developing Interculturally Skilled Counselors, University of Hawaii, 1979a.

Pedersen, P. "Counseling Clients from Other Cultures: Two Training Designs." In M. Asante and E. Newmark (Eds.), *Handbook of Intercultural Communication*. Buffalo: State University of New York, 1979b.

Pedersen, P. "Non–Western Psychologies: The Search for Alternatives." In A. Marsella, R. Tharpe, and T. Ciborowski, *Perspectives in Cross-Cultural Psychology*. New York: Academic Press, 1979c.

Pedersen, P. "The Triad Model: A Cross-Cultural Coalition Against the Problem." In R. Corsini (Ed.), *Innovative Psychotherapies.* New York: Wiley Interscience, 1981.

Pedersen, P. "The Intercultural Context of Counseling and Therapy." In A. Marsella and G. White (Eds.), *Theories of Cross-Cultural Counseling and Therapy* (in press).

Pedersen, P., Holwill, F., and Shapiro, J. "A Cross-Cultural Training Procedure for Classes in Counselor Education." *Counselor Education and Supervision,* 1978, *17* (3), 233–237.

Pedersen, P., Lonner, W., and Draguns, J. G. (Eds.). *Counseling Across Cultures.* Honolulu: University Press of Hawaii, 1976.

Pedersen, P., and others. *Counseling Across Cultures.* (2nd ed.) Honolulu: University Press of Hawaii, 1981.

Peoples, V. Y., and Dell, D. M. "Black and White Student Preferences for Counselor Roles." *Journal of Counseling Psychology,* 1975, *22,* 529–534.

Roberts, D. "Treatment of Cultural Scripts." *Transactional Analysis Journal,* 1975, *5,* 29–35.

Ruiz, R. A., and Casas, J. M. "Culturally Relevant and Behavioristic Counseling for Chicano College Students." In P. Pedersen and others (Eds.), *Counseling Across Cultures.* (2nd ed.) Honolulu: University Press of Hawaii, 1981.

Sananikone, P. Personal communication. Department of Psychology, University of Hawaii, 1980.

Satir, V. *Conjoint Family Therapy.* Palo Alto, Calif.: Science and Behavior Books, 1964.

Seward, G. *Clinical Studies in Cultural Conflict.* New York: Ronald Press, 1970.

Slack, C. W., and Slack, E. N. "It Takes Three to Break a Habit." *Psychology Today,* February 1976, *93,* 46–50.

Strauss, J. S. "Social and Cultural Influences on Psychopathology." *Annual Review of Psychology,* 1979, *30,* 397–416.

Sue, D. W. "Barriers to Effective Cross-Cultural Counseling." *The Journal of Counseling Psychology,* 1977, *24,* 420–429.

Sue, D. W. "Editorial: Counseling Across Cultures." *Personnel and Guidance Journal,* 1978, *56* (8), 451.

Sue, D. W. "Annual Evaluation Report: DISC Training and Field Testing, 1978–1979." California State University, Hayward, 1979.

Sue, D. W. "Evaluating Process Variables in Cross-Cultural Counseling Therapy." In A. Marsella and P. Pedersen, *Cross-Cultural Counseling and Psychotherapy*. Elmsford, N.Y.: Pergamon Press, 1981a.

Sue, D. W. *Counseling the Culturally Different: Theory and Practice*. New York: Wiley, 1981b.

Szapocznik, J., and Kurtines, W. "Acculturation, Biculturalism, and Adjustment Among Cuban Americans." In A. Padilla (Ed.), *Acculturation: Theory Models and Some New Findings*. Boulder, Colo.: Westwood Press, 1980.

Tart, C. "Some Assumptions of Orthodox Western Psychology." In C. Tart (Ed.), *Transpersonal Psychologies*. New York: Harper & Row, 1975.

Triandis, H. C. "Culture Training, Cognitive Complexity, and Interpersonal Attitudes." In R. Brislin, S. Bochner, and W. Lonner. *Cross-Cultural Perspectives on Learning*. New York: Wiley, 1975.

Triandis, H. C. *Interpersonal Behavior*. Monterey, Calif.: Brooks/Cole, 1977.

Tseng, W. S., and Hsu, J. "Minor Psychological Disturbances of Everyday Life." In H. Triandis and J. Draguns (Eds.), *Handbook of Cross-Cultural Psychology*. Vol. 6: *Psychopathology*. Boston: Allyn & Bacon, 1980.

Tucker, M. F. *Screening and Selection for Overseas Assignment: Assessment and Recommendation to the U.S. Navy*. Denver, Colo.: Center for Research and Education, 1974.

Weeks, W., Pedersen, P., and Brislin, R. (Eds.). *A Manual of Structured Experiences for Cross-Cultural Learning*. Chicago: Intercultural Network, 1976.

Weidman, H. "Concepts as Strategies for Change." *Psychiatric Annals*, 1975, *5*, 312–314.

Wintrob, R. M., and Harvey, Y. K. "The Self-Awareness Factor in Intercultural Psychotherapy: Some Personal Reflections." In P. Pedersen and others (Eds.), *Counseling Across Cultures*. (2nd ed.) Honolulu: University Press of Hawaii, 1981.

Wohl, J. "Intercultural Psychotherapy: Issues, Questions, and Reflections." In P. Pedersen and others (Eds.), *Counseling Across Cultures*. (2nd ed.) Honolulu: University Press of Hawaii, 1981.

Wrenn, G. "The Culturally Encapsulated Counselor." *Harvard Educational Review*, 1962, *32* (4), 444–449.

Zuk, G. *Family Therapy: A Triadic-Based Approach.* New York: Behavioral Publications, 1971.

Part Three

Group Leadership Skills Training

"We can do anything in group treatment that we can do in individual treatment—and more . . . . The key throughout all group helping processes is the level of functioning of the leader" (Carkhuff, 1969, pp. 130–131). In the early 1970s, helping skills proponents such as Carkhuff (1969) and Gazda (1973) proposed that a facilitative leader was one who could effectively use the core conditions of empathy, warmth, and genuineness at various stages in a group's development. It was assumed that, "if helpees work intensively and extensively with a high-level–functioning helper, the helpees will improve in a variety of significant ways. If the helper provides an atmosphere in which the helpees can move toward higher levels of functioning, then each individual group member has multiple potential helpers" (Carkhuff, 1969, p. 131).

In addition to their use for treatment purposes, groups have been the predominant context for teaching interpersonal helping skills. For example, in describing his skills training model, Egan (1982, p. 25) stated: "The assumption here is that you will learn the problem-solving model and its skills experientially in the context of a small group." Even though most skills training occurs in groups, the builders of skills models concentrated on identifying and teaching dyadic interpersonal skills and were less concerned about analyzing facilitative skills unique to group leadership. Thus, not they but others whose main orientation is group treatment have taken the inititative to develop skills-based group facilitation models. These group model developers assume that, in addition to high levels of core conditions derived from individual treatment, group-specific skills are also necessary in leading groups.

Although most skills training practice and research have centered on the dyadic helping relationship, many of the services of helpers are offered through groups. Just as it was important at one time to unravel the key interpersonal ingredients of one-to-one therapy, it is now equally imperative that the interpersonal helping field seek to learn about the microskills that underlie effective helping in groups. The multiple interactions and interpersonal dynamics encountered in small groups add complexity to the process of helping. Egan and Cowan (1979) observed that effective group participation requires tailoring the use of basic interpersonal skills to conditions unique to the group, as well as developing a repertoire of group-specific skills. These considerations raise several important questions. Beyond the basic interpersonal skills, what group-specific skills are helpful for facilitating group process and development? Are the skills that are relevant in dyadic helping relationships equally valuable in a group context? Can the microskills of group facilitation be identified, and can they be taught in systematic fashion? In the training of group helpers, should emphasis be placed on the development of skills or the development of knowledge?

This section examines the educational components essential to the training of competent group therapists, explores the microskill base of group leadership, and presents models to illustrate the training of group leaders. Recently, a range of conceptualizations of group leadership skills have been advanced (Bertcher, 1979; Dyer and Vriend, 1977; Egan, 1976; Moreland and Buck, 1979; Shulman, 1979; Trotzer, 1977). These frameworks vary in the type and specificity of their skills, as well as in their training methods. Moreland (1973) was one of the first to develop a taxonomy of group facilitation skills. In Chapter Nine, he and Krimsky discuss their sequential group leadership training model, which highlights the scope and complexity of training group helpers. Those who lead groups must not only master requisite skills but also command a substantive knowledge of how groups function and increase their competency through supervised practice with groups. The authors believe that those responsible for educating competent leaders must define the social and behavioral science base underlying group practice; teach essential behavioral change theories and methods; specify generic as well as group-specific skills basic to helping in groups; and develop mastery of the complex, advanced skills necessary to practice with diverse and specialized groups. In addition to describing the knowledge and skills essential for effective group leadership, the authors focus on key cognitive and experiential training methods.

Although the process of becoming a skilled leader requires substantial training and experience, Ivey (1973) emphasizes that group leader behavior is definable and teachable. However, as Pearson (1981) points out, although the literature contains many formulations of leader functioning, few have been developed specifically for empirical testing and systematic training. Mayadas and Duehn's leadership training program is a notable exception. In Chapter Ten, Mayadas and Duehn present a typology of twelve essential group leadership skills selected for their clinical import, describe an instructional model for their acquisition, and share preliminary results of the application of the model in professional education. These group skills are taught within the context of a unique instructional approach based on social learning theory, and consisting of verbal instructions, videotape presentations modeling effective and ineffective use of the skills, behavioral rehearsal and simulations, performance feedback, and clinical critiques of performance. Among its unique contributions, this skills training program exemplifies education for group competence that is empirically grounded and provides a balanced emphasis on both the scientific and the artistic dimensions of group leadership.

Once a helper has acquired a sound grounding in basic group skills, he or she must learn how to apply them effectively, with sensitivity to the focus, timing, and function of each skill. Skills must be appropriate to the processes and developmental stages of the group. Daniels and Buck illustrate the effect of these factors on skills application in Chapter Eleven, presenting a typology of group process and facilitation skills for leaders of career decision-making groups and describing a program to teach the skills to prospective leaders. Beyond offering a useful typology of group facilitation skills and highlighting the role of generic interpersonal skills in group work, the model illustrates the role that microskills play in relation to broader leadership functions and group processes. The chapter also emphasizes the complexity of the skills application process—for example, the way in which skills are applied in a career decision-making group is affected by the leader's conception of the career development process, as well as his or her understanding of group dynamics and the developmental stages through which groups pass.

The common thread found in each chapter of this section suggests that advancement of the quality of practice with groups requires a conception of the educational components necessary for the preparation of competent group helpers, identification of the core microskills underlying effective group facilitation, and development and testing of instructional models to systematically train group leaders in the essential group skills.

References

Bertcher, H. J. *Group Participation: Techniques for Leaders and Members.* Beverly Hills, Calif.: Sage, 1979.

Carkhuff, R. R. *Helping and Human Relations.* Vol. II. New York: Holt, Rinehart and Winston, 1969.

Dyer, W. W., and Vriend, J. *Counseling Techniques that Work.* New York: Funk & Wagnalls, 1977.

Egan, G. *Interpersonal Living: A Skills/Contract Approach to Human-Relations Training in Groups.* Monterey, Calif.: Brooks/Cole, 1976.

Egan, G. *The Skilled Helper.* (Rev. ed.) Monterey, Calif,: Brooks/Cole, 1982.

Egan, G., and Cowan, M. A. *People in Systems: A Model for Development in the Human-Service Professions and Education.* Monterey, Calif.: Brooks/Cole, 1979.

Gazda, G. M. *Human Relations Development: A Manual for Educators.* Boston: Allyn & Bacon, 1973.

Ivey, A. E. "Demystifying the Group Process: Adapting Microcounseling Procedures to Counseling in Groups." *Educational Technology,* 1973, *13* (2), 27–31.

Moreland, J. "A Descriptive Taxonomy of Group Facilitation Skills." Unpublished paper, Southern Illinois University, 1973.

Moreland, J. R., and Buck, J. N. "Basic Principles of Group Process and Group Facilitation." In V. A. Harren (Ed.), *Career Decision Making for College Students: Facilitators' Handbook*. Carbondale, Ill.: Southern Illinois University, 1979.

Pearson, R. E. "Basic Skills for Leadership of Counseling Groups." *Counselor Education and Supervision*, 1981, *21* (1), 30–37.

Shulman, L. *The Skills of Helping Individuals and Groups*. Itasca, Ill.: Peacock, 1979.

Trotzer, J. P. *The Counselor and the Group: Integrating Theory, Training and Practice*. Monterey, Calif.: Brooks/Cole, 1977.

Chapter 9

Competency-Based Training

John R. Moreland
Eileen Krimsky

Training counseling or therapy occurs in graduate or professional programs in clinical psychology, counseling psychology, counselor education, guidance and counseling, social work, student personnel, and psychiatry. In addition, nonacademic agencies offering social services are training their employees and volunteers in group counseling techniques. The trainees in these diverse training programs include, but are not limited to, graduate level students; postdoctoral students; family practitioners (Stephanos and Auhagen, 1979); college students; psychiatric residents (Salvendy, 1980; Rosenbaum and Berger, 1975); high school, junior high school (Cooker and Chercia, 1976; Pyle, 1977), and elementary school students (Gumaer, 1976); and married couples (Mace and Mace, 1976). Group counselor training programs have also been suggested for professionals in a variety of disciplines (Ohlsen, 1975; Lerner, Horowitz, and Burstein, 1978; Maynard and Long, 1976; Biasco and Redferring, 1976; Collison and Dunlap, 1978; Stephanos and Auhagen, 1979).

Not only do the trainee populations receiving training in group counseling vary in their level of initial competence, sophistication, and prior learning, but the level of competence with which they leave these programs also differs. For the sake of clarity, the goals, content, and training techniques of programs designed to train group counselors and therapists on the one hand, and of programs developed for group facilitators and helpers, on the other, need to be distinguished. The training of group counselors and therapists is consistent with the guidelines developed by the American Group Psychotherapy Association (American Group Psychotherapy Association, 1972) and encompasses both greater breadth and greater depth than that of group facilitators and helpers. The purpose of this chapter is to present a comprehensive, sequential model for training group counselors and therapists (terms that will be used interchangeably). The literature on the training of group facilitators and helpers is included because it provides useful suggestions for content and techniques that can be incorporated into the model.

The model for group therapist training presented in this chapter is based on the sequential mastery of sets of interrelated counseling skills. Competency-based evaluations of group counselor trainees are not a universal component of most training programs. Too often the criteria for evaluating such trainees tend to be based on experience, rather than competency. Trainees receive what amounts to social promotions at the end of particular group practice or training experiences, in part because a specific, sequential model for training is lacking. This presentation serves a heuristic function by encouraging the development of competency-based evaluation criteria where none currently exist and the utilization of those criteria that do. Following presentation of the model, the primary methods used in the training of group counselors are reviewed, and several issues in the selection, training, and evaluation of group therapists are discussed.

Training Model

Our competency-based, sequential model for the learning of group therapy is presented in Figure 1. The novice group counseling trainee brings to his or her initial training experiences a basic facility with individual counseling theories and dyadic helping skills. Although some novice group trainees may be proficient individual therapists, others begin their group training with only minimal individual training. However, no one should begin group training without having developed his or her own conceptualization of human functioning and individual change, for which mastery of the material in courses on individual personality and psychotherapy is probably necessary but not sufficient. Novice group counselors should also have mastered one or more of the sets of basic dyadic helping skills described by Authier and Gustafson, Egan, and McQuellon in previous chapters of this book.

Formal training of group counseling trainees begins with their mastery of concepts of group process and group change. They must be able to compare and contrast dyadic and group change constructs, to describe the different roles and functions served by group therapists, and to identify group leader skills that are used in the performance of those functions.

Mastery of particular theoretical frameworks for group counseling is facilitated by the trainees' prior understanding of general group process principles; competent group counselors have usually mastered a number of group theories. Advanced supervision may help trainees articulate theories and translate them into interventions.

Group counseling is often performed with specific populations that have unique characteristics or problems requiring specific counseling skills. For example, Sharni (1979) describes the leader skills needed to work with groups of disadvantaged mothers, and Malnoti and Pastushak (1980) describe the specific skills needed for group work with the aged. These skills include the acquisition of relevant information about these populations and modifications of existing skills to better meet population needs. Pedersen, in this volume, has discussed the manner in which cultural biases may influence the counseling relationship, and modifications or extensions of his triad training model are necessary and important in the training of group counselors. Increased experience with different group themes and populations enhances the versatility with which a leader can meet the demands of diverse groups. In the remainder of this section, aspects of our group therapist training model will be described.

Figure 1. Learning Tree of Group Counselor Competencies.

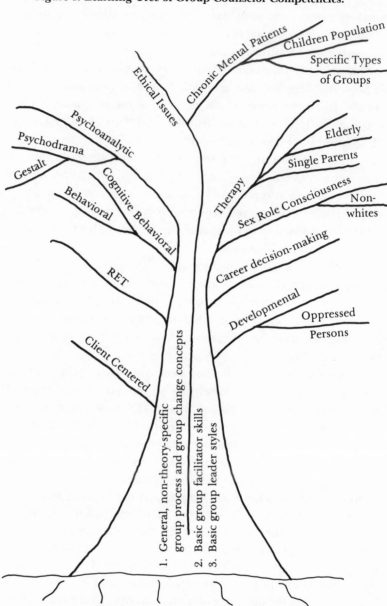

1. Theories of Individual Counseling
2. Non-theory-Specific Dyadic Interpersonal Helping Skills
3. Theory-Specific Individual Change Techniques

Prerequisite Individual Counseling Competence. Many group counselor trainers have recognized the importance of prior training in individual counseling skills. The American Personnel and Guidance Association guidelines for training group counselors recommend a minimum of 200 hours of supervised individual counseling experience prior to beginning group counseling training (Berman, 1975). The American Group Psychotherapy Association requires 400 hours of supervised individual work, with at least 50 of these hours being completed during the course of group counseling training.

Most group training models are based on the assumption that trainees have already acquired both theoretical knowledge and applied skills in individual counseling (Berman, 1975; Horowitz, 1967; Fidler, 1973). However, this assumption is not universally adhered to. Berman (1975) reports, in a comparison study of three sets of group counselors, that, although the least anxious were those with a background in individual therapy, they also proved the most resistant to using group theory and skills in their work. Dies (1980) notes that experience in individual psychotherapy may contribute to the difficulties group counselor trainees have in working with groups and in appyling group process constructs to group events. And Mullan and Rosenbaum (1962) maintain that groups and group dynamics are completely different from individual dyadic relationships and that individual therapy training may interfere with the development of group interaction skills.

Although prior training in individual counseling theories and intervention techniques may make mastery of group principles and concomitant interventions more difficult to learn, we believe that the first step in training group counselors is to help them master individual counseling skills, for several reasons: careful selection and preparation of group members is often needed (Lieberman, Yalom, and Miles, 1973; Yalom, 1975); most groups require that the counselor interact with individual group members; non-theory-specific individual counseling skills are actually effective interpersonal communication skills (Carkhuff, 1969; Ivey, 1971; Egan, 1975; Ivey and Authier, 1979); by using effective interpersonal skills, group counselors provide a model for group members; cognitive mastery of individual theory constructs is the foundation for applying such concepts to groups; and mastery of these interventions with individual clients may facilitate the acquisition of these skills for group application. Methods for teaching and evaluating individual counseling skills have been described elsewhere in this volume by Egan, Authier and Gustafson, and McQuellon.

Group Oriented, Non-Theory-Specific Content. Prior to assuming any supervised group leader functions, trainees need to acquire an understanding of the principles of group process and group change. Lakin, Lieberman, and Whitaker (1969) list and elaborate several goals of a group counselor trainee program:

1. The trainee needs to make explicit his or her own implicit helping model and generate a model appropriate to the group situation.
2. The trainee needs to understand the unique character of the group as a medium for therapy.
3. The trainee needs to understand the relationship between dyadic and group therapy.
4. The trainee needs to become empathically aware of how the patient feels.
5. The trainee needs to become aware of and resolve or control his or her fears of the group.
6. The trainee must have an understanding of how persons are helped in a group.
7. The trainee must learn to operate as a therapist.
8. The trainee needs to become aware of his or her own natural therapeutic role preferences.

Some of these goals are met by mastering individual counseling skills; others require that trainees learn more about themselves. Five of the eight training goals (1, 2, 3, 5, and 6) require cognitive learning and understanding.

Berman (1975) notes that most models assume that beginning group counselors will function more effectively after they have been exposed to a common core of knowledge about group process. However, different programs vary considerably in the depth and breadth of cognitive and experiential training offered to students and in the sequencing of these training components.

Part of the common core referred to by Berman can be acquired through lectures, reading, and discussion. For example, Lieberman, Yalom, and Miles (1973) describe the relationship between group characteristics and non-theory-specific group leader functions and outcomes. Yalom (1975) describes eleven curative factors operative in groups that trainees need to understand before they can lead their own groups.

Another approach is presented by Bascue (1978), who recommends helping trainees learn to discriminate and rate group process on eight different dimensions. Early cognitive training consists of helping trainees recognize the differences on each of these dimensions between various group counseling theories. Trainees can begin to identify their own ideal performance on each dimension prior to their actual experience with groups.

Salvendy (1980) also recommends that group trainees learn about group dynamics early in their education. And Lechowicz and Gazda (1975) surveyed the opinions of 229 group counseling experts who indicated that such learning was important early in the training of group counselors. Cognitive training, then, is a necessary but not sufficient prerequisite for the acquisition of group work competence—trainees also need to demonstrate mastery of the basic group counseling skills required to translate their cognitive understanding into specific counseling behaviors.

Basic Group Facilitation Skills. One reason experienced individual counselors may have difficulty adopting a group focus in their initial group counseling activities is that they have not received training in basic group facilitation skills. Since novice group counselors are not able to automatically translate their recently acquired understanding of group process principles into actual leader behaviors, they frequently rely on the dyadic helping skills currently in their repertoire.

Basic group counseling skills have been identified. Moreland (1975, 1976), Moreland and Hallissey (1979), Bertcher (1979), Carkhuff (1973), Dyer and Vriend (1977), Webster and Cole (1979), Coyne (1975), Egan and Cowan (1979), Ivey (1973), Shulman (1979), Smith (1976), and Mayadas and Duehn (this volume) have identified over 100 discrete counselor skills that are based on attempts to translate basic knowledge of group principles into specific group counse-

lor behaviors. (The skills specified by these authors do overlap
considerably, however.) Daniels and Buck (this volume) present a
skills typology based on a developmental sequencing of the acquisition of group skills. Although their model has been designed for
beginning group facilitators, it is inclusive enough to be used to
train and evaluate advanced group therapists. Table 1 presents a
taxonomy of discrete group counselor skills clustered according to
the four group leader dimensions identified by Lieberman, Yalom,
and Miles (1973). The assignment of specific group counselor skills
to particular functions is arbitrary, and the experienced group therapist will recognize that a number of these skills may be used for
more than one leader function.

The skills contained in Table 1 are behaviors that most group
counselors will use in virtually every group they run. These skills
are specific neither to particular theoretical approaches nor to
particular populations of group members but are basic to almost all
counseling groups. Mastery of these skills through prepracticum
and group practicum experiences is a prerequisite to learning more
advanced group counseling skills. The content of the advanced
skills is determined by the theoretical orientation that the group
counseling trainee is attempting to master and the particular population with which he or she will be dealing.

Although some of these skills resemble individual counseling
skills, they differ in that they are particular to group settings. The
group counselor must learn to attend and be empathic to the group
feeling, to listen to the flow of group content. The taxonomy presented in Table 1 facilitates the teaching of group skills to novice
group leaders prior to their assumption of the group counselor role.
By using modeling, behavioral rehearsal, and feedback, beginning
group facilitators can be taught a set of behaviors that will help
them bridge the gap between their cognitive mastery of group principles and their initial, supervised group practicum experiences.

The skills contained in Table 1 are behaviors that most group
counselors will use in virtually every group they run. These skills
are specific neither to particular theoretical approaches nor to
particular populations of group members but are basic to almost all
counseling groups. Mastery of these skills through prepracticum
and group practicum experiences is a prerequisite to learning more
advanced group counseling skills. The content of the advanced
skills is determined by the theoretical orientation that the group
counseling trainee is attempting to master and the particular population with which he or she will be dealing.

Advanced Mastery. Once group counselor trainees have
adopted a group change orientation and integrated their cognitive
understanding with the non-theory-specific group counselor skills
they have acquired, they are ready for more advanced training. The
branches in Figure 1 show some of the possible areas in which
students can choose to acquire specific expertise. At this point, train-

Table 1. Taxonomy of Basic Group Counseling Skills Assigned to Specific Group Counselor Functions.

Caring	Emotional Stimulation	Meaning Attribution	Executive Functioning
Group attending behavior	Group-oriented, open-ended questioning	Summarizing group content	Starting sessions
Empathy	Inviting participation	Observing group behavior	Gatekeeping
Respect	Immediacy	Group-oriented meaning attributions	Focusing skills
Acceptance	Modeling	Skill instruction to members	External to internal
Understanding	Group-oriented leader self-disclosure	Introducing group exercises	Internal to external
Supporting	Challenging group	Modification of negative labeling in group	Individual to group
Genuineness	Confronting group	Identification and explication of evolving group norms	Group to individual
Reflecting group feeling tone	Catalyzing group interaction		Topic tracking
Responding to group confrontation	Responding to group silence		Group reinforcement skills
	Releasing strong group emotion		Topic development
			Maintaining group focus
			Member assumption of responsibility
			Noncompetitive interaction
			Information management
			Conflict mediation
			Contract negotiation
			Giving directions
			Restraining potentially explosive events
			Perception checking

ees may assume more responsibility for articulating their own learning goals and for defining the sequence of training activities that will enable them to meet those goals.

Needless to say, the priorities of trainees must be considered within the context of their training institution and the interests and strengths of the staff responsible for their training. Specialized training can be used to help the trainee become proficient in a particular technique, gain advanced skills in working with a specific population, or gain expertise in a particular content area. The type of specialization chosen determines the cognitive learning goals that the trainee must master before becoming actively involved in a specific type of group leadership. As the novice group counselor undergoes training with a new type of group, ethical requirements mandate that, regardless of status, he or she must work under the supervision of or in consultation with a group leader with proven qualifications in that area.

A well-trained and competent group counselor will have mastered a number of theoretical perspectives that he or she can apply to many different theoretically oriented groups and to different types of populations. Training in any of the advanced areas mentioned in Figure 1 involves the mastering of new cognitive information and theoretical constructs and the supervised integration of theory with practice and the incorporation of these learnings into the trainee's repertoire of leader behaviors. Trainees usually need to continue their training in specialized areas of group leadership long after they have completed their formal education. While still students in our training programs, trainees must learn to appreciate the skills they have acquired, to accurately assess the level of competence at which they are functioning, and to recognize the limits within which they must function, given the nature and extent of their training.

The discussion to this point has focused on defining the requisite skills of a competent group counselor and the general sequence for teaching them. The remaining sections of this chapter will review the literature describing different methods for accomplishing these goals.

Cognitive Training

In his review of current group training models and issues, Berman (1975) reports that practically all training approaches provide both cognitive and experiential learning opportunities for trainees. Cognitive learning is provided through the use of lectures, discussions, reading assignments, survey courses, and advanced seminars in group theory. Jacobs, Brown, and Randolph (1974), Stone and Green (1978), and Bascue (1978) have spoken to the importance of having trainees acquire factual and theoretical knowledge about group dynamics, specific group intervention techniques, and theoretical approaches to group counseling. Lakin, Lieberman, and Whitaker (1969) suggest that cognitive learning is important but question whether or not the material presented to trainees should be theory-specific, expressing a concern that trainees not be overwhelmed by too many ideas, concepts, constructs, and techniques. This same concern is reflected in the training model presented earlier in this chapter, in which novice group counselors are first presented non-theory-specific concepts and principles. Only after mastering this literature do we recommend cognitive training in specific schools of group counseling.

However, the notion that cognitive training is a necessary precursor to experiential learning is not universally accepted. Lerner, Horowitz, and Burstein (1978) describe a training workshop for analytically oriented group leaders in which the presentation of cognitive material is interwoven with experience in group participation. Coyne (1975) describes a similar mode of presentation for cognitive material. Maynard and Long (1976), in their group training program for school counselors, and Stokes and Tait (1980), in their group training for paraprofessional leaders, do not present cognitive material until after providing trainees with actual group experiences. And Stone and Green (1978) describe a twenty-week training program for graduate student group trainees in which cognitive material is presented only in the last eight weeks.

Nevertheless, we consider it imperative that trainees have a thorough conceptual grounding in basic, non-theory-specific group processes and group principles prior to beginning work with client

groups. Trainees need to be conversant with group process in order
to recognize phenomena as they occur. Ausubel (1967) describes a
cognitive-structural approach to teaching, suggesting that defining
in advance the experiences and information to be given allows students to develop a cognitive map into which they can fit new information as it appears. Without such prior learning, information
appears to have no form or structure and is therefore not as
accessible.

Experiential Techniques

The experiential learning opportunities offered to students
generally take two forms. Trainees in most programs are required to
lead or colead some type of counseling group under the observation
or supervision of a recognized group trainer (Lakin, Lieberman, and
Whitaker, 1969; Berger, 1969; MacLennan, 1971; Smith, 1976;
Roman and Porter, 1978). These experiential training techniques
will be discussed in the section on supervision. In addition, group
trainees are often encouraged to participate in some type of ongoing
sensitivity-training or therapy group (Salvendy, 1980). We would
like to suggest several other experiential training activities that can
be used at this early point in the trainees' education.

Trainers of individual counselors have noted a lag between
trainees' cognitive acquisition of theory and techniques and the
translation of these concepts into actual observations and interventions with clients (Truax and Carkhuff, 1967; Ivey, 1971; Moreland,
Ivey, and Phillips, 1973; Ivey and Authier, 1979). Group trainers
have noted a similar pattern with group trainees. The model presented earlier in this chapter emphasized the importance of systematically teaching trainees discrete group skills early in their training.
To date, however, this has not occurred frequently enough. Perhaps
with the benefit of skills taxonomies, systematic training will become more prevalent.

Roman and Porter (1978) and Malnoti and Pastushak (1980)
have recommended the use of scripted role play groups as an intervening training experience to help their group trainees translate
group constructs into actual observations and interventions. Mini
groups made up of cotrainees are an appropriate vehicle for practic-

ing group-specific skills. Moreland (1975, 1976), Moreland and Hallissey (1979), and Daniels and Buck (this volume) offer examples in their manuals that can be used for initial, structured practice. Roman and Porter's (1978) and Malnoti and Pastushak's (1980) scripted role play groups also allow trainees to master group skills. In addition, cognitive understanding and vicarious recognition of the implementation of these skills can be enhanced by asking trainees to identify and categorize group leader behaviors as they observe groups. Even the reading of transcripts of group sessions can be a useful opportunity for trainees to identify specific interventions using one or more of the available group taxonomies.

Biasco and Redferring (1976) and Krimsky (1978) have recommended that novice group leaders need training in responding to potential group problems. Biasco and Redferring mention group hostility, resistance, and problem members as situations requiring skills training in specific intervention strategies. Krimsky suggested that novice group leaders need to learn both to identify and to respond to collusion between group members, ostracism of one member of the group by the others, scapegoating, and rescuing. The use of structured mini groups or scripted role play groups can help prepare novice group counselors to respond effectively to such problem situations.

Concurrent with experience in the group counselor role, participation as group members is recommended as a way for trainees to learn about themselves (Lakin, Lieberman, and Whitaker, 1969). Berman (1975), Lerner, Horowitz, and Burstein (1978), Salvendy (1980), and Stokes and Tait (1980) also stress the significance of such participation, offering additional rationales for its inclusion in group counselor training models. Participation as a group member can allow trainees to experience the curative or educational influences of a group, learn to become more sensitive and responsive to other people without assuming group leader responsibility, experience the influence of the leader on group members, and increase or initiate their awareness of the group member experience. Nonparticipant observation may also help trainees appreciate the importance of group process, the significance of which is mentioned by Lakin, Lieberman, and Whitaker (1969). In a survey conducted by Stein (1975), practicing therapists agreed that process group membership or actual therapy group membership was an invaluable part of their preparation.

Roman and Porter (1978) have discussed the ethical issues involved in requiring students to "voluntarily" assume the member or patient role, and Berman (1975) also questions demanding that trainees have a group experience prior to or concurrent with group counseling experience as leaders. Generally, a client is not coerced into counseling. Although exceptions to this principle exist (for example, court-remanded counseling), most counselors would be reluctant to accept an unwilling client. The authors believe that to the extent that a trainee feels coerced to assume the group member role, his or her experience of group membership will not be similar to that of voluntary members in the groups he or she subsequently leads, thus subverting several of the reasons for utilizing this training method.

Another important difference between counseling and training groups is that clients in counseling groups are not usually socially or professionally involved with one another outside the group, whereas trainees may spend many of their nongroup waking hours together. Therefore, because the anonymity typical of client groups does not apply within such process groups, trainees may not be willing to share personal concerns and information in the group. In addition, whereas the norm of the group may require the trainee to share problems openly, the trainee needs to appear healthy and intact in order to receive a position evaluation from the supervisor. Nonetheless, process groups can be an effective training modality if appropriate norms are agreed on prior to the group. A nonexhaustive set of recommendations would include keeping the group focused on group counseling issues, keeping the group present-focused, and interpreting trainee issues with the group as learning problems, rather than as personal inadequacies or pathologies. This set of recommendations places responsibility for the process group on the supervisor, who must insist that the trainees adhere to the established norms and principles even when group pressure might lead trainees into other areas.

Peterson, Peterson, and Cameron (1977) and Smith (1976) discuss the use of a supervisory group for counseling trainees as a modification of this required participation. Supervision, within a group setting, gives each trainee an opportunity to receive direct, individual attention from the supervisor while also receiving group support. The universality of trainee problems is spotlighted by this method. These authors note that this type of setting provides a group experience in which many of the phenomena characteristic of counseling groups unfold, requiring the group supervisor to model group interventions without implicitly demanding group trainees to reveal themselves in an actual therapy context. Coché (1977) presents a process model of supervision that focuses equally on group literature, clinical material from ongoing groups, and trainee self-study. He reports that trainee groups can regulate the balance of these three components, thereby increasing the integration of theoretical and affective learning. Daniels and Buck (this volume) use a parallel process model for supervision that allows the trainee group to focus on either the trainees, the groups the trainees are leading, or the didactic material under discussion.

In our own experience as group counselor trainers, we have observed both the potentials and limitations of the training group. Encouraging, rather than requiring, trainees to participate as members in a personal growth group is only a partial solution to this dilemma. Providing training group leaders who are not formally involved in other aspects of the trainees' education is also helpful. We further recommend providing trainees with opportunities to join groups composed of students from other helping profession programs as a means of decreasing the inhibitions to sharing, self-exploration, and confrontation described earlier.

Supervision of Group Counselor Trainees

Although the most common method for facilitating the experiential learning of beginning group counselors is to place them in the group therapist role under supervision, supervision models were not discussed in the section on experiential learning techniques because supervision deserves consideration in its own right and because we wanted to highlight the importance of providing trainees with experiential learning opportunities before requiring them to assume leadership responsibilities. Once trainees have achieved minimally acceptable mastery of both the cognitive group process principles and the counselor behaviors required to apply those principles, some form of supervision must be selected for the trainees' first experience with the group counselor role. Several different supervision models will be described in this section, with the suggestion (Coché, 1977) that effective training programs combine a number of supervision methods, rather than relying on one.

Salvendy (1977) reports that beginning group therapists benefit more from individual supervision than from group supervision. With this approach, novice group cotherapists meet regularly with their supervisor. The topic of these sessions is the trainee's group; the mode of presentation may be the trainee's self-report, audiotape or videotape recordings, or the supervisor's direct observations. Through discussion with the supervisor, trainees receive instruction in or discover for themselves how to better utilize the group setting to facilitate member growth. Reliance on trainee self-report introduces the potential for distortion and selective memory; recordings or direct observation may intrude on the group. Despite these limitations, Dies (1980), summarizing a survey of 171 group counseling trainers, reports that these are the most commonly used methods of supervision.

Another method of supervision is to require trainees to assume a cotherapist role with an experienced group counselor, usually the supervisor. The primary advantages are that the trainee and supervisor share a common set of observations, the experienced group counselor can serve as a role model for the trainee, and the novice group therapist can gradually assume responsibility as his or her competence and confidence increase. Salvendy (1980) notes several disadvantages to this supervision method, including the dilution of the trainee's responsibility and the opportunity for group members to split their projections between the novice, inexperienced trainee and the mature, competent counselor. We have also found that group members tend to view the supervisor as the real therapist and deprive the trainee of the full attention of the group. In addition, the cotherapy training model may inhibit both the trainee and the supervisor. On the one hand, the trainee may be reluctant to attempt innovative interventions because he or she is being evaluated by the supervisor or is afraid of being rescued if the intervention does not work. On the other hand, the supervisor may hold back in an attempt not to intimidate the trainee or to allow the trainee the opportunity to assume the leadership role. Given these potential limitations, cotherapy as a method of supervision may be more effective for advanced trainees who are learning how to work in a particular theoretical framework or with a specific population. For beginning group counselors who are leading their first groups, however, individual or group supervision may be more helpful.

Smith (1976) points out that most group counselor trainees go through similar stages in their professional development and tend to raise similar concerns, including: establishing a trusting relationship with their supervisor and fellow group trainees, learning how to assume a group leadership role, establishing a satisfactory cotherapy relationship, learning how and when to self-disclose, and learning to integrate theory and practice. Smith (1976) and Peterson, Peterson, and Cameron (1977) suggest that the group supervision setting, in which a small group receives supervision together, is the most effective method for training novice group counselors. Group supervision allows trainees to experience the similarities they share and to discriminate these concerns as developmental, rather than personal, deficits. In addition, by listening to reports or tapes of other trainee groups, the novice group counselor can become familiar with methods of responding to group problems that may not have manifested themselves in his or her particular training group. Group supervision affords the trainees an opportunity to see group phenomena unfold and to observe the manner in which their supervisor utilizes the training group to deal with these issues. Coché (1977) describes a group model of supervision that focuses on the group counseling literature, clinical material from the trainees' ongoing groups, and trainee self-study. Group supervision settings appear to offer the greatest promise in addressing the difficulty, noted by Stein (1975), Dies (1980) and Salvendy (1980), that beginning group counselors have in learning to use the group as a distinct therapeutic tool for change.

Gazda, Duncan, and Sisson (1974) report a survey in which one-half of group counselor educators reported that they had limited formal training in group theory or group counseling. Thus, those trainers responsible for training beginning group counselors are primarily self-educated. This lack of formal training does not necessarily limit the effectiveness with which they are training; rather, it is a reminder of the relative newness of group counselor training programs. Muro (1968) reported that few graduate programs for counselor educators offered practica in group counseling, even though APGA guidelines recommended such courses. A study by Zohn and Carmody (1978) reveals little change ten years later. Thus, untrained group counselors are probably facilitating most of the counseling groups offered today. However, the program and the supervisor, regardless of his or her own training, must make decisions about the trainee's appropriateness as a group counselor. The competency-based model described earlier is one safeguard against allowing inadequately trained counselors to run groups and can be used to screen out individuals who have acted in ways that would be counterproductive for groups. Although assessments to prescreen potential group counselors have been attempted (Mace and Mace, 1976), these methods are not yet reliable.

Nevertheless, effective, even competency-based training may allow a trainee to advance to the point of running a group for which he or she is unprepared. The supervisor must then decide between the conflicting needs of the trainee and of the group. This situation also occurs in individual training, but adverse results are minimized by weaning the trainee into counseling with a limited caseload that is carefully screened. Thus, trainee inadequacy can be discovered relatively early, and the supervisor can act to safeguard the client while continuing to train the supervisee. Or, if the trainee is considered harmful to the client, the supervisor can take steps to terminate the relationship, offering the client another counselor and the trainee remedial training to bring him or her up to standard. Because more people are involved in a group, however, the situation becomes more complicated. The group might tend to rally around the trainee and actively resist his or her removal by the supervisor. However, the supervisor is ultimately responsible for clients, as well as trainees, and ethical considerations would demand that the clients be protected and provided with competent professional counseling.

Conclusion

The program presented in this chapter offers a model for a developmental and competence-based training structure. This model can be modified for other programs by considering the unique objectives of the program, the limitations of facilities and faculty, and the specific training techniques favored by the faculty.

This model represents a comprehensive group counselor training program. The chapters that follow offer specific techniques for training within a particular modality. Daniels and Buck discuss a parallel process model for training group leaders of career decision-making groups; and Mayadas and Duehn develop the techniques of microcounseling to train group counselors. Although these methods are effective for their purposes, they are not designed for the total training of group counselors.

More than any other author, Berman (1975) has questioned whether any predoctoral program is capable of providing students with the depth and breadth of cognitive and applied skills required of a mature and competent group counselor. We believe that the diverse and multiple goals of most doctoral and predoctoral programs preclude any such program from producing fully trained group counselors; few in fact would make such a claim. Fortunately, learning does not end with the completion of academic requirements. Nevertheless, master's and predoctoral training programs can make significant contributions toward the acquisition of the competencies required of a comprehensively trained group facilitator.

References

American Group Psychotherapy Association. *Guidelines for the Training of Group Psychotherapists.* New York: American Group Psychotherapy Association, 1972.

Ausubel, D. P. "A Cognitive-Structure Theory of School Learning." In L. Siegel (Ed.), *Instruction: Some Contemporary Viewpoints.* San Francisco: Chandler, 1967.

Bascue, L. "A Conceptual Model for Training Group Therapists." *International Journal of Group Psychotherapy,* 1978, *28* (4), 445-452.

Berger, M. "Experiential and Didactic Aspects of Training in Therapeutic Group Approaches." *American Journal of Psychiatry,* 1969, *126* (6), 845-850.

Berman, A. "Group Psychotherapy Training: Issues and Models." *Small Group Behavior*, 1975, *6* (3), 325–344.

Bertcher, H. *Group Participation Techniques for Leaders and Members*. Beverly Hills, Calif.: Sage, 1979.

Biasco, F., and Redferring, D. "Effects of Counselor Supervision on Group Counseling: Clients' Perceived Outcome." *Counselor Education and Supervision*, 1976, *15* (3), 216–220.

Carkhuff, R. R. *Helping and Human Relations*, Vol. 1: *Selection and Training*. New York: Holt, Rinehart and Winston, 1969.

Carkhuff, R. R. "Human Technology for Group Helping Processes." *Educational Technology*, 1973, *13* (1), 31–38.

Coché, E. "Supervision in the Training of Group Therapists." In F. W. Kaslow and Associates, *Supervision, Consultation, and Staff Training in the Helping Professions*. San Francisco: Jossey-Bass, 1977.

Collison, B. B., and Dunlap, S. F. "Nominal Group Technique: A Process for In-Service and Staff Work." *Counselor Education and Supervision*, 1978, *26* (1), 18–25.

Cooker, P., and Chercia, P. "Effects of Communication Skill Training on High School Students' Ability to Function as Peer Group Facilitators." *Journal of Counseling Psychology*, 1976, *23* (5), 464–467.

Coyne, R. "Training Components for Group Facilitators." In J. E. Jones and J. W. Pfeiffer (Eds.), *The 1975 Annual Handbook for Group Facilitators*. La Jolla, Calif.: University Associates, 1975.

Dies, R. "Current Practices in the Training of Group Psychotherapists." *International Journal of Group Psychotherapy*, 1980, *39* (2), 169–185.

Dyer, W., and Vriend, J. *Counseling Techniques That Work*. New York: Funk & Wagnalls, 1977.

Egan, G. *The Skilled Helper*. Monterey, Calif.: Brooks/Cole, 1975.

Egan, G., and Cowan, M. *People in Systems: A Model for Development of Human-Service Professions and Education*. Monterey, Calif.: Brooks/Cole, 1979.

Fidler, J. "Education for Group Psychotherapy." In L. R. Wolberg and E. K. Schwartz (Eds.), *Group Psychotherapy 1973—An Overview*. New York: Intercontinental Medical Book Corp., 1973.

Gazda, G., Duncan, J., and Sisson, P. "Professional Issues in Group Work." *Personnel and Guidance Journal*, 1974, *49*, 637–643.

Gumaer, J. "Training Peer Facilitators." *Elementary School Guidance and Counseling*, 1976, *11* (1), 27–35.

Horowitz, L. "Training Groups for Psychiatric Residents." *International Journal of Group Psychotherapy*, 1967, *17*, 421–435.

Ivey, A. E. *Microcounseling: Innovation in Interviewing Training.* Springfield, Ill.: Thomas, 1971.

Ivey, A. E. "Demystifying the Group Process: Adapting Microcounseling Procedures to Counseling in Groups." In J. Vriend and W. Dyer (Eds.), *Counseling Effectively in Groups.* Englewood Cliffs, N. J.: Educational Technology Publications, 1973.

Ivey, A. E., and Authier, J. *Microcounseling: Innovations in Interviewing, Counseling, Psychotherapy, and Psychoeducation.* Springfield, Ill.: Thomas, 1978.

Jacobs, E., Brown, D., and Randolph, A. "Educating Group Counselors: A Tentative Model." *Counselor Education and Supervision*, 1974, *13* (4), 307–309.

Krimsky, E. "A Remedial Program in Interpersonal and Group Helping Skills." Unpublished paper, Southern Illinois University, Carbondale, 1978.

Lakin, M., Lieberman, W., and Whitaker, D. "Issues in Training of Group Psychotherapists." *International Journal of Group Psychotherapy*, 1969, *19*, 307–325.

Lechowicz, J., and Gazda, G. "Group Counseling Instruction: Objectives Established by Experts." *Counselor Education and Supervision*, 1975, *15* (1), 21–27.

Lerner, H., Horowitz, L., and Burstein, E. "Teaching Psychoanalytic Group Psychotherapy: A Combined Experiential-Didactic Workshop." *International Journal of Group Psychotherapy*, 1978, *28* (4), 453–466.

Lieberman, M., Yalom, I., and Miles, M. *Encounter Groups: First Facts.* New York: Basic Books, 1973.

Mace, D., and Mace, V. "The Selection, Training, and Certification of Facilitators for Marriage Enrichment Programs." *Family Coordinator*, 1976, *25* (4), 117–125.

MacLennan, B. "Simulated Situations in Group Psychotherapy Training." *International Journal of Group Psychotherapy*, 1971, *21*, 330–332.

Malnoti, R., and Pastushak, R. "Conducting Group Practica with the Aged." *Psychotherapy: Theory, Research, and Practice*, 1980, *17* (3), 352–360.

Maynard, P., and Long, J. "Group Training for Counselors—a One-Year Follow-Up." *Counselor Education and Supervision*, 1976, *15* (3), 225–228.

Moreland, J. "A Taxonomy of Basic Group Facilitation Skills." Paper presented at the American Personnel and Guidance Association Convention, New York, March 1975.

Moreland, J. "Facilitator Training for Consciousness-Raising Groups in an Academic Setting." *The Counseling Psychologist*, 1976, *6* (3), 66–69.

Moreland, J., and Hallissey, J. "Basic Principles of Group Process and Group Facilitation. In V. Harren (Ed.), *Career Decision Making for College Students: Facilitator Handbook*. Washington, D.C.: National Institute of Education, 1979.

Moreland, J., Ivey, A. E., and Phillips, J. "An Evaluation of Micro-counseling as an Interviewer Training Tool." *Journal of Consulting and Clinical Psychology*, 1973, *41* (2), 294–300.

Mullen, H., and Rosenbaum, M. *Group Psychotherapy: Theory and Practice.* New York: Free Press, 1962.

Muro, J. "Some Aspects of the Group Counseling Practicum." *Counselor Education and Supervision*, 1968, 7(4), 371–378.

Ohlsen, M. "Group Leader Preparation." *Counselor Education and Supervision*, 1975, *14* (3), 215–220.

Peterson, C., Peterson, B., and Cameron, C. "Pyramid Groups: A New Model for Therapy and Intern Training." *Professional Psychology*, 1977, *8* (2), 214–221.

Pyle, K. R. "Developing a Teen-Peer Facilitator Program." *School Counselor*, 1977, *24* (4), 278–281.

Roman, M., and Porter, K. "Combining Experiential and Didactic Aspects in a New Group Therapy Training Approach." *International Journal of Group Psychotherapy*, 1978, *28* (3), 371–387.

Rosenbaum, M., and Berger, M. *Group Psychotherapy and Group Function.* (Rev. ed.) New York: Basic Books, 1975.

Salvendy, J. "Education in Psychotherapy: Challenges and Pitfalls." *Canadian Psychiatry Association Journal*, 1977, *22*, 435–440.

Salvendy, J. "Group Psychotherapy Training." *Canadian Journal of Psychiatry*, 1980, *25* (5), 394–402.

Sharni, S. "From Alienation to Admiration—Developmental Stages of Group Leaders in Encounters with Culturally Deprived Mothers." *Human Relations*, 1979, *32* (9), 737–748.

Shulman, L. *The Skills of Helping Individuals and Groups*. Itasca, Ill.: Peacock, 1979.

Smith, E. "Issues and Problems in the Group Supervision of Beginning Group Problems." *Counselor Education and Supervision*, 1976, *16* (1), 13–24.

Stein, A. "The Training of the Group Psychotherapist." In M. Rosenbaum and M. Berger (Eds.), *Group Psychotherapy and Group Function*. New York: Basic Books, 1975.

Stephanos, S., and Auhagen, U. "Reflections on the Qualities of a Balint Group Leader." *British Journal of Medical Psychology*, 1979, *52*, 43–47.

Stokes, J., and Tait, R. "Design of a Short-Term Training Program in Group Facilitation Skills." *Professional Psychology*, 1980, *11*, 298–303.

Stone, W., and Green, B. "Learning During Group Therapy Leadership Training." *Small Group Behavior*, 1978, *9* (3), 373–386.

Truax, C., and Carkhuff, R. R. *Toward Effective Counseling and Psychotherapy: Training and Practice*. Hawthorne, N.Y.: Aldine, 1967.

Webster, E., and Cole, B. "Effective Leadership of Parent Discussion Groups." *Language, Speech, and Hearing Services in Schools*, 1979, *10*, 72–80.

Yalom, I. *The Theory and Practice of Group Psychotherapy*. (2nd ed.) New York: Basic Books, 1975.

Zohn, J., and Carmody, T. "Training Opportunities in Group Treatment Methods in APA-Approved Clinical Psychology Programs." *Professional Psychology*, 1978, *9*, 50–61.

Chapter 10

Leadership Skills in Treatment Groups

Nazneen Sada Mayadas
Wayne D. Duehn

Although the empirical literature on group treatment is extensive, recent reviews of its efficacy are far from conclusive. Galinsky and Schopler (1977) and Abramowitz (1976) provide ample evidence that group intervention must be viewed with caution because a group experience may be as detrimental to some individuals as it is beneficial to others. Similarly, Bednar and Kaul (1978) state that group therapy should be considered a two-edged sword that can both hinder and help clients. Since a central precept of helping is *primum no nocere* ("first of all, do no harm") (Chapman, 1964), the demand for accountability both in practice and in the education of group therapists requires that components that impede and those that facilitate various outcomes be identified and their operational measures assessed in the ongoing context of practice.

Among the problems encountered in addressing this issue are inability to develop individualized outcome measures (Yalom, 1975; Hartford, 1971; Klein, 1972; Galinsky and Schopler, 1977), replicable research designs (Bednar and Kaul, 1978), and explicitly defined group leadership skills. More specifically, the theoretical and empirical literature takes the group therapist or leader as an undifferen-

314

tiated, independent variable so that the factors contributing to deterioration are as uncertain as many of the factors contributing to constructive change. Thus, few educational models exist for imparting leadership skills for group treatment. Of those that do exist, none, to the authors' knowledge, have been empirically tested.

Casper (1970) presents a conceptual framework for assessing the leader in ongoing group processes. His primary vehicle for teaching group processes is an experiential model presented in the classroom situation. Implicit in this approach is the assumption that acquisition of clinical skills occurs through group experiential learning or that skills mastery is outside the purview of courses on group treatment. Schwartz's (1964) contention that one cannot teach the skills of group treatment in the classroom, one can only teach the analysis of skills and modes of theorizing about the nature of the helping process, typifies the latter stance. Competent group treatment requires therapists who not only analyze or theorize but also do. This view is consistent with Truax and Carkhuff's (1967) criticisms that clinical training programs, as a rule, have taught theory and client dynamics, rather than approaches to interacting with patients within the therapeutic process.

In an effort to address the need for educational models for imparting group leadership skills, this paper presents a typology of such skills, together with an educational videotape modeling format by which these skills can be acquired. Further preliminary data are reported on the application of this format to thirty graduate social work students.

Modeling and Group Leadership

Extensive clinical and empirical evidence has accumulated that suggests that modeling can be an effective and efficient method for teaching and modifying complex social behaviors (Bandura, 1969; Bandura, 1971; Bandura, Jeffery, and Wright, 1974; Blanchard, 1970; Doster, 1972; Friedman, 1972; Green and Marlatt, 1972; Gutride, Goldstein, and Hunter, 1973; Hersen and others, 1973; Ivey and Authier, 1978; Marlatt, 1970; McFall and Lillesand, 1971; McFall and Marston, 1970; McFall and Twentyman, 1973; Muzekari and Kamis, 1973; O'Conner, 1972; Rathus, 1973; Young, Rimm, and

Kennedy, 1973). In modeling, a person views the most appropriate interactional behaviors relative to the demands of the situation under examination. Much social learning is fostered by exposure to designed, simulated models in which performance is intentionally patterned in terms of clearly delineated behaviors that can be emulated. Once a learner has developed an adequate behavioral repertoire, increased reliance is placed on the use of verbal or pictorial symbolic models. A modeled performance provides substantially more relevant, clearer cues than a mere verbal description, and a combination of verbal and demonstrational approaches is more effective than either presented alone. The establishment of complex social repertoires is generally achieved through a gradual process in which individuals pass through an orderly learning sequence that guides them in progressive steps toward the desired behavior. Consequently, the efficacy of modeling procedures will depend, to a large extent, on the care with which the modeled performance is programmed (Mayadas and Duehn, 1977a; Ullman and Krasner, 1965). In group treatment and in the education of group therapists, few such programmed models of leadership performance exist.

At a time when clinical practice and education are challenged to give increasing attention to quality control (Duehn and Mayadas, 1977; Bloom, 1978), virtually no research on group therapy has been directed toward examining the comparative effectiveness of various means of instruction in group leadership. Moreover, despite the existence of methodologies for choosing appropriate teaching techniques (Kirkpatrick, 1959), education for group treatment has ignored precise evaluations of teaching methodologies in favor of bland statements of instructor preference unsupported by empirical data. The problem, then, is not only to determine the most effective method for imparting leadership skills for groups but also to identify those factors contributing to actual skills acquisition.

Based on the preceding discussion and on our continuing testing of an empirical, competence-based professional curriculum (Duehn and Mayadas, 1977; Mayadas and Duehn, 1977b), this chapter outlines competence criteria for group leaders. In other words, therapists must demonstrate mastery of leadership skills, as well as a commitment to ethical values of interpersonal helping and responsiveness to evolving practice objectives. Described here is the development of a classification system for categorizing selected group leadership behaviors utilizing videotaped stimulus-modeling procedures. Twelve essential leadership behaviors for groups are operationalized and their reliability statistically established. Further, this instrument is currently being applied to measure the educational effects on leadership skills acquisition of videotape feedback, a combination of modeling and videotape feedback, and verbal instruction. Preliminary findings are discussed in this chapter.

Typology for Group Leadership

Although the literature is filled with anecdotal testimonials of how classroom processes serve as a rehearsal stage for the subsequent leadership of group therapy, both this isomorphism and the extent to which actual leadership skills are transmitted to and internalized by learners have yet to be tested. In order to operationally define concepts alluded to in case examples, twelve behaviors representative of clinical leadership styles were selected on the basis of their importance in the literature and in our clinical experience.

1. *Reinforcement of group's verbal interaction*—leader statements that give recognition, support, and encouragement to member–to–member, rather than leader-to-member, verbal exchanges.

Research indicates that an open, group-centered communication network has positive effects on member morale (Shaw, 1976) and on interpersonal attraction (Cartwright and Zander, 1968) leading to goal achievement. Klein (1972) notes that group cohesion is a function of the efficacy of communication and influences goal attainment activities. Hartford (1971) underscores the importance of "total communication" in both facilitating and symbolizing group cohesion. Through this interactional process, people are joined, act and react together, and arrive at some coalescence that produces "groupness." Konopka (1963) repeatedly provides examples in which the leader's reinforcement of an open communication network is the central principle of group treatment.

2. *Reinforcement of individual responsibility*—leader statements that demonstrate, request, or emphasize member's individual responsibilities toward the group.

Yalom (1975) identifies the importance of each group member being accountable for his or her own actions within the group process. Likewise, Northen (1969) notes that positive change is facilitated when members recognize their respective responsibilities for the group's process and outcome. Indicating that a primary skill of any group leader is to establish the importance of member participation and responsibility, Konopka (1963) views these two components as essential for hastening the interactional process and for giving special status and encouragement to group members. Even more operationally, Klein (1972) advises that the leader is under a mandate to emphasize individual responsibility by explicating procedures whereby members are held responsible for their actions and, ultimately, for group processes and outcomes.

3. *Establishment of leader-member coevaluative functions*—leader comments that make explicit reference to conjoint evaluative and monitoring tasks of all participants.

That all members take part in the evaluative and monitoring processes is an important ingredient, according to Northen (1969), that operationalizes the group as a model of democratic processes. For Yalom (1975), group passivity and dependence, which are antitherapeutic, are more likely to occur when self-evaluation fails to develop. The importance of involving members in evaluative function is also underscored by Gottlieb and Stanley (1967), Levine (1967), Phillips (1957), and Schopler and Galinsky (1974). Coevaluation comprises a complex range of ongoing conjoint leader-member activities that are directed toward monitoring progress, assessing impediments to goal attainment, and reconciling group goals with individual preferences.

4. *Reinforcement of group importance*—leader responses that give higher priority to commitment of both leader and members to the group than to other activities competing with that commitment.

Specifically, these responses relate to group attendance, continuity, punctuality, completion of between-session tasks, and reinforcement of group members' statements pertaining to the usefulness and value of the group experience. Yalom (1975) suggests that the ideal therapeutic posture has been attained when members consider the group experience to have a high priority in their lives. The leader strengthens this belief by utilizing statements that explicitly model the group's importance. Similarly, Hartford (1971) speaks of the necessity for members to be anchored in the group, particularly during the formation phases, in that such anchoring serves as a prerequisite to building interpersonal trust and facilitating treatment outcomes. Rose (1972) notes that a primary means for increasing group attraction is the leader's reinforcement of regular attendance and group task completion.

5. *Negotiation and enforcement of treatment contract*—leader statements that refer to the reciprocal obligations of leader and members.

In these statements, the leader discusses and clarifies definitions of roles, contractual expectations, and the treatment process. So central to treatment are these contracting skills that, according to Croxton (1974), they provide the platform on which the entire therapeutic process is built and by which members' accountability is measured. Northen (1969) notes that the leader's actions are crucial in the determination of group purpose, as is the establishment of a contract with individual members regarding the service to be provided. Additional rationales for leadership skill in this area are provided by Garvin and Glasser (1974), who emphasize that contracting has both ethical and practical roots, the former resting on the therapeutic commitment to self-determination of the client and the latter based on the increasing likelihood of goal attainment and client continuance in treatment. Bernstein (1964), Frey and Meyer (1975), and Konopka (1963) have written extensively on the "working alliance," stressing the importance of distinguishing this agreement from other relationships and advocating clear and precise messages concerning treatment goals, reciprocal obligations relating to means, and ultimate expectations. According to Hartford (1971), "setting a contract" is a crucial aspect of group formation and is essential for establishing criteria for alternative courses of action.

6. *Reinforcement of intragroup focus*—leader comments indicating that immediate interactions within the group take precedence over experiences that are or have been external to the group.

Rose (1972) suggests that the leader's verbal reinforcement of positive statements about persons in the group, group usefulness, and group activities result in the increased frequency of such statements and greater attraction to the group, with intragroup activities taking precedence over other activities. Similarly, Yalom (1975) stresses the importance of an inside focus by emphasizing that the immediate events in the meeting take precedence over events both in the current outside world and in the distant past of the members. For Klein (1972), the group leader plays a major role in constructing a therapeutic milieu by deliberately excluding extra-system inputs that interfere with the group's interpersonal processes. The immediacy and realness of such processes make it possible for positive learning to take place. Events that occurred in the past or outside the group are relevant only insofar as they are manifested in current group interaction. Giving credence to the skills of contract negotiation and enforcement is both an explicit and implicit acknowledgment of the limited range of behaviors that are directly observable and amenable to change.

7. *Reflection of affect*—leader statements that selectively reflect observed affective states of individual group members.

In Rogerian (1951) literature, this concept is viewed as related to empathy, or being one with the client's emotional state. Such statements are considered crucial in the development of empathic understanding. Pernell (1962) identifies empathy as an essential skill for developing group cohesion. More operationally, Klein (1972) states that the group leader should actively invite, accept, and reinforce expressions of feelings and affect. "He operates on the level of feelings, instead of intellectualization, . . . and he reflects the feeling messages, as well as being responsive to them" (pp. 193-194). Vinter (1967) describes the leader as one who relates to feelings, is responsive, and, in so doing, provides rewards or reinforcements to such expressions. Through case illustrations in a variety of settings, Konopka (1963) provides examples in which leaders reflect specific affective states of members.

8. *Reflection of content*—leader responses that inform group members that the content of their preceding verbal statement has been heard.

Consistent with literature on verbal conditioning, client content is, to a large extent, governed by a leader's verbal behavior. Similarly, the group leader directs content focus by selectively reinforcing member verbalizations, thus maintaining the balance between group process and task achievement. Therefore, an effective group leader seeks, through concurrent active listening and modeling, to help individual members improve their communication. Klein (1972) suggests that the leader restate in his own words what individual members have expressed. Northen (1969) outlines the procedures for improving the transmission of content among group members, noting that "the worker is helpful if he knows the power of words to help or to hurt" (p. 179). Likewise, restatement, a therapeutic process suggested by Phillips (1966), is useful when ideas being presented are exceedingly complicated or are distorted by perceptual biases.

9. *Purposive self-disclosure*—leader statements that provide information to members on the cognitive and affective states of the leader and are facilitative of treatment goals.

Expressions of the leader's feelings and cognitions in group sessions are powerful tools for modeling interpersonal openness (Jourard, 1964). Hartford (1971) implies that modeling procedures are a means by which the skilled leader creates a permissive atmosphere, frees informational exchange, and promotes acceptance of cognitive and affective diversity. An important skill, according to Klein (1972), is the leader's use of self, which is translated into verbal behaviors by the group leader's planfully sharing personal feelings and cognitions, rather than assuming an impassive practice stance.

10. *Confrontation of interactional discrepancies*—leader comments that point out discrepancies between attitudes, thoughts, and behaviors of individual members.

Regardless of their theoretical orientation, leaders can use confrontational skills to make group members more aware of behavioral and verbal incongruities. Such skills are of special relevance to group treatment, because perceptual distortions and behavioral discrepancies are less likely to be denied when subjected to the scrutiny of conjoint leader-member confrontation. In Sundel and Lawrence's (1974) approach, confrontation is employed only to observable behavioral discrepancies. Klein (1972) operationalizes leader confrontational techniques by listing a series of questions designed to help members assess the group situation, their behavior in the group, and the appropriateness of behavior to contracted treatment goals. In this process, members become aware of what the situation is, what they actually do, and what they can accomplish.

Vinter (1974) also speaks of the leader's task of confronting group members with inconsistencies between their behaviors and the long-term consequences of such actions. From a behavioral perspective, Rose (1972) suggests that confrontation be used as a punishment procedure to bring deviant behavior into conformity with group norms and goals.

11. *Modification of negative labeling*—leader statements that shift members' negative interpersonal evaluations of each other to situation-specific descriptions of undesirable behaviors.

Such statements provide members safety from fears of unrestrained attack and hostility, create a group norm that distinguishes behaviors from innate personality characteristics, and focus attention on only those interactional behaviors that are directly amenable to modification. Yalom (1975) reports that attaching a negative label to a group member constitutes an attack, and the leader has the responsibility of converting this attack into a constructive confrontation by soliciting descriptive feedback of the interaction in place of the label. Similarly, Klein (1972) states that leaders provide poor examples if they are unable or unwilling to handle labels expressive of hostility and anger. Through their verbal and nonverbal behaviors, leaders must not only model their comfort with these feelings but also shift the focus from an attack to a constructive confrontation. Sundel and Lawrence (1974) note that a requisite norm to be established by therapists in group treatment is that members refrain from hostile confrontation with each other. Thus, members are reinforced when they limit comments to observed behavioral feedback without interpreting unobserved motives for those behaviors. Hartford (1971) indicates that the iatrogenic effects of labeling must be controlled, as they can be used to discredit individual group members. Leadership skills are needed to separate facts from inferences and distortions. Similarly, Konopka (1963) decries group leaders' support of labeling and indicates that it is more profitable to examine the specifics of what an individual does, rather than engage in fanciful guesswork regarding personality.

12. *Reinforcement of noncompetitive individual attributes*—leader statements that explicitly acknowledge and enhance the unique attributes and contributions of members without fostering competition.

This skill operationalizes a central value underlying group treatment—the uniqueness of the individual. Hare (1976) provides ample evidence to support the need for individual recognition in both socioemotional and task-oriented groups. The leader has the responsibility to help meet this need by creating a climate of sharing where individuality is recognized and respected. Konopka (1963) identifies individualization in the group as one of the five key values of group treatment. Similarly, Northen (1969) states that the leader must individualize persons within groups by understanding and taking into consideration their needs, capacities, and environment and recognizing their unique contributions to the group.

Videotapes in Training Methodology

A combination of verbal and demonstrational procedures is most effective in transmitting new patterns of behavior. Bandura's (1969) extensive research highlights factors that increase the efficacy of vicarious learning. Behaviors are more likely to occur when full, accurate, discriminative attention is directed at modeled behaviors; when modeled behavior is vivid, novel, and recurrent; when the model is perceived as having high prestige, expertise, and demographic similarity to the observer; when the model is rewarded for engaging in the depicted behavior; when the model is seen as having interpersonal attractiveness, when the observer has received a specific instructional set; when conflicting, competing, or nonrelevant stimuli are minimized; and when the observer is given feedback and is rewarded for modeling.

Such vicarious learning, or modeling, as well as its procedural implementations, is easily achieved through the use of videotapes. Modeling using videotapes has great potential for training group therapists because the array of complex interpersonal and social skills requisite for leadership can be identified, portrayed, systematically presented, and subsequently imitated, thus eliminating trial-and-error learning inefficiencies so characteristic of many training modalities. Thelen and others (1979) suggest that incorporation of videotaped modeling promotes therapeutic and educational control, convenient use of multiple models, repeated observations of the same model, use of the modeling tape in numerous training situations, and the potential for self-administered learning.

Despite evidence pointing to the efficacy of utilizing videotaped modeling procedures in clinical training, educators and therapists have been reluctant to use these formats, limiting videotape application primarily to confrontational feedback in treatment. Since the prevalent lack of reliable modeling stimuli depicting actual and measurable leadership behaviors is a central concern, the approach discussed in this chapter utilizes videotaped models, behavioral rehearsals, and videotape feedback. The videotapes were developed from the typology of leadership behaviors just described.* Subsequent to typology identification, operational means were necessary for incorporating leadership behaviors into specific, modeled video formats.

In the designing of the videotapes, each of the twelve leadership skills was paired with a contrasting, nontherapeutic behavior presented first in the same context. The presentation of these contrasting skills was based on recent research findings suggesting that portrayal of antithetical behaviors increases acquisition of desired skills (Ivey and Authier, 1978). Each skill and its antithesis was scripted and enacted by coached actors and actresses within the context of a simulated group situation. The advantages of simulations lie in the ability to control factors that increase stimulus cueing and modeling efficacy. Scripts were deliberately written to capture the essence of the modeled leadership behavior; actors were chosen on the basis of their ability to accurately portray the behaviors. Through the use of multiple cameras, zoom lenses, special effects generators, and editing devices, modeled performances were made vivid, discreet, and explicit, and extraneous stimuli were minimized (Mayadas and Duehn, 1981). The need for this approach is confirmed by Thelen and others (1979), who point out that, in modeling complex behaviors and contexts, the responses to be learned must be both simplified and amplified to avoid overwhelming the learner. The time frame for each paired episode was approximately three minutes. Informal rating procedures were utilized as pretest mea-

---

*The authors wish to acknowledge Edward Collier for his effort in developing and testing the instrument.

sures to improve the quality of the modeling tape, and raters were requested to note ambiguous and problematic content and technical flaws. Suggested changes were incorporated into the final tape. The result was a color videotaped production approximately forty minutes in duration. An instrument based on operational definitions of each behavior was employed to assess each vignette, with a scale ranked as follows: -2, definitely does not depict behavior described; -1, may not depict behavior described; 0, uncertain; +1, depicts behavior described to some extent; and +2, definitely depicts behavior described. A consistent "+" rating of behavior for a specific episode indicated a high correlation between definition on the rating instrument and actual demonstration of behavior on the tape.

One question asked by this study concerns the face validity of the taped vignettes—that is, does each vignette demonstrate, in the judges' opinion, the group leadership behavior it is designed to demonstrate. To answer this question two statistical measures were used. First, a one-tailed t was calculated for each vignette (Guilford and Fruchter, 1973). As can be seen from Table 1, which summarizes the reliability scores for each leadership style, there was high interjudge reliability for all twelve vignettes regarding the operational referents of both the positive and negative behaviors modeled on the videotape. Second, high levels of interbehavior reliability were demonstrated by calculating Spearman's Rank Correlation Coefficient for each behavior. The critical calculated value for significance at the .01 level was .661.

Modeling Videotape Formats

The leadership skills typology and the videotape just described served as the major methodological tool in a study measuring the effects of videotaped modeling that incorporated verbal instruction, feedback, and experiential learning through behavioral rehearsal and peer-supervisor critique (Mayadas and Duehn, 1977b). This unique combination of verbal instructions, exposure to modeling tapes, videotaped enactment of demonstrated behaviors by learner, and immediate replay of enacted behavior for learner critique has been found to be an effective mechanism for verifying actual interactional patterns and for providing opportunities for

Table 1. Summary of Interjudge Reliability
for Selected Leadership Behaviors.

Behavior	Vignette	t_1
1. Reinforcement of Group's Verbal Interaction	A. Negative	3.808[a]
	B. Positive	24.974
2. Reinforcement of Individual Responsibility	A. Negative	24.974
	B. Positive	7.658
3. Establishment of Leader-Member Coevaluative Functions	A. Negative	17.750
	B. Positive	24.974
4. Reinforcement of Group Importance	A. Negative	90.909
	B. Positive	14.500
5. Negotiation and Enforcement of Treatment Contract	A. Negative	10.681
	B. Positive	90.909
6. Reinforcement of Intragroup Focus	A. Negative	24.974
	B. Positive	24.974
7. Reflection of Affect	A. Negative	90.909
	B. Positive	24.974
8. Reflection of Content	A. Negative	90.909
	B. Positive	24.974
9. Purposive Self-Disclosure	A. Negative	90.909
	B. Positive	24.974
10. Confrontation of Interactional Discrepancies	A. Negative	90.909
	B. Positive	90.909
11. Modification of Negative Labeling	A. Negative	24.974
	B. Positive	11.454
12. Reinforcement of Noncompetitive Individual Attributes	A. Negative	12.722
	B. Positive	90.909

[a]Critical value for $p < .01$ = 2.681
$p < .005$ = 3.005
$p < .0005$ = 4.318

skills acquisition (Duehn and Mayadas, 1975; Mayadas and Duehn, 1977a).

The preliminary research undertook to examine the results of such procedures in the acquisition of group leadership skills. The sample consisted of thirty second-year students in the Graduate School of Social Work, University of Texas at Arlington. Data were collected over three semesters on three groups of ten students each from a seminar on group dynamics and social work practice.

Table 2. Summary of Interbehavioral Correlation Coefficients.

Behavior	Difference	Spearman's[a] Correlation R_s
1. Reinforcement of Group's Verbal Interaction	9	.777
2. Reinforcement of Individual Responsibility	2	.990
3. Establishment of Leader-Member Coevaluative Functions	1	.998
4. Reinforcement of Group Importance	3	.975
5. Negotiation and Enforcement of Treatment Contract	6	.901
6. Reinforcement of Intragroup Focus	0	1.0
7. Reflection of Affect	1	.998
8. Reflection of Content	1	.998
9. Purposive Self-Disclosure	1	.998
10. Confrontation of Interactional Discrepancies	0	1.0
11. Modification of Negative Labeling	4	.956
12. Reinforcement of Noncompetitive Individual Attributes	4	.956

[a]Critical value for $p < .01 = .661$

The objective of this seminar is to examine contemporary social psychological concepts and small group research for the purpose of testing their applicability to practice propositions and operational principles. The course attempts to enhance the student's awareness of the reciprocal impact experienced by the individual and the group in interaction. Emphasis is placed on factors that promote an understanding of the dynamics of interpersonal and group behaviors encountered in social work practice as they relate to social process groups. A major focus of the seminar is on translating theoretical and empirical knowledge into practice behaviors and techniques for implementing systematic, planned change in and through groups. In an attempt to achieve this objective, the class uses the seminar-laboratory format, with maximum feasible participation by students. An important part of the course design involves the utilization of the classroom group as a laboratory in which to experience, analyze, and study group processes. Frequent use is made of videotape feedback and practice simulations to study various group processes and to test out selected social group work techniques and interventional skills as they apply to behavior management and goal achievement.

This educational program is designed to produce social group workers who can effectively intervene within a variety of group settings. The objective is not new; the innovation is the requirement that the approach to education make itself accountable for turning out social group workers with specific behavioral and cognitive competencies (Duehn and Mayadas, 1977). In other words, students must demonstrate empirical mastery of leadership skills, as well as commitment to the ethical values of the profession and responsiveness to evolving practice objectives.

In class-laboratory sessions, modeling tapes are combined with verbal instruction, behavioral rehearsals, and videotape feedback presented in the following sequence:

1. *Verbal instructions.* Verbal instructions are more likely to facilitate modeling when they both activate a person to respond and describe the relevance and ordering of responses. In order to ensure attention to instructional sets, verbal instructions for the specific skill practiced are provided concurrent with the stimulus cueing and various modeled presentations. Further, Bandura's (1969) research presents consistent and decisive evidence that the subject's attention is a necessary precondition for learning. For example, the rationale, clinical relevance, and empirical validation of the reflection of content skill is presented prior to exposure to the video model.

2. *Modeling videotape presentations.* The videotaped, modeled leadership skill and its antithesis are presented together and discussed. The learner is taught to recognize the appropriate stimuli that elicited the video model's response through a series of questions asking the learner to identify the skill and its appropriateness to a variety of group therapeutic interactions. The modeling tape may be stopped at predetermined intervals in order to emphasize specific cueing and behavioral components.

3. *Behavioral rehearsals and simulations.* The learner practices or rehearses the specific skill in a variety of therapeutic group

simulations, which are videotaped for replay, critique, and subsequent practice.

4. *Performance feedback.* After these behavioral rehearsals are taped, specific feedback procedures provide learners with information on the quality of their performance (learning theory suggests that reinforcement be given for achievement before making suggestions for improvement). During replay, the tape is stopped frequently to focus on selected aspects of predetermined behaviors of concern, and learners in the group are asked to comment on skill performance. Use of videotape feedback not only aids in correcting nontherapeutic behaviors but acts as a potent reinforcement for other desired behaviors already in the therapeutic repertoire.

This unique combination of verbal instruction, viewing of the modeling tape, and the immediate replay and critique of the enacted leadership skill provides learners with a mechanism for verifying skill acquisition. The three steps are repeated until the leadership skill reaches the criterion level of mutual satisfaction for both instructor and learner.

5. *Clinical critiques.* Finally, videotapes of actual group treatment sessions conducted by trainees are submitted for clinical critique. Clinical critiques utilize the interpersonal skills of reinforcement and feedback emphasized in the leadership typology. Thus, the clinical critique serves a dual purpose for the group therapists-in-training: for the therapist whose simulated, videotaped performance is under scrutiny, it provides behavioral feedback from the group; for other group members, it provides an excellent opportunity to practice recently acquired skills in a real-life situation.

Preliminary Findings

Leadership skills acquisition using videotaped modeling procedures was assessed by pretraining and posttraining comparisons of five leadership skills selected arbitrarily from the twelve-item leadership typology: establishment of leader-member coevaluation function, reinforcement of group importance, negotiation and enforcement of treatment contract, reinforcement of intragroup focus, and confrontation of interactional discrepancies. Data on the remaining seven skills are currently under investigation.

The pretraining and posttraining measures for the five leadership skills are displayed in Table 3. These data were collected from videotapes on each student demonstrating the five leadership skills in simulated group sessions at the beginning and end of the semester. To control for contaminating effects (for example, stage of group formation or problem focus), the same group vignette was used as stimulus material in both pretraining and posttraining measures. Percentage of behavioral occurrences were computed from ratings of independent judges and compared using t tests.

As indicated by the results, subjects increased their use of all five leadership skills. However, these are quantitative, rather than qualitative, measures of leadership; although the data suggests that video modeling formats increase leadership behaviors, the question of the appropriateness and relevance of behaviors within the context of ongoing group process is not addressed. In other words, the data only answer the simple question, Are the behaviors in evidence, and to what extent? The results of the present study indicate that not only is it possible to develop a reliable modeling videotape demonstrating leadership skills but also such a technology can be effectively applied to ongoing training situations. Although this study is only a first step in determining the specific microcomponents of leadership behaviors, it is a prerequisite to determining behavioral relevance and to assessing effective leadership styles—areas it leaves for future, more elaborate investigation.

Conclusion

Although the acquisition of leadership skills has been satisfactorily demonstrated by the findings reported in this chapter, establishing the effectiveness of these skills in various group situations still remains a function of clinical judgment. At this point, subjective evidence gleaned from clinical critiques suggests transfer and generalization from simulation to actual practice. Further, subjective ratings of group member satisfaction indicate relevance and contextual appropriateness of the leadership behaviors acquired.

As the findings show, it is possible to develop a leadership typology against which behaviors can be reliably measured. The advantage of developing such a system for training of group thera-

Table 3. Mean and Standard Deviations for Pretraining and
Posttraining Measures.

Measures	Preprogram		Postprogram		$t(df = 27)$
	Mean	SD	Mean	SD	
Establishment of Leader-Member Coevaluative Function	4.18	1.91	6.76	1.46	2.57[b]
Reinforcement of Group Function	5.46	2.36	9.72	3.14	1.96[a]
Negotiation and Enforcement of Treatment Contract	7.12	1.23	9.36	1.41	2.69[b]
Reinforcement of Intragroup Focus	10.63	3.16	15.28	2.39	3.63[c]
Confrontation of Interactional Discrepancies	3.76	1.79	6.91	1.62	4.89[c]

[a] $p < .05$
[b] $p < .01$
[c] $p < .001$

pists is that it reduces a set of complex behaviors to their discrete microcomponents. Further, this typology may be profitably applied in studies of client outcomes, leadership profiles of group therapists, minimum requisites for professional practice, and the relationship of these leadership behaviors to content structuring, stage of group development, member characteristics, and group composition.

The presentation of discrete leadership skills by means of video modeling provides a systematic and structured methodology by which knowledge of group therapy can be applied and, through practice, mastered at identified levels. This methodology is a departure from the more traditional educational approaches, in which didactic content and experiential learning are frequently isolated from each other, and the onus of integration is placed on the learner. Further, traditional approaches rarely identify competence levels explicitly. The educational model explicated in this chapter forms but a first step in the direction of an explicit, competence- and skills-based program for group therapists. This methodology needs to be tested within a variety of group therapy contexts with different theoretical orientations. The differential effects of verbal instruction, video modeling, behavioral practice, and feedback need to be further examined through more controlled experimental procedures. More specifically, research is needed to determine optimal number and length of video presentations consistent with group leaders' capacity for processing information. Likewise, hierarchical ordering of skills, timing of exposure to model behaviors, practice performance, and other format components need to be further identified to ensure maximum learning.

In conclusion, the video modeling methodology explicated here needs to be expanded and more extensively incorporated into training for group therapists. Specifically needed are technological skills for developing a range of modeling tapes, the employment of these materials in explicitly designed treatment formats, and assessment of their effects on clinical group outcomes.

References

Abramowitz, S. I. "Deterioration Effects in Encounter Groups." *American Psychologist*, 1976, *31*, 247–255.

Bandura, A. *Principles of Behavior Modification*. New York: Holt, Rinehart and Winston, 1969.

Bandura, A. "Psychotherapy Based upon Modeling Principles." In A. E. Bergin and S. L. Garfield (Eds.), *Handbook of Psychotherapy and Behavior Change: An Empirical Analysis*. New York: Wiley, 1971.

Bandura, A., Jeffery, R. W., and Wright, C. L. "Efficacy of Participant Modeling as as Function of Response Induction Aids." *Journal of Abnormal Psychology*, 1974, *83*, 56–64.

Bednar, R. L., and Kaul, T. J. "Experiential Group Research: Current Perspectives." In S. L. Garfield and A. E. Bergin (Eds.), *Handbook of Psychotherapy and Behavior Change: An Empirical Analysis*. (2nd ed.) New York: Wiley, 1978.

Bernstein, S. *Youth in the Streets*. New York: Association Press, 1964.

Blanchard, E. B. "Relative Contributions of Modeling, Informational Influences, and Physical Contact in Extinction of Phobic Behavior." *Journal of Abnormal Psychology*, 1970, *76*, 55–61.

Bloom, M. "Challenges to the Helping Professions and the Responses of Scientific Practice." *Social Service Review*, 1978, *52*, 584–595.

Cartwright, D., and Zander, A. *Group Dynamics: Research and Theory.* New York: Harper & Row, 1968.

Casper, M. "The Use of the Class as a Group to Teach Group Process." In Council on Social Work Education, *Teaching and Learning in Social Work Education.* New York: Council on Social Work Education, 1970.

Chapman, A. H. "Iatrogenic Problems in Psychotherapy." *Psychiatric Digest*, 1964, *25*, 23–29.

Croxton, T. A. "The Therapeutic Contract in Social Treatment." In P. Glasser, R. Sarri, and R. Vinter (Eds.), *Individual Change Through Small Groups.* New York: Free Press, 1974.

Doster, J. A. "Effects of Instructions, Modeling, and Role Rehearsal on Interview Verbal Behavior." *Journal of Consulting and Clinical Psychology*, 1972, *39*, 202–209.

Duehn, W. D., and Mayadas, N. S. "The Use of Videotape Feedback and Operant Learning (OIL) in Marital Counseling with Groups." *Group Psychotherapy*, 1975, *28*, 157–163.

Duehn, W. D., and Mayadas, N. S. "Entrance and Exit Requirements of Professional Social Work Education." *Journal of Education for Social Work*, 1977, *13*, 22–29.

Frey, L. A., and Meyer, M. "Exploration and Working Agreement in Two Social Work Methods." In S. Bernstein (Ed.), *Exploration in Group Work.* Boston: School of Social Work, Boston University, 1975.

Friedman, P. H. "The Effects of Modeling, Role Playing, and Participation on Behavior Change." *Progress in Experimental Personality Research*, 1972, *6*, 41–81.

Galinsky, M. J., and Schopler, J. H. "Warning: Groups May Be Dangerous." *Social Work*, 1977, *22*, 89–93.

Garvin, C. D., and Glasser, P. H. "Social Group Work: The Preventive and Rehabilitative Approach." In P. Glasser, R. Sarri, and R. Vinter (Eds.), *Individual Change Through Small Groups.* New York: Free Press, 1974.

Gottlieb, W., and Stanley, J. H. "Mutual Goals and Goal Setting in Casework." *Social Casework*, 1967, *48*, 471–477.

Green, A. H., and Marlatt, G. A. "Effects of Instructions and Modeling upon Affective and Descriptive Verbalization." *Journal of Abnormal Psychology*, 1972, *80*, 189–196.

Guilford, J. P., and Fruchter, B. *Fundamental Statistics in Psychology and Education.* New York: McGraw-Hill, 1973.

Gutride, M. E., Goldstein, A. P., and Hunter, G. F. "The Use of Modeling and Role Playing to Increase Social Interaction Among Social Psychiatric Patients." *Journal of Consulting and Clinical Psychology*, 1973, *40*, 408–415.

Hare, A. P. *Handbook of Small Group Research.* (2nd ed.) New York: Free Press, 1976.

Hartford, M. *Groups in Social Work.* New York: Columbia University Press, 1971.

Hersen, M., and others. "Effects of Practice, Instructions, and Modeling on Components of Assertive Behavior." *Behavior Research and Therapy*, 1973, *11*, 443–451.

Ivey, A. E., and Authier, J. *Microcounseling: Innovations in Interviewing, Counseling, Psychotherapy, and Psychoeducation.* Springfield, Ill.: Thomas, 1978.

Jourard, S. *The Transparent Self.* New York: D. Van Nostrand, 1964.

Kirkpatrick, F. H. "Techniques for Evaluating Training Programs." *Journal of the American Society of Training Directors*, 1959, *13*, 3–9.

Klein, A. F. *Effective Groupwork: An Introduction to Principle and Method.* New York: Association Press, 1972.

Konopka, G. *Social Group Work: A Helping Process.* Englewood Cliffs, N.J.: Prentice-Hall, 1963.

Levine, B. *Fundamentals of Group Treatment.* Chicago: Whitehall, 1967.

McFall, R. M., and Lillesand, D. B. "Behavior Rehearsal with Modeling and Coaching in Assertion Training." *Journal of Abnormal Psychology*, 1971, *77*, 313–323.

McFall, R. M., and Marston, A. R. "An Experimental Investigation of Behavior Rehearsal in Assertive Training." *Journal of Abnormal Psychology*, 1970, *76*, 295–303.

McFall, R. M., and Twentyman, C. T. "Four Experiments on the Relative Contributions of Rehearsal, Modeling, and Coaching to

Assertion Training." *Journal of Abnormal Psychology*, 1973, *81*, 199–218.

Marlatt, G. A. "A Comparison of Vicarious and Direct Reinforcement Control of Verbal Behavior in an Interview Setting." *Journal of Psychology*, 1970, *16*, 695–703.

Mayadas, N. S., and Duehn, W. D. "Stimulus-Modeling Videotape for Marital Counseling." *Journal of Marriage and Family Counseling*, 1977a, *3*, 35–42.

Mayadas, N. S., and Duehn, W. D. "The Effects of Training Formats and Intepersonal Discriminations in the Education for Clinical Social Work Practice." *Journal of Social Service Research*, 1977b, *1*, 147–161.

Mayadas, N. S., and Duehn, W. D. "Stimulus-Modeling Videotape Formats in Clinical Practice and Research." In J. L. Fryrear and R. Fieshman (Eds.), *Videotherapy in Mental Health*. Springfield, Ill.: Thomas, 1981.

Muzekari, L. H., and Kamis, E. "The Effects of Videotape Feedback and Modeling in the Behavior of Chronic Schizophrenics." *Journal of Clinical Psychology*, 1973, *29*, 313–316.

Northen, H. *Social Work with Groups*. New York: Columbia University Press, 1969.

O'Conner, R. D. "Relative Efficacy of Modeling, Shaping, and the Combined Procedures for Modification of Social Withdrawal." *Journal of Abnormal Psychology*, 1972, *79*, 327–334.

Pernell, R. B. "Identifying and Teaching the Skill Components of Social Group Work." In Council on Social Work Education, *Education Developments in Social Group Work*. New York: Council on Social Work Education, 1962.

Phillips, G. M. *Communication and the Small Group*. Indianapolis, Ind.: Bobbs-Merrill, 1966.

Phillips, H. *Essentials of Social Group Work Skill*. New York: Association Press, 1957.

Rathus, S. A. "Instigation of Assertive Behavior Through Videotape-Mediated Assertive Models and Directed Practice." *Behavior Research and Therapy*, 1973, *11*, 57–65.

Rogers, C. R. *Client-Centered Therapy*. Boston: Houghton Mifflin, 1951.

Rose, S. D. *Treating Children in Groups*. San Francisco: Jossey-Bass, 1972.

Schopler, J. H., and Galinsky, M. J. "Goals in Social Group Work Practice: Formulation, Implementation, and Evaluation." In P. Glasser, R. Sarri, and R. Vinter (Eds.), *Individual Change Through Small Groups*. New York: Free Press, 1974.

Schwartz, W. "The Classroom Teaching of Social Work with Groups." In Council on Social Work Education, *A Conceptual Framework for the Teaching of the Social Group Work Method in the Classroom*. New York: Council on Social Work Education, 1964.

Shaw, M. E. *Group Dynamics: The Psychology of Small Group Behavior*. New York: McGraw-Hill, 1976.

Sundel, M., and Lawrence, H. "Behavioral Group Treatment with Adults in a Family Service Agency." In P. Glasser, R. Sarri, and R. D. Vinter (Eds.), *Individual Change Through Small Groups*. New York: Free Press, 1974.

Thelen, M. H., and others. "Therapeutic Videotape and Film Modeling: A Review." *Psychological Bulletin*, 1979, *86*, 701-720.

Truax, C. B., and Carkhuff, R. R. *Toward Effective Counseling and Psychotherapy: Training and Practice*. Hawthorne, N.Y.: Aldine, 1967.

Ullman, L. P., and Krasner, L. "Behavior Modification Through Research Modeling Procedures." In L. P. Ullman and L. Krasner (Eds.), *Research in Behavior Modification*. New York: Holt, Rinehart and Winston, 1965.

Vinter, R. D. "Problems and Processes in Developing Social Work Practice Principles." In E. J. Thomas (Ed.), *Behavioral Science for Social Workers*. New York: Free Press, 1967.

Vinter, R. D. "The Essential Components of Social Group Work Practice." In P. Glasser, R. Sarri, and R. D. Vinter (Eds.), *Individual Change Through Small Groups*. New York: Free Press, 1974.

Yalom, I. D. *The Theory and Practice of Group Psychotherapy*. (2nd ed.) New York: Basic Books, 1975.

Young, E. R., Rimm, D. C., and Kennedy, T. D. "An Experimental Investigation of Modeling and Verbal Reinforcement in the Modification of Assertive Behavior." *Behavior Research and Therapy*, 1973, *11*, 317-319.

Chapter 11

Facilitator Skills in Career Planning Groups

M. Harry Daniels
Jacqueline N. Buck

The purpose of this chapter is to present a typology of group process and facilitation skills for career decision-making groups and to describe a training program that can be used to teach the typology to prospective facilitators. The typology presented is unique in three ways. First, it provides a theory-based approach for designing and conducting career decision-making groups that enables group participants to realize the group's full facilitative potential. Second, the typology provides a systematic and effective model for training leaders of career decision-making groups. Finally, the typology provides a foundation for using nontraditional methods of career counseling.

Ever since Parsons (1909) established a program for helping young adults make career choices based on their occupational interests and aptitudes, career counselors have been attempting to provide effective and efficient career counseling services in one-to-one counseling sessions in which the counselor assisted the counselee to identify the work environment best-suited to his or her personal needs and predilections. When such a work environment was identified, it was assumed, job satisfaction was guaranteed (Miller, 1974). The energies and resources of countless numbers of professionals have been directed toward perfecting this method of career counseling.

Although this traditional method of providing career planning services has a demonstrated utility, current developments suggest that it is no longer the best or preferred treatment program (Babcock and Kaufman 1976; Evans and Rector, 1978; Smith and Evans, 1973). Several reasons can be given in support of this assertion. First, the rapidly changing nature of work in our technological age has necessitated a revision of the career concept (Tofler, 1970). Career no longer refers just to one's vocation; rather, it represents one's course through life. An individual's life course can be defined as a set of multiple, interdependent roles or pathways punctuated over the life span by historical and social events, as well as by personal transitions and turning points (Elder, 1978). The roles one assumes throughout one's life and one's decisions about how to portray those roles define both the life course, or career, and its direction (Buck and Daniels, 1981). Career counseling must consider the various, changing roles that combine to form an individual's career.

Second, new theories about career development (Harren, 1979) and concomitant research studies (Harren and others, 1978, 1979; Lunneborg, 1978) have clarified the process through which career decisions are made. Career decision making may be defined as the prioritization of one's available role alternatives at any given time and involves decisions about one's preferred manner of living, or life-style, not simply decisions about particular job opportunities. In addition, career decision making requires an understanding of the decision maker's personality characteristics and psychological processes, as well as the developmental tasks he or she confronts. In short, career decision making is a complex process that occurs within the context of an individual's social-psychological-historical matrix.

Third, recent advances in our understanding of adult development have required a reassessment of the central importance of the career concept in the life of adults (Buck and Daniels, 1981). The research of Levinson and his associates (1978), Gould (1978), and

Vaillant (1977) provides evidence of three major developmental tasks of adulthood: building and modifying the life structure; working on single components of the life structure; and becoming more individuated. Movement toward the resolution of any or all of these developmental tasks results in concomitant changes in one's life course.

Finally, requests for career planning assistance are being voiced by increasingly diverse subgroups within the population who have not heretofore utilized such services (Smith, 1981)—for example, women, social and ethnic minorities, socially and economically disadvantaged persons, disabled persons, and adults who are experiencing a mid-career change. Traditional career counseling methods have not provided the necessary assistance for these groups.

For all the reasons cited, therefore, new methods of providing career planning services are needed. Alternatives have ranged from a plethora of self-help books (Figler, 1979; Bolles, 1972, 1978; Carney, Wells, and Streufert, 1981; Jackson, 1978; Shingleton and Bao, 1977) to computerized guidance systems (Harris, 1974; Katz, Norris, and Pears, 1978). Other efforts have included the use of age-cohort paraprofessionals (Johnston and Hansen, 1981), mentoring systems (Gardner, 1981), and small group programs (Harren and others, 1979; Figler, 1975).

All of these methods show promise for providing individuals with needed career planning assistance; however, the use of small groups seems particularly promising (Daniels and Buck, 1981). A small group provides a setting in which intragroup interactions can promote the assessment and evaluation by group members of their conflicting values, beliefs, and life-styles, and brings to light the implications of such differences in the work world. All participants, both leaders and members, contribute to the creation of an atmosphere in which group members can actively make explicit for themselves and others what is most important to them, and why.

Career Decision-Making Model for Small Groups

The Career Decision-Making for College Students (CDMCS) program (Harren and others, 1979) is a structured, theory-based, small-group process career development program. The Harren career decision-making model (Harren, 1979) provides a comprehensive, data-based rationale for the program.

As indicated in Table 1, Harren postulates that any career decision requires the consideration of four interrelated parameters: process, characteristics, tasks, and conditions. The core of the model is the process parameter, which consists of four sequential steps in the process of making and carrying out a decision: awareness, planning, commitment, and implementation. Characteristics refer to the relatively stable personality traits that color a person's perception of developmental tasks and environmental conditions. The decision-maker characteristics emphasized in the Harren model are self-concept, decision-making style, and psychological states. Tasks refer to the career-related developmental tasks of college students—autonomy, sense of purpose, and interpersonal maturity. Conditions refer to the environmental and situational factors that affect the decision maker, including interpersonal evaluations, task conditions, and context conditions.

The application of the Harren career decision-making model to the Career Decision-Making for College Students program is based on three assumptions. The first assumption is that one's understanding of self-in-situation is enhanced by one's participation in a small group. One's understanding of self-in-situation—a function of one's developmental history and influenced by self-perceptions, perceptions of others, and the situational context in which the decision is to be made—is the basis for career decision making. The interactions among participants in small group process provide an opportunity for group members to increase their self-understanding (Buck, 1981; Figler, 1975; Rubinton, 1980).

The second assumption is that career decision-making groups have three distinct phases—internal focus, external focus, and synthesis-action focus—and that each phase presents the group with special tasks that must be addressed and resolved. For example, in the internal focus phase, the group must establish and nurture its facilitative potential so that the members may complete their self-evaluation; in the external focus phase, the group must offer feedback as members integrate self-knowledge and knowledge about the work world into a tentative career decision; and in the synthesis-action focus phase, the group must encourage and support its members as they begin to implement their career decisions.

Table 1. Summary of the Harren Career Decision-Making Model.

	Decision-Making Process
Awareness	Appraisal of self-in-situation
Planning	Exploration-crystallization
Commitment	Reintegration of self-concept system; bolstering; action planning
Implementation	Success and satisfaction outcomes; conformity-autonomy-interdependence

	Decision-Maker Characteristics
Self-Concept	
Identity	Level of differentiation and integration of the self-concept
Self-Esteem	Degree of satisfaction with self and degree of self-confidence
Decision-Making Style	
Rational	Objective deliberation and self-appraisal
Intuitive	Emotional self-awareness and fantasy
Dependent	Denial of responsibility; reliance on others; perception of restricted options
Psychological States	Level of anxiety in decision maker; defensive avoidance behaviors under high anxiety

	Developmental Tasks
Autonomy	Limited need for emotional support; instrumentality; cooperative interdependence
Interpersonal Maturity	Tolerance; interpersonal trust; intimacy
Sense of Purpose	Adjustment to college; educational, career, and life-style planning

	Decision-Making Situation
Interpersonal Evaluations	Positive and negative feedback from others
Task Conditions:	
Imminence	Amount of time available before implementation
Alternatives	Number of available, different courses of action
Consequences	Positive and negative effects on self and others
Context Conditions	
Mutuality	A significant other must codecide
Support	Emotional and financial support from others
Probability	Decision by others necessary for implementation

Source: Harren, 1979.

The third assumption underlying the application of the Harren model to the CDMCS program is that group members should pass through all three phases of the career decision-making groups. Each phase has sequential decision-making tasks for group members to do if their decisions are to be satisfying ones. In completing all three group phases, group members are helped to recognize what they think and feel, why they think and feel the way they do, and how they go about synthesizing their knowledge in the form of a career decision.

In order to satisfy these assumptions, the Career Decision-Making for College Students program is comprised of modules that fit together meaningfully and relate to the major components of Harren's model. Each module represents a unit of instruction and consists of the following: the theoretical rationale for the module; the module's goals and objectives; group process goals; activities and discussions to be carried out by the group; and important group facilitation skills. Such a system of program planning provides the continuity of a core of experiences from one session to another, at the same time allowing for special activities to meet the unique needs of a particular group.

Small Group Skills Typology

The skills typology for career decision-making groups described in this chapter represents a reorganization and integration of the works of Harren (1979) on career decision making, Moreland and Buck (1980) on group process, and Egan (1975, 1976) on communication skills. The typology consists of four parameters of group participation that are indigenous to each phase of a career decision-making group: career decision-making group phases; predominant group process; predominant group facilitation skills; and predominant communication skills (see Table 2). Career decision-making group phases are the relatively distinct phases of a career decision-making group that were described in the previous section. Predominant group process encompasses the predictable changes in the group over time and the manner in which the group goes about achieving its goals. Group facilitation skills include the strategies that group facilitators can use to increase the probability that group

Table 2. Skills Typology for Career Decision-Making Groups.

Parameters of Career Decision-Making Groups

Group Phases	Predominant Group Process	Predominant Group Facilitation Skills	Predominant Communication Skills
Internal Focus Identity Self-esteem Decision-making style Personality characteristics Developmental tasks	Norm development Expectation clarification Group cohesiveness	Introduction to activities Expectation clarification External to internal focus Encouraging others to share Stating feelings important to group	Giving directions Attending Open-ended questions Primary-level accurate empathy Genuineness Respect Concreteness Facilitative self-disclosure Summarization
External focus Interpersonal evaluations Task conditions Imminence Alternatives Consequences Context conditions Mutuality Support Probability	Group cohesiveness Group member responsibility Norm development	All of the above plus: Refocus from individual to group Confrontation	All of the above plus: Additive accurate empathy Mutuality Immediacy Confrontation
Synthesis-Action Focus Goals identification Development of action plan Public commitment	Group member responsibility Group cohesiveness	External to internal focus Refocus from individual to group Introduction to activities Confrontation	All of the above

members will interact with each other in helpful and supportive ways. Communication skills refer to the basic interpersonal interventions that group facilitators can use to implement specific group facilitation skills.

The fundamental premise of the skills typology is that, as the group moves from one phase to the next, different group process characteristics, group facilitation skills, and communication skills will predominate. A corollary assumption is that appropriate group process, group facilitation skills, and communication skills must be utilized in each phase if the group is to satisfy its members' needs.

The organization of the typology may be compared to the construction of a house. The phases of a career decision-making group represent the foundation and framework of the typology. Group process, group facilitation skills, and communication skills represent the various kinds of building materials that are needed to complete the typological structure. Just as the carpenter's responsibility is to combine building materials around the framework of a house, the facilitator's responsibility in each phase is to integrate group process, group facilitation skills, and communication skills with the phases of the career decision-making group.

Internal Focus Phase. The purpose of the internal focus phase is to promote among group members clarification of their own decision-making characteristics. For this self-clarification to occur, the group facilitator, working in concert with the members of the group, must establish and nurture the group's facilitative potential. Realization of this goal requires that the group leader attend to the specifics of group process and use group facilitation and communication skills.

The facilitative potential of a career decision-making group is similar to the curative potential of a therapy group (Yalom, 1975)—it emanates from the group members' reasons for joining the group, from their interaction with each other and with the facilitator, and from the facilitator's readiness to lead the group. To enable members to begin self-exploration, the facilitator must work with them to create a safe, open atmosphere. During the internal focus phase, the key to the group's development is the leader's ability to attend to and facilitate group process—for example, introducing group activities, serving as a resource person, identifying the focus of discussion, stating feelings important to the group, facilitating group problem solving—and to model appropriate communication skills (see Table 2).

Career decision making begins with the awareness that one's present situation is unsatisfactory and that new alternatives need to be considered. This sense of awareness provides the stimulus for individual members to reflect on the circumstances and conditions that are contributing to their dissatisfaction and on the consequences of various alternatives. Reflection is an ongoing process in which group members examine their respective decision-making characteristics—for example, identity, self-esteem, decision-making style, personality characteristics, and developmental tasks. Group members' initial efforts at looking inward constitute the internal focus of the group. The leader's ability to utilize appropriate group facilitation skills can help maximize the impact of this phase.

Process characteristics that are important in the internal focus phase include norm development, expectation clarification, and group cohesiveness. Norm development refers to the evolution of agreements among group members that define certain behaviors, events, or activities in the group as appropriate and desirable and others as inappropriate or undesirable. Self-disclosure is an important norm that allows group members to feel free to share with one another their knowledge of themselves. Another valuable norm encourages group facilitators and members to express positive and negative feelings, thereby promoting both genuineness and spontaneity among group members. Giving and receiving feedback is also a desirable norm, enabling members to get a clearer picture of themselves. Finally, punctuality and attendance are essential norms, since a group cannot be effective if members are uncommitted to attending regularly and promptly.

The development of group norms is facilitated by the use of several group facilitation and basic communication skills. An effective introduction to activities includes describing each activity fully, describing the learning objectives or goals, and allowing members to respond to the proposal of the activity. A facilitator encourages group members to share by assisting them in sharing their thoughts and feelings and by helping them feel supported and understood. When using an external-and-internal focus, the facilitator helps members move the focus of discussion from events outside the group to events within the group. These group facilitation strategies may be realized through the selective utilization of all of the communication skills listed in the internal focus phase in Table 2.

The second group process characteristic is expectation clarification. Expectation clarification refers to the need to identify a set of expectations shared by all participants as to what will be accomplished in the group. Even though members enter groups for various personal reasons, if agreement about common goals is not reached, group members will be unable to agree about the importance of particular activities or topics or to invest themselves in the group. On the other hand, if members are able to identify common expectations, they are more likely to feel comfortable in the group and make a commitment to it. Examples of expectations shared by members include identifying a college major, reviewing career-related information, identifying new career alternatives, and improving self-understanding.

The expectation clarification group facilitation skill involves a two step process. First, the leader must help the group acknowledge and accept the diversity of expectations within the group; second, expectations common to all members must be identified. A variety of communication skills, including open-ended questions, primary-level accurate empathy, facilitative self-disclosure, and summarization of the group discussion, can be used for each step.

The third group process characteristic is group cohesiveness. Group cohesiveness refers to the degree of positive feelings group members hold for one another. Cohesive groups tend to be more productive and satisfying than noncohesive groups (Yalom, 1975). Inasmuch as the group is the primary means of promoting members' growth, it is essential that members invest themselves in the group. And, because members are disclosing their thoughts and feelings, strengths and weaknesses, values and beliefs to one another, members need to feel comfortable in making such disclosures.

Group leaders can facilitate group cohesiveness by identifying and stating feelings that group members may be experiencing, thereby enabling members with similar concerns to share their perspectives. Self-disclosures by group members may also be facilitated by relating disclosures to a common theme. Other communication skills that provide structure are giving directions, addressing open-ended questions to the entire group once a major theme has emerged, demonstrating primary-level accurate empathy, modeling self-disclosure, and summarizing.

External Focus Phase. The external focus phase of career decision-making groups is designed to make explicit the interpersonal, sociocultural, and institutional constraints associated with identifying alternatives and implementing decisions. This phase provides group members with the opportunity to field-test their tentative career decisions with other members of the group and to receive and evaluate the group's feedback. This feedback enables individual members either to gain confidence in their respective career decisions or to realize that additional planning may be necessary. Career decisions are not unilateral declarations made in a vacuum. Like most other decisions, career decisions are made within a social context that places very real restrictions on any decision. The purpose of the external focus phase of the group is to help members identify the factors that influence their career decisions and to encourage them to estimate the impact of those factors.

Identification of the factors that may prevent group members from implementing their tentative career decisions requires members to place themselves at risk before the rest of the group by visualizing themselves in a particular major, occupation, or setting; receiving interpersonal evaluations from other group members relative to the suitability of their characteristics for a particular position; identifying and verifying the factors that may prohibit the implementation of their plans; and specifying and evaluating alternative solutions. Members who are able to complete these group activities will be better able to realistically assess the advantages and disadvantages of implementing their decisions. On the other hand, failure to complete these purposefully designed tasks may prevent members from acquiring the information necessary to reach a clear decision in the first place.

In the external focus phase, members must collect and synthesize information external to themselves that is relevant to their decision—in particular, relevant to their relation to the work world. This information is frequently obtained from resource materials (for example, occupational briefs and career interviews), from family and friends, and from others in the group. As members gather and process information, they are encouraged to disclose their intentions and receive the reactions of other group members. In this process, some modifications of their respective decisions may take place. Thus, obtaining and evaluating the reactions of the members of one's group represents an important part of the decision-making process.

The external focus phase provides a unique opportunity for members to clarify their career decisions. The likelihood of group members profiting from this opportunity is directly related to the development of the group's facilitative potential. If the group has not developed its facilitative potential in the internal focus phase, group members will probably not be able to disclose their tentative career decisions or react openly to the plans of others. The group work to be accomplished in the internal focus phase cannot be postponed until the external focus phase.

If the group has achieved its facilitative potential, the emphasis of group process in the external focus phase is on group cohesiveness, norm development, and group member responsibility. The importance of both group cohesiveness and norm development is described in the previous section. The discussion of group process in the external focus phase, therefore, will be limited to group member responsibility.

Group member responsibility refers to members' determining for themselves what occurs in the group. Members typically feel more involved and feel that activities relate more directly to their individual goals if their ideas are incorporated into group activities. In the external focus phase, the career plans of group members constitute the focus of the group. Thus, all members should contribute to the group process.

In addition to using the group facilitation skills identified in the internal focus phase, facilitators may wish to utilize the skill of refocusing attention from the individual back to the group, a skill that involves listening, accepting, and responding to the experiences shared by members and then helping others who have similar concerns to share their perspectives. Career decisions are highly individualized decisions, a fact that the group facilitator and group members need to recognize and respect. Therefore, the group's internal focus must be maintained. On the other hand, the general factors that need to be considered and the steps that are typically employed in making career decisions are similar from one person to the next. These factors and steps, themes that are common to all group members, should be the target of the facilitator's efforts to refocus attention from the individual back to the group.

Because of the personal information being discussed, facilitators need to selectively utilize a number of different communication skills. Experience has demonstrated that additive empathy, mutuality, and immediacy are particularly helpful in moving the focus from the individual back to the group. As an example of mutuality, the group facilitator must communicate an understanding of the learning process of individual members, relating that understanding to the learning process of other group members and to his or her own learning process, as well. Similarly, in communicating to group members, both individually and collectively, an understanding not only of what they actually say but also of what they imply, the facilitator demonstrates additive accurate empathy.

Confrontation is another important group facilitation skill in the external focus phase. Although it is preferable that interactions among members and between individual members and the facilitator be complimentary, occasions will arise when members confront one another or the facilitator with their negative feelings. Confrontation involves challenging the discrepancies, distortions, and games in a member's career decision-making behavior in such a way that the member's self-understanding and, therefore, his or her chances of making satisfactory career choices are increased. With each of the skills mentioned, facilitators must examine and work in the here-and-now of the facilitator-group member interaction.

Synthesis-Action Phase. The purpose of the synthesis-action phase is the identification of action steps that members must take to achieve their career goals, followed by the implementation of those steps. This phase fosters synthesis of the awareness obtained in the previous two phases and formulation of individualized action plans. For example, based on the self-evaluation completed in the internal focus phase and the peer feedback received in the external focus phase, one may elect to enroll in an undergraduate program in social work. That decision is implemented by writing to ten universities that offer such programs to request a packet of admissions materials; evaluating those materials; and then completing and returning the materials to the universities chosen.

The crucial feature of the synthesis-action phase is that the participants' career decision-making behavior becomes more individualized. Having utilized the group process to assist in the identification of a career choice, members are ready to implement their individual decisions. Different members respond to the implementation process differently. For some, the implementation process confirms their decision; for others, the implementation process results in feelings of frustration and confusion. These differing responses place new demands on the group facilitator and group members.

The differential responses of group members to the implementation process necessitates differential treatment in the synthesis-action phase. For members who have their decisions confirmed, the group provides a source of support and encouragement for future work. In contrast, those members who are unsettled by the implementation process may need to talk about their experience in the group. Such a discussion will reflect the group process characteristics of the external focus phase; thus, both the facilitator and members must be prepared to respond to members on a personal basis.

Because of the individualized nature of the synthesis-action phase, the principal group process concern is group member responsibility. Every effort must be made to encourage group members to implement their respective career decisions. At the same time, however, group cohesiveness must also be maintained. Experience demonstrates that group cohesiveness is not a problem in the final group phase if it has been given the necessary attention in the first two phases.

The primary task of the group facilitator in the synthesis-action phase is to strike the appropriate balance between group member responsibility and group cohesiveness by implementing several group facilitation skills. For example, the facilitator may prepare members for participation in this phase by clearly identifying the goals of the activities of this phase and by providing specific directions for those activities. How activities are introduced to the group can prepare group members to take active responsibility for the execution and evaluation of those activities. For example, consider an activity requiring group members to research a career field and report their findings to the group. To ensure that group members complete these assignments, they are asked to commit themselves to their intentions in front of the group. In this way, the group utilizes behavioral group techniques (Thoresen and Potter, 1975) to shape and reinforce the efforts of its members.

Facilitators must also use other group facilitation and communication skills to support the process of group member responsibility. Facilitators must listen and respond to the reports of group members and assist other members having similar experiences or ideas to share their perspectives. Experiences needing to be shared may include discovering a lack of available information, realizing that a tentative career choice is no longer attractive, and identifying job prerequisites. Here again, the facilitator must be able to refocus attention from the individual to the group. However, the group facilitator will also need to help group members relate their individual circumstances and thus will need to use the skill of shifting from an external to an internal focus. For example, the group member who is dismayed to discover that the requirements for admission to a particular course of study are quite stringent may wish to express his or her concerns to the group and to solicit feedback from the other members. Finally, the facilitator or other group members may need to use facilitator-member or member-member confrontation to challenge some members of the group about their lack of willingness to follow through on their stated commitments or to assume more responsibility for the implementation of their tentative career decisions.

The unique characteristics of the synthesis-action focus phase require that facilitators have the ability to differentially utilize each of the basic communication skills, emphasizing different skills for different group member needs. For example, with members who are disappointed by their discoveries, the facilitator may wish to use attending, respect, mutuality, and additive accurate empathy. On the other hand, with members who have not completed their commitment to the group, the facilitator may wish to use open-ended questions, immediacy, and confrontation. The exact communication skill to be utilized will depend on the situation, the particular group member, and the skill level of the facilitator.

In review, the synthesis-action focus phase emphasizes implementation by group members of their tentative career decisions. As members implement their respective action plans, they experience and express differing reactions, which in turn require different responses from the other members of the group. The need for such differential responses places a special stress on the group, since the group must also continue to perpetuate group cohesiveness.

Training and Supervising Facilitators

Training and supervising facilitators of career decision-making groups is of central importance if a group program is to be established. During the past two years, we have conducted a training program designed to prepare graduate students to facilitate career decision-making groups for undergraduates who are undecided as to college major or career. The structure and content of the program are based on Harren's career decision-making model (1979) and utilize instructional materials developed by Harren and his associates (Buck, Daniels, and Harren, 1980, 1981).

The design of the training program is based on three principles (Daniels and Buck, 1981; Daniels and Moreland, 1980): trainees must possess prerequisite competence in the areas of group process, group facilitation skills, and communication skills as indicated in the skills typology for career decision-making groups; the training program should consist of both didactic and experiential components; trainees will learn to apply the skills typology in the career decision-making groups they lead if they first experience the application of the typology in their own training group.

A training program for potential facilitators who do not already possess minimum skills in group process, group facilitation, and basic communication can be developed. However, the training program discussed in this chapter assumes that the facilitator-trainees have had prior instruction in these three areas, as described earlier in this chapter. If trainees lack such preparation, too much of the training time is spent teaching those skills as fundamentals, and less training time is available to teach trainees how to apply the typology to maximize its effectiveness.

After the trainees are selected and before they are asked to lead a group, they should complete a training program in the utilization of skills typology for career decision-making groups. This training program includes the following goals: to acquaint trainees with the parameters of the skills typology, the Harren career decision-making model (Harren, 1979), and the Career Decision Making for College Students program (Buck, Daniels, and Harren, 1980); to provide a review of basic communication and group facilitation skills; to establish an instructional group for trainees that provides a basis of support and encouragement; to create an atmosphere conducive to peer feedback and supervision; and to provide experiential learning of each of the instructional modules, with an orientation toward the identification and resolution of potential problems in module implementation.

The training program used to teach the skills typology is designed to help trainees understand and integrate the parameters of the typology. Specifically, trainees experience the program at three different levels: as individual decision makers, as members of a decision-making group, and as facilitators of career decision-making groups. Each of these three levels provides special learning experiences. As individual decision makers, trainees use the Harren career decision-making model to examine their own career decision-making behavior. By participating in the trainee group, they have the opportunity to learn and practice facilitative group behaviors and to elicit information from other group members. And as group facilitators, trainees learn to differentially select and use the most facilitative interventions for particular situations in career decision-making groups.

The program is separated into four components: career decision-making program orientation and overview; internal focus group phase; external focus group phase; and synthesis-action group phase. Each of the four training program components consists of both didactic and experiential activities, with the amount of time spent on each varying from one component to another. As currently presented, the training program operates concurrently with the Career Decision Making for College Students program.

That is, the group facilitators receive instructions about, and experience with, the modules several days before they conduct the module in their respective groups. A description of each component of the program follows.

Program Orientation and Overview. The purpose of the orientation and overview component is to provide trainees with an introduction to the program and to begin to establish a sense of group cohesiveness. The first goal represents the didactic element of the component, the second the experiential element. The didactic element consists of a presentation of the Harren career decision-making model, the Career Decision Making for College Students program, and the skills typology for career decision-making groups. Get-acquainted activities that allow trainees to discuss their previous training and their expectations for this program comprise the experiential element. The orientation and review component requires two training sessions.

Internal Focus Phase. The purpose of the internal focus training component is to assist trainees in utilizing appropriate basic communication and group facilitation skills to identify and clarify the decision-maker characteristics of themselves and other training group members. This phase of the training program also serves to facilitate group cohesiveness. The component consists of seven two- to three-hour training sessions and includes approximately one-half of the modules of the Career Decision Making for College Student program. The purposes of the component are achieved through completion of the three parts of each training session: skills review and application; experience with the instructional module; and peer feedback and supervision.

The skills review and application section of the training session focuses on a review of the predominant communication skills and group facilitation skills needed to conduct the module. The relationship between the two sets of skills is reviewed didactically and trainees are then provided ample time to practice the skills. The skills are reviewed sequentially: giving directions and attending are reviewed in the first training session, and open-ended questions, empathy, genuineness, respect, concreteness, facilitative self-disclosure, and summarization in the second and subsequent training sessions. At least one-half of the time in each of the training sessions is allocated for skills review and application.

The instructional module provides trainees with a didactic overview of the contents of the module and the opportunity to participate in the activities of the module. To provide facilitator trainees with an opportunity to experience the role of group member, each module is introduced as it would be in the actual career decision-making group. The trainer portrays the role of group facilitator, modeling appropriate uses of group facilitation and basic communication skills, as well as of the skills needed to attend to the predominant group process of that module. Additional advantages of the simulation training technique are that it provides trainees with an opportunity to identify and resolve potential facilitation problems and that it allows trainees to follow group process as members through the evolution of the group. Approximately 30 percent of each training session is allocated for the experiential portion of the module.

Peer feedback and supervision allows an opportunity for trainees to identify the successes and failures of each module after they have conducted it in their respective groups. Attention is drawn to the appropriateness or inappropriateness of activities within each module, to the use or misuse of communication and group facilitation skills, and to the identification of the predominant group process. The feedback and supervision session is primarily experiential and is designed to further the skillful use of appropriate group facilitation and communication skills among the trainees and to promote the cohesiveness of the group. Approximately 30 percent of each training session is reserved for peer feedback and supervision.

External Focus Phase. The purpose of the external focus component is to provide facilitators with the opportunity to utilize appropriate basic communication and group facilitation skills in helping group members identify the interpersonal, sociocultural, and institutional constraints associated with selecting and implementing career decisions. In addition, this component continues to further the development of group cohesiveness. There are four two- to three-hour training sessions in this component, each divided into the same three parts as the internal focus phase: skills review and application; experience with the career decision-making modules; and peer feedback and supervision.

In its basic training format as well, this component is the same as the previous component. The difference between the two centers around the emphasis given to different skills and the utilization of different instructional modules. The skills review and application in the external focus phase emphasizes the skills of immediacy, mutuality, additive empathy, and confrontation.

Synthesis-Action Phase. The purpose of the synthesis-action component is to prepare trainees to help group members identify the action steps that must be taken to achieve career goals and to continue the development of the group. This component consists of three two-and-one-half hour training sessions that are similar in structure to the training sessions in each of the other components.

One of the characteristics of the synthesis-action group phase is the opportunity it provides trainees to practice the differential application of communication and group facilitation skills by role playing a variety of situations that trainees may encounter in actual career decision-making groups. For example, trainees may role play a situation in which they have to confront a group member who is not following through on his or her commitment to complete a task. Trainees not acting in the role play provide feedback to the trainees involved.

The rest of the training sessions, which concentrate on experiencing the career decision-making modules and providing peer feedback and supervision in the synthesis-action focus phase, are similar to the corresponding sessions of the previous training components, except that different career decision-making modules are utilized.

Evaluation

An evaluation of the Career Decision Making for College Students program was conducted over a three-semester period (Buck, 1981). Facilitators were trained utilizing the skills typology for career decision-making groups and the facilitator training program as described in this chapter. The facilitators themselves were not evaluated, but the effectiveness of the groups they led was assessed by a variety of measures. Inferences can be made as to the effectiveness of the training program and the facilitators' skills level by the changes measured in the subjects of the treatment group.

The treatment group consisted of freshman and sophomore students enrolled in a career development course using the Career Decision Making for College Students program as its core. A control group was composed of freshman and sophomore volunteers from an introductory psychology course who participated in the study for grade points.

The two groups were measured on a variety of personality and decision-making characteristics at the beginning and end of each semester. Three decision-making styles—rational, intuitive, and dependent—were assessed, as were self-concept, self-esteem, and anxiety level. These characteristics were further analyzed in relation to: expressed levels of satisfaction and certainty regarding choice of major and occupation; career indecision; and progress in selecting major and occupation. The research design was based on the theory and rationale outlined in the Harren model of career decision making.

Results indicated that the treatment program implemented by the trained facilitators was an effective one. At the end of the course, students in the treatment group indicated less use of the dependent decision-making style, less career indecision, greater satisfaction with selection of major and occupation, and increased certainty about choice of occupation than they did at the beginning of the course. At the same time, the treatment group showed a regression to an earlier stage in the choice of occupation. These results imply that group facilitators were effective in helping dependent decision makers learn other decision-making strategies, thereby enabling them to let go of premature or hasty occupational selections and recommence the process of choosing.

Additional research is needed to assess the effectiveness of group career decision-making programs by focusing not only on the group members but on the facilitators as well. Also, information as to the effectiveness of a particular career decision-making program for students with such specific decision-making problems as low self-esteem must be obtained if facilitators are to be able to maximize the facilitative potential of such groups.

Future Directions

The typology and training program presented in this chapter have great potential for the future because of their broad applicability. Both represent the integration of generic counseling skills with a specific area of content and the subsequent application of the integrated program to a specific kind of structured group. Thus, the skills typology and the training program may appropriately be classified as generic models that may be adapted—by changing the content of the models—to train facilitators to lead structured groups focusing on a variety of topics. The group process, group facilitation skills, and communication skills parameters could either be modified or retained unchanged.

Another contribution of the skills typology and the training program is that they each provide a theoretical foundation for those who wish to conduct research on the effectiveness of structured groups. Because of the generic nature of these two models, research efforts, like training applications, would not have to be limited to career decision-making groups. Moreover, because the skills typology and the training program identify specific group phases, researchers could investigate questions related to either group process or group outcome.

Structured groups will continue to be a popular method used by counselors to meet the needs of their clients. If counselors are to use structured groups effectively, however, they will need to be trained in a systematic framework for designing and facilitating those groups. Additional research will help refine the training program presented in this chapter and develop new training methods.

References

Babcock, R. J., and Kaufman, M. A. "Effectiveness of a Career Course." *Vocational Guidance Quarterly*, 1976, *24* (3), 261–266.

Bolles, R. N. *What Color is Your Parachute?* Berkeley, Calif.: Ten Speed Press, 1972.

Bolles, R. N. *Three Boxes of Life*. Berkeley, Calif.: Ten Speed Press, 1978.

Buck, J. N. "Influence of Identity, Anxiety, and Decision-Making Style on the Career Decision-Making Process." Unpublished doctoral dissertation, Department of Psychology, Southern Illinois University, Carbondale, 1981.

Buck, J. N., and Daniels, M. H. "The Centrality of Career in Adult Development." In V. A. Harren, M. H. Daniels, and J. N. Buck (Eds.), *New Directions for Student Services: Facilitating Students' Career Development,* no. 14. San Francisco: Jossey-Bass, 1981.

Buck, J. N., Daniels, M. H., and Harren, V. A. (Eds.). *Career Decision Making for College Students: Facilitator's Handbook.* Carbondale: Department of Psychology, Southern Illinois University, 1980.

Buck, J. N., Daniels, M. H., and Harren, V. A. (Eds.). *Career Decision Making for College Students: Student's Handbook.* Carbondale: Department of Psychology, Southern Illinois University, 1981.

Carkhuff, R. R., and Anthony, W. A. *The Skills of Helping.* Amherst, Mass.: Human Resource Development Press, 1979.

Carney, C. G., Wells, C. F., and Streufert, D. *Career Planning: Skills to Build your Future.* New York: D. Van Nostrand, 1981.

Daniels, M. H., and Buck, J. N. "Facilitating Career Development Through Small Group Process." In V. A. Harren, M. H. Daniels, and J. N. Buck (Eds.), *New Directions for Student Services: Facilitating Students' Career Development,* no. 14. San Francisco: Jossey-Bass, 1981.

Daniels, M. H., and Moreland, J. R. "Facilitator Training Program." In J. N. Buck, M. H. Daniels, and V. A. Harren (Eds.), *Career Decision Making for College Students: Facilitator's Handbook.* Carbondale: Department of Psychology, Southern Illinois University, 1980.

Egan, G. *The Skilled Helper.* Monterey, Calif.: Brooks/Cole, 1975.

Egan, G. *Interpersonal Living.* Monterey Calif.: Brooks/Cole, 1976.

Elder, G. H. "Family History and the Life Course." In T. K. Hareven (Eds.), *Transitions: The Family and Life Course in Historical Perspective.* New York: Academic Press, 1978.

Evans, J. L., and Rector, A. P. "Evaluation of a College Course in Career Decision Making." *Journal of College Student Personnel,* 1978, *19,* 162–168.

Figler, H. E. *PATH: A Career Workbook for Liberal Arts Students.* Cranston, R.I.: Carroll Press, 1975.

Figler, H. *The Complete Job-Search Handbook.* New York: Holt, Rinehart and Winston, 1979.

Gardner, J. N. "Developing Faculty as Facilitators and Mentors." In V. A. Harren, M. H. Daniels, and J. N. Buck (Eds.), *New Directions for Student Services: Facilitating Students' Career Development,* no. 14. San Francisco: Jossey-Bass, 1981.

Gould, R. C. *Transformations: Growth and Change in Adult Life.* New York: Simon and Schuster, 1978.

Harren, V. A. "A Model of Career Decision Making for College Students." *Journal of Vocational Behavior,* 1979, *14,* 119–133.

Harren, V. A., and others. "The Influence of Sex Roles and Cognitive Styles on Career Decision Making." *Journal of Counseling Psychology,* 1978, *25,* 390–398.

Harren, V. A., and others. "Influence of Gender, Sex Role Attitudes, and Cognitive Complexity on Gender-Dominant Career Choices." *Journal of Counseling Psychology,* 1979, *26,* 227–234.

Harris, J. "The Computer: Guidance Tool of the Future." *Journal of Counseling Psychology,* 1974, *12,* 331–339.

Ivey, A. E., and Authier, J. *Microcounseling: Innovations in Interviewing, Counseling, Psychotherapy, and Psychoeducation.* (2nd ed.) Springfield, Ill.: Thomas, 1978.

Jackson, T. *Guerrilla Tactics in the Job Market.* New York: Bantam, 1978.

Johnston, J. A., and Hansen, R. N. "Using Paraprofessionals in Career Development." In V. A. Harren, M. H. Daniels, and J. N. Buck (Eds.), *New Directions for Student Services: Facilitating Students' Career Development,* no. 14. San Francisco: Jossey-Bass, 1981.

Katz, M., Norris, L., and Pears, L. "Simulated Occupational Choice: A Diagnostic Measure of Competencies in Career Decision Making." *Measurement in Evaluation and Guidance,* 1978, *10,* 222–232.

Krimsky-Montague, E. "A Comparison of Two Approaches to Career Decision-Making Training." Unpublished doctoral dissertation, Department of Psychology, Southern Illinois University, Carbondale, 1978.

Levinson, D. J., and others. *The Seasons of a Man's Life.* New York: Knopf, 1978.

Lunneborg, P. W. "Sex and Career Decision-Making Styles." *Journal of Counseling Psychology*, 1978, *25*, 299-305.

Miller, A. F. "Relationship of Vocational Maturity to Work Values." *Journal of Vocational Behavior*, 1974, *5*, 362-371.

Moreland, J. R., and Buck, J. N. "Basic Principles of Group Process and Group Facilitation." In J. N. Buck, M. H. Daniels, and V. A. Harren (Eds.), *Career Decision Making for College Students: Facilitator's Handbook.* Carbondale: Department of Psychology, Southern Illinois University, 1980.

Parsons, F. *Choosing a Vocation.* Boston: Houghton Mifflin, 1909.

Rubinton, N. "Instruction in Career Decision Making and Decision-Making Styles." *Journal of Counseling Psychology*, 1980, *27*, 581-588.

Shingleton, J., and Bao, R. *College to Career.* New York: McGraw-Hill, 1977.

Smith, D. R., and Evans, J. R. "Comparison of Experimental Group Guidance and Individual Counseling as Facilitators of Vocational Development." *Journal of Counseling Psychology*, 1973, *20*, 202-208.

Smith, E. J. "Career Development Needs for Special Populations." In V. A. Harren, M. H. Daniels, and J. N. Buck (Eds.), *New Directions for Student Services: Facilitating Students' Career Development*, no. 14. San Francisco: Jossey-Bass, 1981.

Thoreson, C. E., and Potter, B. "Behavioral Group Counseling." In G. M. Gazda (Ed.), *Basic Approaches to Group Psychotherapy and Group Counseling.* Springfield, Ill.: Thomas, 1975.

Tofler, A. *Future Shock.* New York: Bantam Books, 1970.

Vaillant, G. *Adaptation to Life.* Boston: Little, Brown, 1977.

Yalom, I. D. *The Theory and Practice of Group Psychotherapy.* New York: Basic Books, 1975.

Part Four

Designing, Conducting, and Evaluating Skills Training Programs

The discussions presented in the first two sections of this book have largely been confined to existing skills training typologies and their accompanying training methods and materials. The purpose of this section is to present a comprehensive framework to guide prospective trainers in the design, delivery, and evaluation of skills training. The section addresses organizational issues, learning factors, training resources, and evaluation, all of which can significantly facilitate skills training.

The field has, for the most part, ignored the influence of organizational factors in the acquisition and subsequent use of helping skills. In Chapter Twelve, Pawlak, Thompson, and Way argue that factors within the delivery system are decisive determinants in the success of helping skills training programs. In addition to highlighting organizational factors that can hinder training, the authors present a range of practical suggestions designed to maximize support of skills training. For example, they describe the importance of conducting a pretraining assessment of critical organizational factors as a basis for establishing a supportive environment for training.

In Chapter Thirteen, Morton and Kurtz examine skills training in the light of widely held theories and current research on teaching and learning effectiveness and propose a contingency model for the design and delivery of skills training. Three dimensions—situational, task, and relationship—are considered to be critical in developing and presenting training. Whereas most skills training models emphasize task factors, the authors focus on the essential training role of the situational and relationship dimensions and identify factors heretofore largely overlooked—factors that merit attention in the refinement of existing training models and the development of new ones.

In Chapter Fourteen, Marshall, Charping, and Hogwood have compiled an up-to-date survey of training materials and resources, including a descriptive list, presented in Appendix B, of packaged programs, audiotapes, videotapes and films, simulation games, and organizations offering training programs. The authors present useful guidelines to assist readers in choosing relevant and appropriate materials from the selective list of over 250 entries.

In the final chapter of this section, Stone addresses two key questions: What needs to be evaluated in skills training, and how can it be evaluated? Suggesting that evaluation is multifocused, he stresses the importance of internal validity and examines different methods and perspectives in measuring and evaluating outcome.

Chapter 12

Assessing Factors that Influence Skills Training in Organizations

Edward J. Pawlak
Ina F. Way
Danny H. Thompson

This training is all well and good, but the supervisors just want us to follow the manual and forget the fancy stuff—A public assistance worker.

I really appreciated the trainer checking with us before the training started. We were given a chance to suggest what should be covered and how—An administrator.

Why did the counseling staff get trained before the supervisory staff? How can we coach or monitor the use of these skills if we haven't been trained yet—A supervisor of social services staff.

The training division at the central office is out of touch with the county staff, who actually work with clients—A county protective services worker.

To be successful, a trainer must not only have a well-conceived instructional design and be a master trainer of interper-

sonal helping skills (IHS)—he or she must also develop competence
in assessing the training request and the organization. Assessment of
the training request includes a study of the purposes and the type of
training desired by the administration. Organizational assessment
consists of an examination of organizational factors that may affect
an IHS training program, including goals, ideology, structure of the
training unit, hierarchy, and operating and governing procedures.
Such factors must be assessed to determine whether they will hamper
or facilitate the training program (Bertcher and Garvin, 1969; Goldstein, 1974; McGehee and Thayer, 1961).

IHS trainers must cope with organizational factors that may
hamper training because they usually have neither the opportunity
nor the leverage to intervene directly in the organization. However,
they may be able to intervene in the organization indirectly by informing the administration of organizational barriers to training. If
even indirect influence is not possible or appropriate, the training
program may be designed to mitigate some of those barriers. In any
case, chances for success are improved if both the planning and
development of the training program include an assessment of the
organization and the training request. Thus, the purpose of this
chapter is to raise the organizational consciousness of IHS trainers,
provide a framework and a set of guidelines to analyze organizational factors that may influence IHS training, and suggest strategies
for coping with those factors.

For the most part, the chapter is directed toward external,
rather than in-house, trainers, but the latter will also find it useful in
structuring an initial analysis of their organization. Not that in-
house trainers with experience in an organization should forego
organizational assessment—organizational assessment is not an
event but a process that must be responsive to organizational and
staff changes. However, as a trainer gets to know an organization, he
or she may not find it necessary to repeat all aspects of the assessment prior to every training program.

Unique Features of IHS Training

Before proceeding to a discussion of the training request and
organizational assessments, we must identify some of the salient

features of IHS training that guided us as we developed this chapter. These features must not only be recognized by the trainer but also conveyed to management in order to gain its support for an instructional design appropriate to the teaching of interpersonal helping skills.

The development of helping skills involves two primary behaviors, perceiving and responding (Gazda and others, 1973). These skills interact—the content of each helper response is influenced by the client comments that precede it. Before responding, the helper must "note those particular cues or clues in a situation needed to evoke one response, rather than another" (English and English, 1958, p. 290). Effective IHS training is participatory, actively involving trainees in discussions, sharing, and feedback (Ivey and Gluckstern, 1976). In contrast to other types of training, which may require only the cognitive participation of trainees, IHS training involves the use of self and requires trainee interaction on a personal level. For example, the public rehearsal of skills involves risk taking on the part of the trainee, who is given feedback and evaluation by fellow trainees or the trainer in a safe learning environment.

IHS training also consists of precise, highly codified material that is taught in a structured progression and must be integrated and practiced. Consequently, IHS training is best delivered incrementally, in a series of sessions; marathon sessions may result in limited trainee learning (Marshall, Charping, and Bell, 1977). Nevertheless, although IHS training involves learning correct responses, the sincerity and timing of responses are as vital as the content. The effective helper combines the objective helping skills with the more subjective use of self in interactions with clients.

In summary, IHS training involves transmission of precise material, participation, use of self, risk taking, practice and integration of skills, and public evaluation of practice trials. These features, as well as the approaches to IHS training discussed in detail elsewhere in this book, have a bearing on organizational assessment and on the planning and implementation of IHS training programs.

Assessment of the Training Request

When an external trainer is invited into an organization to conduct IHS training, two questions must be addressed: What is the purpose of the training? Will the trainer be asked to develop a specialized, individualized training program or to present a standardized, packaged training program that requires little pretraining involvement with the organization? The organization's answers to those questions will influence whether the IHS trainer accepts the offer to train the staff and, if it is accepted, how the training program will be designed and implemented. The flow chart in Figure 1 delineates the interaction of the various possible responses to those questions.

Purposes of Training

A primary factor to be considered by the trainer is the purpose of training, which may be conceptualized from two perspectives, the manifest and the latent. The manifest purpose of training is the official rationale that the administration communicates publicly to its staff. The IHS trainer must ascertain the basis for establishing the training priority for the particular unit or staff within the organization. For example, is IHS training a routine part of staff orientation designed to assist new employees in performing their roles? Is the purpose of training to improve current skills, help staff acquire new skills, overcome performance problems, cope with burnout, decrease mistakes, increase self-esteem as a competent worker, or increase job satisfaction and morale? Is participation in training programs a prerequisite to upward mobility? Occasionally training programs are viewed as perquisites of employment. "Increased skill and knowledge to be gained from training programs have in many cases become important fringe benefits in attracting employees to an organization" (Ackerman, 1968, p. 725). Sometimes a crisis may provoke an administration to undertake a massive training effort—for example, the publicized abuse of two different children while the parents were under the supervision of the department of social services spurred the development of training programs for protective service workers.

The manifest purposes of training must be assessed by the IHS trainer to determine whether IHS training objectives are congruent with those purposes. The organization's reasons for training, as communicated to the staff, influence their commitment to and participation in training.

The purposes of training also influence the construction of needs assessment instruments, the management of communication with prospective trainees, and the design of the training program, including the transfer of training to the work site. For example, IHS training that is part of a routine orientation for new staff would not be approached in the same way as IHS training directed toward workers who are experiencing a crisis. In the latter case, pretraining planning and preparation may require the formation of a staff training advisory committee, careful assessment and management of staff feelings about the crisis that precipitated the training, and careful selection of critical incidents that would facilitate transfer of training.

The latent purposes of training are the reasons for training that the administration may or may not have consciously formulated and that, if consciously formulated, it is reluctant to reveal to the staff. Latent reasons for training that are not consciously articulated are often inadvertently revealed by the administration's comments about the staff or about the training program. For example, an administrator with many new, young, professional staff members privately told a prospective trainer that she was being hired "to hold their hands." Shortly thereafter, the administrator realized what he had said and pledged the trainer to confidentiality. "Don't tell the staff what I said. They'll think I'm a paternalistic, patronizing boss." Some latent reasons for training are consciously formulated by the administration but are not revealed to the staff because disclosure would lead to staff resentment, morale problems, or conflict between management and staff. For example, staff members may be selected for training because they do not know their job or are performing poorly. Or the administration may select staff members for training in order to reduce tensions between supervisors and staff. Some training programs are publicized as routine orientation programs. However, on closer examination, the trainer may discover that educational and testing requirements for appointment to helping roles have been set too low to recruit qualified personnel who can perform competently on entry, and the organization has therefore had to mount a compensatory instructional campaign. Other training programs are developed in a perfunctory manner because

Figure 1. Flow Chart

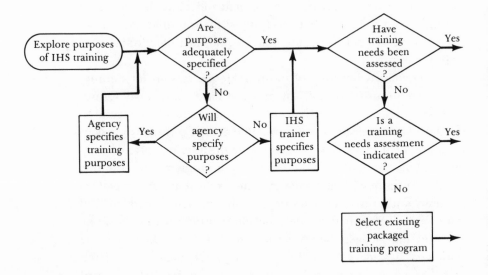

of Pretraining Assessment.

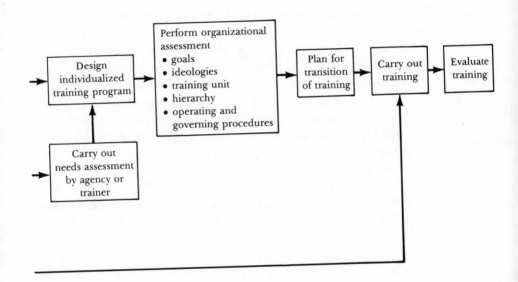

an organization must comply with contracts, personnel policies, or licensing or accreditation requirements.

Administrators do not necessarily have latent purposes for their training programs. Nevertheless, IHS trainers should be sensitive to the existence and staff awareness of such purposes, should anticipate their influence on trainees, and should assess trainees' views of the trainer and the training program. An incident that occurred in a training program led by one of the authors illuminates the importance of being sensitive to latent purposes. The workshop, attended by members of two different agencies, was manifestly intended to facilitate the management of clients served jointly by both agencies. During the second session of a four-session training program, one of the supervisors leaked information that the training was also intended to improve relations and communication between several staff members who were in conflict. The trainer had to discontinue the training temporarily in order to handle staff resentment about the hidden agenda; staff members felt that the administration should have handled the conflict straightforwardly rather than dealing with it indirectly in the context of a training program. The incident diminished the motivation and participation of several trainees.

In summary, the assessment of the request for training includes an awareness of the manifest and latent purposes of training. The manifest purposes of training are usually communicated to the IHS trainer when he or she is invited to develop a training program. The latent purposes may or may not be communicated to the trainer; he or she may only be able to detect them indirectly or accidentally. IHS trainers may discover the presence of latent goals by including in the needs assessment a few direct probes concerning supervisory and staff perceptions of the purposes of training. The value of such probes is revealed in the comment of one prospective trainee: "The management wants us to learn the new technology in order to control us by reducing the discretion we exercise with clients."

Needs Assessment

Needs assessment is a method of evaluating the request for training. Typically, it is a pretraining activity in which a prospective trainer or a training coordinator within the organization determines the needs or desires for training of prospective trainees. This information may be obtained by asking them directly, by conferring with their superiors, or by using both approaches (Morano, 1973). Training needs may be determined by comparing current skills levels with the levels expected by administration and/or staff. Specifically, training needs can be assessed by means of: analysis of practice problems; analysis of tasks staff are expected to perform; observation of staff performance; study of critical incidents; study of clinical records, audiotapes, or videotapes; assessment of formal education and prior training; questionnaires, surveys, inventories, paper-and-pencil tests; interviews or group discussions focused on staff experiences; and training advisory committees (Lawrie, 1979; Alber, 1979; Johnson, 1967).

IHS trainers may think that needs assessments are not necessary for IHS training. If one works with people, one needs IHS skills, the trainees either have or have not received IHS training, or, if they have acquired some skill through their own reading or practice, they will still need formal training to refine that skill. However, the fallacy of this position is that it views training solely from the standpoint of teaching a skill, rather than from the standpoint of a person who works in an organization.

Too often, needs assessments focus solely on the needs and desires of the individual or serve as measures of base-line skills at the time of entry into training. But needs assessments should also include probes as to whether the trainee anticipates any organizational obstacles to the training program and to implementation of the skills acquired during training. Lack of harmony between organizational and training goals, ideological conflict, the attitudes of management toward training, operating and governing procedures, and organizational climate may hamper training and the transfer of skills to the helping situation. (These factors are discussed in detail in the section on organizational assessment.) Needs assessments should also include probes about the unique characteristics of the prospective trainee's helping role and the exigencies of his or her practice. For example, what problems are you currently experiencing in your role as a helper that an IHS training program could help to resolve? The answer to this and other probes should influence the

selection of training exercises that will facilitate the application of
IHS skills to the trainee's work. Finally, needs assessments are a
means of determining staff readiness for and attitudes toward training. What are the consequences of being away from the office? Will
the work pile up? Will someone complete the trainee's tasks in his or
her absence? Can trainees attend training sessions without interrup-
tion? Do staff members take training seriously, or is it viewed as a
day off?

The needs assessment conveys to prospective trainees that
their perspectives are being considered in the development of the
training program. "To be credible in any organization, training has
to be planned properly. Further, it must be seen to be planned properly" (Peterson, 1978, p. 13).

Needs assessments are means of acquiring information about
trainees and their organization in order to plan a training program
responsive to the trainees and the organization. Some organizations
may not have the resources or may not wish to conduct a needs
assessment; other organizations may have their own training units
and personnel who conduct in-house needs assessments; still others
may delegate the needs assessment to the trainer. The importance of
these variations in operation are discussed in subsequent sections of
this chapter.

Individualized Versus Packaged Training Programs

The organization's orientation toward training can also be
assessed by an analysis of whether the organization supports individualized or packaged training programs. The concepts individualized and packaged, as used in this chapter, refer to the overall design,
plan, or approach an organization or trainer follows in the preparation and delivery of IHS training. Individualized training programs
are developed, planned, and implemented in response to the unique
needs of the organization. Packaged training programs are developed for general use with little or no modification from one organization to another or from one presentation to another.

However, packaged training programs are not synonymous
with off-the-shelf training programs. Most IHS trainers use some
form of off-the-shelf training programs, which are self-contained,

replicable, standardized, and available to the public. They typically consist of print and nonprint materials including training manuals, kits, specified training formats, films, and audio and video cassettes (see the list reviewed by Weinrach, 1977; also see Burstein, 1979). Off-the-shelf programs can be offered in a standardized, conventional manner in a packaged training program or in an individualized manner responsive to the needs of the organization. For example, Ivey's microtraining program has been offered in a standardized fashion to counselors (Ivey and Gluckstern, 1974, 1976) and has been adapted and individualized for social work students (Marshall, Charping, and Bell, 1977). Off-the-shelf programs vary in the range of skills taught and in the population toward which they are directed. Some programs focus on a single skill, such as empathy (Milnes and Bertcher, 1980); others focus on a number of skills (Mayadas and Umlah, 1975; Ivey and Gluckstern, 1976; Kagan, 1975). Programs target such various populations as public welfare workers (Marshall and Kurtz, 1980), police officers (Goldstein and others, 1979), and CETA counselors (Lyle and Nyer, 1976).

Thus, the concepts individualized and packaged refer to contrasting types or models of training. Organizational requests for training may correspond to the models described in this section; more frequently, however, such requests will correspond to elements of both models. In any case, the models have heuristic value in helping IHS trainers to structure their assessment of an organization's training request. A comparison of the features of these two approaches to training illuminates their differences.

Organizational support for individualized training programs is a strong indicator that the organization values ongoing training, has carefully defined the objectives of training, and has developed a systematic approach to training within the organization. In contrast, some organizations recognize the need for training but give it halfhearted support. Other organizations neglect training until they have experienced some problems in providing services to clients or until they realize they have not kept abreast of new treatment techniques. In the latter case, a packaged training program is often hastily sought as a short-range solution.

Packaged programs are not necessarily inferior, nor are they inherently ineffective. The instructional point of the comparison is

Table 1. Comparison of Two IHS Training Approaches

Individualized Program	Packaged Program
Pretraining assessment period required.	Little or no pretraining assessment required.
Assessment of request for training.	Training needs and skills levels are assumed, self-evident, or determined in an authoritarian manner.
Needs assessment and baseline measure of skills.	
Organizational assessment.	Little or no organizational assessment.
Training program designed for and adapted to the needs of the trainees and the organization.	Training design predetermined; staff and organization adapt to the training program.
Staff and management involved in planning the training program.	Staff and management involvement in planning is precluded by the fixed format or is voluntarily relinquished.
Transfer of training addressed—it is the responsibility of the trainer.	Transfer of training not addressed—it is the responsibility of the trainee.
Greater time commitment increases training costs.	Reduced time commitment reduces training costs.

that prospective IHS trainers who are asked to deliver a packaged program must at least conduct a modest or brief assessment of the appropriateness of the model for the staff and the organization. Moreover, trainers often wonder on what grounds to select an individualized or packaged approach. The organizational characteristics listed below may be used to help trainers assess whether one or the other approach to training is more appropriate for the organization that seeks their services.

Organizations with inexperienced staff members who have little or no formal education or in-service training in the performance of helping roles may not need an elaborate pretraining assessment. Under such conditions, requests on the part of the administration for a packaged training program may be appropriate. However, organizations with experienced staff who have formal education for helping roles or participate in continuing education programs

Table 2. Organizational Characteristics Supporting the Use of
Individualized or Packaged Training Programs

Individualized Program	Packaged Program
Helpers possessed of substantial or differing levels of formal education in the performance of helping roles.	Helpers possessed of little or no formal education in the performance of helping roles.
Ongoing in-service or continuing education program.	Little or no in-service training.
Experienced staff.	Inexperienced staff.
Availability of funds.	Limited funds.
Decentralized organization, low degree of formalization, participatory management.	Centralized organization, high degree of formalization, bureaucratic management.
Geographical clustering of staff.	Geographical dispersion of staff members into organizational subunits.
Flexible time limits on training.	Strict time constraints on training.

should participate in a pretraining assessment in which the IHS trainer discriminates different levels of skills, assesses the development that is underway, and plans IHS training accordingly.

Some organizations have limited training budgets and may not be able to afford pretraining assessment, whether performed by a staff member or by an external trainer. Occasionally the availability of funds is the decisive determinant of pretraining assessment, regardless of any other organizational characteristics.

Organizations with staff members who expect to participate in decision making and who exercise discretion in their work with clients are likely to respond unfavorably to a packaged program imposed by management. Such staff members are likely to want substantial involvement in the development of training programs. On the other hand, organizations with a bureaucratic, traditional, hierarchical approach to staff and with highly formalized staff-client relations may be able to offer packaged training programs with little or no resistance from staff.

Geographical clustering of staff may facilitate the development of an individualized training program by giving the external trainers access to the staff and its organizations during the pretraining assessment phase. Geographical dispersion limits such accessibility. In addition, strict time constraints on training may preclude the consideration of an individualized approach. For example, an organization that receives funds for a new program may be given a very short start-up time to train staff and launch the program.

The organizational characteristics identified earlier represent polar types of organizations. Although organizations do exist that resemble those types, most organizations do not conform neatly to either of the two models but have some of the characteristics of both. Organizations with most or all of the characteristics of one type are suited for an individualized or a packaged program. However, when an organization has some characteristics of each of the models, the appropriateness of a particular type of training is more difficult to assess. Awareness of the characteristics identified earlier may help them to negotiate accommodations to certain aspects of the pretraining and training activity. Or they may be able to manipulate variables that are under their control to neutralize factors or conditions imposed by management that may have an impact on training. In any case, by using those characteristics, IHS trainers can develop a profile of the organization to use in assessing whether the organization's approach to training is in harmony with its characteristics.

Prospective trainers must also carefully determine at which stage in the training process they have been hired and what organizational resources have been allocated to the pretraining activity. Organizations that have the staff resources to conduct the pretraining activity themselves may contact the prospective trainer only after an organizational and needs assessment has been completed (see the section "Structure of the Training Unit"). Thus, prospective trainers should not infer that an organization is not interested in individualized training just because the trainer is not asked to conduct the pretraining assessment. However, the organization should be willing to share its pretraining assessment with the trainer.

Organizational Assessment

Organizational assessment consists of an examination of the organizational factors that may affect an IHS training program, including goals, ideology, the structure of training units, hierarchy, operating and governing procedures, and the transfer of training. In this section, each factor is discussed, along with its implications for IHS training.

Goals

Organizational assessment begins with a review of the organization's formal and informal goals. Formal goals are usually found in such official statements as policies, bylaws, and planning documents. Informal goals, which are neither written nor official and may even subvert official goals, are reflected in operating procedures or in the intentions or agendas of organizational subunits or informal leaders (Perrow, 1974). IHS trainers must assess the degree of congruence between the formal and informal goals of the organization and the objectives of the IHS training program. Lack of congruence between goals and objectives may be revealed by prospective trainees who question the rationale for acquiring skills they may not be able to use. For example, a juvenile detention home childcare worker reported that it was useless to develop the treatment skills of childcare staff as long as the superintendent supported custodial-punitive, rather than rehabilitative, goals. IHS trainers who discover such incongruence have several options. They may have to confront management with the incongruence if it is marked and likely to lead to low trainee motivation or dissatisfaction. In extreme circumstances, they may even have to refuse to offer the training program. For example, one trainer refused to train volunteers in a young adult offender program because the program was poorly conceptualized and the volunteer handbook suggested that volunteers should inform the police if the offender reveals that he has committed a crime. A refusal to conduct the training program is a dramatic way of informing the organization that a serious problem exists. Such an organizational problem also raises the question of who is the client of the IHS trainer. Is it the organization? The trainees? The clients? Professional norms suggest that the client has preeminence.

Other, less extreme tactics may resolve divergence between goals and objectives. Sometimes the mere revelation of divergence is sufficient to induce an organization to undertake remedial measures.

Or additional consultation or training may be necessary prior to or concurrent with IHS training. If IHS trainers have little or no leverage to influence organizational change, and if training goals are not totally compromised, the IHS training program may still be implemented—in fact, the achievement of training objectives may spur needed organizational change. If nothing else, the divergence between goals and objectives may have to be honestly confronted at the first IHS training session, and trainees may have to discuss how to adapt their interpersonal helping skills in an organization that may not fully promote or support the use of such skills.

Ideological Conflict

To some helpers, theoretical orientation and treatment technologies are not solely means to therapeutic ends nor merely provisional or useful methods under selected contingencies but are also doctrines that bind and guide a group or a social movement. Theories and technologies are often imbued with such ideological and symbolic meaning that the introduction of a new mode of intervention leads to ideological conflict. Discord between group work and casework, treatment and community organization, and psychoanalytic and learning theories are just a few examples of such conflict. The controversy surrounding the introduction of behavior modification into social work is another example of this conflict (Bruck, 1968; Carter and Stuart, 1970). Practitioners who transform their theories and technologies into ideologies often become defensive and protective, viewing different technologies as competing with their own. For example, interpersonal helping skills have been characterized as atheoretical, too technique-oriented, not grounded in a clinical assessment, failing to teach the principles that underlie the appropriateness of a particular technique, and too basic for graduate students or experienced practitioners.

As trainers conduct an organizational assessment prior to the first training session, the views and attitudes of prospective trainees must be examined to assess their theoretical and technological orientation. The IHS trainer must also gain a sense of the ideological position of the organization, as individuals are attracted to organizations with congruent ideologies. Both the cognitive and emotional aspects of this commitment must be considered.

Because an ideology has collective aspects and encompasses not just individuals but whole organizations, the IHS trainer must consider the impact of introducing interpersonal helping skills into the organization. An issue that must be addressed is whether such skills can be assimilated smoothly into the organization's overall functioning or whether the degree of ideological conflict or resistance is too great to surmount. Elaborate means need not be devised to assess ideological commitment; a forthright inquiry may evoke a forthright response. However, indirect probes may have to be made if the IHS trainer senses that the organization or staff are withholding information because they wish to be gracious to a helper from another camp or because they are loath to admit that they are not eclectic. Indirect probes may also be necessary if the trainer detects differences between management and trainees in ideological commitment or in their perceptions of the manifest and latent functions of training. If trainees perceive that the latent function of training is conversion of staff to management ideologies, they are likely to be resentful, and the IHS trainer will undoubtedly experience a strained training session and resistive trainees. Indirect probes may include inquiries about the formal education and training history of prospective trainees; the educational institutions from which they have been recruited; the organization's publications and library acquisitions; and luminaries and schools of thought attractive to the organization or the trainees. The concepts and imagery used to describe and assess clients and the helping process in conversations or in case records also reveal the type and degree of commitment to a particular theory or technology. The inclusion of a few probes on a needs assessment instrument is yet another way of measuring commitment.

Structure of the Training Unit

Specialized organizational training units have different names, functions, staffs, resources, and modes of operation and may be known as personnel, in-service training, staff development, manpower, or continuing education departments. In large organizations, especially those that have geographically dispersed regional or county offices, training personnel may be located not only in the central office but also in local offices, and training units may specialize according to their program area or function—for example, management development, contract compliance, or child welfare. In small organizations, little or no specialization exists, and the training function may be carried out by a supervisor as one task among many administrative assignments. In large organizations, training units usually have one or more persons who perform specialized training functions, and, for our purposes, we shall refer to them as training coordinators.

The responsibilities of training coordinators vary from one organization to another but usually include the development, organization, management, and evaluation of training. The way in which training coordinators conceptualize and perform their roles is not a matter of personal preference but is organizationally determined (DePhillips, Berliner, and Cribbin, 1960). Some training coordinators are bureaucratic functionaries who serve bureaucratic purposes and interests and have an authoritarian approach to the determination of staff training needs that may arouse staff resistance to the training program. Other training coordinators act as staff spokespersons and champion staff development and training needs to the administration. Some training coordinators come up through the ranks with little or no formal education in training but with extensive experience and familiarity with organizational problems. Such coordinators often train personnel from the operational areas in which they were formerly employed and, consequently, can serve IHS trainers as key informants about the knowledge and skills requisites of helping roles in the organization, about the operational and practice problems of helpers, and about reactions to training. Other training coordinators are hired from outside the organization and do little or no training but instead have responsibility for the administration of training activities. Such training coordinators often negotiate the general conditions of the training program with the IHS trainer but rely on other key informants or the prospective trainees themselves to provide information about needs, skills, and problems.

In any case, IHS trainers should recognize that training coordinators may influence the selection of trainers and trainees, the information flow between trainer and trainees, the attitudes of management and trainees toward the training program, and, consequently, the outcomes of the training program. Thus, it is imperative that IHS trainers analyze the role of the training coordinator to assess his or her impact on the training program.

Hierarchy

Organizational assessment must include an analysis of the hierarchical structure of the organization and the impact it may have on IHS training. Hierarchy in helping organizations merits special attention for three reasons: helping organizations typically have several levels of supervisory management—for example, supervisors I, II, and III, or chief psychologist and clinical psychologists I and II; the supervisory management is primarily directed toward enhancement of subordinate helping competencies; and supervisors have substantial power and authority to influence the practice of their subordinates and the adoption of innovations. In short, supervisors have operational control of the development of their staff. Thus, the success of an IHS training program rests heavily on its acceptance by supervisors, especially the first-line supervisors of the helpers who provide direct services to clients.

IHS training should therefore be provided to supervisors before it is provided to subordinates if both groups need the training. There are several reasons for granting priority to supervisors. If the practices and skills taught to subordinate trainees are consistent with the supervisor's, the subordinate trainees will be allowed to apply their new skills to the work situation. Further, the practice of new skills requires coaching and reinforcement. Thus, supervisors should be trained before their subordinates in order to facilitate the effective transfer of training and the diffusion of new skills into the organization's practices (House, 1967).

Supervisors should also receive priority for IHS training because they often jealously guard their prerogatives, do not wish to relinquish their training and coaching roles, and may in fact feel that the training of their subordinates endangers their position. If supervisors master the skills first and have a positive orientation toward the training program, they can acquire a sense of ownership in the training of their subordinates, whereas they are likely to feel resentful if subordinates are trained first.

One could argue that supervisors and subordinates be trained concurrently. Although concurrent training may be appropriate at times, hierarchical mixing—the formation of training groups composed of persons from different hierarchical levels of the organization—has many disadvantages and pitfalls. Although superiors and subordinates might be able to transcend the authority, power, and social distance associated with rank, the quality of interpersonal interaction in skills training, the public nature of the exercises and feedback, and the need for self-disclosure suggest that hierarchical matching may be more appropriate than hierarchical mixing. Hierarchical mixing will most assuredly impede the participation of subordinate trainees if their performance during training is evaluated by supervisors and if past organizational practices indicate that evaluations are used to influence promotion and merit decisions. Thus, hierarchical mixing may inhibit risk taking and participation in IHS exercises. Subordinates who are conscious of status differences may defer to their superiors or may feel they are under scrutiny even if they are not (Gardiner, 1967).

Supervisors may also feel constrained in hierarchically mixed groups. They may be reluctant to engage in exercises lest they reveal their inadequacies and thereby lose credibility as supervisors. On the other hand, supervisors who are quite skilled and demonstrate their helping prowess in the exercises may unwittingly discourage subordinates from engaging in practice trials because they feel that they cannot match the performance. In any case, as the IHS trainer negotiates the composition of training groups with administrators, he or she must assess whether hierarchical matching is necessary or desirable. Administrators may insist on hierarchical mixing when they cannot afford separate training sessions for supervisors and subordinates or when the number of supervisors is too small to justify a separate training session. Experience suggests that hierarchical mixing may be appropriate if both supervisors and subordinates have the same level of formal education or professional orientation and if the organization has egalitarian norms and traditions or an informal structure that transcends the social distancing of rank and office. In any event, IHS trainers can always ask the prospective trainees to express their feelings about hierarchical mixing, although experience suggests that some prospective trainees, who work under a bureaucratic regimen, are reluctant to admit they do not wish to mix. Apart from the hierarchical role problems, homogeneous grouping may be preferred over heterogeneous grouping because the IHS trainer may be able to develop a training program that is geared to the different skills levels of the supervisors and subordinates.

Operating and Governing Procedures

Organizations have rules, routines, procedures, norms, and traditions, collectively known as modes of operation or operating and governing procedures. Operating and governing procedures may be the result of formal official action or of informal agreements or regularities in behavior that evolve without conscious direction but have been accepted as organizational conventions. Organizational assessment includes an examination of operating and governing procedures that may have an impact on training.

Standardization and formalization are dimensions of organizational structure that may affect such operations as client entry into the organization, the flow of clients through the organization, staff-client exchanges and relationships, and staff discretion in work with clients. Standardization refers to the degree to which the organization performs its operations in a uniform, regular, routine manner. Formalization refers to the degree to which the organization has codified its practices and directives in writing in the form of rules, procedures, policies, and sanctions (Hall, 1977). State departments of public welfare are often characterized as the archetype of high standardization and formalization in their handling of eligibility determination with public assistance clients. Some public assistance workers have reported that their department's highly formalized and standardized intake process precludes the use of interpersonal helping skills (Social Security Administration, 1981). In contrast, mental health centers are viewed as exemplars of low formalization and standardization in their handling of patient requests for service. IHS trainers can assess operating and governing procedures by studying agency manuals, policy statements, workbooks, handbooks, forms, or memoranda or by observing the processing of a patient or client through the organization. If a needs assessment instrument is developed, the trainer may include probes concerning the impact of operating and governing procedures on the helping process.

Analysis of operating and governing procedures concerning training also merit the attention of the IHS trainer. How are trainees selected? Is training required or voluntary? What and how does the administration communicate to the staff about the training program? What results does the administration expect, and how are they communicated to the staff? Are trainees given sufficient notice as to the dates of the training? Is the trainee's performance in the training program made known to the administration? IHS trainers can assess the operating and governing procedures concerning training by examining relevant sections of personnel policies, by studying the organization's training manuals or guidelines, and by asking for copies of the administration's or training unit's correspondence with the staff about the prospective IHS training program. Interviews with the administration, the training coordinator, or former trainees are other sources of information.

Transfer of Training to the Work Situation

A vital consideration in the planning of interpersonal helping skills training is the manipulation of both the training effort and the organizational climate in order to facilitate maximum transfer of material and skills. "It is one thing to estimate the results of successfully implementing a training program; it is another to determine the likelihood of a successful implementation in a particular organization. The attitudes and general working environment of employees play a substantial part in producing the practical results that any training effort is intended to achieve" (Hart, 1978, p. 13).

Both the needs assessment and the organizational assessment will determine the potential for this transfer. The IHS trainer must first assess the types of barriers that impede maximum transfer of training and then determine the most productive approach to surmounting them. The IHS trainer may elect to maximize the potential for posttraining transfer of skills by exerting influence indirectly through the administration or directly through the design of the instructional program. The training program design is an excellent starting point to ensure maximum transfer of skills because the design is in the trainer's domain. Goldstein (1974) has reviewed several studies on methods for increasing transfer of learning to new situations. Those that have been adapted for application to IHS training include: maximizing similarity between instructional material and the actual helping situation; providing adequate practice and immediate feedback on performance of skills; presenting a variety of helping situations pertaining to the specific work site to facilitate integration and adaptation—for example, interviews with offenders or child-abusing parents; and identifying organizational and services delivery contingencies that influence the use of various helping skills—for example, formalized intake or the use of formal authority and coercive power in public assistance or correctional settings.

By consciously accounting for both organizational and individual variables, the trainer can develop a training program that facilitates maximum transfer of skills. An awareness of which skills are reinforced in the organization and which are punished is vital—congruence between what is taught and what is reinforced in the work situation will allow for maximum transfer.

Often impediments to the transfer of training cannot be addressed in the instructional design. The IHS trainer must then assess the potential for organizational tinkering with the administration or the trainees (Resnick and Patti, 1980). Frequently, though, the trainer will find that major organizational changes are not possible, and other strategies must then be considered. For instance, it may be desirable to develop an informal support group during the training program to provide continued support for the practice of new skills after the training ends. In one training program, a group of five first-line staff members formed a group that functioned as a vehicle for mutual support and attempted to influence the climate and philosophy of the organization. Involvement by the trainer in this type of activity does pose some obvious risks—management disapproval of an internal support group may generalize to the individual who facilitated its development.

Case Study

Now that each element of organizational assessment has been discussed, examination of a case example will help demonstrate the importance of assessing the training request and the organization.

The director of a county welfare department in a large metropolitan area expressed concern about the way in which eligibility determination was being carried out after receiving complaints about the treatment of individuals applying for public assistance. The director retained the services of an external trainer to conduct an IHS training program for the supervisors and workers. After the meeting with the director, the trainer decided to carry out a brief assessment of the factors relating to the performance discrepancy.

Sometimes organizations seek training because of a perceived performance discrepancy on the part of one or more groups of workers. Training is assumed to be the solution to the problem— that is, a discrepancy is assumed to exist between actual and desired worker performance because of a lack of knowledge or skill on the part of workers, a deficit assumed to be correctable through training. In many instances, such assumptions are warranted, and training of workers can be a solution. Too often, however, performance discrepancy is not affected by training because the workers' knowledge or skill is not the decisive factor; rather, the organization needs to conduct operations research to correct a basic flaw in operations. Therefore, it is important that an accurate assessment be made of the basis for requesting training, and the organization should be encouraged to seek alternative solutions if training is not the appropriate course of action for addressing the performance discrepancy. For example, IHS training would not be successful in ameliorating the performance discrepancy if the problem stemmed from a lack of basic knowledge and skill in substantive areas like food stamps or foster care or from certain administrative rules, regulations, or practices.

As a result of the assessment, the trainer in the case study obtained the following information.

A. *The Performance Discrepancy*
   1. Clients are complaining about the brusque, aloof, brief, and formalized way in which they are being treated when they apply for public assistance.
   2. Client advocate groups and several social agencies and politicians want the public assistance staff to be more responsive to clients.
B. *Organizational Factors*
   1. The state central office has increased its demand for a reduced rate of error in determining eligibility.
   2. The system rewards workers who strictly interpret the regulations governing eligibility, whereas workers who liberally interpret regulations are closely monitored and chastised.
   3. Applications for financial aid have increased dramatically without an increase in staff.
   4. There has been a 15 percent turnover in staff in the past year.
   5. Workers and supervisors have poor relationships, and the work setting is tense.
C. *Helper Knowledge and Skills*
   1. Workers have not received any training on the changes in the eligibility rules and regulations except through supervisory consultation.
   2. Most of the staff participated in workshops on interviewing and the helping process carried out by faculty from a local university during the previous year.

Clearly, organizational problems—the error rate, increased caseloads, staff turnover, and a lack of training on the changes in eligibility rules—are exerting substantial pressures on the staff that contribute to strained relationships with clients and supervisors. The development of an IHS training program under such conditions would only exacerbate the tensions and problems by placing the worker in a double bind—that is, the worker would feel pressure to be more responsive to clients at the same time that the administration is trying to reduce error rates. In this example, formal and informal goals, operating procedures, and hierarchy are the organizational factors that need attention before IHS training is implemented. Failure to identify the reasons for the performance discrepancy in the request for training can result in frustration for the trainer and trainees and in the failure of the training program to achieve its objectives. The results of an assessment can help the organization and the trainer evaluate the appropriateness and timing of IHS training and then engage in informed curriculum development designed to resolve the performance discrepancy.

Conclusion

At this point, the reader may feel overwhelmed by the complexity of assessing the training request and the organization. Pretraining assessment of several organizational factors has been given scrupulous attention in order to sensitize IHS trainers to those that may facilitate or hamper the training program. However, IHS trainers will not necessarily have to contend with all these factors, nor must trainers necessarily have large amounts of time for pretraining assessment. Our experience suggests that certain organizational factors are more decisive determinants than others, and the decisive factors vary among organizations and training situations. Thus, trainers typically have to contend with only one or two organizational factors. In any case, the more factors the trainer must manage, the more time will be needed for an adequate pretraining assessment.

Our experience also suggests that elaborate devices and instrumentation are not necessary in assessing the training request and the organization. Some aspects of the assessment can be completed by reading organizational documents, reports, and memoranda. Needs assessment instruments and brief pretraining surveys can also be used. Much of the assessment can be completed in interviews with the administration, the training coordinator, or a few trainees. In fact, some of the more insightful assessments have occurred during casual, informal talks with staff members. Often the administration or the training coordinator is sensitive to organizational constraints on training and shares them candidly with the trainer. If the organization is reluctant or unwilling to share its own assessments, incremental inquiries are more productive than interrogation begun during training negotiations.

In conclusion, assessment of the training request and the organization provides IHS trainers with an opportunity to control factors that may influence the effectiveness of their training programs. Accordingly, assessment is an activity that is well worth the time and support of IHS trainers.

References

Ackerman, L. "Training Programs: Goals, Means, and Evaluation." *Personnel Journal*, 1968, *47*, 725–727.

Alber, A. F. "How (and How Not) to Approach Job Enrichment." *Personnel Journal*, 1979, *58*, 837–841, 867.

Bertcher, H., and Garvin, C. *Staff Development in Social Welfare Agencies*. Ann Arbor, Mich.: Campus Publishers, 1969.

Bruck, M. "Behavior Modification Theory and Practice: A Critical Review." *Social Work*, 1968, *13*, 43–55.

Burstein, B. "Guidance Formats for Modifying Interpersonal Communications." Unpublished manuscript, Department of Psychology, University of California, Los Angeles, 1979.

Carter, R. D., and Stuart, R. B. "Behavior Modification Theory and Practice: A Reply." *Social Work*, 1970, *15*, 37–50.

DePhillips, F. A., Berliner, W. M., and Cribbin, J. J. *Management of Training Programs*. Homewood, Ill.: Irwin, 1960.

English, H. B., and English, A. *A Comprehensive Dictionary of Psychological and Psychoanalytical Terms*. New York: Longmans Green, 1958.

Gardiner, G. R. "Special programs." In R. L. Craig and L. R. Bittel (Eds.), *Training Development Handbook*. New York: McGraw-Hill, 1967.

Gazda, G. M., and others. *Human Relations Development: A Manual for Educators*. Boston: Allyn & Bacon, 1973.

Goldstein, A. P., and others. *Police Crisis Intervention*. Elmsford, N.Y.: Pergamon Press, 1979.

Goldstein, I. I. *Training: Program Development and Evaluations*. Monterey, Calif.: Brooks/Cole, 1974.

Hall, R. *Organizations: Structure and Process*. Englewood Cliffs, N.J.: Prentice-Hall, 1977.

Hart, S.J.S. "Determining Training Priorities." *Journal of European Industrial Training*, 1978, *2*, 12–15.

House, R. J. *Management Development: Design, Evaluation, and Implementation*. Ann Arbor: Bureau of Industrial Relations, Graduate School of Business Administration, University of Michigan, 1967.

Ivey, A. E., and Gluckstern, N. B. *Basic Attending Skills: Participant Manual*. North Amherst, Mass.: Microtraining Associates, 1974.

Ivey, A. E., and Gluckstern, N. *Basic Influencing Skills: Leader and Participant Manuals*. North Amherst, Mass.: Microtraining Associates, 1976.

Johnson, R. B. "Determining Training Needs." In R. L. Craig and L. R. Bittel (Eds.), *Training and Development Handbook*. New York: McGraw-Hill, 1967.

Kagan, N. *Interpersonal Process Recall: A Method of Influencing Human Interaction* (Rev. ed.) East Lansing, Mich.: Mason Media, 1975.

Lawrie, J. W. "A Guide to Customized Leadership Training and Development." *Personnel Journal*, 1979, *58*, 593–596.

Lyle, B. R., and Nyer, L. *Communication*, CETA Counselor Training Project, University of Texas at Austin, 1976.

McGehee, W., and Thayer, P. W. *Training in Business and Industry*. New York: Wiley, 1961.

Marshall, E. K., Charping, J. W., and Bell, W. J. "Training in Basic Interpersonal Helping Skills: An Adaptation of the Microtraining Model." Paper presented at the showcase session "Teaching of Communication Skills" at the annual program meeting of the Council on Social Work Education, Phoenix, Ariz., Feb. 1977.

Marshall, E. K., and Kurtz, D. *Interviewing Skills for Family Assistance Workers: Instructor's Manual*. Knoxville: Office of Continuing Social Work Education, University of Tennessee, 1980.

Mayadas, N. S., and Umlah, D. *Step-by-Step*. Arlington: Human Resource Center, University of Texas, 1975.

Milnes, J., and Bertcher, H. *Communicating Empathy*. San Diego, Calif.: University Associates, 1980.

Morano, R. "Determining Organizational Training Needs." *Personnel Psychology*, 1973, *26*, 479–487.

Perrow, C. "The Analysis of Goals in Complex Organizations." In Y. Hasenfeld and R. A. English (Eds.), *Human Service Organizations: A Book of Readings.* Ann Arbor: University of Michigan Press, 1974.

Peterson, B. "Training by Design." *Canadian Training Methods,* 1978, *11,* 12-14.

Resnick, H., and Patti, R. *Change from Within: Humanizing Social Welfare Organizations.* Philadelphia, Pa.: Temple University Press, 1980.

Social Security Administration. *Human Relations Skills for Eligibility Caseworkers: Texas Department of Human Resources.* Washington, D.C.: Social Security Administration, 1981.

Weinrach, S. G. "Training Packages." *Personnel and Guidance Journal,* 1977, *55* (10), 612-618.

Chapter 13

Conditions Affecting Skills Learning

Thomas D. Morton
P. David Kurtz

Over two decades ago, Rogers (1957) lamented that the training procedure in the field of psychotherapy was "characterized by a rarity of research and a plenitude of platitudes" (p. 76). A decade later, Matarazzo, Wiens, and Saslow (1966) reviewed the literature on the training of psychotherapists and concluded, "There is essentially no published research regarding the teaching of psychotherapy, the supervisory process, how learning effective psychotherapy takes place, and how to teach psychotherapy efficiently" (p. 608). In recent years, ambitious research into the efficacy of various training procedures has provided significant alternatives to the conventional method for training psychotherapists, which primarily involved the acquisition of a solid theoretical foundation through an intensive series of lectures and seminars prior to engaging in treatment with patients. The experiential component of this method facilitated learning through student recall and analysis of events and processes that transpired in the treatment session and through the therapeutic nature of the supervisory process. Trainee-supervisor sessions were a means for enabling the student to work through the phenomena of transference and countertransference with the supervisor, and learners were expected to generalize this experience to their treatment relationships.

Rogers (1957) was perhaps the first major figure to deviate from the traditional training format. He and his colleagues developed brief, experiential workshops for training psychotherapists and attempted to evaluate the effectiveness of workshops (Blacksma and Porter, 1947). His pioneering model was based on a series of graduated experiences in which trainees listened to tape-recorded interviews of experienced therapists, role played the helper with fellow trainees, viewed live demonstrations by the trainer, participated in group therapy, discussed with their supervisor recordings of their own patient interviews, and received individual therapy. Rogers's original effort was the basis for the human relation training model. Truax, Carkhuff, and their collaborators (Truax, Carkhuff, and Douds, 1964; Truax and Carkhuff, 1967; Carkhuff, 1969) developed and researched a didactic-experiential approach significantly refining Rogers's format. They derived from Rogers's necessary and sufficient conditions of empathy, unconditional positive regard, and genuineness a series of verbal qualities deemed essential for establishing a helping relationship. The initial training format included several central training elements: a therapeutic context led by a trainer who demonstrates a high level of therapeutic conditions; didactic training in the implementation of the helping conditions; discrimination training to enable learners to identify qualities that differentiate successful from unsuccessful helpers; graduated practice experience and structural evaluation of learner performance; and a quasi-group therapy experience in which discussion centered around the difficulties of trainees in their role as therapists.

Ivey and his colleagues (Ivey and others, 1968) developed another significant variant of the didactic-experiential approach called microtraining. Rather than teaching verbal qualities, Ivey identified a set of specific verbal and nonverbal response categories, or interpersonal helping skills. He relied more heavily than his predecessors on principles of learning and the psychoeducational model of helping in formulating microtraining. Perhaps the most significant microtraining innovation was the extensive use of practice accompanied by videotape feedback.

Virtually all systematic interpersonal skills training programs have evolved from either the client-centered, the didactic-
experiential, or the microtraining format, and most follow a format
consisting of some combination of didactic instruction, demonstration, role play, and practice with feedback. Although the field of
psychology has been largely responsible for the development of
these programs, the basic training format has been adapted to train
professionals from a range of fields, such as medicine, education,
nutrition, social work, law enforcement, and business. However, the
extensive application of this format to a variety of settings has, in
many instances, preceded validation of the usefulness of skills in
those settings, particularly in nonpsychotherapeutic helping situations such as public welfare.

Most evaluations of the various models indicate that experimental groups are superior to controls in the acquisition of a range
of interpersonal helping skills. Although Rogers might now be
heartened by the plenitude of training model development and evaluation, Matarazzo (1978) notes that, despite the number of studies,
there has been no "giant leap forward." She attributes the lack of
notable innovations to the great complexity of research in this area.

Toward a Model of Instruction for
Interpersonal Helping Skills Training

Although designers of skills training models have borrowed
heavily from learning theory and especially from social learning
theory, a comprehensive model for instructional development and
skills training has yet to be devised. Most studies of skills training
have been concerned with the relative effectiveness of different training formats and have not examined the processes and factors within
those formats that contribute to different effects. To improve instructional effectiveness, intervening variables must be identified
and sources of variance determined. A contingency model drawing
on leadership research and research into interpersonal influences on
learning seems to offer a cohesive and comprehensive way of approaching the design and delivery of interpersonal helping skills
training and of guiding further research.

Contingency models of leadership stress three sets of factors that determine an appropriate leader response: leader task behaviors, leader relationship behaviors, and situational characteristics. Leadership has been defined as the activity of influencing the behavior of an individual or group toward the attainment of a specified goal in a given situation (Hersey and Blanchard, 1977). Leadership effectiveness is a contingent interaction among leader characteristics and behaviors, follower (individual or group) characteristics and behaviors, the goal, and other situational characteristics. Early research on leadership and teaching sought to determine traits that characterize good or effective leaders and teachers (Witty, 1974; Turbeville, 1965). However, as Jennings (1961) has noted, fifty years of study have failed to produce one personality trait or set of qualities that can be used to discriminate effective from ineffective leaders. As leadership research began to focus on behavior, two sets or dimensions of behavior were discovered that together form a composite of leader behavior. One dimension is called initiation or structure (task) and the other, consideration (relationship) (Fleishman and Harris, 1962). Structure includes leader behaviors that organize and define activities, set goals, plan and assign tasks, and define means of achieving goals. Consideration involves relationship-oriented behavior—including mutual trust, respect, and warmth between the leader and the group—and emphasizes a concern for group members' needs.

In later works, Fiedler (1964), Vroom and Yetton (1973), and Hersey and Blanchard (1977) added to this framework, suggesting that various situational factors determine the extent to which the leader should be task-oriented (structure) or relationship-oriented (consideration). This contingency model of leadership effectiveness stresses that a great number of environmental factors, such as the task maturity of the follower, group cohesiveness, and the nature of the task, determine the type of leader behavior that is more or less effective in a given set of circumstances.

Bidwell (1973) notes that teaching is a social process. "It cannot occur except through interpersonal exchange, and these interpersonal relationships have both a social and a normative structure that are contained within a broader social and moral order" (p. 413). Except for random, trial-and-error learning, almost all formal learning episodes involve some degree of interpersonal facilitation between teacher and learner. "Learning is a change in human disposition or capability which can be retained and which is not simply ascribable to the process of growth" (Gagne, 1965, p. 5). The goal of training or teaching is learning. In light of Bidwell's perspective on teaching as an interpersonal exchange, teaching effectiveness, which is determined by the extent to which the trainer influences learning, can be considered markedly similar to leadership effectiveness, which is determined by the extent to which the leader influences individual or group behavior toward a goal.

According to this perspective, both the design and delivery of training take into account three interacting dimensions: a task or structural dimension, a relationship or consideration dimension, and situational factors that serve to moderate and influence the desired amounts of both task and relationship. In terms of instructional design, structural tasks include the analysis of conditions required for performance, the design of instructional activities and appropriate sequences of learning, and the formulation of objectives for each instructional activity and for the overall sequence. Relationship design tasks include an analysis of issues related to trainer-learner interaction, assessment of learner needs, and analysis of learning activities and materials and their implications for trainer-learner and intragroup relations. Analysis of situational factors in instructional design includes such components as commitment of the sponsoring agency to the training; the circumstances surrounding how the learner came to be involved in the learning experience; the resources available for training, including funding, equipment, room size, and amount of time available for learning; the context of the learner's life situation; and the entering skills level of the learner.

Applied to instructional delivery, each of these three dimensions has similar implications. Task factors include specific trainer behaviors used to guide the instructional process—for example, the cuing of recall of prerequisite learnings; the presentation and sequencing of learning activities; feedback and reinforcement, or group facilitation; and maintenance and generalization of change. Relationship factors include establishing an appropriate climate for learning, building learner-trainer trust and trust among group members, and responding to the learner's needs as the learning process develops. Situational factors include the training environment, changes that occur in this environment, interactions among learners and between the trainer and learners, the impact on the learner of the training pace, learner acquisition of enabling skills, and related variables.

The remainder of this chapter explores each of these three dimensions in more detail, presenting a theoretical perspective for each as it relates to design and delivery of instruction, as well as practical implications for the design of learning experiences.

Situational Considerations in the Design of Instruction

If learners possess prerequisite competencies, adequately developed learning skills and attitudes, and positive attitudes towards the training content, interpersonal helping skills acquisition will proceed efficiently. However, deficits in prerequisite knowledge or competencies (for example, a lack of sensitivity to cultural variations in communication patterns), deficient learning skills and attitudes (for example, strong resistance to participating in role plays), and attitudes in conflict with the effective use of helping skills (for example, the belief that helping entails advice and direction giving but not an empathic ear) can severely hinder or even block learning. "If I had to reduce all of educational psychology to just one principle, I would say this: The most important single factor influencing learning is what the learner already knows; ascertain this and teach him accordingly" (Ausubel, Novak, and Hanesian, 1968, p. 1).

Learners' predispositions include their cultural background, referent groups, developmental stage and age, prior learning experiences, relationships with other learners, expectations about the present training, and overall satisfaction with their job or schooling. These predispositions have critical implications for the design and delivery of the training. For instance, experience with an insensitive trainer can alienate learners from similar programs; in the design of further training for such a group, considerable time and attention would need to be directed toward diffusing this alienation and building credibility. Another example is the considerations involved in planning training for adult learners. In recent years, considerable attention has been given to adult developmental factors and their effects on adult involvement in educational experiences. Adult learning theorists (see, for example, Knox, 1977) advocate the participation of adults in the design and delivery of training. Thus, rather than the traditional, complementary teacher-student roles, symmetrical roles based on an egalitarian relationship may be more appropriate. "Adult learners are usually more effective when an adult-adult relationship, in which the purposefulness of learner's participation and the relationship of the learner role to other adult life roles is recognized, exists among the learners and between the teacher and group members than when a superordinate-subordinate relationship is established" (Irish, 1980, p. 50).

Creativity and thinking, as partly determined by brain hemisphericity, affect learning styles, which in turn have implications for the design of training tasks (Torrance and Mourad, 1979). Experiential learning may be frustrating to cognitively oriented learners but not to persons disposed to experiential learning. Mayadas and Duehn (1977) suggest that a critical learner characteristic in acquiring helping skills is cognitive complexity, which is the individual's ability to make interpersonal discriminations. They discovered that "videotape feedback without modeling is sufficient for training students high in cognitive complexity, . . . whereas their low-scoring counterparts required not only corrective videotape feedback but also the additional external cues displayed in modeling formats in order to incorporate these content skills" (p. 157).

Finally, issues of school and job satisfaction are brought to training settings. Many agency trainers relate spending the beginning hours of training programs diffusing learner hostility to such issues as being ordered to come to training, frustration with supervision and agency policies, perceptions of helplessness on the job, and a reluctance to learn anything new because "it won't make any difference anyway."

The social organizational characteristics of the learning environment have their own impacts on training. "There is now a substantial body of findings apparently demonstrating that colleges or college fields of study have distinctive patterns of social organization, that they also have distinctive effects on students' values and aspirations, and that these effects can be attributed to interaction with teachers or peers" (Bidwell, 1973, p. 440). This same effect is no doubt true of training being conducted for employees of an organization.

A key organizational factor is the commitment of the organization to the instructional program. Lack of commitment is a frequently cited reason for training program failure (Reid and Beard, 1980). College and agency commitment to training is an integral part of the curriculum or staff development program and the adequacy of its resources. One of the most important indications of genuine commitment is the extent to which an agency supports the transfer of skills from the training environment to the field practicum or work situation. The agency's support of skills retention and transfer has implications for the type of tasks that are built into the delivery of instruction. Copeland (1977), for example, found that, although microtraining was sufficient to train prospective teachers to competently use certain attending skills in the training setting, successful transfer of the skills to the student teacher practicum was dependent on either the supervising teacher's modeling of the skills or reinforcement for the student teacher's use of the skills in the classroom. Clearly, if the goal of training is to increase the learner's use of helping skills on the job, the training process cannot terminate with the last hour of formal instruction but must include support from the work environment, which depends in turn on the organization's commitment to the training program.

The social organization also influences the purposefulness with which the learner enters training. Students enrolled in a required course may reflect a different level of interest from those who have selected a course as an elective. Similarly, voluntary participation by agency employees sets the stage for a viable relationship with the trainer and an openness to the learning process. In contrast, if workers are ordered to attend training, the trainer often has significant and in some cases insurmountable barriers to overcome before learning can occur.

Although inherent in the position of trainer is some degree of expert and referent power, the social organization can enhance or detract from the trainer's status and power. Agency-based trainers are largely dependent on the learners' respect for the trainers' expertise and on their ability to develop rapport with learners. At the college level, grades, honors, and the threat of disapproval or expulsion are derived from the socially legitimate power of the school to influence the conduct of its students. Agency-based training must therefore place a higher premium than college-level teaching on the development of personal influence in order to facilitate learning.

Referent groups, as well as the broader culture, set standards for an individual's commitment to education. McClelland (1961), in writing about the "achieving society," comments that, at certain times within certain cultures, one finds a flowering of achievement motivation strongly supported by the society and its institutions. To the extent that culturally determined values and beliefs are shared by trainer and trainee, their relationship is likely to be solid and stable and the trainer's personal influence maximal. However, if values and beliefs are not held in common, then an imbalance in the relationship exists, and training methods for building mutual respect and rapport will need to be incorporated into the delivery of instruction.

The location, time, and length of training and the composition of the training group are also factors influencing teaching effectiveness, particularly for agency staff trainees. Although no documentation exists, experience suggests that training programs located in an agency facility provide a less-conducive learning climate than those given in a setting outside the agency. Apparently, an agency setting occasions work-oriented responses that interfere with participants' undivided attention to the training program.

The training schedule is another situational factor that affects learning. The commonly employed one-day workshop, although compact and transportable, presents serious problems for both trainer and learner and has contributed to much abuse of known principles of learning and instruction. The marketing of programs in a one-day package implies that brief, self-contained learning experiences can facilitate learning that is transferable to the work setting. Although learning certainly does occur under such circumstances, whether such training enhances retention and transfer of learning is questionable. The workshop format does not provide for spaced learning, participants are often subject to fatigue, and virtually no outside instructional tasks, such as readings and homework assignments, are given to supplement the workshop activities. By contrast, college classes and practicums, in which learning episodes are generally short and continue over a period of weeks or months, do not possess these inherent drawbacks.

Another significant aspect of the training schedule is the amount of content included in the session. Typically, the purchaser of the training is concerned with maximizing the amount of material covered in the allotted time, and the trainer may therefore tend to crowd a session with too much content, contributing to a superficial presentation of many complex concepts. Although this approach may enhance the breadth of subject matter, it ignores the role of overlearning in the transfer of newly acquired knowledge and skills. Transfer of learning is the thorniest problem facing training programs. Overlearning through such methods as repeated practice of skills in a variety of circumstances is perhaps the most important ingredient in facilitating transfer. The choice of training program time and length influences the instructional task options open to the trainer.

A frequently overlooked but potent instructional variable is the composition of the training group, particularly when the focus of instruction is interpersonal helping skills, which involve self-exploration, self-disclosure, and possible peer critiques. The group's dynamics—norms, cohesion, roles, power, and communication patterns—significantly influence members' openness to and involvement in training. Cultural similarity, familiarity, and prior relationships among learners affect those dynamics. For example, the inclusion of supervisors with supervisees in training can have a positive or detrimental impact, depending on the nature of their previous interaction and how the trainer intends to involve each in the training program. If the supervisor is permitted to sit back and play a watchdog role, the supervisees may feel stifled in their willingness to open up and be angry at the supervisor's unwillingness to take risks. On the other hand, a supervisor who participates as a peer provides a positive role model to the supervisees.

Frequently training of human services workers involves content that is highly interactive with the self-concepts, personal values, and broad belief systems of learners. The type of content has specific implications for instructional design. For instance, learning objectives imply definite instructional tasks. Skills-oriented training requires significantly different tasks than training focusing on information dissemination (Gagne and Briggs, 1974). Interpersonal skills content, which is based on values and beliefs about helping, also implies a commitment by trainer and trainees to certain expectations. If a discrepancy exists between the values underlying content and the beliefs and values learners bring to training, then task and relationship activities need to be devoted to altering the learners' affective as well as cognitive domain.

Fry (1973) hypothesized that helpers as well as clients have conditioned anxiety responses to closeness. Interpersonal helping skills training, by definition, requires physical and psychological closeness between individuals. Fry discovered that when systematic desensitization is used in combination with role play, role reversal, and concrete feedback, the defenses of learners are alleviated, enabling them to move faster to higher levels of interpersonal functioning.

Increasing emphasis has been placed on needs assessment. Many, especially adult learning advocates, argue that the learner should be actively involved in determining his or her learning needs (Knowles, 1970). Unfortunately, in some cases, needs assessments yield little information that is specifically useful in design beyond a general indication of the content of skills components. Rarely do needs assessments provide meaningful information about the learner's existing knowledge and skills, prior experiences with training, personality factors such as confidence or security with self, and related situational factors—information necessary for adequate instructional planning. Thus, situational factors have typically been dealt with as they arise during the delivery of instruction.

Relationship Considerations in the Design of Instruction

"The relations between one who instructs and one who is instructed is never indifferent in its effect upon learning" (Bruner, 1968, p. 42). Although most of the literature on interpersonal helping skills training focuses on the instructional task dimension, the relationship dimension deserves equal consideration. Rogers (1969) offered three theoretical assumptions that provide the basis for the role of the relationship dimension in learning. The first assumption is that "learning which involves a change in self-organization—in the perception of oneself—is threatening and tends to be resisted" (p. 159). Second, "those learnings which are threatening to the self are more easily perceived and assimilated when external threats are at a minimum" (p. 160). Third, "when threat to the self is low, experience can be perceived in a differentiated fashion and learning can proceed" (p. 161).

An implicit assumption about the role of relationship in the interpersonal helping process is that it is the medium through which the helpee develops trust in the helper and becomes increasingly willing to risk exposure of more protected and potentially vulnerable parts of self. In a parallel way, research on individual and group leadership suggests that relationship has the effect of nurturing cohesion and commitment, as well as increasing participation and goal attainment. In the application of this notion to training, Arndt (1956) points out, "identification with the instructor supports the learner in a more sustained, critical, and balanced scrutiny of self, facilitates the adoption of essential ways of thinking, feeling and acting, and strengthens the integration of learning" (p. 40).

In the training of individuals, particularly helping professionals, much of the interpersonal content is highly interactive with the learner's belief systems and presentation of self and therefore, by definition, with the learner's concept of self—for what could be a more integral part of individuals' concept of self than the way in which they present themselves to other people? Consequently, learning new responding skills is not merely a matter of adding new behaviors to one's repertoire but may also involve changing one's values significantly regarding the acceptability of the client's feelings and personhood, overcoming a personal fear or reluctance to deal with feelings, or even acknowledging one's own affective response to the client's situation and presence. Verbal and physical presentation of self are central to our concept of self. If, as Rogers suggests, learning that involves a change in self-organization is threatening and tends to be resisted, then interpersonal skills training can be a threatening encounter for the learner.

The design stage must include an examination of the learning content and its potential for interacting with and possibly occasioning significant changes in the learner's concept of self. Design must not only take into account the tasks explicitly directed to skills enhancement but also incorporate relationship enhancement strategies to increase individual and group security and reduce the perception of external threats. Consider, for instance, the number of interpersonal skills courses and workshops that, early in the program, have broken trainees into dyads or triads. Reflect on the discomfort the learner experiences in exposing his skills level to or receiving feedback from a relatively unknown coparticipant.

An integral part of designing the relationship dimension of training is appraising and adjusting to situational factors that are likely to influence the development of open, trusting, trainer-learner and learner-learner relationships. The process of relationship enhancement for a class of college students taking an elective interpersonal skills course differs substantially from the process for a group of nurses from the same ward who are directed to attend the training. The college students, although often largely unfamiliar with each other, are purposeful in their intent and apparently place value on course content. Values shared with the students, as well as the status and sanctions bestowed on the instructor by the college, provide the instructor a broad base for personal influence and the development of a stable but not necessarily intimate relationship. On the other hand, the nurses enter training without a clear sense of their interests and their attitudes toward the program. Their prior relationships with each other may help or hinder the growth of a conducive learning climate. The trainer is often devoid of influential status and sanctions in their eyes and thus must rely largely on interpersonal influence, persuasion, and content expertise to move the group.

Task Considerations in the Design of Instruction

Instruction must be planned if it is to be effective. After the overall purpose of training is determined and before objectives can be specified and content determined, Gagne and Briggs (1974) contend, instruction should begin with learning task analysis—an analysis of the requirements for learning. At this stage in planning, the function of learning task analysis is to identify the decisions and associated actions required to implement overall performance capabilities. For example, a microtraining program capability might be to enable the learner to reflect clients' feelings. Further learning task analysis reveals the enabling capabilities or building blocks necessary to acquire the performance capability. In the case of reflection of feelings, enabling capabilities would include the ability to recognize client verbal and nonverbal expression of feelings, appropriately label the feelings expressed by the client, and so on.

Although performance capabilities for interpersonal skills are generally similar across various fields of helping, clear differences are also apparent. Consider, for instance, the difference between the relationship a protective service worker forms with a family in order to be effective and the manner in which a family assistance worker relates to an AFDC recipient. Although empathy is important in both relationships, occasional use of Egan's (1975) primary-level empathy is perhaps more appropriate for the family assistance worker than for the protective service worker, for whom advanced accurate empathy seems necessary. Needs assessment can help identify the individualized performance capability needs of various groups or professions and provide the basis for defining performance objectives. These objectives serve as a guide for the development of training lessons or modules and for devising measures to assess learner performance.

Gagne and Briggs (1974) define another function of learning task analysis as identifying the type of learning implicit in each objective. The purpose of this analysis is to sequence instruction according to hierarchial forms of learning and to identify the conditions necessary to learn each objective. For purposes of planning, objectives may be assigned to five categories of learning: intellectual skills, cognitive strategies, information, attitudes, and motor skills. Although, in general, skills acquisition entails some aspect of each type, the intellectual skills category is the most relevant. It consists of a hierarchy of learning capabilities, beginning with discriminations and followed by concrete concepts, defined concepts and rules, and, finally, higher-order rules or problem solving. These precepts, which follow an information-processing model, suggest that instruction should usually begin with some level of concept formation. Concepts are based in part on the ability to distinguish things as a class. In the context of interpersonal helping skills training, discrimination exercises designed to help the trainee differentiate high-empathy from low-empathy responses reinforce the formation of the concept of empathy (Carkhuff, 1969). Once this concept is developed, the trainee can then be taught to discriminate those instances in which a high-empathy response may be appropriate, thus forming a rule. Practice with feedback facilitates the application of these learned rules, the development of cognitive strategies, and, to some extent, problem solving.

The categorizing of objectives according to their type of learning enables the trainer to identify the optimal conditions for learning. According to Gagne and Briggs, each type of intellectual skill consists of internal conditions, which are composed of capabilities recalled from the learner's memory, and external conditions, which provide appropriate stimulation to the learner by means of pictures, symbols, or meaningful verbal communication. For instance, in teaching discrimination between open and closed questions, the internal condition is merely the ability to cognitively perceive a difference between the skills and to undrstand the concepts of same and different. A key external condition might be the appropriate pairing of a videotaped example of each skill with the response "closed question" or "open question," with reinforcement of correct responses.

One of the essential decisions in the design of training regards the learning activities that will compose the lessons or modules. The learning activities, a set of stimuli or communications to the learner, can take various forms, most commonly verbal and written statements. The key is to match the activities to the conditions of learning identified from the learning task analysis. For instance, verbal instruction generally forms a basis for learning concepts (Gagne, 1965). However, a complex concept like genuineness is extremely difficult to communicate by purely verbal means. Two other strategies can greatly improve the effectiveness of concept formation: modeling, or demonstration; and discrimination exercises. Demonstrations of genuineness and of the absence of genuineness enhance concept formation. Discrimination exercises are helpful in refining the concept and in teaching the learner to distinguish circumstances in which the skill should be used.

The final task consideration in planning training is determining the means of assessing or evaluating learner performance. In Chapter Fifteen of this volume, Stone presents a detailed discussion of assessment. However, it should be mentioned that assessment tools need to be a direct measure of the type of learning stated in the training objectives. Thus, if the objectives state that the learner be able to discriminate among various helping skills responses, the assessment may have learners identify skills demonstrated in videotaped episodes. But the objective of teaching trainees to use whatever helping skills are appropriate to obtain needed information from the client further implies rule learning, the integrated use of skills in a novel situation. In this case, assessment may entail a critique of a videotaped client-trainee interview. Assessment for purposes of learner feedback is always necessary and may not take the same form as summative assessment of training program effectiveness.

Situational Considerations in the Delivery of Instruction

Although instructional design may anticipate and plan for some situational factors, others may not be recognizable until the learners assemble for instruction. Few learning situations allow complete preassessment of prerequisite learner knowledge, skills, attitudes, cognitive processing patterns, and orientation to the training content. It is not uncommon in training situations to discover that learners lack prerequisite capabilities. In these instances, the trainer is faced with the choice of proceeding with the planned instructional design, recognizing that it may not be effective, or providing additional learning sequences in order to develop the prerequisite conditions and skills. Since most learning episodes are time-bound, the inclusion of additional learning sequences may be difficult. Furthermore, when skills instruction occurs in a workshop format, the trainer is frequently unable to produce additional sequences of instruction immediately. Often a refinement of the instructional objectives may be the only realistic solution.

A related problem and complicating situational factor is that individuals learn at different paces. Such design factors as the learner-trainer ratio may preclude meaningful individualization. Where the instructional program is sequenced and earlier skills are necessary for the development of later skills, incomplete learning early in the program is certain to result in ineffective acquisition of later skills. Learning formats that allow for individual pacing and competency attainment prior to moving on to more advanced skills seem to be the most effective instructional approach but usually are more expensive and complex to manage.

Recent events in the lives of learners also constitute a set of situational factors that influence the learning process and may alter the instructional design. Quite often, life events may compete with instructional activities for the learner's attention, thereby limiting reception of incoming stimulation. Relevant events may include pleasurable and painful experiences with family, friends, or work and even occurrences en route to the learning site. Although residential training formats may cloister the learner from disruptive external events and more rapidly facilitate group cohesion, they may also stimulate other competing processes, such as loneliness, worry about family members, apprehension about tasks left undone at work, or fatigue associated with changes in the learner's regular biological schedule. Often trainers must depart from planned instructional activities and respond directly to the learner's experience before effective learning can proceed.

As previously mentioned, factors associated with group membership can also influence learning. The presence in the group of a person perceived as threatening can affect the level of trust the group is able to achieve. Racial and sexual composition can also be a factor—for instance, a single minority member of a group (Davis, 1979) or one male in an all-female group may feel additional pressures against risking self. In the designing of instruction, it is rarely possible to fully anticipate the exact composition of a group. Consequently, the trainer is often in the position of reacting to these situational factors as they develop.

The interaction among learners and between learners and the trainer is also a situational factor that cannot be wholly predicted. Interactions between people invariably stimulate memories of interactions with others. The extent to which these memories are positive or negative may influence the credibility of the trainer and the willingness of learners to participate.

Increasingly, training in interpersonal helping skills relies on sophisticated electronic equipment to augment the instructional program. The availability of videotape equipment not only allows the trainer to present audiovisual models that can be repeatedly viewed but also provides a source of highly accurate and total feedback that can be used for various forms of learner assessment. The incorporation of these technological devices into the instructional program seems to have clear learning advantages. If the devices do not work properly, varying effects may result. Equipment failure may mean only a minor delay in the instructional sequence where backup equipment is accessible. However, when instruction occurs in remote locations, the trainer may suddenly be faced with substituting other learning activities or abandoning the training design altogether. Screen size and distance from a monitor also influence trainee observations during video modeling or discrimination exercises.

Relationship Considerations in the Delivery of Instruction

As discussed earlier, during the design phase of training, the trainer can begin to accommodate the personal and environmental needs of the learner and initiate the communication process. In the delivery of instruction, the trainer focuses on the development of a learning climate in which the learner feels accepted, understood, and secure, willing to take risks and remain committed to the acquisition of helping skills. What are the conditions that make a trainer a source of personal influence and facilitate the development of a healthy learning climate? While this topic is much talked about, the literature is far from definitive, particularly because of the empirical limitations of many studies of teacher-learner transaction.

However, one consistent finding is that trainer rapport with the learner is a crucial factor. Mintzes' (1979–1980) survey of college psychology students revealed that rapport and clarity of expression were two significant dimensions of effective teacher behavior. The quality of the relationship between student and teacher were influenced by the teachers addressing learners by name, showing concern for student progress, and praising them for good ideas. Through direct observation and ratings of 123 vocational education teachers,

Roberts and Becker (1976) found that the communication skills of teacher dynamism, delivery, time spent with students, positive reinforcement of students, and positive attitude toward students differentiated effective from ineffective instructors. Gazda and others (1977) cite several studies conducted on elementary and secondary school students that demonstrate the positive impact of empathy, positive regard, and genuineness on children's adjustment to school, teachers, and peers. In a related study, Berenson (1971) concluded that a group of teachers trained in human relations evidenced clear superiority over untrained teachers on thirty-one different indexes of teacher competence and pupil learning.

Probably no one has written more on this topic than Carkhuff (see, for example, Carkhuff, 1969, 1971). A consistent theme in his writings is that trainers who exhibit high levels of human relations skills are more likely to facilitate high levels of learning in participants than are trainers who display low levels of those skills. "It would appear to be extremely sensible to train teachers on those skills which increase the teacher's effectiveness in his or her role as a functioning mental health professional. Fortunately, these skills are some of the same skills which also have a positive impact on educational achievement" (Anthony and Carkhuff, 1977, p. 112). Thus, trainer use of effective interpersonal skills is not only important from the perspective of modeling effective helping but is also critical in developing a supportive learning environment.

For instance, just as reflections of feelings can facilitate the helping relationship, a trainer who responds empathically to the discomfort a trainee experiences while receiving feedback from a peer enhances the supportive quality of the training and increases the probability that the experience will be perceived constructively. In interpersonal skills training, where the degree of exposure and risk of self is reasonably high, effective trainer communication is especially warranted.

In the case of adult learners, Knox (1980) stresses that "a climate for learning must be quickly established that is supportive, friendly, spontaneous, informal, open, and challenging without being threatening or condescending" (p. 79). Many trainers use climate-developing activities such as breaking the ice, encouraging trainees to reveal something about their personal backgrounds and reasons for participating, allowing participants to formulate or modify program goals, and encouraging members to share relevant experiences in comfortable surroundings. However, for some learners, such activities may provoke, rather than reduce, anxiety. Not everyone warms up in the first five minutes of a workshop or learning activity.

Adult learning theorists further suggest that the training program should be problem-centered, rather than content-centered. Adult learner commitment and involvement is heightened when learners perceive its relevance to their work concerns. For example, a family assistance worker may not be especially interested in the skill of immediacy, but if the skill is taught in the context of how to deal with a hostile client, the worker may be more likely to perceive its value and concentrate on learning it. Irish (1980) suggests that the adult-adult relationship between trainer and learner, which is fostered by encouraging participants to relate their life experiences to the training content, is important for developing trust. Learning discontinuous with the learner's life situations seriously inhibits transfer of learning beyond the immediate setting. The sharing of life experiences also fosters mutual respect and mutual participation—members become aware that they have valuable contributions to make to the learning process.

Although students and adult learners are often presumed to have a commitment to the skills course or workshop they attend, their degree of purposefulness may be no greater than that of the college student fulfilling a degree requirement or the adult learner complying with a directive from a supervisor. A strong sentimental tie or positive relationship between trainer and learner may be the most potent factor in heightening participant commitment to skills training. In addition, the trainer's commitment to the importance of interpersonal skills and his or her enthusiasm in teaching the skills may also influence participation (Bidwell, 1973).

Task Considerations in the Delivery of Instruction

Although the term *skills training* often connotes a rather simple, behavioral form of learning, analysis of even the most basic interpersonal helping skill reveals that it requires a set of enabling capabilities and involves various types of learning. For instance, at one level, a reflection of feeling may simply be viewed as a verbal behavior containing a feeling element, but its competent use involves complex cognitive operations composed primarily of what Gagne and Briggs call intellectual skills. As diagrammed in Figure 1, the cognitive components required to skillfully demonstrate reflection of feelings include recognition and accurate labeling of client feeling, determination that a reflection of feeling would facilitate the goal of the interaction, recollection of a range of interpersonal process goals and selection of the one most appropriate to the situation, recall of the functions of various interpersonal helping skills, selection and formulation of a reflection of feeling to fit the context of the helping process, and delivery of the message in a congruent statement.

The competent use of skills requires a certain cognitive, behavioral, and affective readiness. The importance of the affective component has already been discussed. In most instances, the behavioral component is already present in the learner—learners can readily ask an open question or, on a random basis, may demonstrate a high level of empathic behavior. What most learners lack is the cognitive ability to differentiate among skills, identify the unique functions of each skill, and, based on the goals of the helping situation and the dynamics of the helping process, determine which skill is likely to have the desired impact on the helping process. Instructional tasks are intended to teach cognitive concepts and rules and to sharpen skills behavior. At one level, instructional tasks may take the form of readings, lectures, discussions, live demonstrations, and behavioral rehearsal. On another level, they may include such stimuli as verbal cues, instructions, nonverbal behavior, prompts, and questions. Gagne (1965, 1974) identifies nine instructional events that are related to the learning process and form a framework for the performance of each task. Although the instructional events are presented in the order in which they occur, the sequence is not invariant.

Gaining Attention. Two aspects of gaining the learner's attention are important. One is helping the learner eliminate external distractions. Introductory activities such as warm-up exercises often help the learner disengage from immediate past events and tune into

Figure 1. Enabling Capabilities for Reflections of Feelings or Ideas
(Partial Hierarchy).

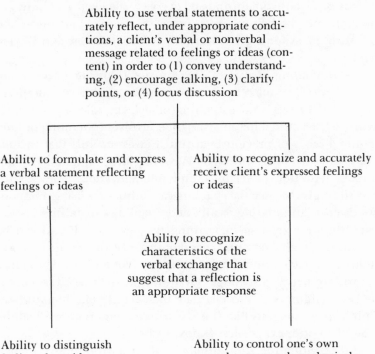

the role of learner. The other is to direct the learner's attention to specific tasks that are about to occur, either with a simple verbal or visual stimulus or, when necessary, with more dynamic activities.

Informing the Learner of the Objectives. Although increasing numbers of training programs provide explicit learning objectives for the entire course, rarely are learners given objectives for specific tasks. For example, learners do not commonly have a precise idea of what they are to learn from viewing a videotaped interview. Is the purpose to improve discrimination of skills, to put the learner in touch with his or her own affective response to the interview situation, or to learn to perform certain skills? Lack of clear direction may result in random learning. Informing the learner of the purpose or objective of the activity might simply involve a statement such as, "Viewing the tape will help you learn the difference between an open and closed question." In addition to statements of objectives, advance organizing and overview statements and advance questions can be helpful in focusing the learners' attention and preparing them for a given learning activity (Hartley and Davies, 1976).

Stimulating Recall of Prerequisite Learning Capabilities. Higher-order learning often involves combining ideas or concepts to form rules. In Ivey's microtraining model, the role of being a responsive listener in a helping situation involves combining or integrating a series of previously acquired ideas or skills that include nonverbal attending, minimal encouragement, questions, paraphrases, reflection of feelings, and summarization. These skills, learned singly, become the enabling capabilities for being a responsive listener. Stimulating recall of the enabling capabilities insures that they are accessible in learning the new rule. Recall can be prompted by verbal or visual cues. For instance, the trainer may ask, "What skills have you studied so far that communicate to the helper that you are actively listening?" Or the learners may be given a list of the key enabling skills to facilitate their recall. The literature on adult learners suggests that it is particularly important with adults to build on prior experiences (Knox, 1980).

Presenting the Stimulus Material. In skills training, a range of verbal and visual stimulus materials are presented. The critical factor is to match the stimulus material to the level of expected performance. For example, if the goal is to teach the learner the concept of immediacy, a rule-example strategy would be effective, in which a definition or description of the skill is followed by a series of examples and nonexamples. However, if the learner is expected to use immediacy in the work environment, the stimulus might involve practice in the use of the skill under conditions similar to the work situation. In the case of a family assistance worker, the optional stimulus condition might be a thirty-minute interview in which the interviewer must seek a range of eligibility information from a hostile client or from one whose culture is different from the interviewer's own.

Providing Learning Guidance. Visual, verbal, and even tactile prompts can be used to guide the learner. Guidance enables the learner to stay on target and to focus on the most important aspects of the task. Many of the skills training models incorporate live or taped demonstrations. A learner viewing such a demonstration is subject to a multitude of stimuli; without adequate guidance, learning may be random and incidental. In a videotaped demonstration, verbal cues can be offered prior to viewing, and, during viewing, visual guidance can be given by pairing the printed name of the skill with the taped model's actual use of the skill. In practice in the use of skills, verbal guidance may be offered through a "bug in the ear" (a simple headset worn by the learner) or with the trainer so positioned as to guide the learner through verbal and tactile cues. Guidance increases the probability that the learner will acquire effective use of the skills with minimal trial and error.

Eliciting Performance. At this stage in instruction, Gagne and Briggs (1974) state that the learners "have 'seen' how to do it! We must now ask them to show that they know how to do it" (p. 162). Virtually all systematic skills training programs include practice of single skills that form the building blocks for the integrated or combined use of the skills. Repeated practice, particularly in situations that closely resemble the work environment, is perhaps the key ingredient in facilitating transfer of learning.

Providing Feedback. Feedback is a valuable tool for guiding learners toward proficient use of skills. In delivering feedback, "the trainer provides descriptive information that assesses the degree to which a trainee's behavior matches or departs from a set of mastery performance criteria. The feedback evaluates a trainee's performance in comparison with publicized criteria with the intent of maintaining, increasing, decreasing, or altering the behavior. To give helpful feedback, a trainer must be able to observe, evaluate, and describe behaviors and then develop suggestions for improving skill performance in a way that discourages a defensive reaction and encourages improved performance by the trainee" (Turock, 1980, p. 216). Some skills training models utilize learner peers to provide feedback. Experience suggests that peers are prone to give global and overly positive feedback. When peer feedback is used, the learners must be trained to accurately recognize and confirm expected behavior and to provide feedback in specific language. Furthermore, the quality of the peer relationship often influences the degree of the feedback's forthrightness.

Assessing Performance. In contrast to feedback, which is offered in many of the learning activities to shape learner responses in the direction of desired performance, assessment determines the success of the training program in terms of learner performance. Chapter Fifteen presents a detailed discussion of the assessment of training. Suffice it to say here that assessment of student performance is necessary to evaluate whether the course or workshop has met the objectives of training and the extent to which each learner has achieved the capabilities defined in the objectives.

Enhancing Retention and Transfer. The Achilles' heel of most training programs is the retention and transfer of skills from the training setting to the helping situation. Preliminary evidence is encouraging but mixed (Haase, DiMattia, and Guttman, 1972; Guttman and Haase, 1972; Hearn, 1976; Scroggins and Ivey, 1976). Spaced practice (Reynolds and Glaser, 1964), practice under various stimulus conditions, reminders or environmental cues, training to criteria, tailoring of the helping skills to the needs of various helping professions, follow-up and refresher training (Gluckstern, 1972), a do-use contract (Weinrach, 1976), learning that is congruent with life situations (Irish, 1980), self-reinforcement, and reinforcement from and modeling by supervisors in the work setting (Copeland, 1977) seem to enhance retention and transfer of skills.

Conclusion

The contingency model of training proposes that three interrelated dimensions—situation, relationship, and task—characterize the design and delivery phases of instruction. Each dimension significantly influences the effectiveness of instruction and must be considered in planning and implementing training. Most models of skills training primarily use task considerations in their design, with less emphasis on situational and relationship factors. Within the task dimension, most of the models tend to cluster around a format that combines didactic instruction with demonstration and rehearsal of skills. Consideration of situational and relationship factors may help account for additional variance in learner outcomes.

References

Anthony, W. A., and Carkhuff, R. R. "The Functional Professional Therapeutic Agent." In A. S. Gurman and A. M. Razin (Eds.), *Effective Psychotherapy.* Elmsford, N.Y.: Pergamon Press, 1977.

Arndt, H. C. "The Learner in Field Work." In *Education for Social Work.* New York: Council on Social Work Education, 1956.

Ausubel, D. P., Novak, J. D., and Hanesian, H. *Educational Psychology: A Cognitive View.* (2nd ed.) New York: Holt, Rinehart and Winston, 1968.

Berenson, D. H. "The Effects of Systematic Human Relations Training Upon the Classroom Performance of Elementary School Teachers." *Journal of Research and Development in Education,* 1971, *4* (2), 70–85.

Bidwell, C. E. "The Social Psychology of Teaching." In R.M.W. Travers (Ed.), *Second Handbook of Research on Teaching.* Chicago: Rand McNally, 1973.

Blacksma, D. C., and Porter, E. H., Jr. "A Short-Term Training Program in Client-Centered Counseling." *Journal of Counseling Psychology,* 1947, *11,* 55–60.

Bruner, J. S. *Toward a Theory of Instruction.* New York: Norton, 1968.

Carkhuff, R. R. *Helping and Human Relations.* Vol. 1. New York: Holt, Rinehart and Winston, 1969.

Carkhuff, R. R. *The Development of Human Resources.* New York: Holt, Rinehart and Winston, 1971.

Copeland, W. D. "Some Factors Related to Teacher Classroom Performance Following Microteaching Training." *American Educational Research Journal,* 1977, *14* (2), 147–157.

Davis, L. E. "Racial Composition of Groups." *Social Work,* May 1979, pp. 208–213.

Egan, G. *The Skilled Helper.* Monterey, Calif.: Brooks/Cole, 1975.

Fiedler, E. E. "A Contingency Model of Leadership Effectiveness." In L. Berkowitz (Ed.), *Advances in Experimental Social Psychology.* Vol. 1. New York: Academic Press, 1964.

Fleishman, E. A., and Harris, E. F. "Patterns of Leadership Behavior Related to Employee Grievances and Turnover." *Personnel Psychology,* 1962, *15,* 43–56.

Fry, P. S. "Effects of Desensitization Treatment on Case Conditioning Training." *Journal of Counseling Psychology,* 1973, *20,* 214–219.

Gagne, R. M. *The Conditions of Learning.* New York: Holt, Rinehart and Wintson, 1965.

Gagne, R. M., and Briggs, L. J. *Principles of Instructional Design.* New York: Holt, Rinehart and Winston, 1974.

Gazda, G. M., and others. *Human Relations Development.* Boston: Allyn & Bacon, 1977.

Gluckstern, N. "Parents as Lay Counselors: The Development of a Systematic Parent Program for Drug Counseling." Unpublished doctoral dissertation, Department of Psychology, University of Massachusetts, 1972.

Guttman, M.A.J., and Haase, R. F. "The Generalization of Microcounseling Skills from Training Period to Actual Counseling Setting." *Counselor Education and Supervision,* 1972, *12,* 98–107.

Haase, R. F., DiMattia, D. J., and Guttman, M.A.J. "Training of Support Personnel in Three Human Relations Skills: A Systematic One-Year Follow-up." *Counselor Education and Supervision,* 1972, *11,* 194–199.

Hartley, J., and Davies, I. K. "Preinstructional Strategies: The Role of Pretests, Behavioral Objectives, Overviews, and Advance Organizers." *Review of Educational Research.* Spring 1976, *46* (2), 239–265.

Hearn, M. "Three Modes of Training Counselors: A Comparative Study." Unpublished doctoral dissertation, Department of Psychology, University of Western Ontario, 1976.

Hersey, P., and Blanchard, K. H. *Management of Organizational Behavior.* Englewood Cliffs, N.J.: Prentice-Hall, 1977.

Irish, G. H. "Critical Decision Making for More Effective Learning." In A. B. Knox (Ed.), *New Directions for Continuing Education: Teaching Adults Effectively,* no. 6. San Francisco: Jossey-Bass, 1980.

Ivey, A. E., and others. "Microcounseling and Attending Behavior: An Approach to Prepracticum Counselor Training." *Journal of Counseling Psychology,* Part 2, 1968, *15,* 1–12.

Jennings, E. E. "The Anatomy of Leadership." *Management of Personnel Quarterly,* 1961, *1* (1), 21–30.

Knowles, M. S. *The Modern Practice of Adult Education*. New York: Association Press, 1970.

Knox, A. B. *Adult Development and Learning: A Handbook on Individual Growth and Competence in Adult Years for Education and the Helping Professions*. San Francisco: Jossey-Bass, 1977.

Knox, A. B. (Ed.). *New Directions for Continuing Education: Enhancing Proficiencies of Continuing Educators*, no. 1. San Francisco: Jossey-Bass, 1980.

McClelland, D. C. *The Achieving Society*. New York: D. Van Nostrand, 1961.

Matarazzo, R. G. "Research on the Teaching and Learning of Psychotherapeutic Skills." In S. L. Garfield and A. E. Bergin (Eds.), *Handbook of Psychotherapy and Behavior Change*. New York: Wiley, 1978.

Matarazzo, R. G., Wiens, A. N., and Saslow, G. "Experimentation in the Teaching and Learning of Psychotherapy Skills." In L. K. Gottschalk and A. Auerbach (Eds.), *Methods of Research in Psychotherapy*. New York: Appleton-Century-Crofts, 1966.

Mayadas, N. S., and Duehn, W. P. "The Effects of Training Formats and Interpersonal Discriminations in the Education for Clinical Social Work Practice." *Journal of Social Service Research*, 1977, *1* (2), 147–161.

Mintzes, J. J. "Overt Teaching Behaviors and Student Ratings of Instructors." *Journal of Experimental Education*, 1979–1980, *48* (2), 145–153.

Reid, W. J., and Beard, C. "An Evaluation of In-Service Training in a Public Welfare Setting." *Administration in Social Work*, 1980, *46*, 71–84.

Reynolds, J. H., and Glaser, R. "Effects of Repetition and Spaced Review upon Retention of a Complex Learning Task." *Journal of Educational Psychology*, 1964, *55*, 297–308.

Roberts, C. L., and Becker, S. L. "Communications and Teacher Effectiveness in Industrial Education." *American Educational Research Journal*, 1976, *13* (3), 181–197.

Rogers, C. R. "Training Individuals in the Therapeutic Process." In C. Strother (Ed.), *Psychology and Mental Health*. Washington, D.C.: American Psychological Association, 1957.

Rogers, C. R. *Freedom to Learn.* Columbus, Ohio: Merrill, 1969.

Scroggins, W., and Ivey, A. E. "An Evaluation of Microcounseling as a Model to Train Resident Staff." Unpublished manuscript, Department of Psychology, University of Alabama, 1976.

Torrance, E. P., and Mourad, S. "Role of Hemisphericity in Performance on Selected Measures of Creativity." *The Gifted Child Quarterly,* 1979, *23* (1), 44–55.

Truax, C. B., and Carkhuff, R. R. *Toward Effective Counseling and Psychotherapy: Training and Practice.* Chicago: Aldine, 1967.

Truax, C. B., Carkhuff, R. R., and Douds, J. "Toward an Integration of the Didactic and Experiential Approaches to Training in Counseling and Psychotherapy." *Journal of Counseling Psychology,* 1964, *11,* 140–147.

Turbeville, G. "A Teacher Rating Scale." *Peabody Journal of Education,* 1965, *43* (2), 78–88.

Turock, A. "Trainer Feedback: A Method for Teaching Interpersonal Skills." *Counselor Education and Supervision,* 1980, *19,* 216–222.

Vroom, V. H., and Yetton, P. *Leadership and Decision Making.* Pittsburgh, Pa.: University of Pittsburgh Press, 1973.

Weinrach, S. "A Model for the Systematic Generalization of Counseling Skills." *Counselor Education and Supervision,* 1976, *15,* 311–314.

Witty, P. "An Analysis of the Personality Traits of the Effective Teacher." *Journal of Educational Research,* 1974, *40,* 662–671.

Chapter 14

Selecting and Using Skills Training Materials and Resources

Eldon K. Marshall
John W. Charping
Pamela A. Hogwood

For those engaged in interpersonal skills training, the task of keeping abreast of the continually expanding body of training resources is a demanding one. A cursory review of the field reveals a vast array of available print and nonprint resources and a maze of organizations offering various programs relevant to the interests of trainers. Training programs are offered by both well-established and lesser-known organizations. Comprehensive, multi-media–based skills training packages exist alongside those with a narrower focus. Audiotapes, videotapes, and films abound, and a range of communication simulation games are available.

The wealth of skills training resources is reflected in such volumes as *Audiovisual Market Place 1982: A Multimedia Guide*

(1982); *The Directory of Directories* (Ethridge and Marlow, 1980); *Educational Film Locator* (1978); *The Guide to Simulations/Games for Education and Training* (Horn and Cleaves, 1980); *Nonprint Materials on Communication* (Buteau, 1976); *Reference Encyclopedia of American Psychology and Psychiatry* (Klein, 1975); *The Seed Catalogue* (Schrank, 1974); *Seminars: The Directory of Continuing and Professional Education Programs* (1981); and *Training's Yellow Pages of Software and Services* (1980).

In this rapidly expanding field, consumers and trainers are challenged to keep abreast of available resources and to determine which resources are most appropriate for their needs. One aim of this chapter is to selectively survey available resources in the following interpersonal skills training areas: training packages; audiotapes, videotapes, and films; simulation games and exercises; and organizations offering training programs, consultation services, and a variety of print and nonprint materials.* Since the purview is large, the survey must, of necessity, be selective and highlight the richness of existing resources. Qualitative evaluations of resources are beyond the scope of this chapter and must be left to the consumer; inclusion of a given resource does not imply the authors' endorsement. The second purpose of this chapter is to present considerations and guidelines for the selection and use of training resources—the variety of available resources necessitates such guidance.

Training Packages

As earlier chapters of this book reveal, the past ten years have witnessed the proliferation of programs for enhancing the interpersonal performance of helpers from varied professional disciplines. That this growth includes the emergence of a host of media-based training packages is of little surprise in an age in which the medium has become the message (McLuhan, 1964). Media-based programs discussed in this chapter refer to those packages that combine some

*A summary of surveyed resources from each of the four skills training areas, as well as a list of the sources for materials, programs, and services, is presented in Appendix B.

form of written training guide with one or more supportive media. Although supportive media most frequently consist of films, videotapes, and audiotapes, other material components may involve: participant workbooks, manuals and self-study guides; group leader discussion guides and lecture notes; slides and transparencies; supplemental aids, such as charts, article reprints, and bibliographies; written exercises; and evaluation and assessment forms. Training packages presented in this chapter fit Burstein's (1979) criteria—they are "self-contained, standardized, replicable, and available to the public, as distinguished from training programs whose sole description can be found in a journal article" (p. 2).

Survey Procedures. Since information on packaged programs tends to be scattered among many different sources, locating these resources required a systematic search of publisher and distributor catalogues of print and nonprint materials oriented to skills training; brochures of major organizations engaged in the human relations and resource development field; and advertisements in journals publishing in the skills training area.

Each training package has been classified into one of four broad categories to reflect its overall scope and focus. (1) The comprehensive training systems category includes the more publicized and empirically tested programs for the development of core helping skills relevant to a wide range of helpers. (2) The interviewing or counseling skills category focuses on skills that are either generic and applicable to diverse helping professionals or tailor-made to the needs of such specific trainee populations as nurses or public welfare workers. Many of these are adaptations of existing models like microtraining or systematic human relations training. (3) Packages in the interpersonal communication skills category are oriented to the development of basic communications skills that are generally applicable to both human services workers and nonprofessionals. Although the skills taught in these programs may be used by all helpers, they are not formally labeled and taught as helping skills, unlike the skills in the preceding package classifications. (4) Packages in the last category focus on communication theory and process and tend to have generic relevance to professional and paraprofessional audiences, although they may be suited for lay persons, as well. Emphasis is not on skills development per se.

Excluded from the survey are self-instructional or programmed texts with no accompanying media. Many of these can be found in the references section. For each packaged training program, Appendix B, Part One, presents a program description, a media description, the fee for the program, and the program distributor.

Scope. Programs vary greatly in focus, nature, and range of skills taught, training model being implemented, training methods used, types of media incorporated, and cost. The number of skills taught ranges from as many as fourteen to as few as one. The extent of media support also varies substantially—one comprehensive training package contains twenty-two separate videotapes; programs of lesser scope may include just a single videocassette. Cost of program materials may range from as low as $9 for an audiocassette series to as high as $2700 for an entire comprehensive training package. Promotional materials also vary: some brochures provide detailed descriptions of a given program, whereas others include only sketchy information. Of the fifty-one programs listed, seven are distributed through university centers, the majority through commercial firms. Overall, the diversity in programs surveyed resembles the variability found in Burstein's (1979) analysis of twenty packaged programs, in which the number of skills at focus ranged from two to twenty-two, the number of training sessions from three to thirty, and the duration of training from 6 to 100 hours.

Guidelines for Selection and Use. Given the variety of existing packaged programs, consumers are beset with a number of important questions concerning which programs to use for what purposes, to what advantage, and at what cost. To assist trainers in selecting from available packaged training programs, an evaluation checklist for packaged programs is presented in Table 1. The evaluation criteria listed in the checklist are guidelines, rather than hard and fast rules for selection. Specific criteria assume differing degrees of importance depending on the intended use of a particular program. For example, one is apt to be more stringent in appraising a program intended to serve as a basic skills course for graduate students than in appraising a training package envisioned as only one supplementary portion or module of a more comprehensive training program. In addition to providing some reference point for program selection, the criteria listed in Table 1 represent standards that may be used to guide the development of packaged training programs. In weighing the relative merits of different programs and determining their suitability for particular training needs, trainers should consider a program's demonstrated training effectiveness, the fit between trainees' needs and what a program can actually deliver, and the training conditions required for effective program delivery.

In considering the demonstrated effectiveness of training packages, trainers should note that some programs presented in Appendix B, Part One, have not been evaluated, whereas others have been the subject of numerous investigations (Carkhuff, 1969; Kasdorf and Gustafson, 1978; Kagan, 1975). Although current research does not confirm the unequivocal superiority of one skills training model over another (Marshall, Charping, and Bell, 1979), most of the experimental methods seem to produce results superior to the results of control groups (Matarazzo, 1978). In addition to a packaged program's effectiveness from the perspective of statistical significance, consumers should also consider the reported practical significance or usefulness, particularly since a substantial number of seemingly well-designed programs have not been systematically evaluated. In such cases, previous users constitute a valuable source of information on program effectiveness.

The usefulness of packaged programs inevitably hinges on the "goodness of fit" between trainee needs and program capability (Danish and Brock, 1974). According to Danish and Brock, to determine a program's suitability for a particular trainee population, trainers need to evaluate: the compatibility between established program goals and trainer objectives; the adequacy of trainer resources to support such program requirements as duration, cost, and number of trainees; the capability of trainers to deliver a given program; and flexibility in adapting program format to the unique needs of the trainee population without compromising program quality. To protect consumer interests, Ginsberg and Danish (1976) recommend that training manuals provide essential information related to program purpose, intended trainee audience, prerequisites for participation, optimal time for training, procedures to be used, studies documenting program validity and effectiveness and evaluation techniques. As can be seen from a review of disseminated mate-

Table 1. Evaluation Checklist for Packaged Programs.

Yes	No	Evaluation Criteria
		Theory
____	____	Are the assumptions or theory underlying the program clearly identified?
____	____	Is the theory base consistent with trainer philosophy or orientation?
____	____	Is the theory base compatible with the philosophy and orientation of the service setting?
		Content
____	____	Are the skills included appropriate to the trainees' level of competence?
____	____	Are the skills taught clearly defined?
____	____	Is there sufficient breadth to the skills taught?
		Population
____	____	Are skills relevant to helper and helpee?
____	____	Are skills generalizable to work with different helpee populations?
____	____	Does the program evidence sociocultural bias?
____	____	Does the program evidence racial-ethnic sensitivity?
		Training Materials—Written
____	____	Do written materials contain essential information about purpose, nature of program, target population, and instructional prerequisites?
____	____	Are procedures for overall program implementation clearly defined?
____	____	Is a written manual provided for trainees?
____	____	Are training activities sufficient for effective implementation?
____	____	Are useful design alternatives or adaptations provided?
____	____	Are optimum time frames established for the different activities?
		Training Materials—Audiovisual
____	____	Are the video and audio materials clear?
____	____	Is the video material well integrated with the manual?

Table 1, (cont'd.)

Yes	No	Evaluation Criteria
___	___	Are sufficient audiovisual resources included?

Training Activities

Yes	No	
___	___	Are activities provided for presenting theory, conceptual frameworks, or underlying assumptions of the skills model being used?
___	___	Are skills adequately demonstrated?
___	___	Is there a range of relevant skill models?
___	___	Can the population being trained identify with the models provided?
___	___	Does the program provide for ample skills practice?
___	___	Does the program afford sufficient videotape or audiotape feedback?
___	___	Does the program assure ample peer-instructor feedback?
___	___	Does the program deal with social class and cultural differences?
___	___	Does the program teach discrimination of effective and ineffective skills use?
___	___	Are exercises provided to further the integration of skills?
___	___	Are activities provided that are oriented to furthering transfer or generalization of learning?

Evaluation

Yes	No	
___	___	Has the program been field-tested?
___	___	Has the validity of the training model been established?
___	___	Are instruments for evaluation of trainee performance provided?
___	___	Is trainee evaluation incorporated throughout the program?
___	___	Is there provision for program modification in response to evaluative feedback?

Practical Considerations

Yes	No	
___	___	Are the training materials easily accessible?
___	___	Is the program adequately and conveniently packaged?

Table 1, (cont'd.)

Yes	No	Evaluation Criteria
___	___	Is more than one trainer required for implementation?
___	___	Is the required audiovisual equipment extensive?
___	___	Is the program reasonably priced?

rials on the various training packages, many programs fall short of these standards.

As Morton and Kurtz discuss in this volume, enhancing learning through skills training requires that trainers strive to arrange the most optimal conditions for learning. Although some packaged programs specify the conditions requisite to program effectiveness (Carkhuff and Pierce, 1977; Ivey and Gluckstern, 1974a, 1974b, 1976a, 1976b; Kagan, 1975; Marshall and Kurtz, 1980; Morton, 1979), many neglect this area. Burstein (1979) highlights this problem in observing that, "with notable exceptions, few program developers detail the situations and conditions under which training is to take place or should optimally take place" (p. 35). Leaving these important matters to the judgment and expertise of less experienced trainers may jeopardize training effectiveness. In an effort to make their programs more "trainer-proof," some developers have given greater attention to specifying the essential conditions for effective program implementation. Manuals accompanying these packages include essential information pertaining to: training logistics, such as numbers of trainees that can be accommodated, the most desirable context for training, needed resources, and optimal time schedules; leader requirements; essential training procedures; and difficulties that may be encountered in the training process (Danish and Brock, 1974).

In general, the development of innovative training packages has notably advanced contemporary training technology. Burstein (1979) observes that the use and proliferation of packaged training programs to serve traditional and nontraditional helper populations offers the enormous social advantages of mobility, quality control, and cost-effectiveness. The more broadly based comprehensive training packages offer the additional advantages of basic helping skills systems relevant to diverse populations; competence-based frameworks for interpersonal learning; well-defined and replicable instructional procedures; educational models based on established learning principles; liberal amounts of practice and behavioral experimentation without endangering client populations; and educationally accountable learning systems using behavioral learning goals and built-in means for learning assessment.

Audiotapes, Videotapes, and Films

Over the past forty years, the development and use of audiovisual media have increased substantially. Films and tapes have been used extensively in a variety of settings to train helping professionals and paraprofessionals (Berger, 1978; Bonn, 1977; Buteau, 1976; Klein, 1975; Rufsvold, 1977), and the specific use of audiovisual media in interpersonal helping skills training is well documented throughout this book.

Until recently, little attention was given to the theoretical considerations underlying the use of audiovisual media. As Rodwell (1978) observes, "over the past few decades the audiovisual movement has forged ahead of its own volition, media development and utilization tending to be an ad hoc process determined more by the availability of the new technology than by any clear theoretical rationale" (p. 44). Over time, however, theory supporting the use of films and tapes became increasingly sophisticated, drawing on developments in learning and communications theory and relevant research findings in educational practice. By the early 1960s, this sophistication prompted an effort to redefine audiovisual instruction, resulting in the widely recognized use of the term educational technology (Hitchens, 1979) to describe a newly developing field that has advanced far beyond the mere use of films, tapes, and electronic equipment as innovative teaching methods to become a science in itself, with its own evolving theoretical constructs.

Survey Procedures. The selection of tapes and films presented in Appendix B, Part Two, was based on a review of catalogues from major university media centers, private companies, training institutes, and professional associations and includes only those tapes and films that are unaccompanied by other training materials. A list of distributors from which selections were made appears in Appendix B, Part Five. Specific information concerning each of the items listed can be obtained from these distributors.

Based on its overall focus, each tape or film has been classified into one of four broad categories: (1) *interpersonal/communication skills* category encompasses media pertaining to interpersonal relations, interpersonal communication skills, communications theory and practice, and nonverbal communication; (2) *interviewing skills* contains films and tapes describing essential skills needed in a variety of interviewing situations; (3) *individual treatment modalities* refers to demonstrations of skills used by helpers applying differing modalities of individual therapy; and (4) *group treatment modalities* includes demonstrations of skills by group leaders applying different group treatment modalities.

All tapes and films are listed in alphabetical order by title. If a particular film or tape is part of a series, the title of the series appears in parentheses directly beneath the title of the film or tape. The content description describes the focus of the film or tape and is immediately followed by the date of release in parentheses, if known. Media produced before 1960 are excluded. The media description indicates the type of audiovisual material—film, videocassette, video reel-to-reel, audiocassette, or audio reel-to-reel—the viewing or listening time, and any other pertinent technical information. The fee column provides an estimate of cost, and the distributor column lists the source or sources from which the material can be obtained. As indicated in the table, many of the films and tapes are available from more than one distributor. An alphabetical listing by letter codes of distributors and their addresses appears in the Appendix.

Scope. A total of 125 films, 45 audiotapes, and 32 videotapes are presented in Appendix B, Part Two, with viewing times ranging from a few minutes to several hours. Films and tapes presenting different treatment modalities are included to demonstrate the differential use of interpersonal skills. When a number of tapes and films demonstrating the same treatment modality are available, an attempt has been made to include those media that offer the best overall presentation of the given approach or that compare the treatment modality with other modalities.

Guidelines for Selection and Use. Incorporating audiovisual media into a skills training program requires the development of an educationally sound rationale. Among their educational functions, filmed and taped media may be used to heighten motivation and interest in a given topic area, illustrate important theoretical and skills concepts, model behaviors being taught, provide stimuli for skills practice, and facilitate a focus on specifics in the learning situation. Although these educational gains can be furthered through the use of other instructional practices, audiovisual media offer unique advantages. In discussing the instructional uses of media, Roeske (1978) identifies three distinct contributions of audiovisual materials. First, tapes and films assure the ready availability of the teaching resource for immediate, precise representation of material, thereby reinforcing learning through repetition. Second, audiovisual materials allow flexibility in responding to particular training needs. Media can be used in large and small groups and by individuals in self-instructional programs. Finally, audiovisual materials can provide multiple stimuli for different kinds of learning experiences. For example, the same film or tape might be used to model specific interviewing techniques or to teach about the interviewing process.

A major task confronting trainers centers on how to make the most effective educational use of available tapes and films. For substantive discussions of the theory and methodology of media utilization, see Gagne and Briggs (1979), Gerlach and Ely (1971), Carey and Prieto (1980), Gropper (1976), Diamond (1977), Turner (1977), Locatis and Atkinson (1976), and Kingston (1975).

Simulation Methods and Games

Simulation technology has long been a part of the skills trainer's repertoire. In the context of skills training, simulation methods involve the creation and controlled use of representations of real-life situations that resemble or approximate in varying degrees some aspects of the realities confronted by the helping practitioner (Miller, 1972; Shay, 1980; Spivack, 1973).

Simulation methods include taped or filmed models of helping behavior (Eisenberg and Delaney, 1970; Mayadas and Umlah, 1975; Miller, 1972; Thayer, 1977); taped or filmed vignettes of critical incidents encountered in counseling (Marshall and Kurtz, 1980; Spivack, 1973; Thayer and others, 1972); interviews with coached clients (Finn and Rose, 1981; McIlvaine, 1972; Shymko and Weiser, 1973; Stillman and Sabers, 1977; Whitely and Jakubowski, 1969); structured role plays (Ivey and Gluckstern, 1974a, 1976a; Marshall and Kurtz, 1980; Spector, 1969); affect simulation vignettes (Danish, 1971; Danish and Brodsky, 1970; Kagan, 1975; Resnikoff, 1969); enactments of selected aspects of the helping process (Beaird and Standish, 1964; Kinney, 1976, 1977; Maslon, 1973; Tarrier, 1972); and communication games and exercises (Horn and Cleaves, 1980; Ruben, 1980).

Applied for different purposes in different training contexts, simulation techniques have been employed to develop response repertoires through behavior modeling (Beaird and Standish, 1964; Delaney, 1969; Eisenberg and Delaney, 1970; Marshall and Kurtz, 1980; Mayadas and Umlah, 1975; Stone, 1975); to teach qualitative discriminations of behavior (Beaird and Standish, 1964; Carkhuff, 1969; Ivey and Gluckstern, 1974a, 1976a); to develop skills for coping with critical incidents (Marshall and Kurtz, 1980; Spivack, 1973; Thayer, 1972); to facilitate self-awareness and sensitivity to one's feelings, thoughts, and behavior and their impact on interpersonal communication (Grzegorek, 1970; Kagan, 1975; Spivack, 1973); to provide occasions for practicing behavior (Kinney, 1976, 1977; Maslon, 1973; Miller, 1972; Spector, 1969; Tarrier, 1972; Thayer, 1977); to promote competence in dealing with human emotion (Danish, 1971; Danish and Brodsky, 1970; Kagan, 1975; Resnikoff, 1969); and to standardize interviewing behavior for research and evaluation purposes (Finn and Rose, 1981; McIlvaine, 1972; Stillman and Sabers, 1977; Whiteley and Jakubowski, 1969).

Since the late 1950s and early 1960s, interest in the use of simulation games and exercises in education and training has grown (Horn and Cleaves, 1980; Zuckerman and Horn, 1973); in the late 1970s, Gohring (1978) reported that "a comprehensive bibliography of books on simulation and gaming in education . . . contains over 125 listings" (p. 46). In discussing the proliferation of games and simulations, McLean (1978) comments on their expanded use in many disciplines, the appearance of specialized periodicals and books in the field, and the increased interest in simulations and games in various professional journals. *Journal of Experiential Learning and Simulation, Simulation/Gaming News,* and *Simulation and Games* are among the periodicals devoted specifically to simulation. Of the simulation resources that have emerged, many are applicable to the teaching of interpersonal communication skills (Barbour and Goldberg, 1974; Covert and Thomas, 1978; Cruickshank and Telfer, 1979; Gibbs, 1974; Grove, 1976; Horn, 1977; Horn and Cleaves, 1980; Johnson and Johnson, 1975; Krupar, 1973; Learning Resources Center, 1979; Myers and Myers, 1980; Pfeiffer and Jones, 1973–1979; Ruben, 1980; Ruben and Budd, 1975; Werner and Werner, 1969; Zuckerman and Horn, 1970).

When applied in a training context for the purpose of skills development, simulation games and exercises consist of structured activities designed to resemble, in whole or in part, specific aspects of the real world confronting helping practitioners in order, typically, to facilitate learning important aspects of communication and the processes of interpersonal change. In their strictest and most traditional use, simulation games involve well-defined objectives, constraints, roles, resources, and rules of conduct (Beck and Monroe, 1969; Cruickshank, 1977; Spannaus, 1978). In their broadest use, simulation activities may extend from the more highly controlled formal games to structured role plays and exercises that center on some facet of interpersonal communication (Ruben, 1980; Beck and Monroe, 1969). To the extent that the important realities confronting helping practitioners can be meaningfully replicated, simulation technology constitutes a useful instructional medium for teaching about the process of interpersonal helping and for developing the interactional competencies of participating trainees.

The Listening Triads game (Myers and Myers, 1980), a good example of the relevance of simulation media for interpersonal skills training, affords trainees an opportunity to learn about the nature of effective communication. Participants are grouped in triads and assigned the roles of speaker, listener, and judge. Speakers are asked to talk for a specified time on some designated personal theme—for example, communication strengths and major problems in interacting with others—while listeners and judges listen attentively. When time is called, listeners are asked to recall as much as possible of what was said, while judges interrupt to point out errors in understanding, or information omitted by the listener. Roles are then rotated, with each person assuming all three roles during the process. Discussion can highlight barriers to effective listening, requirements for accurate understanding, and the importance of feedback in the communication process. The game's demands for effective listening partially resemble those of any helping process and thus serve to promote transfer of learning to actual helping situations.

Scope. Simulation games and exercises in the communication field are used in classes, seminars, and workshops with groups differing in age and educational level and may range from brief (ten- to fifteen-minute) exercises focused on single topics, such as feedback or self-awareness, to extended (semester-long or longer) activities focusing on a number of themes.

Given the number and variety of available resources, Appendix B, Part Three, presents only a sample of the many and various resources available, divided into six broad categories developed for organizing simulations in the communication field (Ruben, 1980; Buteau, 1976; Horn and Cleaves, 1980): (1) intrapersonal games highlight the processes of message selection and interpretation and the factors affecting those processes; (2) interpersonal games focus on the dynamics of dyadic interactions; (3) group simulations focus on group processes, relationships, and interactions; (4) cross-cultural simulations center on the dynamics of communication between culturally different persons; (5) self-development games and exercises focus on aspects of self-awareness and personal growth; and (6) human services games are designed to heighten participant sensitivity to the unique issues and dynamics involved in working with populations encountered in specific service contexts—for example, persons who are handicapped or on welfare.

For each simulation activity selected, Appendix B, Part Three, presents the focus, the number of players (participants) involved, the structure, the time or duration necessary for implementation, and the source. Structure indicates whether a given game is at a low (L), medium (M), or high (H) level of organizational complexity and reflects the overall configuration of such variables as rules, leadership tasks, necessary materials, and minimum number of participants required.

Guidelines for Selection and Use. Trainers are responsible for applying simulation games and exercises to further the interpersonal learning of trainees. Among other educational applications, simulation games and exercises may be used to heighten motivation and involvement in the training process; to offer a variety of interactional contexts for examining one's interpersonal effectiveness; to cultivate insight into and sensitivity toward one's thoughts, feelings, and behavior and their impact on interactions with others; to further cognitive learning and understanding of important communication concepts; and to facilitate the transfer of skills learning through practice in simulated real-life situations.

Two established games further illustrate the training uses of simulation. *The Memory Game* (Ruben, 1978) has been designed to teach how one's past experience influences perception, attention, memory, and recall. Objects symbolizing activities common to most participants—for example, work activities—are assembled, numbered, and covered. After a brief two-minute exposure, items are recovered and participants are instructed to list the items they recall displayed on the table. Patterns in the selection process are then distinguished and explained, and discussion centers on the way in which previous experience influences what is noticed and recalled.

Agitania, Meditania, Solidania (Ruben and Budd, 1975) is a game that teaches about cross-cultural differences and their consequences for communication. Participants are asked to assume roles from one of three cultural groups, each with its own cultural and communication characteristics. Throughout the interactions, participants become more sensitive to cross-cultural differences, their implications for communication, and the effects of cultural stereotyping on communication patterns.

Ruben (1980) and Weinrach (1978) have suggested criteria, or guidelines, applicable to the selection of simulation activities. In appraising the quality and suitability of simulation games and exercises for given training purposes, trainers should consider: the activity's purpose and its relevance to training objectives; the extent to which an activity focuses on significant aspects of the interpersonal communication process; the probability of similar outcomes resulting from different applications; compatibility with the background, education, and experience of the trainee population; quality of the simulation package; adequacy of users' guide in presenting purpose, intended audience, overall description, instructions for implementation, and results of testing; and cost and accessibility of materials. Although not all simulation resources measure up in every dimension, these criteria offer some basis for more discriminating selection and use.

Organizational Resources

In addition to colleges and universities, which assume a vital role in the education and training of helping professionals and paraprofessionals, a variety of other organizations offer skills training resources directed both to trainers and to those interested in furthering their own professional development. Many of these resources are useful to educators and trainers in formal educational settings, as well as to those in in-service training and continuing education. This section presents a selective survey of organizations offering interpersonal skills training resources ranging from consultation services, training programs, and workshops to print and nonprint materials.

Survey Procedures. Selected from listings in reference books and professional directories and from advertisements in professional journals, over 300 professional associations and organizations were surveyed, including professional associations; human relations training organizations serving business, higher education, and the human services (American Society for Training and Development, 1980; *Seminars* . . . , 1981; and *Training's* . . . , 1980); and a sampling of growth centers (Association for Humanistic Psychology, 1978).

Questionnaires were distributed to each of the 300 identified associations and organizations. The decision to include an organization in Appendix B, Part Four, was based both on a review of returned questionnaires and descriptive brochures and on whether the organization: offered services in interpersonal and communications skills development, interviewing, and/or group leadership training; provided training or consultation services in at least one of those areas; and served at least one helping professional or paraprofessional population. Omitted from the survey were organizations offering specialized training exclusively in a particular modality of counseling or therapy, such as gestalt, rational-emotive, or behavioral.

Appendix B, Part Four, profiles the skills training resources available from the selected organizations in the areas of: consultation services, training programs and workshops, packaged training programs, audiotapes and videotapes, films, and simulation games and exercises.

Scope. Among the organizations listed in Appendix B, Part Four, most serve more than one of the following disciplines: social work, medicine, nursing, psychiatry, psychology, counseling, and education. In most cases, organizations offer not just one but a combination of skills training resources. Certain organizations, such as Human Resource Development Press or Microtraining Associates, market established models of interpersonal skills development; resources available through such organizations range from consultation, training programs and workshops, and videotapes to training manuals and a variety of publications. Other organizations offer resources of a broader and less-specialized type, extending beyond just one theoretical framework or model. In addition, some professional associations provide resources relevant to skills development.

Appendix B, Part Four, is useful to those in search of organizational resources for particular training needs; however, prospective consumers are also advised both to write for current brochures to better evaluate the suitability of a given resource and to contact previous users for further information.

References

American Society for Training and Development. *Buyer's Guide and Consultant Directory.* Madison, Wisc.: American Society for Training and Development, 1980.

Association for Humanistic Psychology. *AHP Growth Center List 1978.* San Francisco: Association for Humanistic Psychology, 1978.

Audiovisual Market Place 1982: A Multimedia Guide. New York: Bowker, 1982.

Barbour, A., and Goldberg, A. A. *Interpersonal Communication: Teaching Strategies and Resources.* Falls Church, Va.: Speech Communication Association, 1974.

Beaird, J. H., and Standish, J. T. *Audio Simulation in Counselor Training.* Monmouth, Ore.: Teaching Research Division, Oregon System of Higher Education, 1964.

Beck, I. H., and Monroe, B. "Some dimensions of simulation." *Educational Technology,* 1969, *10,* 45–59.

Berger, M. M. (Ed.), *Videotape Techniques in Psychiatric Training and Treatment.* (Rev. ed.) New York: Brunner/Mazel, 1978.

Bonn, T. L. *A Guide to Audio-Visual References: Selection and Ordering Sources.* Cortland, N.Y.: State University of New York, 1977. (ERIC No. ED 148 371.)

Burstein, B. "Guidance Formats for Modifying Interpersonal Communication." Unpublished manuscript, Department of Psychology, University of California, 1979.

Buteau, J. D. *Nonprint Materials on Communication.* Metuchen, N.J.: Scarecrow Press, 1976.

Carey, J. O., and Prieto, E. M. "Guidelines for Incorporating Nonprint Media into Social Work Education." *Journal of Education for Social Work,* 1980, *16* (3), 96–100.

Carkhuff, R. R. *Helping and Human Relations.* 2 Vols. New York: Holt, Rinehart and Winston, 1969.

Carkhuff, R. R., and Pierce, R. M. *The Art of Helping III: Trainer's Guide.* Amherst, Mass.: Human Resource Development Press, 1977.

Covert, A., and Thomas, G. L. *Communication Games and Simulations.* Falls Church, Va.: Speech Communication Association, 1978.

Cruickshank, D. R. *A First Book of Games and Simulations.* Belmont, Calif.: Wadsworth, 1977.

Cruickshank, D. R., and Telfer, R. A. *Simulations and Games: An ERIC Bibliography.* Washington, D.C.: ERIC Clearinghouse on Teacher Education, 1979. (ERIC No. ED 177 149.)

Danish, S. J. "Film-Simulated Counselor Training." *Counselor Education and Supervision,* 1971, *11* (1), 29–35.

Danish, S. J., and Brock, G. W. "The Current Status of Paraprofessional Training." *Personnel and Guidance Journal,* 1974, *53,* (4), 299–303.

Danish, S. J., and Brodsky, S. L. "Training of Policemen in Emotional Control and Awareness." *American Psychologist,* 1970, *25,* 368–369.

Delaney, D. J. "Simulation Techniques in Counselor Education: A Proposal of a Unique Approach." *Counselor Education and Supervision,* 1969, *8,* 183–188.

Diamond, R. M. "Piecing Together the Media Selection Jigsaw." *Audiovisual Instruction,* 1977, *22* (1), 50–52.

Educational Film Locator. New York: Bowker, 1978.

Eisenberg, S., and Delaney, D. J. "Using Video Simulation of Counseling for Training Counselors." *Journal of Counseling Psychology,* 1970, *17,* 15–19.

Ethridge, J. M., and Marlow, C. A. (Eds.). *The Directory of Directories: An Annotated Guide to Business and Industrial Directories, Professional and Scientific Rosters, and Other Lists and Guides of All Kinds.* Detroit, Mich.: Gale Research, 1980.

Finn, J., and Rose, S. "Development and Validation of the Interview Skills Role-Play Test." Manuscript submitted for publication, 1981.

Gagne, R. M., and Briggs, L. J. *Principles of Instructional Design.* (2nd ed.) New York: Holt, Rinehart and Winston, 1979.

Gerlach, V. S., and Ely, D. P. *Teaching and Media: A Systematic Approach.* Englewood Cliffs, N.J.: Prentice-Hall, 1971.

Gibbs, G. I. (Ed.). *Handbook of Games and Simulation Exercises.* Beverly Hills, Calif.: Sage, 1974.

Ginsberg, M., and Danish, S. J. "Evaluating Skill Dissemination Programs." Report submitted to the Professional Affairs Committee, Division 17 (Counseling Psychology), American Psychological Association, Washington, D.C., 1976.

Gohring, R. J. "A Beginner's Guide to Resources in Gaming/Simulation." *Audiovisual Instruction*, 1978, *23* (5), 46-49.

Gropper, G. L. "A Behavioral Perspective on Media Selection." *AV Communication Review*, 1976, *24* (2), 157-186.

Grove, T. G. *Experiences in Interpersonal Communication*. Englewood Cliffs, N.J.: Prentice-Hall, 1976.

Grzegorek, A. A. "A Study of the Effects of Two Types of Emphasis in Counselor Training Used in Conjunction with Simulation and Videotaping." Unpublished doctoral dissertation, Department of Counselor Education, Michigan State University, 1970.

Hitchens, H. "The Evolution of Audiovisual Education in the U.S.A. Since 1945." *Educational Media International*, 1979, *3*, 6-12.

Horn, R. E. *The Guide to Simulations/Games for Education and Training*. (3rd ed.) Cranford, N.J.: Didactic Systems, 1977.

Horn, R. E., and Cleaves, A. (Eds.). *The Guide to Simulations/Games for Education and Training*. (4th ed.) Beverly Hills, Calif.: Sage, 1980.

Ivey, A. E., and Gluckstern, N. *Basic Attending Skills: Leader Manual*. North Amherst, Mass.: Microtraining Associates, 1974a.

Ivey, A. E., and Gluckstern, N. *Basic Attending Skills: Participant Manual*. North Amherst, Mass.: Microtraining Associates, 1974b.

Ivey, A. E., and Gluckstern, N. *Basic Influencing Skills: Leader Manual*. North Amherst, Mass.: Microtraining Associates, 1976a.

Ivey, A. E., and Gluckstern, N. *Basic Influencing Skills: Participant Manual*. North Amherst, Mass.: Microtraining Associates, 1976b.

Johnson, D. W., and Johnson, F. P. *Joining Together: Group Theory and Group Skills*. Englewood Cliffs, N.J.: Prentice-Hall, 1975.

Kagan, N. *Interpersonal Process Recall: A Method of Influencing Human Interaction*. (Rev. ed.) East Lansing, Mich.: Mason Media, 1975.

Kasdorf, J. A., and Gustafson, K. "Research Related to Microtraining." In A. E. Ivey and J. Authier (Eds.), *Microcounseling: Innovations in Interviewing, Counseling, Psychotherapy, and Psychoeducation*. (2nd ed.) Springfield, Ill.: Thomas, 1978.

Kingston, R. D. "The Selection and Use of Audiovisuals." *American Vocational Journal*, 1975, *50* (8), 58-60.

Kinney, T. J. (Ed.). *Enhancing Interviewing Skills of Income Maintenance Workers: A Training Manual.* Albany: School of Social Welfare, State University of New York, 1976.

Kinney, T. J. (Ed.). *Enhancing Interviewing Skills of Medical Assistance Workers: A Regulation and Procedures Supplement for Trainers.* Albany: School of Social Welfare, State University of New York, 1977.

Klein, B. T. (Ed.). *Reference Encyclopedia of American Psychology and Psychiatry.* New York: Todd Publications, 1975.

Krupar, K. R. *Communication Games.* New York: Free Press, 1973.

Learning Resources Center. *Catalogue of Non-Computerized Simulations and Games.* Granville, Ohio: Denison University, 1979.

Locatis, C. N., and Atkinson, F. D. "A Guide to Instructional Media Selection." *Educational Technology,* 1976, *16* (8), 19–21.

McIlvaine, J. F. "Coached Clients as Raters of Counseling Effectiveness." *Counselor Education and Supervision,* 1972, *12* (2), 123–129.

McLean, H. W. "Are Simulations and Games Really Legitimate?" *Audiovisual Instruction,* 1978, *23* (5), 12–13.

McLuhan, M. *Understanding Media: The Extensions of Man.* New York: McGraw-Hill, 1964.

Marshall, E. K., Charping, J. W., and Bell, W. J. "Interpersonal Skills Training: A Review of the Research." *Social Work Research and Abstracts,* 1979, *15* (1), 10–17.

Marshall, E. K., and Kurtz, D. *Interviewing Skills for Family Assistance Workers: Instructor's Manual.* Knoxville, Tenn.: Office of Continuing Social Work Education, University of Tennessee, 1980.

Maslon, P. J. *Preparing Counselors for Disadvantaged Students Using Videotape and IPR.* New York: New York University, 1973. (ERIC No. ED 095 441.)

Matarazzo, R. G. "Research on the Teaching and Learning of Psychotherapeutic Skills." In S. L. Garfield and A. E. Bergin (Eds.), *Handbook of Psychotherapy and Behavior Change.* (2nd ed.) New York: Wiley, 1978.

Mayadas, N. S., and Umlah, D. *Step-by-Step.* Arlington, Tex.: Human Resource Center, University of Texas, 1975.

Miller, T. V. "Simulation and Instructional Objectives in Counselor Education." *Counselor Education and Supervision,* 1972, *12* (2), 83–87.

Morton, T. M. *Casework Interviewing Effectiveness.* Athens, Ga.: Office of Continuing Social Work Education, University of Georgia, 1979.

Myers, G., and Myers, M. T. *The Dynamics of Human Communication* (3rd ed.) New York: McGraw-Hill, 1980.

Pfeiffer, J. W., and Jones, J. E. (Eds.). *A Handbook of Structured Experiences for Human Relations Training.* 7 Vols. San Diego, Calif.: University Associates, 1973–1979.

Resnikoff, A. "The Use of Simulation in Counselor Education." Paper presented at meeting of the American Personnel and Guidance Association, Washington, D.C., March 1969.

Rodwell, S. "Audiovisual Media." In D. Unwin, R. McAleese, and R. Morton, (Eds.), *The Encyclopedia of Educational Media Communications and Technology.* Westport, Conn.: Greenwood Press, 1978.

Roeske, N. A. "Videotapes as an Educational Experience." In M. M. Berger (Ed.), *Videotape Techniques in Psychiatric Training and Treatment.* (Rev. ed.) New York: Brunner/Mazel, 1978.

Ruben, B. D. *Human Communication Handbook: Simulations and Games.* Vol. 2. Rochelle Park, N.J.: Hayden, 1978.

Ruben, B. D. "Communication Games and Simulations: An Evaluation." In R. E. Horn and A. Cleaves (Eds.), *The Guide to Simulations/Games for Education and Training.* (4th ed.) Beverly Hills, Calif.: Sage, 1980.

Ruben, B. D., and Budd, R. W. *Human Communication Handbook: Simulations and Games.* Vol. 1. Rochelle Park, N.J.: Hayden, 1975.

Rufsvold, M. I. *Guides to Educational Media.* (4th ed.) Chicago: American Library Association, 1977.

Schrank, J. *The Seed Catalog.* Boston: Beacon Press, 1974.

Seminars: The Directory of Continuing and Professional Education Programs. Madison, Wis.: Creative Communications, 1981.

Shay, C. "Simulations in the Classroom: An Appraisal." *Educational Technology,* 1980, *20* (2), 26–31.

Shymko, D. L., and Weiser, J. C. "The Use of Coached Clients in Summer Practicum Programs." *Canadian Counselor,* 1973, 7 (3), 200–205.

Spannaus, T. W. "What is a Simulation?" *Audiovisual Instruction,* 1978, *23* (5), 16–17.

Spector, P.A.J. "An Application of the Behavior Change Principles of Role Playing and Shaping to the Training of Counselors." Paper presented at meeting of the American Personnel and Guidance Association, Washington, D.C., April 1969.

Spivack, J. D. "Critical Incidents in Counseling: Simulated Video Experiences for Training Counselors." *Counselor Education and Supervision,* 1973, *12* (4), 263–270.

Stillman, P. L., and Sabers, D. L. "Use of Trained Mothers to Teach Interviewing Skills to First-Year Medical Students: A Follow-Up Study." *Pediatrics,* 1977, *60,* 165–169.

Stone, G. L. "Effect of Simulation on Counselor Training." *Counselor Education and Supervision,* 1975, *14,* 199–203.

Tarrier, R. B. *Videotape Learning Exercises.* New York: Guidance Laboratory, City University of New York, 1972. (ERIC No. ED 149 715.)

Thayer, L. "Video Packaging: Integrating Simulation Techniques and Systematic Skill Training." *Counselor Education and Supervision,* 1977, *16* (3), 217–223.

Thayer, L., and others. "Development of a Critical Incidents Videotape." *Journal of Counseling Psychology,* 1972, *19* (3), 188–191.

Training's 1980 Yellow Pages of Software and Services. Minneapolis, Minn.: Lakewood Publications, 1980.

Turner, P. M. "Is Misuse of Media Giving Us a Black Eye?" *Audiovisual Instruction,* 1977, *22* (8), 24.

Unwin, D., McAleese, R., and Morton, R. (Eds.). *The Encyclopedia of Educational Media Communications and Technology.* Westport, Conn.: Greenwood Press, 1978.

Weinrach, S. "Guidelines for the Systematic Selection, Evaluation, and Use of Simulated Guidance Materials." *American Personnel and Guidance Journal,* 1978, *56* (5), 288–292.

Werner, R., and Werner, J. T. *Bibliography of Simulations: Social Systems and Education.* La Jolla, Calif.: Western Behavioral Sciences Institute, 1969.

Whiteley, J. J., and Jakubowski, P. A. "The Coached Client as a Research and Training Resource in Counseling." *Counselor Education and Supervision,* 1969, *9,* 19–28.

Zuckerman, D. W., and Horn, R. E. *The Guide to Simulation Games for Education and Training.* Cambridge, Mass.: Information Resources, 1970.

Zuckerman, D. W., and Horn, R. E. *The Guide to Simulations/ Games for Education and Training.* Lexington, Mass.: Information Resources, 1973.

Chapter 15

Evaluating the Effectiveness of Skills Training Programs

Gerald L. Stone

One of the most prominent debates in the counseling field concerns the question of what constitutes an acceptable methodology for counseling research and evaluation (Gelso, 1979; Goldman, 1978). Two interrelated facets of this debate are worth considering: protests against scientism and demands for more evaluation instead of more research.

The first facet concerns objections to the blind application of physical science procedures to the study of interpersonal counseling. Critics argue that the use of quantification, random assignment, control groups, and the artificial conditions of the laboratory precludes any meaningful application of counseling research to practice. This protest, often associated with a greater emphasis on more humanistic and qualitative research methods, has contributed to the development of evaluation research. Recent writers (for example, Burck and Peterson, 1975), calling for more evaluation instead of more research, are convinced that traditional research strategies cannot respond to the practical issues of accountability raised by legislators and consumers in a society facing limited resources and dominated by powerful interest groups. Instead, they argue for evaluation methods that are more concerned with providing information for practical decision making. In response to these practical issues, evaluation researchers, in contrast to their colleagues who aim at describing cause-and-effect relationships among a few variables within the laboratory, do their evaluation in the field to establish the effectiveness and efficiency of multicomponent programs. Clearly, the amount of experimental control is a salient dimension in distinguishing between evaluation and research, since the complexities of field settings result in less control and precision.

Before discussing the evaluation of training programs, let us address these two facets or issues. (Actually, the debate is multifaceted and involves more than the two issues.) As in most debates, both sides are partially right. The critics of scientism are generally correct when they point to the use of laboratory procedures, operationalism, and statistics without a recognition of the irreducible, subjective components and illogic often involved in such procedures (Mahoney, 1976). On the other hand, the linking of scientism with science and an uncritical promotion of more humanistic approaches is throwing out the proverbial baby with the bathwater. To do so is to give up the prospect of generating reliable information. Moreover, those advocating subjective, qualitative strategies often fail to recognize that problems encountered in experimental studies are not limited to such studies—the threats to validity outlined by Campbell and Stanley (1963) and updated by Cook and Campbell (1979) also arise in the more humanistic investigations. Studies using the more qualitative methods, such as observational strategies, are plagued by problems of bias. For example, when we consider a person we observe to be quite orderly to be more interested in computer science than in social work, we are being influenced by stereotyping (Kahneman and Tversky, 1973), a bias that yields unsatisfactory results.

Some of the arguments advanced by the proponents of evaluation research are also well taken, Limiting research to laboratory settings in which single experiments investigate a few variables overlooks alternative methods and variables of interest. At the same time, care must be taken in balancing demands for relevance and the importance of making scientifically meaningful statements. Too often, program evaluators have underestimated the costs of being wrong and overestimated the value of producing timely, relevant results—as in the premature decision about the harmful effects of Head Start. In this chapter, evaluation is considered within the context of scientific research that uses experimental methods and at the same time recognizes the limitations of such methods.

What to Evaluate?—The Focus of Evaluation

A major question in the evaluation of training programs for professionals or nonprofessionals is one of focus: Are we primarily interested in attributing the training effects to the program? Is the critical impact of a training program assessed in terms of the trainee, client, or society? Do we concentrate on skills or on the personal development of the trainee? Do we record data by means of self-report, rating scales, or the counting of behaviors?

These and other questions suggest that the evaluator needs to be concerned with three issues: different sources of influence in producing the outcome (internal validity), different perspectives in evaluating the outcome, and different ways of measuring the outcome. Although the issue of internal validity logically takes precedence, the discussion will begin with outcome perspectives, since this issue has been neglected in the skills training literature.

Perspectives. Evaluators may overlook the diverse effects of training if they select only one perspective from among the many available for viewing training outcome. A program may teach trainees to produce facilitative responses, but such responses may have little impact on other domains: the client is interested in experiencing a sense of well-being; society is interested in the client's behavior becoming more socially useful; the trainee is interested in self-development; the trainer is interested in making contributions to psychological theory. Can the training be considered effective if we only concentrate on producing the expected skills performances?

Unfortunately, many interpersonal skills training programs continue to rely solely on a behavioral skills curriculum that focuses on teaching discrete behaviors using an input-output instructional strategy that emphasizes modeling, practice, feedback, and evaluation. Students are expected to acquire specific skills and demonstrate them after training. Although such an input-output model of training may enhance the scientific precision of skills acquisition, it typically ignores other important dimensions of training, such as consumer needs, social benefits, and conceptual and professional development.

An overemphasis on skills acquisition can lead to training that is experienced by trainees as stilted, mechanical, and unrelated to their personal development. Moreover, because of the emphasis on skills production, trainees may experience a great deal of evaluation anxiety and be preoccupied with negative feedback. The training environment can become an unduly stressful one in which the main objective of trainer and trainee is to avoid making errors, rather than to creatively pursue issues of self-development that may involve confronting and dealing with errors and inappropriate expectations. To reduce human relations training programs to skills only is to neglect professional development, including the development of personal beliefs and attitudes.

Another unfortunate consequence of relying on single behavioral outcomes is the paucity of conceptual development. Typically, the questions of interest in skills training evaluation have concerned technology, rather than psychological theory. Recently, Stone (1980b) found that supervisors in a skills training situation make few conceptual planning statements. Such findings support the notion that skills acquisition issues dominate the training literature, resulting in an impoverished model of training and evaluation.

Preoccupied with demonstrating skills acquisition, trainers and researchers have given most of their attention to the performance of trainees without adequately assessing the impact of such performance on clients. A trainee may learn to produce empathic responses, but such responses may have little impact on the client's sense of well being and may not be perceived and experienced by clients in the expected way.

In a discussion of client needs, the social benefits of training also emerge as a legitimate evaluation perspective. Human services educators have been troubled by the issue of social responsibility because of the implication that practitioners can easily become agents of social control (Szasz, 1970). In part, this concern of educators results from preoccupation with training methods, rather than with the client and his or her behavior in society. Although the value conflicts involved certainly deserve consideration, it is nonetheless naive and simplistic to rely on trainee outcome without considering the benefits to society in terms of client behavior and costs of training. As the taxpaying public becomes increasingly responsible for financing professional and paraprofessional training, and as insurance companies increasingly provide reimbursement for the delivery of therapeutic services, issues of training can quickly become issues of accountability.

Recommendations. Certainly, skills acquisition is not unimportant. Skills that have not been learned are unavailable to the counselor, with consequent reduction in flexibility and creativity. Without a specified training outcome, evaluation can easily become little more than exaggerated promotional statements without evidence, resulting in a return of therapeutic training to the realm of the mystical and mysterious. On the other hand, the predominance of skills acquisition in the literature has led many trainers to ignore a more mediational approach to professional development (Stone, 1980a). Thus, the following recommendations and suggestions are intended to redress this omission.

The first suggestion concerns the multiple focus of training and evaluation. Training evaluation needs to consider each of the perspectives mentioned in the previous section, using multiple measures to ensure that each perspective is adequately represented. The following discussion, however, will focus on only one example for each perspective.

Trainee Performance. As discussed earlier, trainee performance has served as a major outcome perspective. Several procedures are available for analyzing trainee performance, including content knowledge measures and performance measures involving highly structured situations analogous to face-to-face interviews. In later sections, these measures will be discussed as different methods for recording data; this section will focus on the content-analytical approach to trainee interview performance. In this approach, samples of a trainee's interview behavior—including interviews conducted before, immediately after, and some time after training—are recorded on audiotape or videotape, randomly ordered, and transferred to typescript. Raters then classify each interviewer statement according to a particular system. Of the many systems available, two are worth mentioning. The first, Hill's Counselor Verbal Response Category System (Hill, 1978), which incorporates many of the major categories of other systems, consists of fourteen categories that are nominal (with no implications of ranking), mutually exclusive, and operationally anchored for judging counselor verbal behavior: minimal encouragement, approval-reassurance, information, direct guidance, closed question, open question, restatement, reflection, nonverbal referent, interpretation, confrontation, self-disclosure, silence, and other. A written definition and four client-counselor examples are available for each category. Recent results (Hill, Thames, and Rardin, 1979) suggest the usefulness of the system, especially in detecting patterns of skills use and theoretical orientations.

The second analytical system for categorizing counselor statements, Ivey's microskills taxonomy, consists of three major categories: attending skills (closed question, open question, minimal encouragement, paraphrase, reflection of feelings, and summary), influencing skills (directive, expression of content, expression of feelings, interpretation, influencing, and summary), and focus analysis (client, others, topic, helper, mutual, and cultural-environmental). The first two categories are similar to other systems in which raters categorize counselor statements based on content definitions and examples. The third category provides an opportunity for raters to score each statement in terms of focus, as well as skill. Ivey and his colleagues (Ivey and Simek-Downing, 1980) have also stressed the relationship between theoretical orientation and skills usage. For example, Ivey suggests that Rogerians mainly restate, reflect, and encourage the client to talk, whereas rational-emotive therapists primarily use directive skills like interpretation. Such suggestions are congruent with the respective theories and appear to be validated by interviews conducted by Rogers and Ellis (Hill, Thames, and Rardin, 1979). Ivey's procedure may help trainers link skills learning and performance with conceptual development. In addition, Ivey's matrix may help students articulate their implicit theories and may provide evidence of their theories in action.

Cognitive Activity. Although skills performance has value as an outcome measure, it neglects the cognitive activity of trainees and its influence on performance. Typically, new trainees are troubled by doubts about their competence: "I must be able to do therapy without error"; "I should know what to do, but I don't"; "I should be able to help more clients"; "I shouldn't feel angry, powerful, anxious, or bored." Evaluators need to assess the impact of training on trainee attitudes and the interaction between these attitudes and helping skills usage. One way of making such assessments is to obtain cognitive response data—by using a structured, thought-listing procedure (Cacioppo and Petty, in press) that records participants' thoughts about aspects of training. In this procedure, participants are given a thought-listing form with separate spaces for the listing of each individual thought. After listing their cognitive responses, participants may be asked to do a number of tasks, including rank ordering their thoughts on a separate sheet on the basis of importance and estimating the certainty of their cognitive responses. A reaction-to-skills-training procedure developed by one of my students included the following instructions: "Please list your thoughts and feelings about the skill you have just learned and practiced. Specifically, include any thoughts or feelings you have about using them in an interview. Please list each comment separately in one of the spaces below. You may or may not use all of the spaces. You have three minutes to complete the task."

Cognitive responses can be scored along a number of dimensions—including polarity, origin, target, saliency, emotionality, and reality—by external judges and trainees. In the example mentioned in the previous paragraph, thought listings were classified by judges into one of the following referent categories: thoughts about the skill, thoughts about skill usage, and other thoughts. In addition, trainees and naive judges independently categorized each response by placing a plus next to the thoughts that were favorable, a minus next to those that were unfavorable, and a zero next to neutral thoughts. After the interrater reliability of the judges was checked, analyses were performed on the frequency of each type of response per referent category along the polarity dimension.

Client Perspective. After the evaluation of trainee performance and cognitive activity, it is necessary to address the question of whether trained helpers actually help clients. To determine the client perspective, both the behavior and internal states of experience of clients must be assessed. A popular procedure that provides a form of accountability is Goal Attainment Scaling (GAS) (Kiresuk and Sherman, 1968). With counselor assistance, the client uses the GAS to list his or her behaviorally oriented outcomes, ranging from the worst possible outcome through the expected outcome to the best possible outcome. For example, Smith (1976) had each client report his or her outcome in terms of a five-point scale; if the reported behavior was not at the expected level, it was assigned to one of the four remaining categories (worse, much worse, better, much better).

The influence of behavioral psychology has increased the popularity of overt behavioral change as a counseling outcome, but such change is not universally accepted as the most important outcome. Some devices have been constructed and used in outcome studies to assess internal criteria of consumer satisfaction. For instance, the Therapy Session Report (Orlinsky and Howard, 1966) has been used to assess client satisfaction and perceptions of therapeutic effectiveness. In such postinterview questionnaires, clients are asked several questions—such as, "How do you feel about the session that you just completed?"—and asked to rate their response to the session as a whole.

Social Benefits Model. A final perspective to consider is the social benefits model. One aspect of social benefits that has not been given much attention in training is cost-effectiveness. In an era of shrinking resources, training programs need to improve their efficiency by using a cost-effectiveness analysis, in which training inputs (trainees, trainers, material resources, curriculum, and others) are priced in terms of dollars, and outputs (for example, growth in knowledge and skills) are quantified. However, costs should be viewed not in terms of input alone but in terms of potential benefits to be derived from a given program.

A major responsibility of training administrators is to structure and organize the training resources efficiently to achieve training goals. Although resources and ways of combining human and material resources are numerous, the use of time is of central importance in the learning process (Brophy, 1979). Perhaps training psychologists need to investigate the costs of involving educational technology, particularly computer-assisted programs, programmed manuals, and instructional videotapes, in accomplishing skills acquisition objectives. Such procedures may lead to significant time savings without affecting the skills acquisition level of trainees, at the same time enabling trainers to allocate more time to the issues of personal development, conceptual understanding, and the integration of discrete skills into a therapeutic style.

Another facet of the social benefits perspective has to do with how society perceives the social value of the effects of treatment. One approach to gathering these data is to involve significant others, collect reports from several informants, and use pooled judgments. Measurement of the views of relevant others has grown, especially in the area of marital and family therapies. In collecting such data, one may provide an observation checklist, such as the Spouse Observation Checklist (Weiss, Hops, and Patterson, 1973), that includes numerous discrete behaviors that relevant others can check for presence or absence, as well as quality.

Another way of assessing social validation is the social comparison method, in which the client's behavior before and after exposure to a trained helper can be compared with the behavior of a desired reference group. Moreover, the social comparison method can be used to measure trainee outcome, as well as client change, by comparing trainee performance with the performance of an appropriate reference group.

In sum, many potential changes can result from training. In order to emphasize multiple training effects, training outcome must be viewed from the vantage point of society, the client, and the trainee, and, within each perspective, additional outcome questions need to be assessed. The perspectives and outcomes presented in this section are outlined in Table 1.

Although methods for evaluation have been recommended, each has its limitations: taxonomies need clear, detailed definitions; cognitive responses may reveal reconstructive information, rather than thought processes during the event; GAS provides a framework for stating client goals, rather than for insuring their relevance and specificity; self-report questionnaires and reports from others are susceptible to bias; and, finally, it is difficult to quantify training

Table 1. Perspectives and Outcomes.

Perspective	Outcome	Description
Trainee		
Skills	Hill's Counselor Verbal Response Category System; Ivey's Microskills Taxonomy	Classification of trainee verbal behavior
Cognitions	Thought-listing technique	Listing of cognitive responses
Client		
Behavioral	Goal Attainment Scaling	Structured goal-setting procedure
Satisfaction	Therapy session report	Self-report questionnaire
Society		
Efficiency	Cost-benefits analysis	Quantification of inputs, alternatives, and outputs
Social Validation	Social comparison method	Comparison of outcomes with appropriate reference group

inputs and outputs and to determine the appropriate reference groups in making social comparisons.

Although the suggested assessment procedures are limited and time-consuming and often provide different, even contradictory data, I still favor the use of multiple measures from a variety of viewpoints. In addition to providing a broader picture of the effects of training, assessment of training from different perspectives may reduce bias and may stimulate continued interactions between training psychology and experimental, especially cognitive, psychology.

Sources of Influence. For most training programs, the main interest in evaluation is in determining whether the program is effective. The determination of program effectiveness, it has been suggested, involves not one outcome but multiple outcomes from different perspectives. In this section, the concern shifts from the dependent to the independent variable—that is, from training effects to the training program and its relationship to training effects. This concern is associated with internal validity; although it follows the discussion of outcome perspectives in this chapter for conceptual reasons, it should probably be explored first when making causal inferences about training programs. If other factors cannot be ruled out as causal factors, then outcomes become less than meaningful indices of program effectiveness. On the other hand, the selection of an outcome from a single perspective may yield inadequate evidence for training program evaluation, regardless of how rigorous the methodology. Perhaps it is wise to consider both outcome perspectives and internal validity as equal in priority in planning and conducting a program evaluation.

The first task in attempting to make valid statements about the relationship of a training program to outcome is to ensure that the training program described fits the training program as implemented and experienced by the trainees. Training components and measures are selected from a well-defined theoretical context so that the specific procedures will be congruent with theory. For example, client-centered theory emphasizes the role of subjective experience and facilitative conditions in learning to be a therapeutic person. Thus, following theory, the trainer would use methods and measures that reflect these emphases, such as using facilitative supervisors, experiential methods, and assessment of the impact of training on the trainee through self-report indices. After the conceptual work and during the evaluation process, data need to be collected from a number of sources regarding the training program as implemented. For example, if the purpose of a training program evaluation is to compare a structured and an unstructured format in skills training, the dimension of training structure would need to be assessed by obtaining random excerpts from training experiences and asking experts to rate training structure or by having trainees rate the level of structure experienced. Such validation is necessary in relating training to outcome because inadequate specification of training precludes unambiguous conclusions and results in a lack of replicability.

A second task is to provide a strong test of the relationship between training and outcome through the adoption of a set of research procedures designed to rule out alternative explanations. One set of procedures, randomization, makes this task easier. When trainees are randomly assigned to training groups, many alternatives are ruled out. With other procedures, such as quasi-experimentation, the evaluator has to rule out alternatives one by one, instead of relying on randomization. Randomization does not solve all problems, but randomized experiments generally yield more interpretable results than quasi-experiments. Of course, the complexity and restraints of field settings need to be recognized, but the decision as to whether to use randomized experiments or quasi-experimental designs should be based on which design alternative in this specific training situation will enable the evaluator to make the clearest statements about the relationship of training to outcome.

Given randomization, other experimental design procedures can be used to enhance internal validity. One procedure concerns the use of representative designs in which the evaluator takes samples from populations of trainees and from populations of training stimuli, most often human stimuli such as trainers, models, experimenters, and clients. Usually evaluators sample from trainee populations but not from populations of human stimuli. Instead, single individuals are used to represent training constructs, yielding an inadequate representation of the construct and, consequently, confounding and limiting generalization. For instance, in single stimulus designs, the influence of a particular trainer or supervisor may interact with a particular program, resulting in difficulties in attributing outcome. The same can be said for using only one method of training, such as written simulation or any other single operation.

Another design procedure is to include appropriate control groups, such as active, instructional training groups, whose trainers have been informed about the target skills and whose training can demonstrate credibility and ability to influence trainee expectations without providing the relevant training components. In addition, other control group procedures, such as a Solomon Four-Group Design and negative expectancy sets, can be considered in light of the questions of measurement reactivity and trainee expectations, respectively.

A final set of procedures to be discussed involves the systematic gathering of data for purposes of conducting several check analyses. Some of these check analyses have already been mentioned, including a manipulation check in which the evaluator gathers data from participants and relevant others concerning the independent variable or variables. Other empirical checks are necessary concerning demand characteristics, trainee expectations, trainer expectations, curriculum materials, and facets of the outcome evaluation, such as differences between role-played clients.

In terms of check analyses, training research has relied on stimulus-defined designs and has neglected information from a response-defined orientation. That is, under the influence of behavioral psychology, training researchers have been preoccupied with externally defined research variables without considering the phenomenological experience of the trainees undergoing evaluation. Researchers may use external ratings to establish that trainers were either high-level or low-level empathic communicators during supervision, but trainees may not necessarily experience their supervisors in the same way. Thus, evaluators are advised to obtain data for check analyses from several sources.

Estimating the impact of various sources of influence on the relationship between training and outcome is a complex process. Alternative explanations can be ruled out through experimental designs that include the use of randomization, representative designs, and appropriate control groups. Moreover, some influences can be reduced through statistical analyses of data collected to verify the independent variable and to check the operation of nonspecific influences. In addition, these extraneous influences can be dealt with through logic and theory, and alternatives sometimes ruled out on the basis of implausibility. Whatever procedures are adopted, if evaluators are interested in linking training to outcome, internal validity must be a primary consideration.

How to Evaluate: Strategy and Measurement

The development of an effective training program is usually guided by evaluation and research conducted in three stages. First, a series of outcome evaluations are carried out using treatment–no-treatment control studies to determine the promise of the proposed program. Further studies comparing appropriate control groups and traditional training groups are conducted to ascertain the relationship of the outcome to the experimental training program in the context of outside influences (so-called nonspecific effects) and established training programs. Given evidence that a training program achieves good results, the second stage involves component studies that are conducted to determine the relevance of the various training components in producing the training outcomes. The component approach uses an analytical method in which a composite program is dismantled into its training components. These components are isolated and examined, either singly or in combination with appropriate control groups, to determine the significant ingredients. Finally, training programs are matched to different personality and cognitive dimensions of the trainee in hopes of enhancing effectiveness and discovering learning processes that may mediate training effects.

Generally, most skills training programs have followed this threefold strategy. In the case of microcounseling, early studies were done using outcome analyses (Guttman and Haase, 1972; Toukmanian and Rennie, 1975). Later studies used component analyses (Stone and Vance, 1976), and more recent research has concerned individual differences (Berg and Stone, 1980). In program evaluation, it seems important to establish the effectiveness of the training program before conducting studies of components and individual differences.

Figure 1 summarizes the major components of an evaluation of trainee outcomes. As in the discussion of perspectives, a multidimensional approach is appropriate. Many training researchers assume that training assessment involves little more than an evaluation of the trainee's overt behavior in either a naturalistic or a laboratory situation. On the contrary, however, trainee evaluation can involve multiple response channels, methods, and operations. Although this section focuses primarily on the trainee, other sources of information need also to be considered: clients, significant others, and cost-benefit data.

In terms of the trainee, the first measurement dimension involves assessment of three response channels: self-report, motoric, and physiological. The first two channels have been discussed previously in relation to cognitive response data and skills outcomes. Physiological data can also be collected in training investigations.

Figure 1. A Model for Evaluating Trainee Outcome.

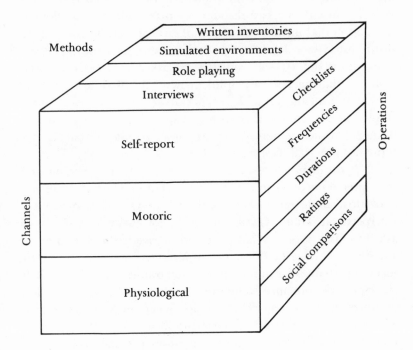

For example, Kagan and his colleagues (Archer and others, 1972) have used physiological feedback in their stimulated recall methodology, recording and videotaping a trainee's physiological activities as he or she observed simulated vignettes of an actor or actress portraying various intense emotions. The physiological responses were played back to the trainees and used as an additional feedback mode for understanding their interpersonal behavior. Although such data can be helpful, physiological evaluation has its limitations (for example, reactivity, costs, measurement difficulties), as does evaluation of the other response channels, and the inconsistent correlations among physiological responses and between such responses and self-report and motoric indices warrant caution in interpreting findings.

A second measurement dimension concerns the various methods used to obtain information relevant to training effectiveness, including written inventories, simulated environments, role playing, and interviews. Content knowledge of particular therapeutic skills are usually assessed through a written, audio, or audiovideo simulation that includes a number of critical incidents from therapeutic interviews. In these simulations, such as Carkhuff's Communication Index (1969), trainees are asked to respond to client stimulus statements in a helpful manner. A criterion is generally used to indicate the trainee's level of skill acquisition—for example, 80 percent acquisition at level-three response—but research has indicated that such content knowledge measures may not predict performance very well (Gormally and Hill, 1974).

Performance assessments use role-played interviews, naturalistic interviews, or a simulated environment in which the trainee is asked to demonstrate certain skills. In the Group Assessment of Interpersonal Traits (Goodman, 1967), for example, trainees are asked to disclose a personal issue and to give feedback in a group situation. Whether the format is an interview or a simulation, the focus of such assessment procedures is on trainee performance. Deficiencies in performance evaluations may emerge from the contrived nature of the situation, including lack of ego involvement of trainees and lack of demand characteristics, and from the unknown relationship between the trainees' performance and experience in the controlled and natural environments.

When data can be gathered from multiple channels using a number of techniques, evaluators can score it in various ways, including checklists, frequency and duration counts, ratings, and social comparison procedures. Checklists assess the presence or absence of a behavior; frequency counts reflect the number of occurrences of a behavior; duration counts involve the length of time a behavior occurs or the latency of a specific response; and ratings indicate the intensity or quality of a behavior.

In scoring a trainee's performance, for example, audio or audiovisual recordings of the trainee's interviews can be transcribed and put on typescripts. Raters can then use a verbal response category system that includes definitions of relevant responses to check the presence or absence of these skills, count their occurrences, assess the amount of time (number of clauses) spent on these skills versus the time (number of clauses) spent on nonrelevant interaction, or rate the quality of the verbal responses with ratings of 1 (not helpful) to 5 (very helpful). Such information can then be compared with outcomes derived from an appropriate norm group.

These operations also present problems, however. The quantitative indices rely on sound definitions and replicable rater protocols. In addition to such definitions and protocols, the rating scales need specific and unambiguous descriptions for each scale point, as well as psychometric soundness—unidirectionality and appropriate range, among other factors. Finally, the comparison procedure must deal with the problem of selecting an appropriate reference group.

Needless to say, many other facets of measurement could be discussed. For instance, in terms of the time of measurement, a multiple operational strategy is relevant, with evaluations scheduled to occur before, during, and immediately after training, with a follow-up evaluation scheduled some time after training has ended. In addition, evaluation could address other ecologically relevant dimensions, instead of focusing on the individual trainee. It is hoped that the first section of this chapter helped broaden the focus of training evaluations.

Conclusion

In conclusion, it will be helpful to examine a recent study (Stone, 1981) in relation to some of the points made in this chapter. The purpose of the study was to determine whether teaching and supervision had an impact on reflective communication development within a microtraining situation. The experimental strategy involved an analytical approach in which certain components, including cognitive learning, supervision, and teaching, were systematically varied among four groups: full treatment group (learning, supervision, teaching), partial treatment group (learning, supervision, reading a programmed manual), supervision group (learning and supervision), and learning group (learning). Two comparisons were of interest: comparison of the full and partial treatment groups involved the question of teaching, and comparison of the supervision and learning groups examined the impact of supervision. Multiple measures representing three sources—counselor behavior, client participation, and client evaluation—were used in evaluation.

Some features of the study are worth noting here. First, the research strategy adopted, including proper controls for exposure time (for example, reading the programmed manual), would be classified as a component-analytical approach that assumes the overall effectiveness of microtraining. Given that assumption, I attempted to see if supervision and teaching are effective ingredients. In so doing, I adopted a multidimensional assessment approach in which several measures were used, including a written inventory, a role-played interview, and four self-report measures (Counselor Effectiveness Scale, Barrett-Lennard's Relationship Inventory, Satisfaction Scale, and Helpfulness Scale). The measures were conceptualized in terms of three sources and the plausibility of such a conceptualization was empirically verified. This is the second feature worthy of note—the use of a multifocused evaluation in which client and trainee outcome perspectives were assessed.

In carrying out the study, I used a number of methodological procedures to reduce the viability of alternative hypotheses, including random assignment and several check analyses. One check analysis, using audiotape ratings, verified that the supervision process was implemented as described. Another analysis was done to rule out client differences across groups. Other methodological procedures used to enhance the representatives of the design included the use of multiple video models, multiple training methods (videotape, manuals, live supervision), and multiple ways of recording data. These methodological procedures—randomization, verification, and representativeness—represent the third feature: internal validity.

As described earlier, the study also used a multiple approach to the measurement of the selected dependent variables. In addition to trainee, client, and rater perspectives, several channels were used in assessing client outcomes: self-referenced verbalization and self-report (for example, Counselor Effectiveness Scale). Moreover, cognitive response data collected from the full treatment trainees (Stone, 1980b) made the trainee evaluation multifaceted, as well (skills and cognitive response data). Multiple methods, including written inventories and role-played interviews, were used to obtain information, which was scored in terms of frequency counts (Ivey and Authier, 1978) and quality ratings (Carkhuff, 1969). The final feature worthy of note, then, is the study's multidimensional approach to measurement, including multiple sources, channels, methods, and operations.

Of course, the study did not meet all the criteria discussed, such as the examination of social benefits and the use of multiple measures over time. Nevertheless, as this chapter has made clear, investigators planning to evaluate skills programs must consider the following three points: evaluation can be viewed from many perspectives; evaluation needs to be concerned about making interpretable statements (internal validity); and evaluation should use multiple operations in assessing training outcome.

References

Archer, J., and others. "A New Methodology for Education, Treatment, and Research in Human Interaction." *Journal of Counseling Psychology*, 1972, *19*, 275–281.

Berg, K. S., and Stone, G. L. "Effects of Conceptual Level and Supervision Structure on Counselor Skill Development." *Journal of Counseling Psychology*, 1980, *27*, 500–509.

Brophy, J. E. "Teacher Behavior and Student Learning." *Educational Leadership*, 1979, *37*, 33–34.

Burck, H. D., and Peterson, G. P. "Needed: More Evaluation, Not Research." *Personnel and Guidance Journal*, 1975, *53*, 563–569.

Cacioppo, J. T., and Petty, R. E. "Social Psychological Procedures for Cognitive Response Assessment: The Thought-Listing Technique." In C. R. Glass and M. Genest (Eds.), *Cognitive Assessment*. New York: Guilford Press, in press.

Campbell, D. T., and Stanley, J. C. "Experimental and Quasi-Experimental Designs for Research on Teaching." In N. L. Gage (Ed.), *Handbook of Research on Teaching*. Chicago: Rand McNally, 1963.

Carkhuff, R. R. *Helping and Human Relations*. 2 Vols. New York: Holt, Rinehart and Winston, 1969.

Cook, T. D., and Campbell, D. T. *Quasi-Experimentation: Design and Analysis Issues for Field Settings*. Chicago: Rand McNally, 1979.

Gelso, C. J. "Research in Counseling: Methodological and Professional Issues." *The Counseling Psychologist*, 1979, *8*, 7-35.

Goldman, L. *Research Methods for Counselors: Practical Approaches in Field Settings*. New York: Wiley, 1978.

Goodman, G. C. "An Experiment with Companionship Therapy: College Students and Troubled Boys—Assumptions, Selection, and Design." *American Journal of Public Health*, 1967, *57*, 1772-1777.

Gormally, J., and Hill, C. E. "Guidelines for Research on Carkhuff's Training Model." *Journal of Counseling Psychology*, 1974, *21*, 539-547.

Guttman, M., and Haase, R. "The Generalization of Microcounseling Skills from Training Period to Actual Counseling Setting." *Counselor Education and Supervision*, 1972, *12*, 98-107.

Hill, C. E. "Development of a Counselor Verbal Response Category System." *Journal of Counseling Psychology*, 1978, *25*, 461-468.

Hill, C. E., Thames, T. B., and Rardin, D. K. "Comparison of Rogers, Perls, and Ellis on the Hill Counselor Verbal Response Category System." *Journal of Counseling Psychology*, 1979, *26*, 198-203.

Ivey, A. E., and Authier, J. *Microcounseling: Innovations in Interviewing, Counseling, Psychotherapy, and Psychoeducation*. (2nd ed.) Springfield, Ill.: Thomas, 1978.

Ivey, A. E., and Simek-Downing, L. *Counseling and Psychotherapy: Skills, Theories, and Practice*. Englewood Cliffs, N.J.: Prentice-Hall, 1980.

Kahneman, D., and Tversky, A. "On the Psychology of Prediction." *Psychological Review*, 1973, *80*, 237-258.

Kiresuk, T. J., and Sherman, R. E. "Goal Attainment Scaling: A General Method for Evaluating Community Mental Health Programs." *Community Mental Health Journal*, 1968, *4*, 443-453.

Mahoney, M. J. *Scientist as Subject: The Psychological Imperative*. Cambridge, Mass.: Ballinger, 1976.

Orlinsky, D. E., and Howard, K. T. *Therapy Session Report, Form P and Form T*. Chicago: Institute for Juvenile Research, 1966.

Smith, D. L. "Goal Attainment Scaling as an Adjunct to Counseling." *Journal of Counseling Psychology*, 1976, *23*, 22-27.

Stone, G. L. *A Cognitive-Behavioral Approach to Counseling Psychology: Implications for Practice, Research, and Training.* New York: Praeger, 1980a.

Stone, G. L. "Effects of Experience on Supervision Planning." *Journal of Counseling Psychology,* 1980b, *27,* 84–88.

Stone, G. L. "Effects of Different Strategies Within a Microtraining Situation." *Counselor Education and Supervision,* 1981, *20,* 301–311.

Stone, G. L., and Vance, A. "Instructions, Modeling, and Rehearsal: Implications for Training." *Journal of Counseling Psychology,* 1976, *23,* 272–279.

Szasz, T. S. *The Manufacture of Madness.* New York: Harper & Row, 1970.

Toukmanian, S., and Rennie D. "Microcounseling vs. Human Relations Training: Relative Effectiveness with Undergraduate Trainees." *Journal of Counseling Psychology,* 1975, *22,* 345–352.

Weiss, R. L., Hops, H., and Patterson, G. R. "A Framework for Conceptualizing Marital Conflict, a Technology for Altering It, Some Data for Evaluating It." In F. W. Clark and L. A. Hamerlynck (Eds.), *Critical Issues in Research and Practice: Proceedings of the Fourth Banff International Conference on Behavior Modification.* Champaign, Ill.: Research Press, 1973.

Part Five

Training Clients in Interpersonal Skills

Within the past decade, interest has grown in educational training as a therapeutic modality. The psychoeducational approach is based on the assumption that individuals with psychological problems are not sick but rather have failed to learn facilitative skills or have learned deviant behavior patterns. In either case, skills training, rather than healing, is warranted. Unfortunately, few helpers conceptualize their role in educational terms, although many of the activities they perform are educative. What helper does not provide guidance, modeling, and feedback? Are not information sharing and evaluation of performance common elements of helping? Are not clients frequently instructed to carry out "homework" assignments?

The movement from a medical to a teaching orientation has been accompanied by the lack of a clear theoretical foundation. Rather than standing on its own conceptual framework, the skills training movement is seen, as Ivey laments in Chapter Sixteen, an appendage to more accepted approaches to treatment. Using the microtraining paradigm as a backdrop, Ivey attempts to move the field one step closer to the establishment of its own theoretical base.

Ivey's conceptual chapter is followed by the presentation of two skills training models: Guerney's relationship enhancement approach and Gazda's life-skills training program. Both illustrate the delivery of helping through training, rather than treatment. For two decades, Guerney has pioneered his skills training approach to

469

helping. In Chapter Seventeen, he elucidates his model, describes its application to helping contexts ranging from marital and family groups to foster parents and senior citizens, and provides empirical documentation for its effectiveness. In Chapter Eighteen, Gazda proposes an approach that encompasses eleven generic skills areas over the course of the life span. His comprehensive training program has been used as a preventative curriculum with elementary school children and for remedial purposes with patients at Veterans Administration hospitals.

Chapter 16

Skills Training: a Model for Treatment

Allen E. Ivey
Maryanne Galvin

Skills training is rooted in both theory and pragmatism. Carkhuff's human relations development (1969) and Guerney's filial therapy (1964) are based on a client-centered approach. Goldstein's structured learning therapy (1973) and Ivey's microcounseling (1971) most closely relate to a social learning model, whereas Kagan's interpersonal process recall (1972) is influenced by psychodynamic thinking. Common to all, however, is a basic pragmatism—skills training has been consistently effective for over fifteen years, combining theory and practice in a unique working combination in which individual trainers and trainees can immediately test whether the concepts have validity.

Therapists of differing treatment orientations tend to use skills and manifest empathy in different forms. An examination of Figure 1 reveals, for example, that classical psychoanalysts may most frequently use the skill of interpretation, whereas nondirective therapists tend mainly to use paraphrases and reflections of feelings.

Figure 1. Twelve Counseling and Psychotherapy Theories: Their Use of Quantitative, Qualitative, and Focus Skills.

Theory	Microskills: Quantitative Dimensions											Focus						Empathy: Qualitative Dimensions								
	Closed Question	Open Question	Minimal Encouragers	Paraphrase	Reflect Feeling	Summarization	Directive	Express Content	Express Feeling	Interpretive Summarization	Interpretation	Helpee	Others	Topic	Helper	Mutual	Cultural Environment	Primary Empathy	Additive Empathy	Positive Regard	Respect	Warmth	Concreteness	Immediacy	Confrontation	Genuineness
Psychodynamic	○	○		○						●	●	○						○	●	○	○		○	P	○	
Behavioral	●	●	○	○	○	○	●	●		○		●	○	●				○	○	●	○	○	●	F	○	
Nondirective			○	●	●	○						●						●		●	●	●		H	○	○
Modern Rogerian			○	●	●	○		○				●			○	●		●	○	●	●	●		H	○	●
Existential-Humanistic	○		○	○	○			○				●	●	○	○	○	○	○	○	○	●	○		H	○	○
Gestalt	○	○					●	○				●	●					●	○				○	H	●	○
Transpersonal	○	○	○	○	○	○	●	●	●	○	○	●	●	○	○	○	○	●	○	●	●	●	○	F	○	●
Trait and Factor	○	●	○	○	○	○	○	○	●	○	○	●			●			○	○	○	○	○	●	F	○	○
Rational - Emotive	○	○				○	●	○	●	●		●						○	○	●	○	○	○	PH	○	
Transactional Analysis	○	○	○	○	○	○	●		○	●	●	●						○	●	○			○	PH	●	○
Reality Therapy	○	○	○	○	○	○	○	●	○	○	○	●	○	●	○	○	●	○	○	●	○	○	○	PF	○	●
Strategic	○	○					●					○	●	○				○	●	○		●		PH	●	

Legend

● Most frequently used dimension.
○ Frequently used dimension.
□ Dimension may be used but is not a central aspect of theory.
P Primary emphasis on past tense immediacy.
H Primary emphasis on present tense immediacy.
F Primary emphasis on future tense immediacy.

Adapted from Ivey, A., and Gluckstern, N. *Basic Attending Skills.* North Amherst, Mass.: Microtraining, 1974, p. 198.

By contrast, questions are a prominent skill used in the trait-and-factor, behavioral, and Gestalt modes.

Skills training has made valuable contributions to the practice of a wide array of treatment modalities. Therefore, it should cease viewing istelf as a theoretical appendage to these modalities and focus on its own contributions to treatment approaches in psychology, counseling, and social work. The purpose of this chapter is to draw from experience with microtraining and other skills models in order to present some common elements that may ultimately lead to a general theory of skills training with clients. Skills training is now a significant movement with a substantial research history—research whose results are possibly more impressive than the results of outcome research in counseling and psychotherapy. Skills training has the potential for contributing to answering the basic question: "What treatment, by whom, is most effective for this individual with that specific problem, and under which set of circumstances?" (Paul, 1967, p. 111).

Toward a Theory of Skills Training

Microtraining, human relations development, assertiveness training, values clarification, or any others from a wide array of skills training and psychoeducational programs—all focus on the development of intentionality and an increased response repertoire. "The person who acts with intentionality has a sense of capability. He or she can generate alternative behaviors in a given situation and 'approach' a problem from different vantage points. The intentional, fully functioning individual is not bound to one course of action but can respond in the moment to changing life situations and look forward to longer term goals" (Ivey with Simek-Downing, 1980, p. 8). Generating increased response capability is a metagoal of the microtraining framework and, it may be suggested, a metagoal of skills training in general. The major premise and commonality of skills training is that all skills training programs are ultimately concerned with developing intentionality and freeing clients to generate an ever-increasing array of sentences, metaphors, and behaviors that will enable them to commit themselves in the world from a standpoint of options rather than limitations. The word *generate* is particularly important and may be considered analogous to Chomsky's (1965) generational grammar. Clients come to skills training programs (or psychotherapy) unable to generate the full array of sentences and behaviors that they are capable of generating. Fritz Perls's inelegant term *stuckness* is perhaps most descriptive of the immobility of clients unable to cope with difficult situations. Psychotherapy helps clients deal with certain types of stuckness, such as logical inconsistencies (rational-emotive therapy), behavioral deficits (behavioral therapy), polarities (psychodynamic therapy), and rigid scripts (transactional analysis). Skills training has a similar objective but provides a broader framework for problem solving in more areas. Skills training can be highly therapeutic but, because of its broader base, is perhaps more able than traditional therapy to increase client alternatives.

The relationship of skills training to traditional treatment is at present still tentative. Skills training has largely served as an adjunct to traditional therapies but has been demonstrated to be a viable treatment approach in itself (Goldstein, 1973; Ivey, 1973). Training indeed can be treatment. Whereas research on the effectiveness of therapy (Gurman and Razin, 1977; Garfield and Bergin, 1978) has had mixed results, research on the effectiveness of skills training seems more positive and hopeful. Skills training may indeed be the treatment of choice.

The following assumptions, based on the major premise stated earlier, may be useful in leading to a general theory applicable to the many alternative skills training programs.

Assumption 1: The major alternative approaches to skills training may be considered systematic constructs for construing the world and acting more intentionally. These systematic constructs permit the alteration of actions and the generation of new sentences and behaviors by the client.

The identification and acquisition of new behaviors through skills training is similar to the fixed-role therapy of Kelly (1955). A specific role is identified, and the key constructs associated with that role are made explicit. In skills training, the client can test out the role or behavior in a simulated situation with little danger to himself or others. This process is similar to the process whereby clients engaged in Rogerian, behavioral, or Gestalt therapy generate constructs in accord with that view of the world.

A special merit of skills training is that constructs are measurable and immediately tested in the training program. Furthermore, plans are made for generalization beyond the training setting. All skills training programs, although based on different theoretical constructs, are likely to encourage the generation of new behaviors, and the acquisition and usefulness of these behaviors is more easily tested in skills training than in traditional therapeutic modes.

Assumption 2: Skills training programs have in common rigorous specification of the alternative sentences, metaphors, and behaviors they wish to teach. With this specificity of objectives is an instructional system that ensures that learned constructs may be tested first in the laboratory environment of the training program and then generalized systematically to the home environment.

One of the reasons that skills training works is that specific and limited objectives are established prior to training. Each program has an established instructional technology that has been demonstrated over time to produce changes that can be generalized to the home environment.

Assumption 3: Different modes of skills training will be of varying degrees of utility with people who present different types of issues, come from different backgrounds, and have special histories of person-environment transaction.

If a basic assumption of a skills training theory is that different people may require different training, then perhaps we can avoid the tiresome question of which training modality is most effective and ask instead, Which training modality is most effective for what? Specific goals and objectives need to be defined as we move toward comparing the relative merits of the several training programs. A corollary is that we can expect some clients to benefit more from traditional psychotherapy or counseling than from skills training—for example, the person raised in a culture that believes in the medical model of healing.

All the skills training programs have experienced resistance and difficulty with some client populations. This in turn has resulted in a flexibility of training and an effort on the part of trainers to offer something to every person in a training group. This ability to adapt programs to meet special needs is a unique strength of skills training. Although some competition between programs has arisen from time to time, trainers have generally respected differences and learned from one another, recognizing that no one skills training program has all the answers. With research and theory (Goldstein and Stein, 1976; Berzins, 1977) suggesting that systematic planning of appropriate treatment modes may be possible, a major challenge for skills training over the next few years is to determine the specific methods and techniques that are most suitable for clients presenting differing concerns.

Despite differences, all skills training programs tend to follow some variant of the psychoeducational model. Authier and his colleagues (1975) have perhaps said it best: "Most of the advocates of such an approach (psychoeducation/skills training) agree that the educational model means psychological practitioners seeing their function not in terms of abnormality (or illness) $\rightarrow$ diagnosis $\rightarrow$ prescription $\rightarrow$ therapy $\rightarrow$ cure; but rather in terms of client dissatisfaction (or ambition) $\rightarrow$ goal setting $\rightarrow$ skill teaching $\rightarrow$ satisfaction or goal achievement. The person being served is seen as analogous to a pupil, rather than a patient" (p. 31). This distinction leads to another basic assumption of the skills training model.

Assumption 4: Skills training is concerned with teaching, rather than remediation, with prevention, rather than cure. This, however, does not mean that skills training is not therapeutic. It is a distinct alternative or supplement to traditional therapy.

Most skills trainers come from traditional therapeutic backgrounds. Microtraining and human relations development evolved from attempts by counseling psychologists to understand therapy. Through their investigations, the generic aspects of the process were uncovered, and the psychoeducational skills training approach was developed.

Assumption 5: Skills training programs generally rest on a systematic technology. Through experience and research, the technology has been shaped and adapted to many types of individuals and groups. Most skills training technologies contain: cognitive information about a construct; sample experiential exercises to illustrate the construct; practice experiential exercises to try out the construct; and systematic practice leading toward generalization beyond the skills training program.

Although the influence is not universal, some form of the social learning model seems to pervade skills training. In Kelly's work, the theoretical concepts are seldom explicit, but, in skills training programs, a scientific view of human relations is emphasized, the knowability of one's own constructs is taught, and the need to test out constructs through some form of role play or practice is considered essential. Further, skills trainers seldom consider themselves to have the final answer to all questions but emphasize that the skills learned are just a part of the solution to the clients' problems.

Assumption 6: Skills training is generic in nature, teaching a basic set of human interactions that may be used by many people in differing settings.

Microtraining has been used with patients and parents, physicians and paraprofessionals, in settings ranging from the Canadian Arctic to aboriginal Australia. The universal application of skills training inevitably results in resistance from specialists who deny the ability of psychologists and counselors to generalize behavior to multiple settings and emphasize the professionalization of psychology and the importance of unique contributions that can be "owned." Skills trainers are often interested in sharing basic generic concepts with the lay population and making psychology public and available to all. An intent of skills training is the demystification of the helping process.

Assumption 7: Skills training, like psychotherapy, is a cultural phenomenon primarily representative of Western culture. As such, increased awareness of cultural uniqueness and cultural differences is needed as skills training becomes more broadly available.

Pedersen (this volume) has described the issues of cross-cultural communication and skills training. Experience with microtraining has revealed that microtraining works—but works differently—in different cultures. For example, skills of questioning, popular in the white, middle-class population, turn out to be inappropriate in many native cultures where a more subtle approach is better suited. Because of a tolerance for vague language, psychotherapy often flounders when dealing with cultural differences. In contrast, the precision of skills training allows specific differences in behaviors and attitudes to be identified, specified, and eventually taught. A true frontier for skills training is to accurately outline effective modes of cross-cultural communication.

The major premise and the seven basic assumptions should be considered only the beginning of a comprehensive theory of skills training. We are still left with Paul's question, cited earlier in this chapter, (1967) "what treatment, by whom, . . . under what set of circumstances?" (p. 111). We do not yet know which skills training programs can substitute for therapy, which will be most effective for different types of individuals, or even which are most cost-effective given a certain goal. Perhaps these questions will serve as a basis for further research and investigation.

Future Directions

This chapter has outlined and suggested some beginning theoretical formulations for an integrated view of skills training. Key issues for the future include:

1. Comparative analysis of the skills approach and traditional approaches to therapy. This issue is difficult to address because psychotherapy is generally individual in nature, and skills training is most often a group process. However, individual work in structured learning therapy and microtraining, for example, is clearly possible. Can we demonstrate that such approaches are viable alternatives to individual therapy? Such evidence will be necessary if supporting funds and insurance payments are to be made available to enable further growth of skills training as a viable movement.

2. Given the back-to-basics movement of the late 1970s and early 1980s, skills training, as a relatively new phenomenon, will

have to prove its validity and win a more secure place in the educational curriculum of universities and colleges. Simply because it is new on the scene, skills training may have difficulty maintaining momentum in a time of budgetary cutbacks.

3. Skills training to date has been conducted among many professional groups, including social workers and the various divisions of the American Psychological Association. However, skills trainers have had little contact among themselves. Is it time for a national association of skills trainers to help further the movement? Or perhaps it is more appropriate to work within existing organizations to further our views.

4. Can skills training develop its own independent theory? At present, skills training remains an appendage to other theoretical frameworks but, in many instances, may be more powerful than the framework within which it functions. A separate, theoretically based movement would pose problems for the counseling, social work, and psychological establishments. Among such problems might be redefining present theoretical frameworks, allowing the risk of larger systems changes by giving skills to the public; communicating and maintaining criteria for effective services delivered by professionals and paraprofessionals.

We believe skills training is the treatment of choice for the future. The research data, the explicitness of the various programs, the promising patterns of cost-effectiveness, the ease and simplicity of training, all point to the viability of skills training. Yet it is difficult to convince a person who has gone through a lengthy psychotherapy training program that an approach as clear and obvious as skills training could be more effective than traditional treatment approaches. The clarity and power of skills training may be its own undoing. We recall a conversation with a famous psychologist who said that he was fully aware of the power and impact of skills training but had turned away from it because it made psychology too clear and easily available to the public, and "we are a profession." Skills training clearly faces a challenge in the future. Impressive beginnings have been made in a short time, but they are only beginnings.

The ability of skills training to blend theory and practice in programs that clarify a wide variety of complex issues to our client populations is perhaps our greatest asset. The pragmatism of this approach cannot be argued; what is now needed is a more comprehensive and dynamic theory of social skills training itself. Skills training works—we now need to show how and why it works so effectively.

References

Authier, J., and others. "The Psychological Practitioner as a Teacher." *The Counseling Psychologist,* 1975, *5,* 31–50.

Berzins, J. "Therapist-Patient Matching." In A. Gurman and A. Razin (Eds.), *Effective Psychotherapy.* Elmsford, N.Y.: Pergamon Press, 1977.

Carkhuff, R. R. *Helping and Human Relations.* 2 Vols. New York: Holt, Rinehart and Winston, 1969.

Chomsky, N. *Aspects of the Theory of Syntax.* Cambridge, Mass.: M.I.T. Press, 1965.

Garfield, S. L., and Bergin, A. E. (Eds.). *Handbook of Psychotherapy and Behavior Change.* New York: Wiley, 1978.

Goldstein, A. *Structured Learning Therapy.* New York: Academic, 1973.

Goldstein, A. P., and Stein, N. *Prescriptive Psychotherapies.* Elmsford, N.Y.: Pergamon Press, 1976.

Guerney, B., Jr. "Filial Therapy." *Journal of Consulting Psychology,* 1964, *28,* 303–310.

Gurman, A., and Razin, A. *Effective Psychotherapy.* Elmsford, N.Y.: Pergamon Press, 1977.

Ivey, A. E. *Microcounseling.* Springfield, Ill.: Thomas, 1971.

Ivey, A. E. "Media Therapy: Educational Change Planning for Psychiatric Patients." *Journal of Counseling Psychology,* 1973, *20,* 338–343.

Ivey, A., and Gluckstern, N. *Basic Influencing Skills: Participant Manual.* North Amherst, Mass.: Microtraining Associates, 1974.

Ivey, A. E., with Simek-Downing, L. *Counseling and Psychotherapy: Skills, Theories, Practice.* Englewood Cliffs, N.J.: Prentice-Hall, 1980.

Kagan, N. *Influencing Human Interaction*. East Lansing: Michigan State University Press, 1972.

Kelly, G. *Psychology of Personal Constructs*. New York: Norton, 1955.

Paul, G. "Strategy of Outcome Research in Psychotherapy." *Journal of Consulting Psychology*, 1967, *31*, 109–119.

Chapter 17

Relationship Enhancement

Bernard Guerney, Jr.

Relationship Enhancement (RE) is systematic instruction in a set of skills designed to achieve personal or group goals, to improve personal and interpersonal adjustment, and to help participants help others do the same. It is applicable as therapy, as a method of training to do therapy, as a means of problem prevention, and as an enrichment program. The skills are useful, and may be taught, to professionals and paraprofessionals, to individuals and groups of individuals, and to members of a family or familylike group (for example, coworkers).

In RE's application to the training of professionals, paraprofessionals, coworkers, and similar groups, the appropriateness of fit between the program and needs of the participants is generally made clear before the initial contact, just as the general nature of a course or workshop is understood by participants before they come to the first session.

With therapy clients, each person, before beginning RE, has the opportunity to express his or her problems or the goals to which he or she aspires, as well as his or her perception of the problems or goals of any others involved, after which it is jointly determined whether RE is appropriate to those needs. RE would be appropriate whenever better relationships with others would be of help. The only criterion for excluding a client is lack of sufficient reality contact to attend to instruction. At the time of initial contact with clients, the instructor also determines whether additional types of treatment or enrichment programs ought to be encouraged.

The skills are then explained in terms of how they will be useful in resolving the problems or achieving the goals of each client. An illustration of an attempt to try to solve a conflict or problem without the use of skills is usually contrasted with an illustration of how the same problem can be better resolved when RE skills are used. Usually this is done with selections from specially prepared audio cassette tapes containing illustrations appropriate to a wide variety of client situations (Guerney and Vogelsong, 1981).

Once RE has begun, and the skills are being practiced, clients select the specific topics for practice according to criteria explained by the leader. The topics chosen are to be progressively more serious as mastery of skills improves and more skills are learned. Training begins with about twenty minutes of practice of empathic skill on nonproblematic issues not involving intimates. Then empathy skill is practiced with positive perceptions and feelings as the topic. Next, relatively noncontroversial topics designed to improve the relationship serve as topics for skill usage, with the other skills added at appropriate times. By the time problem-solving skills have been mastered—a point generally reached after each participant has had about two hours of supervised practice—there are no longer any restrictions on the difficulty of the topics that may be discussed or the types of problems that may be rehearsed through role playing.

Wherever feasible, outside assignments begin early, immediately on mastery of empathic skill. As the other skills are mastered, assignments are also made for their use in real-life settings, with the nature of the outside assignment matched to the skill level attained.

The final phase of therapy, problem prevention, or enrichment concentrates heavily on rehearsal and real-life assignments, with feedback from the therapist designed to bring the skills into regular usage outside the session. Outside usage includes both using skills at designated times and using skills spontaneously in the course of everyday living. Therapy terminates successfully when the presenting problems have been resolved or goals attained and when the skills have become part of the client's permanent behavioral repertoire, to be used whenever appropriate to resolve conflicts or problems, prevent problem development, or enrich a relationship.

Basic Assumptions and Theory

The underlying assumptions and theoretical perspectives for the application of RE may be considered in three parts. The first part pertains to the use of skills training as the medium for therapy; the second, to the rationale for choosing the particular skills taught; and the third, to the rationale for the manner in which the skills are taught.

Rationale for Skills Training as Therapy. The assumptions of this rationale are the following.

1. Personality—defined here as relatively enduring, preferred ways of dealing with emotions, people, and self-concept–related thoughts—is based on the interplay over time of one's biochemistry (including genetic components) and the environment.
2. The effects of all nonbiochemical interventions depend on the individual's interaction with the environment—that is, on learning.
3. The best models for therapy come not from the institution of the clinic and the practices and procedures of physicians (medical model) but from the institution of the school and the practices and procedures of teachers (educational model). Only the latter model is both efficient and effective in producing the learning and relearning that constitutes personality change.
4. In addition to greater relevance, speed, and enduring effect in accomplishing personality change, an educational model of intervention can reach much greater numbers and a much broader range of people than a medical model. The main reasons for this are the high degree of public acceptance of educational procedures, as distinct from psychiatric ones, and the feasibility of using paraprofessionals and mass-produced aids (for example, audio and video training tapes) within the educational model.
5. Significant and enduring personality change is achieved most effectively through an educational program that combines cog-

nitive instruction—which may include principles, attitudes, and values—and behavioral instructions—which may include emotional self-reconditioning and guided practice or rehearsal of new ways of handling emotions, interpersonal interactions, and self-concept–related thoughts. This dual approach is here defined as skills training.

Skills training is distinct from traditional, predominantly introspective analytic therapy—which consists largely of unsystematic instruction—and from those types of behavioral therapy that may be systematic but do not involve knowledge/principle/attitude/value transformation, relying instead on the conditioning of a relatively passive client, and/or seek only to remedy a specific problem or deficit and do not seek to implant the knowledge and skill necessary to resolve the entire class of problems or deficits of which the client's symptom or complaint is but one example. Skills training therapies preserve many of the principles and methods of both of these older approaches but integrate them in such a way that the client is consciously involved in the choice of therapeutic or enrichment goals. In skills training therapies, the clients themselves are consciously concerned with mastering those skills that effect personality change and are themselves in charge of the use of those skills during the intervention process and in their daily lives. Clients also develop the ability to use these new skills in resolving problems and achieving goals in future situations.

Rationale for Choosing RE Skills. The particular skills selected for RE training are based on the following assumptions and rationale.

1. Personality is formed, expressed, and continuously re-formed mainly by the nature of our relationships with significant others.
2. As set forth in the writings of Rogers, Anna Freud, Horney, and others, our ability to avoid the reality-distorting effects of psychological defense and escape maneuvers and our ability to achieve productivity and self-acceptance depend mainly on the nature of our relationships to significant others.

3.   The ability to acknowledge and appreciate our wants, our emotions, and the way we want to relate to others and want to have them relate to us is an essential first step toward avoiding the crippling effects of psychological defense mechanisms and dealing with emotional and interpersonal realities in such a way as to satisfy our wants.

4.   To achieve lasting satisfaction, we must also be able to communicate such thoughts, emotions, and wants effectively to other people. That is, we must communicate them to others in a manner that maximizes the probability that they too will appreciate these realities and be willing to cooperate in helping us achieve our emotional, personal, and interpersonal goals.

5.   As set forth in Leary's interpersonal theory of personality (1957), based on the theories of Harry Stack Sullivan (1947), the interpersonal responses we make to other people trigger certain kinds of responses in them. Usually this triggering takes place automatically and unconsciously—that is, outside our awareness. That reaction in turn automatically or semiautomatically triggers our next response, and so on. By teaching people this principle, by teaching them the central roles that self-concept and psychological defense play in such interactions, by making them acutely aware of interactions that had hitherto been unconscious, and by training them to understand and alter their responses accordingly, we can help them gain control over what had previously been mysterious and had operated mainly at an unconscious, reflexive level.

6.   As initially determined by Leary (1957) and then by Shannon and Guerney (1973), such "interpersonal reflexes" are largely reciprocal in nature, with like eliciting like on certain critical dimensions of attitude and behavior. Affection, love, openness, cooperativeness, and positive statements in general tend to elicit positive responses from others. Hostility, deception, competitiveness, uncooperativeness, and negative statements in general likewise tend to elicit negative responses from others.

7.   The capacity to consciously control and generate our interpersonal responses and generate desired responses from others

allows us to better achieve our interpersonal goals, serving, in the long run, to modify personality in desired directions.

8. The capacity to generate responses from others that improve a relationship and facilitate personal growth also depends on another factor—our ability to consistently meet the emotional and interpersonal wants of significant others.

9. The ability to consistently meet the emotional needs of others depends on our knowledge and appreciation of their emotional, interpersonal wants.

10. Understanding and appreciating the emotional, interpersonal wants of others depends on the capacity to generate responses from them that reveal those wants.

11. Generally, others will risk revealing their emotions and wants to us, thereby placing us in a position to meet them, to the degree to which they trust us to understand and appreciate those feelings and wants, rather than raising challenges about them.

12. Generally, it is possible to instruct people systematically and successfully in the principles, attitudes, and behaviors that will encourage others to understand, appreciate, and trust them.

13. Similarly, it is possible to instruct people systematically and successfully in attitudes and behaviors that will increase their ability and inclination to compassionately understand and appreciate the emotions and wants of significant others.

14. Interpersonal conflict and problem resolution rests mainly on the capacity to generate honest and compassionate communication as described in the preceding assumptions. However, additional principles and guidelines may also be used to promote realistic and lasting resolution of interpersonal conflicts and problems. These problem-solving skills are cognitive in nature and comparatively simple to teach.

15. Principles and practices that promote generalizations of skills, their transfer from the teaching situation to the real world, and their maintenance over time can be systematically taught to people.

Rationale for the Manner in Which Skills are Taught. In general, the most efficient way to teach the principles, attitudes, and behaviors mentioned earlier in this chapter, including skills of maintenance and generalization, is a systematic educational method that is programmatic (that is, procedurally systematic and replicable); allows for a wide range of individual differences; takes cognizance of psychodynamic principles, especially the use of defense mechanisms to protect and enhance the self-concept; and makes use of both traditional methods of instruction (for example, motivating, encouraging, and demonstrating) and modern methods of instruction (for example, modeling and social reinforcement). The following are some of the more important specific assumptions and perspectives underlying the manner in which RE skills are taught.

1. Inducing a high level of motivation is essential to teaching skills that are difficult to learn, require change of previously automatic or semiautomatic behaviors, or have a high ratio of long-term gains to immediate gains.

2. A high level of motivation is best achieved by building high expectations that, when the behaviors being learned eventually are applied, gratification of significant personal needs will be achieved and by convincing the client that a high level of success is or will be attained as the result of a reasonable expenditure of energy. (The gratification of personal needs mentioned here includes the resolution of conflicts or problems and the fulfillment of personal and interpersonal aspirations.)

3. The degree to which the client will perceive the new behaviors as meeting his or her needs is largely a function of the degree to which the instructor makes evident the causal relationship between the new behaviors and the fulfillment of the client's perceived wants.

4. Inducing high motivation also depends on the therapist or instructor's credibility as an individual and upon his or her capacity to provide a convincing rationale to the client for adopting the principles, attitudes, and behaviors being taught. Personal credibility is generally a function of the client's perception of the instructor's competence, enthusiasm, warmth, genuineness, and empathy.

5. An important motivation of continued effort and practice is the client's feeling of success in learning. The client should feel that

his or her level of success is high in proportion to the effort he or she is expending. Such a high success-effort ratio is best achieved if the instructor, among other things, reduces the time spent in activities not essential to the learning process; arranges the role-played and real-life practice experiences in a hierarchy so as to maximize chances of success and minimize chances of failure; provides ample social reinforcement for effort, as well as for any successes in learning actually attained; and minimizes behaviors that even hint of criticism or serious incapacities or failures on the client's part.

6. The therapist or instructor is in the best position to induce strong feelings of success if he or she adopts and displays the attitude in interactions with clients that failures stem from deficiencies in the instructor's performance, rather than from deficiencies of the client, and successes stem mainly from the client's efforts and abilities.

7. A high level of encouragement and reward for learning and practice needs to be supplied by the therapist or teacher during the acquisition of such skills. This support remains necessary until skills levels and generalization/transfer levels afford a reward-effort ratio in the natural environment that is high enough to make skills use self-sustaining.

8. Performance of skills in the natural environment can be significantly increased if the process of generalization/transfer is treated in every way as a skill in itself. That is, the principles, attitudes, and behaviors underlying generalization/transfer and the importance of generalization/transfer in meeting personal needs should be explained and demonstrated to clients, rehearsed with them, and reinforced in the same manner as any other skill. Moreover, the client should be instructed in when and how to elicit from others in the environment overt social reinforcement for his or her performance of the skill being used.

Goals of RE

The goals of RE apply to any aspect of the client's functioning involving interactions with other people. In my view, that arena includes most of the variables that affect the client's psychological and emotional well-being.

The major goals of RE are to impart to each client skills that will:

1. Deepen the client's understanding of his or her self-concept, emotions, conflicts, problems, desires, and goals, and of the most realistic way for him or her to achieve personal and interpersonal goals.
2. Increase the client's ability to elicit help and cooperation from others that will enable the client to deepen self-understanding and better meet personal goals.
3. Increase the client's personal attractiveness to others.
4. Increase the client's ability to understand others' self-concepts, emotions, conflicts, problems, desires, and goals.
5. Increase the client's ability to help others effectively by promoting their self-understanding, providing compassionate understanding and appreciation of their needs, and offering his or her own insights and possible solutions to their problems at appropriate times and in appropriate ways.
6. Increase the client's ability to understand and resolve problems between himself or herself and others in a constructive and enduring way that takes all realities, including emotional ones, into account and comes closest to mutually satisfying all parties.
7. Increase the client's ability to enhance his relationships with those who are significant to him in love, work, and play—that is, enable him to find more ways to increase the enjoyment and productivity he derives from such relationships.
8. Give the client the ability to generalize/transfer these and other desired skills into his or her daily life and to maintain them over time.
9. Give the client the ability to teach significant intimates the skills necessary to increase the various abilities outlined here.

Skills of Relationship Enhancement

Expressive Skills. Expressive skills serve two major purposes. First, they increase clients' sensitivity to and understanding of their own self-regarding attitudes and their own emotions, conflicts, problems, desires, and goals. Second, they increase clients' ability to communicate their awareness of those aspects of themselves to others in ways that will increase the probability that others will understand them and respond to them in a compassionate and cooperative manner.

The subskills for this mode of behavior may be outlined as follows:

1. Before expressing your own views, feelings, and goals, try to make a statement to the other person that acknowledges your respect and compassion for his or her views and desires. (This will make the other more responsive to your own views and needs.)

2. If the statement you are about to make implies anything negative about the other person or about your attitudes toward him or her (for example, anger), when the time is right, search for and express the implicit positive attitudes or feelings (for example, affection) that are often more basic than and may even give rise to the negative ones. (This also increases the probability that the other will be compassionate and understanding of your viewpoint and capable of perceiving its validity.)

3. Whenever there is even the remotest possibility that the other person might disagree with your perceptions, state your views subjectively ("I think," "I believe," "in my view," "it seems to me," and so on), rather than presenting them as objective, factual, morally valid, or normatively correct.

4. If your feelings are an important aspect of the problem or its solution, describe them to the other person. (This allows him or her to concentrate on all major dimensions of the problem and often increases the probability that the other's response will be an understanding, compassionate one.)

5. Instead of or in addition to making generalizations, describe the particular events and behaviors that cause you to think and feel as you do. This is helpful whether you are focusing on your own reactions or those of others. When focusing on your own feelings and behavior, such specificity helps prevent you from exaggerating and overgeneralizing and helps focus your atten-

tion on problems more accurately, thereby increasing the probability that you will actually do something constructive about them. When the focus of the discussion is on the other person, this guideline is even more important in that it helps prevent name calling—either plain (character description) or fancy (motivational analysis)—which can easily lead to exaggerations, diversions, recriminations, and general deterioration of the discussion's relevance to problem-solving. Like many of the other guidelines, this guideline reduces the probability that the other person will become threatened and defensive.

6.   At the proper time, usually at an advanced stage of the dialogue, present an interpersonal message to the other person—a request for new, more satisfying attitudes and behaviors. Its formulation requires the use of many of the other skills just mentioned—for example, being positive and including important feelings, such as the anticipated positive feelings the other person's compliance with your request would generate in you. An interpersonal message allows the other person to understand precisely what you would like of him or her, thereby increasing the probability that he or she will consider your suggestion realistically and carefully. Your expression of anticipated positive effects gives the other person an incentive to cooperate.

Empathic Skills. The first purpose of empathic skill is to help the client elicit self-revealing statements from others in order to understand the others' self-regarding attitudes and their emotions, conflicts, problems, desires, and goals. The second purpose is to increase the client's attractiveness in the eyes of the other person. Empathy facilitates the attainment of both these objectives by making the other person feel that he or she is well respected and understood and that his or her communications are appreciated by the client. The client's increased attractiveness causes the other person to more carefully and cooperatively consider the client's own views, attitudes, opinions, and suggestions. A third purpose is an altruistic one: to help the other person better understand his or her own emotions, self-regarding attitudes, conflicts, problems, desires, and goals and more effectively explore and appropriately select realistic courses of action with the purpose of increased self-satisfaction and goal achievement.

The empathic mode is based largely on the attitudes and behaviors of a traditional Rogerian psychotherapist. The following are specific guidelines (highly abbreviated) aimed at implementing these attitudes and effectively communicating them to the other person.

1. Listen intently.
2. Show interest and understanding while the other person is talking.
3. Absorb the other's mood.
4. Concentrate on the other's internal world.
5. Put yourself in the other's place by asking yourself the following questions: "If I were the other, what would I be thinking, pro or con, about myself as a person? What would I be feeling? What would I be wishing? What would I be thinking about doing? What conflicts would I be experiencing?"
6. Consider possible differences between your reactions (answers to the preceding questions) and the reactions of the other.
7. Formulate a tentative statement that incorporates answers to one or more of those questions.
8. Put yourself in the other's place again to hear your own tentative statement.
9. Screen out nonempathic words and phrases.
10. Make your statement declaratively.
11. Monitor the length of your statement.
12. Accept corrections readily.

Mode Switching. The purposes of mode-switching skill are to give the client the ability: always to keep in mind which of the above modes of behavior (empathic or expressive) is being employed at any given time; to employ each of the modes at the appropriate times; to move from one mode to the other in coordination with the needs and statements of the other person; and to know when and how to switch from one mode to the other in order to resolve conflicts and problems most effectively, to enrich self-understanding, to promote self-improvement, and to enhance relationships with others.

The guidelines for mode switching vary in accord with the mode of behavior (expresser, responder, or facilitator) that the person is engaged in at the moment. Mode switching may be employed unilaterally (only one person is skilled), dyadically (two people are skilled), or multilaterally (some or all of the persons involved have RE skills). Briefly, the guidelines are the following:

1.   As expresser, switch modes when you have already expressed your most important thoughts, feelings, and suggestions on the topic under discussion or when you want to know the other person's views, feelings, or suggestions.
2.   As empathic responder, switch modes when you have already repeated the other's deepest thoughts and feelings on an issue twice; when your own thoughts and feelings begin to impair your ability to be empathic; or when you have something to say that might favorably influence the other's perceptions, help resolve their conflict or problem, or facilitate their efforts toward goal attainment or that might help resolve a problem or conflict between you and the other.
3.   As facilitator, suggest a mode switch when you think that any of the preceding conditions characterize the individuals whose discussion you are trying to facilitate.

Interpersonal Conflict and Problem Resolution. The purpose of interpersonal conflict and problem resolution skills is to enable the client to resolve conflicts and problems between himself and one or more other persons in a manner that takes into account all pertinent realities, including emotional ones, and promotes a resolution that comes as close as possible to mutually satisfying the wants and goals of all parties, thus increasing the probability that the solution will be an enduring one.

The guidelines for interpersonal conflict and problem resolution skills are:

1.   Make sure that you and the other people involved are satisfied that you have expressed and have had understood by the others all that is pertinent to the issue under discussion concerning

each person's views, self-concept, emotions, conflicts, problems, desires, and goals.

2. Determine whether this seems to be the most appropriate time and place for you and the others to attempt to reach a solution or whether different circumstances or more time for private deliberations would be more auspicious.

3. Try to think of solutions that will satisfy the needs of everyone involved. Do not settle for mere compromise (splitting the difference) until you have spent considerable time thinking about the possibility that more creative solutions might come closer to meeting the needs of all persons involved.

4. Communicate your suggested solutions, making use of all expressive skills, with emphasis on the interpersonal message.

5. Use your empathic skills when responding to the suggestions and reactions of others.

6. Use unilateral, bilateral, or multilateral mode switching frequently in discussing solutions.

7. In working toward an agreement in principle, make sure that you have used the specificity guideline of expressive skills to work out in detail the time, place, frequency, and so on.

8. When the tentative agreement has been reached consider ways in which exceptions and difficulties might arise that might lead to misunderstandings or negative feelings. Modify the agreement to eliminate such possibilities.

9. To cement the actual agreement, make sure that the same specificity is used to review in detail the behaviors (including time, place and frequency) each person will henceforth adopt.

10. Set a time when everyone involved will meet again to evaluate the adopted plan and to make such further modifications as may be necessary.

Facilitation. The purpose of facilitation skills is to enable the client to elicit from others interpersonal responses that will help them resolve their conflicts or problems; enrich their relationships; foster their personal growth; and foster the client's own personal growth. The client's instruction of others in appropriate kinds of responses may be either systematic or limited to modifying responses in a given situation. Facilitation can be done with others just once—

for example, in a particularly critical situation—or can involve a long-term, systematic shaping of another's behavior.

Guidelines for facilitation skills are:

1. With respect to skilled interpersonal responses, make an example of yourself, a model to be emulated.
2. Use expressive skills, especially interpersonal messages, to elicit the desired type of response.
3. With a relatively unskilled partner, and frequently with a skilled partner also, couple the interpersonal message with modeling responses. (That is, suggest a specific response to be copied by the other person.)
4. Request only such responses as you believe the other person would be willing and able to provide at the time.
5. Use expressive skills to express appreciation of any sincere attempt at compliance with your request. Similarly, reinforce any unsolicited approximations of skilled responses.
6. Where your partners are skilled and cooperative, develop nonverbal symbols as quick and efficient cues to elicit skilled responses.
7. Where your partners are skilled and motivated, take the initiative in setting up regular times at which to use the skills to express positive perceptions and feelings and to work through conflicts and problems.

Generalization and Maintenance. The purpose of teaching generalization and maintenance skills is to enable clients to make regular use of their RE skills for the rest of their lives and to provide them with the basic concepts and skills necessary to train themselves similarly in other desirable behavior patterns. (Substituting "desired behaviors" for "skills" in the following guidelines will show the usefulness of the guidelines for patterns of behavior other than RE skills.)

The guidelines for generalization and maintenance skills are:

1. Recognize that all complex new skills initially seem unnatural, discomforting, awkward, ungratifying, and lacking in spontaneity and self-expression but can later become a part of

you and a vehicle for spontaneous and more complete self-expression and gratification.

2. When acquiring a skill, practice for the sake of practice. This means to regard each mistake or mishap not as a failure but as a success in the process of learning.

3. When acquiring a skill, set aside regular times and/or occasions when you will practice your skills.

4. Compliment yourself and/or imagine your instructor or others complimenting you for your effort and for any approximation of successful skill performance, regardless of outcome.

5. As your confidence and skills grow, find new and more challenging situations in which to practice your skills.

6. When acquiring a skill, ask others, if appropriate, to compliment you on your new behaviors or solicit expression of their appreciation if your use of the skill has a favorable impact on them.

7. When acquiring a skill, increase your awareness of the times when you might use it by keeping a log, preferably daily and preferably in writing, in which you look back over the day and note times when you might have used your skill but did not or when you did in fact exercise your new behavior (for which you should compliment yourself).

8. When your skill level is high enough to lead to successful real-world outcomes, mentally contrast the outcome with what probably would have happened had you not used your skill, in order to increase your appreciation of the beneficial effects of your new behaviors.

9. When first acquiring a skill, place unusual objects in your surroundings to serve as reminders to implement your new skills.

10. Learn to identify those situations that generally elicit behaviors contrary to skilled behaviors. Try to make conscious the previously unconscious or taken-for-granted self-statements you make at those times, and substitute new self-statements that are more appropriate to the use of your skills and the attainment of your goals, thereby replacing cues for unwanted behavior with cues for wanted behavior.

11.   Recognize that entropy is a law of nature—that is, that skilled
      behaviors generally require more effort than unskilled ones
      and that the promise of short-range relief or quick gratifica-
      tion is constantly opposing the attainment of long-range satis-
      factions and goals. Therefore, continue to set aside regular
      times and occasions for skills usage, rather than relying solely
      on their spontaneous use; continue to consciously monitor
      your skills at some regular interval; and, if feasible, enlist the
      cooperation of others to help maintain skills usage.

Training of Clients

Relationship Enhancement therapies had their beginning in
the early 1960s with Filial therapy, which teaches parents of emotionally disturbed children therapeutic skills and attitudes to apply
with their children. In nearly twenty years of clinical use, Filial
therapy has proven itself to be applicable in an extremely wide
variety of cases, including hyperactive and aggressive children.

With adults, RE therapy has been used with disturbed marital
couples, with troubled family dyads (parent-adolescent), and with
disturbed families seen as a unit. (The preferred minimum age for
the children is twelve in such family units, but children as young as
seven have on occasion been incorporated quite successfully.) When
others in the family are unwilling or unable to attend, such RE
methods as extensive role playing and carefully rehearsed and monitored home assignments can nevertheless be used for marital and
family therapy with only one member of a family unit.

RE therapy has also been adapted for the purposes of problem prevention and enrichment. For example, Filial therapy led to
the development by Louise Guerney of the Foster Parent Training
Program, which includes training manuals for trainers (Guerney,
1976) and parents (Guerney, 1975b, 1979), as well as training films
(Guerney, 1973, 1974). The program incorporates not only empathic, reinforcement, and some expressive skills but also skills in setting
limits, structuring, and setting priorities in complex child-rearing
situations. Louise Guerney then adapted this program for training
parents to work with their own natural children, with a manual and
a training program that are appropriate for parents of low socioeco-

nomic and educational levels and middle-class parents, as well as for training high school students in parenting skills (Guerney, 1979).

RE problem prevention and enrichment programs have been successfully used with groups of parents, groups of teenagers, groups of parents with their own teenagers, married couples, dating couples, premarital couples, and cohabiting couples. Cassette audio tapes which exemplify the use of the skills are available for these groups as well as for disturbed couples and families (Guerney and Vogelsong, 1981). They have been used successfully to improve communication, decision making, supervision, and the general quality of staff relationships and morale in groups ranging from public schools to computer-manufacturing firms.

Training for Professionals

In the past ten years, hundreds of psychologists, psychiatrists, social workers, and mental health counselors have been trained to administer RE therapy. In addition, many types of professionals and paraprofessionals in mental health and related fields have been trained in RE skills to use as part of their armamentarium of general helping skills or to apply in preventative and enrichment programs. Among others, such trainees have included rehabilitation counselors, drug and alcohol counselors, consultation and education specialists, family physicians, nurses, daycare workers, preschool teachers, dormitory counselors, special educators, speech therapists, ministers, and high school and elementary school teachers.

Instruction in RE skills has also been used as the practicum component for undergraduate courses in counseling and therapy skills. Students practice the skills for their own self-improvement in a context that makes clear how they can use the RE skills alone or in conjunction with other psychotherapeutic and counseling skills to help future clients.

Training and certification in RE therapy is available from two sources: annual workshops conducted at The Pennsylvania State University; and supervision and certification available through a tax-exempt, nonprofit educational institute, IDEALS (the Institute for the Development of Emotional and Life Skills).

IDEALS also conducts on-site training for agencies anywhere in the country.

Formats for RE Training

Any type of Relationship Enhancement therapy, prevention, or enrichment program can be used with an individual, with a dyad, or with a group. For example, family therapy can be applied with only one member of a family if the others are unwilling or unable to attend; with a subgroup from the family; with the entire family as a unit; or with groups comprised of two or more whole family units or of subunits of two or more families.

Such groups can be seen in either an intensive or an extensive time format. The intensive format consists of marathon (eight-hour or week-end) or minimarathon (three- or four-hour) sessions. The extensive format involves one- or two-hour sessions occurring once or twice weekly for many weeks. Combinations of intensive and extensive formats may also be used. RE problem prevention and enrichment programs are typically time-limited—that is, they run for a predetermined length of time. For example, a marital or premarital enrichment program usually lasts for one weekend.

The typical program for training professionals in RE therapy consists of a three-day beginning workshop, followed by one or more additional days of advanced training. Trainees then assume coleadership of treatment groups with a trainer or receive supervision based on audiotapes of therapy mailed to the supervisor and discussed through return tapes, in person, or by phone.

Training Procedures

RE training methods rely on age-old teaching principles and practices. The need to induce motivation in learners is given highest priority. The paradigm sequence is: explain, demonstrate, model, supervise skills practice within the training sessions, prepare the learner to be successful with homework, supervise homework, prepare the learner to use the skills spontaneously in everyday living, and supervise the transfer process.

Social reinforcement is of paramount importance in the supervisory process. An effort is made to make reinforcement at least 90 percent of the feedback received. Social reinforcement is used in its traditional, contingent sense to strengthen specific types of responses. However, an even more important aspect of social reinforcement in the RE method is to provide encouragement and the general feeling of success. That is, a major function of the therapist's use of social reinforcement responses is not to shape specific responses, but to provide motivational impetus.

Two major methods of providing constructive feedback to help trainees improve their skills are demonstration and modeling, which are distinguished in the RE approach. *Demonstration* refers to the use of illustration followed by analysis and discussion to demonstrate concretely the rationale and principles being taught. A part of demonstration is structuring, which entails relating the specific responses used in the demonstration to the guidelines or rules that define the skills. *Modeling* refers not only to the therapist demonstrating the skills but also, more importantly, to giving the trainee specific words he or she can say when struggling to make or improve a response.

Less frequently, and only after a high level of skill has been attained by trainees, prompting techniques are used. Prompting techniques provide a general cue to the trainee—for example, "What is the implicit interpersonal message he is giving you?" or "It seems like a mode switch would be appropriate here." Prompting is used only when the leader feels certain that the trainee will immediately be able to provide an appropriate response.

Other special techniques are used as they are needed. Troubleshooting, one such technique, is used in two types of situations: when trainees question or resist the rationale, guidelines, or assignments made and when the system breaks down because one or more of the persons involved are emotionally overcome. Troubleshooting involves a series of empathic responses made directly to the trainee, followed, at an appropriate time, by therapist expressive and/or administrative responses designed to bring the trainee back to the usual RE practices and procedures.

Doubling, another special technique, is a specialized facilitation skill in which the facilitator does not model or prompt the person he or she is facilitating but instead repeats his or her expressive empathic responses, trying, in the process, to make them even more skillful, if possible, but, in any case, always restating or rephrasing them. Doubling, another special technique, is a type of facilitation that promotes empathy on the part of a person who is not at the moment assigned the empathic mode of responding and equalizes what would otherwise be a psychological imbalance of power and attention in the eyes of one or more group members. This method is used primarily when there are parents and their adolescent children in the same group, as, for example, in some formats of RE family therapy.

The therapist is responsible for maintaining psychological equality in the attention he pays to each individual in the group, as well as for maximizing the amount of time spent in skills practice by preventing any digression into general discussion in which skills are not employed. He or she is also responsible for guiding clients to select for discussion the most significant topics in their lives, as distinct from those issues that are merely the most salient—for example, salient because of some recent emotional impact on the participant. In other words, the therapist does not merely follow the here and now but sees to it that the here and now reflects issues of fundamental importance. Therapist responses used to accomplish these goals are termed administrative responses.

The fact that RE leaders are trained to avoid certain responses is perhaps as important as the fact that they are trained to use the responses outlined thus far. With respect to the specific content under discussion by the group members (as distinct from the manner in which the content is discussed), leaders are trained to remain impartial and unintrusive and, unlike therapists from almost any other form of therapy with the exception of traditional Rogerian psychotherapy, generally avoid such common therapeutic responses as directive leads, interpretations, suggestions, explanations, advice, encouragement, approval, and reassurance. The goals usually sought by such responses are achieved instead by RE techniques. Of course, leaders also avoid anything the client might interpret as personal criticism.

Although, in many circumstances, certain errors in client performance are allowed to pass without correction, it is considered a critical error for the therapist to accept without correction responses that violate key RE guidelines and thereby lead to unnecessary threat, defensiveness, or argumentativeness.

The topics that trainees select are kept appropriate to the types of skills they have already acquired and the level of skills they have achieved. For example, a client first learning empathic skill is likely to have considerable difficulty mastering it with topics that are personally threatening to him. Thus, when members of the same family are present, they begin by discussing topics that do not involve other members of the family at all; they then proceed to discuss positive perceptions and feelings about other family members, then enhancement or enrichment issues, and, finally, conflict or problem issues.

In the training of student counselors, the trainees produce a hierarchy of personal goals, including enlisting others to be of help, establishing or enriching a relationship, and resolving conflicts or problems with others. These goals are then arranged from least to most difficult, and skills practice proceeds as follows: preparation of planning sheets for the achievement of those goals, role rehearsal, implementation of the goal in real life, and a recapitulation and feedback session afterwards.

In the training of professionals, the professionals generally role play situations they have encountered or would expect to encounter with their clients, with the issues again proceeding from the least to the most difficult.

Termination Criteria

As stated earlier, a time-designated format is used in RE therapy, in distinction to the time-limited format frequently used in RE problem prevention and enrichment programs. At a time designated at intake, therapist and clients together evaluate progress achieved. Although written questionnaires might serve a purpose in this regard, to date such evaluations have been conducted orally. The questions discussed include the following:

1. Has a level of skill mastery been reached that is high enough to assure success in resolving conflicts and problems? Would any

further refinement of skills fail to justify the cost of additional supervision?

2. Have times been set aside for the continued regular use of the skills? Have the skills been integrated into daily living?
3. Have all the critical presenting relationship conflicts and problems been resolved?
4. Would any noncritical problems still remaining fail to justify the cost of additional supervision by the therapist?
5. Are the skills generalized sufficiently that they could be used not only to resolve problems and conflicts but also to enrich relationships?

Research with Clients

The research summarized in this section spans almost twenty years. Various types of formats are covered. The samples studied vary widely in age. The goals of the programs studied include problem prevention, treatment, and enrichment.

Group Filial Therapy and Related Prevention and Enrichment Programs. After pilot work (Guerney, 1964), a three-year National Institute of Mental Health–supported study of group Filial therapy was conducted. The study involved mothers and their fifty-one children, mostly boys between four and ten years of age (mean, eight years) who were experiencing serious emotional difficulties but were not organically impaired, retarded, or psychotic. Mothers participating in the Filial study attended an average of fifty sessions and conducted an average of forty home play sessions. For long-term therapy, the dropout rate was extremely low. Twenty-five percent did not complete the program, whereas similar studies conducted with traditional approaches to child therapy showed a 93 percent dropout rate for long-term treatment (Hunt, 1961). The children showed highly significant improvement on all measures of adjustment used: Problem Checklist, Wichita Guidance Checklist (including each of the subscales: inner tension, school failure, parent conflict, teacher conflict, and peer conflict), Des Moines Parent Ratings, Children's Adjustment Inventory, and Parental Dissatisfaction. Levitt (1957), in summing twenty studies of child therapy, concluded that, in a period comparable to the treatment time of the

Filial study, at least some improvement was to be expected in 70 percent of untreated cases. In the Filial study, clinicians' ratings on the Rutgers Maladjustment Index showed that 100 percent of the children were at least somewhat improved, and 78 percent were "much" or "very much" improved.

Oxman (1971) studied a comparison group of seventy-seven children matched to the Filial treatment group for geography, age of parents and children, size of family, and socioeconomic status. Change over a comparable period of time indicated that the variables studied—symptomatology (the Problem Checklist) and maternal dissatisfaction (ICL Discrepancy)—differed significantly in favor of the Filial group. In a more recent study of Filial therapy with a shorter treatment interval (six months), Horner (1974) found a significant 59 percent reduction in the number of problems.

The children's spontaneous interactions with their parents were coded over the course of the therapy. Naive coders made 49,000 observations covering some 600 play sessions. Changes observed were very consistent with theoretical expectations. Also, comparisons with other studies (Moustakas and Schlalock, 1955) showed that, whereas the children's play behavior before therapy was similar to that of disturbed children, their behavior at the close of treatment was similar to that of normal children. Early in the training process, mothers' behavior in the play sessions manifested all the skills they were expected to learn.

In a study by Sywulak (1977), nineteen mothers or fathers and their emotionally disturbed, nonpsychotic children served as their own controls. Significantly greater gains were found during the four-month treatment period than during the four-month wait period on two measures of children's adjustment (the Filial Problem List and the Wichita Parent Checklist). A third measure, the Des Moines Parent Rating Scale, narrowly missed significance ($p < .06$). Parents showed the same pattern of relatively greater change with treatment in parental acceptance as measured by the Porter Parental Acceptance Scale. Sensué (1981) tested the participants in Sywulak's study after six months of treatment. The clients continued to gain on all measures from the fourth to the sixth month and, in the sixth month, the Des Moines Parent Rating Scale measure also

reached the point of statistically significant gains over the pretreatment and prewait testings.

A follow-up study of the first large-scale study of Filial therapy mentioned earlier (Guerney and Stover, 1971) was conducted by
questionnaire approximately fifteen months after completion
(Guerney, 1975a). Of the forty-one parents who responded to the
question concerning the child's adjustment, only one reported that
the child had a problem greater than when he or she entered therapy
or that they had since sought additional psychotherapy. Only four
of the children were reported to have shown a decrease from their
level of adjustment at termination, four were at the same level as at
termination, and thirty-two were said to have continued to improve
after termination.

Sensué (1981) did a follow-up study on the participants in
Sywulak's study approximately three years after termination of
treatment. Sensué used a normative group comprised of neighbors
of the clients to determine whether, after three years, the disturbed
children as assessed on objective tests by their parents had remained
at a normal level of adjustment. She found that they had. In addition, the follow-up sample and the normative sample did not differ
on measures of child adjustment and parental acceptance. Questionnaire data further indicated that the parents considered their
children's posttherapy adjustment as having continued to be normal
and acceptable to them. Other questionnaire data indicated that the
parents felt they had learned valuable childrearing skills and that
they continued to use them in their interactions with their children.
Interviews conducted by the researcher with the parents supported
these findings. Interviews with the children showed that, with near
unanimity, they regarded the therapeutic play sessions very
positively.

Group Family RE

Ginsberg (1977) studied group family RE in a parent-
adolescent relationship development (PARD) program format consisting of ten two-hour meetings in which father-son pairs were
generally seen in groups of three pairs. Fourteen father-son pairs
comprised the randomly assigned experimental group, and fifteen

pairs comprised the no-treatment control group. Results from the Acceptance of Other and Self/Feeling Awareness questionnaire, along with unobtrusive observations of naturalistic interactions between fathers and sons, indicated that treatment subjects made significant gains on the scales of empathic acceptance and expressive communication. The RE-trained pairs also showed greater improvement in patterns of general communication as measured by the Adolescent-Parent Communications Checklist (Beaubien, 1970). The hypothesis that the general quality of the relationship would show greater improvement in RE participants than in untrained fathers and sons was confirmed by means of the Family Life Questionnaire.

The most definitive study compared a family RE (PARD format) group to a traditional (discussion-based) treatment group and a no-treatment control group (Guerney, Coufal, and Vogelsong, 1981). Fifty-four mother-daughter pairs were randomly assigned to one of these three conditions. The groups met approximately thirteen times for two hours weekly in groups of three pairs. On a wide variety of measures, the three basic hypotheses were confirmed. The RE participants were superior to both the traditional treatment and the no-treatment groups in: specific empathic and expressive communication skills as measured both behaviorally and on paper-and-pencil measures; general patterns of communication between the mothers and daughters; and the quality of the general relationship. The traditional and RE methods were carefully equated in every way, and the leaders, who were the same for both groups, were perceived by the clients as being extremely close on all variables measured—empathy, warmth, genuineness, enthusiasm, and competence. This study conclusively rules out the idea that generic factors (attention, placebo effect, and so on) could fully account for any of the various types of improvement shown as a result of RE training.

Six months after termination of treatment in this study, mothers and daughters in the traditional treatment group showed no greater gains over pretreatment in specific communication skills, general communication patterns, or the general quality of their relationship than mothers and daughters in the no-treatment control group. Participants in RE showed significantly greater gains in all of these areas than both the other groups. These results demonstrate not only that the method is superior to the type of traditional treatment studied but also that a significant portion of such gains are treatment-specific.

Group Marital RE

The first study of group marital RE therapy (then called conjugal therapy) was conducted with twenty-three couples seen in groups of approximately three couples (Ely, Guerney, and Stover, 1973). Only the training phase (the first eight to ten sessions) of the therapy was studied. The objective was primarily to determine whether the couples were able to learn the skills taught in the program. Comparisons of the experimental group with the control group showed that, when couples responded to hypothetical, critical incidents on a questionnaire, and when their behavior in role-played incidents was coded, they made more use of the skills being taught than did a control group.

Collins (1977) studied group marital RE therapy over a full course of treatment. Data from the Primary Communication Inventory suggested that the forty-five couples participating in the study were more poorly adjusted than normal couples but not so seriously maladjusted as the typical marital couple seeking counseling at a psychiatric clinic. The findings were as follows: in comparison to an untrained group, couples in RE showed greater gains in marital communication as measured by the Marital Communication Inventory (Bienvenu, 1970) and in marital adjustment as measured by the Marital Adjustment Test (Locke and Williamson, 1958).

Rappaport (1976) studied an intensive group marital RE format using an own-control design: twenty married couples were tested, waited two months, then were tested again just prior to beginning the two-month, four-session program. The sessions, conducted on weekends and alternating between four and eight hours, totaled twenty-four hours. On all variables studied, the clients showed greater gains during the treatment period than during the waiting period. Specifically, the following results were found. In discussions of emotionally significant topics with their partner (Guerney, 1977), clients expressed themselves in ways deemed more sensitive to their own feelings and less likely to induce argument from their partners, as determined by coding their audiotaped performance on the Verbal Interaction Task using the Self/Feeling Awareness Scale (Guerney, 1977). Clients also showed more empathic acceptance of their partners as determined by behavioral coding using the Acceptance of Other Scale (Guerney, 1977), greater improvement in marital adjustment on the Marital Adjustment Test (Locke and Wallace, 1959), greater improvement in marital harmony on the Family Life Questionnaire (Guerney, 1977), greater improvement in their general patterns of marital communication on the Marital Communication Inventory, greater gains in trust and intimacy as measured by the Interpersonal Relationship Scale (Guerney, 1977), greater rate of change in their overall relationship patterns on the Relationship Change Scale (Guerney, 1977), greater improvement in their satisfaction with their relationships on the Satisfaction Change Scale (Guerney, 1977), and greater improvement in their ability to resolve relationship problems satisfactorily on the Handling Problems Change Scale (Guerney, 1977).

The first direct comparison of group marital RE with another, equally credible and competently administered program was conducted by Wieman (1973), who compared RE with his reciprocal reinforcement program. The reciprocal reinforcement program drew upon principles and techniques used by Knox (1971), Rappaport and Harrell (1972), and especially Stuart (1969a,b). The RE program was an abbreviated one (eight weeks). Participants in both treatments showed significant improvement over a waiting list control group in measures of marital communication, marital adjustment, and cooperativeness. Ratings on sixteen semantic differential scales were mostly positive for both treatments but also differed in a number of ways. Clients in the reciprocal reinforcement program saw their experience in treatment as lighter, safer, easier, colder, and calmer than did clients in the RE program. Clients in the RE program perceived their treatment as being significantly deeper, better, more worthwhile, more exciting, stronger, fairer, more important, more comfortable, and more professional than did the clients in the reciprocal reinforcement program. An empirical assessment ten weeks after the close of treatment showed that married couples in both programs maintained their gains extremely well.

Since these were both highly credible treatments, such results are not attributable to nonspecific treatment variables.

Another study pertinent to this question was conducted by Jessee and Guerney (1981). Thirty-six couples were randomly assigned to group marital RE or to a group gestalt relationship facilitation treatment. Each small-group treatment was conducted two-and-one-half hours per week for twelve weeks. Significant gains were made by the participants in both groups on all variables studied: marital adjustment, communication, trust and harmony, rate of positive change in the relationship, relationship satisfaction, and ability to handle problems. RE participants achieved greater gains than Gestalt relationship facilitation participants in communication, relationship satisfaction, and ability to handle problems.

Research on Training Paraprofessionals

Foster Parents. The foster parent skills training program developed by Louise Guerney (1977) is not an RE program—it does not include all the skills in RE and does include additional skills. It has its own manuals for the trainer (Guerney, 1976) and for the foster parents (Guerney, 1975b), as well as its own training films (Guerney, 1974), and it does not use play sessions with actual children, as Filial therapy does. Nevertheless, the principles taught and the way in which they are taught have much in common with Filial therapy and with other RE programs. Thus, the program seems well worth considering in this review.

A study was conducted, in the first year of the broad-scale application of the program (Guerney, Vogelsong, and Wolfgang, 1977), of the persons trained to be trainers of foster parents—mainly caseworkers in child welfare agencies and, less frequently, other foster parents. A control group matched to the paraprofessionals being trained did not receive training during a comparable period.

A Training Problems Situation measure developed by Louise Guerney (1975a) assessed the ability of the trainees to deal effectively with a variety of frequently encountered situations and problems in leading skills training groups. The trained group showed superior gain on this measure in comparison to the control group.

The trainees were also rated by supervisors who watched them conduct training sessions with foster parents. Ratings were done by means of the Trainer's Supervisory Form developed by Louise Guerney (1975a), which provides twenty ratings assessing various positive aspects of leadership and the ability of the trainees to avoid making mistakes of various specific kinds. The supervisors judged the trainees to be weak in none of the areas covered and to be very strong in friendly, noncompetitive relationships between co-leaders of groups; the ability of leaders to encourage questioning and expression of disagreement by the participants; the sensitivity of leaders to the feelings of the foster parents in the group; their knowledge of appropriate techniques; their willingness and ability to reinforce the participants; and their ability to avoid creating defensiveness in the participants.

In interviews, trainees indicated that the skills they had learned for conducting these training sessions were beneficial to them not only in leading the groups but also in other aspects of their lives and working careers. The caseworkers indicated that these skills were helpful to them in relating to clients in a variety of situations, including intake, home visits, interviews with prospective foster parents, and daily relations with clients. They also felt that, as a result of the skills they had learned, they were more effective in relating with other staff members in staff meetings and in relating with family and friends in their personal lives.

The ability of the trainees to effect changes in the foster parents they trained was also investigated. In comparison with an untrained control group, the foster parents showed significantly greater gains on all three aspects of parental acceptance as measured by the Porter Parental Acceptance Scale (Porter, 1954): acceptance of the child's feelings, valuing of the child's uniqueness, and acceptance of the child's autonomy. Parent perceptions of their skills in parenting was assessed by the Foster Parent Opinion Questionnaire—Skills (Guerney, Vogelsong, and Wolfgang, 1977). The foster parents trained by the trainees showed the expected significant improvement in their perceptions of their skills as foster parents. In comparing their pretraining and posttraining status, they saw themselves as superior in coping with children's withdrawal, making and enforcing rules, reinforcing appropriate behavior, structuring appropriately, understanding feelings, and coping with misbehavior.

Seven months to approximately a year and a half after training, Guerney, Wolfgang, and Vogelsong (1978) followed up thirty-two foster parents who had participated in their earlier study (Guerney, Vogelsong, and Wolfgang, 1977). The parents showed no significant decline in their perceptions of their own competence as described earlier. A Parenting Program Follow-Up Questionnaire (Guerney, Wolfgang, and Vogelsong, 1978) indicated general acceptance and use of each of the skills as a result of training. Also, 84 percent of the parents indicated that what they learned in the foster parent skills training program "much" or "very much" affected the way they acted with their foster children in a variety of ways. In a Problem Situations Questionnaire completed at follow-up, the trained group showed no significant decline in their performance and remained superior to the control group.

Resident Hall Counselors. Avery (1978) adopted the marital family relationship enhancement program for paraprofessional training and trained twenty potential residence hall counselors, with an additional fifteen serving as a control group. The training was conducted over a nine-week period in groups of approximately six. Each potential counselor in both groups conducted a fifteen-minute audiotaped interview with a trained confederate of the experimenter at the outset of the study and again following the training. The trained group showed significantly greater improvement on the Carkhuff Scale for Empathic Understanding (Carkhuff, 1969). In a follow-up (Avery, 1978), it was found that the superiority of the trained over the untrained prospective dormitory counselors was maintained six months after the completion of training.

Drug Rehabilitation Staff. Cadigan (1980) trained former drug addicts, who had become staff members in a residential, therapeutic, community drug rehabilitation center, to conduct a program (RETEACH) he adapted from RE to suit this setting and population. The sixteen residents these staff members then proceeded to train were compared with a nonrandomly assigned, untrained control group of twenty-four residents later determined to be an equivalent group in terms of initial scores on the dependent variables. The trained residents achieved greater improvement in mean scores on every measure used. Some of these superior gains were statistically significant: more positive written interpersonal responses to hypothetical peer problem situations and more positive perceptions of the way staff members behaved toward them. Perceptions of the quality of their relationships with "squares" and with peers also showed strong trends toward greater gains ($p < .10$).

Probation Workers. A study was conducted in which probation officers were trained to provide family RE therapy. The probation workers were given one week's training in RE methods and weekly supervision. The uncontrolled empirical evaluation (Guerney, Vogelsong, and Glynn, 1977) assessed 17 members of five families completing treatment. Improvement was shown in questionnaire measures of family harmony (Family Life Questionnaire), family satisfaction (Satisfaction Change Scale), and ability to handle family problems (Handling Problems Change Scale).

Senior Citizens. A group of senior citizens was trained in play session skills using the principles and techniques of Filial therapy (Levine, 1977). Using twelve trainees as their own controls, investigators coded behavioral interactions during play sessions with children in a daycare center. As hypothesized, Levine found significant increases in trainees' positive involvement, empathic behavior, and capacity to allow the children self-direction. A quasi-behavioral measure confirmed the hypothesized generalization of empathic skills to situations other than play.

Future of Skills Training as Therapy

Stimulated and encouraged by the views, theories, and methods of such writers as Albee (1959), Bandura (1969), Szasz (1961), Ellis (1963), Sanford (1955), Hobbs (1964), and, more recently, Miller (1969) and Armstrong (1971), I have for two decades been expressing the view that skills training would become the treatment of choice for the great majority of problems now dealt with by other methods of individual and family therapy. If this comes to pass, mental health centers (except for biochemically oriented treatment programs) will become, in effect, mental health schools.

As I have explained in this chapter and elsewhere (Guerney, 1977), such a revolution would, I believe, bring about equally bene-

ficial developments in personality testing and therapy outcome evaluation. Such changes will afford these fields the same kinds of
validity and utility now generally found in the fields of aptitude and
educational achievement testing.

In addition, as these changes come to pass, the exaggerated
and generally harmful (or, at best, nonheuristic) distinctions between prevention, enrichment, and therapy will tend to fade away,
to be replaced by the overriding conception of improving one's self
and one's relationships. This development may take place as the
paradigm for psychological intervention derived from the individual practice of medicine is replaced by the paradigm derived from
the practice of mass education—that is, as the paradigm "sickness or
maladjustment → prescription → therapy → cure" is replaced by
the paradigm "dissatisfaction or ambition → goal setting → selection of preexisting paradigm → psychosocial skills training → satisfaction, achievement, or goal attainment" (Authier and others,
1975).

References

Albee, G. *Mental Health Manpower Needs.* New York: Basic Books,
     1959.
Armstrong, H. E., Jr. *Of Cabbages and Kings:* "A Conversation
     About the Adult Development Program." KUOW (Seattle radio
     station), September 16, 1971.
Authier, J., and others. "The Psychological Practitioner as a
     Teacher: A Theoretical-Historical Practical Review." *The Coun-
     seling Psychologist,* 1975, *5* (2), 31-50.
Avery, A. W. "Communication Skills Training for Paraprofessional
     Helpers." *American Journal of Community Psychology,* 1978, *6,*
     583-592.
Bandura, A. *Principles of Behavior Modification.* New York: Holt,
     Rinehart and Winston, 1969.
Beaubien, C. O. "Adolescent-Parent Communication Styles." Un-
     published doctoral dissertation, Department of Human Devel-
     opment and Family Studies, Pennsylvania State University, 1970.
Bienvenu, M. "Measurement of Marital Communication." *The
     Family Coordinator,* 1970, *19,* 26-31.

Cadigan, J. D. "RETEACH Program and Project: Relationship Enhancement in a Therapeutic Environment as Clients Head Out." Unpublished doctoral dissertation, Pennsylvania State University, 1980.

Carkhuff, R. R. *Helping and Human Relations.* Vol. 1. New York: Holt, Rinehart and Winston, 1969.

Collins, J. D. "Experimental Evaluation of a Six-Month Conjugal Therapy and Relationship Enhancement Program." In B. G. Guerney, Jr., *Relationship Enhancement: Skill-Training Programs for Therapy, Problem Prevention, and Enrichment.* San Francisco: Jossey-Bass, 1977.

Ellis, A. *Reason and Emotion in Psychotherapy.* New York: Lyle Stuart, 1963.

Ely, A. L., Guerney, B. G., Jr., and Stover, L. "Efficacy of the Training Phase of Conjugal Therapy." *Psychotherapy: Theory, Research, and Practice,* 1973, *10* (3), 201–207.

Ginsberg, B. G. "Parent-Adolescent Relationship Development Program." In B. G. Guerney, Jr., *Relationship Enhancement: Skill-Training Programs for Therapy, Problem Prevention, and Enrichment.* San Francisco: Jossey-Bass, 1977.

Guerney, B. G., Jr. "Filial Therapy: Description and Rationale." *Journal of Consulting Psychology,* 1964, *28* (4), 303–310.

Guerney, B. G., Jr. *Relationship Enhancement: Skill-Training Programs for Therapy, Problem Prevention, and Enrichment.* San Francisco: Jossey-Bass, 1977.

Guerney, B. G., Jr., Coufal, J., and Vogelsong, E. "Relationship Enhancement Versus a Traditional Approach to Therapeutic/Preventative/Enrichment Parent-Adolescent Programs." *Journal of Consulting Psychology,* 1981, *49,* 927–931.

Guerney, B. G., Jr., and Stover, L. *Filial Therapy: Final Report on MH 1826401.* State College, Pa. 1971. (Mimeographed.)

Guerney, B. G., Jr., and Vogelsong, E. *Relationship Enhancement.* University Park: Individual and Family Consultation Center, Catharine Beecher House, Pennsylvania State University, 1981. (Cassette tapes.)

Guerney, B. G., Jr., Vogelsong, E., and Glynn. *Evaluation of the Family Counseling Unit of the Cambria County Probation Bureau.* State College, Pa.: IDEALS, 1977. (Mimeographed.)

Guerney, B. G., Jr., Vogelsong, E., and Wolfgang, G. *Foster Parent Skills Training Program: First-Year Evaluation.* State College, Pa.: IDEALS, 1977.

Guerney, B. G., Jr., Wolfgang, G., and Vogelsong, E. *Second-Year Evaluation of Foster Care Systems Training Project.* State College, Pa. IDEALS, 1978.

Guerney, L. F. *What Do You Say Now?* University Park: Pennsylvania State University, in cooperation with the Pennsylvania Department of Public Welfare, 1973. (16mm film.)

Guerney, L. F. *The Training of Foster Parent Trainers.* University Park: Pennsylvania State University, in cooperation with the Pennsylvania Department of Public Welfare, 1974. (16mm film.)

Guerney, L. F. *A Follow-Up Study on Filial Therapy.* Paper presented at the annual convention of the Eastern Psychological Association, New York, April 1975a.

Guerney, L. F. *Foster Parent Training: A Manual for Parents.* University Park: Pennsylvania State University, 1975b.

Guerney, L. F. *Foster Parent Training: A Manual for Trainers.* University Park: Pennsylvania State University, 1976.

Guerney, L. F. "A Description and Evaluation of a Skills Training Program for Foster Parents." *American Journal of Community Psychology,* 1977, *5* (3), 361-371.

Guerney, L. F. *Parenting: A Skills Training Manual.* State College, Pa.: Institute for the Development of Emotional and Life Skills, 1979.

Hobbs, N. "Mental Health's Third Revolution." *American Journal of Orthopsychiatry,* 1964, pp. 822-833.

Horner, P. "Dimensions of Child Behavior as Described by Parents: a Monotonicity Analysis." Unpublished master's thesis, Department of Human Development and Family Studies, Pennsylvania State University, 1974.

Hunt, R. G. "Age, Sex, and Service Patterns in a Child Guidance Clinic." *Journal of Child Psychology and Psychiatry,* 1961, *2,* 185-192.

Jessee, R., and Guerney, B. G., Jr. "A Comparison of Gestalt and Relationship Enhancement Treatments with Married Couples." *The American Journal of Family Therapy,* 1981, *9,* 31-41.

Knox, D. *Marriage Happiness: A Behavioral Approach to Counseling.* Champaign, Ill.: 1971.

Leary, T. *Interpersonal Diagnosis of Personality.* New York: Ronald, 1957.

Levine, E. T. "Training Elderly Volunteers in Skills to Improve the Emotional Adjustment of Children in a Day-Care Center." Unpublished doctoral dissertation, Department of Human Development and Family Studies, Pennsylvania State University, 1977.

Levitt, E. "The Results of Psychotherapy with Children: An Evaluation." *Journal of Counseling Psychology,* 1957, *21,* 89–196.

Locke, H. J., and Wallace, K. M. "Short Marital Adjustment and Prediction Tests: Their Reliability and Validity." *Marriage and Family Living,* 1959, *21,* 251–255.

Locke, H. J., and Williamson, R. C. "Marital Adjustment: A Factor Analysis Study." *American Sociological Review,* 1958, *28,* 562–569.

Miller, G. A. "Psychology as a Means of Promoting Human Welfare." *American Journal of Psychology,* 1969, *24,* 1063–1075.

Moustakas, C. E., and Schlalock, H. D. "An Analysis for Therapist-Child Interaction in Play Therapy." *Child Development,* 1955, *26,* 143–157.

Oxman, L. "The Effectiveness of Filial Therapy: A Controlled Study." Unpublished doctoral dissertation, School of Psychology, Rutgers University, 1971.

Porter, B. "Measurement of Parental Acceptance of Children." *Journal of Home Economics,* 1954, *46* (3), 176–182.

Rappaport, A. F. "Conjugal Relationship Enhancement Program." In D. H. Olson (Ed.), *Treating Relationships.* Lake Mills, Iowa: Graphic Publishing, 1976.

Rappaport, A. F., and Harrell, J. "A Behavioral Exchange Model for Marital Counseling." *Family Coordinator,* 1972, *21,* 203–212.

Sanford, F. H. "Creative Health and the Principle of Habeas Mentem." *American Journal of Psychology,* 1955, *10,* 829–835.

Sensué, M. E. "Filial Therapy Follow-up Study: Effects on Parental Acceptance and Child Adjustment." Unpublished doctoral dissertation, Department of Human Development and Family Studies, Pennsylvania State University, 1981.

Shannon, J., and Guerney, B. G., Jr. "Interpersonal Effects of Interpersonal Behavior." *Journal of Personality and Social Psychology*, 1973, *26* (1), 142-150.

Stuart, R. B. "Operant-Interpersonal Treatment for Marital Discord." *Journal of Consulting and Clinical Psychology*, 1969a, *33*, 675-682.

Stuart, R. B. "Token Reinforcement in Marital Therapy." In R. D. Rubin and C. M. Franks (Eds.), *Advances in Behavior Therapy*, 1968. New York: Academic Press, 1969b.

Sullivan, H. S. *Conceptions of Modern Psychiatry*. Washington, D.C.: William Alanson White Psychiatric Foundation, 1947.

Sywulak, A. E. "The Effect of Filial Therapy on Parental Acceptance and Child Adjustment." Unpublished doctoral dissertation, Department of Human Development and Family Studies, Pennsylvania State University, 1977.

Szasz, T. *The Myth of Mental Illness: Foundations of a Theory of Personal Conduct*. New York: Hoeber-Harper, 1961.

Wieman, R. J. "Conjugal Relationship Modification and Reciprocal Reinforcement: A Comparison of Treatments for Marital Discord." Unpublished doctoral dissertation, Psychology Department, Pennsylvania State University, 1973.

Chapter 18

Life Skills Training

George M. Gazda

The life-skills training model represents an attempt to focus treatment on the whole person. But according to what parameters does one view the whole person? The position taken in this chapter is somewhat arbitrary, as are the positions assumed by others. For example, Lazarus (1982) has chosen to compartmentalize the whole person according to seven major areas of personality functioning: behavior, affective responses, sensations, images, cognitions, interpersonal relationships, and biological functioning—what Lazarus calls BASIC I.D. Goldstein, Sprafkin, and Gershaw (1976), on the other hand, have used patient and staff surveys, clinical experiences, reviews of relevant professional literature, and research on structured learning therapy to develop a list of fifty-nine specific life-skills areas involving social, personal, and interpersonal functioning.

In the life-skills training model, the person is viewed in terms of the seven areas of human development for which developmental stages have been identified: psychosocial (Erikson, 1963; Havighurst, 1972); physical-sexual (Gesell, Ilg, and Ames, 1956; Gesell and others, 1946); cognitive, in the manner of Piaget (Flavell, 1963; Wadsworth, 1971); moral (Kohlberg, 1973; Kohlberg and Turiel, 1971); vocational (Super, 1963; Super and others, 1957);

ego (Loevinger, 1976); and emotional (Dupont, in press). Within each of these areas of human development, the authorities just cited have identified certain life-coping skills appropriate for certain ages or stages of development. From this population of skills, families of related skills, referred to as generic life-skills, can be determined.

At the time of this writing, the generic life-skills have not been identified empirically. However, a research model is underway to determine and name them. In the meantime, families of life-skills have been suggested based on literature reviews and clinical evidence. As early as 1918, the Commission on the Reorganization of Secondary Education (Shane, 1977) developed the "cardinal principles of secondary education": health, command of fundamental processes, worthy home membership, a vocation, good citizenship, worthy use of leisure time, and ethical character. The National Assessment of Educational Progress (1975) cited seven skills areas recommended by a national planning committee as basic skills, in addition to the three Rs: consumer, health maintenance, interpersonal, citizenship, family relationship, community resource utilization, and career and occupational development skills. The similarity of these seven skill areas to the earlier cardinal principles is remarkable.

The life-skills training approach includes the generic life-skills of: family relationships, physical fitness/health maintenance, interpersonal communication, career/vocational development, consumer resource utilization, leisure, identity/purpose-in-life, emotional awareness, problem solving, group relationships, and self-evaluation. These life-skills have been developed from a review of the literature and from a classification, by a panel, of the life-coping–skills of the seven areas of human development. In addition, within each generic life-skill have been identified a number of related subskills that are necessary to perform the developmental task for a given stage and sex. For example, within the generic life-skill family relationships are subskills of marriage relationship, parenting, and sibling relationships.

Theoretical Basis of Life-Skills Training

A basic assumption of the life-skills training model is that most people become emotionally or mentally disturbed because they have never mastered certain basic life-skills necessary to cope with the daily requirements of living. These life-skills deficits generally occur because appropriate training models are not available.

Lazarus (1982) concurs with the position outlined above but adds the blockage model to explain conflicts and upheavals in individuals. Exemplified by psychoanalytic and Rogerian therapies, this model holds that people become disturbed because of some perceived or actual trauma in the course of their lives that leads to a barrier or blockage of normal or effective functioning. The removal of the barrier is the goal of these forms of therapy. By contrast, instruction in skills deficits is the goal of the life-skills training model.

Although I accept the trauma-blockage explanation for personal disorders of some individuals, I contend that this explanation fits far fewer people than most therapists assume. Even if one accepts the explanation, the question of the susceptibility of the person to trauma is still left unanswered. The position taken here is that, if the individual's life-skills are strong or well developed, he or she will not be as susceptible to trauma.

Certainly, this world holds many opportunities for personal tragedy. However, is it enough to attack problems with a blockage removal approach? Rarely have just removing the blockage and assuming that the suffering person will be restored to adaptive functioning been sufficient. Much more frequently, the dysfunctional person must not only be able to understand and accept the nature of his or her problem but must also have skills training to contend with and overcome it.

Prevention. As a viable model for mental health prevention, life-skills training can be conceptualized as the fourth R in education. A curriculum can be developed around each of the seven developmental areas or, more functionally, around the eleven generic life-skills. Since the life-skills paradigm is based on the seven areas of human development, which are related either to age or to stage, a developmental curriculum can be constructed by identifying and teaching the appropriate coping skills to facilitate attainment of developmental tasks.

For example, assume that we decide to teach the generic life-skill of interpersonal communication to elementary school children. To do so requires identifying the coping skills of interpersonal communication in each of the seven areas of human development. The skills are grouped into subcategories for purposes of instruction, such as initiating a conversation, requesting information, expressing a compliment, and listening for understanding. For each subcategory, we assess the children for their skill level, note their strengths and deficits, and choose activities that are developmentally appropriate for use in a group setting. Following this format, a developmental curriculum can be devised for each of the generic life-skills for each age level, including adults.

The following assumptions are inherent in the preventative application of life-skills training:

1.   In each of the seven areas of human development are identifiable stages through which individuals must progress if they are to function effectively.

2.   Specific coping skills that assist in achieving developmental tasks are optimally learned during certain periods of life (Havighurst, 1972).

3.   The capacity for learning is inherited. The degree to which individuals achieve their potential is closely related to their environment or life experiences.

4.   Life-skills can be taught most efficiently and effectively in small groups whose members are developmentally at the peak of readiness.

5.   Life-skills will be learned best and transferred to everyday life situations when an entire life-skills curriculum is taught at the age of maximum readiness for each stage.

Remediation. The remedial application of life-skills training is referred to as Multiple Impact Training (MIT). Essentially, treatment is the training of clients in life-skills in which they are deficient. The life-skills training paradigm seems to be most effective when the client receives training simultaneously in two or more areas of life-skills deficits (Gazda, 1981a, 1981b) and when the training is accomplished in small groups. The primary assumptions of the remedial application of life-skills training include the six assumptions of the preventative application and the four assumptions that follow.

1. Neuroses and functional psychoses are primarily the result of failure to learn basic life-skills.
2. Clients, with the help of counselors, can determine which life-skills are deficient (and also which are adequate or well developed).
3. Clients suffering from neuroses or functional psychoses typically have more than one life-skill deficit.
4. Neuroses and functional psychoses can be most effectively and efficiently overcome by directly training clients in the generic life-skill in which they are deficient, especially when they receive training concurrently in two or more life-skills areas.

The Training Process

The most distinctive features of the life-skills training model include the following:

1. The life-skills comprising the model are gleaned from the coping behaviors appropriate to the developmental task of a given age and sex across the seven areas of human development.
2. A mastery learning model is employed whenever the life-skills are hierarchical or progressive.
3. Activities are varied throughout training to accommodate the three basic modes of learning: auditory, visual, and kinesthetic.
4. Generic life-skills are viewed as a family of related skills that are taught, much as other subjects, according to the developmental readiness of the trainee.
5. Essentially the same training procedures are applied when teaching the life-skills for prevention and when teaching them for remediation.
6. Extensive, supervised practice through role rehearsal and simulation training is utilized to ensure skills development.
7. Homework assignments are given to facilitate transfer of learned skills to trainees' lives.
8. Peer trainers are utilized whenever possible to increase credibility and transfer of learning.

9. Self-monitoring is emphasized and, where possible, self-rating scales are used.
10. Trainees may repeat the training program to increase and to solidify skills levels.
11. The training utilizes an educational, rather than a treatment, approach.
12. A wide variety of training materials and methods is employed.
13. The most theoretically sound and operationally efficient model for teaching a given life-skill is employed.
14. Typically, cotrainers are used.
15. The training time, including length of sessions, spacing of sessions, and duration of training, is flexible and can accommodate trainees at different levels of readiness.
16. Training is conducted in small groups of six to twelve clients.
17. Client/trainers are taught in a four-step pyramid sequence encompassing generic life-skills training, cotraining with a "master" trainer, training with supervision by a master trainer, and training alone.

The client/trainer is expected to have mastered the generic life-skill and the family of subskills that he or she is to teach in order to effectively model the skill and monitor its development in trainees. Roles assumed by the trainer include teacher, modeler, monitor/evaluator, motivator, encourager, facilitator, protector, and methods and materials developer.

Although clients generally assume the role of trainee or learner, some may advance to be cotrainers, and then become trainers under the supervision of a master trainer. Finally, those who reach an effective skills level may even serve as self-sufficient trainers.

Training Pyramid. The training activities can be imaged in a pyramidal structure because more training is done in the first steps, which provide the broad foundation on which succeeding ones are based. The activities most frequently used in each of the four steps include:

Stage 1. Training in generic life-skills.

1. Didactic presentations of the rationale of the model for the given generic life-skill to be mastered—"tell."

2. Modeling or demonstration of the behavior or response to be learned—"show."
3. Practice by trainees of the skill to be mastered—"do."
4. Homework application of the new skill to daily living—"transfer."
5. Monitoring and assessment, by self and others, of skill level achieved.
6. Peers helped by peers in developing their skills.

Stage 2. Cotraining with master trainer.

Stage 3. Training under supervision of master trainer.

Stage 4. Training alone.

Stages 2, 3, and 4 contain the six elements of Stage 1, but in each case the former trainee is now serving as trainer in some capacity.

Materials Required. The amount and kinds of materials required vary with the generic life-skill taught. For example, when teaching physical fitness/health maintenance, one may use printed handouts or slides pertaining to the basic food groups or to the effects of certain drugs on the body. In addition, for the exercise routines, exercise equipment may be employed, along with monitoring devices for measuring physical stress, blood pressure, body weight, and changes in body conformity. The Health Hazard Appraisal may be given to assess and give computer feedback on a person's health assets and health hazards.

In teaching the interpersonal communication life-skill, books are frequently used as are videotaped and live lectures on the communication model to be learned. Live and videotaped models of appropriate and inappropriate interpersonal communications are also available. In addition, clients' skills practice can be videotaped to provide feedback, and clients can be taught how to use a rating scale to evaluate themselves and other group members. The trainer is expected to accommodate the preferred learning styles of everyone by providing a balanced use of materials that appeals to auditory, visual, and kinesthetic learning modes.

Organizational Support and Resources Needed. For life-skills training to be introduced into helping settings like schools and hospitals, the administration, staff, and community must be receptive. In schools, life-skills training can be taught daily at every grade level. Student personnel services specialists, such as counselors, school psychologists, and social workers, serve as the backbone of the program, but they cannot do all the instruction and training— other expertise should be utilized. For example, the school nurse, dietician, and physical education director can team to teach the physical fitness/health maintenance life-skill; the counselor, social worker, and social studies teachers can team to teach the family relationships life-skill; and the vocational development/career awareness life-skill can be taught by counselors, with assistance from both the vocational and academic subject teachers. Given the limited number of student personnel specialists, trainers must of necessity assume a counseling and coordinating role and be empowered to draw upon the entire school staff and even other experts from the community to serve as trainers.

To train teachers, counselors, social workers, and other school personnel to be life-skills trainers, a combination of preservice training and in-service training is recommended. For the present, however, only in-service training is available, because no complete life-skills training programs have yet been applied to the education of teachers, counselors, or social workers.

When life-skills training is utilized for remediation, again interdisciplinary cooperation is the key to its success. A motivating aspect of interdisciplinary cooperation is the opportunity it provides for professionals and paraprofessionals from the various disciplines to choose a life-skills area of special interest to them and to develop their expertise in that area, usually working with someone else from a different discipline but with similar interests. For example, in a Veterans Administration program in Augusta, Georgia, a clinical nurse specialist, a social worker, and a psychologist coordinate the life-skills training program. A dietician and a corrective therapist teach the physical fitness/health maintenance skill, a nurse, a psychologist, and a social worker teach the interpersonal communication skill, and a chaplain teaches the purpose-in-life skill. In-service training was provided for all the trainers prior to initiating the life-skills training model. A similar model can be used in training community health personnel.

Interdisciplinary cooperation is necessary for the success of life-skills training used for remediation or prevention. A positive side effect is the increased communication and respect that develops between specialists from different disciplines and the increase in staff morale that follows. Adequate space, materials, and personnel are also necessary for a successful life-skills training program, and the assistance of an audiovisual specialist to provide such services as videotaping and video playback is very useful, if not essential.

Trainer Competence in Generic Life-Skills

Since the life-skills training model is based on at least a dozen generic life-skills areas, trainers must decide in which of the areas they will become specialists. Although a trainer could possibly become a specialist in all of them, most trainers will not be able to develop expertise in more than three or four rather closely related areas. For example, for a trainer who may wish to specialize in family relationships life-skills training, related life-skills areas would include interpersonal communication and problem solving. A trainer who is especially interested in developing the vocational/career development area may find it closely related to purpose in life and use of leisure time. However, regardless of the generic life-skills area or areas to be studied, all prospective trainers are expected to be trained first in interpersonal communication.

Once the prospective life-skills trainer has knowledge of the subject area, he or she must then learn certain generic group leadership skills in order to teach the content. Since life-skills training typically involves didactic instruction, modeling, and practice, the group skills required of trainers include those of an instructor, as well as those of a facilitator or counselor.

Leader as Instructor and as Facilitator or Counselor. As instructor, the counselor's first task is to determine the skill deficits of potential group members through interviews, psychological and other tests, and case history notes. A second instructor function is to select printed, audiovisual, and other training materials appropriate to the readiness level of the clients. Next, the training materials must be organized according to a training schedule based on the length of time for training and the frequency of training sessions. Finally, some systematic approach, such as a lesson plan, dictated by the nature of the skills to be taught, should be developed for each training session. Bloom's (1976) mastery learning model provides the structure and rationale for instruction.

Carkhuff (1969) contended that the effective facilitator must offer high levels of the "core conditions" of empathy, warmth, and respect and the more action-oriented conditions of concreteness, genuineness, appropriate self-disclosure, confrontation, and immediacy. Life-skills trainers are first trained systematically to effective levels in these core and action dimensions. Without well-developed interpersonal communication skills, other group and leadership skills are, for the most part, unteachable.

Leader as Model. Bandura (1977) has identified four processes that explain the success of observational learning: attention, retention, motor reproduction, and motivation. Characteristics of the model observed, such as interpersonal attractiveness, warmth, nurturance, perceived competence, perceived social power, age similarity, sex, and socioeconomic status, influence the observers' attending behavior. Observer characteristics, such as dependency, level of competence, sex, race, socioeconomic status, and previous social learning experiences, also affect learning.

The observed behavior must be symbolically coded to be retained, and this coding can be either imaginal or verbal. Once coding has occurred, retention can be enhanced by rehearsal strategies (Holland and Kobasigawa, 1980).

Motor reproduction of the images and thoughts acquired through observation depends on the availability of the motor skills to the observer. In situations where several components are to be mastered for motor reproduction, the missing or deficient skills must first be developed by observation and practice.

Motivation is influenced by external reinforcement. Learned responses that are likely to result in some direct, external, positive consequences will be expressed overtly, whereas those that lead to neutral consequences or are negatively reinforced may not be translated into behavior. In addition, modeled behavior may be acquired if the observed person is positively reinforced, whereas, if the observed person is punished, the behavior may be suppressed (Holland and Kobasigawa, 1980). The observer may also manifest or inhibit an observed behavior based on comparisons of his or her own behavior to standards that have been assimilated through observation (Bandura and Kupers, 1964).

The use of modeling in the teaching of life-skills takes into account the characteristics just outlined. In some instances, the models are presented on videotape, with prior orientation given to trainees as to the rationale for the behavior to be modeled. Both positive and negative reinforcement are shown. When modeling is live, a similar program is followed. Frequently peers are used as models to accommodate sex and age similarity.

Leader Use of Role Playing. According to Shaw and others (1980), no one has yet provided a completely satisfactory theory to explain the value of role playing in changing human behavior. Nevertheless, role playing includes several features that appear to help change behavior: emphasis on personal concerns or problems, emphasis on personal behavior, active participation, feedback, and practice.

In order to avoid training procedures that are too hypothetical or impersonal, role plays are based on relevant, personal concerns of trainees. Bradford (1945) stresses the importance of the concreteness of the role play and its relevance to the role player. Thus, when the role play is relevant to the trainee's own concerns or behavior, he or she is motivated to experiment with effective approaches suggested in trainer critiques and feedback.

Bohart (1977), French (1945), and Moody (1953) cite, in addition to the specific or concrete features of role playing, the importance of the active involvement of the role player, contending that role playing breaks through the verbal barriers and generates insight and skill where other methods fail. Research by Huyck (1975), O'Donnell (1954), and Planty (1948) supports their contention. Role playing therefore provides the client opportunity to participate actively in the subject matter being studied through exploration and experimentation (Shaw and others, 1980).

Moody (1953) has found that role playing can be used to expand social awareness, and Stahl (1953), Speroff (1953), and Cohen (1951) have shown that it can be used to increase personal respect for the feelings of others. These characteristics are related to the feedback dimensions of role playing. Feedback helps clients identify their blind spots and receive the kind of information that they ordinarily fail to see or hear. Clients can check their perceptions against the perceptions of others and can evaluate their own and others' behavior. Alternative ways of behaving explored under feedback conditions can be evaluated instantly. By testing various reactions, clients can learn to be more comfortable when practicing new behaviors (Shaw and others, 1980).

Finally, role playing allows clients to practice more effective methods of relating to others (Stahl, 1953). "The idea of skill practice is as appropriate in improving human relationships as it is in learning any new physical skill" (Shaw and others, 1980, p. 22). A major deficit in current counseling and therapy procedures is the almost total lack of opportunity for clients to practice and perfect new responses or behaviors prior to using them in their day-to-day circumstances. Frequent use of role playing and behavioral rehearsal in life-skills training circumvents this problem.

Leader Facilitation of Transfer of Training. Several features of the life-skills training model are aimed at ensuring the transfer of training to the trainee's home environment. First, the use of small groups of approximately ten members permits a degree of personal intimacy and cohesiveness that contributes to support and motivation. From a learning point of view, the small group represents a microcosm of society and helps to ensure stimulus variability—that is, the group composition is representative of the client's larger world. Therefore, skills learned in this context are more likely to transfer to a variety of situations encountered in daily living.

Second, homework assignments between training sessions facilitate transfer. These assignments vary from workbook exercises intended to increase cognitive understanding of the model for a given life-skill to assignments that involve practice of the skill with significant others. The use of personal journals facilitates self-monitoring of behavior between training sessions, and self-rating devices are taught so that the trainee can monitor his or her own performance against a standard. For example, in the interpersonal communication life-skill model, a scale for rating one's global level of functioning is taught (see Global Scale in Gazda, Walters, and Childers, 1975; Gazda and others, 1977). In the physical fitness/

health maintenance life-skill model, trainees are taught how to monitor their pulse rate during exercise activities.

Third, training is given to all members of a specific work, family, or educational unit in order to build external monitoring and mutual reinforcement into the system. In other words, training is directed toward subsystems to enable them to play a constructive role in enhancing the transfer of life-skills.

Finally, trainees are encouraged to attend intermittent "booster shot" training sessions—analogous to in-service education for professionals—in order to maintain their skills level. Learning life-skills is considered to be a life-long endeavor; as with other skills, disuse can lead to deterioration.

Overview of Program's Effectiveness

The ultimate criterion of the effectiveness of any mental health training program is the ability of trainees to effect positive change in their clientele. Both preventative and remedial life-skills training programs have been evaluated: a preventative, partial life-skills program offered to elementary school children (Robinson, 1976; Bixler, 1972) and the remedial Multiple Impact Training (MIT) program used to treat patients in a Veterans Administration hospital (May, 1981; Powell and Clayton, 1980).

In the elementary school study, three randomly selected third-, fourth-, and fifth-grade experimental classes were compared with three randomly selected, comparable control group classes against the standardization sample on the Barclay Classroom Climate Inventory (BCCI) (Barclay, 1978). The females in the experimental group showed less impulsivity and considerably more energy, effort, sociability, and enterprising dominance than females in the control group; they were about the same on task-order achievement and slightly more introverted. Males in the experimental group were more task-order oriented, controlled, extroverted and outgoing, and sociable and demonstrated more effort. Both experimental and control group teachers rated the students more positively and less negatively than the standardization group. Regarding the diagnostic categories on the BCCI, the experimental classrooms had less need for career awareness and far more children who could serve as peer tutors. None of the experimental children were targeted for special attention or remediation. By contrast, eighteen children from the control classrooms were identified as needing special attention. Graduates (at the end of the fifth grade) of the experimental school scored significantly higher at the end of the sixth grade on all categories of the Iowa Test of Basic Skills. They also scored significantly higher on a teacher-rated questionnaire on the following four dimensions: responsibility, respect, resourcefulness, and responsiveness. The groups did not differ on the Piers-Harris Children's Self-Concept Scale.

An intensive study at a Veterans Administration psychiatric hospital was conducted by May (1981) to assess the effectiveness of the MIT remedial model. Patients were provided concurrent training in three life-skills areas—interpersonal communication, physical fitness/health maintenance, and purpose in life—and compared with a traditionally treated control group. The MIT subjects received twelve hours of training in interpersonal communication, six hours in purpose in life, and ten hours in physical fitness/health maintenance, including instruction in diet and nutrition, as well as practice in an exercise program. The MIT subjects increased their interpersonal communication skills significantly ($p < .001$) over the traditional treatment control group. The patients trained in the purpose-in-life group were significantly ($p < .025$) higher on the Purpose-in-Life Test than controls. Both MIT-trained patients and controls showed physical fitness improvements on forced vital capacity, blood pressure, and heart rate. (It was discovered after the study that controls received as much health maintenance training on an individual basis as experimentals received in small groups.) Both experimentals and controls showed a decrease in psychopathology as measured by ward staff on the Nurses's Observation Scale for Inpatient Evaluation. The experimental group of patients also showed a trend ($p < .10$) toward greater satisfaction with treatment than the control group as measured on a Semantic Differential. Staff reports indicated that participating patients were returning less often to the hospital and, when they did return, were remaining in the hospital for shorter periods of time.

Powell and Clayton (1980) studied the effect of interpersonal communication training on the patients' length of stay in the hospital. A comparison of the duration of hospital stays over two-year pretreatment and posttreatment periods revealed that experimental patients reduced their length of stay from thirty-two to fifteen weeks. By contrast, Hawthorne control group subjects increased their duration from forty-five to fifty-one weeks. Powell and Clayton also found that experimental patients obtained more gainful employment or productive work than control patients.

Conclusion

In sum, the life-skills training model offers a learning approach for preventative and remedial treatment. Further model development is necessary to expand the life-skills curriculum to make it truly comprehensive. Evaluation findings from the initial application of the model are encouraging; however, continued development of life-skills training models and intensive research will be necessary before life-skills training can gain wide acceptance.

References

Bandura, A. *Social Learning Theory*. Englewood Cliffs, N.J.: Prentice-Hall, 1977.

Bandura, A. and Kupers, C. J. "Transmission of Patterns of Self-Reinforcement Through Modeling." *Journal of Abnormal and Social Psychology*, 1964, *69*, 1–9.

Barclay, J. R. *Manual of the Barclay Classroom Climate Inventory*. Lexington, Ky.: Educational Skills Development, 1978.

Bixler, J. "Influence of Trainer-Trainee Cognitive Similarity on the Outcome of Systematic Human Relations Training." Unpublished doctoral dissertation, Department of Counseling and Human Development Services, University of Georgia, 1972.

Bloom, B. S. *Human Characteristics and School Learning*. New York: McGraw-Hill, 1976.

Bohart, A. C. "Role Playing and Interpersonal-Conflict Reduction." *Journal of Counseling Psychology*, 1977, *24*, 15–24.

Bradford, L. "Supervisory Training as a Diagnostic Instrument." *Personal Administration*, 1945, *8*, 3–7.

Carkhuff, R. R. *Helping and Human Relations.* Vols. 1 and 2. *Selection* and *Training.* New York: Holt, Rinehart and Winston, 1969.

Cohen, J. "The Techniques of Role-Reversal: A Preliminary Note." *Occupational Psychology,* 1951, *25,* 64–66.

Dupont, H. "Meeting the Emotional-Social Needs of Students in a Mainstreamed Environment." *Counseling and Human Development,* 1978, *10,* 1–12.

Dupont, H. "Affective Development: Stage and Sequence." In R. L. Nosher (Ed.), *Adolescent Development in Education.* Berkeley, Calif.: McCutchen, in press.

Erikson, E. H. *Childhood and Society.* (2nd ed.) New York: Norton, 1963.

Fabry, J. A. *The Pursuit of Meaning.* New York: Harper & Row, 1980.

Flavell, J. H. *The Developmental Psychology of Jean Piaget.* New York: D. Van Nostrand, 1963.

French, J.R.P. "Role Playing as a Method of Training Foremen." *Sociometry,* 1945, *8,* 410–422.

Gazda, G. M. "Multiple Impact Training." In R. J. Corsini (Ed.), *Innovative Psychotherapies.* New York: Wiley, 1981a.

Gazda, G. M. "Multiple Impact Training: A Model for Teaching/ Training in Life-Skills." In G. M. Gazda (Ed.), *Innovations to Group Psychotherapy* (2nd ed.) Springfield, Ill.: Thomas, 1981b.

Gazda, G. M., Walters, R. P., and Childers, W. C. *Human Relations Development: A Manual for Health Sciences.* Boston: Allyn & Bacon, 1975.

Gazda, G. M., Walters, R. P., and Childers, W. C. *Realtalk: Exercises in Friendship and Helping Skills.* Atlanta, Ga.: Humanics, 1980.

Gazda, G. M., and others. *Human Relations Development: A Manual for Educators.* (2nd ed.) Boston: Allyn & Bacon, 1977.

Gesell, A., Ilg, F. L., and Ames, L. B. *The Years from Ten to Sixteen.* New York: Harper & Row, 1956.

Gesell, A., and others. *The Child from Five to Ten.* New York: Harper & Row, 1946.

Goldstein, A. P., Sprafkin, R. P., and Gershaw, N. J. *Skill Training for Community Living: Applying Structured Learning Therapy.* Elmsford, N.Y.: Pergamon, 1976.

Havighurst, R. J. *Human Development and Education.* (3rd ed.) New York: Longmans, 1972.

Holland, C. J., and Kobasigawa, A. "Observational Learning." In G. M. Gazda and R. J. Corsini (Eds.), *Theories of Learning.* Itasca, Ill.: Peacock, 1980.

Huyck, E. T. "Teaching for Behavioral Change." *Humanist Educator,* 1975, *14*, 12–20.

Kohlberg, L. "Continuities and Discontinuities in Childhood and Adult Moral Development Revisited." In P. L. Baltes and K. W. Schaie (Eds.), *Lifespan Developmental Psychology: Personality and Socialization.* New York: Academic Press, 1973.

Kohlberg, L., and Turiel, P. "Moral Development and Moral Education." In G. Lesser (Ed.), *Psychology and Educational Practice.* Glenview, Ill.: Scott, Foresman, 1971.

Lazarus, A. A. "Multi Modal Group Therapy" In G. M. Gazda (Ed.), *Basic Approaches to Group Psychotherapy and Group Counseling.* (3rd ed.) Springfield, Ill.: Thomas, 1982.

Loevinger, J. *Ego Development: Conceptions and Theories.* San Francisco: Jossey-Bass, 1976.

May, H. J. "The Effects of Life-Skill Training Versus Traditional Psychiatric Treatment on Therapeutic Outcome in Psychiatric Patients." Unpublished doctoral dissertation, Department of Counseling and Human Development Services, University of Georgia, 1981.

Moody, K. A. "Role Playing as a Training Technique." *Journal of Industrial Training,* 1953, *7*, 3–5.

National Assessment of Educational Progress. *Draft of Basic Skills Objectives.* Denver, Colo.: National Assessment of Educational Progress, a Division of the Commission on the Education of the States, 1975.

O'Donnell, W. G. "Role Playing in Training and Management Development." *Journal of the American Society of Training Directors,* 1954, *8*, 76–78.

Planty, E. G. "Training Employees and Managers." In E. G. Planty, W. S. McCord, and C. A. Efferson (Eds.), *Training Employees and Managers for Production and Teamwork.* New York: Ronald, 1948.

Powell, M. F., and Clayton, M. "Efficiency of Human Relations Training on Selected Coping Behaviors of Veterans in a Psychiatric Hospital." *Journal of the Association for Specialists in Group Work,* 1980, *5,* 170–176.

Robinson, E. H., III. "Student's Perceptions of Teachers' Abilities to Provide Certain Facilitative Conditions and Their Relationship to Language Arts Achievement Gains." Unpublished doctoral dissertation, Department of Education, University of North Carolina at Greensboro, 1976.

Shane, H. G. *Curriculum Change Toward the 21st Century.* Washington, D.C.: National Education Association, 1977.

Shaw, M. E., and others. *Role Playing.* San Diego, Calif.: University Associates, 1980.

Speroff, B. J. "The Group's Role in Role Playing." *Journal of Industrial Training,* 1953, *7,* 17–20.

Stahl, G. R. "Training Directors Evaluate Role Playing." *Journal of Industrial Training,* 1953, *7,* 21–29.

Super, D. E. "Vocational Development in Adolescence and Early Adulthood: Tasks and Behaviors." In D. E. Super, *Career Development: Self-Concept Theory.* New York: College Entrance Examination Board, 1963.

Super, D. E., and others. *Vocational Development: A Framework for Research.* Monograph 1. New York: Teachers College Press, 1957.

Wadsworth, B. J. *Piaget's Theory of Cognitive Development.* New York: McKay, 1971.

Epilogue

Future Directions for Interpersonal Skills Training

Eldon K. Marshall
P. David Kurtz

When one looks at the current state of the science and art of skills training, one encounters many critical but unanswered questions that must be addressed if the field is to advance. Is skills training, as Calia (1974) suggests, a technology in search of a theory? What is the relationship between the skills used in therapy and treatment outcomes? What is the status of skills training research and evaluation methodology? What helping professions can benefit from skills training? What level of skills competence must trainees acquire in order to be effective helpers? Do skills training programs create a bunch of look-alikes? What is the relative effectiveness of various training methods in teaching skills? What factors facilitate the transfer of skills from the training environment to the work world? How effective are skills training programs in teaching responses that endure? How useful are skills programs in preparing helpers to work with ethnically and culturally different individuals? Are the skills for working with individuals similar to those for working with groups? Assuming that Matarazzo (1978) is correct and that skills programs have adequately explored the more basic skills of helping, what are the future directions of the field? The responses to these and related questions are complex and varied. Discussion in this chapter will focus on key issues not addressed in other sections of this book.

Is It Feasible to Define the "Necessary and Sufficient" Skills for Helping?

Although Rogers's "necessary and sufficient" hypothesis was perhaps the major factor for stimulating sustained empirical interest in the helper conditions that facilitate the helping process, the more recent literature reflects the sobering realization that the helping process is extremely complex and that it is exceedingly difficult to determine which conditions are necessary. Investigators have all but given up on determining which conditions are sufficient.

The large number of distinct skills labels (138) cited in the studies surveyed in Chapter One reflects the lack of consensus regarding the necessary or core facilitative skills. The skills identified differ drastically in their complexity and actual behavioral referents and range from discrete units of behavior, such as eye contact, restatements, and reflections of feelings, to global behaviors and attitudes, such as intimacy, respect, friendliness, and politeness. Several writers (Bohart and others, 1979; Gormally and Hill, 1974; Matarazzo, 1978; Reivich and Geertsma, 1969) cite the need for increased operationalization of interpersonal skills as the basis for more effectively determining which skills are critical to the helping process, to improving training, and to providing a sound basis for evaluating training effectiveness. Goodman and Dooley (1976) call for the identification of irreducible "prime number type skills." However, most programs tend to combine discrete, measurable behaviors like eye contact with global behaviors like problem solving (see, for example, Egan, 1975)—what Goodman refers to as the "beebees and boulders" dilemma. This dilemma raises a number of issues: Can the boulders be reduced, if not to beebees, at least to pellets? Can boulders be as effectively taught as beebees? Are boulders measurable? Can programs that teach boulders be satisfactorily evaluated?

Rather than converging, approaches to interpersonal skills training are becomingly increasingly divergent. A cursory look at the models included in this book reveals that each has its own set of skills. True, some of the more recent models have built on the earlier ones. However, rarely do the new and the old exactly correspond. As more professions discover the relevance of skills training for their service delivery, as a wider diversity of scholars engage in model building and research, and as model builders seek to develop increasingly more advanced skills, the multiplicity of skills and their uses will only increase. The area of group psychotherapy, group counseling, and social group work, which cuts across many professions, is a prime example of how skills models and training methods continue to expand. Relevant skills schema are emerging, most of which focus on group leadership and group facilitation.

As a result of its growing popularity, the field is caught in a dilemma. "The field is moving, albeit slowly, away from the linear strategy toward studying a broader range of therapist activities as they interact with differentiated patient groups under a variety of specified treatment conditions" (Parloff, Waskow, and Wolfe, 1978, p. 252). The differential treatment or helping needs of clients require the differential use of a range of interpersonal helping skills. The question to be addressed is not, What are the necessary and sufficient skills for helping? but rather, What skills by whom are most helpful for this individual with this specific problem in this set of circumstances? (Paul, 1967).

Is It Possible to Teach Helpers How to Form a Helping Relationship?

Strupp (1974) questions the feasibility of systematically teaching specific core conditions. "The art, which is to some extent teachable, consists of knowing when and how to communicate interest, respect, understanding, empathy, etc. . . . some people undoubtedly know these things intuitively and others can be trained. Still others, because of their life history and personality makeup, cannot benefit from such training" (p. 3). Two questions emerge: Is relationship composed of diffuse qualities embodied in helpers' attitudes and values? and, Are these qualities largely intuitive? The contributors to this volume would almost certainly reply in the negative to both points. Each contributor proposes certain teachable, measurable, relationship enhancement skills. Although opinions differ somewhat in the choice of significant skills, Matarazzo (1978) concludes that, "with regard to what interviewing skills to teach, there seems to be convergence among programs on at least a few basic measured variables" (p. 962). However, she also stresses that these programs have not attempted to measure more subtle, advanced-level skills such as self-disclosure, interpretation, and confrontation.

In general, skills training programs seem to produce favorable outcomes (Matarazzo, 1978). Trainees who participate in such training programs typically demonstrate substantial improvement in their use of helping skills. However, the results are not unequivocal. Mahon and Altman (1977) caution, "It has been our experience (both as trainees and trainers) that not all individuals respond equally well to training, that not all skills are equally 'trainable,' that not all approaches to training are consistently effective, and that trained skills frequently do not transfer to nontraining settings" (p. 42).

Does Learning How to Be an Effective Helper Simply Entail Acquiring Interpersonal Skills?

Rogers (1957a) observes that learning involves a change in one's self. How one interacts with others is closely related to one's perception of self and the environment, and helping is a dynamic process that depends on how one uses self. Since an individual's interpersonal response patterns and corresponding belief systems have developed over the years into entrenched habits and attitudes, Rogers believes that learning how to be an effective helper entails much more than simply acquiring specific behaviors—development of the individual is also essential.

Combs (1969) suggests that attitudes, beliefs, and values are the underlying basis for skills. Mahon and Altman (1977), however, question this assumption: "Do the skills essential for effective communication consist of behavioral expressions of certain attitudes and values that are not easily acquired or maintained, as some might assume?" (p. 42). For those who answer this question affirmatively, skills training takes a back seat to transmission of professional knowledge and values and the internalizing of the professional role.

In contrast, Fischer (1976), although acknowledging that skillfulness is related to values and knowledge, does not believe that skills performance naturally follows from one's affective and cognitive orientation. Skills training is essential. Ivey (1974) makes a similar observation, suggesting that intentionality is an important dimension of skills training: "Underlying any single act are a multitude of possible intentions. It is vital that those who teach behavioral skills pay special attention to underlying motivation and intent" (p. 108). Another aspect of intentionality is that the helper can generate alternative behaviors and respond to problems from different vantage points (Ivey and Rollins, 1972). Ivey proposes that a limited skills repertoire may result in stereotypical helper responses and recommends microtraining to overcome the behavioral deficit. Although Ivey's model increases helper response repertoires, it does little more than acknowledge the motivational and intentional dimensions. Seemingly, an approach such as Kagan's (1975) IPR program, which, in addition to teaching explicit skills, focuses on in-depth inquiry into self in the helping process, may have considerable potential as a method for addressing the underlying values, attitudes, and motives of trainees. If skills training is to avoid the creation of mechanistically oriented practitioners, programs need to give greater attention to intentionality and motivation and teach skills within conceptual frameworks to further their meaningful integration within broader professional roles and tasks.

Does Skills Training Produce "Therapeutic Technicians?" Do Skills Trainees Become Mechanical Look-Alikes?

Jourard (1973) expresses concern that concentration on skill or technique may result in substituting the goal of helping the client for the aim of simulating the "correct" use of skills. Do trainees become so enmeshed in the appropriate use of skills that they lose sight of the skills' function? Does the helping process supersede treatment outcome in importance? Furthermore, are trainees so enamored with Carkhuff, Ivey, Egan, and others that they attempt to emulate the models, rather than work to achieve an integration of skills into their own self and their unique style of helping? Calia (1974) quips, "Is SHRT nurturing humans or humanoids?" (p. 92). A critical question to raise concerns whether the focus and instructional technology of skills programs are focused so narrowly on the skills per se that trainees do not grasp the broader role of skills in the helping process. To be sure, some established training programs do view the development and use of skills within a context of the broader helping process. For example, the skills at focus in SHRT are viewed as instrumental in facilitating the helping processes of exploration, understanding, and action (Carkhuff and Pierce, 1977). Gazda and others (1977) focus on skills within a developmental perspective of helping, and Egan, in this volume, presents skills in the context of a problem-solving orientation. On the other hand, if one takes certain skills manuals, such as Danish and Hauer (1973) and Ivey and Gluckstern (1974), at face value, one finds there an exclusive focus on the acquisition of specific skills without an overall frame of reference for their use. That is not to say that these manuals are without merit. However, in using such programs, trainers must be keenly aware of this deficit and adapt their teaching to the context of the helping environment of each trainee group. Emphasis must not be simply on the rote production of skills but on the integration of skills to fit client needs, agency realities, the helping orientation of a professional discipline, and the trainee's personal style of helping. For instance, although common skills are likely to be used across disciplines and service settings, the mix of skills used by a public assistance worker may differ markedly from those of a school counselor. In the words of Rogers (1957b):

> The student should develop his own orientation to psychotherapy out of his own experience. In my estimation, every effective therapist has built his own orientation to therapy within himself and out of his own experience with his clients or patients. It is quite true that this orientation as finally developed may be such that it closely resembles that of others or closely resembles the orientation to which he was exposed. Nevertheless, the responses made by the effective therapist in his interviews are not made in a certain way because that is the psychoanalytic way or the client-centered way or the Adlerian way, they are made because the therapist has found that type of response effective in his own experience. Likewise, he does not put on certain attitudes because those are the attitudes expected of an analyst or

client-centered therapist or an Adlerian. He discovers and uses certain attitudes in himself which have developed because they have been rewarded by the effective outcome of earlier experiences in carrying on therapy. Thus, the aim of a training program in therapy should be to turn out individuals who have an independent and open attitude toward their own therapy and continually formulate and reformulate and revise their own approach to the individuals with whom they are working in such a way that their approach results in more constructive and effective help (p. 87).

What Are the Characteristics of a Comprehensive Skills Training Program?

The fact that many programs reported in Chapter One are of short duration, focus on a limited number of skills, use training methods selectively, and reflect limited conceptual frameworks raises important questions concerning their relevance for practice and their overall impact on practitioner roles. It seems warranted to urge the implementation of programs of sufficient practice relevance and breadth to heighten the probabilities of a meaningful impact on the interpersonal performance of helping practitioners and to promote a significant level of skills integration and retention. In working toward this objective, those in the training field would do well to bear in mind the principles of training design formulated by Havelock and Havelock (1973). Actualizing these principles would move trainers to do the following: (1) define a program structure that encompasses well-formulated objectives and a specified sequence of activities; (2) provide high levels of specificity in the formulation of goals and training activities; (3) assure the relevance of the program to the objectives, social and on-the-job needs, and background of trainees; (4) provide content that is general enough in its application to benefit a range of people and situations; (5) offer high levels of reinforcement for effective performance in the training process; (6) maintain flexibility and openness in making program adjustments that accommodate unanticipated needs of trainees and unanticipated circumstances in the training process; (7) promote linkage of trainees with appropriate resources and resource persons inside and outside the training context; (8) foster high levels of trainee involvement through activities that capture attention and maintain motivation; (9) provide for a level of redundancy that reinforces key instructional points in varied ways and contexts and through different media; (10) train for psychological wholeness through emphasis on integration and internalization of skills, knowledge, and attitudes; (11) train for transfer of learning to performance in the work setting; (12) assure reasonable compatibility or fit between the training experiences and the cultural background, work experience, and future work situation of trainees; and (13) work toward cost effectiveness in providing programs of greatest benefit to the most trainees at the lowest expense.

Do Individual Characteristics of Trainees Affect Skills Acquisition?

One of the impressive trends in skills training is the application of skills training programs to a wide array of helping groups. Some training programs have been broadly administered to trainees who may differ significantly in personality style, cultural and ethnic background, sex, cognitive style, expectations and motives, and helping experience.

Most trainers have experienced great variability in the way participants engage themselves in any given training process. For example, there is typically a cluster of trainees who can be characterized as less involved, less responsive, and less open to the training experience. Looking at one's performance and contending with feedback from others can be overly threatening, thereby generating resistance to the entire process. As Mahon and Altman (1977) point out, "Not all individuals respond equally well to training" (p. 42). The existence of this familiar phenomenon raises questions concerning the suitability of persons for training. Who can learn best from a skills training experience? For whom is training likely to be least valuable? Are there selection procedures to screen those most suited for a particular skills learning process?

Some studies do suggest a link between individual characteristics and learning outcomes from training. Although not sufficient to support definitive generalizations, the evidence to date indicates that the success of training may relate to such individual variables as level of interpersonal functioning (Carkhuff, 1969), cognitive functioning or style (Mayadas and Duehn, 1977), conceptual development (Rosenthal, 1977), level of neuroticism or trait anxiety (Rennie and Toukmanian, 1976), tolerance for ambiguity (Jones, 1974), need for order (Jones, 1974), openness or readiness to change (Passons and Dey, 1972), trainability (Anthony and Hill, 1976; Anthony and Wain, 1971), and level of anxiety (Fry, 1973). Furthermore, some research reveals that attitudinal orientation may predispose individuals toward one training approach instead of another (Blair and Fretz, 1980) and that one's conceptual style differentially influences predisposition toward given training methods (Berg and Stone, 1980). As Ivey and Authier (1978) suggest, further research appears warranted to determine more precisely how and to what extent individual characteristics interact with training experiences to influence participant learning.

What Are the Ethical Issues in Training That Require Attention?

For the most part, the role of ethical issues in skills training has been largely neglected in the literature. Material from most training programs does not touch on the subject. Although devoting only a page and one half to the discussion of ethical matters, Ivey and Authier (1978) go further than most in highlighting the importance of trainers' keeping information shared by volunteer clients confidential; providing referral and follow-up services to volunteer clients and trainees, when needed; obtaining formal authorization for taping interviews and using taped material with others; and assuring adequate supervision for student and paraprofessional trainers.

The need for trainers to be sensitive to ethical issues derives from the unique features of the training process itself. Training may require participants to practice with volunteer clients (either real or role played by fellow trainees) who may present problems requiring professional help. Any process involving trainee sharing of sensitive personal and interpersonal concerns should provide protection, along with the professional regard and respect typically afforded clients.

Prior to committing themselves to a training experience, prospective trainees should be given sufficient information concerning the nature of the program, the expectations for member participation, the kinds of personal sharing required, as well as the unique demands of the practice process. Literature promoting training programs should realistically portray the experience to be encountered.

When volunteer clients are to be taped, informed consent should be obtained, and protection of rights to confidentiality and safeguards in the use of taped materials should be provided. Intended uses and restrictions on use of materials should be known to trainees and clients.

Referral and follow-up resources should be assured for clients and trainees evidencing problems of a personal nature not manageable in the training process. Since training experiences may surface the personal vulnerabilities of participants, trainers should be prepared to refer participants for professional service, when warranted.

Finally, given the diverse settings in which training is conducted, along with the great variation in trainer experience and competence, supervision for those implementing programs becomes an important issue, especially for programs conducted by student and paraprofessional trainers. Adequate supervision is necessary to insure that ethical standards are maintained.

Conclusion

This book has drawn together significant interpersonal helping skills models and proposed ideas to advance skills training, but it is only a step in the development of the field. The authors' discussions raise more questions than the helping professions can presently answer. Hopefully, this work will kindle interest in addressing those many knotty, unanswered questions, which must be examined if the field is to progress.

The growing interest in the use of interpersonal helping skills is encouraging. Skills training and skills use are evident in virtually every helping profession. Seemingly, it would be wonderful if society were full of helpers who were not only skilled themselves but were also capable of teaching others high levels of interpersonal helping skills. However, such a proliferation of skills usage must be accompanied by critical thinking and continued scrutiny. Without such an ongoing commitment to empiricism, the field will be turning its back on its roots. The resolve must continue for "easing the artificial distinction between research training and therapy training, . . . researching the therapeutic process and its outcomes in order to explicate its effective ingredients, training persons to provide higher levels of these ingredients, and researching the resultant process and outcome to determine if indeed there is a significant improvement" (Truax and Carkhuff, 1967, p. 225).

References

Anthony, W. A., and Hill, C. E. "A Student Evaluation of Systematic Human Relations Training." *Counselor Education and Supervision*, 1976, *15* (4), 305-309.

Anthony, W. A., and Wain, H. J. "Two Methods of Selecting Prospective Helpers." *Journal of Counseling Psychology*, 1971, *18* (2), 155-156.

Berg, K. S., and Stone, G. L. "Effects of Conceptual Level and Supervision Structure on Counselor Skill Development." *Journal of Counseling Psychology*, 1980, *27* (5), 500-509.

Blair, M. C., and Fretz, B. R. "Interpersonal Skills Training for Premedical Students." *Journal of Counseling Psychology*, 1980, *27* (4), 380-384.

Bohart, R. C., and others. "Two Methods of Interpersonal Skills Training: Conceptual Versus Response-Oriented Training." *Small Group Behavior*, 1979, *10*, 299-312.

Calia, V. F. "Systematic Human Relations Training: Appraisal and Status." *Counselor Education and Supervision*, 1974, *14*, 85-94.

Carkhuff, R. R. *Helping and Human Relations*, Vols. 1 and 2. New York: Holt Rinehart and Winston, 1969.

Carkhuff, R. R. "Principles of Social Action in Training for New Careers in Human Services." *Journal of Counseling Psychology*, 1971, *8* (2), 147-151.

Carkhuff, R. R., and Pierce, R. M. *The Art of Helping III: Trainer's Guide*. Amherst, Mass.: Human Resource Development Press, 1977.

Combs, A. W. *Florida Studies in the Helping Professions*. University of Florida Social Science Monograph, No. 37. Gainesville: University of Florida Press, 1969.

Danish, S., and Hauer, A. *Helping Skills: A Basic Training Program*. New York: Behavioral Publications, 1973.

Egan, G. *The Skilled Helper*. Monterey, Calif.: Brooks/Cole, 1975.

Fischer, J. *The Effectiveness of Social Casework*. Springfield, Ill.: Thomas, 1976.

Fry, P. S. "Effects of Desensitization Treatment on Core-Condition Training." *Journal of Counseling Psychology*, 1973, *20* (3), 214–219.

Gazda, G. M., and others. *Human Relations Development: A Manual for Educators*. (2nd ed.) Boston: Allyn & Bacon, 1977.

Goodman, G., and Dooley, C. D. "A Framework for Help-Intended Communication." *Psychotherapy: Theory, Research and Practice*, 1976, *13*, 106–117.

Gormally, J., and Hill, C. E. "Guidelines for Research on Carkhuff's Training Model." *Journal of Counseling Psychology*, 1974, *21*, 539–547.

Havelock, R. G., and Havelock, M. C. *Training for Change Agents: A Guide to the Design of Training Programs in Education and Other Fields*. Ann Arbor, Mich.: Center for Research on Utilization of Scientific Knowledge, 1973.

Ivey, A. E. "Microcounseling and Media Therapy: State of the Art." *Counselor Education and Supervision*, 1974, *13*, 172–183.

Ivey, A. E., and Authier, J. *Microcounseling: Innovations in Interviewing, Counseling, Psychotherapy, and Psychoeducation*. Springfield, Ill.: Thomas, 1978.

Ivey, A. E., and Gluckstern, N. *Basic Attending Skills: Leader and Participant Manuals*. North Amherst, Mass.: Microtraining, 1974.

Ivey, A. E., and Rollins, S. A. "A Behavioral Objectives Curriculum in Human Relations: A Commitment to Intentionality." *The Journal of Teacher Education*, 1972, *23*, 161–165.

Jones, L. K. "Toward More Adequate Selection Criteria: Correlates of Empathy, Genuineness, and Respect." *Counselor Education and Supervision*, 1974, *14* (1), 13–21.

Jourard, S. M. "Changing Personal Worlds." *Cornell Journal of Social Relations*, 1973, *8*, 1–11.

Kagan, N. *Interpersonal Process Recall: A Method of Influencing Human Interaction* (Rev. ed.) East Lansing, Mich.: Mason Media, 1975.

Mahon, B. R., and Altman, H. A. "Skill Training: Cautions and Recommendations." *Counselor Education and Supervision*, 1977, *17* (1), 42–50.

Matarazzo, R. G. "Research on the Teaching and Learning of Psychotherapeutic Skills." In S. L. Garfield and A. E. Bergin (Eds.), *Handbook of Psychotherapy and Behavior Change*. (2nd ed.) New York: Wiley, 1978.

Mayadas, N. S., and Duehn, W. D. "The Effects of Training Formats and Interpersonal Discriminations in the Education for Clinical Social Work Practice." *Journal of Social Service Research*, 1977, *1* (2), 147–161.

Parloff, M. B., Waskow, I. E., and Wolfe, B. E. "Research on Therapist Variables in Relation to Process and Outcome." In S. L. Garfield and A. E. Bergin (Eds.), *Handbook of Psychotherapy and Behavior Change*. (2nd ed.) New York: Wiley, 1978.

Passons, W. R., and Dey, G. R. "Counselor Candidate Personal Change and the Communication of Facilitative Dimensions." *Counselor Education and Supervision*, 1972, *12*, 57–62.

Paul, G. L. "Strategy of Outcome Research in Psychotherapy." *Journal of Consulting Psychology*, 1967, *31*, 109–119.

Reivich, R. S., and Geertsma, R. "Observational Media and Psychotherapy Training," *Journal of Nervous and Mental Disease*, 1969, *148*, 310–327.

Rennie, D., and Toukmanian, S. "Effects of Counselor Trainee Extroversion and Neuroticism on Empathy Gain During Training." Unpublished manuscript, Toronto, York University, 1976.

Rogers, C. R. "The Necessary and Sufficient Conditions of Psychotherapeutic Personality Change." *Journal of Consulting Psychology*, 1957a, *21*, 95–103.

Rogers, C. R. "Training Individuals to Engage in the Therapeutic Process." In C. R. Strother (Ed.), *Psychology and Mental Health*. Washington, D.C.: American Psychological Association, 1957b.

Rosenthal, N. R. "A Prescriptive Approach for Counselor Training." *Journal of Counseling Psychology*, 1977, *24* (3), 231–237.

Strupp, H. H. "On the Basic Ingredients of Psychotherapy." *Psychotherapy and Psychosomatics*, 1974, *24*, 249–260.

Truax, C. B., and Carkhuff, R. R. *Toward Effective Counseling and Psychotherapy*. Hawthorne, N.Y.: Aldine, 1967.

Resource A

Skills Training Research, 1970-1981

This Resource presents a summary of the skills training research published between 1970 and 1981. The survey includes information pertaining to (1) trainee population; (2) duration of training; (3) model used, purpose of study, and skills at focus; and (4) training methods and evaluation design employed.

Counseling

Author	Trainee Population	Duration	Model/Purpose/Skills	Training Methods/Evaluation Design
Altmaier and Bernstein, 1981	Counselor trainees	9 hours	Eclectic. To evaluate the effectiveness of training program in teaching nondirective core conditions of attending, empathy, concreteness, genuineness, respect, confrontation, disclosure, and immediacy; and directive interviewing skills of asking concrete questions, eliciting elaboration, formulating behavioral alternatives, obtaining client commitment, and working with the difficult client.	P[a]: Cognitive input, skills demonstration, role-play practice with leader, feedback, and didactic and experiential homework assignments. E[b]
Anthony, Gormally, and Miller, 1974	Graduate counseling students	40 hours	SHRT[c]. To assess the prediction of training outcomes by traditional and nontraditional selection indices. Skills assessed include responsive and initiative conditions.	P: (1) Systematic human relations training; and (2) control. PE[b]
Boyd, 1973	Graduate counseling students	4 hours	Eclectic. To evaluate factors for teaching affective-cognition, understanding-nonunderstanding, specific-nonspecific, and exploratory-nonexploratory.	CS[a]: (1) Reading of manual, simulation-model exercise, and recall interrogation supervision or behavioral supervision; and (2) same as (1) except includes practice interview. E

Bradley, 1974	Graduate counseling students	36 hours	IPR[c]. To evaluate training program on level of teaching regard, empathic understanding, unconditionality of regard, and congruence.	PC[a]: (1) IPR, individual supervision, and group supervision; and (2) individual and group supervision. QE[b]
Butler and Hansen, 1973	Graduate counseling students	10 hours	SHRT. To evaluate the effect of didactic-experiential training on the acquisition and retention of core facilitative skills.	P: (1) Didactic-experiential training; and (2) control. E
Carkhuff, Friel, and Kratochvil, 1970	Beginning clinicians	30 hours	SHRT. To evaluate the effects of the sequence of training on counselor-responsive conditions (empathy and respect) and counselor-initiated conditions (confrontation and immediacy).	PC: (1) 15 hours of didactic-experiential training in responsive conditions followed by 15 hours of training in initiative conditions; and (2) 15 hours of didactic-experiential training with initiative conditions followed by 15 hours of training in the responsive conditions. E
Carlson, 1974	Graduate counseling students	N S[d]	SHRT. To evaluate 3 factors for teaching empathy.	CS: (1) Didactic, counseling session, and immediate feedback; (2) didactic, counseling session, and random feedback or instructions; (3) didactic, counseling session, and no feedback but feedback equipment present; and (4) control. E
Cash and Vellema, 1979	Graduate and undergraduate psychology students	N S	SHRT. To compare the effectiveness of conceptual and competence-based human relations training centering on interpersonal discrimination and communication skills. Skills NS.	PC: (1) Pre-1974, conceptually oriented human relations training; (2) competence-based systematic human relations training; and (3) control. QE

Author	Trainee Population	Duration	Model/Purpose/Skills	Training Methods/Evaluation Design
Cormier, Hackney, and Segrist, 1974	Graduate counseling students	16 hours	Eclectic. To evaluate 2 models for teaching attending, use of silence, and opening and closing an interview.	PC: (1) T-group focus on feelings and attitudes; (2) systematic training of defined skills using video models, role-play practice, and video counseling sessions; and (3) control. E
Dalton, Sundblad, and Hylbert, 1973	Undergraduate rehabilitation students	1 3/4 hours	Behavioral. To evaluate the effect of videotaped, modeled learning experience on the acquisition and transfer of communication of empathy.	CS: (1) Modeled learning experience consisting of modeled counseling interviews and content practice sessions; (2) readings about counseling behavior; and (3) control. E
DiMattia and Arndt, 1974	Graduate counseling students	N S	MIC[c] and reflective listening. To evaluate 2 models for teaching attending.	PC: (1) MIC manual, models of appropriate and inappropriate attending, and videotaped practice interview with feedback; and (2) reflective listening, dyad interview, and in-group practice with feedback. PE
Dooley, 1975	Paraprofessional counselors	45 minutes	Eclectic. To evaluate method for teaching reflective responses.	P: (1) Written and audiotape discrimination training, practice, and instructions; and (2) control. E
Dowd and Blocher, 1974	Graduate counseling students	5 hours	Behavioral. To evaluate 2 factors for teaching responses of relationship-speculative, personal-confrontive, and relationship-confrontive.	CS: (1) Interviews with immediate reinforcement; (2) interviews with prior awareness of desired interviewer behavior; and (3) control. QE

Eisenberg and Delaney, 1970	Graduate counseling students	N S	Behavioral. To evaluate 2 factors for teaching counselor verbal tacting response leads.	CS: Trainee views 40 client episodes followed by either (1) modeling, (2) reinforcement of trainee responses to client, or (3) modeling and reinforcement of trainee responses; and (4) control. PE
Eskedal, 1975	Graduate counseling students	30 minutes	Eclectic. To evaluate the effects of symbolic role modeling on teaching genuineness, warmth, and empathy.	CS: (1) Symbolic role modeling with attentional variables; (2) symbolic role modeling; (3) control with attentional variables; and (4) control. E
Gade and Matuschka, 1973	Graduate counseling students	14 hours plus practicum	Interactional analysis. To evaluate the effect of interaction analysis on indirect influence (accepting feelings, praising, accepting or using ideas of counselee), direct influence (asking questions, giving information, giving directions, and criticizing), responding, and initiating.	PC: (1) Interactional analysis training and practicum; and (2) discussion and practicum. PE
Genthner and Falkenberg, 1977	Graduate clinical psychology students	40 hours	SHRT. To evaluate model for teaching empathy, genuineness, specificity, immediacy, and confrontation.	P: (1) Didactic-experiential; and (2) control. E
Gormally and others, 1975	Graduate clinical and counseling psychology students and undergraduates from varied fields	40 hours	SHRT. To evaluate model for retention of skills (empathy responses) 6-9 months after training and evaluate the effect of educational level on skills retention.	P: (1) Didactic-experiential. QE

Author	Trainee Population	Duration	Model/Purpose/Skills	Training Methods/Evaluation Design
Gutman and Haase, 1972	Graduate counseling students	N S	MIC. To evaluate model on generalization of attending, reflection of feelings, and summarization.	P: (1) Microcounseling; and (2) control. E
Harris, 1973	Professional counselors	N S	SHRT. To evaluate model for teaching genuineness, empathy, respect, concreteness, and acceptance of others.	P: Sensitivity exercises and discrimination training. PE
Hart, 1973	Graduate counseling students	N S	Programmed instruction. To evaluate the effect of self-teaching program on open-mindedness.	P: (1) Self-teaching program including written exercises with instructor reinforcement; and (2) control. E
Hector and others, 1981	Graduate counseling students	30 minutes	Eclectic. To evaluate several factors for teaching responding to negative client feelings.	CS: (1) Verbal practice with modeling; (2) verbal practice without modeling; (3) didactic and modeling; (4) supervision model; and (5) control. E
Hector and others, 1979	Graduate counseling students	N S	Eclectic. To evaluate videotaped modeling and lecture on teaching affective responding.	CS: (1) Read interview transcript and view videotaped interviews; (2) outline of lecture and videotaped lecture; and (3) control. E
Hill, Charles, and Reed, 1981	Graduate counseling students	3 year longitudinal study	Longitudinal evaluation of doctoral program in counseling psychology on minimal encouragers, directives, questions, complex responses, activity level, and self-composure.	P: No specific skills training described. PE
Kelley, 1971	Graduate counseling students	4 hours	Eclectic. To evaluate use of supervisor or peer reinforcement for teaching attending, questions,	CS: (1) Supervisor reinforcement, reading of manual, discussion with supervisor, audiotaped in-

Author/Date	Population	Duration	Purpose	Method
			pace of interview, short responses, and use of silence.	terview with feedback from supervisor; (2) self-reinforcement, reading of manual, audiotaped interview but no feedback from supervisor; and (3) control. E
Kuna, 1975	Undergraduate counseling students	1½ hours	Eclectic. To evaluate 3 factors for teaching restatement of client response.	CS: (1) Lecture; (2) lecture and reading; (3) lecture, reading, and modeling; and (4) control. E
McCarthy, Danish, and D'Augelli, 1977	Undergraduate counseling students	30 hours	Helping skills training. To evaluate effect of model on teaching continuing, leading, and self-referent responses.	P: Skills defined, modeled, and practiced; and homework assigned. PE
Markey and others, 1970	Undergraduate counselors	N S	Eclectic. To compare the effect of playback techniques on counselor performance. Skills NS.	CS: (1) Audiotape and videotape playback; (2) audiotape playback; (3) videotape playback; and (4) no playback. PE
O'Toole, 1979	Graduate counseling students	3 hours	MIC. To evaluate factors for teaching silence, questions, and tacting.	CS: (1) Video model and practice; (2) video model; (3) written model and practice; (4) written model; and (5) control. E
Pedersen, Holwill, and Shapiro, 1978	Graduate counseling students	64 hours	Triad model and eclectic. To compare the effectiveness of 2 models in teaching cross-cultural sensitivity and empathy, respect, and congruence.	PC: (1) Traditional prepracticum including readings, lectures, role play, and supervised counseling; and (2) same as (1) plus cross-cultural triad exercises. PE
Peters, Cormier, and Cormier, 1978	Graduate counseling students	45–135 minutes	MIC. To evaluate 4 factors for teaching goal setting.	CS: (1) Written and video models; (2) written and video models and practice; (3) written and video models, practice, and feedback; and (4) written and video models, practice, feedback, and remediation practice. E

Author	Trainee Population	Duration	Model/Purpose/Skills	Training Methods/Evaluation Design
Pierce and Schauble, 1970	Graduate counseling students	70 hours	Eclectic. To evaluate 2 factors for teaching empathy, regard, genuineness, and concreteness.	CS: Compare levels of supervisor and supervisee performance. QE
Robinson, Froehle, and Kurpius, 1979	Graduate counseling students	15 minutes	Eclectic. To evaluate the use of different media for teaching counselor tacting response leads.	CS: (1) Video model and practice; (2) written model and practice; and (3) audio model and practice. E
Robinson, Kurpius, and Froehle, 1979	Graduate counseling students	N S	Eclectic. To evaluate the effects of feedback on teaching counselor tacting response leads.	CS: Video model of client to which trainees respond, followed by either (1) immediate feedback from expert; (2) self-generated feedback; or (3) no feedback. E
Robinson, Kurpius, and Froehle, 1981 (Study 1)	Graduate counseling students	16 minutes	Eclectic. To evaluate the effect of 3 factors on teaching tacting response leads.	CS: (1) Video models and oral response to videotaped clients; (2) typescript of videotape and oral response to videotaped clients; and (3) written serial script of videotape and oral response to videotaped clients. E
Robinson, Kurpius, and Froehle, 1981 (Study 2)	Graduate counseling students	16–24 minutes	Eclectic. To evaluate the effect of 4 factors on teaching reflection of feelings.	CS: (1) Written model and oral response to videotaped clients; (2) written model and written response to videotaped clients; (3) video model and written response to videotaped clients; and (4) video model and oral response to videotaped clients. E

Reference	Sample	Time	Description	Method
Ronnestad, 1977	Graduate counseling students	N S	Supervision models. To evaluate the effect of modeling, feedback, and experiential methods of supervision on the learning of empathy.	CS: (1) Modeling supervision; (2) feedback supervision; (3) experiential supervision; and (4) control group. E
Rosenthal, 1977	Graduate counseling students	6 hours	Structured learning training. To evaluate 2 methods for teaching confrontation and their relationship to trainee conceptual level.	CS: (1) Guided instruction (high structure); (2) self-instruction (low structure); and (3) brief instruction. E
Saltmarsh, 1973	Graduate counseling students	4 hours	Programmed instruction. To evaluate model on teaching of empathy.	PC: (1) Programmed instruction including printed material, tape, and directed interaction; and (2) readings and videotape discussion of Adlerian views. E
Saltmarsh and Hubele, 1974	Graduate counseling students	N S	MIC. To evaluate and compare the effects of 3 microcounseling instructional programs on self-giving (here-and-now verbalization), taking (amount of response latency) and seeking behavior (open-ended verbalizations).	PC: (1) Instructional program teaching self-giving behavior; (2) instructional program teaching taking behavior; and (3) instructional program teaching seeking behavior. PE
Shapiro and Gust, 1974	Graduate counseling students	66 hours	Eclectic. To evaluate the effect of a didactic and experientially oriented prepracticum course on self-actualization and counseling skill. Skills NS.	PC: (1) Sensitivity group and class sessions consisting of readings, lectures, modeling, tapes, role play, and supervised counseling; and (2) control. PE
Spivack, 1972	Graduate counseling students	N S	IPR and eclectic practicum. To evaluate 2 models for teaching sensitivity to own feelings and client communication and for teaching effective communication,	PC: (1) IPR; and (2) lecture with discussions and demonstration. E

Author	Trainee Population	Duration	Model/Purpose/Skills	Training Methods/Evaluation Design
Stillman, 1980	Graduate counseling students	45 hours	including affective, understanding, specific, and exploratory responses. Eclectic. To examine whether level of trainee communication performance prior to and after training is related to ratings of counseling effectiveness in a later practicum. Skill NS.	P: Lectures, discussion, readings, communication in group interaction, role play, feedback exercises, and videotape, audiotape, and instructor demonstrations. PE
Stone, 1975	Undergraduate counseling students	N S	Simulation modeling. To evaluate the effect of high-fidelity and low-fidelity models and practice on tacting response leads.	CS: (1) Instructional manual model; (2) audiotaped model; (3) live model; and (4) videotaped model. QE
Toukmanian and Rennie, 1975	Undergraduate counseling students	48-72 hours	SHRT and MIC. To compare effectiveness of systematic human relations training and microtraining on empathy, open evaluations, closed questions, interpretation, and advice.	PC: (1) Microtraining, including initial 5-minute videotaped interviews; manual; videotaped role-played interviews modeling high and low frequencies of skills at focus; and final videotaped interviews; (2) human relations training, including discrimination training; community center training involving audiotaped role-played interviews; group review; and critique; and (3) control group. QE

Truax and Lister, 1971	Professional counselors	40 hours	SHRT. To evaluate the effect of short-term didactic-experiential training on accurate empathy and nonpossessive warmth.	P: Therapeutic supervisory content, didactic use of research scales, and quasi-group therapy. PE
Ward, Kagan, and Krathwohl, 1972	Graduate counseling students	N S	IPR. To compare the effect of 2 IPR formats on behavioral and feeling responses.	CS: (1) Videotape-IPR training process; (2) audiotape-IPR training process; and (3) supervision using audiotape of regular counseling session. E

Medicine

Adler, Ware, and Enelow, 1970	Psychiatry students	10 hours	Programmed instruction. To compare effectiveness of videotaping and closed circuit television in teaching interviewing, including facilitative communication, cooperative communication, supportive educational atmospheres, questions, and attempt of verbal activity.	PC: (1) Simulated response to videotaped client statements with feedback; (2) videotaped interviews with peer and trainer feedback. PE
Anthony and Wain, 1971	Medical corpsmen	72 + 120 hours	SHRT. To evaluate 2 methods for teaching empathy.	CS: (1) Didactic-experiential, 12 weeks, 10 hours per week; and (2) didactic-experiential, 12 weeks, 16 hours per week. QE
Authier and Gustafson, 1976	Registered nurses, licensed practical nurses	6 hours	MIC. To evaluate the effect of supervised and nonsupervised microcounseling paradigms on the learning of open initiations,	CS: (1) Supervised microcounseling training; (2) nonsupervised microcounseling format; and (3) control. QE

Author	Trainee Population	Duration	Model/Purpose/Skills	Training Methods/Evaluation Design
Barbee and Feldman, 1970	Medical students	N S	reflection of feelings, questions with statements, confrontation, feedback, and self-disclosure. Eclectic. To conduct a 3-year longitudinal evaluation of interviewing skills (data collection, interview structure, communication, and role appropriateness) and relationship of skills to performance in clinical medicine.	P: Total training in clinical medicine. PE
Bartnick and O'Brien, 1980	Healthcare professionals	N S	SHRT. To evaluate the effect of a special course/workshop on counseling and empathy skills.	PC: Course/workshop including small group self-exploration, didactic presentation, and mini supervised practicum. PE
Blair and Fretz, 1980	Medical students	3 hours	IPR and SHRT. To determine student receptivity and differential reactions to IPR (including exploration, listening, affective and honest-labeling responses) and SHRT (including attending, responding, and confrontation skills).	PC: (1) Interpersonal process recall; and (2) systematic human relations training. E
Brown and O'Shea, 1980	Medical students	3 hours	Eclectic. To teach interviewing skills of social feedback, responsiveness to patient concerns, and open-ended questions.	P: (1) Videotaped interviews, didactic sessions, instructor feedback, and readings; (2) feedback, videotaped interviews; and (3) videotaped interviews. E

Source	Population	Duration	Description	Method
Carroll, Schwartz, and Ludwig, 1981	Medical students	4-week course	Simulated patient approach. To evaluate effectiveness practice with simulated patients on acquisition of inquiry, listening, facilitation, and closure skills.	P: Videotaped interviews with simulated patients, videotaped interview critiques, simulator- and student-completed content checklists and process rating forms. PE
Cline and Garrard, 1973	Medical students	12–18 hours	Eclectic. To teach interview skills, including attention to process, observation of behavior, encouragement to explore problem, and creation of support.	P: Programmed text, instructor demonstrations, audiotaped interviews, live interviews, role-played interviews, instructor/peer feedback. PE
Engler and others, 1981	Medical students	9-week course	Eclectic. To evaluate effectiveness of course in teaching establishing trust; facilitating patient self-exploration and student understanding of patient; and providing information, reassurance, support, and direction.	P: Lectures, live and videotaped skills demonstrations, discrimination training, peer dyads with structured practice and videotape feedback, trainer feedback, and tutor practice and feedback. PE
Farsad and others, 1978	Medical students	1½ hours	Eclectic. To compare interviewing skills of interns with clinical faculty and evaluate the effect of training on communication style, such as the use of questions, support, and reassurance.	P: (1) Videotaped interview with coached client and feedback and evaluation session; and (2) videotaped interview with coached client. E
Fine and Therrien, 1977	Medical students	12 hours	Eclectic. To evaluate effectiveness of a systematic skills training program on empathy, immediacy, and personal-meaning responses.	P: Communication training, role playing, triad practice sessions, and instructor/peer feedback. QE
Goldstein and others, 1971	Registered and practical nurses and hospital attendants	30 minutes	Behavioral. To evaluate the effects of modeling and social class structuring on empathy and warmth.	CS: (1) Lower-social-class, high-attraction model; (2) lower-social-class, neutral-attraction model; (3) lower-social-class, low-attraction model; (4)

Author	Trainee Population	Duration	Model/Purpose/Skills	Training Methods/Evaluation Design
				middle–social class, high-attraction model; (5) middle–social-class, neutral-attraction model; (6) middle–social-class, low-attraction model; (7) no-class-structure, high-attraction model; (8) no-class-structure, neutral-attraction model; and (9) no-class-structure, low-attraction model. E
Goldstein and Goedhart, 1973	Student nurses	10 hours	Structured learning. To evaluate model for teaching empathy and the training of trainers.	P: (1) Discussion, Carkhuff Empathy Scale, initial modeling, initial role playing and modeling–role playing–social reinforcement; and (2) control. E
Goroll, Stoeckle, and Lazare, 1974	Medical students	N S	Eclectic. To evaluate the effect of an experiential course on history-taking and interviewing techniques. Skills NS.	P: Videotaped interviews, counterviewing, small group tape sessions, and readings. PE
Grayson, Nugent, and Oken, 1977	Health associate students	18 hours	Eclectic. To evaluate the effectiveness of the program for teaching sensitivity to patient feelings, social amenities, interchange of information, organization of interview, and arrangement of interview environment.	P: Sensitivity exercises, readings, lectures, videotaped practice and feedback, and discussions. PE

Hayes, Hutaff, and Mace, 1971	Medical students	64 hours	Eclectic. To teach interviewing, including awareness of student-patient interactions, and establishing relationships. Skills NS.	P: Lectures on principles of interviewing, panel questions and class discussion, demonstration interviews with class observation and discussion; role playing in small groups; supervised patient interviewing including peer and supervisor observation and feedback, along with written reports of interviews; special seminars; and personal interviews with students. PE
Hutter and others, 1977	Child health associate students	N S	Eclectic. To evaluate the effects of a comprehensive approach to teaching interviewing skills (content-gathering and process-oriented skills).	PC: (1) Practice-oriented interviewing course extending 4 or 5 academic quarters; and (2) 20-hour interview course. PE
Kalisch, 1971	Nursing students	12½ hours	Eclectic. To evaluate the effectiveness of a short-term program on empathy.	P: (1) Didactic training including ratings of psychotherapy interviews, verbal and written responses to taped clients, and feedback on taped role-played interviews, with peer ratings and discussions and experiential group; and (2) control group with lecture, discussion, films, and tapes. E
Kauss and others, 1980	Interns and residents	N S	Follow-up study of subjects from 24 schools. To examine long-term effectiveness of skills training on teaching exploratory, affective, and listening responses, questions, empathy, gathering of med-	PC: (1) Skills course with videotape feedback; (2) skills course without videotape feedback; and (3) little or no skills training. PE

Author	Trainee Population	Duration	Model/Purpose/Skills	Training Methods/Evaluation Design
Kauss and others, 1981	Interns and residents	N S	ical data, and opening of an interview. Eclectic. To compare the effectiveness of 2 programs in teaching psychosocial, affective, and empathy responses.	PC: (1) 1-month course including lecture, practice, and videotape of physician-client interviews with supervision and feedback; (2) brief written instructions; and (3) controls. E
La Monica and others, 1976	Nurses	N S	SHRT. To evaluate the effect of human relations training on trainee skill in perceiving and responding with empathy.	P: (1) Short-term human relations training program consisting of training in perceiving with empathy; expressing anger; role playing situations; observing and analyzing nonverbal behavior; perceiving feelings and responding with empathy; and recognizing ineffective communication styles; (2) pretest-posttest controls; and (3) posttest controls only. QE
Moreland, Ivey and Phillips, 1973	Medical students	N S	MIC. To compare the effectiveness of microcounseling with traditional interview teaching procedures on minimal encouragers, open and closed questions, paraphrases, reflection of feelings, and summarization.	PC: (1) Microcounseling; and (2) traditional interview training. QE

Pacoe and others, 1976	Medical students	40 hours	SHRT. To increase comfort in dealing with emotionally intense material and skill in core facilitative conditions of empathy, nonpossessive warmth, and genuineness.	P: Role feedback sessions, including 10 taped simulated interviews, small group discussion and feedback, ratings of counselor behavior, taped interview replay, written alternative responses by trainees, client feedback to responses, and exploration of response characteristics; and experiential sessions including warm-up exercises and discussion of personal issues. PE
Rasche, Bernstein, and Veenhuis, 1974	Medical students	64 hours	Electic. To evaluate the effects of interviewing course on understanding, evaluative, reassuring, hostile, and probing responses.	P: Readings, interviews with actual patients, videotaped interviews; small group reviews and discussion of interviews, and demonstration interviews conducted by instructor. PE
Robbins and others, 1978	Medical students	10–20 hours	IPR. To teach interpersonal skills, including elements of effective communication and responding to affect.	P: (1) Lectures, films, demonstration interviews, exercises, videotaped interviews, process recall sessions with instructors, learning elements of facilitative communication, and the use of affect simulation films; and (2) control with traditional didactic instruction. E
Robbins and others, 1979	Medical students	N S	IPR. To teach effective interviewing, including the use of facilitative response modes (exploring, listening, affective responding,	P: (1) Videotaped patient-doctor interactions, videotape recall process with instructor, taped demonstrations, group discus-

Author	Trainee Population	Duration	Model/Purpose/Skills	Training Methods/Evaluation Design
			honest labeling), and dealing with strong affect and common patient fears.	sions, sensitivity exercises, and programmed videotapes of desirable and undesirable interviewing behaviors; and (2) control with traditional didactic program. QE
Rogers and Rasof, 1975	Psychiatric residents	N S	Eclectic. To evaluate a teaching drill to teach communication of psychiatric concepts to nonpsychiatric physicians and parents of disturbed children. Skills NS.	P: Role play with supervision drill consisting of referral source, supervision of interpersonal interview conducted with parents, resident supervisor critiques of interview, and case discussions conducted by resident with supervisor and observer. PE
Scott, Donnelly, and Hess, 1976	Medical students	2 years	Eclectic medical school curriculum. To evaluate the direction and extent of change in student interviewing, including skills in explanation of rationale, initial exploration, directed clarification, social amenities, open-ended clarification, reassurance, empathy, supportive/facilitative behavior, effective silence, miscellaneous procedures, uncommon words and concepts, and negative verbal and negative nonverbal responses.	P: 2-year medical school curriculum. PE

Smith, Hadac, and Levesee, 1980	Medical students	15 hours	Eclectic. To evaluate the effectiveness of a course taught at 3 different campuses on teaching probing, understanding, supportive, evaluative, and interpretive responses.	P: Lectures, demonstration interviews, and personal interviews with patients. PE
Stillman, Sabers, and Redfield, 1976	Medical students	1½ hours	Eclectic. To evaluate the effect of a first interview and training session on teaching interviewing skills such as attending behavior, questions, social reinforcement and summarization.	P: (1) Videotaped interview with coached client in role of a mother, client ratings of students on process and content, and videotape replay with client critique; and (2) control. E
Taylor and Berven, 1974	Medical students	11–12 hours	Eclectic. To develop effective, personal style of interviewing and teach methods of observing behavior and feelings. Skills NS.	P: Videotaped student interviews with patients, cointerviewing by student and instructor, small group videotape review sessions, and instructor and peer feedback. PE
Vaughn and Marks, 1976	Medical students	15 hours	Eclectic. To compare 2 methods of teaching interviewing skills, including open and closed questions, facilitation, clarification, reassurance, confrontation directives, and nonverbal cues.	PC: (1) Videotape training group focused on discussion of videotaped interviews conducted by students and experienced psychiatrists; and (2) traditional training group emphasizing observation of experienced physicians. QE
Werner and Schneider, 1974	Medical students	20 hours	IPR. To teach interaction skills including affective, exploratory, listening, and confronting responses.	P: Precourse test, didactic presentations, group discussions, demonstration interviews, videotaped simulated interviews, process recall and small group

Author	Trainee Population	Duration	Model/Purpose/Skills	Training Methods/Evaluation Design
				discussion sessions, instructor and peer feedback, and completion of written interview evaluation forms. PE
Wolraich and others, 1981	Pediatric residents	N S	Eclectic. To evaluate effect of simulated interviews with videotape feedback on teaching reinforcement, reassurance, questions, and discussion of etiology.	P: Simulated interviews with videotape feedback. PE

Social Work

Author	Trainee Population	Duration	Model/Purpose/Skills	Training Methods/Evaluation Design
Clubok, 1978	Undergraduate social work students	N S	Helping skills training. To each basic interpersonal helping skills, including nonverbal attending, content and affective responses, open and closed questions, influence, advice, self-disclosure, and self-involving.	P: Lecture, group discussion, modeling, practice, and audiotaped role-played interviews. PE
Fischer, 1975	Graduate social work students	44 hours	SHRT. To determine the effect of intensive training in the core conditions on student communication of empathy, warmth, and genuineness.	P: Systematic human relations training. E
Fry, 1973	Social caseworkers, probation officers,	40 hours	Eclectic. To evaluate the effect of desensitization on learning of core facilitative skills, including em-	CS: (1) Preliminary experiential training, systematic desensitization, and advanced experiential

	and youth workers		pathy, respect, concreteness, and genuineness.	training; and (2) preliminary and advanced experiential training. E
Katz, 1979	Graduate social work students	N S	Eclectic. To increase awareness of interaction styles, teach a developmental model of helping, and develop a basic repertoire of interview skills, including nonverbal attending, genuineness, respect, sensitivity, mutuality, warmth, verbal following, exploratory responses, understanding responses, summarizing primary empathy, responses, self-disclosure, advice, confrontation, advanced empathy, immediacy, and concreteness.	P: Simulated practice interviews, videotaped interviews, peer/instructor feedback, structured exercises, and group process experience. PE
Keefe, 1979	Graduate social work students	N S	Experiential-didactic and structured meditation. To compare 2 methods of teaching empathy.	PC: (1) Didactic presentations, role play, and observer ratings; and (2) instructions and practice in structured Zen meditation. E
Larsen and Hepworth, 1978	Graduate social work students	24 hours	SHRT. To teach skills of empathy, respect, and genuineness.	P: (1) Lecture, discrimination training, group discussion, modeling, role playing, written communication training, videotaped interviews, and peer/instructor feedback; and (2) traditional didactic instruction. QE
Mayadas and Duehn, 1977	Graduate social work students	18 hours	Focused videotape feedback, modeling, and process recording. To compare the effectiveness of 3 different programs in training for open and closed questions, con-	PC: (1) Focused videotape feedback; (2) modeling; and (3) process recording. QE

Author	Trainee Population	Duration	Model/Purpose/Skills	Training Methods/Evaluation Design
Rose, Cayner, and Edleson, 1977	Graduate social work students, volunteer social workers, and psychiatric nursing students	12 hours	tent and affect reflections, and content and affect expressions. Behavioral. To develop skills for dealing with problem situations presented by clients, including identifying and expressing feeling, seeking and giving clarification, appropriate affect, appropriate response latency, appropriate volume, and appropriate fluency.	P: Lecture, modeling, overt/covert rehearsal, goal setting, peer feedback, coaching, role playing, behavioral assignments, delegation of leadership skills. E
Schinke and others, 1978	Graduate social work students	4 hours	Behavioral. To evaluate the effect of behavioral training on nonverbal behaviors (forward trunk lean, eye contact, smiles, and head nods) and verbal behaviors (open and closed questions, affect and content summarizations, stimulus-response congruence, and distance from client).	P: (1) Lecture modeling, role playing, skills practice, feedback, and cueing; and (2) control. E
Schinke and others, 1980	Graduate social work students	N S	Helping skills training. To evaluate a field-based program on teaching eye contact, forward body lean, head nods, open questions, content and affect summarization, influencing responses, advice-giving responses, and self-involving responses.	P: Didactic and Socratic methods, including skills demonstration, role play with videotape, supervisor/peer feedback, and homework assignments. PE

Spielberg, 1980	Undergraduate and graduate social work students	N S	SHRT. To evaluate the effects of undergraduate and graduate professional education in psychology and social work on development of the core faciliative conditions of empathy, respect, genuineness, and concreteness.	P: Global comparison of professional education programs in psychology and social work. PE
Wells, 1975	Undergraduate and graduate social work students, telephone volunteers, and probation officers	6–54 hours	SHRT. To compare the effects of brief and extended systematic training in developing the facilitative conditions of empathy, respect, and genuineness.	PC: (1) Brief systematic human relations training and (2) extended systematic human relations training, each using didactic preventatives, group discussion, discrimination training, peer feedback, small group practice, and role playing. PE

Nonprofessional Helpers

Alssid and Hutchison, 1977	Peer counselors	20 minutes	Eclectic. To compare pure and corrective models for teaching open-ended questions.	CS: (1) Video model of desired behavior; and (2) video model of inappropriate behavior and video model of desired behavior. E
Anthony and Hill, 1976	Psychology students	7 hours	SHRT. To evaluate trainees perception of SHRT and usefulness of Trainability Index.	P: Didactic-experiential. QE
Berg and Stone, 1980	Undergraduates	N S	MIC. To evaluate the effects of trainee conceptual level and degree of structured supervision on teaching reflections.	CS: (1) Low conceptual level plus high-structure supervision; (2) high conceptual level plus high-structure supervision; (3) low conceptual level plus low-structure supervision; (4) high conceptual level plus low-structure supervision; and (5) didactic only. E

Author	Trainee Population	Duration	Model/Purpose/Skills	Training Methods/Evaluation Design
Brockhaus, Marshall, and Dustin, 1973	Psychiatric aides	12 hours	Eclectic. To evaluate the effect of training on empathic ability, including awareness and understanding of own feelings with clients and empathy with clients.	P: (1) Training manual, role playing, group discussion, and training tapes; and (2) control. E
Canada, 1973	State employment interviewers	40 minutes	Eclectic. To evaluate types of reinforcement for teaching open-ended leads.	CS: (1) Trainee interview, immediate reinforcement, and videotape recall exercise; and (2) trainee interview, delayed reinforcement, and videotape recall exercise. E
Carkhuff, 1971	Lay trainers and casework aides	110 hours (lay) 500 hours (aides)	SHRT. To train lay trainers to train aides in empathy, respect, concreteness, genuineness, confrontation, immediacy, self-exploration, self-experiencing problems, self-understanding, and constructive action.	P: Didactic-experiential. PE
Carkhuff and Griffin, 1970	Human relations specialists	60 + 150 hours	SHRT. To train specialists in empathy, respect, concreteness, genuineness, confrontation, and immediacy and in developing courses of action to enable them to help in school adjustment of black children.	P: Didactic-experiential. PE
Carkhuff and Griffin, 1971	Employment counselors	110 hours	SHRT. To train trainers in empathy, respect, concreteness, genuineness, confrontation, and	P: Didactic-experiential. PE

Collingwood, 1971	Undergraduate students	10 hours	immediacy to enable them to train workers. SHRT. To evaluate the effect of retraining on the retention of facilitative communication skills, including empathy, respect, genuineness, and concreteness.	CS: (1) Large group of trainees receiving 2½ hours of retraining; (2) large group of trainees not receiving retraining; (3) small group of trainees not receiving retraining; and (4) small group of trainees receiving retraining. E
Cook, Kunce, and Sleater, 1974	Psychiatric aides	4½ hours	Eclectic. To evaluate the effects of vicarious behavior induction in teaching interpersonal skills.	CS: (1) Written lesson handouts and group discussion; (2) written lesson handouts and 5-minute videotaped lecture; and (3) written lesson handouts and 5-minute videotaped demonstrations of skills discussed in written materials. QE
Dalton and Sundblad, 1976	Residence hall advisers	10 hours	SHRT. To evaluate modeling and SHRT on teaching empathy.	CS: (1) SHRT only; (2) SHRT and modeling; and (3) traditional training program. E
Danish, D'Augelli, and Brock, 1975	Human services students	30 hours	Helping skills training. To evaluate model for teaching effective nonverbal and verbal behavior, using self-involving behavior, understanding others' communication, and building helping relationships.	P: Skills defined, modeled, and practiced; and homework assigned. PE
D'Augelli, Danish, and Brock, 1976	Human services students	30 hours	Helping skills training. To evaluate model for assessing use of continuing, leading, and self-referent responses.	P: Skills defined, modeled, and practiced; and homework assigned. PE

Author	Trainee Population	Duration	Model/Purpose/Skills	Training Methods/Evaluation Design
Elsenrath, Coker, and Martinson, 1972	Residence hall assistants	N S	MIC. To evaluate audio programmed method for teaching silence and reduced length of counselor responses.	CS: (1) Live interview, audiotaped interview, reinforcement, and audiotaped interview conducted by trainee; (2) same as (1), but trainee conducts interview 7–10 days after training; and (3) same as (1), but no audiotape component. PE
Emener, 1974	Undergraduate education students	25 hours (leader-led) 9 hours (programmed)	Leader-led group training (SHRT) and programmed instruction. To compare effectiveness of 2 programs in teaching empathy, respect, genuineness, concreteness, and self-disclosure.	PC: (1) Leader-led SHRT, including lecture, readings, audiotape recordings, role play, and group experience; (2) programmed instruction, including videotaped lectures, workbook and videotaped client stimulus statements, and electronic and instructor feedback; and (3) controls. E
Evans, Uhlemann, and Hearn, 1978	Hotline volunteers	20 hours	MIC and sensitivity training. To compare programs for teaching attending, paraphrase, reflection of feelings, questions, and minimal encouragers.	PC: (1) MIC; (2) sensitivity training weekend experience; and (3) control. QE
Frankel, 1971	Undergraduate psychology students	1½ hours	Eclectic. To evaluate 3 methods of teaching attending to client feelings.	CS: (1) Read manual, interview peer, and view video model; (2) read manual, interview peer, and view videotape playback; and (3) read manual, interview peer, and read about empathy. E

576

Gantt, Billingsley, and Giordano, 1980	Human services students	70 hours	Eclectic. To evaluate a course for teaching listening, empathy, questions, value goals, and decision making.	P: Lecture, modeling, and supervised role play. QE
Ginsberg and Danish, 1979	Undergraduate and graduate human development students	25 hours	Helping skills training. To evaluate effectiveness of program in teaching continuing responses to groups of self-selected students with low, medium, and high entry-level use of continuing responses.	P: Skill definition, modeling, and skill practice and homework. PE
Gormally, 1975	Undergraduates	20 hours	Eclectic. To evaluate 3 methods for teaching empathy, respect, immediacy, confrontation, interpretation, advice giving, and questions.	CS: (1) Structured group with trainer feedback and focus on skills; (2) structured group with videotape feedback and focus on skills; and (3) encounter group with no direct focus on skills. E
Gulanick and Schmeck, 1977	Psychology students	N S	Eclectic. To evaluate 3 factors for teaching empathy.	CS: (1) Praise; (2) criticism; (3) modeling; (4) praise and modeling; (5) criticism and modeling; (6) criticism, praise, and modeling; and (7) control. E
Haase and DiMattia 1970	Guidance support workers	12 hours	MIC. To evaluate model for teaching attending and expression and reflection of feelings.	P: Diagnostic videotape, manual, models, review of diagnostic videotape, videotaped interview, and review of videotaped interview. PE
Haase, DiMattia, and Guttman, 1972	Support personnel	4 hours	MIC. 1-year follow-up evaluations to assess the retention of skills (attending, reflection of feelings, and expression of feelings) learned in a previous program.	P: Overview of skills taught earlier, review of manuals, and role-played practice sessions. PE

Author	Trainee Population	Duration	Model/Purpose/Skills	Training Methods/Evaluation Design
Hart and King, 1979	Undergraduate students	6 hours	Eclectic. To evaluate the impact of trainee entry-level skills competence and training program on teaching empathy, warmth, genuineness, and concreteness.	CS: (1) High entry-level competence and training; (2) random-level competence and training; (3) high level of competence but untrained; and (4) control. E
Hodge, Payne, and Wheeler, 1978	Psychology students	N S	Eclectic. To evaluate training method and supervisor experience on teaching empathy.	CS: (1) Individual professional supervision; (2) individual peer supervision; (3) audio programmed training by professional; (4) audio programmed training by peer; and (5) control. E
Kramer, Rappaport, and Seidman, 1979	Undergraduate students	2½ hours	Eclectic. To evaluate interaction of trainee entry skills level (high versus low) and brief interview training on interviewer effectiveness. Skills NS.	CS: (1) Problem-solving training with high-skills trainees; (2) problem-solving training with low-skills trainees; (3) diagnostic interview training with high-skills trainees; (4) diagnostic interview training with low-skills trainees; (5) no training with high-skills trainees; and (6) no training with low-skills trainees. E
Levant, Slattery and Slobobian, 1981	Foster parents	30 hours	Eclectic. To evaluate effect of program for teaching attending, empathy, genuineness, respect, and sharing of own feelings.	P: (1) Introduction and definition of skill, videotaped and live demonstrations, role-play practice, and homework assignments; and (2) controls. QE

Mitchell and others, 1971	Undergraduate residence hall assistants	6 hours	SHRT. To evaluate the effect of didactic training on empathy, warmth, and genuineness.	P: Empathy training, including didactic interaction, group discussion, listening to role-played interviews, use of research instruments to rate empathy level, and role-played interviews with trainees rating each other on empathy and giving feedback. PE
Newton, 1974	Residence hall staff	12 hours	Eclectic. To teach staff empathy, respect, and communication accuracy.	P: Communication exercises, practice triads, stimulus vignettes, role-play practice, and videotape playback. QE
Nicoletti and Flater, 1975	Volunteer community mental health workers	N S	Eclectic. To evaluate course for teaching empathy and narrowing.	P: Discrimination training. PE
O'Connell, 1974	Psychology students	30–60 minutes	Eclectic. To evaluate feedback and perceptual cues for teaching interpersonal inquiry.	CS: (1) Delayed feedback; (2) videotape feedback; (3) immediate feedback; (4) perceptual cue; and (5) delayed feedback and perceptual cue. E
Payne, Weiss, and Kapp, 1972	Undergraduate psychology students	N S	Eclectic. To evaluate 2 factors on teaching empathy.	CS: (1) Didactic supervision; (2) experiential supervision, (3) didactic supervision and modeling; and (4) experiential supervision and modeling. PE
Perkins and Atkinson, 1973	Residence hall assistants	N S	Eclectic. To evaluate lecture and 3 factors on teaching attending, reflection of feelings, and summarization.	CS: (1) Lecture and discussion; (2) lecture and modeling; (3) lecture and role play; and (4) control. E
Perry, 1975	Ministers	N S	Eclectic. To evaluate modeling and instructions on teaching empathy.	CS: (1) High-empathy model; (2) low-empathy model; (3) instructions; (4) high-empathy

Author	Trainee Population	Duration	Model/Purpose/Skills	Training Methods/Evaluation Design
				model and instructions; (5) low-empathy model and instructions; and (6) control. E
Rappaport, Gross, and Lepper, 1973	Psychology students	N S	Sensitivity training and modeling. To evaluate 2 models for teaching interpersonal openness and understanding of the problems and feelings of others.	CS: (1) Sensitivity training and general instructions; (2) sensitivity training and specific instructions; (3) videotaped modeling and general instructions; (4) videotaped modeling and specific instructions; and (5) control. E
Reck and Behar, 1976	Psychiatric outpatient clinic support staff	8 hours	Eclectic. To evaluate program for teaching friendliness, interest, politeness, and informativeness.	P: Didactic presentation, discussion, problem sharing and solving, and role play. PE
Richardson and Stone, 1981	Undergraduate psychology students	N S	Cognitive-behavioral, behavioral, and programmed learning. To compare effectiveness of three programs in teaching empathy and confrontation.	PC: (1) Cognitive-behavioral including manual with cognitive strategies, videotaped models of skills, and supervision in small groups consisting of explanation, playback of section of pretest interview, written response, practice, feedback, and written summary; (2) same as (1), except no cognitive strategies; and (3) programmed learning including programmed manuals and videotaped models of skills. E

Schinke and others, 1979	Residence hall assistants	4 hours	Crisis intervention workshop. To evaluate effectiveness of crisis intervention training on knowledge and skills, including smiles, nods, influencing responses, advice responses, content summarizations, affect summarizations, questions on suicide plans and attempts, and crisis intervention competence.	P: (1) Crisis intervention workshop consisting of lectures, description and modeling of interviewing and helping techniques, practice in triads, videotapes, role-played crisis interviews, videotape playback with feedback, reinforcement, and discussion; and (2) untrained controls. E
Schroeder and others, 1973	Residence hall counselors	18 hours	SHRT. To evaluate model on teaching empathy, respect, genuineness, confrontation, immediacy, and specificity of expression.	P: Didactic-experiential. QE
Stone, 1981	Undergraduate psychology students	70 minutes	Eclectic. To evaluate the effect of learning through serving as teachers on the acquisition of reflective skills.	CS: (1) Full-treatment group included videotaped instructions and skills models, supervision with didactic, role-play, and discussion components, and teaching through supervision; (2) partial treatment group same as (1), except read programmed manual instead of teaching; (3) supervision group included videotaped instructions and skills models, as well as supervision from full-treatment subjects; and (4) learn group included videotaped instructions and skills models. E
Stone and Vance, 1976	Undergraduate psychology	12–36 minutes	Eclectic. To evaluate 3 factors on teaching empathy.	CS: (1) Modeling; (2) instructions; (3) rehearsal; (4) modeling and

Author	Trainee Population	Duration	Model/Purpose/Skills	Training Methods/Evaluation Design
	students			instructions; (5) modeling and rehearsal; (6) instructions and rehearsal; (7) modeling, instruction, and rehearsal; and (8) control. E
Teevan and Gabel, 1978	Crisis-call workers	9 hours	MIC. To evaluate model and supervision on teaching questions and reflection of feelings.	CS: (1) Lectures, group discussions; (2) live model, role play; and (3) control. E
Thompson and Blocher, 1979	Undergraduate volunteers	N S	MIC and cocounseling supervision. To compare effectiveness of 3 programs in teaching open-ended questions and reflection of feelings.	PC: (1) Standard microcounseling format, including reading of manual, audiotape modeling of skills, practice, supervised audiotape replay of interview; (2) same as (1) plus cocounseling interview with client; and (3) written instructions on use of questions and reflection of feelings. E
Tyler and others, 1978	Undergraduate counseling volunteers	80 hours	Eclectic. To compare the effectiveness of a didactic and an experiential-didactic program in teaching affective, understanding, and exploratory responses.	PC: (1) Didactic training, including lectures and readings; (2) experiential-didactic program consisting of lectures, readings, role playing, and communication and feedback exercises; and (3) controls. QE
Uhlemann, Hearn, and Evans, 1980	Hotline volunteers	16 hours	MIC and programmed instruction. To evaluate 2 models on teaching attending, open inquiry,	PC: (1) MIC; (2) programmed instruction and role-played interviews with feedback. E

			and reflection of feelings and content.	
Uhlemann, Lea, and Stone, 1976	Undergraduate psychology students	30 minutes	Eclectic. To evaluate the effects of instructions and modeling on the reflection-of-feelings training of individuals low in interpersonal communication skills.	CS: (1) Instruction; (2) modeling; (3) combined instructions and modeling; and (4) control. E
VanderKolk, 1973	Psychiatric attendants	24 hours	Eclectic. To evaluate programs for teaching empathy.	PC: (1) Integrated didactic-experiential; (2) sequential didactic-experiential; and (3) control. PE

[a]P—program evaluation; PC—program comparison; CS—component studies.
[b]PE—preexperimental; QE—quasi-experimental; E—experimental.
[c]SHRT—systematic human relations training; IPR—interpersonal process recall; MIC—microtraining.
[d]NS—not specified.

References

Adler, L. M., Ware, J. E., and Enelow, A. J. "Changes in Medical Interviewing Style After Instruction with Two Closed-Circuit Television Techniques." *Journal of Medical Education*, 1970, *45*, 21–28.

Alssid, L. L., and Hutchison, W. R. "Comparison of Modeling Techniques in Counselor Training." *Counselor Education and Supervision*, 1977, *16*, 36–41.

Altmaier, E. L. and Bernstein, D. N. "Counselor Trainees' Problem-Solving Skills." *Counselor Education and Supervision*, 1981, *20*, 285–290.

Anthony, W. A., Gormally, J., and Miller, H. "Prediction of Human Relations Training Outcome by Traditional and Nontraditional Selection Indices." *Counselor Education and Supervision*, 1974, *14*, 105–111.

Anthony, W. A., and Hill, C. E. "A Student Evaluation of Systematic Human Relations Training." *Counselor Education and Supervision*, 1976, *15* (4), 305–309.

Anthony, W. A., and Wain, H. J. "Two Methods of Selecting Prospective Helpers." *Journal of Counseling Psychology*, 1971, *18* (2), 155–156.

Authier, J., and Gustafson, K. "Applications of Supervised and Nonsupervised Microcounseling Paradigms in the Training of Registered and Licensed Practical Nurses." *Journal of Consulting and Clinical Psychology*, 1976, *44* (5), 704–709.

Barbee, R. A., and Feldman, S. E. "A Three-Year Longitudinal Study of the Medical Interview and Its Relationship to Student Performance in Clinical Medicine." *Journal of Medical Education*, 1970, *45*, 770–776.

Bartnick, R. W., and O'Brien, C. R. "Health Care and Counseling Skills." *Personnel and Guidance Journal*, 1980, *58* (10), 666–667.

Berg, K. S., and Stone, G. L. "Effects of Conceptual Level and Supervision Structure on Counselor Skill Development." *Journal of Counseling Psychology*, 1980, *27* (5), 500–509.

Blair, M. C., and Fretz, B. R. "Interpersonal Skills Training for Premedical Students." *Journal of Counseling Psychology*, 1980, *27* (4), 380–384.

Boyd, J. D. "Microcounseling for a Counseling-Like Verbal Response Set: Differential Effects of Two Micromodels and Two Methods of Counseling Supervision." *Journal of Counseling Psychology*, 1973, *20* (1), 97-98.

Bradley, F. O. "A Modified Interpersonal Process Recall Technique as a Training Model." *Counselor Education and Supervision*, 1974, *14*, 34-39.

Brockhaus, J. P., Marshall, J. C., and Dustin, R. "The Effect of a Training Program on the Empathic Ability of Psychiatric Aides." *Journal of Community Psychology*, 1973, *4*, 431-435.

Brown, J. E., and O'Shea, J. S. "Improving Medical Student Interviewing Skills." *Pediatrics*, 1980, *65* (3), 575-578.

Butler, E. R., and Hansen, J. C. "Facilitative Training: Acquisition, Retention, and Models of Assessment." *Journal of Counseling Psychology*, 1973, *20* (1), 60-65.

Canada, R. M. "Immediate Reinforcement Versus Delayed Reinforcement in Teaching a Basic Interview Technique." *Journal of Counseling Psychology*, 1973, *20* (5), 395-398.

Carkhuff, R. R. "Principles of Social Action in Training for New Careers in Human Services." *Journal of Counseling Psychology*, 1971, *8* (2), 147-151.

Carkhuff, R. R., Friel, T. and Kratochvil, D. "The Differential Effects of Sequence of Training in Counselor-Responsive and Counselor-Initiated Conditions." *Counselor Education and Supervision*, 1970, *9*, 106-109.

Carkhuff, R. R., and Griffin, A. H. "The Selection and Training of Human Relations Specialists." *Journal of Counseling Psychology*, 1970, *17* (5), 443-450.

Carkhuff, R. R., and Griffin, A. H. "Selection and Training of Functional Professionals for Concentrated Employment Programs." *Journal of Clinical Psychology*, 1971, *27*, 163-165.

Carlson, K. W. "Increasing Verbal Empathy as a Function of Feedback and Instruction." *Counselor Education and Supervision*, 1974, *14*, 208-213.

Carroll, J. G., Schwartz, M. W., and Ludwig, S. "An Evaluation of Simulated Patients as Instructors: Implications for Teaching Medical Interview Skills." *Journal of Medical Education*, 1981, *56*, 522-524.

Cash, R. W., and Vellema, C. K. "Conceptual Versus Competency Approach in Human Relations Training Programs." *The Personnel and Guidance Journal*, 1979, *58* (2), 91-94.

Cline, D. W., and Garrard, J. N. "A Medical Interviewing Course: Objectives, Techniques, and Assessment." *American Journal of Psychiatry*, 1973, *130* (5), 574-578.

Clubok, M. "Evaluating the Effectiveness of a Helping Skills Training Program." *The Journal of Applied Social Sciences*, 1978, *2* (1), 33-41.

Collingwood, T. "Retention and Retraining of Interpersonal Communicational Skills." *Journal of Clinical Psychology*, 1971, *27*, 294-296.

Cook, D. W., Kunce, J. T., and Sleater, S. M. "Vicarious Behavior Induction and Training Psychiatric Aides." *Journal of Community Psychology*, 1974, *21*, 293-297.

Cormier, L. S., Hackney, H., and Segrist, A. "Three Counselor Training Models: A Comparative Study." *Counselor Education and Supervision*, 1974, *14*, 95-104.

Dalton, R. F., and Sundblad, L. M. "Using Principles of Social Learning in Training for Communication of Empathy." *Journal of Counseling Psychology*, 1976, *23* (5), 454-457.

Dalton, R. F., Sundblad, L. M., and Hylbert, K. W. "An Application of Principles of Social Learning to Training in Communication of Empathy." *Journal of Counseling Psychology*, 1973, *20* (4), 378-383.

Danish, S. J., D'Augelli, A. R., and Brock, G. W. "An Evaluation of Helping Skills Training: Effects on Helpers' Verbal Responses." *Journal of Counseling Psychology*, 1975, *23* (3), 259-266.

D'Augelli, A. R., Danish, S. J., and Brock, G. W. "Untrained Paraprofessionals' Verbal Helping Behavior: Description and Implications for Training." *American Journal of Community Psychology*, 1976, *4* (3), 275-282.

DiMattia, D. J., and Arndt, G. M. "A Comparison of Microcounseling and Reflective Listening Techniques." *Counselor Education and Supervision*, 1974, *14*, 61-64.

Dooley, D. "Effect of Automated Reflection Response Training in the Group Assessment of Interpersonal Traits." *Journal of Counseling Psychology*, 1975, *22* (6), 535-541.

Dowd, E. T., and Blocher, D. H. "Effects of Immediate Reinforcement and Awareness of Response on Beginning Counselor Behavior." *Counselor Education and Supervision*, 1974, *14*, 190-197.

Eisenberg, S., and Delaney, D. "Using Video Simulation of Counseling for Training Counselors." *Journal of Counseling Psychology*, 1970, *17*, 15-19.

Elsenrath, D. E., Coker, D. L. and Martinson, W. D. "Microteaching Interviewing Skills." *Journal of Counseling Psychology*, 1972, *19* (2), 150-155.

Emener, W. G. "Improving Interpersonal Communication Skills by Programmed-Machine Training." *Rehabilitation Psychology*, 1974, *21*, 95-100.

Engler, C., and others. "Medical Student Acquisition and Retention of Communication and Interviewing Skills." *Journal of Medical Education*, 1981, *56*, 572-579.

Eskedal, G. A. "Symbolic Role Modeling and Cognitive Learning in the Training of Counselors." *Journal of Counseling Psychology*, 1975, *22* (2), 152-155.

Evans, D. R., Uhlemann, M. R., and Hearn, M. T. "Microcounseling and Sensitivity Training with Hotline Workers." *Journal of Community Psychology*, 1978, *6*, 139-146.

Farsad, P., and others. "Teaching Interviewing Skills to Pediatric House Officers." *Pediatrics*, 1978, *61* (3), 384-388.

Fine, V. K., and Therrien, M. E. "Empathy in the Doctor-Patient Relationship: Skill Training for Medical Students." *Journal of Medical Education*, 1977, *52*, 752-757.

Fischer, J. "Training for Effective Therapeutic Practice." *Psychotherapy: Theory, Research, and Practice*, 1975, *12* (1), 118-123.

Frankel, M. "Effects of Videotape Modeling and Self-Confrontation Techniques on Microcounseling Behavior." *Journal of Counseling Psychology*, 1971, *18*, (5), 465-471.

Fry, P. S. "Effects of Desensitization Treatment on Core-Condition Training." *Journal of Counseling Psychology*, 1973, *20* (3), 214-219.

Gade, E., and Matuschka, E. "Effects of Verbal Interaction Analysis Training with Counseling Practicum Students." *Counselor Education and Supervision*, 1973, *13*, 184-189.

Gantt, S., Billingsley, D., and Giordano, J. A. "Paraprofessional Skill: Maintenance of Empathic Sensitivity After Training." *Journal of Counseling Psychology*, 1980, 27 (4), 374–379.

Genthner, R. W., and Falkenberg, V. "Changes in Personal Responsibility as a Function of Interpersonal Skills Training." *Small Group Behavior*, 1977, 8 (4), 533–539.

Ginsberg, M. R. and Danish, S. J. "The Effects of Self-Selection on Trainee's Verbal Helping Skills Performance." *American Journal of Community Psychology*, 1979, 7, 577–581.

Goldstein, A. P., and Goedhart, A. "The Use of Structured Learning for Empathy Enhancement in Paraprofessional Psychotherapist Training." *Journal of Community Psychology*, 1973, 1 (2), 168–173.

Goldstein, A. P., and others. "The Effects of Modeling and Social Class Structuring in Paraprofessional Psychotherapist Training." *The Journal of Nervous and Mental Disease*, 1971, 153 (4), 47–55.

Gormally, J. "A Behavioral Analysis of Structured Skills Training." *Journal of Counseling Psychology*, 1975, 22 (5), 458–460.

Gormally, J., and others. "The Persistence of Communications Skills for Undergraduate and Graduate Trainees." *Journal of Clinical Psychology*, 1975, 31 (2), 369–372.

Goroll, A. H., Stoeckle, J. D., and Lazare, A. "Teaching the Clinical Interview: An Experiment with First-Year Students." *Journal of Medical Education*, 1974, 49, 957–962.

Grayson, M., Nugent, C., and Oken, S. L. "A Systematic and Comprehensive Approach to Teaching and Evaluating Interpersonal Skills." *Journal of Medical Education*, 1977, 52, 906–913.

Gulanick, N., and Schmeck, R. R. "Modeling, Praise, and Criticism in Teaching Empathic Responding." *Counselor Education and Supervision*, 1977, 16, 284–291.

Guttman, M.A.J., Haase, R. F. "Generalization of Microcounseling Skills from Training Period to Actual Counseling Setting." *Counselor Education and Supervision*, 1972, 12, 98–108.

Haase, R. F., and DiMattia, D. J. "The Application of the Microcounseling Paradigm to the Training of Support Personnel in Counseling." *Counselor Education and Supervision*, 1970, 10, 16–23.

Haase, R. F., DiMattia, D. J., and Guttman, M.A.J. "Training of Support Personnel in Three Human Relations Skills: A Systematic One-Year Follow-Up." *Counselor Education and Supervision,* 1972, *11,* 194–199.

Harris, G. A. "Training and Evaluation of School Counselors' Communication with Students." *Counselor Education and Supervision,* 1973, *13,* 200–205.

Hart, G. "A Programmed Approach to Increased Counselor Open-Mindedness." *Journal of Counseling Psychology,* 1973, *20* (6), 569–570.

Hart, L. E., and King, G. D. "Selection Versus Training in the Development of Paraprofessionals." *Journal of Counseling Psychology,* 1979, *26,* 235–241.

Hayes, D. M., Hutaff, L. W., and Mace, D. R. "Preparation of Medical Students for Patient Interviewing." *Journal of Medical Education,* 1971, *46,* 863–868.

Hector, M. A., and others. "Teaching Counselor Trainees How to Respond Consistently to Client Negative Affect." *Journal of Counseling Psychology,* 1979, *26,* 146–151.

Hector, M. A., and others. "Helping Counselor Trainees Learn to Respond Consistently to Anger and Depression." *Journal of Counseling Psychology,* 1981, *28,* 53–58.

Hill, C. E., Charles, D., and Reed, K. G. "A Longitudinal Analysis of Changes in Counseling Skills During Doctoral Training in Counseling Psychology." *Journal of Counseling Psychology,* 1981, *28,* 428–436.

Hodge, E. A., Payne, P. A., and Wheeler, D. D. "Approaches to Empathy Training: Programmed Methods Versus Individual Supervision and Professional Versus Peer Supervisors." *Journal of Counseling Psychology,* 1978, *25* (5), 449–453.

Hutter, M. J., and others. "Interviewing Skills: A Comprehensive Approach to Teaching and Evaluation." *Journal of Medical Education,* 1977, *52,* 328–333.

Kalisch, B. J. "An Experiment in the Development of Empathy in Nursing Students." *Nursing Research,* 1971, *20* (3), 202–211.

Katz, D. "Laboratory Training to Enhance Interviewing Skills." In F. W. Clark, M. L. Arkava, and Associates, *The Pursuit of Competence in Social Work: Contemporary Issues in the Definition,*

Assessment, and Improvement of Effectiveness in the Human Services. San Francisco, Calif.: Jossey-Bass, 1979.

Kauss, D. R., and others. "The Long-Term Effectiveness of Interpersonal Skills Training in Medical Schools." *Journal of Medical Education,* 1980, *55,* 595–601.

Kauss, D. R., and others. "Interpersonal Skills Training: Comprehensive Approach Versus Brief Instruction." *Journal of Medical Education,* 1981, *56,* 663–665.

Keefe, T. "The Development of Empathic Skills: A Study." *Journal of Education for Social Work,* 1979, *15,* 30–37.

Kelley, J. D. "Reinforcement in Microcounseling." *Journal of Counseling Psychology,* 1971, *18* (3), 268–272.

Kramer, J. A., Rappaport, J., and Seidman, E. "Contribution of Personal Characteristics and Interview Training to the Effectiveness of College Student Mental Health Workers." *Journal of Counseling Psychology,* 1979, *26,* 344–351.

Kuna, D. J. "Lecturing, Reading, and Modeling in Counselor Restatement Training." *Journal of Counseling Psychology,* 1975, *22* (6), 542–546.

LaMonica, E. L., and others. "Empathy Training as the Major Thrust of a Staff Development Program." *Nursing Research,* 1976, *25* (6), 447–451.

Larsen, J., and Hepworth, D. H. "Skill Development Through Competency-Based Education." *Journal of Education for Social Work,* 1978, *14* (1), 73–81.

Levant, R. F., Slattery, S. C. and Slobobian, P. E. "A Systematic Skills Approach to the Selection and Training of Foster Parents as Medical Health Paraprofessionals, II: Training." *Journal of Community Psychology,* 1981, *9,* 231–238.

McCarthy, P. R., Danish, S. J., and D'Augelli, A. R. "A Follow-Up Evaluation of Helping Skills Training." *Counselor Education and Supervision,* 1977, *17,* 29–34.

Markey, M. J., and others. "Influence of Playback Techniques on Counselor Performance." *Counselor Education and Supervision,* 1970, *9,* 178–182.

Mayadas, N. S., and Duehn, W. D. "The Effects of Training Formats and Interpersonal Discriminations in the Education for Clinical Social Work Practice." *Journal of Social Service Research,* 1977, *1* (2), 147–161.

Mitchell, K. M., and others. "Effects of Short-Term Training on Residence Hall Assistants." *Counselor Education and Supervision,* 1971, *10,* 310–319.

Moreland, J. R., Ivey, A. E., and Phillips, J. S. "An Evaluation of Microcounseling as an Interviewer Training Tool." *Journal of Consulting and Clinical Psychology,* 1973, *41* (2), 294–300.

Newton, F. B. "The Effect of Systematic Communication Skills Training on Residence Hall Paraprofessionals." *Journal of College Student Personnel,* 1974, *15* (5), 366–369.

Nicoletti, J., and Flater, L. "A Community-Oriented Program for Training and Using Volunteers." *Community Mental Health Journal,* 1975, *11* (1), 58–63.

O'Connell, M. "Immediate Feedback, Delayed Feedback, and Perceptual Cues and Inquiry During Verbal Interactions." *Journal of Counseling Psychology,* 1974, *21* (6), 536–538.

O'Toole, W. M. "Effects of Practice and Some Methodological Considerations in Training Counseling Interviewing Skills." *Journal of Counseling Psychology,* 1979, *26* (5), 419–426.

Pacoe, L. V., and others. "Training Medical Students in Interpersonal Relationship Skills." *Journal of Medical Education,* 1976, *51,* 743–750.

Payne, P. A., Weiss, S. D., and Kapp, R. A. "Didactic, Experiential, and Modeling Factors in the Learning of Empathy." *Journal of Counseling Psychology,* 1972, *19* (5), 425–429.

Pedersen, P., Holwill, C. F., and Shapiro, J. "A Cross-Cultural Training Procedure for Classes in Counselor Education." *Counselor Education and Supervision,* 1978, *17,* 233–237.

Perkins, S. R., and Atkinson, D. R. "Effect of Selected Techniques for Training Resident Assistants in Human Relations Skills." *Journal of Counseling Psychology,* 1973, *20* (1), 84–90.

Perry, M. A. "Modeling and Instructions in Training for Counselor Empathy." *Journal of Counseling Psychology,* 1975, *22* (3), 173–179.

Peters, G. A., Cormier, L. S., and Cormier, W. H. "Effects of Modeling, Rehearsal, Feedback, and Remediation on Acquisition of a Counseling Strategy." *Journal of Counseling Psychology,* 1978, *25,* 231–237.

Pierce, R., and Schauble, P. "Graduate Training of Facilitative

Counselors: The Effects of Individual Supervision." *Journal of Counseling Psychology,* 1970, *17,* 210-215.

Rappaport, J., Gross, T., and Lepper, C. "Modeling, Sensitivity Training, and Instruction: Implications for the Training of College Student Volunteers and for Outcome Research." *Journal of Consulting and Clinical Psychology,* 1973, *40* (1), 99-107.

Rasche, L. M., Bernstein, L., and Veenhuis, P. E. "Evaluation of a Systematic Approach to Teaching Interviewing." *Journal of Medical Education,* 1974, *49,* 589-595.

Reck, J. J., and Behar, T. "Impact of a Personnel Workshop on the Behavior of Support Employees Toward New Patients in a Psychiatric Outpatient Clinic." *Community Mental Health Journal,* 1976, *12* (1), 95-98.

Richardson, B., and Stone, G. L. "Effects of a Cognitive Adjunct Procedure Within a Microtraining Situation." *Journal of Counseling Psychology,* 1981, *28,* 168-175.

Robbins, A. S., and others. "Teaching Interpersonal Skills in a Medical Residency Training Program." *Journal of Medical Education,* 1978, *53,* 988-990.

Robbins, A. S., and others. "Interpersonal Skills Training: Evaluation in an Internal Medicine Residency." *Journal of Medical Education,* 1979, *54,* 885-894.

Robinson, S. E., Froehle, T. C., and Kurpius, D. J. "Self-Instructional Modules: Comparison of Modeling and Feedback Media." *Counselor Education and Supervision,* 1979, *18,* 251-259.

Robinson, S. E., Kurpius, D. J., and Froehle, T. C. "Self-Generated Performance Feedback in Interviewing Training." *Counselor Education and Supervision,* 1979, *18,* 91-100.

Robinson, S. E., Kurpius, D. J., and Froehle, T. C. "A Two-Study Comparison of Written and Video Modeling and a Written and Oral Assessment." *Counselor Education and Supervision,* 1981, *21,* 45-56.

Rogers, R. R., and Rasof, B. "A Teaching Drill in Child Psychiatry." *American Journal of Psychiatry,* 1975, *132* (2), 158-162.

Ronnestad, M. H. "The Effects of Modeling, Feedback, and Experiential Methods on Counselor Empathy." *Counselor Education and Supervision,* 1977, *16,* 194-201.

Rose, S., Cayner, J. J., and Edleson, J. L. "Measuring Interpersonal Competence." *Social Work,* 1977, *22* (3), 125-129.

Rosenthal, N. R. "A Prescriptive Approach for Counselor Training." *Journal of Counseling Psychology,* 1977, *24* (3), 231-237.

Saltmarsh, R. E. "Development of Empathic Interview Skills Through Programmed Instruction." *Journal of Counseling Psychology,* 1973, *20* (4), 375-377.

Saltmarsh, R. E., and Hubele, G. E. "Basic Interaction Behaviors: A Micro-Counseling Approach for Introductory Courses." *Counselor Education and Supervision,* 1974, *13,* 246-249.

Schinke, S. P., and others. "Developing Intake-Interviewing Skills." *Social Work Research and Abstracts,* 1980, *16,* 29-34.

Schinke, S. P., and others. "Interviewing-Skills Training." *Journal of Social Service Research,* 1978, *1* (4), 391-401.

Schinke, S. P., and others. "Crisis-Intervention Training with Paraprofessionals." *Journal of Community Psychology,* 1979, *7,* 343-347.

Schroeder, K., and others. "Systematic Human Relations Training for Resident Assistants." *Journal of College Student Personnel,* 1973, *14* (4), 313-316.

Scott, N., Donnelly, M., and Hess, J. "Longitudinal Investigation of Changes in Interviewing Performance of Medical Students." *Journal of Clinical Psychology,* 1976, *32* (2), 424-431.

Shapiro, J. L. and Gust, T. "Counselor Training for Facilitative Human Relationships." *Counselor Education and Supervision,* 1974, *14,* 198-206.

Smith, C. K., Hadac, R. R., and Levesee, J. H. "Evaluating the Effects of a Medical Interviewing Course Taught at Multiple Locations." *Journal of Medical Education,* 1980, *55,* 792-794.

Spielberg, G. "Graduate Training in Helping Relationships: Helpful or Harmful?" *Journal of Humanistic Psychology,* 1980, *20* (3), 57-70.

Spivack, J. D. "Laboratory to Classroom: The Practical Application of IPR in a Master's Level Prepracticum Counselor Education Program." *Counselor Education and Supervision,* 1972, *12,* 3-16.

Stillman, P. L., Sabers, D. L., and Redfield, D. L. "The Use of Paraprofessionals to Teach Interviewing Skills." *Pediatrics*, 1976, *57* (5), 769–774.

Stillman, S. M. "Early Training Facilitative Level as a Predictor of Practicum Performance." *Counselor Education and Supervision*, 1980, *19*, 173–176.

Stone, G. L. "Effect of Simulation on Counselor Training." *Counselor Education and Supervision*, 1975, *15*, 199–203.

Stone, G. L. "Effects of Different Strategies Within a Micro-Training Situation." *Counselor Education and Supervision*, 1981, *20* (4), 301–311.

Stone, G. L., and Vance, A. "Instructions, Modeling, and Rehearsal: Implications for Training." *Journal of Counseling Psychology*, 1976, *23* (3), 272–279.

Taylor, M. K., and Berven, D. M. "An Evaluation for Teaching Interviewing in Multiple Settings." *Journal of Medical Education*, 1974, *49*, 609–612.

Teevan, K. G., and Gabel, H. "Evaluation of Modeling—Role-Playing and Lecture-Discussion Training Techniques for College Student Mental Health Paraprofessionals." *Journal of Counseling Psychology*, 1978, *25* (2), 169–171.

Thompson, A.J.M., and Blocher, D. H. "Co-Counseling Supervision in Microcounseling." *Journal of Counseling Psychology*, 1979, *26* (5), 413–418.

Toukmanian, S. G., and Rennie, D. L. "Microcounseling Versus Human Relations Training: Relative Effectiveness with Undergraduate Trainees." *Journal of Counseling Psychology*, 1975, *22* (4), 345–352.

Truax, C. B., and Lister, J. L. "Effects of Short-Term Training Upon Accurate Empathy and Nonpossessive Warmth." *Counselor Education and Supervision*, 1971, *10*, 120–125.

Tyler, M., and others. "A Brief Assessment Technique for Paraprofessional Helpers." *Journal of Community Psychology*, 1978, *6*, 53–59.

Uhlemann, M. R., Hearn, M. T., and Evans, D. R. "Programmed Learning in the Microtraining Paradigm With Hotline Workers." *American Journal of Community Psychology*, 1980, *8* (5), 603–612.

Uhlemann, M. R., Lea, G. W., and Stone, G. L. "Effect of Instructions and Modeling on Trainees Low in Interpersonal-Communication Skills." *Journal of Counseling Psychology,* 1976, *23* (6), 509-513.

VanderKolk, C. J. "Comparison of Two Mental Health Counselor Training Programs." *Community Mental Health Journal,* 1973, *9* (3), 260-269.

Vaughn, M., and Marks, J. N. "Teaching Interviewing Skills to Medical Students: A Comparison of Two Methods." *Medical Education,* 1976, *10,* 170-175.

Ward, R. C., Kagan, N., and Krathwohl, D. R. "An Attempt to Measure and Facilitate Counselor Effectiveness." *Counselor Education and Supervision,* 1972, *11* (3), 179-186.

Wells, R. A. "Training in Facilitative Skills." *Social Work,* 1975, *20* (3), 242-243.

Werner, A., and Schneider, J. M. "Teaching Medical Students Interactional Skills." *The New England Journal of Medicine,* 1974, *290,* 1232-1237.

Wolraich, M., and others. "Teaching Pediatric Residents to Provide Emotion-Laden Information." *Journal of Medical Education,* 1981, *56,* 438-440.

Available Skills Training Resources and Materials

This section presents the training resources discussed in Chapter Fourteen. Resources are organized into four major categories: (1) training packages (Part One); (2) audiotapes, videotapes, and films (Part Two); (3) simulation games and exercises (Part Three); and (4) organizations (Part Four). Part Five provides names and addresses of sources for materials, programs, and services listed in the other categories.

Part One: Training Packages.

Title	Program Description	Media Description[a]	Fee[b]	Distributor
Human Resource Development Videotape Series	*Comprehensive Training Packages*	Videotapes with trainer's guide	PH	Human Resource Development Press
Background Videotapes:				
1. Carkhuff as a Person	Presents interview with Carkhuff to introduce the person behind the model.	30 minute videocassette	PH	
2. The Evolution of Systematic HRD Models	Reviews history of the human resources development model.	60 minute videocassette	PH	
Life-Skills Model Videotapes:				
1. Helping Model Module	Introduces basic interpersonal skills, including nonverbal attending, responding to content and feelings, personalizing meaning, problems and goals, and defining goals and steps to goals.	60 minute videocassette	PH	
2. Problem-Solving Model Module	Introduces decision making and seven steps in effective decision making.	60 minute videocassette	PH	
3. Program Development Model Module	Reviews the program development model and skills involved in setting goals and developing systematic plans for their achievement.	60 minute videocassette	PH	

Art of Helping Training Videotapes:

1. Attending Skills Module	Provides thorough explanation of attending, observing, and listening skills.	30 minute videocassette	PH
2. Responding Skills Module	Explores in-depth responding to content, feeling, and meaning.	30 minute videocassette	PH
3. Personalizing Skills Module	Demonstrates 2 steps of personalizing: laying a base and personalizing the meaning.	30 minute videocassette	PH
4. Initiating Skills Module	Teaches initiating skills, with emphasis on program development skills, goal setting, and first and intermediary steps.	30 minute videocassette	PH

Demonstration Videotape Series:

1. The Case of Jane	Demonstrates the process of exploration, understanding, and action.	30 minute videocassette	PH
2. The Case of Manny	Demonstrates uses of responsive and immediacy skills in real-life interview.	45 minute videocassette	PH
3. The Case of Jerry	Demonstrates the integration of interpersonal skills with decision-making and program development skills.	60 minute videocassette	PH

Microtraining Series	Videotapes with trainer and trainee manuals	Microtraining Associates

Part One: Training Packages (cont'd.).

Title	Program Description	Media Description[a]	Fee[b]	Distributor
1. Microcounseling: An Introduction	Presents the microtraining framework, including relevant background information.	1 hour videotape	PH R	
2. Basic Attending Skills	Focuses on effective listening and nonverbal skills, including attending behavior, questions, paraphrasing, reflection of feelings, summarization, and integration of attending skills.	2½ hour videotapes	PH R	
3. Basic Influencing Skills	Teaches interpersonal influencing skills, including self-expression, directions, self-disclosure, interpretation, direct mutual communication, use of video in assertion training, and integration of microtraining skills.	2½ hour videotapes	PH R	
4. Highlights of Influencing and Attending Skills	Models influencing and attending skills in interview situations through vignettes.	1 hour videotape	PM	
Interpersonal Process Recall: Influencing Human Interaction Series		Videotapes with trainer's manual		Mason Media
Elements of Facilitating Communication	Defines and illustrates exploratory responses, listening responses, affective and honest labeling responses.	52 minute videocassette	PH	
Affect Simulation: The Process	Helps students increase sensitivity to themselves and recognize some of their "interpersonal allergies."	16 minute videocassette	PL	

Affect Simulation: Vignettes	Presents series of brief scenes of actor looking directly at viewer and making emotionally charged statements.	49 minute film only	PL
Series A—Individual Recall Videotapes:	Demonstrates the interviewer recall process implemented with different professionals.		
1. Psychotherapist, Client		39 minute videocassette	PM
2. Psychotherapist, Ongoing Therapy		23 minute videocassette	PM
3. Resident Adviser, Colleague		14 minute videocassette	PL
4. Curriculum Director, Teacher		28 minute videocassette	PM
Series B—Client Recall Videotapes:	Demonstrates the client recall process with a student as inquirer.		
1. Client, Ongoing Therapy		18 minute videocassette	PL
2. Student, Junior High School Principal		6 minute videocassette	PL
3. Couple, Man and Woman		54 minute videocassette	PH
4. Discussion Tape	Provides further cognitive frameworks for understanding experiences in the interpersonal process recall program.	14 minute videocassette	PL
Series C—Mutual Recall Videotapes:	Following an interview, both student and client recall interview as tool for understanding client and facilitating growth.		

601

Part One: Training Packages (cont'd).

Title	Program Description	Media Description[a]	Fee[b]	Distributor
1. Client and Therapist		9 minute videocassette	PL	
2. Supplement, Psychiatrist and Patient		31 minute film only	PH	
3. Physician and Patient		32 minute videocassette	PM	
4. Supplement, Physician and Woman		12 minute film only	PL	
5. Man and Woman		5 minute videocassette	PL	
6. Health Team		8 minute videocassette	PL	
7. Family I		21 minute videocassette	PM	
8. Family II		13 minute videocassette	PL	
9. Junior High School Classroom		16 minute videocassette	PL	
10. Military		60 minute videocassette	PH	
Interviewing/Counseling Skills Development Packages				
The Art of Interviewing	Presents interviewing principles and techniques, such as interview structure, questions, opening, and closing.	4 audiocassettes and teacher's guide	PM	Lansford Publishing Company
Basic Counseling Skills	Presents basic counseling skills of attending, clarification, and self-	3 videocassettes and instructional manual	PM	George Warren Brown School of Social Work, Washington

Title	Description	Media	Code	Publisher
Casework Interviewing Effectiveness	Focuses on interviewing in public welfare using the microtraining model, with emphasis on skills of attending, reflection, use of questions, information giving, directions and advice, summarization, self-disclosure, empathy, respect, and genuineness. ... expression through scenes of workers using these skills in client interviews. (From series entitled, "Videotaped Training Package for Child Abuse Workers.")	10 videotapes, leader's guide, exercises, and trainee handouts	PH	Office of Continuing Social Work Education, University of Georgia
Counseling Skills	Provides an instructional system for development of counseling skills emphasizing communication barriers, attending, reflection, questioning, confrontation, and advanced-level communication skills.	Audiocassette, leader's guide, participant's manual, and test instruments	NS	Learning Dynamics
Crisis Intervention Counseling	Presents the primary purposes and stages of crisis counseling.	15 transparencies and teacher guide	PM	Lansford Publishing Company
Crisis Intervention and Suicide Prevention	Helps teach proper interview techniques to professional and lay helpers working with people in crisis.	6 audiocassettes, instructor's guide, and student response sheets	PL	Charles Press
The Dynamics of Face-To-Face Communication	Teaches ABCs of interviewing, use of probes, directive and nondirective questions, latent and manifest meanings, a communications model, and communication barriers.	Audiocassette, leader's guide, participant's manual, and handouts	PL	Training House

Part One: Training Packages (cont'd).

Title	Program Description	Media Description[a]	Fee[b]	Distributor
Helper Effectiveness Learning	Structures experiences to develop participant counseling and interpersonal skills.	Audiocassette and 260-frame program booklet	PL	Human Development Institute
Incidents from Medical Assistance Interviews	Portrays 6 client incidents providing opportunity for participants to enhance skill in attending, questioning, reflection, expression, interpretation, managing the interview process, and identifying service needs.	Audiocassette with manual for trainer	PL	School of Social Welfare, State University of New York at Albany
Incidents from Income Maintenance Interviews	Portrays 6 client incidents providing participants opportunity to enhance skill in attending, active listening, self-management, questioning, identifying service needs, and managing the interview process.	Videotape with manual for trainer	PL	School of Social Welfare, State University of New York at Albany
Interviewing and Crisis Intervention Techniques	Teaches skills for interviewing clients in crisis situations.	6 audiocassettes, instructor's guide, and 30 response sheets	PM	Lansford Publishing Company
Interviewing Skills for Family Assistance Workers	Applies a microtraining model to teach basic responsive and initiative skills, including nonverbal attending, minimal encouragers, open and closed questions, reflection of feelings, paraphrase, information sharing, directions, encouragement, self-disclosure, and immediacy.	5 videocassettes (color), instructor's manual, and trainee manual	PM	Office of Continuing Social Work Education, University of Tennessee

Title				
Nurse-Patient Communication: A Skills Approach	PH	Microtraining Associates	Videocassette (color), instructor's guide, and student workbook	Applies microtraining model to teach 6 communication skills, including nonverbal attending, questioning, minimal encouragers, reflection of feelings, paraphrasing, and summarization.
SASHAtapes	PL	University of California, Los Angeles, Extension	6 audiocassettes (2 hours each) and 10 instructional manuals	Consists of a self-led, automated instructional program oriented to the enhancement of "help intended" communication responses including questions, advisement, silence, reflection of feelings, interpretations, and self-disclosure.
Step-by-Step	PH	Human Resource Center, University of Texas at Arlington	Videocassette and instructor's manual	Uses a skills transfer model to teach nonverbal attending, minimal encouragers, open and closed questions, and reflection skills through step-by-step process integrating instructor, participant, and video feedback tape.
Tell Me About Yourself	PH	Roundtable	Film, trainer's package with audiotape, role-play exercises, interview critique sheets, and discussion leader's guide	Demonstrates questioning techniques that help with common interviewing problems like probing for negatives, maintaining control, and handling moments of silence.
Vantage Point	PH	University of Tennessee Research Corporation	7 videocassettes and trainer manual	Presents a series of "original scene" protective service interviews, ensuing supervisory conferences, and expert commentaries.

Part One: Training Packages (cont'd.).

Interpersonal Communication Skills Packages

Title	Program Description	Media Description[a]	Fee[b]	Distributor
Basic Interpersonal Relations	Furthers development of effective interpersonal relations through guided interactions designed for small groups.	Texts and coordinator's manual	PL	Human Development Institute
Body Language	Alerts viewers to messages given through nonverbal body language.	15 transparencies and teacher's guide	PM	Lansford Publishing
Communicating Empathy	Teaches verbal empathic responses through a self-instructional process and helps participants evaluate effectiveness of own empathic reactions.	2 audiocassettes, participant's manual, and response forms	PL	University Associates
Communicating Skills	Emphasizes importance of and opens discussion about the keys to effective communication.	6 audiocassettes and leader's guide	PL	Resources for Education and Management
Communication: Process in Perspective	Focuses on key factors in communication, self-assessment, effective and ineffective communication, and stimulus-response analysis of communication.	Audiocassette, leader's guide, participant's manual, and handouts	PL	Training House
Communications	Focuses on nurse-patient verbal and nonverbal communication, defines communication goals, and shows how communication can break down. (From series entitled "The Nursing Process.")	4 audiocassettes, 170 slides, and 25 response booklets per module	PH	Harper & Row College Media

Title	Description	Components		Publisher
Effective Interpersonal Relationships	Emphasizes the development of basic interpersonal skills, such as active listening, self-expression, feedback, and interpersonal risk taking, through a 10-session program.	4 audiocassettes and facilitator's guide	PL	University Associates
Effective Listening	Discusses problems that hinder effective listening and offers suggestions for improved listening.	12 transparencies, teacher's guide, workbook, and supplements	PM	Lansford Publishing Company
An Experience in Successful Communication	Presents programmed series of interpersonal exchanges permitting each person to experience insights and skills of effective communication.	3 audiocassettes and leader's guide	PL	Mass Media
Improving Self-Esteem and Relationships	Presents specific and effective ways of interacting in relationships.	2 audiocassettes, 18 transparencies, and teacher's guide	PM	Lansford Publishing Company
Improving Your Helping and Communication Skills with Mental Practice	Provides experiential situations through which individuals can practice communication or counseling skills.	3 audiocassettes and user's guide	PL	Lansford Publishing Company
The Jones-Mohr Listening Test	Provides feedback on listening accuracy through tape-assisted evaluation tool and serves as a motivator toward skill improvement.	Audiocassette, test forms, and facilitator's guide	PL	University Associates
Listening: Sharpening Your Analytical Skills	Emphasizes 6 guidelines to listening analytically and discusses barriers to listening, a communication enhancement model, and use of questions.	Audiocassette, leader's guide, participant's workbook, exercises, self-assessments, role plays, case studies, and games	PL	Training House

Part One: Training Packages (cont'd).

Title	Program Description	Media Description[a]	Fee[b]	Distributor
Nonverbal Communication	Facilitates awareness of nonverbal messages sent by self and others.	Videocassette (color), leader's guide, 20 participant's worksheets, and book	PH R	Salenger Educational Media
The Power of Listening	Develops effective listening through multimedia modules that facilitate learning key communication skills.	Facilitator's guide, videocassette, audiocassettes, and participant's workbook	PH	CRM McGraw-Hill Films
Project Listening	Teaches empathic listening based on Rogerian model and 12 general styles of listening.	Leader's guide, 3 audiocassettes, and participant handouts	PH	Sales Distribution Center, Unitarian-Universalist Association
The Way I See It	Provides methods for improving reliability of perception and controlling misperceptions that can influence communication and job performance.	Film and participant's workbook, *Getting Your Signals Straight*	PH	Roundtable
	Communication Theory/Process-Oriented Packages			
Case Studies in Communication	Presents 2 dramatized case histories illustrating major barriers to effective communication.	Film or videocassette, leader's guide, charts, bibliography, and participant worksheets	PH	Salenger Educational Media
Communication	Provides introduction to the role and scope of communication in daily living and stresses theory and function of communication in society.	12 transparencies, teacher's guide, and reprints	PM	Lansford Publishing Company

Title	Description	Materials		Publisher
Communication Lectures	Includes 4 lectures covering the communication process, persuasion and attitude change, human listening, and audience analysis.	4 audiocassettes, student handbook, lecture notes, and test booklet	PL	Lansford Publishing Company
Hidden Communication Barriers	Describes barriers to communication, such as ethnic and cross-cultural protective mechanisms, that are often ignored.	15 transparencies and lecture notes	PM	Lansford Publishing Company
Human Relations Fundamentals	Presents important human relations principles that permeate training programs in a variety of disciplines.	22 transparencies and lecture notes with reprints	PM	Lansford Publishing Company
Intercultural Communication	Defines and identifies characteristics of culture and suggests ways to develop cross-cultural sensitivity.	20 transparencies, teacher's guide, exercises, and reprints	PH	Lansford Publishing Company
Interpersonal Communication	Defines interpersonal communication from a developmental perspective, including cultural, sociological, and psychological levels of information.	Videocassette (color) and instructor's manual	PM	Instructional Media Center
Interpersonal Communication	Examines factors that influence contact with others and explores ways to deepen communication.	6 audiocassettes, 2 books, and lecture guide	PL	Lansford Publishing Company
A Measure of Understanding	Shows causes of communication breakdown and principles for preventing it, ways to recognize the "double level" of a verbal message, and reliable ways to clear up conflicting messages.	Film with participant's workbook, *Getting Your Signals Straight*	PH	Roundtable
Non-verbal Communication	Explores the importance of nonverbal cues (mannerisms, gestures, audio and tactile messages) in human communication.	15 transparencies with leader's guide	PM	Lansford Publishing Company

Part One: Training Packages (cont'd.)

Title	Program Description	Media Description[a]	Fee[b]	Distributor
Non-verbal Communication And Interaction	Defines the fundamentals of nonverbal communication and its functions, focusing on body motion, language of distance, voice language, environmental language, and other features of nonverbal interaction.	Audiocassettes, 14 transparencies, games, and leader's guide	PM	Lansford Publishing Company
The Psychology of Communication	Examines key aspects in communicating with others, including non-verbal messages, communication of feelings, and styles of communication.	2 audiocassettes and self-guide	PL	Learning Consultants

[a]Where a program is available in both videotape and film, description and fee are based on the videotape.
[b]The fee column indicates whether a given program is available for rental (R) and/or purchase (P). Purchase price is designated as follows: PL (up to $99), PM ($100-$199), and PH ($200 and above).

Part Two: Films, Videotapes, and Audiotapes.

Title[a]	Content Description	Media Description	Fee[b]	Distributor Code[c]
	Interpersonal/Communication Skills			
Bip at a Society Party (Art of Silence Series)	Illustrates Western cultural signs through a mime by Marcel Marceau. (1975)	Film, color, 16mm, 14 minutes	R	IU, UC
Bridging the Gap	Discusses such needs as identity, honest recognition of feelings, and straightforward action as a method of communicating. (1974)	Film, color, 16mm, 30 minutes	R	UA
Communication Feedback	Shows the need for and results of the use of feedback and discusses why feedback may be ignored. (1965)	Film, color, 16mm, 21 minutes	R	IU, UA, UW
Communications Primer	Presents and illustrates conceptual theories of communication. (1965)	Film, color, 16mm, 23 minutes	R	IO
Communication: The Nonverbal Agenda	Discusses the importance of recognizing nonverbal messages. (1975)	Film, 16mm, videocassette, color, 30 minutes	R PH	McGH, UW, PSU
A Communications Model	Considers the way a message is delivered and the ways it can be perceived or received. (1967)	Film, black-and-white, 16mm, 30 minutes	R	PSU, IU
Communications Fundamentals: Five Basic Skills (Communications Skills Series)	Shows through a series of humorous skits in communication: reading, writing, speaking, listening, and nonverbal communication. (1977)	Film, color, 16mm, 16 minutes	R	IU

611

Part Two: Films, Videotapes, and Audiotapes (cont'd.).

Title[a]	Content Description	Media Description	Fee[b]	Distributor Code[c]
Doubletalk	Reveals through overlapping soundtracks what each person is really thinking as they speak. (1976)	Film, color, 16mm, 9 minutes	R PL	LCA
Effective Listening	Demonstrates the importance and techniques of effective listening habits. (1961)	Film, black-and-white, 16 mm, 17 minutes	R	IO
Emotional Communications	Explores various forms of emotional communication and particularizes how our bodies reflect them.	Audiocassette, 27 minutes	PL	CCS
If I Was Sure I Could Manage (Making a Sensitive Response Series)	Demonstrates sensitive and nonsensitive interaction between 2 nurses and a patient when nonverbal cues do not correspond with what is said. (1970)	Film, color, super-8 and 16mm, 14 minutes	R PR	McGH, IU
Information Processing (Psychology Today Series)	Uses a cocktail party and the interaction between a psychologist and an actor to illustrate the basic principles of human information processing. (1972)	Film, color, 16mm, 29 minutes	R	UI-ISU, UW
The Interview	Presents a satirical interview between a TV announcer and rock musician demonstrating interpersonal noncommunication. (1960)	Film, color, 16mm, 5 minutes	R	MM UC
Introduction to Feedback	Examines the meaning of the term *feedback* and utilizes a variety of mechanical and social examples to illustrate the concept. (1974)	Film, color, 16mm, 10 minutes	R	IU, UI-ISU

612

Title	Description	Format		Source
Invisible Walls	Demonstrates the dependence of American social interactions on nonverbal communication. (1969)	Film, black-and-white, 16mm, 12 minutes	R PL	PSU
The Joy of Communication	Depicts communication between people of all ages and shows reciprocal joys of sharing values and experience. (1976)	Film, color, super-8 and 16 mm, 18 minutes	R PM	UN
Kinesics	Presents linguistic kinesics through a lecture defining facial expressions, posturing, and gestures in terms of communicative meaning. (1964)	Film, black-and-white, 16mm, 73 minutes	R PH	PSU
Listening Skills: An Introduction	Demonstrates what could be going through one's mind, as opposed to what should be going through one's mind, when listening. (1969)	Film, color, 16mm, 11 minutes	R	UA, UI-ISU
Making a Sensitive Response: Stimulus Film (Interpersonal Relationships In Nursing: Making a Sensitive Response Series)	Shows 5 communication situations that require nurses to give immediate responses to patients' questions. (1970)	Film, color, super-8 and 16mm, 14 minutes	R	UN, IU
Meanings Are in People (Berlo Effective Communication Series)	Demonstrates how meaning in communication is not in words but in the experience which people bring to interpretation. (1965)	Film, color, 16mm, 24 minutes	R	MSU-UM, UW
Meeting (Social Seminar Series)	Depicts various obstacles to honest communication that hamper effective collaboration in a community drug prevention program. (1971)	Film, color, 16mm, 30 minutes	R	UC

Part Two: Films, Videotapes, and Audiotapes (cont'd).

Title[a]	Content Description	Media Description	Fee[b]	Distributor Code[c]
Message to No One	Uses a family's experience to show the differences between listening and hearing. (1960)	Film, color, 16mm, 26 minutes	R	UI-ISU, FSU
Nonverbal Communication	Presents research and theory on communication through gestures, body posture, intonation, eye contact, and facial expression. (1976)	Film, color, 16mm, 22 minutes	R, PM	HR, PSU
Oral Communication (You in Public Service Series)	Applies important aspects of oral communication to 3 types of interaction: person-to-person interaction, informal interviews, and group discussion. (1977)	Film, color, 16mm, 28 minutes	PL	GSA
The Orator	Presents the circular nature of communication, emphasizing the importance of sensitivity and adaptation to feedback. (1969)	Film, black-and-white, 16mm, 11 minutes	R	IO
Perception and Communication	Shows concrete examples of how human perception affects the communication process. (1968)	Film, black-and-white, 16mm, 32 minutes	R, PL	PSU, SUNYB
Person-to-Person Relationships (You in Public Service Series)	Explores skills and attitudes of getting along well with others in one-to-one situations. (1977)	Film, color, 16mm, 28 minutes, workbook	R, PL	GSA
The Power of Listening	Demonstrates through a lively listening workshop the full meaning and benefits of active listening.	Film, 16mm, videocassette, color, 26 minutes	R, PH	McGH, UW

614

Title	Description	Format		Source
The Process of Communication (The Communication Theory and The New Education Series)	Examines the communication process, first with an animated theoretical model and then with sequences that progressively elaborate and illuminate the process. (1968)	Film, black-and-white, 16mm, 46 minutes	R PL	UI-ISU, PSU
Role Playing in Human Relations Training	Illustrates the techniques of role playing for gaining insight into human relations problems.	Film, black-and-white, 16mm, 27 minutes	R	MSU-UM
Sexuality and Communication	Explores communication and sexuality as they relate to doctor–patient and husband-wife relationships.	Film, color, 16mm, 55 minutes	R	UA
Signals Without Words	Discusses communication through many different forms of non-verbal signals. (1973)	Film, videocassette, color, 15 minutes	R PL	FI
Some Personal Learnings About Interpersonal Relationships	Discusses the mysterious business of relating with other human beings and compares effective and ineffective listening. (1967)	Film, videotape, 33 minutes	R PM	IU, MSU-UM
They Don't Hear What I Say (Interpersonal Relationships in Nursing: Making a Sensitive Response Series)	Demonstrates through appropriate and inappropriate nurse interactions how communication is more effective when emotions are dealt with before content is addressed. (1970)	Film, color, 16mm, 14 minutes	R	IU
Viewpoint: Believe Me	Examines communication in its many forms as a way of building and maintaining our social beliefs and customs. (1975)	Film, color, 16mm, 18 minutes	R	UI-ISU

Part Two: Films, Videotapes, and Audiotapes (cont'd).

Title[a]	Content Description	Media Description	Fee[b]	Distributor Code[c]
Why We Listen	Discusses attentive listening and the importance of minimizing interruptions in the listening process. (1965)	Film, color, 16mm, 6 minutes	R	CAFC
Without Words: An Introduction to Nonverbal Communication	Demonstrates examples of nonverbal communication related to kinesics, pupillometrics, and proxemics. (1977)	Film, color, 16mm, 23 minutes	R	UW
	Interviewing Skills			
The Art of Interviewing (Part 1)	Explains the most effective technique in preparing for 3 phases of an interview and how to conduct a job interview.	Audiocassette, 30 minutes	PL	CCS
The Art of Interviewing (Part 2)	Analyzes some of the barriers encountered in interviewing.	Audiocassette, 35 minutes	PL	CCS
Essential Elements of Interviewing: A Series	Teaches eligibility workers the essential elements of interviewing prospective or current welfare recipients. (1975)	7 films, black-and-white, 16mm, 11–23 minutes	PH	GSA
Initial Assessment Interviews	Demonstrates an initial assessment interview with 2 clients. (1978)	Videocassette, 60 minutes	PL	VRL
Initial Interview	Reenacts the initial interview between a case worker and an applicant for public welfare and demonstrates	Film, black-and-white, 16mm, 20 minutes	R	UW, PSU

Title	Description	Format		
	specific techniques, such as putting the client at ease and questioning. (1965)	Film, color, 16mm, 14 minutes	R	FSU
Initial Interviews	Depicts a variety of on-the-job police interviews to demonstrate successful basic interviewing techniques. (1961)	Film, color, 16mm, 35 minutes	PL	GSA,UW
The Interview (We Can Help Series)	Presents an interview between a parent and a pediatrician revealing social history information and offering commentary. (1977)	Film, color, 16mm, 27 minutes	R	CAFC
Interviewing: Basic Communication Skills	Teaches important nonverbal and verbal interviewing skills. (1970)	Film, black-and-white, 16mm, 25 minutes	NC	SPF
Interviewing a Child	Discusses problems involved in interviewing a child for the purpose of learning the causes of medical or psychosocial difficulties. (1970)	Film, color, 16mm, 28 minutes	R PL	GSA
Interviewing Skills (You in Public Service Series)	Discusses how to obtain the right information at the right time. (1977)	12 films, black-and-white, 16mm, 12–20 minutes	PL (each) PH (series)	GSA
Program Instruction in Medical Interviewing: A Series	Demonstrates facilitation, confrontation, silence, accuracy in communication, control, creating an emotional climate, and building confidence in an interview. (1970)	Videocassette, 35 minutes	PL	VRL
Social Work Interviewing: The Exploration Phase	Demonstrates an assessment interview conducted by a social worker with a woman who has a child with cerebral palsy. (1978)			

Part Two: Films, Videotapes, and Audiotapes (cont'd.).

Title[a]	Content Description	Media Description	Fee[b]	Distributor Code[c]
Social Work Interviewing: The Involvement Phase	Presents an interview between a social worker and a young woman with multiple problems. (1978)	Videocassette, 22 minutes	PL	VRL
Studies in Interviewing: A Series	Demonstrates, in 4 different versions of 2 different interview situations, how interviewer skills and attitudes affect the interviewee and determine the success of the interview. (1965)	4 films, black-and-white, 16mm, 140 minutes (total)	R PL (each) PM (series)	USC
Unmarried Mother Interview	Demonstrates how interviewer skills and attitudes affect the interviewee, as well as the overall outcome of the interview, and highlights the importance of nonverbal communication. (1965)	4 films, black-and-white, 16mm, 17 minutes (each)	R	FSU, UW
Individual Treatment Modalities				
AAP Research Tape: Six Therapists	Compares different therapist approaches to psychotherapy, including those of Ellis, Felder, Levitsky, Progoff, Rogers, and Rosen.	Audiocassette, 57 minutes, monograph by N. Raskin, scripts	PL	AAP
Actualization Therapy: An Integration of Rogers, Perls, and Ellis (Three Approaches to Psychotherapy Series)	Presents 3 styles of therapy and describes how actualization therapy is an attempt to integrate all 3.	Film, color, 16mm, 27 minutes	R PM	PsyF

618

Title	Description	Format		
Adlerian Therapy: Two Interviews	Illustrates Adlerian therapy as demonstrated by Bernard Shulman.	Audiotape, 69 minutes, script	PL	AAP
Allen Case	Presents segments of 5 interviews with a mother receiving AFDC assistance. (1965)	Film, black-and-white 16mm, 75 minutes	R	FSU
The Allen Case	Provides a sample family services case to consider how social workers can increase their skill in treatment-oriented interviewing.	Film, black-and-white, 16mm, 26 minutes	R	IU
Applying Communication Theory to Work with Patients	Discusses communication theory and research and its application to therapy and provides exercises to improve communication skills.	Videotape, color, 60 minutes	PM	AVMM
An Approach to Understanding Dynamics	Depicts an interview between a patient and a psychiatrist and analyzes the dynamics of the interview. (1976)	Film, black-and-white, super-8 and 16mm, 34 minutes	PL	GSA, UN
Behavior Therapy	Demonstrates behavior therapy, including the use of relaxation and reciprocal inhibition.	Audio reel, 65 minutes, script	PL	AAP
Behavior Therapy: An Introduction	Demonstrates 3 models of learning—operant, classical, and observational—and 3 basic processes—contingency management, counterconditioning, and role playing.	Film, color, 16mm, 23 minutes	R PM	HR
B. F. Skinner and Behavior Change: Research, Practice, and Promise	Reviews briefly the developmental stages of behaviorism, its philosophies, and its application. (1975)	Film, color, 16mm, 45 minutes	R	UW, UI-ISU

Part Two: Films, Videotapes, and Audiotapes (cont'd.).

Title[a]	Content Description	Media Description	Fee[b]	Distributor Code[c]
Chalk Talk on Counseling	Documents the special skill of charisma, competence, and commitment necessary to be an effective counselor. (1977)	Film, color, 16mm, 21 minutes	R	UI-ISU
Communication: Difficulties in Speaking, Listening, Hearing, Understanding, Interrupting, and Interacting	Discusses 6 significant activities in psychotherapy.	Film, color, 16mm, 60 minutes	PM	AVMM
Composite A, B, C	Shows an edited composite of 34 selections from a 3-year course in analytically oriented therapy conducted by Levitsky.	3 audio reels, 247 minutes (total), script	PL	AAP
Conversations on Casework	Discusses 3 important aspects of casework—relationship, the problem, and diagnosis.	6 videotapes, black-and-white, 30 minutes (each)	PL (series)	UCSSSA, UTA
Counseling Interaction Profile Training Tape	Demonstrates the Counseling Interaction Profile (CIP) system of recording and analyzing interaction between counselor and counselee.	Audiotape	PL	PAA
Creating Specialized Relationships	Discusses 3 types of specialized relationships with clients—stabilizing, stimulating, and synthesizing.	Film, black-and-white, 16mm, 30 minutes	R	IU

620

Title	Description	Format	Source	
Crisis Intervention Training Series	Presents a comprehensive model of crisis intervention covering such topics as characteristics of crisis, understanding-listening skills, assessment skills, action skills, and others.	12 audiotapes, 18–30 minutes (each)	PL (series)	UTA
Critical Counseling Incidents	Consists of a stimulus-response film dramatizing 9 open-ended incidents calling for a response from viewers. (1975)	Film, color, 16mm, 25 minutes	R PM	EMC, UW
Doing Casework (Casework in Public Welfare Series)	Discusses and outlines steps in problem solving that must take place jointly between client and caseworker. (1969)	Film, black-and-white, 16mm, 30 minutes	R	IU
Four Psychotherapies	Presents the same client interviewed by Drs. Murray (client-centered therapy), Ellis (rational-emotive therapy), Cautela (behavior therapy), and Seidenberg (psychoanalytic).	Audio reel, 79 minutes	PL	AAP
Frederick Perls and Gestalt Therapy	Presents the essence of Gestalt therapy and demonstrates the model.	2 films, black-and-white, 16mm, 39 and 36 minutes	R PH PM (used)	PsyF
Identifying the Problem	Depicts a behavioral counselor translating a problem into behavioral terms and helping a client to express feelings.	Film, color, 16mm, 21 minutes	PM	APGA

Part Two: Films, Videotapes, and Audiotapes (cont'd).

Title[a]	Content Description	Media Description	Fee[b]	Distributor Code[c]
Inner World of Counseling with Dr. Carl Rogers, Session I and Session II	Demonstrates how to practice client-centered therapy in a one-to-one session. (1981)	2 films, color, 16mm, 40 minutes (each)	R PM (each) PH (series)	APGA
An Introduction to Behavioral Counseling	Demonstrates through a case study how a behavioral counselor works with a client (teen-ager), parents, and teachers. (1975)	Film, color, 16mm, 26 minutes	R	PSU
Language and Meaning (Language and Linguistics Series)	Shows how linguistic science can be applied to the analysis of the psychiatric interview.	Film, black-and-white, 16mm, 30 minutes	R	SUNYB, UA
Listening	Provides an overview of concepts involved in crisis intervention by telephone. (1971)	Film, color, 16mm, 30 minutes	R	UC
Lowen and Bioenergetic Therapy	Describes the key ideas of bioenergetic therapy and presents a demonstration of the model with a young female client.	Film, color, 16mm, 48 minutes	R PH	PsyF
The Natural and the Unnatural	Discusses the unconscious and conscious acts engaged in by the caseworker. (1969)	Film, black-and-white, 16mm, 30 minutes	R	IU
An Observation System for Analysis of Social Work Practice	Introduces a system developed by Lawrence Shulman that allows an observer to view a video-	Videotape, color, 55 minutes	R PL	SU

Title	Description	Format	Code	Source
	tape of practice and characterize the interaction observed by recording a number every 3 seconds.			
Perception and Problem Solving	Presents a discussion by Allen Pincus and Michael Heus on the relationship between perceptions and the ability to problem solve in social work practice. (1977)	Videotape, color, 30 minutes	PR	UTA
Rational-Emotive Therapy: Two Interviews	Demonstrates the application of rational-emotive therapy.	Audiocassettes, 69 and 56 minutes, script	PL	AAP
Short-Term or Brief Psychotherapeutic Techniques	Examines the fundamental components of the psychotherapy process. (1975)	Film, super-8 and 16mm, videocassette, color,	PR	UN
Simple Problem Ideas	Demonstrates an intake interview in a voluntary family services agency.	Audiotape, 60 minutes	PL	CSWE
Social Work Practice Behavior in Two Child Welfare Agencies (The Helping Process in Social Work Series)	Describes the 9 treatment behavior groupings isolated by Lawrence Shulman, including such skills as contracting, demand for work, sharing worker feelings, and others (Part 1), and examines the relationship between these behaviors and a number of practice outcome measures (Part 2).	2 videocassettes, color, 55 and 52 minutes	R PM (set)	McGU, SU
Social Work Theory and Practice (The Helping Process in Social Work Series)	Outlines and illustrates the mediation theory of William Schwartz (Part 1) and discusses the advanced-level skills of contracting,	2 videocassettes, color, 52 and 38 minutes	R PM (set)	McGU, SU

Part Two: Films, Videotapes, and Audiotapes (cont'd.).

Title[a]	Content Description	Media Description	Fee[b]	Distributor Code[c]
	dealing with affect, and making a demand for work (Part 2).			
Task-Centered Casework, Part I	Demonstrates task-centered interviewing with 2 role-played clients.	Videocassette, 60 minutes	PL	VRL
Task-Centered Casework, Part II	Demonstrates task-centered interviewing with 2 role-played clients.	Videocassette, 50 minutes	PL	VRL
Teaching and Learning in Casework	Presents many concepts and techniques for the beginning caseworker and furthers understanding of the relationship between caseworker, client, and supervisor.	3 audiocassettes, 60 minutes (each)	PL	SI
Three Approaches to Psychotherapy I	Presents the same client interviewed by three different therapists—Carl Rogers (client-centered therapy), Frederick Perls (Gestalt therapy), and Albert Ellis (rational-emotive therapy). (1965)	3 films, color or black-and-white, 16mm, 48, 32, and 38 minutes, respectively	R (each or series) PM (each) PH (series) PM (series-used)	PsyF, PSU
Three Approaches to Psychotherapy II	Presents the same client interviewed by three different therapists—Carl Rogers (client-centered	3 16mm films or ¾ inch videocassette, color, 48 minutes (each)	R (each or series)	PsyF

Group Treatment Modalities

			(each) PH (series)	
therapy), Everett Shostrom (actualizing therapy), and Arnold Lazarus (multimodal behavior therapy).				
Actualization Group	Consists of a series of seven authentic, unrehearsed group therapy sessions illustrating Everett Shostrom's actualizing therapy. (1966)	7 films, black-and-white, 16mm, 25–44 minutes (each)	R (each)	PSU
Behavioral Group Counseling	Demonstrates the use of behavioral counseling techniques in a group setting. (1973)	Film, 16mm, color, 28 minutes	R	PSU, IU
Broad-Spectrum Behavior Therapy in a Group	Depicts some of the active behavioral methods used by Arnold Lazarus in groups. (1969)	Film, black-and-white, 16mm, 29 minutes	R PL	PSU
Carl Rogers Conducts an Encounter Group	Demonstrates the various phases of group process, ranging from superficial expression at the beginning through tentative explorations of feelings to free emotional encounter.	Film (two reels), color, 16mm, 70 minutes	R PH	APGA
Carl Rogers on Facilitating a Group (Distinguished Contributors to Counseling Series)	Discusses important factors in facilitating a group, including the role of the group leader, levels of group operation, and physical contact. (1970)	Film, color, 16mm, 30 minutes	R PM	APGA, UI-ISU
Casework with Groups	Describes how the elements of social casework with individuals are applicable to a group. (1969)	Film, black-and-white, 16mm, 30 minutes	R	IU
Children in the Hospital	Illustrates social group work carried on with children in a hospital (1962)	Film, black-and-white, 16mm, 44 minutes	R	IU

Part Two: Films, Videotapes, and Audiotapes (cont'd.).

Title[a]	Content Description	Media Description	Fee[b]	Distributor Code[c]
Circle of Love	Illustrates the methods and problems involved in the use of encounter group techniques as a means of improving interpersonal understanding and relations.	Film, color, 16mm, 25 minutes	R PM	McGH
Communication Problems of Couples	Reviews, analyzes, and discusses the communication patterns and systems of four couples participating in a mini-marathon couples group.	Videocassette, ¾ inch, color, 60 minutes	PM	AVMM
Group Therapy (Parts I and II)	Reproduces the social, psychological, and interpersonal aspects of a group session. (1968)	2 films, black-and-white, 16mm, 30 minutes (each)	R	BYU
How T-Groups Work	Demonstrates the process of a T-group, illustrating varied leadership and behavior styles. (1973)	Film, color, 16mm, 25 minutes	R	IO
Intensive Adolescent Group	Presents a composite tape of a week-end of intensive psychotherapy conducted with adolescent wards of the court.	Audio reel, 64 minutes, script	PL	AAP
Journey into Self	Documents a 16-hour encounter group of 8 adults led by Carl Rogers and Richard Farson. (1968)	Film, black-and-white, 16mm, 47 minutes	R	UC, UW
Multiple Family Therapy	Demonstrates the process and technique through which 5–6 families are brought together in regular group sessions. (1975)	Film, black-and-white, super-8 or 16mm, 17 minutes	PR	SPF, UN

Title	Description	Format	Type	Source
A Multicouple Group Therapy Meeting Conducted by Married Cotherapists	Illustrates work with 4 couples during a 6 hour mini-marathon group session.	2 videocassettes, ¾ inch, color, 120 minutes	PM	AVMM
Principles of Psychoanalytic Group Psychotherapy	Details the theory and practice of psychoanalytic group psychotherapy.	12 audiotapes, 60 minutes (each)	PL	SI
Rational-Emotive Group Psychotherapy	Discusses the use of RET in group psychotherapy and in encounters.	Film, color, 16mm, 30 minutes	PM	IRL
The Scream Inside: Emergence Through Group Therapy	Covers the basics of group process in an analytic psychotherapy group emphasizing group composition, the function of the leader, promotion of interaction, and the introduction of art and movement therapy. (1969)	Film, black-and-white, 16mm, 47 minutes	PR	SPF, AGPA
Sharing the Leadership	Explores 3 categories of action—self-serving, task and group-serving functions—and their relationship to group leadership. (1963)	Film, black-and-white, 16mm, 30 minutes	R	FSU
Therapist(s)-Couple Communication	Focuses on the what, how, when, and why of communications between psychotherapists and 4 couples in a group situation.	Videocassette, ¾ inch, color, 60 minutes	PM	AVMM
Three Approaches to Group Therapy (Parts I, II, and III)	Demonstrates 3 different approaches to group therapy, including Everett Shostrom's actualizing therapy (Part I), Albert Ellis's rational-emotive therapy (Part II), and Harold Greenwald's decision therapy (Part III).	3 16mm films or videotapes, color, 38, 40, and 38 minutes	R (each) PM (each) PH (series)	PsyF, UW

Part Two: Films, Videotapes, and Audiotapes (cont'd.).

Title[a]	Content Description	Media Description	Fee[b]	Distributor Code[c]
Two Faces of Group Leadership	Captures the dynamics of group process using selected growth groups and demonstrates basic leader functions of mobilizing and managing.	Film, 16mm, or video-cassette, color, 30 minutes	R PM	PsyF
Two Group Sessions	Contains the major portions of 2 group sessions that have an interesting thread of continuity, although they occur 4 months apart.	Audio reel, 60 and 59 minutes, script	PL	AAP
Video Replay in Group Psychotherapy	Presents excerpts from a 1-day analytically oriented psychotherapy group session in which many uses of videotape replay are demonstrated.	Film, black-and-white, 16mm, 50 minutes	PL	AVMM AGPA
When Strangers Meet	Demonstrates 4 women and 2 men going through the process of initial explication of problems, goals, and reactions to one another and to the group.	Audio reel, 53 and 44 minutes, script	PL	AAP

[a]Film and tape titles appear in alphabetical order.
[b]Fee codes: **R** (rental, $10–$50), **PL** (low-cost purchase, under $200), **PM** (medium-cost purchase, $200–$400), **PH** (high-cost purchase, over $400), **NC** (no charge), **PR** (prices available on request).
[c]Names and addresses of distributors appear in Part Five in alphabetical order by letter code.

Part Three: Simulation Games and Exercises.

Title	Focus	Players[a]	Structure[b]	Time[c]	Source
Intrapersonal					
Learning Game	Illustrates the nature of the dynamics involved in learning and the problems in modifying established patterns.	V	L	20 minutes	*Human Communication Handbook: Simulations and Games* (Ruben and Budd, 1975)
The Listening Game	Demonstrates how listening is functionally selective and affected by mental-set and personal needs.	V	M	NS	Didactic Systems
Listening Triads	Furthers understanding of the problems and importance of listening.	V	L	45 minutes	*A Handbook of Structured Experiences for Human Relations Training.* Vol. 1 (Jones and Pfeiffer, 1974)
Meanings Are in People: Perception Checking	Demonstrates that meanings are found in more than words and illustrates how our perceptions of words affect the meanings ascribed to them.	2–10 or groups of 4–6	H	1–3 hours	*A Handbook of Structured Experiences for Human Relations Training.* Vol. 7 (Pfeiffer and Jones, 1979).
Memory Game	Highlights the influence of past personal life experience in perception, attention, memory, and recall.	5–25	M	1–1½ hours	*Human Communication Handbook: Simulations and Games.* Vol. 2 (Ruben, 1978).

629

Part Three: Simulation Games and Exercises (cont'd).

Title	Focus	Players[a]	Structure[b]	Time[c]	Source
No Cause for Alarm	Demonstrates the nature of assumptions and the barriers to understanding, such as ambiguity and need for closure.	2–20	M	45 minutes	Dynamics of Human Behavior
Zif	Illustrates the nature of category formation and memory processes.	V	L	1–1½ hours	*Human Communication Handbook: Simulations and Games.* Vol. 2 (Ruben, 1978)
		Interpersonal			
The Abelson-Baker Interview	Focuses on important concepts and skills in interpersonal communication.	V	M	NS	Didactic Systems
Active Listening: A Communication Skills Practice	Teaches the nature of emotional message and offers practice in listening skills.	V (dyads)	H	1½ hours	*A Handbook of Structured Experiences for Human Relations Training.* Vol. 7 (Pfeiffer and Jones, 1979)
Ernstspiel (Kit)	Focuses on teaching specific communication concepts and skills—for example, nonverbal and one-way and two-way communication. (Game consists of 8 kits, each focusing on a different concept or skill.)	5–30	M	1–1½ hours	MUST, Research Division, Center for Educational Policy and Management
Exercise Communication	Facilitates analysis of the different channels of communication.	V	L	1 hour	Didactic Systems

Name	Description	Group	Level	Time	Source
Helping Relationships	Facilitates understanding of the effects of posturing and eye contact on helping relationships, highlights the effect of nonverbal behavior on others, and teaches basic attending skills.	2–20	L	30 minutes	*A Handbook of Structured Experiences for Human Relations Training.* Vol 5 (Pfeiffer and Jones, 1975)
The Information Game	Demonstrates where communication can break down and the nature and effects of selective perception.	V	L	NS	Didactic Systems
Mixed Messages: A Communication Experiment	Explores the dynamics of discrepancies in verbal and nonverbal behavior and the importance of congruent messages.	Minimum of 4 triads	M	45 minutes –1 hour	*A Handbook of Structured Experiences for Human Relations Training.* Vol. 7 (Pfeiffer and Jones, 1979)
Not Listening: A Dyadic Role Play	Provides experience in not being heard and orients persons toward more effective listening.	V (dyads)	L	30 minutes	*A Handbook of Structured Experiences for Human Relations Training.* Vol. 3 (Pfeiffer and Jones, 1971)
One-Way Two-Way Feedback	Emphasizes the importance of feedback and checking out in the communication process.	V	L	45 minutes	*A Handbook of Structured Experiences for Human Relations Training.* Vol. 1 (Jones and Pfeiffer, 1977)
Telephone	Focuses on problems in the accurate transmission of information from one person to another and the ease	V	L	45 minutes	*Human Communication Handbook: Simulations and Games.* Vol. 1 (Ruben and Budd, 1978)

Part Three: Simulation Games and Exercises (cont'd.).

Title	Focus	Players[a]	Structure[b]	Time[c]	Source
	with which facts are subtracted, added, or distorted.				
Ungame	Facilitates openness and self-disclosure.	2–6	M	V	Ungame Company
	Group				
Ball Game: Controlling and Influencing Communication	Explores the dynamics of assuming leadership in a group.	6–12	M	30 minutes	A Handbook of Structured Experiences for Human Relations Training. Vol. 4 (Pfeiffer and Jones, 1973)
Helping Hand Strikes Again	Assists others to perform in a group situation.	11–50	M	2–3 hours	Didactic Systems
I'll Grant You That	Identifies elements that hinder and facilitate communication between individual group members and between groups.	V	M	3 1-hour sessions	Communication Games and Simulations (Covert and Thomas, 1978)
Pins and Straws: Leadership Styles	Highlights three general styles of leadership and their effects on others.	V (groups of 6)	M	2 hours	A Handbook of Structured Experiences for Human Relations Training. Vol. 5 (Pfeiffer and Jones, 1975)
Poems	Focuses on group dynamics and what members do or do not to work creatively together.	V (groups of 6–8)	M	1–1½ hours	The 1977 Annual Handbook for Group Facilitators (Jones and Pfeiffer, 1977)

Part Three: Simulation Games and Exercises (cont'd.).

Title	Focus	Players[a]	Structure[b]	Time[c]	Source
Toothpicks: An Analysis of Helping Behaviors	Demonstrates different ways to assist others in a task and illustrates the effects of differing helping approaches on task accomplishment and interpersonal relations.	10–20	M	1 hour	*A Handbook of Structured Experiences for Human Relations Training.* Vol. 4 (Pfeiffer and Jones, 1973)

Cross-Cultural

Title	Focus	Players[a]	Structure[b]	Time[c]	Source
Agitania, Meditania, Solidania	Highlights some problems and challenges encountered in cross-cultural communication, along with the nature and effects of cultural stereotyping.	15–45	M	Several hours to several days	*Human Communication Handbook: Simulations and Games.* Vol. 1 (Ruben and Budd, 1975)
Bafa Bafa	Highlights the nature and meaning of culture and affords participants experience in interacting with a different culture.	V	M	1–1½ hours	Simile II
Culture Contact	Focuses on the potential for conflict when persons of differing cultures come together.	30	M	1½–2 hours	ABT Associates
Lobu-Abu	Sensitizes to the problems of communication between those not sharing the same language and highlights the importance of nonverbal communication in intercultural understanding.	V (dyads)	M	1 hour	*Human Communication Handbook: Simulations and Games.* Vol. 1 (Ruben and Budd, 1975)

Part Three: Simulation Games and Exercises (cont'd).

Title	Focus	Players[a]	Structure[b]	Time[c]	Source
The Shoe Game	Teaches awareness of communication in discrimination situations.	12–50	V	45 minutes	Catalogue of Noncomputerized Simulations and Games (1979)
Human Services					
The End of the Line	Develops awareness of and sensitivity to the aging process and problems confronting the elderly.	16–30	M	1½–2 hours	Institute of Gerontology
Everybody Counts	Develops sensitivity to the needs and problems of the handicapped.	25–60	M	Individual activities of 30 minutes or more	The Council for Exceptional Children
Ghetto	Highlights the problems and pressure experienced by the urban poor and the choices confronting them.	7–10	M	2–4 hours	Didactic Systems
Hang-Up	Facilitates participant awareness of psychological hang-ups experienced in stress situations and highlights racial stereotyping.	V	M	1 hour	Synectics Education System
Horatio Alger (A Welfare Simulation Game)	Introduces players to the realities of the welfare system.	13–32	M	2 hours	Citizens for Welfare Reform

Name	Description	Participants	Level	Time	Source
Tracy Congdon	Facilitates understanding of the complexities of social problems.	6–30	M	2 hours	Community Service Volunteers
Welfare Week	Facilitates development of empathy for those on public welfare and demonstrates ways the system can be supportive or destructive of clients.	5–500	M	6 hours or more	Gamed Simulations

Self-Development

Name	Description	Participants	Level	Time	Source
Auction	Develops awareness of own values underlying choices made during a simulated auction.	7–17	M	1–2 hours	Creative Learning Systems
Can of Squirms	Facilitates self-understanding through analysis of one's handling of pragmatic dilemmas presented in the simulation process.	2–40 (in teams)	M	5 minutes –2 hours	Contemporary Drama Service
Power Play	Furthers understanding of how one's own self interest (values and goals) influences use of power.	6–200 (3 or more teams)	M	4–10 hours	Powerplay
Process	Furthers participant understanding of self and others (series of 8 exercises).	5–9	M	2–3 hours per exercise	Didactic Systems
The Sharing Game	Develops greater self-awareness through a simulation process requiring participants to risk, think, do, or make some decision.	2–6	L	1 hour	Psych-Ed Associates

635

Part Three: Simulation Games and Exercises (cont'd.).

Title	Focus	Players[a]	Structure[b]	Time[c]	Source
Shrink	Furthers insights into one's self-perceptions.	3–8	L	1 hour	Art Fair
Value Bingo	Sharpens participant awareness of values underlying varied statements made and actions taken.	2–40	L	45 minutes	Pennant Educational Materials

[a]V indicates that the optimal number of players is not specified and may vary with a given context and use.

[b]Letters indicate the degree of organizational complexity of a given simulation game or exercise—low (L), medium (M), or high (H). Judgments about the nature of structure required are to some degree subjective.

[c]NS signifies that the time required to implement a particular simulation activity is not specified.

636

Part Four: Organizational Resources for Skills Training.

Organization		Kind and Focus of Resource[a]					
	Consultation Services	Training Programs, Workshops	Packaged Training Programs	Audiotapes Videotapes	Films	Simulation Games, Exercises	Publications[b]
American Group Psychotherapy Association	1,2,3	1,2,3	1,2,3				J(1,2,3),TM(1,2,3), M(1,2,3)
American Personnel and Guidance Association		1,2,3			1,2,3		B(1,2,3),J(1,2,3), M(1,2,3)
Amherst Consulting Group	1,2,3	1,2,3	1,2,3	A, V (1,2)	1,2	1,2,3	B(1,2,3)
Applied Leadership Technologies	1,2,3	1,2,3	1,2,3			1	TM
Applied Skills Press		1	1			1	B(1,2)
Cambridge House	1,2,3	1,2,3		A (1,2)	1,2,3		B(1,2,3)
Center for Human Communication	1,2,3	1,2,3		V (2,3)	1		B(1,2),M(1,2)
The Center for Organizational and Personal Effectiveness (C.O.P.E.)	1,2,3	1,2,3				1,2,3	B(1,2,3)
Center for Studies of the Person	1,3	1,3					B(1,3)

Part Four: Organizational Resources for Skills Training (Cont'd).

Organization	Kind and Focus of Resource[a]						
	Consultation Services	Training Programs, Workshops	Packaged Training Programs	Audiotapes Videotapes	Films	Simulation Games, Exercises	Publications[b]
Choice Awareness Programs Development Center	1	1	1	A, V (1)			B(1),M(1)
Communication Services	1,2,3	1,2,3					
Consultants' Network	1,3	1,2	1,2			1,2,3	
Creative Learning Systems	1,2,3	1,2,3	1,2,3			1,2,3	
Dynamics of Human Behavior	1,2,3	1,2,3	1,2,3	A (1,2,3), V(1,3)		1,2,3	B1
Education and Training Consultants	1,3	1,3	1,3			1,3	B(1,3)
Educational Technologies	1	1	1	A, V(1)		1	TM(1)
Encounters: Workshops in Personal and Professional Growth		1,2,3					
Esalen Institute		1,3		A (1)			M
Explorations Institute	1,3	1,3	3	A (1)			B(1,3),M(3),TM(3)
FOCUS Consulting	1,2,3	1,2,3	1,2,3			3	B(1,3),TM(1,3),M
Health Professional Resources	1,2,3	1,2,3					

Organization							
Human Resource Development Press	1,2,3	1		A (1,2),V(1,2)			TM(1),B(1,2,3)
Humanistic Psychotherapy Studies Center	1,2,3	1,2,3					
IDEALS	1,2,3	1,2,3		V(1,3)			B(1,3),M(1,3), TM(1,2,3)
Impact Consultants/ Impact Publishers	1,3	1,2,3				3	B(1,3),M(1)
Institute for Sociotherapy	1,2,3	1,2,3					
Instructional Dynamics/ Human Development Institute	1		1,2,3	A (1,2,3), V (1)	1	1,3	TM(1,3)
Interpersonal Communication Programs		1,3	1,3				B(1,3),TM(1,3)
LEAD Associates	1,2,3	1,2,3				1,2,3	M(1,3)
Learncom	1,2,3	1,3					
Learning Consultants	1,2,3	2					
Learning Dynamics	1,2,3	1,2	1,2	A (1,2)			TM(1,2)
Mainland Institute	1,2,3	1,2,3					
The Menninger Foundation, Division of Continuing Education	1,2,3	1,2,3					B,M
Microtraining Associates	1,2,3	1,2,3	1,2,3	V(1,2,3)			B,M(1,2,3)

Part Four: Organizational Resources for Skills Training (Cont'd).

Organization	Consultation Services	Training Programs, Workshops	Packaged Training Programs	Audiotapes Videotapes	Films	Simulation Games, Exercises	Publications[b]
				Kind and Focus of Resource[a]			
NTL Institute for Applied Behavioral Science	1,2,3	1,2,3	3				J(1,3),TM
Oasis Center for Human Potential	1,3	1,3					
Performance and Communication Associates	1,3	1,3	1	A (1)			TM(1)
Personal Growth Foundation	1,3	1,3	1	A (1)		1	
Postgraduate Center for Mental Health	1,2,3	1,2,3	1,2,3				M(1,2,3),B(1,2,3), J(1,2,3)
Psychology Associates		1,3					
Resource	1,3	1,3	1,3	A, V (1,3)	1,3		B(3),TM(3)
Resources	1,3	1,3					
Sagamore Institute	1,2,3	1,2,3	1,2,3		1,2		B(1,2,3),M(1,2,3)
Seminars Directory		1,2,3					
Social Psychiatry Research Institute		1,2		A, V (1,2)			B(1,2,3)
Southwest Center for Human							

Stanford Institute for Intercultural Communication	1,3	1,3	1,3	A (1,2,3)	1,2,3	B(1,2,3)
Training House		1,2,3	1,2,3			
University Associates	1,3	1,3	1,3	A (1)	3	B(1,2,3),J(3)

[a]Numbers indicate whether the focus of a given resource is an interpersonal and communication skills (1), interviewing (2), or group leadership training (3).

[b]Published resources include books (B), journals (J), training manuals (TM), and miscellaneous (M), which encompasses monographs, articles, and reports.

Part Five: Sources for Materials, Programs, and Services.

Packaged Programs

The Charles Press Publishers, Inc.
Bowie, Md. 20715

Continuing Education Program
School of Social Welfare
State University of New York at
  Albany
135 Western Avenue
Albany, N.Y. 12222

CRM/McGraw-Hill
110 Fifteenth Street
Del Mar, Calif. 92014

George Warren Brown School of
  Social Work
Learning Resources Center
Campus Box 1196
Washington University
St. Louis, Mo. 63130

Harper & Row College Media
2350 Virginia Avenue
Hagerstown, Md. 21740

Human Development Institute
666 North Lake Shore Drive
Chicago, Ill. 60611

Human Resource Center
Graduate School of Social Work
University of Texas at Arlington
Arlington, Tex. 76019

Human Resource Development
  Press
22 Amherst Road
Amherst, Mass. 01002

Instructional Media Center
Marketing Division
Michigan State University
East Lansing, Mich. 48824

Lansford Publishing Company
P.O. Box 8711
San Jose, Calif. 95155

Learning Consultants, Inc.
6600 North Lincoln Avenue
Lincolnwood, Ill. 60645

Learning Dynamics, Inc.
P.O. Box 323
Needham, Mass. 02192

Mason Media, Inc.
1265 Lakeside Drive
East Lansing, Mich. 48823

Mass Media
1720 Chouteau Avenue
St. Louis, Mo. 63103

Microtraining Associates, Inc.
Box 641
North Amherst, Mass. 01059

Office of Continuing Social Work
  Education
Tucker Hall
University of Georgia
Athens, Ga. 30602

Office of Continuing Social Work
  Education
University of Tennessee
1838 Terrace
Knoxville, Tenn. 37916

Resources for Education and
  Management, Inc.
544 Medlock Road
Decatur, Ga. 30030

Roundtable Films, Inc.
113 North San Vicente Boulevard
Beverly Hills, Calif. 90211

Salenger Educational Media
1635 Twelfth Street
Santa Monica, Calif. 90404

Sales Distribution Center
Unitarian-Universalist Association
Beacon Press
25 Beacon Street
Boston, Mass. 02108

Training House, Inc.
100 Bear Brook Road
Princeton, N.J. 08550

University Associates
8517 Production Avenue
San Diego, Calif. 92121

The University of Tennessee
Research Corporation
Room 404, Andy Holt Tower
University of Tennessee
Knoxville, Tenn. 37916

UCLA Extension, Department K
P.O. Box 24901
Los Angeles, Calif. 90024

Films, Audiotapes, and Videotapes

AAP
The American Academy of
Psychotherapists
A.A.P. Tape Library
300 Gaffey Road
Watsonville, Calif. 95076

AGPA
American Group Psychotherapy
Association, Inc.
1995 Broadway, Fourteenth Floor
New York, N.Y. 10023

APGA
American Personnel and Guidance
Association
Two Skyline Place, Suite 400
5203 Leesburg Pike
Falls Church, Va. 22041

AVMM
Audio Visual Medical Marketing,
Inc.
850 Third Avenue
New York, N.Y. 10022

BYU
Educational Media Services
290 HRCB
Brigham Young University
Provo, Utah 84602

CAFC
Central Arizona Film Cooperative
Arizona State University
Tempe, Ariz. 85281

CCS
The Center for Cassette Studies,
Inc.
8110 Webb Avenue
North Hollywood, Calif. 91605

CSWE
Council on Social Work Education,
Inc.
111 Eighth Avenue
New York, N.Y. 10011

EMC
Educational Media Corporation
Box 21311
Minneapolis, Minn. 58421

FI
Films Incorporated
8124 North Central Park Avenue
Skokie, Ill. 60076

FSU
Instructional Support Center
Instructional Systems Development
Center
Florida State University
Tallahassee, Fla. 32306

GSA
General Services Administration
National Archives and Records
Service
National Audiovisual Center
Washington D.C. 20409

Films, Audiotapes, and Videotapes (cont'd.)

HR
Harper & Row College Media
Order Fulfillment/Customer Service
2350 Virginia Avenue
Hagerstown, Md. 21740

IO
AVC Media Library
Audio Visual Center
The University of Iowa
Iowa City, Iowa 52240

IRL
Institute for Rational Living
45 East Sixty-fifth Street
New York, N.Y. 10021

IU
Indiana University
Audio-Visual Center
Bloomington, Ind. 47401

LCA
Learning Corporation of America
1350 Avenue of the Americas
New York, N.Y. 10019

McGH
McGraw-Hill Films
1221 Avenue of the Americas
New York, N.Y. 10020

McGU
Instructional Communications Centre
McGill University
815 Sherbrooke Street West
Montreal, P.Q. H3A 2K6

MM
Mass Media
2116 North Charles Street
Baltimore, Md. 21218

or

1270 Chouteau Avenue
St Louis, Mo. 63103

MSU-UM
Audio-Visual Education Center
The University of Michigan
416 Fourth Street
Ann Arbor, Mich. 48103

or

Instructional Media Center
Michigan State University
East Lansing, Mich. 48823

PAA
Paul S. Amidon & Associates, Inc.
1966 Benson Avenue
St. Paul, Minn. 55116

PSU
The Pennsylvania State University
Audio-Visual Services
University Park, Pa. 16802

PsyF
Psychological Films
205 West Twentieth Street
Santa Ana, Calif. 92706

SI
Sigma Information, Inc.
240 Grand Avenue
Leonia, N.J. 07605

SPF
Sandoz Pharmaceuticals
Film Department
East Hanover, N.J. 07936

SU
Film Rental Center
Syracuse University
1455 East Colvin Street
Syracuse, New York 13210

SUNYB
State University of New York at Buffalo
Educational Communications Center
Media Library
Foster Annex
Buffalo, N.Y. 14214

UA
University of Arizona
Film Scheduling Office
Bureau of Audiovisual Services
Tucson, Ariz. 85721

UC
University of California
Extension Media Center
Berkeley, Calif. 94720

UCSSSA
University of Chicago School of
  Social Service Administration
The Media Center
969 East Sixtieth Street
Chicago, Ill. 60637

UI-ISU
The University of Iowa
Media Library
C-5 East Hall
Iowa City, Iowa 52242

or

Iowa State University
Media Resources Center
121 Pearson Hall
Ames, Iowa 50011

UN
Biomedical Communications
  Division
University of Nebraska Medical
  Center
Forty-second and Dewey Avenue
Omaha, Nebr. 68105

USC
University of Southern California
Division of Cinema
Film Distribution Section
University Park
Los Angeles, Calif. 90007

UTA
Sam Houston
School of Social Work
The University of Texas at Austin
Austin, Tex. 78712

UW
Bureau of Audio Visual Instruction
University of Wisconsin-Extension
P.O. Box 2093
Madison, Wis. 53701

VRL
Video Resource Library
School of Social Work Media Center
University of Wisconsin—Madison
425 Henry Mall
Madison, Wis. 53706

645

Simulation Materials

Abt Associates, Inc.
55 Wheeler Street
Cambridge, Mass. 02138

Art Fair, Inc.
18 West Eighteenth Street
New York, N.Y. 10011

Citizens for Welfare Reform
305 Michigan Avenue
Detroit, Mich. 48226

Community Service Volunteers
237 Pentonville Road
London N1 9NG England

Contemporary Drama Service
Arthur Merriwether, Inc.
Box 457
Downer's Grove, Ill. 60515

Council for Exceptional
    Children
1920 Association Drive
Reston, Va. 22091

Creative Learning Systems, Inc.
936 C Street
San Diego, Calif. 92101

Denison Simulation Center
Denison University
Granville, Ohio 43023

Didactic Systems, Inc.
Box 457
Cranford, N.J. 07016

Dynamics of Human Behavior
34 Tenth Avenue
San Mateo, Calif. 94402

Gamed Simulations, Inc.
Suite 4H
10 West Sixty-sixth Street
New York, N.Y. 10023

Institute of Gerontology
University of Michigan
520 East Liberty
Ann Arbor, Mich. 48109

MUST
Research Division
Center for Educational Policy and
    Management
1472 Kincaid Street
Eugene, Oreg. 97403

Pennant Educational Materials
8265 Commercial Street
La Mesa, Calif. 92041

Powerplay, Inc.
Box 411
Naperville, Ill. 60540

Psych-Ed Associates
P.O. Box 2091
Lawrence, Kans. 66045

Simile
218 Twelfth Street
P.O. Box 910
Del Mar, Calif. 92014

Synectics Education Systems
121 Battle Street
Cambridge, Mass. 02138

Ungame Co.
Division of Au-Vid, Inc.
761 Monroe Way
Placentia, Calif. 92670

American Group Psychotherapy
Association, Inc.
1995 Broadway, Fourteenth Floor
New York, N.Y. 10023

American Personnel and Guidance
Association
5203 Leesburg Pike, Suite 400
Falls Church, Va. 22041

Amherst Consulting Group
Box 649
North Amherst, Mass. 01059

Applied Leadership Technologies,
Inc.
554 Bloomfield Avenue
Bloomfield, N.J. 07003

Applied Skills Press
200 South Bemiston, Suite 202
St. Louis, Mo. 63105

Cambridge House, Inc.
1879 North Cambridge Avenue
Milwaukee, Wis. 53202

Center for Human Communication
15405 Los Gatos Boulevard, Suite
201
Los Gatos, Calif. 95030

Center for Human Development
221 Shady Avenue
Pittsburgh, Pa. 15206

Center for Organizational and
Personal Effectiveness, Inc.
55 West Jersey Street
Elizabeth, N.J. 07202

Center for Studies of the Person
1125 Torrey Pines Road
La Jolla, Calif. 92037

Choice Awareness Programs
Development Center
1307 South Killian Drive
Lake Park, Fla. 33403

Communication Services
2102 Sycamore Road
LaGrange, Ky. 40031

Consultants' Network
57 West Eighty-ninth Street
New York, N.Y. 10024

Creative Learning Systems, Inc.
936 C Street
San Diego, Calif. 92101

Dynamics of Human Behavior
34 Tenth Avenue
San Mateo, CA 94401

Educational Technologies
1007 Whitehead Road
Trenton, N.J. 08638

Education and Training
Consultants Company
Box 2085
Sedona, Ariz. 86336

Encounters: Workshops in Personal
and Professional Growth
5225 Comm Avenue, N.W.
Washington, D.C. 20015

Esalen Institute
Big Sur, Calif. 93920

Explorations Institute
1711-A Grove Street
Berkeley, Calif. 94709

FOCUS Consulting
P.O. Box 12
Belmont, Mass. 02178

Health Professional Resources
Village of Mainland
Harleysville, Pa 19438

Hughs-Chakiris Incorporated
755 Lincoln Avenue
Winnetka, Ill. 60093

Human Resource Development
Press
22 Amherst Road
Amherst, Mass. 01002

Organizational Resources (cont'd.)

Humanistic Psychotherapy Studies
Center
2127 Pine Street
Philadelphia, Pa. 19103

IDEALS, Inc.
P.O. Box 391
State College, Pa. 16801

Impact Consultants/Impact
Publishers
P.O. Box 1094
San Luis Obispo, Calif. 93406

Institute for Sociotherapy
116 East Twenty-seventh Street
New York, N.Y. 10003

Instructional Dynamics/Human
Development Institute
666 North Lake Shore Drive,
Suite 924
Chicago, Ill. 60611

Interpersonal Communication
Programs, Inc.
1925 Nicollet Avenue, Suite 102
Minneapolis, Minn. 55403

LEAD Associates, Inc.
P.O. Box 4455
Charlotte, N.C. 28204

Learncom, Inc.
113 Union Wharf
Boston, Mass. 00100

Learning Consultants, Inc.
6600 North Lincoln Avenue
Lincolnwood, Ill. 60645

Learning Dynamics, Inc.
P.O. Box 323
Needham, Mass 02194

Mainland Institute
Village of Mainland
Harleysville, Pa. 19438

The Menninger Foundation
Division of Continuing Education
Box 829
Topeka, Kans. 66601

Microtraining Associates, Inc.
Box 641
North Amherst, Mass. 01059

NTL Institute for Applied
Behavioral Science
1501 Wilson Boulevard, Suite 1000
Arlington, Va. 22209

Oasis Center for Human Potential
7463 North Sheridan
Chicago, Ill. 60626

Performance and Communication
Associates
884 West End Avenue, Suite 144
New York, N.Y. 10025

Personal Growth Foundation,
Incorporated
4257 Forty-sixth Avenue
Number 207
Minneapolis, Minn. 55422

Postgraduate Center for Mental
Health
124 East Twenty-eighth Street
New York, N.Y. 10016

Psychology Associates
Professional Building
Suite 318
120 Oakbrook Center Mall
Oak Brook, Ill. 60521

Resource, Inc.
13902 North Dale Mabry
Tampa, Fla. 33618

Resources
423 East Seventy-eighth Street
New York, N.Y. 10021

Sagamore Institute
110 Spring Street
Saratoga Springs, N.Y. 12866

Seminars Directory
525 North Lake Street
Madison, Wis. 53703

Social Psychiatry Research Institute
150 East Sixty-ninth Street
N.Y.

Southwest Center for Human
   Relations Studies
University of Oklahoma
Building 4
555 Constitution
Norman, Okla. 73019

Stanford Institute for Intercultural
   Communication
P.O. Box A-D
Stanford, Calif. 94305

Training House, Inc.
P.O. Box 3090
Princeton, N.J. 08540

University Associates
8517 Production Avenue
San Diego, Calif. 92126

Name Index

Subject Index